21507

1125

AN INTRODUCTORY
LOGIC

AN INTRODUCTORY LOGIC
Second Edition

William J. Kilgore

Baylor University

HOLT, RINEHART AND WINSTON

New York   Chicago   San Francisco   Dallas
Montreal   Toronto   London   Sydney

To
Barbara
and
Sally

Library of Congress Cataloging in Publication Data

Kilgore, William Jackson, 1917–
  An introductory logic.

  Bibliography: p. 455
  Includes index.
  1. Logic. I. Title.
BC108.K5 1979   160   78-26568
ISBN 0-03-022626-0

PREFACE

In revising this work for a second edition I have sought to make it a more useful teaching and learning instrument. One basic objective was to make the presentation of the material clearer and simpler for freshmen and sophomore students. But I also wanted introductory students to have a good foundation in logic.

The difference in ability of students to grasp the essentials of deductive logic is a primary source of difficulty in teaching this material. Some students grasp the material quickly. Others appear to remain in a state of bewilderment. Moving on too soon can add to the confusion of some. Failure to do so can result in the boredom of others. In this work I have sought to present the material in a way that those who have some difficulty in grasping basic logical concepts and operations can do so with reasonable effort. And I have sought to present the subject matter with sufficient depth and variety so that those who grasp it more readily can find the material interesting and stimulating.

In this work there is a treatment of the topics usually found in first courses in logic. There also are supplementary materials that can help either to motivate interest in the subject or to show different ways of applying logic in language analysis, in scientific inquiry, in decision making, and in critical common sense. One assumption I have made is that most students studying this material will not take additional work in logic. Yet I also have sought to provide the fundamentals needed for further work either in logic or in philosophy for students who wish to take other courses in these subjects.

This work is a complete revision of the first edition. I have reorganized and rewritten most of the sections. There are four new chapters dealing with meaning and language, analyzing arguments, logic and moral issues, and arguments and policy making. I have omitted four chapters from the previous edition and I have condensed some of this material and placed it in other chapters. Many examples found in the exercises of the original edition are in this revised edition, but I have both changed and added to some of these exercises.

My reason for such extensive revision of this material is that I believed it would improve the quality of the work. It also would add to the ease with which some students could learn this material.

There is more material in this work than classes are likely to cover in a semester course. I have sought to organize the material throughout the work with a view to allowing for flexibility in the way a teacher presents different topics. In completing a three-hour course there will be a need to skip some of the sections or chapters. It is possible to study most of the chapters in the divisions on informal logic and on the logic of induction independently of the others.

One approach could present the material in the first nine chapters and then proceed to the section on the logic of induction. The last chapter on challenging arguments and on constructing them provides a review of the work.

Another approach could study Chapters 1 and 6 and proceed to Chapters 10, 11, and 12, omitting traditional logic. However, in this approach it may be desirable in some cases to review the sections on categorical statements in Sections 7.1 and 8.2 and on the dilemma in Section 9.6. It is also possible to use other combinations of chapters in the first and third divisions.

There are good reasons for studying the logic of truth functions and the logic of quantification at the beginning of the course. By following this procedure it is possible to analyze the other materials in a more rigorous manner. My reasons for delaying treatment of this material are various. Many logic classes omit some of this material. Likewise, some teachers prefer to cover such material after a class has developed interest in the subject matter, has some sense of need for the more formal approach in dealing with logic, and has some feeling of having made progress in dealing with the other materials. But views on the methods best suited to attain the objectives of a basic course in logic will vary.

There is no claim for innovative contribution to the theory of logic in presenting this work on this level. I have sought in the first and third divisions to justify the presentation of the materials around a context approach to issues related to the development and use of logical techniques.

Similarly to other authors in this area I am indebted to many writers who have worked on the topics treated in this work. In the division on language these sources include Ludwig Wittgenstein and John L. Austin. In the division on deductive logic, they include the works of Aristotle, George Boole, Gottlob Frege, Bertrand Russell, A. N. Whitehead, and W. V. Quine. The chapter treating the logic of quantification uses techniques developed in the tradition of natural deduction.

In the division on inductive logic the writings of Carl S. Hempel, Ernest Nagel, and Karl R. Popper, along with others, have had an influence in my development of the material. Philosophers such as W. David Ross and Arthur E. Murphy have influenced my approach in the section on logic and moral issues. Writers such as C. I. Lewis, Stephen Pepper, and David L. Miller, along with others, have contributed to my general approach to philosophical issues.

In the preparation of this edition I am indebted to my colleagues Robert

M. Baird, William F. Cooper, and Elmer H. Duncan, who have read chapters of drafts of this work and made suggestions for its improvement. I likewise am indebted to some of my family for their assistance. Barbara E. (Sally) Kilgore helped extensively in writing the final drafts for the chapter on Statistics. She also made helpful suggestions on the chapter on arguments and policies. Carol Isensee Kilgore and Frank J. Kilgore helped in reading some chapters on the logic of induction. I also am grateful to students who read portions of the final drafts and who made suggestions about improvements of this work. In addition I acknowledge the help of my assistant, Marilyn R. Ender, who helped to type the manuscript.

The publishers, Holt, Rinehart and Winston, gave excellent assistance in various stages of this work. The comments and criticisms of at least seven reviewers provided by the publishers who read drafts of this edition have been quite helpful. These reviewers are Robert Ackermann (University of Massachusetts), Bruce W. Hauptli (Florida International University), Jerry Henson (Eastfield College), Raymond Lyons (San Bernardino Valley College), James D. McCarthy (San Antonio College), Richard L. Oliver (San Antonio College), and John Richards (University of Georgia). In no way are any of these reviewers responsible for any shortcomings found in this work.

I also wish to thank the editors of the *National Geographic Magazine* and of the *Editor and Publisher* for permission to quote material from their publications. Many other sources have been used as a basis for illustrative materials. *Science News* was a valuable source of information in providing illustrations related to contemporary use of scientific methods.

I remain indebted to Mrs. Eugenia Rayzor and to her late husband J. Newton Rayzor, Sr., for support that made possible the preparation of the first edition. Likewise, a sabbatical provided by Baylor University made possible, in part, my having time to make many of the extensive revisions found in this second edition.

Waco, Texas   W. J. K.

CONTENTS

PART II: DEDUCTIVE LOGIC   115

PART I

INFORMAL LOGIC

CHAPTER 1

INTRODUCTION

argument = prem + concl

1.1 WHAT ARE ARGUMENTS?

The subject of this work is arguments, which seek to show that one has rational grounds to justify a conclusion. To provide rational grounds for an argument we need evidence. In an argument we present evidence in the form of statements. We seek to show that such evidence justifies our accepting another statement, which is a conclusion.

Let us look at some statements. What would count as evidence to justify our making such statements? That is, how would we go about giving evidence, in a stated context, in support of each of these statements as a conclusion to an argument?

The door is locked.

The football field is in good shape.

The car is a good buy.

The Cuba policy needs to be changed.

In each of these cases we need to know something about the conditions that have some relevance as evidence. How can we determine if a door is locked? How do we tell if a football field is in good shape? What do we look for when buying a good car? What is the Cuba policy? How do we determine if a policy is good?

Let us look at a different set of statements that can occur as parts of arguments. Evidence to support a judgment about the truth of these statements is difficult to identify. We are making no claim that these statements are true. But what are some of the kinds of evidence that we would look for if we wanted to determine if they are true?

That is, the beginning of philosophy is this:
  the being sensible of the disagreement of men with each other;
  an inquiry into the cause of this disagreement
  and a disapprobation and distrust of what merely seems;
  a careful examination into what seems, whether it seems rightly;
  and the discovery of some rule which shall serve like a balance, for the determination of weights; like a square for distinguishing straight and crooked.

(*Epictetus*, c. A.D. 60)

The passions that incline men to peace are fear of death, a desire of such things as are necessary to commodious living, and a hope by their industry to obtain them.

(*Thomas Hobbes*, 1588-1679)

Virtue, then, is a habit or trained faculty of choice, the characteristic of which lies in moderation or observance of the mean relative to the persons concerned, as determined by reason, that is, by the reason by which the prudent man would determine it.

(*Aristotle*, 384-322 B.C.)

Words are only the breaths of the voice.

(*Roscellin*, c. 1050-1120)

A wise sentence shall be rejected when it comes out of a fool's mouth; for he will not speak it in due season.

(*Jesus Sirach*, c. 200 B.C.)

A virtue which perfects the will, as charity or justice, also causes one to make good use of speculative habits.

(*Thomas Aquinas*, 1225-1274)

Whatever is the object of any man's appetite or desire, that it is which he for his part calls "good"; and the object of his hate and aversion, "evil"; and of his contempt "vile." For these words of good, evil, and contemptible are ever used with relation to the person that uses them.

(*Thomas Hobbes*, 1588-1679)

Now the law of nature is so unalterable that it cannot be changed even by God himself. For although the power of God is infinite, yet there are some things to which it does not extend. Because the things so expressed would have no true meaning, but imply a contradiction. Thus two and two must make four, nor is it possible to be otherwise; nor, again, can what is intrinsically evil not be evil.

(*Hugo Grotius*, 1583-1645)

To point out the evidence for or against these claims would require an extensive discussion that is beyond our immediate purpose. But we are at least alerted to the need to search for reasons to back up a claim in an argument.

Any statement we make can become a conclusion of an argument, if someone asks for our reasons for accepting the statement, and then we proceed to state those reasons. Mary tells her roommate, "It is time to go to class." The roommate asks, "Why?" Mary can reply, "The class meets in fifteen minutes and it takes almost fifteen minutes to get to the class-room." Most arguments are not so simple. And we have to make many distinctions. John says, "Prices are going up." George asks, "Why?" John replies, "Well, wholesale prices are going up, wages are going up, the costs of services are going up, and we are not doing enough to stop inflation." We have an argument. We shall be interested in finding out if it is a good one.

The arguments above are not complete. They assume a context. More-over, we might claim that the statements giving the evidence are false or that they are not relevant. Or we might claim that the conclusion does not follow from the evidence.

Someone can claim that we are not showing good faith. This work is supposed to be about logic and, indeed, it is about logic. But logic, the study of how we make and analyze arguments, provides us with the tools to tell good arguments from poor ones. It studies the reasons we can give for saying that one argument is correct and another one is incorrect.

What do we mean when we talk about "arguments"? There are many different uses of the concept of an argument. And the interest of the logician focuses primarily on one of these uses. Sometimes "argument" denotes a fuss, a hassle, a dispute, or a sharp difference of views. But such usage does not represent the way a logician uses this word. Rather we are inter-ested in the way we can justify a conclusion by evidence. And we expect that other rational persons can judge the logical merit of an argument by the way they find the evidence related to the conclusion.

An argument in logic is a series of statements having two parts. One part is a conclusion. The other part is evidence given to justify the conclu-sion. A specific interest of the logician is the way the different parts of the evidence fit together and relate to the conclusion. We want to know if the way these parts fit together logically justifies the conclusion. Let us look at some examples:

(1) EVIDENCE: If the rate of inflation decreases, interest rates will stabi-lize. The rate of inflation decreases.

CONCLUSION: Hence, interest rates will stabilize.

(2) EVIDENCE: All heads of agencies are persons held accountable for their agencies' practices. The Director of the CIA is the head of an agency.

CONCLUSION: Hence, the Director of the CIA is a person held accountable for that agency's practices.

Are these arguments good? This question has various possible meanings. We could be asking if the statements used in the arguments are true.
If one of these statements is false, then obviously something is wrong with
the argument. In a general way the logician is interested in how we determine whether such statements are true. But determining whether such
statements are true is not his primary task.

When we ask if the arguments above are good, we could be asking
whether they are fitting for the occasion where they are used. Will they do
the job that the speaker wants done when she makes the argument? Will
they move someone to take action? But the strict interest of the logician is
not in how fitting an argument is in persuading people to act.

When he asks if the arguments above are good, the logician is primarily
interested in the way the parts fit together to justify the conclusion. We are
talking about parts in a loose way. Exactly what parts in the arguments
above do we mean? By letting capital letters like A, B, and C stand for
some words in the above cases we find these schemes.

(3)   If A, then B.
                 A.
                 Hence, B.

(4)   All C is D.
                 All E is C.
                 Hence, all E is D.

The parts of the argument consist of the letters A and B in the first
scheme and C, D, and E in the second. "If . . . then ———" is another
part of the first argument. And "All . . . is ———" is a part in each instance
in which it occurs in the second argument. "If . . . then ———," "all" and
"is" in the above cases also show us how other parts fit together. That is,
their job is to help connect the parts of the argument.

The way these parts fit together and the order in which they occur can
loosely be called the *form* of these arguments. The strict job of the logician
is to determine if such forms yield valid arguments. For reasons that we
shall go into later, the above forms do yield valid arguments. It should come
as no surprise that a basic interest of the logician is in the logical evidence
presented in arguments.

Logical evidence refers to two factors about the way the evidence in
an argument relates to the conclusion. One factor is an analysis of the parts
of the argument's statements. The second factor is an analysis of the way
the parts of these statements fit together in the total argument. We also can
refer to this second factor as the analysis of the form of the argument as a

whole. We shall be dealing with the forms of argument in many sections of this work. And the notion of the form of an argument should become clearer as we proceed.

1.2 WHAT DO WE STUDY IN LOGIC?

What is logic? We use this term in a strict sense and not in its broader popular meaning. In ordinary language one may refer to a "logical plan," a "logical step," a "logical idea," or a "logical person." In such cases logic means roughly "workable," "well-thought-out," "well-grounded," or "reasonable." Such uses are in contrast to "a poorly constructed plan," "a rash step," "an unclear idea," or "a prejudiced person." However, we shall not develop these uses of "logic" in this work.

Logic is an analysis and evaluation of the ways of using evidence to derive correct conclusions. We develop and analyze those argument forms that yield correct conclusions. We distinguish a correct form of argument from an incorrect one. If someone claims the form of an argument is correct, the logician is interested in identifying the logical evidence to support that claim. If someone holds that the form of an argument is incorrect, the logician's task is to identify the reason that the form is incorrect. In this work we shall develop ways to identify and make correct arguments. But in a broader sense we shall be examining related areas that bear upon our interest in deriving sound conclusions.

Sometimes logic is referred to as the art of reasoning. If we want to call logic an art, then we are talking more about the skill one employs in making arguments than about a strict analysis of the form of an argument. Likewise, we need to restrict the meaning of "reasoning" more to what the logician is doing. Reasoning can refer to many things. It may mean our explanation of why we take certain actions. Or it can refer to our explanation of the social context in which someone accepts certain beliefs. But the logician's strict interest is not in reasoning in that sense. We are interested in reasoning as it relates to making correct arguments and to knowing why other arguments are incorrect.

In this work, we shall consider various types of arguments. Part I will examine further how to identify the basic types of arguments and clarify some disputes. We shall look at some incorrect arguments whose fault is a lack of relevance between the conclusion and the evidence given in its support. Some expressions that are used in logic will be clarified. We shall seek to determine how we go about finding out what words, phrases, and statements mean when they occur as parts of arguments. Some basic uses of language will be explored. Finally we shall study different ways to clarify what words mean by use of definitions.

In Part II the focus will be on deductive arguments. Categorical statements and their use in arguments will come under analysis. Also, we shall look at some types of mediate inference in which only one statement provides evidence for justifying another statement. The use of compound statements will be explained, as well as the way we can use them in making arguments. We shall discuss a way to combine various types of arguments into a system.

Part III will be devoted to inductive arguments—how one uses them in critical common sense and in science. We shall study the use of evidence to confirm hypotheses and to support sound decisions. There will be discussion of what a cause is and how to identify one. The notion of probability will be examined, both as it relates to statements and to events. The statistical use of arguments will be considered, as will the way arguments are used in advancing claims about moral issues and policy decisions. In the final chapter we review how to make good arguments and to refute others.

In this chapter we have seen that logic is about arguments. We opened a discussion about argument forms. In the next chapter we shall continue our discussion about what arguments are.

EXERCISES

Make some suggestions about what one might look for as evidence, either that any one of the following statements is true or that any one statement is false. (There are comments on these examples at the end of these exercises.)

1. Professor Beta is a good teacher of math.

2. Miss Jones is an efficient administrator.

3. This TV set is a good buy.

4. Commercial air flight is the safest form of public transportation.

5. A witness testifying against a defendant charged with taking a bribe needs to have the advice of a lawyer while he is on the witness stand.

6. "How selfish soever man be supposed, there are evidently some principles in his nature which interest him in the fortunes of others and render their happiness necessary to him, though he derives nothing from it except the pleasure of seeing it."

Adam Smith (1723–1790)

7. "At a certain level of development it [petty industry] brings into being the material agencies for its own dissolution." [A petty industry for Marx in this context refers to situations in which a laborer owns a small piece of property together with the tools needed for making goods which he helps to produce.]

Karl Marx (1818–1883)

8. "I say that democracy can never prove itself beyond cavil, until it founds and luxuriantly grows its own forms of art, poems, schools, theology, displacing all

that exists, or that has been produced anywhere in the past under opposite influences."

Walt Whitman (1819–1892)

9. "The essential characteristic of philosophy, which makes it a study distinct from science, is *criticism*. It examines critically the principles employed in science and in daily life; it searches out any inconsistencies there may be in these principles, and it only accepts them when, as the result of a critical inquiry, no reason for rejecting them has appeared."

Bertrand Russell (1872–1970)

10. "Schools and colleges are not intended to foster genius and to bring it out. Genius is a nuisance, and it is the duty of schools and colleges to abate it by setting genius-traps in its way. They are as the artificial obstructions in a hurdle race, tests of skill and endurance, but in themselves useless. Still, so necessary is it that genius and originality should be abated that, did not academics exist, we should have to invent them."

Samuel Butler (1835–1902)

COMMENTS ON EXERCISES

1. Has knowledge of subject; presents subject in an orderly and interesting way; motivates students to learn and understand material; students learn material, can show relations of basic notions to each other, and in relevant cases are in position to do more advanced work.

2. Plans and organizes in an efficient manner; encourages and motivates others to carry out their jobs; supports good achievements; eliminates waste and inefficiency; relates work to what others in organization are doing; completes successfully work that lies in area of administrative responsibility.

3. Price is competitive; picture and sound are relatively good; upkeep of model is relatively satisfactory; guarantees backed by reliable dealer and company; replacement parts readily available; service readily available with trained technicians at competitive costs; set suitable for location where it is to be placed.

4. Relative accidents per passenger mile; relative seriousness of injuries per passenger mile; likelihood of safely reaching destination per passenger mile in comparison with alternative forms of public transportation; adequate regulations and enforcement to provide basis for expecting continuation of safety features.

5. This is a controverted view. But one can point out that a witness has legal rights that need protection. Ignorance of witness about some phases of the law could place him or her in some kind of jeopardy. Witness may need advice on propriety of some questions or on the need to limit the scope of some questions. One may need advice on a need to divide some questions. Witnesses may incriminate themselves without knowing that they are doing so. But there is a need for the court to know the facts of the case.

The intent of the quotations 6, 7, 8, 9, and 10 is to evoke discussion about examining the meaning of statements and the context in which they occur. No short answer is satisfactory. Some suggestions may be relevant.

6. What is the meaning of man's "nature"? Can generalizations be based upon such vague notions? What assumptions is the author making and what grounds are there for holding to them? For example, is the author assuming some kind of "harmony of interests" or pointing out that "man is a social and political animal"?

7. Does Marx presuppose some "laws of history"? Can such a view be supported? What are some examples and counterexamples of petty industries that fail to survive in an industrialized society? What material agencies do they help to support? For example, do they tend to bring about both competition in providing goods and services and social organizations that recognize their legitimacy? Do such competition and organizations then require that such industries perish?

8. There is need to clarify meaning of "democracy." Are there not some good things, such as common law in some countries, that are the heritage of the past and worthy of preserving (with some flexibility for development)? And are not art, education, and the forms religion takes expressive of many different factors rather than merely an economic or a political factor?

9. One would need to point to past and present philosophers to see what they sought to do and what they actually did. Philosophers have sought rational grounds for advancing and evaluating views on various issues. These include, with acknowledgment to Immanuel Kant, such matters as "'What can one know?''; "What ought one to do?"; "What can one hope?"; and "What can one appreciate?" But there are, of course, significant differences, not only within Western philosophy, but between Western and Eastern philosophy. And these differences relate both to one's view of what philosophy is and to how philosophers are to do their job.

10. We need to recognize the type of discourse in this example as social criticism. The notions of "genius" and "originality" need to be clarified. Are there any conditions that appear essential to their appearance? Or do they tend to appear more frequently under some conditions than others? What appears to be the relation of schools and colleges to these conditions? Is there any uniformity in the way that schools and colleges work such that as a group they never stimulate and they always repress the developing of originality and genius?

CHAPTER **2**

INFORMAL FALLACIES

2.1 INTRODUCTION

In the previous chapter we saw that our basic interest in this work is in arguments. In this chapter we shall look at a group of arguments called informal fallacies.

A fallacy is an error in an argument that results from a flaw in the form of the argument or from a lack of relevance of the evidence to the conclusion. An informal fallacy is an error in argument due to faulty assumptions or to irrelevances occurring in stating the evidence for a conclusion. Informal fallacies occur as a result of errors in the broader context of the argument. Errors in such arguments have other causes than those used strictly to judge the form of a deductive argument. That is, an informal fallacy is a "nonformal" fallacy.

The following examples can help us distinguish between formal fallacies and informal fallacies.

(1) The winner of the conference title will have strong reserves on its football team.
Smoky College will have strong reserves on its football team.
Therefore, Smoky College will be the winner of the conference title. (Invalid formal fallacy)

(2) Since John's family is highly respected in the community, John is highly respected in the community. (Informal fallacy)

In the first example the flaw in reasoning is due to a fault in the form of the argument. Any proposed argument having this form is invalid and has a formal fallacy.

The second example makes a false assumption: that any part of a whole also has the characteristics of the whole. This is an informal fallacy. The basis for the purposed claim is the faulty assumption that characteristics of a whole also apply in the same way to any part of that whole. In informal fallacies the evidence given to justify the conclusion is deficient on such grounds as the use of faulty assumptions, the misuse of language, and other types of irrelevances.

The claim that an argument constitutes an informal fallacy needs to be examined carefully. In a strict sense a logical fallacy has to do with an error in an argument rather than an error in the use of language. A statement may be loaded. It may have obvious double meanings. It may raise improper questions. Such errors in the use of language or in inquiry are logical fallacies only if they relate to a further error in argument. That is, they must have some bearing on a faulty or unjustified claim made in an argument.

Schemes for classifying informal fallacies tend to occur in overlapping groups. An example of one fallacy can also be an instance of other kinds of errors in argument. Moreover, we could extend the list and division of these fallacies beyond what is given in this chapter, or use other schemes to classify them. This discussion is organized under two divisions: informal fallacies of faulty assumptions and informal fallacies of irrelevance.

2.2 FALLACIES OF FAULTY ASSUMPTIONS

In a fallacy of a faulty assumption one presumes some unwarranted conditions in the context of presenting the argument. The evidence stated does not justify the argument. The conclusion has as its basis a faulty assumption on which the argument rests. Consider the following example:

(3)   *Ed:* The strongest motive always is the motive that determines a person's decision to act.
Art: But how do you identify the motive that determines a person's decision to act?
Ed: We identify the motive that determines a person's decision to act as the strongest motive.

In identifying the strongest motive as the motive that determines a person's decision to act and in identifying the motive that determines a person's decision to act as the strongest motive, Ed is not proving anything. It is like saying, "the motive that determines a person's acts is the motive that determines a person's acts." This type of argument is circular and the conclusion depends on a faulty assumption made in stating the argument.

1. Faulty Assumptions and Exceptional Cases

Accident.   General principles or rules can have exceptional or "accidental" cases to which they do not apply. In law the possibility of such exceptions led to the forming of courts of equity. Such courts deal with cases where the use of a legal rule appears harsh, cruel, or unfair. And to apply the legal rule in such cases could result in grossly unfair or inequitable outcomes.

The informal fallacy of *accident* is the use of a general principle in exceptional or accidental cases to which the general principle does not apply. That is, there is the faulty assumption that a general principle covers instances to which it is not applicable. This fallacy occurs in the following examples.

(4) Discrimination on the basis of sex is wrong.
     Therefore, a meeting limited to teenage girls who can be accompanied by an adult woman in order to discuss how to cope with sexual assaults on females is wrong.

(5) A citizen should be allowed to express his own views freely.
     Therefore, he should be permitted to yell "Fire!" in a crowded theater if he chooses to do so.

In these examples we apply principles (with restrictions on their use) to cases which the principles do not cover.

Converse Accident.   The fallacy of converse accident uses an exceptional situation as the basis for making a general rule or principle. In this case we form a general principle on the basis of an accidental state of affairs. This fallacy occurs in the following examples.

(6) Since deceit is permitted in protecting a small girl from being attacked by a mentally deranged man, the use of deceit for the advancement of self-interest is socially acceptable.

(7) Since it is permissible for a student to delay handing in his assignment if he is called home in an emergency, it is permissible for a student to delay handing in an assignment whenever he wishes to do so.

We need to recognize exceptions in such cases as exceptions. They do not constitute a basis for making a general principle to guide actions.

2. Faulty Assumptions about Characteristics of Wholes and Parts

A whole or composite entity such as an orchestra consists of parts or individual entities such as the first violinist. Fallacies in arguments can occur if we assume that we can switch the characteristics applied to parts and wholes.

The Fallacy of Division.   The fallacy of division is an argument based on the mistaken assumption that a characteristic of a whole also applies to its separate parts. Consider the following cases of this fallacy:

(8)   Since Professor Smith is on the faculty of an outstanding department of physics, he is an outstanding professor of physics.

(9)   The Supreme Court practices a strict interpretation of the Constitution. Therefore, Justice Smith, who is a member of this Court, practices a strict interpretation of the Constitution.

The fallacy of division also occurs when the meaning of a word shifts from referring to a group as a whole to referring to any individual member of the group. We can talk about "students," "scientists," or "physicians" as a group or we can talk about a specific person who is a student or a scientist or a physician. The following fallacy of division shifts the meaning of a word from a group as a composite entity to a separate individual in the group as a discrete entity.

(10)   Since professors have supported the rights of students to protect the confidentiality of academic records, Smith, who is a professor, has supported the rights of students to protect the confidentiality of academic records.

As a group professors, lawyers, or bakers may act in one way. But it does not follow that each individual professor, lawyer, or baker also acts in that way.

The Fallacy of Composition.   The fallacy of composition is an argument using the assumption that the characteristics of the parts of a whole also apply to the whole. This fallacy also occurs when we apply the characteristics of an individual member of a group to the group as a whole. Consider the following examples:

(11)   Since the members of the all-star team are the best players of their respective positions in the conference, a team composed of these players would be the best team in the conference.

(12)   Since individual athletes grow too old to compete for new records, athletes as a group will grow too old to compete for new records.

3.   Faulty Assumption of the Point at Issue

Fallacies of faulty assumption of the point at issue have a concealed assumption in the premises which is made explicit in the conclusion. The conclusion in such cases is a statement of something presupposed in the premises but not established by the argument.

Begging the Question (Petitio Principii).   In a general sense, begging the question can refer to any faulty assumption of the point of issue in an argument. In this chapter it will have a more limited meaning. It refers to arguments whose premises have an unexpressed assumption and a conclusion that makes this assumption explicit. To claim that a person is naive and to offer as evidence that he is liberal, with the assumption that being a liberal is sufficient grounds to call a person "naive," is to beg the question. Begging the question can occur even though the technical form of the argument does not violate any formal rule of inference. Consider a simplified form of an argument that could be advanced where the first premise expresses an assumption of the point that needs to be proven in the argument:

(13)   All abnormal behavior is a result of guilt feelings.
John's behavior is abnormal.
Thus, John's behavior is a result of guilt feelings.

In this argument the premise, "All abnormal behavior is a result of guilt feelings," not only is controversial and an assumption but it would be rejected by many psychologists. The conclusion merely makes explicit what is implicit in the assumption. Yet to claim that this type of argument commits the fallacy of begging the question does not provide a basis for holding that the proposed conclusion is false. But it does emphasize that we have not justified the conclusion in this case by satisfactory evidence, since one of the premises is a questionable assumption.

Arguing in a Circle.   The fallacy of arguing in a circle is a special case of the fallacy of begging the question; it is listed separately here for emphasis. A premise is used as evidence to establish a conclusion and this conclusion is used as evidence to establish the original premise. Arguing in a circle has the form, "A is true because B is true, and B is true because A is true." Consider the proposed argument:

(14)   Democracy is desirable because it promotes freedom of inquiry. But why is freedom of inquiry desirable? It is desirable because it promotes democracy.

Arguing in a circle is also called circular reasoning. It may be more complex than the form given above: "A is true because B is true. B is true because C is true. Thus, C is true because A is true."

Complex Question.   A complex question is posed in such a way as to assume certain states of affairs. Any answer to the question assumes the acceptance of the states of affairs. In answering the question, "Have you stopped telling lies?" you would be accepting the assumption that you have been telling lies. A complex question is not strictly a fallacy of argument. Rather it represents a defective or improper manner of pursuing an investigation.

A leading question can be a special case of a complex question. However, in addition to being loaded with an assumption, a leading question also suggests or "plants" a proposed answer. The question, "You turned out of your traffic lane only after you saw that an accident could not be avoided, did you not?" suggests the answer, "Yes, I did." A frequent scene in TV court cases has one attorney protesting to the judge that the other attorney is "leading the witness." Judges rule complex questions out of order when an attorney uses them in examining a witness in court.

4.   Faulty Assumptions in Interpreting Language

A discussion of the many types of faulty assumptions made in interpreting language requires a more extended treatment than is possible within the scope of this section. We could discuss the following types simply as informal fallacies in the use of language. But they make faulty assumptions regarding language use and are included in this section for reasons of convenience. We shall focus our attention on five informal fallacies of this type.

The Fallacy of Equivocation.   Equivocation is the use of a word or phrase in a given context with the shifting of the meaning of the word from one occurrence to another. In informative discourse equivocation is a misuse of language. A fallacy of equivocation occurs if one attempts to justify a faulty conclusion by the shift in meaning of an expression in a given context. Consider the following argument:

(15)   Everything subject to law is subject to a lawgiver.
The natural order is subject to law.
Therefore, the natural order is subject to a lawgiver.

In this argument "law" is used in two different senses. In the first case it refers to statutory "law." In the second it refers to a natural or statistical uniformity that provides a basis for prediction and control of events in the natural order. One reaches the faulty conclusion by blurring these different meanings of "law."

In the example above a formal fallacy also occurs in the use of the phrase "subject to law." It is a four-term fallacy to be discussed under the rules of the categorical syllogism.

The example about the shift in the meaning of "professor" in an earlier part of this chapter also can be called "equivocation."

In ordinary discourse, some words lend themselves readily to shifts in meaning. Expressions used in the same context in figurative and nonfigurative senses, or moral and nonmoral ones, are especially subject to this error.

The Fallacy of Simple Ambiguity. A sentence is ambiguous if it can have more than one meaning in a given context. The fallacy of simple ambiguity is to justify a faulty conclusion by the use of a statement having more than one possible meaning. However, in this case the ambiguity does not have as its source errors of grammar or of punctuation. The following statement is an example of this fallacy:

(16)   We cannot expect John to cooperate in this project since he said, "Nothing will deter me from cooperating with you."

The fallacy of simple ambiguity results from an effort to justify a conclusion by interpreting an ambiguous sentence in a manner not supported by the context. In some cases the context does not provide a basis for clarifying a statement. An interpretation of the statement in a manner consistent with the context does not commit this fallacy. Other persons with different views, still can raise questions about the interpretation. Usually the fallacy of simple ambiguity occurs only if the faulty interpretation is either deliberate or careless. (We shall analyze ambiguity in greater detail after we have made further distinctions about word meanings.)

The Fallacy of Amphiboly. A special case of a fallacy of ambiguity is the fallacy of amphiboly. A sentence is amphibolous if it is ambiguous as a result of errors of grammar or punctuation. The fallacy of amphiboly occurs if a faulty conclusion is due to an ambiguity based on errors of syntax or punctuation of a sentence. An example of this fallacy is the following:

(17)   No cat has nine tails.
       Any cat has one more tail than no cat.
       Therefore, any cat has ten tails.

The erroneous conclusion is a deliberate distortion of the meaning of the statements presented as evidence in the argument.

The Fallacy of Accent.   The fallacy of accent occurs by placing improper emphasis upon a word, a phrase, or a sentence and using this distorted emphasis to make a faulty conclusion. One may commit this fallacy by stressing a word or phrase, by using italics or boldface type, by underlining, by inflection of the voice, or by taking a statement out of context ("excerpt lifting").

The fallacy of accent occurs in the following examples. A theme was returned to a student with the notation, "Some parts of this theme are good and other parts interesting. The interesting parts are inaccurate and the good parts were copied." The student commented to his classmates, "The grader wrote that my theme was 'good' and 'interesting.' " A newspaper headline declares, "NATIONAL EMERGENCY ARISES." The accompanying story recounts an interview with a congressman who stated, "If inflation is not held in check, a national emergency can arise." The statement, "You look well" reads with apparently a clear meaning. However, pausing after saying "look" and using different vocal inflections in saying "well" can give different meanings to the sentence when it is spoken aloud. Mere inflections or pauses change the meaning and thus can result in an error in argument.

The Fallacy of Ambiguity of Significance.   Ambiguity of significance occurs in the making of a faulty conclusion when relevant factors are ignored within the broader context of a statement. A speaker could argue as follows:

(18)   A period of higher unemployment is developing, since a .5 percent increase in the rate of unemployment occurred in June.

If a 1 percent decline in employment during June were customary, a decline of .5 percent represents a relative increase rather than a relative decline in employment rate. Evidence not only is insufficient to support the proposed claim, but use of other data needed for the argument may justify an opposing conclusion.

We could discuss other fallacies that use faulty assumptions. Some of these would overlap with the informal fallacies already presented; some are discussed elsewhere in this work; and others would unduly extend this discussion. Such fallacies include arguments based on evidence that is too restricted (hasty generalization), false cause, false analogies, limiting choices only to one of two opposite and extreme options, and contradictory assumptions. We also could discuss other fallacies, such as presenting only those cases supportive of a favored view (special pleading or card-stacking), confusing labels with characteristics of individuals or movements (name-tagging), and ignoring the merits of an argument by discrediting the source advancing the argument (poisoning the wells).

The following suggestions can be helpful in identifying or classifying informal fallacies:

1. A given example can represent several different informal fallacies.

2. Find the proposed conclusion of the argument.

3. Examine the evidence given as statements in support of the conclusion.

4. Seek to determine the general principle whose misuse accounts best for the error in the argument in that context. (Is a faulty assumption present? What kind of faulty assumption is it?)

5. Make as specific identification of the informal fallacy as possible (for example, arguing in a circle).

EXERCISES

A. Identify the informal fallacies or misuse of language in the following examples. (Answers to every other example are at the back of this work.)

   1. Since the government is permitted to exercise forms of censorship during times of war, it is permissible for the government to exercise censorship during any national emergency. *Converse acc.*
   2. Since there was a 4 percent drop in enrollment during the second semester, there must be a decline in enrollment in the college. *ambig signif*
   3. Jan alone cannot walk in the park at night. *amphiboly*
   4. Each member of the committee on civic improvement is a hard-working person; therefore, we can be assured that the committee on civic improvement is a hard-working committee. *composition*
   5. The natives here must be barbarians, since John heard one of them say that as they were eating a friend the nephew of their chief came in. *amphiboly*
   6. A person is entitled to use what is his own property. This automobile is the property of John's uncle, who is drunk. Therefore, John's uncle is entitled to the use and possession of the automobile now. *accident*
   7. "You must accept my belief in the freedom of speech, since freedom of speech is the cornerstone of liberal principles. But why should one accept liberal principles? One should accept liberal principles because this assures freedom of speech." *Circular*
   8. Any student has the right of a citizen. Students have an obligation to do the right thing. Citizens have a right to protest the actions of government. Therefore, students have an obligation to criticize the actions of government. *equivocation*
   9. The officer put the case of liquor in his car as evidence and opened the case.
   10. Since this rope is strong, each piece of twine in the rope is strong. *division*
   11. Did not Emerson say, "A foolish consistency is the hobgoblin of little minds, little statesmen, and little divines"? Therefore, you should not be concerned if all my statements are not consistent. *accent*
   12. Professor Jones must be a good man since he is a good teacher. *equiv.*
   13. Since a mother survives on very little sleep to take care of a sick child, she can be expected to survive at any time on very little sleep. *conv. acc.*

14. A crumb is better than nothing. Nothing is better than strawberry shortcake. Therefore, a crumb is better than strawberry shortcake. *amphib*

15. Any great musical composition is beautiful because if it isn't beautiful, then it is not a great musical composition. *simple ambig*

16. Since attorneys are professional persons concerned with the defense of human rights, Attorney Smith is a professional person concerned with the defense of human rights. *division*

17. Since the officer said that no more leaves would be given, we can expect a leave next weekend, since we have been getting leaves on weekends in the past. *conv acc*

18. Since each premise in this argument is relevant, we can expect the argument to be relevant. *comp*

19. Ignorance is bliss. Why? Is the saying not true that "if ignorance is bliss then it is foolish to be wise"? *circular*

20. Have you decided to begin to pay attention in class? *complex q*

B. Identify any words or expressions used equivocally in the following statements:
   1. Any free man is free to do as he pleases.
   2. Not all is well that ends well.
   3. Some poor workers come from poor families.
   4. Anything that is according to nature is right. "An eye for an eye and a tooth for a tooth" is according to nature. Therefore, "an eye for an eye and a tooth for a tooth" is right.
   5. Honesty is the best policy. This is the best policy. Therefore, it is honest.
   6. The best things come to those who wait. Death comes to those who wait. Therefore, death is the best thing.
   7. Business is business.
   8. Any profitable undertaking increases income. Studying logic is profitable. Therefore, studying logic increases income.

2.3 FALLACIES OF RELEVANCE

Fallacies of relevance are arguments that are faulty because of some failure of the evidence to bear directly on the conclusion with sufficient grounds to establish the conclusion. That is, fallacies of relevance are faulty arguments in which the evidence given to establish a claim is lacking some essential factor needed to justify the claim. These fallacies are in opposition to the principle of relevance, which holds that the evidence given to support a conclusion needs to provide essential and sufficient grounds to justify the conclusion the argument is making.

In a broad sense many of the informal fallacies already discussed in this chapter are also types of fallacies of relevance. The fallacies dealt with in this section represent a cluster of faulty arguments that by tradition have fallen under the heading of "fallacies of relevance." But there is some sense of "irrelevance" applicable to any informal fallacy.

Fallacies of relevance are not always obvious. New views or added information can affect our judgments about the relevance of evidence given in support of a conclusion.

Some irrelevances in arguments with informal fallacies are internal and others are external. If the irrelevance is internal to the argument, the evidence lacks some point needed to complete the proof of an argument. If the irrelevance is external to the argument, the evidence is "beside the point at issue," and a conclusion other than the one given can be suggested. We shall discuss two general types of irrelevance later in this chapter. The first, the fallacy of *ignoratio elenchi* ("ignoring or missing the point at issue"), deals with external irrelevance. The second, the fallacy of *non sequitur* ("it does not follow" or jumping to a conclusion), deals with internal irrelevance. These names are usually reserved for fallacies whose contexts are developed at some length. No hard and fast line can be drawn in all cases with regard to the internal or external character of the irrelevance.

1.   Fallacies of Misuse of Appeal to Emotions

The misuse of appeal to emotion occurs if an argument appeals to emotion as a substitute for evidence, or as a means of distracting attention from inadequate evidence or of making evidence appear more significant than it actually is.

We do not claim here that expression of emotion is a logical fault. We find such expression in healthy social interaction, in great works of literature, and in other art forms. We judge these cases by standards fitting for such situations. The use of emotion to motivate us to do something is not only a normal action; we accept it as proper in some cases. We respect emotions in cases where its expression has a basis in personal relations or events, reflects honestly the feeling of the persons involved, and is fitting in degree and manner. Even David Hume claimed that nothing great is achieved without passion.

The fallacy of the misuse of emotion occurs with cases of avoiding, replacing, or distorting the significance of evidence in advancing a conclusion of an argument. Feeling replaces evidence as a basis for supporting a claim. The appeal to emotion can be reassuring in some forms of persuasive speech, but in justifying arguments it is not a substitute for evidence. An example of the misuse of emotion is evident in an anecdote of a janitor who found the trial notes of an attorney. At one point in the summary outline was the notation, "The case is weak here; appeal to the sympathies and biases of the jury."

Three types of fallacies of misuse of appeals to emotion can be singled out for emphasis.

The Appeal to Pity (Argumentum ad Misericordiam).   The appeal to pity attempts to elicit the emotional response of sympathy in an audience, so that they will accept a conclusion. Consider the example:

> (19)   John deserves a ''B'' in this class since his parents have made great sacrifices to send him to college and he will not gain admission into a good professional school if he receives a lower grade.

Appeal to pity can be more indirect. For example, during his final argument a lawyer can find occasion to relate to a jury an incident in which a car runs over a small boy's dog. Or a speaker seeking to secure acceptance of his views can digress to tell an emotional story about his mother's hardships in caring for her children.

The fallacy of appeal to pity rests on the replacement of relevant evidence for a conclusion by a bid for the sympathy of an audience. We recognize sympathy as an appropriate emotional response under proper circumstances, and it can provide motivation for praiseworthy acts. But it does not count as a rational substitute for evidence in making an argument.

Appeal to Laughter.   Humor is an excellent means of securing the attention of an audience. Anyone who is active in public affairs finds the use of humor an effective means of gaining acceptance. The art of telling a humorous story is a skill mastered by many successful politicans, executives, salesmen, and clergymen. Humor can help relieve tensions at a critical point of a discussion. And it can help to focus attention on issues of serious moment. For example, in one of his fireside chats Franklin D. Roosevelt once compared the position of his opponents to that of a group who believed that ''the tail wags the dog.''

Use of humor also has another side. It can be misused to introduce irrelevant matters into an argument. It also can divert attention from basic issues and can stifle serious thought and analysis. The use of humor in such cases becomes a misuse of the appeal to emotions. A laugh rather than a sound argument becomes the basis for making a claim.

Appeal to the Gallery (Argumentum ad Populum).   Experienced speakers usually seek a way to persuade a lay audience to relate to them. They want their audience to be aware of a mutual sharing of some common interests, concerns, and experiences. They are aware that if they do not achieve this sense of a common bond, many persons in the audience will ''turn them off.'' Achieving this sense of a common bond is a skill, one that can be abused. It is the abuse of appealing to the gallery that will concern us in this discussion.

An appeal to the gallery seeks acceptance of a claim through the emotional support of values, traditions, interests, prejudices, or provincial concerns shared widely by members of an audience. In making this appeal the speaker frequently uses the talk and clichés that are common to the discourse of the group. A speaker at a political rally in a blighted neighborhood might seek to secure approval of his program not by offering evidence in its support, but by appealing to the prejudices against "big business" or "vested interests" or "Wall Street." A speaker at a luncheon for a business club might dwell on his opposition to government control of business to secure support for his position on wildlife conservation. Likewise, a speaker to a labor group might condemn sweatshops and scabs in order to win support for his views on agricultural reform. A candidate for public office might stress the hardships she had in getting an education as a basis for persuading the audience to accept the claim that she is the most qualified candidate to represent them in Congress.

2.   Fallacies Misusing Appeals to Authority
(*Argumentum ad Verecundiam*)

To use the views of authorities as evidence to support a conclusion is not in itself a fallacy of argument. The views of qualified authorities can count as good evidence in proper settings. Problems do emerge if the point at issue is in dispute among different competent authorities. In such cases we may need to appeal to original data. In basic research we do not accept an appeal to an authority relative to a point at issue as a proper way to resolve a dispute.

Fallacies based on misusing appeals to authority use as supporting evidence the statements of a source that is not qualified or is not germane to deal with the point at issue. Such sources can be well-known persons or generally held beliefs. The statements of a physician about matters of health, of an attorney about law, or of an economist about finance can be relevant in an argument dealing with these areas. However, the use of a physician's statements to support a conclusion regarding astronomy is a fallacy of misuse of authority (assuming such a physician has achieved recognized professional competence only in medicine). If persons have achieved competence in the field to which reference is made, the appeal is to an authority on astronomy who is also a physician, an authority in economics who is also a lawyer, or a scientist who is also a historian.

For purposes of analysis we can identify three major types of the fallacies misusing appeals to authority. The first is the *appeal to misplaced authority*. In this case the views of an authority in one field are given as evidence on a point at issue in another subject area, for which the alleged authority has no particular competence. Consider the following argument:

(20)   We need to support the formation of a common market among the countries of Latin America because the great nuclear scientist, Juan Fulano, stated that this would help strengthen the economy of these countries.

Appeal to celebrity is a second kind of fallacy of the misuse of appeal to authority. This consists in the proposed settlement of a point at issue in an argument by reference to a well-known or popular public figure, relying upon his fame or popularity rather than his competence on any given subject matter. Some testimonials in TV commercials and other advertising are further examples of this type of fallacy. Consider the following example:

> (21)   Flying saucers carrying creatures from outer space have landed in this country because the great TV star, John Doe, reported in an interview that this was a fact.

Appeal to consensus is a third kind of misuse of appeal to authority. This appeal seeks to resolve a point at issue in an argument by introducing evidence based on an alleged general belief of mankind. The following argument might be made:

> (22)   Man must be immortal because this belief has tended to be present in such large numbers of societies in widely divergent conditions over such a long span of history.

A widespread belief may or may not be well supported by basic evidence. The point at issue is not whether there is a consensus about a view but rather whether there is solid evidence to support the claim.

3.   The Appeal to Force (*Argumentum ad Baculum*)

The *argumentum ad baculum,* or the appeal to force, substitutes force or the threat of its use for rational evidence in the support of a claim. The fallacy of appeal to force takes the form "If you do not accept this claim, then certain misfortunes will come your way." Consider the example given below:

> (23)   You should accept the view that our protection society can strengthen the sales of your product. Otherwise you might find that your machinery has been damaged and that your labor troubles increase.

Although the appeal to force may be effective in achieving a limited goal, it abandons rational procedures in gaining an objective. In some instances this kind of appeal may be successfully opposed by rational argument. Rather than might making right, the threat of the use of power can spark a further strife and even violence.

4.   The Appeal to the Man (*Argumentum ad Hominem*)

The fallacy of the appeal to the man discredits one claim and advances another by verbal attacks on the character, reputation, or social situations of the person proposing the original claims. An *ad hominem* argument shifts the point at issue from evidence related to the claim of the argument to the person making it. The effort is made to have one claim rejected by impugning the character or situation of the person making the claim.

Two forms of *ad hominem* arguments are usually made: the abusive and the circumstantial. The abusive *ad hominem* seeks to discredit the person proposing an argument by an attack upon his character. Charges that the other person lies, deceives, cheats may be advanced. One may accuse another of guilt by association by charging that she is a friend of hoodlums or by pointing to corrupt actions taken by her relatives or close associates. Consider the following abusive *ad hominem* arguments:

(24)   My opponent's view that we should increase taxes is wrong, since he gave support to Senator Doe who was a party in a scandal over improper use of funds raised at testimonial dinners.

(25)   One cannot accept the statement of this witness as reliable, since as a student he was accused of cheating and it was widely held that some of his friends had other persons write their term papers for them.

Abusive *ad hominem* appeals also can attempt to direct social prejudice against the person advancing an opposing argument. [Attack character]

(26)   The views of Mr. Smith cannot be sound, since he sought refuge in Canada rather than serve as a draftee in the war in Vietnam.

Circumstantial *ad hominem* arguments try to discredit the person advancing an argument by charging that he participates in some situation or movement for reasons based on self-interest concerns. The reason given to discredit the evidence is that the persons holding to these views are expressing the kinds of opinions one expects to find in someone with the speaker's social or professional background. Consider the following argument: [Attack situation]

(27)   The recommendations of Attorney Smith to file suit for damages in this case are unsound, since he is a lawyer and lawyers are expected to recommend that suits be filed when persons claim to have been injured by the action of another party.

A special case of a circumstantial *ad hominem* argument is the *tu quoque* (you also or you are another one) or appeal to similar conditions. This attack seeks to discredit views of an opposing party by charging that the opposing party does the kind of thing he claims to be against or that he has advocated the same views that he is now rejecting. The following case illustrates the *tu quoque* attack:

(28)   You cannot believe what you say in favor of desegregating housing, since you live in a neighborhood where there is *de facto* segregated housing.

Some arguments that bring in evidence relevant to the character or situation of a person advancing a claim may not constitute a fallacy of relevance. If a person is shown to distort and misrepresent evidence habitually, his testimony can be discredited. The appeal to similar circumstances can show the bad faith or hypocrisy of another party. However, there is need to justify a given charge by evidence rather than merely by name calling. The relevance of the charges to the issue at hand is a critical factor in determining the merits of such charges. It is the unusual case if such an attack does not introduce matters irrelevant to the point at issue.

5.   The Appeal to Ignorance (*Argumentum ad Ignoratiam*)

The fallacy of appeal to ignorance uses the false assumption that if one cannot show that the claim of an argument is false, then one can accept the claim as true. It has the form "*P* is true because you are unable to show convincingly that *P* is false." Consider the following example:

> (29)   Since you cannot disprove that there are flying saucers, you should accept as reliable the reports of those claiming to have seen such objects.

A fault with arguments using appeals to ignorance is that the same kind of argument can be used to establish opposing views. Consider a reply to one of the above arguments:

> (30)   Since you cannot prove that there are flying saucers, you should agree that there are no objects of this kind.

Furthermore, cases in which a party has not established a given conclusion do not provide evidence that the opposing view is worthy of acceptance. What we have is only an unjustified claim.

Are legal procedures which assume a defendant innocent until he is proven guilty instances of appeal to ignorance? Legal guilt requires proof in our judicial system. The prosecution has the burden to show that the accused is guilty "beyond a reasonable doubt." The legal status of the accused remains what it was prior to the accusation unless legal proof and court action change the status to guilty. Prior to such action the defendant remains legally innocent. Both "guilt" and "innocence" in this case have technical meanings. They do not refer merely to specific actions of the accused but rather to an official action taken by a court. The accused becomes legally guilty only after proper court action declares her to be such. Before such court action can occur, the state through its public advocate must prove that the accused is guilty beyond reasonable doubt by using the rules of evidence accepted in a court of law. Unless the state provides such evidence, or the accused pleads guilty in a manner acceptable to the courts, no change occurs in the legal status of the defendant.

6.   The Fallacy of Missing the Point at Issue (*Ignoratio Elenchi*)

The fallacy of missing the point at issue is an example of an external irrelevance in an argument. The evidence of the argument supports a claim other than the issue at hand. The Latin name for this fallacy, *ignoratio elenchi*, simply means "ignoring the point at issue."

Suppose the issue at hand is the claim that price ceilings should be placed on all products. A speaker could argue that inflation is a terrible burden on retired persons and on anyone else with a fixed income. He also might tell about several families suffering from extreme hardship as a result of having to pay more for goods, without the means to increase their income to secure these goods.

What the speaker says can be true. But what conclusion does it establish? It can provide a basis for holding that some measures are needed to help control inflation. However, it does not justify the claim that price controls should be initiated by Congress.

Consider another case in which one makes the claim, "Any high school graduate should be admitted to any university supported by taxes in his state." A speaker then makes a case for the need both for well-educated citizens and for equal opportunities for all citizens. Such evidence can support a policy that provides for additional college or vocational training for qualified graduates of high schools. But it does not justify the claim that any high school graduate, regardless of grades and national test scores, should be admitted to any state-supported university of his choice.

The fallacy of missing the point at issue can include various other informal fallacies such as appeals to the gallery and other forms of appeals to emotion. However, in practice the classifying of a fallacy under this heading tends to be limited to those with a developed context. The fallacy occurs with some frequency in illustrations, digressions, and repetitions. The issues tend to become obscured by a constant flow of words and a sense of bewilderment created about the central topic. Irrelevant conclusions are a favorite device of persons resorting to emotional appeals if they are hard pressed to justify a conclusion or to offer an effective counterargument.

7.   The Argumentative Leap (*Non Sequitur*)

The fallacy of an argumentative leap is a flaw due to an irrelevance internal to an argument. The Latin phrase (*non sequitur*) means "it does not follow." In its broadest sense any fallacy can fall under the general

look at conclusion — is evidence related or not?

"jump to concl"

heading of having a conclusion that does not follow from its premises. But in this discussion the meaning of *non sequitur* argument is restricted to an argument where the premises do provide evidence in support of a conclusion, but where they are not sufficient to establish the conclusion. One or more premises are missing, and a gap remains in the argument. *Non sequitur* fallacies tend to occur primarily in arguments that are developed at some length.

Consider the following example, which is oversimplified:

> (31)   The president of the United States should be elected by direct popular vote rather than by the electoral college. The electoral college permits the election of a president who has not received the most popular votes. It gives a few states with a large number of voters too much power. It also gives too much power to minority groups who vote in blocks in the higher populated states.

It may well be the case that the electoral college is not the best way to elect the president. But the argument above does not establish this claim. The evidence is relevant to the issue, yet something is missing. The argument does not show that election of the president by popular vote would be an improvement over the electoral college system.

In concluding this section there is need to emphasize that fallacies can be alleged to apply to an argument without good reasons to support this claim. The use of information relative to a disputant's background can be relevant in limiting the weight of his argument without being a circumstantial *ad hominem* fallacy. To show that a person in a given situation is restricted to one point of view can have bearing on an argument he advances. Pointing out this limited view does not establish that the opposing party has made an error in argument, but it emphasizes that whatever the evidence may be, he would be willing to accept only one conclusion. When a general principle is applied to a specific case, the case chosen may be extreme without being either exceptional or a fallacy of accident. If we hold to the general principle that all adult citizens can vote in national elections, then we may regard the applying of this principle to persons unable to read as an extreme case. But this is not an example of the fallacy of accident. Rather it is an extreme (rather than an exceptional) case.

Because some errors in reasoning may be instances of several different kinds of fallacies, the context needs to be examined for the main thrust of the proposed argument. Determining the primary kind of error may be a matter of judgment. It is preferable in making such judgments to restrict fallacies of irrelevant conclusion and.argumentative leap primarily to cases with a developed context, and to use names of other fallacies where these apply. We need to bear in mind that any given example can be an instance of more than a single type of informal fallacy.

A review of the suggestions given at the end of Section 2.2 may be helpful.

EXERCISES

Identify the informal fallacies or misuses of language in the following examples. (There are answers to even-numbered examples in the back of this work.)

1. Prosecutor to defendant: "When did you begin to make false entries in your account books?" *Complex question*

2. Research has failed to prove that some dyes and sugar substitutes used in food products are really harmful to health. Therefore, it is reasonable to conclude that if they are used in moderation they are not harmful. *appeal to ignorance*

3. If you don't support my candidacy for Congress, then I will see to it that no new reservoirs are built in your area. *appeal to force*

4. Man must be free, since this has been a commonly accepted view for centuries. *consensus, authority*

5. Students are anxious to get a good education. They also want qualified teachers and interesting classes. Therefore, students should be permitted to receive a college degree only by taking four years of undergraduate courses regardless of the selection of courses they might take. *Misses point - external*

6. This ruling of the Supreme Court is unfair to reporters, since reporters keep the public informed and a well-informed public is necessary for justice. *leap* *Insufficient evidence*

7. You cannot accept his view that there is need to increase the size of the armed forces, since he is a military officer and military officers are expected to recommend an increase in military personnel. *Circumstance - appeal to man*

8. "Informed people do not believe that the treaty is a good one."
"But Correspondent Beta does believe the treaty is a good one." *circular*
"But I said 'informed people.' And Correspondent Beta obviously is not informed since he does believe that the treaty is a good one."

9. In a famous debate on evolution one of the speakers asked the opposition a question of the following kind: "Would you please tell the audience whether you were descended from apes on your mother's side or your father's side of the family?" *emotions*

10. Teacher to the student: "If you don't accept my reason for marking your answer wrong, I shall regrade your paper; but you can be sure that your score will not be as high as it is now." *force*

11. Since you cannot prove intelligence tests are inaccurate, they must be accurate. *ignorance*

12. Books are expensive and books are necessary for making good grades in college. Therefore, the government should provide texts for all college students. *Misses point*

13. Obviously you cannot believe what Congressman Delta said because everyone knows he will knife people in the back if they get in his way. *abusive appeal to man*

14. What Julian Huxley said about religion must be true because he was a great scientist. *Authority*

15. "You must agree that these students did not cheat on the exam. Think what effect their failure in the class would have on their subsequent careers." *Pity*

16. Councilman Smith's plea that the city needs more industry cannot be accepted as worthy of serious consideration, since he is a member of the Chamber of Commerce and any member of the Chamber of Commerce is expected to make this kind of plea. *misses pt / Circumstantial appeal to man / Circular*

17. "My client must be innocent. He worked hard to get through school. He has gone to church all his life. He has taken good care of his mother. He takes his son to the Little League ball games. He is an ordinary citizen and would do only those things that you, as self-respecting citizens, would do." *Gallery*

18. What right do you have to advise me that cigarette smoking is bad for one's health. Did you not smoke for many years? *Circumstantial Appeal to Man / to Q vague*

19. Our chances of winning the game must be good since the coach said that our chances of winning were not slim. *Ignorance*

20. It is good to help other persons when they need your assistance. Therefore, you should help me answer these questions on this exam since I need your help. *Accident*

21. Why is the study of logic valuable? Because it helps you learn how to think. And why is knowing how to think so important? Because you can reason better. And why is learning how to reason important? Because then you can study logic. *Circular*

22. How do you account for the existence of the Abominable Snowman? *Complex*

23. Beta: "I find it difficult to believe that Smith is double-crossing me."
Beta's enemy to Smith: "Beta claims that you are double-crossing him." *Accent*

24. Department store sales are down 4 percent this month in comparison to department store sales last month. *Ambig of Significance*

25. "You must believe that I told the truth. Do you want me to be convicted of perjury and have to spend several years in jail?" *Pity*

26. Anyone who does not agree that this decision is the one we should make is both incompetent and uninformed. *abusive appeal to man*

27. Candidate: "We cannot lower taxes until we cut back on government spending."
Rival candidate: "My opponent has said specifically that we cannot lower taxes." *Accent*

28. Each member of the Supreme Court had an outstanding record as a judge or as an attorney prior to appointment to the highest court in the land. Therefore, this Supreme Court should have an outstanding record as the highest court in the land. *Composition*

29. Man's actions are determined solely by his own self-interests because people everywhere believe this is true. *Consensus / Authority*

30. After you read this report I am confident you will have the same view of it as I have. *Ambiguity*

31. Since the government needs to increase its spending during times of economic depressions, it should increase its spending regardless of unemployment rates and business conditions. *Converse accident*

32. Since all of our attitudes are fixed by the time we are six years old, your present attitudes about gambling can be explained by what happened to you in your childhood. *Begging Question*

33. We have an apartment for rent to a couple with many built-ins and new light fixtures. *Amphiboly*

34. The rule that one should not covet one's neighbor's wife does not apply in my case since the woman I am seeing lives in another city. *Accent / Rule out of context*

35. No news is good news and tension in the Middle East is no news. Thus, tension in the Middle East is good news. *Amphiboly*

36. If you do not agree that this business merger is a good deal you may find yourself in a price war. *Force*

37. When are you going to admit that you did the wrong thing? *Complex question*

38. The patient is not seriously injured since each of his injuries taken separately is not serious. *Comp*

39. You should accept Einstein's view on philosophical analysis since was he not one of the greatest physicists of modern times? *Misplaced Authority*

40. Since everything is material, man's soul also must be material. *Begging Question*

41. What the prisoner tells us about birds cannot be true. After all if he was stupid enough to steal, he is too stupid to know what he claims to know about birds. *Abusive ad Hominem*

42. Since it is all right to fight in self-defense it also is all right to fight whenever one's self-interests are threatened. *equiv*

43. Our region is entitled to the use of all water in this river basin, because the development of both agriculture and industry in this area is dependent upon our having available every drop of this water for our own use. *miss pt*

44. Exercise is excellent for health. Therefore, Charles Jones who has a serious heart ailment ought to take more exercise. *Accident*

45. Democratic institutions are to be supported. Therefore, the Democratic Party is to be supported. *equiv*

46. The increase in the cost of living is inevitable in an expanding economy. Therefore, it is a good thing for the economy. *Missing Point at Issue*

47. Morphine is habit-forming; therefore, physicians should not use this drug in easing pain. *Appeal to Ignorance acc*

48. Every book in his library is a good book. Therefore, he has a good library. *Composition*

49. She ran to meet her mother, happy and excited. *simple ambig*

50. Of course you do not have to accept my decision just as I do not have to keep you on the payroll. *force*

51. Glistening Glitter is the most revolutionary toothpaste on the market. Ima Starr stated on television that she had been trying this for six months and that no other toothpaste had ever cleaned her teeth so effectively. *celebrity*

52. Salesman to undecided customer: "Shall I charge this TV set to your account or do you wish to pay cash?" *complex ?*

53. You can't possibly accept his views that the employees need a raise. After all, he is the executive secretary of the labor union, and he is paid to make these kinds of statements. *circum*

54. Since many persons claim to have extrasensory perception, we must conclude that they have extrasensory perception, since no one has ever disproved that they do not have this ability. *ignorance*

55. Our prices are cheap and our values are great every day except Sunday. *amphib*

56. You can be sure that I am behind you, yes, far behind. *equiv*

57. Since inflation hurts people on fixed incomes and decreases the purchasing power of the dollar, inflation is always bad for the economy. *eqp*

58. You did throw the revolver in the river, did you not? *complex ?*

59. The men of the Executive Committee exercise superior judgment in their personal affairs. Therefore, we can be assured that the Executive Committee will exercise superior judgment in handling the affairs of the club. *comp?*

60. Since I shall demonstrate for you beyond any possibility of a doubt that my client is a strong, upstanding, red-blooded American, you must agree that he cannot have been involved in any way with the falsification of records. *gallery*

61. The judge did not sleep during the hearing this afternoon. *ignorance*

62. Since no one has proved that there is life on Mars, we can conclude that there is none.

63. We know that all social scientists believe that right and wrong are reflections of what any given society approves or disapproves, since if they do not believe this they are not social scientists.

64. Since the national government can get the country out of a depression by spending more money, I can get out of my personal depression by spending more money. *equiv*

65. Since you believe in the freedom of the press you also should believe that the press can print any libelous statements it wants to regardless of how incorrect the statement is and how much it damages someone's reputation or business. *acc*

66. Your view that farmland should not be taxed according to its economic value is absurd since you are a farmer and all farmers believe this. *circum*

67. Sorority Alpha has the highest scholastic average of any sorority on campus. Therefore, each person in Sorority Alpha is a superior student. *div*

68. Since our candidate for Congressman is not a member of the establishment he will have new and innovative ideas. But how do you know that the members of the establishment will not have new and innovative ideas? Because they are members of the establishment. *beg ?*

69. We must reduce the size of the public debt, since George Stradivarius, the great orchestral conductor, pointed out that this is essential. *celebrity*

70. Political speaker to a group of student activists: "I have emphasized the need for respect for student rights. I believe students should have a voice on the Board of Regents of their colleges. I believe students should determine all the rules they are expected to observe in college and to be the jury and judge in cases involving violations of these rules. I am confident that you will agree that I would make a good member of the state legislature." *gallery*

71. When you know the applicant as well as I do, you will be as convinced of his abilities as I am. *ambig of sig*

CHAPTER 3

SOME ELEMENTS OF STATEMENTS

We have seen that in logic we analyze and evaluate arguments. And that some bad arguments result when a person presents evidence not relevant to her claim.

Arguments use statements, and statements have elements. In this chapter we shall look at statements and their elements in various ways. We shall examine the meaning of a sign, as well as the notion of a class, of a property, and of a term. The meaning of connotation and denotation will be considered. The chapter concludes with a discussion of different kinds of ambiguity and vagueness.

3.1 NATURAL AND CONVENTIONAL SIGNS

There are many ways to convey meanings. Let us call a sign an object used to convey some meaning related to some object other than itself. We use the word "object" in this context to cover the broadest range of matters. It includes any subject of discourse and anything one says about a subject of discourse. Anything or any happening can be an object in this sense. The movement of the limbs of a tree can be an object, or it can be a sign of movements of currents of air. A yellow light can be a sign for caution; a groan can be a sign of pain; the clinching of a fist can be a sign of anger or of disapproval. Each word used in this sentence is also a sign.

We can classify signs in many different ways. For our purposes we shall distinguish between natural signs and conventional signs. Natural signs indicate meanings derived from the relation of the physical character of a sign to its physical environment. We base the meaning that we associate with a natural sign with some feature of the way things happen in our natural environment: we associate one feature of the physical world with another feature in it. A dark cloud with lightning may be a natural sign of a thunderstorm. Smoke may be a natural sign for fire. A ripple in fast-moving water may be a natural sign that indicates a rock or a log close to the surface. Breathing or a beating pulse may be a sign of life. Prints on a sandy beach may be a sign that birds have walked on the shore. The surfacing of shad in a lake may be a sign of larger fish feeding in the area. Natural signs signify some meaning by some condition or happening in the physical world. What they signify is not contingent upon conventions about how we talk.

Conventional signs derive their meanings from social usage and custom. In some respects meanings associated with them are arbitrary. A yellow light may signify caution but it might be used to signify "full speed ahead." We can use words like "dolls" and "wax" or "running" and "kicking," but such words derive their meaning from social usage. Sometimes we refer to conventional signs as artificial signs to contrast them with natural signs.

We can further divide conventional signs into linguistic and nonlinguistic signs. Linguistic signs are oral or written language expressions such as words or phrases used to indicate meanings. Nonlinguistic conventional signs are objects with meanings conveyed by social practices other than by direct language expressions, such as waving the hand, a pat on the back, a siren sounding, or the blinking of red and blue lights. We also refer to conventional signs as symbols.

Sometimes we consider the way a sign presents itself by its sensible qualities. In such cases we talk about the token of a sign—its physical character or physical behavior. A verbal token refers to the physical character of a spoken or written word. We also can refer to a sentence token as the physical character of a sentence. Each word in this sentence is a sign token. If one reads the sentence aloud, the sound of each word is a sign token. Each occurrence of a sign is a separate token of the sign. For example, if "fox . . . fox" occurs in a sentence, we find only one word but two sign tokens in the expression.

We also need to distinguish between those cases in which a conventional sign or symbol refers back to itself and those cases in which it has some other use. Consider what is wrong with the following sentences. "Logic is spelled with five letters and logic is the study of the principles and procedures of good arguments. Therefore, the study of the principles and procedures of good arguments is spelled with five letters."

The above error is that the first time the word "logic" occurs it refers to the word itself; the second time it occurs it refers to a subject matter. In the first instance there is the mention of the word; in the second instance there is the use of the word. If we mention a word, we need to place it in quotation marks or italicize it.

If we mention a word, its referent is the word itself. If we use a word, the referent is something other than the word itself. Mention of the word *red* (or "red") occurs in the sentence, "*Red* begins with an r and *red* has fewer letters than *blue*." Use of the word "red" occurs in the following sentence: "Red is a bright color and red is a warm color."

However, we should recognize that quotation marks or italics also have other functions. They may indicate citations, emphases, or unusual meanings.

EXERCISES

Determine which words are mentioned and should have quotation marks in the following examples:

1. War is evil and war begins with a "w," so some things beginning with a "w" are evil.

2. Poliomyelitis is more difficult to spell than polio.

3. Mary had written had had where Tom had had had; had had had had the approval of the instructor.

4. Some words used to express numbers are one, five, and ten.

5. Words of commendation are good, excellent, splendid, and bravo.

3.2   STATEMENTS

We communciate with each other by conventional signs. We learn to use these conventions by interaction with other persons who are using them. We combine these signs into sentences and use sentences to make arguments. In this section we shall look at how logicians use expressions like "utterance," "sentence," "statement," and "proposition" in their talk about arguments. Let us begin by looking at an utterance.

An utterance in its simplest sense is some noise or sound made by humans in talking. Utterances may be without sense, such as the sounds "ba," "ta," "na." They can make sense, as does the utterance "stop."

In its broadest sense an utterance is any human talk originating from a common source and having pauses or sequences of pauses before and after the sounds that are made. Examples of utterances are the sounds made by the use of the following syllables or expressions:

yipee

ho hum

la, le, li, lo, lu

The table is set.

Dolphins breathe when they surface.

In a derived sense an "utterance" also can signify the written form of such human talk.

We put utterances together to make a linguistic unit that makes complete sense. In short we make sentences. But "sentence" is not easy to define. A traditional definition states that a sentence is a series of words, constructed according to accepted grammatical rules, which express a complete and independent thought and which usually have a subject and predicate. In some cases we expand the definition to say that such expressions state, ask, request, command, or exclaim something. In this traditional use the notion of "a complete thought" is difficult to clarify. Likewise, we use sentences to do many other jobs in addition to those listed above. We also use sentences to perform acts, to advise, to give instructions, to praise, to warn, to admonish, to blame, and to do many other things. But the notion that a sentence expresses something complete and independent is basic to what a sentence is. For our purposes we shall refer to a sentence as the smallest grammatically independent linguistic unit which has a complete meaning. Use of the notion of "complete meaning" distinguishes a sentence from words and phrases. But we grant that it shares some of the difficulties of the notion of "complete thought." The notion of "smallest independent unit" distinguishes a sentence from a larger linguistic unit such as a paragraph.

Some sentences are simple; others are compound. A simple sentence contains no other sentence as a part. A compound sentence is one whose components are two or more sentences. "All men are mortal" is a simple sentence. Some compound sentences are: "Life is beautiful and life is precious." "Either we go to class or we go on a picnic."

Some expressions have incompletely expressed sentences. To analyze such expressions as sentences we have to make explicit the words that are unexpressed but understood in that context. For example, such imperatives as, "Say something" or "Just don't sit there," require a grammatical subject such as "you" to complete their meaning.

There are many kinds of sentences. But in this work, we are primarily interested in the kind used as assertions. Sentences are used as assertions

assertions

when they have a claim internal to their meaning. In this claim, certain conditions, happenings, states of affairs, relations, or connections expressed by the ordering of the elements in the sentence hold with regard to what the sentence is about. Consider the statement, "The sky is clear." The statement claims that one of its elements, "is clear" characterizes another of its elements, "the sky."

We expect statements used in arguments to meet two conditions. First, any given statement in an argument needs to be one that is true or false. But it cannot be both true and false in that context. This condition does not require that we know whether or not any given statement is true. It does require that with sufficient knowledge we could apply fittingly either the expression "true" or the expression "false" to the statement. Consider the statement: "The assassination of President Kennedy was a part of a conspiracy originating in Cuba." We may not know whether the statement is true or false. However, we can know that it is either one or the other. The use by a clergyman of the sentence, "I pronounce you husband and wife," is not a statement in the restricted sense in which we are using the word. One does not say that such sentences are true or false. But one judges them as proper or improper, duly authorized or not duly authorized. Yet, the following sentence is a statement: "The clergyman said, 'I pronounce you husband and wife.'" Either this sentence is true or it is false.

There is a second condition required for statements used in arguments. They need to be assertions with complete and independent sense. We need to have some way of understanding what it is that one is asserting by making the statement. An expression which reads, "The green circle tripped on its four blue corners," does not make complete sense. (Or, if it makes sense, it is trivially false.) A sentence which reads, "He flipped his lid," in some contexts, can make complete sense and would count as a statement.

A statement is a meaningful sentence that is either true or false and that makes an assertion. It is true if what it asserts tells how things are. A true statement asserts what is the case in the domain of objects about which the statement is made. The denial of a true statement is a false statement. What is asserted by a false statement does not hold in the domain of objects that the sentence is about.

The denial of a false statement yields a true statement. One denies different kinds of statements in different ways. And we discuss these ways later in this work. However, we may note that in denying a statement, we need to deny the sense of the complete statement.

Many logicians use the word "proposition" instead of "statement." We have no basic dispute with some of them and we could replace the term "statement" by "proposition" in this work. But one proposed view of a proposition would not be satisfactory for this purpose. This view holds that a proposition is the meaning of a declarative sentence which is either true or false. Consider these sentences in three languages:

It is raining.
Es regnet.   [German for, "It is raining."]   Il pleut.
Se llueve.   [Spanish for, "It is raining."]

These three sentences have a common meaning and they express one proposition. However, we are concerned not only with what a sentence means,
as important as this is. We are concerned with what it asserts to be the
case. It is not the meaning of "It is raining" that we find true or false. But
rather it is what the sentence asserts that is true or false. If we regard a
proposition as a meaningful true-or-false sentence that makes an assertion,
then the use of this word makes no difference for our purposes. Some
logicians hold that the use of the notion of proposition makes a needless
addition to the domain of abstract entities. Others prefer to use the term
since it is the one used traditionally. Our preference for "statement" has
some basis on the grounds of its greater simplicity and its more frequent
use in ordinary discourse.

We shall see that several different kinds of statements occur in the
making and in the analyzing of arguments. The following statements illustrate these basic types.

All tax cuts are economic stimulants.

Smith's energy policy is better than Jones' policy.

If we conserve energy, then we are less dependent on foreign imports of fuel.

Either we control inflation or we face continued social unrest.

It is not the case both that we have sufficient energy for our growth and that
we fail to develop new sources for energy supplies.

If and only if we solve our energy crisis can we increase our production
significantly.

We develop new sources of energy and we develop means to conserve energy.

Some of these statements are simple. They focus on one primary assertion.
Some of them are compound and consist of two separate statements joined
together. These compound statements use statement connectors like "If . . . ,
then ———," "Either . . . or ———," "——— if and only if . . . ,"
" . . . and ———," "It is not the case both that . . . and that ———."
These statement connectors also have a job to do in telling us how the
different parts of these compound statements relate to one another. When
we view these connectors from the point of view of the job they do in
making arguments, we refer to them as logical operators. Such operators

have a logical function in determining whether our arguments are good ones. Later we shall analyze the logical use of these operators in developing arguments.

3.3 TERMS, CLASSES, AND PROPERTIES

We need to analyze the statements used in arguments in various ways. For one thing we need to be able to identify the subject term and the predicate term of a statement. We also need to make further distinction about singular terms, class terms, and property terms in order to determine their proper logical use. We shall examine the meaning of "term," "class," and "property" in this section.

We have noted that sentences are made up of elements ordered in a way that makes sense. A statement has basic units of meaning. Let us refer to the different units of linguistic meaning within a simple statement as the terms of that statement. In the statement, "The house is burning," we can note two basic units of meaning or terms. These are "the house" and "is burning." The job of one of the terms is to stand for the subject of an assertion. The job of the other term is to stand for the predicate that tells us something about the subject.

In analyzing statements we use the notions of class and property. A class can be any grouping of objects, but we shall be using the notion of class in a more restricted sense to stand for a group or set of objects having one or more identifiable characteristics in common. We can talk about a class of college students. Such a class consists of all members of the group that are college students. We also can talk about the class of all radios, or the class of all dragons. If a term stands for a class, we call it a class term.

A property is anything ascribed to a class or to individuals. Words or phrases like "hard," "fast," "yellow," "climbing the wall," "reading the logic book" refer to properties. In popular usage we sometimes say "characteristic" rather than property to refer to some of the notions expressed by the word "property."

The notions of class and property tend to be interrelated. A class is a group of individuals that share one or more common properties. Properties are conditions we can ascribe to individuals or to classes. To simplify, classes have properties and properties are something classes have.

A class term is a unit of discourse that stands for a group or a set of individuals that we consider to have one or more properties in common. "Rocks," "hair," "trees," "coats," "electrons," "genes," "wax," "students" are examples of expressions used as class terms. A property term is a unit of discourse that stands for an expression that ascribes anything to a class or to individuals. "Working" and "reading" can be expressions used as property terms.

A complementary class consists of everything to which the original class does not include. The complementary class of "houses" is "non-houses" or "all things that are not houses." The complementary class of "rational animals" is "all things that are not rational animals." In forming a complementary class, we need to include all classes of things in the universe of discourse other than the original given class as a member of the complementary class. Many words with prefixes such as "in-," "ir-," "un-" may not exclude every class or object other than the original class. In such cases they may form a contrary, but not complementary, class. Consider the classes "rational persons" and "irrational persons." The use of one of these expressions precludes a consistent use of the other to a given individual in the same context. But these are not complementary classes. They are contrary classes. In contrary classes a member of one class cannot be a member of the other class in a given context. But a class and its contrary class, unlike a class and its complementary class, do not jointly exhaust all other classes in the universe of discourse. "The class of all round things" is a contrary class to "the class of all square things." But they are not complementary classes. Some things are not members of one class or the other. Other examples of contrary classes are "cooperative persons" and "uncooperative persons," "competent judges" and "incompetent judges." Some prefixes, such as "in-," may not significantly change the fundamental meaning of a word. Consider the expressions "flammable gas" and "inflammable gas."

Different words can be used to stand for the same class. Consider expressions like "man" (in English) and "hombre" (in Spanish). The same word can signify different classes, as does the word "flies" in the following statements. "Some flies are crawling on the table." "Some flies are foul balls." "Some flies help to catch big trout."

In analyzing some simple statements we have seen that a predicate ascribes a property to a subject. We also may call the expression used as the subject term of statements a name. A name may refer to any subject of discourse and to anything whether actual or otherwise. We may talk about John Jones, atoms, hats, elves, bears, irrational numbers, or slowness as a subject of discourse. But an attempt to unravel many of the complex issues about names is outside the purpose of this chapter.

Some expressions used as class terms are general and others are singular. An expression used as a general term identifies a collection of individuals that hold one or more properties in common. But in such cases we are talking about individuals in a group rather than a singular entity.

An expression used as a singular term identifies a single individual or entity, actual or fictitious. There are different kinds of singular terms.

Some singular terms are proper names, such as "John," "Mary," "Martin Luther King, Jr." Other words used as singular terms are personal pronouns such as "he," "she," "it."

Definite descriptions are other kinds of expressions used as singular terms. A definite description is the use of a general or class name together with a word or phrase that limits the scope of an expression to a singular entity, for example, "the author of *Tom Sawyer*," "my closest friend," and "that house on the hill."

In other instances, some words used as singular terms are proper names that refer to a group as a single entity. Such a unit has a separate identity. Examples of such expressions are "The Boston Trio" and "The Organization of American States."

Some expressions used as singular terms are collective nouns that refer exclusively to an entity or species without regard for the distinct parts of the entity or species, for example, "dinosaur," "army," and "mankind." Such collective nouns have use as singular terms in the following contexts: "The dinosaur [as a species] is an extinct reptile." "The army [as an entity] is a major branch of the national security forces." "Mankind will disappear from the earth."

Imaginary or fictitious entities may be represented by words used as singular terms. We may write a story about Jack and Jill or discuss the roles of Hamlet and Othello. Zeus, Hera, or Hercules may be used as singular terms in discussing Greek mythology.

We shall see that many technical decisions in logic turn on identifying and using words used as terms in an accurate way. In talking about terms in the context of this discussion we are referring to a linguistic unit of meaning in a sentence.

EXERCISES

A. Identify the types of terms italicized in the following examples as a general class term or as a singular term.
  1. *Jim* is working. *Sing*
  2. *Watches* are *instruments*. *general*
  3. *The president of the student body* is an English major. *singular*
  4. *Running* can be fun. *General*
  5. *Elves* are happy *creatures*. *general*

B. Determine which of the following pairs are complementary terms.
  1. Strong arguments and weak arguments *No*
  2. Animate and nonanimate things *yes*
  3. Athletes who are professional golfers and athletes who are amateur golfers *No*
  4. Veterans and all things not veterans *yes*
  5. Theists and atheists *No*
  6. Jurists and nonjurists *yes*
  7. Repairable losses and all things not repairable losses *yes*
  8. Serious issues and trivial issues *No*
  9. Dent and indent *No*
  10. Payable accounts and paid accounts *No*

ANSWERS

A. Singular terms: (1) "Jim"; (3) "The president of the student body."
   General class terms: (2) "Watches," "instruments"; (4) "Running" (derived from a property term); (5) "Elves," "creatures."
B. Complementary terms: 2, 4, 6, 7.
   Noncomplementary terms: 1, 3, 5, 8, 9, 10.

3.4   CONNOTATION AND DENOTATION

To continue our analysis of words used as class terms, we need to know whether such words refer to all individuals in any given class or only to some individuals in that class. We also need to distinguish between the entities to which words used as a class term apply and the properties which such entities have in common. Logicians use the notions of denotation and connotation to make this distinction.

The denotation of a word used as a class term consists of every entity designated by that word. "House" denotes every object that is a house—all the objects that one can point to and say, "that is a house." The denotation of "students" consists of every person that one can call a student.

The connotation of a word used as a class term is the properties held in common by the objects to which it applies. The connotation of "square" includes such properties as "a plane figure," "four equal sides," "each side with a straight line," and "four right angles." The connotation of "human being" includes such properties as: "an animal who stands upright"; "an organism with a highly developed brain"; "an animal with well-developed vocal cords"; "a tool maker and tool user"; and "an animal that develops a highly complex language system."

We need to distinguish the objective connotation of a word used as a class term from its subjective connotation. The objective connotation refers to the properties that a qualified person can recognize as applicable to members of the class to which the expression applies. The properties given for "square" and "human being" are examples of objective connotations. The subjective connotation of an expression refers to the properties associated with words used as a class term and based on varying feelings, moods, and attitudes of different people. Consider the subjective connotation of the word "cat." Some persons may be reminded of a small, cuddly pet, others of a bird-killing pest that also carries diseases. Persons interested in changing or influencing attitudes and actions of others may use subjective connotations of words to help persuade others to accept their point of view. We may respond differently if one calls public officials public servants rather than government snoopers.

We also need to distinguish between the strict objective connotation of a word and its general objective connotation. The strict objective connotation refers to those properties that are sufficient and essential for including an object as a member of the class covered by a given expression. But what we regard as sufficient and essential may vary with the purpose we have in using a given expression. For a work on medicine, we may propose one set of properties for the class of human beings. But we may want to offer a differing set of characteristics for a work about art or language or religion.

The general objective connotation of a word used as a class term includes all the properties shared in common by the class of objects covered by the expression. All human beings may have lobes on their ears. But in ordinary cases we would regard this property as a general objective connotation of the expression "human being" but not as a property of its strict connotation.

The notion of the strict connotation of a work used as a class term has basic significance in one kind of definition. In a connotative definition one seeks to identify the properties that are essential in distinguishing a given class from any other class. We shall see that expressions used in such areas as science or law can be defined more easily in this manner than others such as those used in a political debate.

Logicians also talk about the extension of expressions used as general terms and about the intension of such expressions. To some degree the distinction between extension and denotation or between intension and connotation has historical usage as its basis and is arbitrary.

The notion of the extension of an expression used as a general term, like the notion of denotation, applies to the individuals covered by an expression used as a general term. But we also use the notion of extension to distinguish between all the members of a class and some of its members or between classes that are fully extended and those that are partially extended. This distinction is basic to working many problems in logic. For example, an expression used as a completely extended term includes all the members of its class. Consider the use of the expressions "dogs," "circles," and "students." They have complete extension when they occur as "all dogs," "all circles," and "every student." They have only partial extension when they occur as "many dogs," "some circles," and "various students." These latter uses do not include all members of the classes of "dogs," "circles," and "students."

The intension of an expression used as a general term, like the notion of connotation, applies to the characteristics held in common by the individuals found in any given class. But we also use the notion of intension to stand for cases in which we may want to add to the properties of an expression used as a general term or to take away properties from such an expression. We talk about increasing or decreasing the intension of such expressions. The connotation and intension of the expression "plane figure" are the same. Suppose we want to add to the intension of "plane figure." We can add "enclosed by four straight lines," as a property, and this newly formed class has an increased intension. We can add other properties like "with each line equal in length," and "with four right angles." Again we have a newly formed class with increased intension. We now have the expression, "a plane figure enclosed with four straight and equal lines, and with four right angles." In the above example, with the adding of each new property we reduced the number of objects in the class to which the given expression applies.

Although the rule usually holds that as we increase the intension of an expression used as a class term we decrease its extension, we cannot apply this rule in all cases. Suppose we continue to talk about the plane figure mentioned above, which turns out to be a square. Once we have identified the properties sufficient and essential for the class of squares we could continue to add additional properties such as "consisting of two pairs of parallel lines." We would have increased the stated intension of the original class without having decreased its extension.

We also shall find that in the next section there is a relation between expressions that are ambiguous or vague and the intension or extension of such expressions.

EXERCISES

A. Arrange each of the following series in order of increasing intension.
   1. Teacher, logic teacher at State College, human being, logic teacher.
   2. Symbolic logic textbook, book, logic textbook, textbook.
   3. Plane figure, quadrilateral, square, figure.
   4. Constitutional monarchy, political system, constitutional government, social organization, British constitutional monarchy.
   5. Philosophy of science, philosophy of natural science, philosophy, philosophy of physics.

B. Determine the extension of the italicized classes in the following statements:
   1. Some exceptional *students* are industrious *persons*.
   2. Every *dog* has his day.
   3. Many *prizes* are not worthy *goals* of endeavor.
   4. All *roses* are *shrubs* and most *varieties* have prickly stems.
   5. Most *rules* of syntax are not difficult *things* to master.

C. Provide examples of the denotation and connotation of the following expressions:
   1. "desk"
   2. "chair"
   3. "window"
   4. "blackboard"
   5. "student"
   6. "democratic institution"

7. "constitutional government"
8. "bureaucracy"
9. "physicist"
10. "custom"

3.5 AMBIGUITY AND VAGUENESS

In analyzing an argument we need to know what its statements assert. But to know what a statement asserts we need to know about the denotation and the connotation of the words used as class terms. A court of law expects that a given law be sufficiently explicit for a "reasonable person" to know what kinds of situations it covers. (For example, in what situations is a given person the head of a household for income tax purposes?) Such courts also require that a reasonable person can know if a given kind of act is a violation of the law. (For example, can the head of a household know whether it is lawful in a given case to deduct payments for the care of her invalid mother for income tax purposes?) In dealing with such issues we are touching upon the use of ambiguous or vague expressions.

We have seen that a word or phrase is ambiguous if in a given context it can have more than one meaning. A word or phrase is vague if we have no way of determining the range of entities to which it applies. Ambiguity is concerned with the notion of double meanings; vagueness is concerned with borderline cases. But some words may be both vague and ambiguous. The difference of range of entities to which a vague expression applies in borderline cases can be so wide that double meanings also may be present. Some parts of a sentence may be vague and other parts may be ambiguous. One or both of the possible meanings of an ambiguous term also may be vague.

In the 1976 presidential campaign the candidates of each major political party made many ambiguous and vague statements. President Gerald Ford committed what even his friends recognized as a serious political blunder when he made the following statement in a TV debate: "There is no Soviet domination of Eastern Europe and there never will be under a Ford Administration."

Note the ambiguities. By "Eastern Europe" Ford intended to refer to each country in Eastern Europe as a separate entity of a geographic area. He could point to Albania and Greece as cases where the Soviets did not dominate the governments. But his critics chose to interpret the phrase "Eastern Europe" as a geographical and political unit and in a collective sense. Ford intended to use "no Soviet domination" in the sense that "the Soviets do not exercise complete control over internal, national, and local affairs in political, economic, and security matters in each country of Eastern Europe." As cases in point he could refer to practices and policies in these countries which were contrary to the preferences of officials of the Soviet Union. However, his critics chose to interpret "no Soviet domination of" in the sense of "no Soviet sphere of influence" and "making sure Eastern Europe is a Communist Zone" subject to the pressures and in some cases the intervention by the army of the Soviet Union. They could point to events in Czechoslovakia, Hungary, and Poland to support their claim. After efforts to clarify his position, Ford retracted the ambiguous statement.

We have noted that in handling cases that are ambiguous or vague we are dealing with issues related to connotation and denotation. Once we clarify what properties characterize a given general class we can eliminate many ambiguous or vague uses of language. Let us consider the following example.

Professor Joe Smith is a liberal educator.

In this case "liberal educator" can have multiple meanings. And we can attribute such ambiguity to different connotations related to the phrase "liberal educator." For example, which of the following properties do we want to ascribe to a liberal educator? "Liberal" can refer to an "educator" who emphasizes the study of the humanities and sciences as subject areas to be pursued for their own sake as a means of personal enrichment and enjoyment rather than as means to getting a better-paying job. "Liberal" also can refer to an "educator" who seeks to use the most recently developed techniques and aids in teaching his students. "Liberal" also could signify an "educator" who shows a permissive attitude toward students. What he expects students to do in a given course varies with their interests and abilities. "Liberal" educator also could signify that the "educator" holds certain social and political attitudes and that he supports more government planning and action in attaining a wider sharing of the goods of an affluent society. Given such multiple meanings of "liberal," the above expression is ambiguous.

Once we eliminate in a given context an ambiguity based on such an expression as "liberal," we may need to clarify issues of borderline cases. And we may need to make more explicit the connotation of an expression. Would someone who teaches computer languages or who supervises students in fieldwork be a liberal educator?

We also have issues related to possible borderline cases about what characteristics we are to ascribe to persons who are educators. Is the property of "teaching others how to teach" essential for someone to be an educator? Is the property of "directly teaching students in a classroom situation" required to be an educator? Is a craftsman who teaches an apprentice the art of printing an educator? Are those who administer educational programs but do not teach students educators? Are administrators of state or federal programs in primary education or in universities also educators?

Ambiguity regarding the extension of a term also is present in the above cases. As one revises the intension of the phrase "liberal educator," so the individuals covered by "educator" vary.

Let us consider another example of ambiguity:

All freshmen are not required to take math courses.

The ambiguity here turns on the indefiniteness of the sentence form "All . . . are not ————." We have to determine which of the following meanings apply.

Some freshmen are not required to take math courses.

No freshmen are required to take math courses.

This is a case of deciding the extension of the expression "freshmen." If "some freshmen" is the extension, then a given student would need to make further inquiry to determine whether the program he is following does or does not require that a math course be taken. If "no freshmen" is the proper meaning, then we find the expression used as a class term fully extended. And all freshmen are free of such a requirement. Taking a math course would be left up to the wishes of the student regardless of the program she is following. Given the requirements of some degree programs, we have grounds for holding that in the above cases, the proper interpretation of the ambiguous phrase would be the form that "some freshmen are not required to take the math course." But one bases this rendering of the meaning on a context in which such a statement likely would occur. The original statement taken by itself does not provide the clue for such an interpretation to follow. It is ambiguous since it does not make clear the extension of the class of "freshmen."

In some cases ambiguity permits evasion of issues. Consider the letter of recommendation that states, "When you come to know this person as well as I know him, you will have the same regard for him that I do." We do not know what properties characterize the person for whom the recommendation is made.

Let us consider some other examples of vague expressions. Mr. Jones, a political candidate, could claim, "We need to reduce the size of our armed forces." His opponent could immediately ask, "How much of a reduction in the size of the armed forces do you propose?" Jones responds, "By a number sufficient to significantly decrease the budget for military appropriations but not to the degree that it would weaken our military capability of defense." In this case we still do not know how much he plans to cut back. But we can surmise that he is hedging or being deliberately vague on this issue. These ambiguities and vague statements are due to the lack of clarity about the extension of the class to which a key word refers.

Consider the case of a member of the governing board of a major state university system who seeks to justify some arbitrary and perhaps capricious acts of the board by declaring, "He who pays the piper calls the tune." Apart from what some persons may regard as an unusual analogy which suggests the legalizing of the prostitution of universities, the question remains, "Who does pay the piper?" in such cases.

On some occasions speakers deliberately choose to be vague. If they appeal to "the American way of life" politicans are not likely to divide their followers. On the other hand, if they extend the range of "the American way of life" to include the "great experiment" in government as proposed by Thomas Jefferson, some listeners might regard them as too liberal. If they restrict "the American way of life" to the economic and social system championed by major nineteenth century investors, they might alienate other followers.

The use of vague terms is not always a critical matter. If we are told that there is bad weather to the east but we are driving west, we may not raise any further questions. But if we are driving east, we likely will want more specific information.

The precise legal meaning courts have given to a word determines the outcome of many legal cases. In some cases a job of the court is to provide further clarification of the legal meaning of a word or phrase. Let us consider some examples. How is discrimination on the basis of race or of sex to be identified? Under what conditions is a movie or a magazine pornographic? When is a statement libelous? What constitutes false advertising? What constitutes the pollution of a stream? When is a labor practice unfair? We have noted that in a strict sense an expression is clear only if those situations to which it applies can be singled out from those cases to which it does not apply.

We have seen that ambiguity has to do with a context in which an expression may have several different meanings. Vagueness occurs in contexts in which there are borderline instances about the objects covered by a word. Both the intension and the extension of a word may be the source of the ambiguity or vagueness. In a given context an expression may be both ambiguous and vague.

In this chapter we have looked at how we distinguish natural signs and conventional signs. We have made other distinctions about word usage. The meaning of statement was analyzed, and a distinction was made between terms, classes, and properties. We also discussed connotation and denotation and saw how these notions relate to ambiguity and vagueness.

EXERCISES

Analyze the following expressions for ambiguity. Show two different interpretations that might be made in each case.

1. We have a liberal government.
2. Are you a conservative student? *good use of resources*
   strict morals
3. Popular education is the best assurance of an informed electorate.
4. We support the rights of the oppressed.
5. We need to have better employment opportunities.
6. Professor Smith is a good teacher.
7. Jones is a religious person.
8. Nothing is good enough for you. *amphib, ambig*
9. John stroked his hair with his fingers and took out his pipe. *amphib*
10. All who sow do not reap. *amphib*

CHAPTER **4**

MEANING AND LANGUAGE

4.1 MEANING IN ORDINARY DISCOURSE

This chapter deals with the theory of meaning and some of the different ways that "meaning" is used. We shall examine various proposed theories of meaning and some language expressions with meaning-related faults.

In attempting to define "meaning" we are faced with the variety of ways in which this word is used. Ludwig Wittgenstein, the Austrian philosopher who taught at Cambridge, noted that we tend to take for granted that we know what meaning is. But we are hard-pressed to provide a fitting response to the question, "What is meaning?" A part of the difficulty becomes apparent when some of the multiple uses that "meaning" or similar expressions like "meant" and "mean" have in actual usage. Let us consider a few examples of the many uses of these expressions:

(1)   1. Does life have any meaning?

      2. Did you really mean to ignore the warning?

      3. I really meant what I promised.

      4. I have sought to find a mean between the extreme alternatives presented to me.

      5. You can't really mean what you are saying.

6. Your failure to call means that you don't care about me.

7. What is the meaning of the streak of bad luck that we have had?

8. You should not have cheated. Doesn't your reputation mean anything to you?

9. John has a mean disposition.

10. What is the meaning of his feelings of anxiety, depression, and guilt?

11. What is the meaning of three consecutive monthly increases in the prime interest rate?

12. What is the meaning of this lipstick on the collar of your shirt which was clean when you left for work?

The above sentences can be restated in other ways without using "meaning," or "meant," or "mean." The effort required to restate these sentences shows how hard it is to convey the sense that these words have in different contexts. It also points to the vagueness that many uses of "meaning" have in various sentences. The following sentences show some of the different ways of recasting the original expressions.

(2) 1. Does human existence have a purpose that transcends material well-being and that is basically moral or spiritual in character?

2. Did you intend to ignore the warning?

3. My promise was sincere and I plan to keep it.

4. I have sought a moderate position on this issue.

5. What you are saying does not appear reasonable.

6. Your failure to call justifies my belief that you don't care about me.

7. Is the streak of bad luck we have had some type of omen about the future?

8. You should not have cheated. Isn't your reputation of any concern to you?

9. John responds in a harsh or cruel manner to persons he does not like.

10. Do his feelings of anxiety, depression, and guilt indicate some serious mental problem?

11a. How do you explain the three consecutive monthly increases in the prime interest rates?

11b. What do you expect to be the effect of three consecutive monthly increases in prime interest rates on plant expansion and other economic growth?

12.   What is the source of the lipstick that was not on your shirt collar
when you left home this morning?

The different senses of meaning and its variants help to emphasize that
the task of finding a fitting sense of meaning is difficult. But our interest in
the sense of "meaning" is different from its use in the above examples.
Rather we shall focus on "meaning" as it applies to language use in words,
phrases, and sentences. When we are asked to state the meaning of a
linguistic expression, what are we being asked to do?

4.2 THEORIES OF MEANING

In trying to clarify what linguistic meaning is we shall consider five
views or theories. These theories are: (1) the idea theory, (2) the reference
theory, (3) the behavioral theory, (4) the use theory, and (5) a context
theory. Each of these views accounts for some notions we wish to convey
in some contexts where linguistic meaning is discussed. We shall propose
a context theory of linguistic meaning for use in this work. This will be a
simplified discussion; further analysis of these views could be made. Likewise, persons who hold to a given theory of meaning have ways of answering
criticisms of any of these views.

1.   The Idea Theory of Meaning

Historically we associate the idea theory of meaning with views attributed to John Locke. In his *Essay Concerning Human Understanding* (Book
III, Chapter 2, Section 1) Locke wrote:

(3)   The use, then, of words is to be the sensible marks of ideas; and the ideas
they stand for are their proper and immediate signification.

In this view linguistic expressions such as words and marks are regularly
associated with ideas. Each word in the expression, "The pine tree has
green needles," would have an idea associated with it. The idea expressed
by the person making the statement would become clear and properly
associated in her consciousness by a decision to focus her attention on the
idea. In this view, meaning is the idea that we associate with the expression.
It can become the focus of attention in someone's consciousness.

The idea theory of meaning has several difficulties. Some linguistic
expressions can have more than one meaning, and different expressions can
have similar meanings. It is difficult to determine the conditions under
which two persons are known to share the same ideas or thought. Disputes
can become difficult to resolve if the meanings disputants are using are

simply ideas in their own "stream of consciousness." Some words do not appear to have any definite idea associated with them. And the sense of basic notions like "idea," "image," "thought," "consciousness" is not clear in this approach.

To illustrate some of these problems let us consider the following sentence:

> (4) The aspiration for a greater share in the distribution of goods and services in the Third World will continue to be a source of major unrest in developing countries.

"Goods" can signify various "ideas." The "Third World" and "developing countries" may or may not convey "similar ideas." Some persons would find several of the expressions so vague that they would not be able to associate a definite idea with them. Different persons could accept the above statement as being accurate but their "ideas" about what the statement asserts could differ. If two parties did agree that the above statement is correct, how can we determine if they are accepting similar views? If different parties have a dispute about the truth of the statement, how can we determine if they are talking about the same idea in their dispute? What ideas are expressed by such words as "the," "a," "in," "major," "services," and "unrest"?

If "idea" signifies some kind of mental image or picture, then there are likely to be many different mental images on the part of persons reading the expression. Some would deny that they have any mental images at all. The claim that the meaning of the linguistic expressions in the above statement is in the "sensible marks of ideas" results in notions as vague and indefinite as the notion of meaning itself. That is, one type of vagueness merely replaces another. The meaning of "meaning" remains unclarified.

2. Reference Theories of Meaning

In its simplest form, the reference theory of meaning identifies the meaning of a term with the object or entity which it signifies. The analysis of the relation of proper names to the objects bearing the proper name appears to have influenced the development of this view. Consider the name Abraham Lincoln. It refers to the person bearing this name. We also can talk about the dog whose name is Fido. In the above cases the meaning of the name is its object of reference. But names not only refer to individuals, they also refer to classes of individuals.

By using the model of naming in individual cases we can develop a more advanced theory of meaning. Names like "dog" can be extended to refer to all animals that have the common characteristics of the dog, Fido, and to other animals that we want to put in this class. The meaning of a word becomes the object it designates. And the object can be a class of objects identified because they share a common characteristic. The meaning of words like "bees," "birds," "roads," and "houses" is what we designate by these words. The meaning of a word in this view is what it refers to. We identify the difference in meaning between linguistic expressions by the difference in what they designate as referents.

This theory has the advantage of being simple. What is meaning? It is the referent of an expression. But the view is too simple. Let us consider some objections to it. One basic objection to the reference theory is the claim that any meaningful expression refers to some nonlinguistic object or class of objects. By this theory it is hard to account for the meaning of such expressions as "furthermore," "about," or "elves." Such apparent meaningful expressions as "the present king of France," "the only woman president of the United States in the nineteenth century" do not have nonlinguistic referents in any clear sense. Referring is a basic function of some words, and identifying referents helps us to understand the differences among expressions. Yet this approach does not provide a test for the meaning of some expressions we regard as meaningful. The reference theory does not appear to be able to do some jobs we expect a theory of meaning to do.

A second problem with the simplest form of the reference theory of meaning has to do with words having different meanings but the same referent. This problem was pointed out by Frege, who noted that "the morning star" and "the evening star" have different meanings but refer to the same planet, Venus. Likewise, the expressions "the first president of the United States to resign during a term of office" and "the president of the United States who won election victories over both Hubert Humphrey and George McGovern" have different meanings but refer to the same person, Richard Nixon. In each of these cases expressions with different meanings have the same referent. The simpler reference theory would require that they have the same meaning since they refer to the same object.

A third objection to the reference theory of meaning is its neglect of the role that language use has in determining meaning. By focusing basically on external functions of meaning, that is, on the referents of words, it bypasses basic issues having to do with how words function to express meaning in a community of language users. Separated from such a community, language expressions would be mere noises, scratches, or marks. Both meaning and reference depend upon a community of language users. Such language users and the language customs in which they participate help to determine the meaning and reference given to linguistic expressions.

3.   Behavioral Theories of Meaning

Behavioral theories of meaning use a stimulus-response model. Meaning is associated with the activities which set off a given utterance and with the responses or response tendencies which are set off as a result of the utterance.

Consider the meaning of the expression, "Lunch is ready." The activities which set off such an utterance include the speakers seeing prepared foods, some tableware, and containers for eating food spread on a table, and some place to eat the food. The response which is set off would have the concerned parties going to a table, sitting down, serving their plates, and eating the food.

The meaning of an expression (in this view) consists in those kinds of activities that tend to evoke its utterance and in the range of responses or tendencies to respond that we expect to follow that utterance. Behavioral theories of meaning react against the idea theory and reject attempts to find linguistic meaning in the mind of the language user. In contrast to reference theories behavioral theories rightly emphasize that language use occurs in a social context which gives rise to the notion of linguistic meaning.

Some behavioral theories of meaning develop in great detail the notion of response. Such views emphasize notions of "implicit response" or "disposition to respond." An implicit response has various internal organic activities such as contraction of muscles and physical movement within the nervous system. One obvious problem with this view is the difficulty we have in identifying internal movements that do not lend themselves to our observation.

Some behavioral theories emphasize the notion of disposition to respond and they refine the notion of condition for a response. An expression satisfies a condition for a response if a given type of response can be expected with the presence of an identified cluster of added conditions. Let us consider the utterance, "The Superbowl game is on TV this afternoon." To utter these words would provide a condition to expect certain responses in the presence of other conditions. The added conditions include a working TV set placed in a convenient place and the time to watch the televised game. Given these conditions sufficient to set off the disposition to watch the game, we can expect that a named person would sit down in front of the set and watch the game.

The above view still has problems. Some expressions such as "the planet Pluto" or "whereas" may not arouse any disposition to respond. Other utterances such as "It is snowing" may arouse different responses in different persons in similar situations. And the disposition of a named person to respond to a given utterance even under a list of specific conditions can vary. If responses in specified situations are not always predictable, the notion of disposition to respond has added problems requiring further analysis.

Behavioral theories of meaning continue to be refined. A common emphasis in these views appears to be basic to any theory of meaning. This emphasis is that meanings develop in a social context as persons interact with and respond to each other.

4.   Use Theories of Meaning

We associate the use theory of meaning with Ludwig Wittgenstein, but we are not limiting our interpretation of this position to his views. Advocates of the use theory seek to correct some of the defects found in the other theories and to advance a more tenable view. Put in its simplest terms, which are readily subject to distortion, the theory holds that the meaning of a linguistic expression is its use. "Use" in this view has a broad sense and includes the purpose of the language user in making an utterance in a social setting. The use theory of meaning takes seriously the way in which we learn meanings of expressions.

We learn the meaning of words in ordinary cases by taking note of their use and by using them in similar contexts. A child hears the word "dog" and sees a parent point to a dog. He may confuse the meaning of the word and use the word "dog" to refer to another pet such as a cat. The parent corrects the child by pointing to a dog and saying "dog," then imitates the bark of a dog and strokes the pet. Next the parent points to the cat, says "cat," and imitates the purring or the meowing of the cat. The child associates the conditions for using "dog" and "cat" with objects to which the names apply.

Learning to use a word is something like learning to mount a horse or to adjust the picture on a TV set. We learn to perform an appropriate act in part by watching others, by being instructed in doing the act and receiving suggestions on how to improve our performance. As we mature we can seek help in knowing the meaning of words by finding how a wider circle of people uses these expressions and how others have used them in the past.

We also learn the meaning of words by the use of clarifying examples or paradigm cases in which the word occurs. Consider the following examples:

> When someone borrows ten dollars from you and promises to repay you on Saturday, and after he meets you on Saturday he not only does not pay you back but asks to borrow another ten dollars, that is *gall*.
>
> The growth you see on my right hand is a *wart*.
>
> Companies like American Telephone and Telegraph, United States Steel, and General Motors are *giant corporations*.

To contrast basic views of use theories of meaning with views of other related theories may assist in clarifying some of the basic notions in dispute.

(1)   Use theories of meaning hold that we find meaning in the function that language fulfills in human activities. They reject the notion that (linguistic) meaning is some special form of entity, such as an idea.

(2)   Use theories hold that referring applies to a function of some but not all expressions. They reject the view that meaning requires every linguistic expression to have a referent, in the sense that the expressions always are directly or indirectly naming something.

(3)   Use theories hold that language has countless uses. They reject the view that the use of language is limited to a few restricted functions such as informing, requesting, asking, exclaiming, and directing. Language use includes the purpose a language user has in making an utterance.

(4)   According to most use theories, we relate meaning to a set of conditions. When we clarify these conditions we can determine the acceptable use of an expression for doing a definite job. In most cases one may set forth other conditions for use of an expression to clarify other meanings that an expression has.

(5)   Use theories hold that linguistic meaning relates to the way we use language in human behavior. But in contrast to some strict behavioral approaches they insist that the purpose of the language user in making the utterance is a critical issue in determining meaning. They reject the view that a behavioral or stimulus-response model applies to all cases of linguistic meaning.

In developing the view of meaning as use, the analysis of a speech act adapted from John L. Austin can be helpful.[1] One may distinguish various elements in performing a speech act. Suppose a student says to a roommate who is dozing in bed, "Your class meets in thirty minutes." We can note these phases in the act:

(1)   The act of uttering noises

(2)   The act of uttering expressions in accordance with social conventions of grammar

(3)   The act of making a linguistic utterance with some identifiable sense

(4)   The act of the utterer doing something other than saying something in making the utterance (such as reporting or advising)

(5)   The act of the utterer exerting some influence on some state of affairs by making the utterance (such as the roommate getting up, dressing, leaving, going to class)

[1] John L. Austin, *How To Do Things with Words* (New York: Oxford University Press, 1965), p. 108. For a discussion of the views of Wittgenstein and Austin and of some other topics treated in this chapter see William P. Alston, *Philosophy of Language* (Englewood Cliffs, N.J.: Prentice-Hall, 1964).

Austin called these phases of the speech act:

typically other theories

(1) Phonetic

(2) Phatic

(3) Locutionary

(4) Illocutionary

(5) Perlocutionary

In use theories of meaning all these phases of a speech act are relevant to determining meaning. The fourth phase, that of the speaker doing a job in making the utterance, is a highly controversial feature of this view. Reference theories and idea theories tend to emphasize the third phase, that of the utterance making identifiable sense. Behavioral theories emphasize among other things something close to the fifth phase, which relates to the response made to the utterance. But some behavioral theories also permit the language user to expect some response. And the expected response becomes a part of the meaning of the expression.

In what practical way does the use theory of meaning help us in determining the meaning of an expression? It guides us to look at how one uses an expression. By looking at such uses we also are looking for conditions of its use and to the social conventions related to its use. Any given expression can have various uses and various conditions for each of its uses. Consider the different types of conditions and social conventions associated with the expression "fire" in the following examples:

To inform as "fire" in the case of describing a happening

To warn as in "Fire!" in the case of a burning building with people still inside it

To guide to shelter as "Fire!" in the case of persons lost in a blizzard

To caution as "Fire!" in the case of a scouting party approaching a campsite of unknown origin

To seek help as "Fire!" in the case of a field of grass burning near houses

To signal an act as "Fire!" in the case of target practice

To change a relationship as "I fire you"

To express some belief as "Fire is a symbol of change," "Fire is a symbol of the divine," or "Fire is a symbol of freedom"

In works of science and other technical fields the conditions of use of many language expressions are more restrictive than in ordinary talk. Consider the conditions of use of the word "triangle" as this word is used in plane geometry:

a geometrical figure

a plane figure

a three-sided figure with straight lines

a figure with three and only three angles

Words used in ordinary discourse require a listing of many different conditions to accord with many different uses. Consider the conditions of use of the expression "brother":

a male

persons having the same parents

The expression also can be used under these conditions.

a male

a member of a religious or fraternal order

a member of an order whose members address each other by a word used to apply to persons who have the same parents

It also can be used under these conditions.

a male

a member of a minority ethnic group

a person who actively seeks equal rights and opportunities for members of his or her ethnic group

a member of a group whose members address other group members by a word used to apply to persons who have the same parents

Other sets of conditions can be given for use of this word in other contexts.

New meanings and language expressions are given meaning in a language community. These changes occur as we become aware of how to use such expressions to get some job done.

Many linguistic expressions apply to a wide range of cases. If we try to specify all possible sets of conditions for such uses, the task will be time consuming and may never be completed. The conditions for use of language expressions vary from one generation to another and also from one region to another.

In setting forth conditions for language use we usually are concerned with those that apply to the time and region of the language user. We also list the uses of those sets of conditions that most adequately state the meaning of the expression. Language remains open ended, making possible new meanings for given expressions while other meanings fade away.

The set of conditions sufficient for the use of a word frequently is not an object of immediate attention. Neither is it always feasible to expect a person who knows how to use a word to be able to list the conditions sufficient for its use. However, the gaining of technical or scientific knowledge may help to develop the ability to identify the conditions sufficient and essential for the use of technical words relevant to a given area of inquiry.

The use theory of meaning has several difficulties. One problem is that some language expressions appear to have some connotations not dependent on our knowing the conditions for their use. And to know the conditions relative to the use of an expression appears to presuppose that the expression already has some sense for us. This sense it has for us is not merely knowledge of the conditions for the use of a word. Otherwise how would we be able to list a set of conditions of its use in various contexts?

A second objection relates to a distinction we sometimes make between the meaning of an expression and its use. In some cases, when we ask the meaning of a word we do not appear to be asking merely how the word is used. Rather we appear to be asking an extralinguistic question. That is, we want to know the distinguishing elements of the classes of objects, relations, acts, or states of affairs to which the word applies. A response about how the word is used does not on its face appear to answer the question. That is, we are not directing such a question toward language use but toward conditions in an extralinguistic world that we try to signify by the use of language. Let us consider the apparent difference between these two questions:

Do you know that "the fat's in the fire"?

Do you know what conditions are sufficient to justify the use of the expression "the fat's in the fire"?

Let us assume that in some cases the answer to the first question is "Yes" and to the second question is "No." Why can this happen? In the first case we can be asking something about a nonlinguistic state of affairs. In the second case we are talking about our knowledge of a linguistic convention related to the use of an expression.

Consider a possible conversation regarding the meaning of the Spanish word *simpático*:

What is the meaning of *simpático*?

There is no English word that expresses its meaning.

Well, tell me what it means.

Let me tell you the condition for its use. We use the term to describe:
a person who is pleasant
one who is considerate and friendly
one who is sensitive to the feelings of others
one who acts so as to make others feel at ease
one who acts to show regard for the dignity of others.

But I did not ask how you use the word. I asked about the character a person must have that would justify your saying that such a person was *simpático*.

Well, at least you know the conditions for using the word.

Yes, you have helped me to know when I use the word according to certain language conventions. Can I assume that you also are saying something about a person that we describe as *simpático*?

A third objection to the use theories of meaning relates to the kind of job such theories actually do. What is it that they do? They help us to identify the use that language expressions have, to clarify conditions for their use, and to distinguish between their different uses. This is a much-needed job. And in many cases the analytic tools provided by the use of this approach to language are of great aid. But the fact that these tools are helpful does not establish that the view of meaning found in these theories is complete. Briefly put, this objection states that some use theories fail to draw a line between useful techniques for identifying and distinguishing language meaning, and the meaning they are clarifying.

Those who follow use theories of meaning can reply to these objections. We can accept the view that in some cases, when we ask the meaning of an expression we are asking how we go about using it in a language community. What we are objecting to is the view that this is the question we are always asking when we raise such an issue. But we shall recommend a view of meaning that has many elements of use theories in it.

5. Meaning and Context

We have seen that problems emerge with any theory of meaning we have discussed. So we can expect any theory we adopt to have problems. A part of the difficulty in finding a theory of meaning is the variety of jobs we expect a theory of meaning to do.

Let us review some of the things we may be asking when we inquire about the meaning of a given linguistic expression. We can be asking about one or several of the following matters.

The ideas, images, abstractions associated with the expression

The referent of an expression

The function a word has in relating different parts of an expression to each other

The use a word has in a given context

The conditions for using a word to get a given job done

The act the language user is doing when he makes a linguistic expression

The kinds of situations that tend to give rise to these expressions

The responses or conditions that the language user expects to bring about by using this expression

The social conventions that relate to the use of the expression

The kinds of objects, characteristics, relations, feelings, actions, states of affairs to which we can apply this expression

What kind of response can we make to the question, "What is the meaning of the linguistic expression x?" In this case x covers any given linguistic expression that we might use. There does not appear to be any single or simple answer to such a question. We have to examine both the context in which the question arises and the context relevant to making a satisfactory response. We shall call such an approach to linguistic meaning a "context theory of meaning."

What does context theory of meaning signify for us? It means that when we want to find the meaning of a given linguistic expression the total situation has to be taken into account before we can answer the question, "What is the meaning of the linguistic expression x?" We have to dig the meaning out of the context in which the expression occurs.

Linguistic meaning, in this view, is the sense of an expression used in a given context. By sense we mean what a linguistic utterance conveys or does in a complete and independent linguistic expression. What are some of the things language utterances convey or do? We have seen that they express ideas, images, and abstractions; they talk about classes, properties, and relations; they signify expectations and feelings; they express actions, states of affairs, and conditions; and they signify how elements of language expressions are connected and how they function.

By the context of an utterance we are signifying, in part, the conditions of a situation that elicit our making a given linguistic utterance. We wish to include in such situations matters like the following:

The general states of affairs present when the utterance is made

Happenings prompting the utterance

The utterance made and any emphasis given in its making

The act done by the language user in making the utterance

The job which the language user expects to do in making the utterance

The responses or changes occurring as a result of making the utterance

Units of meanings are combined according to social conventions to produce a complex unit of meaning. These complex meanings usually occur in a sentence, although what a sentence is remains in dispute among some logicians. In determining meanings we may need to refer not only to the sentence in which the expression occurs but to its larger context—a paragraph, a chapter, or a book, as well as the social conventions relative to meaning regarding the matter under consideration.

We have many different ways to determine meanings. Some of the usual ways to determine meanings of linguistic expressions include the following procedures:

Pointing to an object and repeating the expression, as in pointing to a dog and saying "dog."

Performing an act characteristic of the object or happening, as the act of kicking several different objects and saying "kick."

Drawing an object, as in drawing a chair and saying "chair."

Describing a situation to which a word applies, as in referring to dampness, limited visibility, and reduced range of a beam of light and saying "fog."

By use of a typical case to illustrate a meaning and saying "example" or "paradigm."

By use of similar words, as "By 'mix' I mean a blend, a putting together, a joining together."

By giving a class term and a restricting identifying property, as in "By 'vertebrates' I mean animals with spinal columns or backbones."

By providing sentences in which one finds the expression, as in "The libel suit has a *chilling* effect on the freedom of the press," and "The policies of the Nazis had a *chilling* effect on lectures given by professors in German universities."

By providing conditions for the use of an expression, as in the conditions for using "cough" as a sudden expulsion of air from the lungs, air passages, or the thorax originating either as an involuntary spasm of throat muscles or as an effort to clear the throat, air passages, or lungs.

By providing an explication that further restricts and classifies the use of a word whose general meaning is known but whose use is being limited for a special purpose.

In a context theory of meaning we need to distinguish between the meaning that a word or phrase can have in general, the meaning that such words or phrases have in a given sentence, and the meaning a given sentence has in the context of its use. These three factors cannot be taken in isolation. But in analyzing any given language expression, we begin with the context, which provides the basis for judging what a given expression means.

In dealing with arguments, we are concerned with something specific—the assertive meaning of statements. This type of meaning is what the statement tells us about how things are, what relations or characteristics hold in the realm of objects to which our discourse applies. Although sentences can be about words and phrases, we normally use words and phrases in statements to tell us something about a nonlinguistic matter. The assertive meaning of a statement is what it is saying about a given subject.

We determine the meaning of words and phrases in our discourse by reference to their conventional usage in the type of context that we are considering. Even in giving new meanings to words, we use conventional meanings in trying to convey the context for understanding the new meaning we are creating. The meaning of a word or phrase in a sentence is the range of what it connotes, of what it denotes, of what it relates, of what it connects, and of how it functions in the context of its use.

4.3 EXPRESSIONS WITH MEANING-RELATED FAULTS

Some expressions appear not to make any sense. Other expressions that apparently make no sense do make sense when we further examine their context. Let us consider the following expressions:

Don't buy a pig in a poke.

Don't buy a pig in a zoke.

Each of these expressions may appear senseless. However, using a dictionary one finds that "poke" can mean a (burlap) sack, but that "zoke" is not listed as a word and no conditions are given for its use. The former statement would then have some meaning but the latter would not. However, the literal meaning of "Don't buy a pig in a poke" does not seem to be the speaker's intended advice. Further inquiry could show that his advice meant, "Make sure of what you are buying and of its condition before you buy it." The second expression as a whole does not make sense. We are unable to tell people how to use "zoke" or what its basic properties are. And we would not know what advice, if any, is being given or whether it is good or bad.

We shall look at several different kinds of language expressions that have meaning related faults. The expression as a whole in these cases does not make sense and we have no way of judging what the language user intends to say. The fault is in the way the language expression is put together.

Some cases of faulty expressions of meaning are a result of uniting elements without meaning in an expression. Other faults occur when some elements are missing from an expression so that as a whole it does not make any sense. Another fault is the combining of the meaning of elements in such a way that a proposed sentence does not make sense. Let us consider these faults separately.

1.   Expressions with Elements Having No Meaning

The simplest form of expressions with meaningless elements is the use of nonsense syllables or of uniting syllables that do not make an accepted word. Consider these expressions:

> da ra ga vo ro wo

> The nookeria is niftidade.

These expressions make no sense. But some word of caution is in order: codes or abbreviations can use nonsense syllables. In such cases they can be constructed into sentences with meaning for persons who know how to use them. Likewise, the mixture of sense and nonsense expressions with a view to entertain or to satirize can have a meaning in the context of their use. Lewis Carroll's *Alice in Wonderland* is an example of this. Such cases need to be judged by their context and by the standards of meaning relevant to that form of talk.

Some apparent nonsense expressions also can have meaning in the context in which they occur. Consider some of the following cases. "Ho hum" can signify, "I am bored," or "What you say is trivial." "Fiddle-de-de" can signify, "What grounds does he have to say that or do that?" "Tra-la-la" can signify, "Mind your own business," or "I'll be seeing you."

2. Expressions with Missing Elements

In some cases expressions have no meaning because of missing elements. A series of words is present but the larger unit fails to make complete sense. Consider a string of words as in the following cases:

Whereas, we are among

The dried flowers are between

But a word of caution again is in order. In some cases an expression may not be complete, but the context in which it occurs can provide a basis for its completion. Consider the word "cake." Standing alone it does not express a completed meaning. Yet consider its use in the following context: "Do you prefer pie or cake for dessert?" "Cake." In this use the context provides a basis for completing the expression in the form, "I prefer cake." And the expression "Cake" makes sense.

3. Expressions with Faulty Ways of Mixing Elements

Sometimes expressions do not make sense when combined with other expressions. The elements in the expression do not mix because of the properties, actions, or conditions that the combined meanings signify as holding. The mixing of elements does not work because the elements in the complete expression do not relate to each other in a way that results in meaning. Let us consider some examples. We can describe flowers by their color such as red, blue, green, and purple. We also can describe football games as hard-fought, defensive, wide-open, fast-moving, mistake-ridden, high-scoring. However, a wrong mixture of meanings would occur if we made statements like the following:

The purple football game is a wide-open contest.

The mistake-ridden orchid is a beautiful gift.

The meanings of elements in these sentences do not go together.

In some cases expressions using verb forms are mixed with other elements whose meaning does not fit. Consider the following cases where the meaning of the verb form is applied in a literal sense:

The dogs conspired against their enemy.

The building is longing for occupants.

The beach bristled with anger as the globs of grimy oil oozed into the pores of its sandy shores.

Some logicians would regard the sentences in the last two sets of examples as meaningless. Others would acknowledge that a mistake in meaning is present. They hold that the expressions are meaningful, but that as literal statements they are trivially false. We shall take a view in agreement with W. V. Quine that the latter position has fewer difficulties and is preferable.[2]

Other cases of a wrong mixing of the meanings of expressions occur when different elements of an expression signify a state of affairs that cannot go with another meaning within a single sentence. Consider the following expression:

> The barefoot boy now spreading peanut butter on a slice of bread in the kitchen at this moment is climbing the roof in his tennis shoes.

The meaning expressed by the first part of the sentence cannot go with the meaning expressed by the latter part.

Sometimes we use expressions in a figurative or poetic way to add color, to make a point, or to express feelings. Suppose the following statements are made during a football game:

> The football field is a gladiator's arena.

> The football field is square in shape.

In the first statement the use of "gladiator's arena" is figurative. The announcer might be trying to give color to his description of the force of impact in the blocking and tackling that is taking place. The second sentence saying that the football field is square is meaningful. The football field does have a geometrical shape, but the shape is not that of a square. This statement is false. This sentence would not be a clear example of the fault of mixing the meaning of elements that do not fit together.

Let us consider the expression, "The football field is a feathered creature." This is a clearer example of the fault of mixing the meaning of elements that do not fit. There is a lack of relevance in using expressions like "feathered creature" in either a literal or figurative way when describing a football field. And we can say this statement also is trivially false.

Suppose someone made the statement, "This car is the only car I own and this car is not the only one I own." This statement is meaningful but it cannot be true. It is a compound sentence that joins two units of meaning with the connective "and." The first part of the original sentence can be made into a separate sentence, "This is the only car I own." The second part also can be made into a complete sentence. Each of these separate

[2] W. V. (sometimes W. V. O.) Quine, *Methods of Logic*, 3d ed. (New York: Holt, Rinehart and Winston, 1972), p. 215.

sentences are meaningful. But they both cannot be true at the same time and in the same place and circumstances. In the above sentence (about the car) each of the separated sentences can be meaningful. But when they are joined together by "and," the statement is false.

Let us consider another case and assume that some writer is expressing his feelings in an article about a conflict he has seen. Somewhat in a poetic vein he writes,

> The trees drooped their branches in horror at the blood spewed out beneath their gnarled trunks.

Taken in any literal sense, this would not be a meaningful expression. But we would say that the expression could have meaning in a figurative or poetic way.

We can consider another example in a statement reported in the news media. A person was unhappy about some minority groups not being fully represented in President Carter's initial Cabinet appointments. He claimed that some people got pure peanuts, others got peanut butter, and some got peanut hulls. We would hold that this expression is meaningful and that its purpose was to make a point. Its intent probably was to bring further pressure on Carter's staff to recommend more persons from minority groups for key positions in the administration.

In this chapter we examined various theories of meaning and noted that each has difficulties. But we argued that perhaps a context theory has fewer difficulties than the others. We also reviewed some of the types of expressions with meaning-related faults.

In the next chapter we shall look further into the problem of meaning and shall glance at some traditional language uses. Then we shall analyze some methods for clarifying meaning by definitions.

EXERCISES

A. Give a set of conditions sufficient for using the following expressions. (Please note that several sets of such conditions could be made for these expressions.)
1. Circle
2. Sister-in-law
3. Book
4. Physician
5. Mention of a word
6. Politician
7. Legal right
8. Human rights

B. Identify three different kinds of things a speaker might be doing in making the following statements:
  1. It is very late.
  2. I have a date tonight.
  3. The economy is in a mess.
  4. We have been fiddling while Rome is burning. (A figurative expression)
  5. The chemistry course is hard.

C. Name or illustrate five different procedures to show the linguistic meaning of the following expressions:
  1. Skiing
  2. A teacher
  3. A planet
  4. Defendant
  5. Due process

D. Identify the type of meaning-related faults in the following expressions:
  1. The calculator is angry.
  2. The man now sitting in the chair in the living room is now walking in the next block.
  3. The do re mi is ho de te.
  4. He is beside.
  5. He dumped his agreement to pay me the two round squares he owes me.

CHAPTER 5

LANGUAGE USES AND DEFINITIONS

5.1 SOME CONVENTIONAL USES OF LANGUAGE

In the preceding chapter we looked at various uses of "meaning." In this chapter we shall examine some conventional uses of language and some ways we express what a word means by definitions. Guidelines for good definitions will be set.

We have found that constructing a theory of linguistic meaning is difficult and that any theory of meaning will need to take into account the uses of a linguistic expression in a given context. The meaning of a linguistic expression varies with its context. In ordinary discourse language use is not as simplistic as a partial survey of some examples may appear.

Wittgenstein emphasizes the multiple and varied purposes of language use in Section 23 of his *Philosophical Investigations*. There are "countless kinds" of sentences, symbols, and words. Language use is constantly changing. "New types of language . . . come into existence, and others become obsolete and get forgotten."[1] He provides the following cases of linguistic uses among many other possible examples.

---

[1] Ludwig Wittgenstein, *Philosophical Investigations,* trans. by G. E. M. Anscombe, 2d Ed. (New York: Macmillan, 1958), pp. 11-12.

Giving orders, and obeying them—

Describing the appearance of an object or giving its measurements—

Constructing an object from a description (a drawing)—

Reporting an event—

Speculating about an event—

Forming and testing a hypothesis—

Presenting the results of an experiment in tables and diagrams—

Making up a story; and reading it—

Play-acting—

Singing catches—

Guessing riddles—

Making a joke; telling it—

Solving a problem in practical arithmetic—

Translating from one language into another—

Asking, thanking, cursing, greeting, praying.

We note that a close relation holds between the use of an expression and its meaning. In determining such meaning we need to consider what a language user expects to accomplish in making an utterance. Furthermore, we need to know the kind of response elicited by the expression. What meaning does the following expression suggest by its use? "A little learning is a dangerous thing." What does a person who makes this statement expect to accomplish? What kind of response does one expect? Is the speaker merely reporting on a number of cases and making a generalization? Is she seeking to discourage inquiry unless it is done in depth? Is she motivating someone to make a more thorough inquiry about those views about which she expresses an opinion? Is the speaker poetically vague to provoke a variety of reactions?

We shall consider various language uses under the conventional labels of influencing, asking, emoting, conforming, performing, evaluating, and informing. Such a list is highly restrictive and refers only to a few of many different uses of language. For each different kind of language use we also can find a corresponding kind of meaning. We shall also discuss these language uses from the point of view of the person who makes the utterance. We cannot determine uses of language solely by grammatical form.

1. Influencing Use of Language

The influencing use of language has as its purpose some change in the courses of action of other persons. In its most common form it expresses a command or request. But it also occurs as suggestions, questions, reports, or advice. The following examples show this type of use.

Put the book on the desk.

Will you help me with this problem?

The room is too stuffy.

I would suggest that you leave before the rain starts.

Some writers refer to this type of language use as the directive use of language. It often occurs with other types of language use.

2. Asking Use of Language

The asking use of language raises a question. We can illustrate its use in the following examples:

What time is it?

Who do you believe will be our next president?

Some writers refer to this type as the interrogative use of language.

3. Emotive Use of Language

The emotive use of language expresses our feelings, attitudes, or emotions. We often combine this use with other forms of language uses. Sometimes this use also is called the expressive use of language. Some examples of this use are the following:

A thing of beauty is a joy forever.

We won the game!

Peace be with you!

In ordinary discourse words or phrases can vary widely in the degree to which they convey any emotive meaning in contrast to essentially a neutral meaning. We shall consider the following examples:

Smith is open to new ideas in his views on politics.

Smith is a weird radical in his views on politics.

Smith supports a major role for private enterprise in his political views.

Smith is a bigoted supporter of reactionary power groups in his political views.

The words used in the first and third statements are basically neutral in that they are trying to tell us something about Smith's political views. But they do not appear to be used to influence directly our attitude toward Smith. Some of the words used in the second and fourth statements have obvious emotive overtones. And they appear to be trying to influence our attitudes and feelings toward Smith.

Emotive words express feeling and many of them are used with a view to influence the feelings and attitudes of other persons. Neutral or non-emotive expressions tell us how things are or at least how we believe things are. But they are not in themselves the kinds of utterances that usually give direct expression to how we feel about things or how we would like others to feel. Yet we are aware that some words taken apart from a context are not subject to an immediate labeling regarding their use as an emotive expression. "Damn" is usually an emotive word. But in the expression, "'Damn' is a word used to express strong feelings of disapproval," "damn" is mentioned rather than used. And in this context it is neutral.

Emotive words vary in the degree to which they express feelings. Some words that tend to have an emotive meaning are "rascal," "pigheaded," "true-blooded," "fink," "hocum," and "hoodlum." Some words that one expects to be neutral are "book," "ocean," "microscope," "atom," "germ theory," "history," "building," and "oxygen." Some words that may be emotive or neutral words depending on the context are "liberal," "conservative," "cynical," "sly," "pigeon," and "smooth."

The use of emotive words to influence the attitudes, feelings, and actions of audiences varies widely. The kind of response made to such use also varies with the dominant interests and concerns of the group. In some cases subtle use of emotion can be effective with an informed audience. If a speaker calls his opponent a fool or a liar, he may be thought to be speaking too harshly. In other cases he may be regarded as "telling it like it is."

We expect to find emotive words used in good novels and poetry. In some cases the ability to express views with an emotional overtone is an essential part of what we expect a good writer or speaker to do. If a person is reporting her reactions to a tragic subway accident, to the rescue of some children from a flood, or to the closing seconds of a closely fought athletic contest, we would be surprised if emotive words were not used. We have standards for evaluating good reporting that are appropriate to these types of acts. And these standards include the manner of dealing with the emotions of the situation.

The logician is primarily interested in the use of nonemotive words. Emotive words can be ambiguous and vague when used to describe what the evidence holds and how well it supports a claim. The use of emotive elements also provides a means to digress from the claim an argument makes.

4. Conforming Use of Lanugage

The conforming use of language has social custom as its basis. Writers also refer to this type as the ceremonial use of language. Within limits, this use of language helps us to interact with one another. It can serve to "break the ice" in meeting other persons. Also, it can be a means of relating to other persons in a social setting. The following examples illustrate this use of language.

> Good morning.
>
> Have a good day!
>
> I'm so sorry that I have made other plans for that evening but please call me again.
>
> It is a pleasure to meet you.
>
> Your home-cooked meal was great.

We judge ceremonial uses of language as fitting or unfitting or as in good taste or in poor taste, but we do not judge them as true or false.

5. Performing Uses of Language

In making an utterance we are performing an act. In a broad sense we could say that any speech act is a performing use of language. But we want to narrow what we mean by the performing use of language to cases in which the speech act itself changes some relationship. It can mark the beginning of a new state of affairs, the ending of an old one, or some variation in a continuing one. We also can indicate some change in obligations that we recognize. This is more restricted than the view of what is sometimes referred to as the performative use of language. Some examples of the performing use of language are the following:

> I declare this meeting adjourned.
>
> I proclaim this week "Be Kind to Students Week."
>
> I confer on you the degree of Bachelor of Arts.
>
> I pronounce you husband and wife.

I free you from your promise.

I increase my offer by $100.

We judge such language uses as fitting or unfitting, proper or improper, but not as true or false.

6. Evaluating Use of Language

In the evaluating use of language we make judgments about the worth of things or events. An act is judged to be right or wrong; a painting is judged to be excellent, average, or poor; some policies are good—others are bad. Some examples of this use of language are the following:

Cheating is wrong.

The play is great.

The sunset is beautiful.

The air pollution is terrible.

7. The Informing Use of Language

[handwritten: always either true or false.]

The informing use of language tells us how things are. We are letting this type of language use cover a very broad range. It will be used to include any sentence that can be said to be either true or false. When other language uses that we have already discussed are also regarded as true or false, they also are using language to inform. Other cases of this language use are the statements about what we know, what we report, how we explain, how we interpret, how we relate materials or ideas. Some examples of this view of the informing use of language are the following:

Lead is heavier than water.

Isaac Newton was a physicist.

The clock stopped because of a power failure.

If the energy shortage continues, we shall have more persons without jobs.

The informing use of language is the type in which we have a basic interest in logic and in the study of arguments. We shall return to comment further on this use of language in other sections of this work.

Many of our utterances have more than one use in a given context. Such instances are called the mixed use of language. If we have a mixed use of language, then we also need to identify the basic types of uses which we find in the given case.

EXERCISES

A. Identify the type of conventional language use in the following examples. In the case of mixed uses, give more than one traditional use.
   1. The door is locked. *Inform   Influence*
   2. Turn in your papers. *Influence*
   3. What did you eat for lunch? *Ask*
   4. I declare this meeting adjourned. *Perform*
   5. Lying is wrong. *Evaluate*
   6. We have had a wonderful time. *conforming*
   7. My political opponent is a do-gooder. *emotive*
   8. Your father is arriving. *inform*
   9. Where are the car keys? *ask*
   10. The movie is unsuitable for children. *evaluate*
   11. I withdraw my offer. *perform*
   12. There is a mouse under the cabinet in the kitchen. *inform, influence, emotive*
   13. He did a lousy job. *evaluate*
   14. "With a little time, we'll all find that switching to metric is indeed no big *influence* deal—except, perhaps, for the worried farm wife who said she wasn't sure she could get her hens to lay eggs in metric sizes!"[2]

B. Determine which of the following words or statements are usually emotive, which are usually neutral, and which are emotive only in some contexts.
   1. "Battered," "puppy," "underdeveloped," "culturally deprived," "moralizing," "stupid," "sturdy," "hillbilly," "illiterate," "donkey," "fair-haired boy," and "emotive."
   2. "Provincial," "purloin," "pusillanimous," "lonely," "scrape," "scroll," "taxes," "territorial integrity," "vocal cords," "youthful," "crook," "freckle," and "cheese eater."
   3. "Smoke the cigarette of the thinking man." *E - appeal to prejudice*
   4. "Your fee is exorbitant." *E*
   5. "All triangles are plane figures." *N*

5.2 SOME FAULTY NOTIONS ABOUT THE USE OF WORDS

In this section we discuss several errors found in popular beliefs about the use of words. One of these is that the use of a word in some sense

[2] Kenneth F. Weaver, "How Soon Will We Measure in Metric?" *National Geographic,* Vol. 152, No. 2, August 1977, p. 294.

assures that there is some nonlinguistic thing to which it applies. A variation of this view is that there is some essential connection between labels given objects and those objects having the characteristic ascribed to them. A third view is that the mere saying of some words brings about certain other events in some magical way.

We can use words to do a great many jobs but there are many things they cannot do. For example, they cannot create nonlinguistic objects. But we use words in some domain of discourse. The fact that we have a domain of discourse does not assure us that there is a nonlinguistic world that corresponds to our talk about such a world.

A domain of discourse is the order or the level on which a given language use occurs such that we can test its concepts and statements for clarity and consistency. For example, in talking about fairy tales for children we may use words like "elves," "ghosts," and "fairies." This is one domain of discourse. In a discussion of mathematics we may use words like "positive integer" and "negative integer." This is another domain of discourse. Some physics terms are "atoms," "electrons," "gravity," and "mass." We can attempt to make the language of two levels of discourse consistent with each other. We may also develop a language to talk about other domains of discourse—the language of logic or math or ethics.

Domains of discourse are linguistic devices. They do not provide us any assurance that the world of fact or of nonlinguistic entities corresponds to our world of talk. Our use of a word on one level of discourse does not signify that what we intend that word to mean has existence in space and time. Words cannot bring objective entities into existence nor can they do away with them. Our language may influence the way we think about the world and even how we try to control what happens. But if we claim that an objective entity must exist because we have a word for it, we have committed a logical fault called the fallacy of reification. This fallacy consists in the claim that a given object has some type of physical existence on the basis that we have a word or phrase for such an object. We cannot claim that linguistic objects like "ghosts" and "demons," "fairies" and "elves" have an objective existence merely because we have a word for them. If atoms and molecules exist, it is for reasons other than our having words for them. Things have objective existence independently of our language use. Talking about things cannot make them exist. We reify a word if by using it we claim that some fictitious individual or class of linguistic objects must exist merely because we have a given word for it.

A related linguistic fault is that the mere use of words can create conditions that characterize things or relations. Simply stating that a public figure is a radical does not make him a radical. The labeling of a painting as a "creative work" does not make it a creative work. "A thing is what it is" and labeling it does not change its character. Obviously a label may influence the way we react to an object. If a label on a box reads "poison" and we have no other way of knowing about the contents, it would be foolish to eat its contents. But the mere label does not make what is in the box poison.

Using words as if they had some special nonlinguistic power to influence the course of events is called the fault of the magical power of words. The use of words as a means of communication may enable us to move mountains. But as physical objects or tokens, words have no physical force other than the vibrations made in their being uttered. The number 13 has no power to influence any event. But the fact that many people believe that 13 is an unlucky number has resulted in the omission "floor thirteen," from many buildings. If an announcer assumes that reference to a pitcher's having a "no-hit" game going has a relation to the pitcher's completing a "no-hit" game, he is deferring to a popular belief in the magical power of words. Likewise, knocking on wood to avoid a state of affairs referred to in a conversation is an instance of a superstition based, in part, on belief in the magical power of words.

5.3 NOMINAL AND REAL DEFINITIONS -vary according to context

One way we try to clarify what a word or phrase means is by definition. But the meaning of "definition" itself is not easy to state. A reason for the difficulty in stating an accepted meaning for "definition" is that we use so many different procedures in trying to clarify the meaning of a word. Words also are used in particular contexts and their meaning can vary with the context.

Suppose we are asked, "What is the meaning of 'clever'?" We likely would ask, "What was the context or sentence in which it was used?" And the reply is, "Mary was quite clever in the way she responded to the question asked her in class." Various responses to the original query about the meaning of "clever" could be made. "Well, Mary was just neat in the way she handled the matter." "She was ingenious in pointing out the different types of answers that had been given to this question and in focusing on the best one." "She was able to make some humorous responses that diverted attention from the fact that she was beating around the bush and not actually dealing with the question." And "Mary was quick-witted and showed good grasp of the subject in the response that she made." None of these replies provides a strict definition of clever. But each of them makes an attempt to clarify what "clever" could mean in the above context. These efforts to clarify either provide substitute words for "clever" or they suggest some conditions in which the word is used in such a context. For ordinary conversation, these meanings may suffice for our purposes. But in some cases we need more refined procedures for stating what words mean.

In general, a definition clarifies and makes explicit the meaning of an expression in a given context. A definition frequently gives the range and limits of the linguistic meaning of a word in a stated setting.

We are confronted with an issue by Plato and Aristotle. Do definitions describe some essences of objects to which a word applies? Or do they state simply a meaning ascribed to a linguistic sign and in this sense clarify the meaning of a word, without stating the essence of the class of objects for which the word is used? To explain these questions would require a lengthy treatment of "real" and "nominal" definitions. Adding to such a job is the highly varied manner in which different writers treat "real" and "nominal" definitions.

One approach holds that real definitions describe the actual nature or essence of the thing being described. Thus, if a definition were asked for words such as "house" or "good," a real definition would state the "actual nature" of a house or of good—that is, it would tell us the essence found in the objects to which such words apply. Writers holding this view have difficulty in showing how a verbal definition actually sets forth the essence of a nonverbal object merely by the use of words. Some writers question the usefulness of the notion of real definitions.

We shall take the position that definitions are nominal in the sense that they tell us primarily about the meaning of words in a context. A definition of "house" sets forth the meaning this word has in a given case. A definition of "good," if such is possible, states a common meaning of this word in different contexts (such as "something worthy of praise") rather than describing the "essence of good."

5.4 DEFINITIONS BY EXAMPLES

Some definitions are efforts to clarify meanings of words by use of examples. We say that such definitions are helpful or not helpful, or accurate or inaccurate. But usually we would not claim that they are true or false. Let us consider different types of such definitions.

1.   Examples by a Physical Act of Pointing to Objects

If we are asked what is meant by a "caboose" we can point to the last car on a freight train and say that is a "caboose." This type of defining is an _ostensive_ definition. An ostensive definition gives an example of the meaning of a word by the act of pointing to an object or to several different objects that are examples of things to which the word applies.

(handwritten: Substitution)

2.   Examples by Use of Words to Designate Objects

We can also use words to designate objects to which the word applies. In this case we have a verbal denotative definition. We could say, ''The last car on that freight train is a caboose.'' We also can give examples of several different cases to which a word applies. We could say, ''By 'van' I mean the kind of truck you see that is parked at that curb, or that is stopped at that light, or that is moving in front of that house.''

3.   Examples by Descriptive Phrases

We also can use descriptions to indicate the type of things to which a word applies. We could say that by ''truck'' we mean the kind of vehicle that moves furniture from one house to another, that moves freight on highways, that is used to deliver cattle by highways to stock yards, or that delivers food to grocery stores. Anyone with a basic knowledge of a language can use this technique. And it can be quite helpful in learning a language. But such a method also can have its limits of use. We can become confused about borderline cases, and may associate the wrong kind of objects or activities with the examples that are given. Also, we have a need for stating the meanings of words in more precise and inclusive ways.

5.5 STIPULATIVE DEFINITIONS

(handwritten: decision, not true or false, clarifying or muddling)

Stipulative definitions are meanings stated to restrict or to make more precise the way a word is used in a given context. A language user makes known that in a given context he or she made a decision to use a word in a given way. Stipulative definitions have the form, ''Let us use the word x to mean. . . .'' Since these definitions represent decisions, one judges them to be useful or not useful, clear or obscure, but not true or false. If some speaker also recommends the use of their stipulated meaning to others, the recommendations can be regarded as acceptable or unacceptable. Stipulative definitions that come to have general acceptance become reportive definitions. We shall consider three types of stipulative definitions. These types have to do with introducing new words, proposing new meanings for words in use, and making more precise the meaning of a conventional word.

1.   Introducing New Words

A language user may have occasion to introduce a new word into a language to convey a meaning not covered by conventional word usage. After the discovery of a sweet-tasting chemical substitute for sugar, some name was needed for it. The new name given this compound was "saccharin," based on a Latin word. A stipulative definition of "saccharin" was made. After common acceptance of the word, a lexical definition meaning came to be used with a popularized meaning given for the original stipulative meaning of the word.

2.   New Meanings for Words in Use

We also can stipulate new meanings for words already in use. At one time the word "cybernetics" meant the art of steering ships. The physicist Ampère provided a stipulated meaning for the term to refer to the science of social control. In 1948 Norbert Wiener stipulated another meaning for "cybernetics" as the science of communication that compares the functioning of the human nervous system and complex electronic calculating machines. But there was an extension of this meaning. And the study of cybernetics now includes an analysis and evaluation of communication and ways of using it to control living organisms, mechanistic devices, and organizations. In the above example we have a case of a stipulative definition proposed by Ampère that remained a stipulated definition since it did not become commonly accepted. The stipulative definition of Wiener became a lexical definition. But the word came to have a wider range of meaning than it had at the time of its initial common acceptance.

We also can consider another example of how words develop new meanings. At one time the word "planet" referred to any body in the heavens that appeared to move, in contrast to the stars that appeared to be fixed. It came to mean any celestial body that moves around the sun and reflects the sun's light. In modern astronomy it came also to include what are called minor planets, such as asteroids, which move in orbits between the major planets of Mars and Jupiter. An old word came to have a new meaning. Our language meanings develop and change as new meanings develop and some previous meanings fade out of use.

We also coin types of new words by use of abbreviations for a more complex meaning. A common example of this procedure is the way we may refer to some government agencies: HUD for the Department for Housing and Urban Development, and HEW for the Department of Health, Education and Welfare.

3.   Making the Meaning of a Word More Precise

We also use stipulative definitions to make the meaning of a word more precise. Some definitions of this type are known as explicative definitions. An explicative definition states some of the common characteristics associated with the use of a word and then places added restrictions on its use in a given context. Many definitions using legal or regulatory statements are of this type. We shall consider, for example, the meaning of "head of household." As this word is used in ordinary language it is vague. But the Internal Revenue Service provides an explicative definition for this phrase for use in income tax purposes. For this agency, "head of household" means "a person who both maintains a household and contributes over half the cost of maintaining the household, who is unmarried on the last day of the tax year and who has at least one relative using the household as his or her principal residence for the entire year." Other stipulative definitions are then provided to determine the way "maintaining a household" and "relative" are to be applied in the above case. (Such stipulated definitions can be subject to change in future years.)

5.6 REPORTIVE DEFINITIONS

Reportive definitions provide us with information about how a word is used or how it has been used. We can evaluate reportive definitions as true or false by adding a statement about the relevant context in which the defined word occurs. The following definition is true or false. In nineteenth century dictionaries, one meaning of the word "liberal" was "a characteristic of a person who sought to assure the exercise of certain basic personal and civil rights by limiting the powers of government." Reportive definitions are found in works on particular subjects and in dictionaries. There are five types: synonymous, historical, classifying, lexical, and stating conditions for use.

1. Synonymous Definitions

A synonymous definition uses a word with a meaning similar to the word being defined. These definitions, which are found in abridged or bilingual dictionaries, state the meaning of words by using other words with meanings generally known. Examples of synonymous definitions are the following: "Vagabond" means "vagrant." "Logic" means the same thing as the Spanish word "lógica." This method of definition is helpful in learning or in expanding a vocabulary. In many cases synonymous definitions do not have equivalent meanings. In the case of slang expressions a proposed synonym can be misleading. For example, a citizens' band operator states on his radio that he needs to stop and get some "motion lotion." Such an expression for gasoline likely would not be found in an abridged dictionary.

2. Historical Definitions

Historical definitions give the meaning that a word or phrase had at some time in the past. Language use changes from one period to another. Historical definitions help us to understand such past uses and, at times, the current use of such words. The definition of a "liberal person" given previously in this section is an example of a historical definition. Another example would be a historical definition of "economics." "In classical Greek one sense of the word 'economics' means the art of administering a household, an estate, a village or a state." Another example would be a historical definition of "cosmos." "In its historical meaning as developed by the Greeks, 'cosmos' means an orderly universe whose different parts worked together harmoniously to form a complete system."

3. Defining by Classification

Sometimes we make definitions by classifying or ordering the major types of objects which one finds covered by a given expression. We shall call this procedure "definition by classification." We could define "a company with public common stock" as a "corporation whose equities are bought and sold openly and competitively on national or regional exchanges and that engages in some form of industry, utility, transportation, merchandising or finance or in some combination of these activities."

4. Lexical Definitions   *in good unabridged dictionary*   *true or false*

A lexical definition states in some detail the current meaning that a word has in a given context. This kind of definition occurs in the better dictionaries, which illustrate the use of such words by quotations using these words in primary sources. One lexical definition for a current use of the word "jack" is the following. "A jack is a portable tool to lift heavy loads for a short distance by use of force originating in a movement by the hands of a screw, of a lever, or of a hydraulic instrument." Some lexical definitions are connotative definitions and these are discussed in the next section.

Many technical definitions used in science come to have acceptance as lexical definitions for special subject areas. Physicists define such words as "mass," "force," "field," "stress," and "strain" in ways understood primarily by serious students in this subject area. Technical definitions tend to occur in a context in which other words also have highly precise meanings. Consider a technical definition of "enzymes." "Enzymes are special kinds of protein that control the different steps in the synthesis or breakdown of an organic molecule." Technical definitions are often used as a part of a series of other definitions which, taken in their entirety, are essential to an understanding of the theoretical system of which they are a part.

Other technical definitions relate to the performance of a skill. A builder may refer to a floor joist for which he could give the technical definition, "A floor joist is a beam used to support the direct weight of the floor of a building and joined to adjacent materials such as girders as a means of providing support for the load carried by the beam."

A special case of technical definition is an operational definition. We associate operational definitions with P. W. Bridgman, a physicist. Operational definitions tend to connect the use of a word with some observable condition or act. The presence of such conditions or acts is essential for the technical use of the expression. An operational definition for "acid" would state the test for determining if a given solution is acid. A person making the definition would state that if a solution is acid, it will meet the following test: a piece of litmus paper placed in a solution turns red. In some cases the person giving an operational definition carries out the indicated "operation" while verbalizing the definition. Some writers use the following type of operational definition for "is harder than." "'Is harder than' means that if one rubs two unscarred objects, A and B, against one another and B is scarred and A is not, then it holds that 'A is harder than B'."

Many experiments in psychology require the use of operational definitions. For example, one may state the meaning of an "aggressive act" so that the technical use of the word requires that there is some type of physical attack on or verbal abuse of other persons or their property. This would be in contrast to an assertive act, in which a person sets forth personal claims or rights to satisfy specific interests. Then she takes steps to satisfy such claims or to express such rights but without using physical attacks or verbal abuses.

Operational definitions become reportive definitions only when they have recognition within a system and have use as statements within a context that makes possible their appraisal as true or false.

5. Defining by Stating Conditions for Use

Another way of defining a word is by forming a list of the conditions required for its use in a given instance. For example, in medicine, the word "syndrome" has the following conditions for its use:

A group of symptoms

Appearing in typical cases

Relating to abnormal organic conditions

Occurring in cases of a specific disease.

Another example: the term "jet stream" in reference to the upper atmosphere has the following conditions for its use:

A current of wind

Wind speed equal to or greater than 50 knots (approximately 58 miles per hour)

Direction of current usually from west to east

Altitude of current from 10,000 to 50,000 feet

Originates usually from currents around one of the earth's poles.

5.7 GUIDELINES FOR CONNOTATIVE DEFINITIONS

We have seen that there are numerous ways of making definitions. The way we go about defining depends, in part, on the purpose we have in stating the meaning of a word, and also on the level of understanding of our audience.

In this section we shall consider some conventional rules for making connotative definitions. We associate these rules with Aristotle. But we want to apply these rules primarily to the meaning of the words that we are defining rather than to some essence that objects covered by the use of such words may have.

One way of identifying the parts of a definition is by reference to the *definiendum* and the *definiens*. The *definiendum* is the word we are defining. The *definiens* is the part of the definition that clarifies the meaning of the word in a given context. Let us consider the definition, "A human being is a rational animal." The definiendum is "human being"; the definiens is "rational animal."

A connotative definition states the meaning of a word by specifying a larger (general) class to which a word applies. It then gives an essential and identifying property of the specific class to which the expression applies. Sometimes one refers to this type of definition as "definition by genus and difference." The genus is the general class noted in the definiens. The difference identifies an essential property of the members of the specific class to distinguish them from other members of the larger class. In the definition "A human being is a rational animal," the genus is "animal" and the difference is "rational." Sometimes we refer to the difference as the *differentia*.

The following guidelines for definitions apply to connotative definitions, but they can be helpful in judging other types of definitions as well.

1. Essential Characteristics

A good connotative definition should state the general class and basic identifying properties of the word we are defining. What are regarded as such essential characteristics may vary to some degree from one case to another, depending on the intended use of the definition. Unless we are focusing on the role of humor, a definition of "man" as "the animal that laughs" would fail to state the essential characteristics of the definiendum. The following definition of "galaxy" does state the essential characteristics of the word being defined: "A galaxy is a grouping of millions of stars together with gases and dust in a gravitational system with a disk-like shape, whose diameter approaches 90,000 light years, and whose thickness approaches 15,000 light years." But a definition of "habit" as "a practice that is hard to break" fails to state the essential characteristics of the word which is being defined.

2. Proper Range

The definiens needs to include all cases covered by the definiendum, but only those cases. Another way of stating this guideline is that a definition should not be too broad or too narrow. It should cover all cases to which the defined word applies, but no others. A definition is too broad if it includes other matters which are not a part of the meaning of the word. It is too narrow if the definition excludes some cases covered by the word. An example of a definition that is too broad is: "A square is a plane figure with four straight sides and four right angles." Rectangles are not excluded by this definition. A definition that is too narrow is: "A kibitzer is someone who is watching a card game and offers one of the players unwanted advice about how to play his or her hand." One can kibitz at games other than cards. Some definitions are too broad in one sense and too narrow in others. The definition "A novel is a narrative story" is too broad in the sense that some narrative stories are not novels. It also is too narrow in that some novels, such as those dealing with the absurd, may not be properly covered by the phrase "a narrative story."

3. Clear and Neutral Language

A definition needs to be stated in language that is clear, precise, and neutral. An acceptable definition of an "expert" could be the following: "An expert is a person who by training, experience, and knowledge is highly qualified to provide information, to render a judgment, or to perform a skill in a specialized field." The definition "An expert is an ordinary 'pert' who is away from home'' would not be satisfactory as a definition, but it might serve as a means of entertainment.

In stating definitions in clear, precise, and neutral language, we should not use expressions that are vague, obscure, poetical, figurative, facetious, sarcastic, cynical, or verbose. We find some examples of such faults in the following cases.

> Time is the moving image of eternity (Plato).
>
> A fanatic is a person who intensifies his efforts after he has lost his bearings.

Persuasive definitions are special cases of definitions which are not stated in neutral language. Persuasive definitions offer proposed meanings of words with a slant or bias so as to condition the emotions or attitudes of an audience in a way sought by the language user. In some cases the purpose of such definitions is to secure support for one position and to arouse a bias against another view. Some examples of persuasive definitions are the following:

> A conservative is a person who wishes to preserve the best of the past for future generations.
>
> A liberal is a person who seeks to change the defects of the past to maximize the enjoyment of the good life for future generations.
>
> A compromise is the sacrifice of a basic principle for personal gain.
>
> Social Security is a racket of taking money from hard working people to pay money to persons too lazy to work or too short sighted to save for their old age.

Such definitions tend to appeal to the emotions and prejudices of people. Many times they also fail to follow other guidelines for good definitions such as the need to state the essential characteristics of the objects for which the word is used.

4. Affirmative Manner

Definitions are to be stated in an affirmative manner where this can be done in a manner consistent with the use of an economy of language. That is, definitions should avoid needless negative statements or statements that tell us under what types of conditions a word does not apply. We need to know the conditions for using the word. An example of failing to state a definition in an affirmative manner is, ''A vice is a habit that is not good.''

Occasionally we may need to define a word that basically has a negative type of meaning. In such cases we can properly use a definition that has a negative element. For example, an empty class may be defined as ''the denotation of a set of objects ascribed to have one or more properties in common but the set of indicated objects has no actual members." Such cases of a permissible negative element in an acceptable definition are unusual. Examples of other definitions that needlessly refer to negative factors are:

> A simple substance is something that is not compound.

> A good teacher is one that is not just average or poor.

> Human beings are bipeds without any feathers.

Most definitions with negative elements are usually too broad. They also tend to omit the essential characteristics of the objects covered by the word which is being defined.

5. Avoiding Needless Circularity

A good definition avoids needless circularity. A circular definition defines one word by use of a second word, which in turn derives its meaning from the original word. This fault is evident in the definition, "A scientist is one who engages in scientific activity." Use of a synonym for the word defined is another example of this fault, for instance, "A cat is a feline creature." A circular definition also occurs when we define an original word by a second word and then define the second word by reference to the first, for example, "An effect is something that has a cause and a cause is something that has an effect."

It is permissible to repeat a part of a phrase of a definiendum in the definiens if one already has clarified that part in the general context in which the new definition also occurs. We can define "premise" as "a statement in an argument that provides relevant evidence in the support of a conclusion." It is permissible in such a case to define "major premise" as "the premise in a categorical syllogism that has as one of its terms the term that also occurs as the predicate term of the conclusion." This definition is not needlessly circular. Rather it is a move for economy of word and avoids needless repetition of a definition that already appears in the general context of the discussion.

Other examples of definitions that show needless circularity are:

> A normal person is one who acts normally.

> A rat is a rodent.

> A husband is someone who has a wife and a wife is someone who has a husband.

In summary, in making acceptable connotative definitions, we need to take into account the context in which we give a definition. This context includes our purpose for giving the definition and the level of understanding of our audience. A good definition should enable us to distinguish cases where a word applies from those where it does not.

This chapter has reviewed some of the traditional uses of language. We noted that in making definitions we are attempting to state the meaning of a word rather than the essence of the class of objects to which a word refers. We looked at various ways of making definitions and developed some guidelines for connotative definitions.

EXERCISES

A. Use the guidelines for good connotative definitions to evaluate the following proposed definitions:
   1. A square is a plane figure with four right angles. *range*
   2. Politics by consensus is the policy of substituting mediocrity in leadership for initiative in decision-making. *essential char*
   3. A star is any stellar object. *circular*
   4. A postman is the government employee who comes most frequently to residences. *range*
   5. Communism is a form of government that is in control of the Communist party. *circular*
   6. A conservative is a person who wants to live in the past. *essen, narrow pers.*
   7. A clock is an instrument for keeping time.
   8. A student is someone who studies. *circ.*
   9. Darkness is the opposite of light. *negative*
   10. A Democrat is a man who wants to exploit the miseries of the poor to gain political power. *persuasive, not clear & neutral*
   11. A Republican is a person who wants to have the rich get richer and the poor get poorer. *not essential char. persuasive not clear & neutral*
   12. "Beauty is the flower of virtue." (Zeno, c. 336–265 B.C.)
   13. "By moral reasoning, I understand all reasoning that is brought to prove that such conduct is right, and deserving of moral approbation; or that it is wrong; or that it is indifferent, and, in itself, neither morally good nor ill." (Thomas Reid, 1710–1796) *circular*
   14. ". . . Duty is the obligation to act from reverence for law." (Immanuel Kant, 1724–1804)
   15. "Sensations are those internal feelings of the mind, which arise from the impressions made by external objects upon the several parts of our bodies." (David Hartley, 1705–1757)
   16. ". . . the cost of a thing is the amount of what I will call life which is required to be exchanged for it, immediately or in the long run." (Henry D. Thoreau, *Walden*; 1817–1862)

B. Identify the types of definitions found in the following examples.
1. "Still another definition of the foot comes from a 16th-century German regulation: 'Stand at the door of a church on Sunday, bid 16 men to stop, tall ones and short ones as they happen to pass out as the service is finished, then make them put their left feet one behind the other and the length obtained shall be a right and lawful rod, and the 16th shall be a right and lawful foot.' "[3]
2. "Capital is that part of the wealth of a country which is employed in production, and consists of food, clothing, tools, raw materials, machinery, etc., necessary to give effect to labor." (David Ricardo, 1772–1823)
3. "For scientific use, temperatures are measured in kelvins starting with absolute zero ($-273.15°C$). A kelvin is equal to a degree Celsius. In addition, the meter has been redefined, for even greater accuracy, as 1,650,763.73 wavelengths of orange-red light emitted by the krypton-86 atom."[4]
4. "The *will* is the causality of living beings in so far as they are rational. *Freedom* is that causality in so far as it can be regarded as efficient without being *determined* to activity by any cause other than itself. Natural *necessity* is the property of all nonrational beings to be determined to activity by some cause external to themselves." (Immanuel Kant, 1724–1804)
5. "There is often a great deal of difference between the will of all and the general will; the latter regards only the common interest, while the former has regard to private interests, and is merely a sum of particular wills; but take away from these same wills the pluses and minuses which cancel one another, and the general will remains as the sum of the differences." (Jean Jacques Rousseau, 1712–1778)

Negative definitions are too broad
"null set" – w/out members; fail to state EC

null set – has no members
– fails to have a member
– is w/o members

---

[3] Weaver, "How Soon Will We Measure in Metric?", p. 288.
[4] Weaver, "How Soon Will We Measure in Metric?", p. 289.

CHAPTER 6

ANALYZING ARGUMENTS

6.1 DEDUCTIVE AND INDUCTIVE ARGUMENTS

In this chapter there will be a further analysis of arguments. We shall distinguish between deductive and inductive arguments as well as valid and invalid arguments. We shall also look at ways of analyzing arguments and of distinguishing issues in disputes.

As we have seen, arguments contain a series of sentences or of elements that can be expressed as sentences. In fully expressed arguments sentences should be in the form of statements.

Premises are the statements of an argument which provide evidence for justifying a conclusion. The conclusion is the statement set forth as derived from the premises and as justified by them. In making an argument one is making a claim. This claim is that a conclusion holds on the basis of the evidence given in its support.

One can assert, "All Athenians are Greeks," and "All Greeks are rational persons." He can make the inference and state the claim of the argument as "Thus, all Athenians are rational persons."

Logicians also extend the use of the notion of a claim of an argument to include the argument's conclusion. This is done without requiring that reference to a person making such a claim be stated explicitly in the context. Thus, we can say that the claim of the above argument is "All Athenians are rational persons."

In deriving a conclusion from the premises of an argument, we are making an inference. Many logicians restrict the notion of inference to this instance. In this view it is incorrect to say that the evidence given by the premises in the above argument infers the conclusion, "All Athenians are rational persons." It would be correct to say that Jan or Tom makes this inference, based on the stated reasons.

Sentences used to express an argument are usually statements. But other types of sentences occur in some implicit arguments. We shall need to recast such sentences as statements to analyze them in the types of arguments we shall study in this work. Some examples of arguments whose original forms have sentences that are not statements are the following:

(1) What a beautiful spring day!
We have the time.
So let's take a walk in the park along the dogwood trails.

(2) Take your topcoat.
The weather forecaster announced a cold front moving this way.
Do you want to catch a cold?

There are several ways in which we can restate the above arguments in the form of statements to make their claims more apparent. In such cases some of the force of the original sentences is lost. The above two arguments can be restated in the following manner:

(3) If we have both a beautiful spring day and the time, then we need to take advantage of the opportunity to walk in the park along the dogwood trails.
We have both a beautiful spring day and the time.
Therefore, we need to take advantage of the opportunity to walk in the park along the dogwood trails.

(4) If the weather forecaster announces a cold front moving this way, then you need to avoid taking a chance on catching a cold.
If you need to avoid taking a chance on catching a cold, then you need to take your topcoat.
The weather forecaster announces a cold front moving this way.
Therefore, you need to take your topcoat.

Many sentences occurring in a common context do jobs other than make arguments. The following sentences neither make an argument nor present evidence to justify a conclusion.

(5) John slouched into the chair and mumbled to himself. He glanced at the floor and then at the ceiling. He fumbled for a cigarette, lit it, and drew a few puffs. As he twiddled his fingers, his eyes roamed aimlessly about the room.

Deductive- premises true, conclusion true

Inductive- premises true conclusion probably true

Let us move toward analyzing the difference between inductive and deductive arguments. We shall state what this difference is and then attempt to clarify it.

We have seen that logic is a study of ways to justify and evaluate arguments and to analyze the elements found in arguments and in argument forms. Deductive logic is the logic of necessary inference. It is the analysis of arguments whose form requires that in all cases in which the conclusion is false, at least one premise be false.

Inductive logic is the logic of probable inference. It is the analysis of arguments that can yield conclusions that are unlikely to be false when the statements presenting the evidence are true.

In making a distinction between deductive and inductive arguments, we focus on the logical relation holding between the statements giving the evidence and the statement giving the conclusion. The argument is deductive if there is a claim internal to the argument that accepting the statements presented as evidence as true also requires the acceptance of the conclusion as true. The argument is nondeductive if there is a claim internal to the argument that by accepting the statements presented as evidence as true it is highly unlikely, yet possible, for the conclusion to be false. For our purposes we shall regard a nondeductive argument as an inductive one. But in a more technical study we would make some exceptions to this last statement.

Let us look at the relation of the conclusion to the premises in the following arguments.

(6)   All presidents are politicians.
Some presidents are persons of good judgment.
Thus, some persons of good judgment are politicians.

(7)   If we increase taxes, we lose purchasing power.
We increase taxes.
Thus, we lose purchasing power.

Do these arguments hold that in accepting the premises as true, it is necessary also to accept their conclusion as true? They do. And they are deductive arguments.

Let us examine some other arguments.

(8)   *A* is a satellite and it has an elliptical orbit.
B, C, D, and *E* also are satellites and they have elliptical orbits.
Hence, all satellites have elliptical orbits.

(9)   The last five times we have had ice storms, John has been late to work.
We have an ice storm today.
Hence, John will be late to work today.

Are these arguments inductive or deductive? Do the arguments appear to hold that if the statements presenting the evidence are true, then the conclusion is necessarily true? They do not. The arguments appear to hold that given the evidence, it appears unlikely that the conclusion is false. Therefore, they are inductive.

Inductive arguments can take various forms. One form is enumeration. A second form is analogy. And a third form is the use of hypotheses and testing. We shall discuss inductive logic in the third section of this work.

As we have seen, a critical way to distinguish deductive arguments from inductive ones is to determine whether the argument holds that acceptance of the truth of the premises necessitates accepting the truth of the conclusion. If the claim of the argument holds to this position, the argument is deductive. If it does not, it is nondeductive. But we cannot make the above distinction merely by the confidence with which we advance a conclusion. Someone may advance a correct deductive argument with some reservations regarding the truth of a premise. Such reservations may appear to a beginner in logic to make the argument a nondeductive one, but they have no bearing on the strict logical correctness of the argument. However, the use of such reservations may lead a person mistakenly to call the argument an inductive one.

On the other hand a nondeductive argument can be stated so that the conclusion appears to be presented as true, without any reservations. Yet the mere conveying of this impression does not make the argument a deductive one. When distinguishing between deductive and inductive arguments some guidance can be found in the deductive and nondeductive arguments presented in this chapter. But some understanding of materials discussed later in this book is essential to be able to make such distinctions with greater skill.

Some popular ways of defining induction and deduction are faulty. Consider the wrong claim that a deductive argument is one whose statements proceed from matters of wider generality in the premises to those of greater particularity in the conclusion. The following deductive argument illustrates this view.

(10)   All men are mortal.
        Socrates is a man.
        Hence, Socrates is mortal.

But the statement in the conclusion, "Socrates is mortal," is a statement of wider generality than the preceding statement, "Socrates is a man." Surely, we find no notion of wider or lesser generality in the following

Induction: by enumeration – from particular to general or from one particular to another particular

deductive argument:

(11) A is equal to B.
       B is equal to C.
       Thus, A is equal to C.

The above way of identifying deductive arguments will not do.

The account of induction as arguments in which the order of generality proceeds from statements of greater particularity to those of greater generality also has problems. The following type of model sometimes is the basis for illustrating this view.

(12)   Cretan A lies.
       Cretan B lies. . . .
       Cretan L lies. . . .
       Cretan W lies.
       Thus, all Cretans are liars.

But notice an apparent assumption that is missing. This assumption is that "All Cretans are persons who misrepresent things like the Cretans with whom I have talked." If we grant this assumption, then look at what happens. A proposed inductive argument now has a statement assumed as evidence and that statement has the degree of generality found in the conclusion.

The limited generalization from the statements given above would permit the forming of the sentence, "All Cretans with whom I have talked are liars." Note that this limited generalization is simply a summary statement of common properties shared by a limited number of persons who are members of a larger group. This limited generalization is not the conclusion of any argument. It reports on what has been found.

Note also what has happened to our inductive argument. In seeking to clarify the evidence to justify the conclusion, we found an assumption. And when we express this assumption as a statement in the argument we find that it now has a deductive argument as a part of the total argument.

Let us look at the following restatement of the argument:

(13)   All persons who misrepresent things like the Cretans with whom I have talked are liars.
       All Cretans are persons who misrepresent things like the Cretans with whom I have talked.
       Therefore, all Cretans are liars.

The popular view, that one can identify induction as an argument whose order of statements proceeds from those of lesser generality in the premises to those of greater generality in the conclusion, also is faulty.

The purpose of the above discussion is not to discredit inductive logic. Rather its purpose is to show that some popular views about induction do not meet the conditions claimed to apply to them. In a later section we shall see that induction is the most effective method we have in carrying out some types of inquiry. Its use is basic both in science and in critical common sense.

symmetrical relation - (reflexive) equals
if premises are true, conclusion is true.

EXERCISES

A. Which of the following sets of statements are arguments? Identify the conclusion of any argument.
   1. The lab is open. The experiment is ready. The assistant is away. *no - concl no*
   2. If we go to the lab now we can do the experiment. We cannot do the experiment. Thus, we cannot go to the lab. *yes*
   3. We are eighty miles from home. We are averaging forty miles an hour. Hence, we can be home in two hours. *yes*
   4. Are you prepared for the test? I heard that the teacher is out of town. *no*
   5. If John is lying, he says Jones is a lawyer. And if John is telling the truth, he says Jones is a lawyer. Either John is lying or he is telling the truth. Hence John says Jones is a lawyer. *yes*

B. Identify the deductive arguments and the nondeductive arguments in the following examples.
   1. Some political issues are divisive issues.
      All ~~divisive~~ *political.* issues are controversial issues.
      Hence, some controversial issues are divisive issues.
   2. Primitive societies in the South Seas have a language.
      Primitive societies in jungles in Brazil have a language.
      Primitive societies in Central Africa have a language.
      Primitive societies in Southeast Asia have a language. *inductive generalization*
      Primitive societies in the Arctic have a language.
      Therefore, all primitive societies have a language.
   3. If the conference is successful, there will not be increased spending on arms.
      There is increased spending on arms.
      Therefore, the conference is not successful. *deductive*
   4. Oil fields in California, Texas, and Alaska have sedimentary rocks with an upward thrust followed by a downward thrust of the rocks' structure. These rocks also have buried in them decayed organic materials of plants or animals from past geological ages. The Beta region also has similarly shaped rocks in its structure. There is reason to believe also that these rocks have buried in them organic materials of decayed plants and animals from past geological ages. Therefore, there is oil in the Beta region. *inductive*
   5. The last four times there has been an excessive build-up in inventories we have had a slowdown in production. We now have an excessive build-up in inventories. Thus, we shall have a slowdown in production.

inductive

6. Either you speak in jest or you speak in earnest.
   You do not speak in jest.
   Thus, you speak in earnest.
7. Susan is a better swimmer than George.
   George is a better swimmer than James.
   Therefore, Susan is a better swimmer than James.
8. Roman civilization passed through periods of Spring, Summer, Fall, and Winter (decay).
   Western civilization has passed through periods of Spring, Summer, and Fall.
   Therefore, it will pass through the period of Winter.
9. It is not the case both that you do make a good grade in this course and that you do not learn how to analyze arguments.
   You do make a good grade in this course.
   Therefore, you do learn how to analyze arguments.

6.2   ARGUMENT FORMS, VALID ARGUMENTS, AND SOUND ARGUMENTS

In this section we shall look at what we mean by the form of an argument, by valid arguments and by sound arguments.

What is the form of an argument? We talked about this in the first chapter, but we need a more exact statement about this. The form of an argument is the way the elements of an argument are ordered and connected in seeking to justify a conclusion. That is, the form of an argument is the internal structure of its logical elements. But let us read on to understand what this means.

Let us look at the following deductive arguments: (The first example is a good argument and the second argument is a poor one.)

(14)   All logic students are persons who study arguments.
       All students in this class are logic students.
       Thus, all students in this class are persons who study arguments. (Valid)

(15)   All history students are liberal arts students.
       All philosophy students are liberal arts students.
       Thus, all philosophy students are history students. (Invalid)

Let us use the capital letters *F*, *G*, and *H* to refer to subjects and predicates of these sentences. And we shall use these letters in the order of their appearance as subjects and predicates in the original sentences. The first argument has the following form:

(16)   All *F* is *G*.
       All *H* is *F*.
       Thus, all *H* is *G*.

For reasons we shall discuss in a later chapter, this argument is correct. Any argument having this form must have a true conclusion if the sentences stating the evidence are true.

Let us look at the form of the second argument. This argument is a deductive one. But it looks phony even to common sense. Why is it incorrect? Look at its form:

(17)   All F is G.
       All H is G.
       Thus, all H is F.

Invalid - form improper - yield false conclusion. true premises can yield false conclusion

The form does not require that any member of G also be a member of both F and H. Consider the following counterexample. "All Democrats are U.S. citizens. All Republicans are U.S. citizens." It is obviously wrong to conclude that we could then claim that "All Republicans are Democrats." The fact that all F is G and all H is G does not provide for our inferring some other relation holding strictly between F and H. The fact that all Democrats are U.S. citizens and that all Republicans are U.S. citizens does not permit us to draw other conclusions about other conditions holding only between Republicans and Democrats.

We can use the form of a deductive argument as a commonsense way of seeking to determine if the form is a correct one. If we can construct an argument by the use of a form that has true premises and a false conclusion, we can know that the form of the argument is incorrect. Consider the incorrect argument:

(18)   If interest rates go up, the price of common stocks goes down.
       The price of common stocks goes down.
       Therefore, interest rates go up. (Invalid)

We can show the form of this argument by the following scheme:

(19)   If F, then G.
       G.
       Thus, F.

Can we find a counterexample with this argument form that has true premises and a false conclusion? We can. Consider the following one:

(20)   If Jean wins swimming contests, she keeps in training.
       Jean keeps in training.
       Thus, she wins swimming contests. (Invalid)

Anyone familiar with swimming knows that things like skill and practice also are essential to winning contests in that sport. But what this argument by a counterexample shows is that any deductive argument using this form is also a bad argument.

We can look at another incorrect argument:

(21)   All radial tires are gas savers.
No radial tires are cheap in price.
Thus, no tires which are cheap in price are gas savers. (Invalid)

A counterexample that shows this form of this argument to be incorrect is the following:

(22)   All college teachers are adults.
No college teachers are persons who cannot read.
Thus, no persons who cannot read are adults. (Invalid)

Such counterexamples can be helpful in showing incorrect arguments in everyday discourse. But we also need to be able to analyze the form of arguments by rules of deductive logic. We shall study such rules in the second part of this work.

If a deductive argument has a correct form, it is valid; if it has an incorrect form, it is invalid. But what do we mean by "valid" and "invalid" in such cases?

A valid deductive argument is one whose logical form requires that in all cases in which the conclusion is false that at least one premise is false. An invalid deductive argument is an argument whose logical form permits a conclusion to be false in some cases in which all of the premises are true.

In ordinary language we hear talk about a valid idea, a valid procedure, a valid license, or a valid contract. In such cases the talk can be about well-founded ideas, useful procedures, licenses that are still in force, or legally binding contracts. We are not proposing that such uses of "valid" be stricken from talk of this kind. But in matters of deductive logic, the limiting of the meaning of "valid" and "invalid" to finding about a correct form or an incorrect form of an argument helps to prevent confusion.

We also want deductive arguments to be sound. And a sound deductive argument must meet two conditions: it must be valid, and its premises must be true. Consider these two arguments:

(23)   All icy roads are roads with driving hazards.
This road is icy.
Thus, this road is a road with driving hazards.

(24)   Either you drive safely or you risk an accident.
You do not drive safely.
Hence, you risk an accident.

For the above arguments to be sound, they must be valid. These arguments are valid (for reasons discussed later). But look what happens if we alter the second argument as follows:

(25)   Either you drive safely or you risk an accident.
       You drive safely.
       Therefore, you do not risk an accident. (Invalid)

Is this argument sound? It is not. It is invalid. Both premises are true but the argument is invalid because it has a faulty argument form. We know by common sense that sometimes safe drivers do have accidents through no fault of their own. But common sense does not always provide us with insight to spot faulty arguments or to identify good ones. We need more definite rules to be able to judge the argument form.

The second condition for a sound deductive argument is that the premises must be true. Normally we would determine the truth of the above premises by common sense. To judge if the roads are icy, we would look at the roads, listen to weather reports, make inquiries regarding driving conditions, and watch for sliding and spinning of the wheels on other cars.

Assume that one makes the argument listed as (23) during the summer in clear weather in a region with daily temperature ranging from 50 to 90 degrees (Fahrenheit). The argument would be valid since it has a valid form. But the argument would not be sound since its second premise would be false.

How do we usually go about determining if statements are true? We test commonsense judgments, as has just been described. But we also need to raise questions about commonsense judgments. The moon may appear to be as large as the sun to the naked eye. We have to correct our commonsense view by use of more exact sources of knowledge.

We also consult the views of persons with good training and successful experience in the field of the subject matter in question. For certain types of issues the views of a physicist, chemist, or biologist will be sought out. For other questions we may want to consult a mechanic, an engineer, a coach, an attorney, or a cook. Testing common sense and finding out what informed persons say about things in the area of their competence do not resolve many issues related to the truth of statements. But they do offer a point of beginning and a means of resolving some issues.

In this section we have analyzed what we mean by the form of an argument. We also described valid arguments and sound arguments.

EXERCISE

The following arguments are invalid. Write counterarguments for them.

1. If we lose the game, then we make mistakes. We do not lose the game. Thus, we do not make mistakes.

2. Some students are good learners. All persons in this class are students. Thus, some persons in this class are good learners.

3. Either we go to the apartment or we do not watch TV. We go to the apartment. Thus, we watch TV.

4. No rats are welcome visitors. All rats are rodents. Thus, no rodents are welcome visitors.

5. If we work this problem, we shall take a rest. We take a rest. Thus, we work this problem.

6. All vacations are relaxing things. All vacations are enjoyable things. Thus, all relaxing things are enjoyable things.

6.3 WAYS OF ANALYZING ARGUMENTS

In this section we shall look at how to analyze arguments and consider some things we expect to find in a good argument.

Arguments can occur in almost any context, such as in editorials, essays, speeches, conversations, reports, advertisements, and even comic strips. Generally, in analyzing an argument we need to identify its conclusion and the evidence given to justify it. And we need to determine how well the evidence supports the conclusion. We also want to know whether the argument is inductive or deductive. A complex argument has a series of different arguments, some of which may be inductive and others deductive. In many cases statements not relevant to the conclusion are mixed in with the statements providing the evidence.

Let us consider some steps relative to the analysis of an argument.

1. Internal Analysis of Arguments

Identifying the Conclusion. The first step in analyzing an argument is identifying the conclusion. We find that in arguments in use, the premises and conclusions can occur in any order. Some sentences may be restating something appearing elsewhere in the argument. Some premises or even the conclusion may be missing. But how do we go about finding the conclusion?

In many cases signal words such as "therefore," "thus," or "hence" introduce the conclusion. However, such words may occur in ordinary speech without being followed by a conclusion. Use of such signal words may alert us to the summary of a view. In some arguments where the conclusion occurs without use of any signal words, we have to try to identify the conclusion by analyzing the context. In conversations we sometimes ask, "What's the point?" or "What are you driving at?" to try to make a conclusion explicit.

Identifying the Statements Used as Evidence.   Once we identify the conclusion, we seek the reasons given to justify the argument. Signal words such as "since," "because," and "given that" may introduce evidence. In many cases no signal words occur. We may have to write out some premises assumed in the argument. Let us look at some examples found in deductive arguments.[1]

(26)   If the anchovies are not as large as sardines, then the Peruvian fishermen don't fish.
If the Peruvian fishermen don't fish, a shortage of protein develops for livestock and poultry feed.
The anchovies are not as large as sardines.
Therefore, a shortage of protein develops for livestock and poultry feed.

(27)   Inflation will continue since the Fed is increasing the money supply. (Assumed premise: If the Fed increases the money supply, inflation will continue.)

(28)   Because John is a freshman, he cannot be expected to solve problems in advanced math.
No students that can be expected to solve problems in advanced math are freshmen.
Only students with adequate background in math can be expected to solve advanced math problems.

Ordering and Clarifying Statements.   In the proper ordering of the statements in an argument we place the conclusion last. And we place the premises in an order that will make the argument flow clearly. Some statements will need to be restated to make their meaning clear. The meanings of the words will need to be examined to make sure they are not used in different senses.

Identifying Logical Relations.   We have to make precise the way in which the expressions like "if . . . then———," "either . . . or ———," "all" and "is" signify the logical relations in the sentence. We then

[1] In the first example (26) "therefore" introduces the conclusion which occurs as a final statement in the argument. And the premises occur in the previous statements. They do not have any signal words to alert us that they are premises. In the second example (27), the conclusion occurs first. A part of the evidence occurs in the clause after "since." One premise also is missing. It is assumed. In the third example (28), the conclusion is "he (John) cannot be expected to solve problems in advanced math." One premise is the clause introduced by "because." A second premise is the second separate and complete sentence. The last statement is not essential to establishing the conclusion. However, if one questions the truth of the second premise, then the last sentence could serve as a part of another undeveloped argument to justify accepting one of the premises.

need to find ways to analyze the logical relations holding in the argument. (This will be developed in other chapters.)

Evaluating the Truth of the Evidence.   We want to know if the evidence given to support the conclusion is true. As we have seen, the determining of the truth of statements (outside the field of logic) is not strictly the responsibility of a logician. But the logician is interested in knowing how we determine whether a statement is true. (And in using an argument in everyday life, she can be as interested as anyone else in using premises that are well founded.)

Making a Decision About the Merits of the Argument.   We need to determine whether the argument justifies the conclusion.

The remainder of this work develops in greater detail the matters set forth in this review of how to analyze an argument internally. We are interested not only in analyzing arguments of others, but in making and analyzing our own arguments.

2.   External Use of Arguments

We shall consider briefly some external considerations about the use of arguments.

Clarifying the Flow of an Argument.   To make an argument flow clearly, we can alert audiences to the major points we plan to establish. In addition, we can make precise the logical relations we are using in an argument and we can make clear our points of transition from one argument to another.

Holding the Attention of an Audience.   If no one pays any attention to our arguments, they do not get the job done that we expect. We have to recognize that what holds one person's attention may bore someone else. In some cases we may need to determine the specific group in an audience to which we want to direct an argument. Illustrations either at the end or the beginning of a major transition can be useful in creating interest and providing insight into the claim of an argument.

Choosing the Right Level of Language.   The language in which we present an argument should be appropriate for its intended audience. Technical language is appropriate for persons trained in the use of such words. Use of analogies to illustrate a technical point to a lay audience can be helpful. For audiences with mixed backgrounds, the use of simpler language forms usually is desirable.

Keeping a Proper Balance.   In advancing an argument we can be sensitive to the need for correct and accurate statements. We can be fair in representing the views of others as well as in the way we select material in support of our argument. What is fair can vary with the context of our argument. But deliberate confusing of issues or distorting of evidence does not appear to be fair. Presenting only one side of a case stacks the cards. Yet there are occasions to take an advocate's position. One expects lawyers to make the best legal case they can for their clients. And as citizens we can be advocates for those policies and practices we prefer. The forum in which advocates work tends to provide for expressing other views. It is to be hoped that we can be advocates to keep such forums open.

Persuading Others to Accept our Conclusions.   Arguments have a purpose. One basic purpose is to advance knowledge and to make the truth known. Another is to advance those interests which we believe are well-founded. We can hope to persuade others by the use of sound arguments. But we also have to recognize that in a public forum some persuasion also has a subjective basis. Adapting an argument to the interests and concerns of an audience can aid in persuading them not only to see the logical force of our argument but to be willing to accept it and act upon it.

In making these suggestions about the external use of arguments, we have moved outside the field of logic in its strict sense, and have entered the domain of common sense and the art of communication.

In this section we have looked at how to analyze the internal structure of an argument. Some ways to use arguments in presenting our views to others have been considered. In the next section we shall look at different types of disputes and how some of them may be resolved.

EXERCISES

Identify the conclusion in the following arguments taken primarily from the history of philosophy.

1. "Everything which happens either happens in such wise as you are formed by nature to bear it, or as you are not formed by nature to bear it. If, then, it happens to you in such a way as you are formed by nature to bear it, do not complain, but bear it as you are formed by nature to bear it. But if it happens in such wise as you are not formed by nature to bear it, do not complain, for it will perish after it has consumed you. Remember, however, that you are formed by nature to bear everything, with respect to which it depends on your own opinion to make it endurable and tolerable, by thinking that it is either your interest or your duty to do this." (Marcus Aurelius, 121–180)

2. "The ceaseless efforts to banish suffering accomplish no more than to make it change its form. It is essentially deficiency, want, care for the maintenance of life. If we succeed, which is very difficult, in removing pain in this form, it immediately assumes a thousand others, varying according to age and circumstances, such as lust, passionate love, jealousy, envy, hatred, anxiety, ambition, covetousness, sickness, etc., etc. If at last it can find entrance in no other form, it comes in the sad, grey garments of tediousness and boredom, against which we then strive in various ways. If finally we succeed in driving this away, we shall hardly do so without letting pain enter in one of its earlier forms, and the dance begins again from the beginning; for all human life is tossed backwards and forwards between pain and boredom." (Arthur Schopenhauer, 1788–1860)

3. "Moral rules need a proof; ergo, not innate. —Another reason that makes me doubt of any innate principles, is, that I think there cannot any one moral rule be proposed whereof a man may not justly demand a reason; which would be perfectly ridiculous and absurd, if they were innate, or so much as self-evident; which every innate principle must needs be, and not need any proof to ascertain its truth, nor want any reason to gain it approbation." (John Locke, 1632–1704)

4. "Let the reader imagine a steel spring, bent together. There is doubtless in the spring a tendency to repel the pressure, hence a tendency outwards. Such a spring is the picture of an actual willing, as the *state* or condition of a rational being; but of it I do not speak here. Let me now ask what is the first *ground* (not condition) of this tendency, as a real and determined manifestation of the spring? Doubtless an inner action of the spring upon itself, a self-determination. For no one surely will say that the outward force which presses the spring is the ground of the spring's reacting against it. This self-determining is the same as the mere *act* of willing in the rational being. Both together would produce in the spring, if it could contemplate itself, the consciousness of a will to repel the pressing force. But all these moments are possible only on condition that such an external pressure is actually exercised upon the spring. In the same way the rational being cannot determine itself to an actual willing, unless it stands in reciprocal relation with something external (for as such the rational being *appears* to itself)." (Johann Gottlieb Fichte, 1770–1831)

5. "The autopilot can't be used on a runway that does not have an Instrument Landing System; there's no electronic ramp for the gadget to lock on to. Here the pilot flies the entire approach. He descends to a specified height where, according to the regulations, he must see the 'approach threshold of that runway, or approach lights or *other markings identifiable with the approach end of the runway. . . .*'

   "There's been a fuss over the phrase I've italicized, even among the guys who make these rules in FAA's [Federal Aviation Administration] Flight Standards. 'The phrase . . . is ambiguous to the extreme,' an internal memorandum stated. 'A motel sign, building, or other object could possibly be established in a pilot's mind as being "identifiable" with the end of the runway, and this is not the intent of the rule.' "[2]

[2] Michael E. Long, "The Challenge of Air Safety," *National Geographic,* Vol. 152, No. 2, August 1977, p. 228.

facts
difference of views about given issue
6.4 DISPUTES AND ARGUMENTS
using evidence to support a conclusion

In this section we shall discuss different types of disputes and ways of resolving some of them when those who differ show good faith.

We have different views on issues that relate to the general goals toward which we move, and to specific ways for meeting such goals. We may talk about these differences and seek ways of resolving these disputes.

What is the difference between a dispute and an argument? A dispute is a disagreement between two or more persons or groups about the correct resolution of a discussed issue. An argument is the setting forth of reasons which seek to justify a claim. Arguments are something we use in seeking to resolve some disputes.

Sources of disagreement that lead to disputes vary. A source of many disputes is a difference of interest. That is, some disputes arise between persons and groups whose primary or exclusive interest is to satisfy their own goals. And practical resolution of such disputes awaits some way of finding a common interest which will enable such groups to share some common goals and agree on common means to achieve these goals.

Our concern in this section is to focus on those disputes in which the disputants have not locked themselves into a closed position. They are least willing to consider some way of resolving their differences through an open and free exchange of ideas. But we recognize that in some cases we may want to argue that the other parties have locked themselves into an inflexible position.

To resolve a dispute we first have to find what it is about. The sources of the dispute may not be obvious to the disputants. We shall seek to identify some of these sources. In these cases, we shall assume that the disputants are reasonable persons. We can hope that they are willing to persuade others or to be persuaded by rational arguments.

We shall focus on five different sources of disputes. Disputants can differ on what the facts of the case are. They can differ on the evidence relevant to the issue in dispute. They can differ on the meaning of a key word or phrase in the dispute. They can differ on the evaluation made in the dispute. And they can differ on their expectancies about the results that would follow from the different ways of resolving the dispute.

1. Disputes about Facts

A factual dispute is a disagreement about what happens, what characterizes a state of affairs, or what relations hold in the world about us. We may dispute about the speed of a car or the condition of the road at the time of an accident. We also may dispute about the position of two cars in relation to each other at the time of collision. To get at the facts we look, we probe, we inquire, we sort out evidence, we test, and we make findings.

2.   Disputes about Relevance of Evidence

A dispute about the relevance of evidence is a disagreement about what facts or ideas are essential and sufficient to justify the claim of an argument. We can dispute about whether past discrimination against persons of a given race or sex justifies a present policy that may appear to discriminate against groups that did not undergo such unfair treatment in the past. In many disputes the factors that we choose as evidence relevant to resolving an issue make the difference in the kind of conclusion that we reach. In a trial in a court of law, the rules about admissible evidence can be crucial to the outcome of a case.

3.   Disputes about Words

A verbal dispute is a disagreement based on the use of a key word or phrase to which the disputants give different meanings in an argument. The persons in the dispute are not talking about the same thing although they are using the same word. For example, we hear disputes about whether men are created equal. But one person may be using "equal" to refer to legal rights and privileges which any citizen enjoys. And the other person may be using "equal" to refer to the financial power necessary to gain something one wants through the use of the law.

4.   Disputes about Evaluating

An evaluative dispute is a disagreement about the worth of something. Whether a novel is good literature can be a subject for dispute. So can the issue of whether we should give greater priority to the protection of wildlife, trees, flowers, and hills or to the development of our energy resources. In such cases disputants can appear to be talking about facts. But the source of their differences may relate to whether something is good or bad, fitting or not fitting. Our evaluations may reflect our attitudes and interests. Our judgments about values are relative to some standard which we apply in making decisions about what is better or worse.

5.   Disputes Based on Different Expectancies

A dispute over expectancies is a disagreement based on different views about the future consequences of acting on different options that one can choose in the present. Managers of a pension fund can differ on how to invest money under their control today, because they have different expectancies about the state of the economy several years hence. Our beliefs about the capabilities of other nations to threaten our security in the years ahead influence our views about current national defense policies.

Several of these sources of disputes can be present in the same discussion. Consider the following case. Ron and Rick are having a dispute regarding inflation and its possible effects on their future life-styles. Ron states, "The present annual rate of inflation is four percent." Rick replies, "It is five percent." They can be differing about what the facts are. But they may also have a second difference. If they explore how they are going about determining an annual rate of inflation, they may be using different points of reference and different formulas to determine it. In this case their dispute would be about relevant evidence.

The dispute continues. Ron states, "A cause of the inflation is too much money chasing too few goods." Rick replies, "Money does not chase anything. The real source of inflation is the high cost of goods and services." At this point, they may be having a verbal dispute regarding the meaning of "money chasing" something. But they also may have an unexpressed disagreement about relevance. What factors are relevant to determining why the rate of inflation is so high?

Ron points out, "A moderate inflation can be a stimulus for further expansion of business and industry. As the economy grows inflation also grows." Rick replies, "With inflation, the dollar is able to buy fewer goods and the economy becomes depressed. People living on fixed incomes such as pensions have less purchasing power each year and this reducing of spending power also results in less demand for goods and in lower production." In this case they are having an evaluative dispute based on different views held with regard to whether the existing inflation rate is good or bad for the economy. They also may have different expectancies about the future consequences of inflation. And they may be disputing about the facts of the case.

Ron says, "The economic obligations of the government require a continuing inflationary trend. Such an inflation is essential to service the public debt and to meet the costs of welfare programs." Rick replies, "At the existing inflation rate the price of goods and services will more than double every fifteen years. And the economy cannot continue to bear this type of load. Rather than spending our way to prosperity we are throwing away an opportunity to provide a stable economy in which our basic freedoms are secure." The dispute at this point is being directed, in part, toward what is relevant in determining obligations of government. In addition, Rick and Ron are making evaluations. These differences also could be based on both factual and verbal matters. We see that they have different expectancies of what the consequences of inflation will be.

This illustration is not designed to teach any economics. Its purpose is to focus on the kinds of issues that arise in disputes. Such disputes can be resolved only by identifying what kind of issue is being dealt with. These issues need to be clarified. And the kind of evidence relevant to resolve such disputes needs to be identified. The dispute may not be resolved, but agreement on some matters may be reached. A resolution of a dispute requires that the disputants be aware of what it is that they need to resolve.

Let us consider the possible types of disputes that can occur on the basis of only three of the factors we have mentioned. In this case we can have eight possible variations of agreement and disagreement; these are illustrated in Table 6.1. If we included a fourth factor, we would have sixteen possible variations. And a fifth factor would provide for thirty-two variations.

The second row in the table indicates that the disputants agree on the factual matters in the argument and on the meaning of the words used in the argument. But they differ on evaluations reflected in the discussion. The sixth row indicates that the disputants disagree about the factual matters and in their evaluations. But they agree on the meaning of words used in the discussion.

Table 6.1   Possible Variations of
Agreement and Disagreement

Facts	Words	Evalua-tions
Agree	Agree	Agree
Agree	Agree	Disagree
Agree	Disagree	Agree
Agree	Disagree	Disagree
Disagree	Agree	Agree
Disagree	Agree	Disagree
Disagree	Disagree	Agree
Disagree	Disagree	Disagree

This table may obscure other significant features of disputes. Differences about the facts related to the dispute may be wide or limited. There may be several verbal disputes. Evaluations may range from deploring any inflation to supporting an "accommodation to the inevitable." Their expectancies of the effect of inflation on future economic conditions may range widely. One may hold that the consequences would be totally disastrous. And the other may believe that inflation is the only alternative to widespread loss of jobs, an alternative which he rejects.

We need to consider how to resolve verbal disputes. John and Doris are discussing the value of the study of logic. "A syllogism," according to John, "does not really provide you with any information you do not already have." Doris disagrees: "But it most certainly does." The key words in this dispute are "provide you with information." John argues that a conclusion is implicit in some sense in the premises of a syllogism. And the conclusion does not provide any added information. Doris holds that the conclusion may not have been known explicitly. Moreover, she can point out that new knowledge is gained by showing that a sound argument justifies the conclusion.

In clarifying such verbal dispute, we can take the following steps:

1. Identify the specific words giving occasion for the dispute.

2. Restate the meanings of key words in the dispute in order to make explicit the interpretations given to them.

3. Apply restated meanings of key words to the original statements.

4. Render a decision on the basis of each explicit interpretation of the statement in question.

This chapter has dealt with how to identify different arguments. We have seen that a deductive argument requires that its form yields a false conclusion in all cases where one premise is false. It was shown that induction is the logic of probable inference. Internal and external ways of analyzing arguments were considered. We analyzed sources of disputes in arguments and showed how to clear up a verbal dispute.

This chapter concludes the first part of this work. Our study of logic focuses on arguments. Because arguments use statements, we have sought to analyze statements from various points of view. We have examined the terms of statements, the meaning of statements, and the words used in statements. We also have dealt with ways of clarifying the meaning of words used in statements.

The next part of this work analyzes ways of making valid deductive arguments.

EXERCISES

A. Analyze the following examples to determine if they are about disputes. Identify the kind of dispute that is present when such occurs. In cases of verbal disputes propose a clarification according to the rules recommended.
   1. George bets John a dollar that John cannot throw a rock across the river. John throws a flat-surfaced rock, which skips across the top of the water, to the far bank. John declares himself winner. George claims that the rock was not thrown across the river but was skipped across. Who won the bet?
   2. William James related an incident about a hunting trip. One hunter saw a squirrel dart behind a tree. As the hunter walked to different positions around the tree, the squirrel kept a limb of the tree between himself and the hunter. Later the hunter remarked that if he had been able to walk around the squirrel, he could have shot him. A companion argued that the hunter did walk around the squirrel, since he walked around the tree into which the squirrel had climbed. Did the hunter walk around the squirrel?

3. Two newspapers entered into an agreement with a typographical union that local advertising would be reproduced by the members of the union in the composing rooms of the newspapers. National advertisements could be used without local reproduction. In a court case in 1966 the newspapers claimed that advertising with the newspapers through local firms might constitute national advertising if the specific material that an advertisement featured was also featured on a national basis. The representatives of the union claimed that national advertising required that the organization doing the advertising distribute the specific content of an advertisement to news media throughout the country and that this distribution was to be done either directly or through an agency. Show how this dispute was verbal. (It obviously also was a legal one.) (Source: *Editor & Publisher,* March 12, 1966, p. 18)

4. Jones: "This is an unbearably hot summer." Smith: "The temperature is about normal for summers in this part of the country." No dispute

5. Joe: "We are confronted with the possibility of massive destruction of human life by nuclear explosions and fallout." Linda: "The probability of mass attacks by nuclear weapons is decreasing with the growing realization that their use would involve also the destruction of the populations of the countries who use them." No dispute

6. Carl: "The Middle East crisis has provided a basis for a more durable peace in that area." David: "The Middle East crisis has sown the seeds for future armed conflicts." resolution depends on context — could be expectancies of diff aspects of compatible view

7. Jim: "The financial deals of congressmen, as exposed through investigations, destroy the confidence of the public in Congress." Tom: "There is nothing new in the kinds of financial deals made by members of Congress. We have survived public scandals in the past and we shall continue to do so." dif exp

8. Mary: "The television industry provides the kinds of programs in which the majority of the viewing public are interested." Nan: "The television industry provides the kinds of programs that will assure their producers of the greatest profit in the long run." no

9. Susan: "We are having a delicious lunch but it will result in my gaining weight." Harry: "We are having a nourishing lunch that will provide the food value I need to compete in strenuous athletic contests." word

10. Jim: "The defendant's car did not stop at the intersection at Main and First Streets before the accident." George: "The defendant's car stopped at that intersection before the accident." fac

11. Mary: "Cigarette smoking is injurious to health, as many experiments show conclusively." Tom: "We do not know yet that cigarette smoking is injurious to health since the experiments on this issue lead to confusing results." rel of evi

B. The following problems are adapted from sources that go back to Lewis Carroll and beyond. Some of the problems require a focusing on the concepts related to the stating of the problem. Some of the problems require eliminating some factors so as to identify another.

1. A bucket is placed under a leak. The amount of water in the bucket doubles

each hour. In twelve hours the bucket is full. How long does it require for the bucket to be half full of water?

2. Three men who are either lawyers or crooks meet on the street. The lawyers tell only the truth. The crooks tell only lies. The first man identifies himself to the second and the second tells the third that the first man said he was a lawyer. The third replies that the first man was not a lawyer but a crook. How many lawyers are there in the group? Show that your answer is correct.

3. A mother is on a picnic with three children. She has 30 ounces of punch in one jar, and she has three empty jars that hold 16 ounces, 14 ounces, and 4 ounces. How can she divide the punch equally for the children?

4. Smith, Brown, and Jones have numerals placed on their backs. Each is unable to see his own number. Smith and Brown are permitted to see the numbers the others are wearing, but Jones is not. They are told that at least two of the numbers are even. The person who first determines whether he has an odd or an even number and shows how he knows he is correct wins an expense-paid trip to the World Series. Smith and Brown say they cannot make such a determination but Jones says he can. Is Jones wearing an odd or an even number, and how does he know?

5. Three couples are skiing. There is only one lift, which carries only two persons. It is agreed that until all persons are at the top of the hill, at least one person must always ride in the ski lift. The men distrust each other and insist that no man can ride on the lift or be left at the base or the top of the hill with a girl that is not accompanied by her date. How can everyone get to the top of the lift in these circumstances?

6. An airline company flies a plane nonstop each hour from Rome to New York. Exactly eight hours are required from the time the plane leaves the terminal until it stops at the terminal of destination. How many planes of this company on this nonstop New York to Rome flight will a given pilot meet while he is making the flight?

7. Ann, Betty, Carol, and Dorothy are married to Frank, Earl, George, and Henry, but not necessarily in that order. George's sister-in-law has a new car, which she bought from Frank. Carol and her husband visit frequently with Earl and his wife. Ann is the only sister of Earl's wife. Henry is married to the sister of Earl's wife. Betty and George do not have any brothers or sisters. Identify the wife of each husband.

8. Herbert, John, Kelly, Louis, and Marty are in the following professions but not necessarily in this order: physician, engineer, attorney, architect, and dentist. The engineer is a bachelor and he plays golf with Kelly. Louis is 5 feet 6 inches tall; he is shorter than Kelly and 6 inches shorter than Herbert. Herbert is taller than John but shorter than Marty. John is 3 inches taller than Kelly. The physician is the tallest member of the group; his nearest neighbor is the shortest of the group. Herbert's wife is a social worker. John swims frequently in Herbert's pool. The nearest neighbor of the physician is an attorney. The architect does not have a swimming pool. Who is the architect?

9. Give the value of a different number from 0 through 9 for each letter type in the following scheme. Add the resultant columns in the first two lines. What

is the sum of these two lines found in the third line? (There are at least two answers.) (Hint: find what values will need to hold for the letters "M" and "R" and "O".)

	(a)	(b)	(c)	(d)	(e)
Line 1	M	A	J	O	R
Line 2	M	I	N	O	R
Line 3	T	E	R	M	S

M < 5

sample
question
for
test

DEDUCTIVE LOGIC

CHAPTER 7

SYLLOGISTIC LOGIC

7.1 ANALYSIS OF CATEGORICAL STATEMENTS

The second part of this work discusses and develops deductive logic. We shall study syllogistic logic, truth-functional logic, and logic using quantifiers.

This chapter analyzes categorical statements. And it shows their use in forming valid categorical syllogisms.

We have seen that deductive logic analyzes the forms of valid arguments. An argument is valid if the form of the argument requires that in all cases in which a conclusion is false, at least one premise is false.

We can illustrate the need for analyzing the form of categorical syllogisms by studying the following proposed arguments.

(1) All colleges are schools of higher education.
   No colleges are schools of propaganda.
   Thus, no schools of propaganda are schools of higher education. (Invalid)

(2) All philosophers are rationalists.
   All logicians are philosophers.
   Therefore, all logicians are rationalists.

Each of these arguments uses statements composed of different elements.

These statements have a subject term, a predicate term, and a relation expressed as holding between these terms.

The first argument above is invalid. It is possible for its logical structure to have true premises and a false conclusion. The second argument is valid. Its structure requires that in any case in which the premises are true that the conclusion also be true.

The statement found as the conclusion in the first argument can be true. But the argument does not justify its acceptance as true. The conclusion in the second argument can be false. But if it is false, then one of the premises also must be false.

The issues relevant to determining if the premises are true are important. But such issues lie outside the focus of our direct attention in this chapter.

1. Kinds of Categorical Statements

Examples of categorical statements, which we also can call categorical propositions, are the following:

(3) All civil rights are rights protected by the constitution.

(4) Some moral obligations are not legal obligations.

The subject terms in the above examples are "civil rights" and "moral obligations." The predicate terms are "rights protected by the constitution" and "legal obligations."

Categorical statements have two terms, a subject term and a predicate term. But we shall restrict the meaning of "predicate term" to a greater degree than we did in our previous discussion. In syllogistic logic the predicate term refers only to the class term expressed in the predicate of the categorical statement.

A form of the copula "to be" connects the two terms of a categorical statement. That is, the verb "is" or "are" connects the terms. This use of the verb form "is" or "are" also requires the notion of class inclusion, or in cases of negation, of class exclusion. In the first instance above "all members of the class of civil rights" are included in "the class of rights protected by the constitution." In the second instance above, "some members of the class of moral obligations" are excluded from (are not included in) "the class of legal obligations."

We also distinguish categorical statements as affirmative or negative. If the verb form specifies the relation of "class inclusion" of the subject term in the predicate term, the statement is affirmative. If the verb form specifies the relation of class exclusion, the statement is negative. In this case a sign of negation such as "no" or "not" occurs as a part of the meaning of the copula (is, are). The statement "All whales are mammals" is affirmative. And the statement "Some sharks are not hammerheads" is negative.

We are now in position to state what a categorical statement in syllogistic logic is. It is a statement making a claim that a relation of class inclusion or of class exclusion holds between the members of the class expressed by the subject term and the members of the class expressed by the predicate term.

We also need to identify the distribution of the subject term. A categorical statement is universal provided the subject term includes all members in its class. If reference is made to fewer than all the members of the subject class, then the statement is particular. The statement "All logicians are philosophers" is universal. And the statement "Some logicians are birdwatchers" is particular. A distributed term is fully extended. And an undistributed term is only partly extended. (See Section 3.4.)

Categorical statements using singular class terms as subject terms are universal. And there is full distribution of the class expressed by the subject term. In this case statements using such expressions as the following have distributed subject terms: "Ann," "Mr. Jones," "she," "the first man to walk on the moon," "The New York Jets," and "that boy running across the street."

When we talk about a categorical statement as affirmative or negative we use the word "quality." To talk about such statements as universal or particular we use the word "quantity." In classifying categorical statements on the basis of quality and quantity, four different types become evident.

Quantity	Quality	Example
Universal	Affirmative	All politicians are statesmen.
Universal	Negative	No politicians are statesmen.
Particular	Affirmative	Some politicians are statesmen.
Particular	Negative	Some politicians are not statesmen.

EXERCISES

Classify the following categorical statements as universal or particular and as affirmative or negative.

1. Some chemicals are not volatile substances.

2. All eyeglasses are instruments made of shatterproof materials.

3. No hearsay evidence is evidence admitted as primary evidence.

4. Some used cars are not cars in good shape.

5. Some legal risks are risks that are all right to take.

(handwritten annotations in top margin: "Variables)", "Placeholders", "F - any term", "Subject term - any predicate", "G - term")

6. Mr. Jones is an artist.

7. Some books that are not read widely are technical works.

8. All good chess players are persons who do not seek to play beginners.

2.   Distribution of Terms

We use the vowels **A**, **E**, **I**, and **O** to refer to four different kinds of categorical statements. These vowels are adapted from the first vowels in the Latin word "affirmo" for the affirmative categorical statements. They are adopted from the comparable vowels in the Latin "nego" for the negative categorical statements. To analyze the form of categorical statements we shall use initially the letter *F* as a letter serving as a place holder for the subject term of any categorical statement. By a letter serving as a place holder we mean in this context that any letter so designated is a symbol for a term of any categorical statement. It "holds the place" for that term. In the above case we designate the letter *F* as a place holder for any subject term of a categorical statement for the following analysis.

We shall let the letter *G* serve in this context as a place holder for the predicate term of any categorical statement. Consider the statements "All seniors are students" and "All politicians are adults." They both have the statement form "All *F* is *G*."

By using these letters we can analyze the four kinds of categorical statements in the following manner.

Type	Quantity	Quality	Statement Form	Example
A	Universal	Affirmative	All *F* is *G*.	All Feds are Gurus.
E	Universal	Negative	No *F* is *G*.	No Feds are Gurus.
I	Particular	Affirmative	Some *F* is *G*.	Some Feds are Gurus.
O	Particular	Negative	Some *F* is not *G*.	Some Feds are not Gurus.

We noted that the distribution of the subject term determines whether a given categorical statement is universal or whether it is particular. We also need to know how we determine the distribution of the predicate term. We interpret the predicate term of affirmative categorical statements as undistributed. That is, we interpret such terms to refer to fewer than all of the members of its class. In such statements as "All biologists are scientists" and "Some professors are scientists" the predicate term "scientists" is undistributed. In each case we are referring only to some scientists rather than to all scientists. The class of all biologists does not constitute the class of all scientists. And "some professors" does not comprise the class of all scientists.

But the predicate term of all negative categorical statements is a dis-

[handwritten margin note: undistributed - but at least one of the class, less than all of the class / distributed - all of that class]

tributed term. Consider the statements "No logic students are seal hunters" and "Some Eskimos are not seal hunters." In each case we refer to the class of all seal hunters. In the first example we are saying that "All members of the class of logic students are excluded from all members of the class of seal hunters." In the second example we are holding that "Some members of the class of Eskimos are excluded from all members of the class of seal hunters."

Let us use the small letter d to indicate a distributed term. And let us use the small letter u for an undistributed term. We can look at the use of these small letters in the following table:

Statement Type	Statement Form	Term Distribution	Example
A	All F is G.	Fd is Gu.	All Feds are (some) Gurus.
E	No F is G.	No Fd is Gd.	No Feds are Gurus.
I	Some F is G.	Fu is Gu.	Some Feds are (some) Gurus.
O	Some F is not G.	Fu is not Gd.	Some Feds are not Gurus.

We can use the symbol $<$ to mean "included in the class of." And we can use the symbol $\not<$ to mean "is excluded from the class of" (or "is not included in the class of"). The following table gives an analysis of four different types of categorical statements.

Statement Type	Term Distribution	(Adapted) Aristotelian Form
A	Fd is Gu.	$Fd < Gu$
E	No Fd is Gd.	$Fd \not< Gd$
I	Fu is Gu.	$Fu < Gu$
O	Fu is not Gd.	$Fu \not< Gd$

We base the convention that the predicate term of an **A** proposition is undistributed on a decision rule. This decision rule is that by using the more restricted interpretation of a meaningful expression we shall avoid errors that otherwise would result from a broader interpretation of the expression. We might hold that a statement such as "Mr. Smith's favorite chair is the easy chair in his den" has a distributed predicate term. Such categorical statements would require special treatment and (as categorical statements) do not occur with great frequency. For purposes of this introductory treatment we shall follow the usual procedure of regarding the predicate term of affirmative categorical statements as undistributed.

The use of the notion of an empty or null class developed by Boole makes possible added analyses of categorical statements. Let us draw two overlapping circles to represent the class designated by the subject term, F, and the class of the predicate term, G. The overlapping (which is common

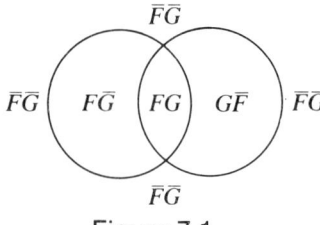

Figure 7.1

to both classes) is the class of FG. (See Figure 7.1) We use a bar, "—," meaning "not" over the F or G to designate "not F" or "not G." We note the three classes shown within the circles as the class of $F\bar{G}$, the class of FG and the class of $G\bar{F}$. (The part outside both circles can be designated as the class of $\bar{F}\bar{G}$ but it is not relevant to the immediate analysis.) We refer to these classes as the class of F and not G, the class of FG, and the class of G and not F. Figure 7.1 illustrates these circles for Boolean analysis.

A null class is empty. It has no members. A class that is not null has at least one member (and possibly more than one member). If we designate a class as null, then we shade the class so designated in the circles. This indicates that the class has no members. If we state that a class is not null, then we place an x within the indicated class in the circles. Figures 7.2, 7.3, 7.4, and 7.5 illustrate the manner of drawing these circles to represent the four different types of categorical statements.

A universal-affirmative categorical statement holds that the part of the circle designated as F and not G ($F\bar{G}$) is null; it has no members. The section designated as $F\bar{G}$ is shaded in the diagram. A universal-negative categorical statement holds that the part of the circle designated F that is common to G (FG) is null. This area also is shaded. A particular-affirmative categorical statement holds that the part of the circle designated F that is common to G (FG) is not null; it has at least one member. An x is marked

All F is G

$Fd < Gu$

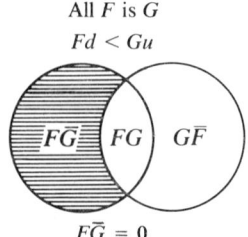

$F\bar{G} = 0$

The class of F and not G is null.

Figure 7.2. Universal affirmative

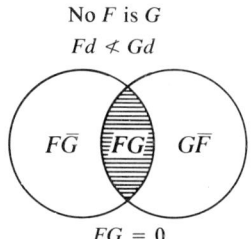

No *F* is *G*

Fd ⊀ *Gd*

$F\bar{G}$ FG $G\bar{F}$

FG = 0

The class of *FG* is null.

Figure 7.3.   Universal negative

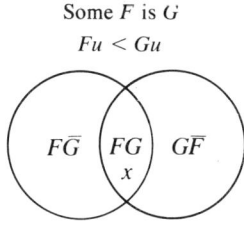

Some *F* is *G*

Fu < *Gu*

$F\bar{G}$ FG $G\bar{F}$
        x

FG ≠ 0

The class of *FG* is not null.

Figure 7.4.   Particular affirmative

Some *F* is not *G*

Fu ⊀ *Gd*

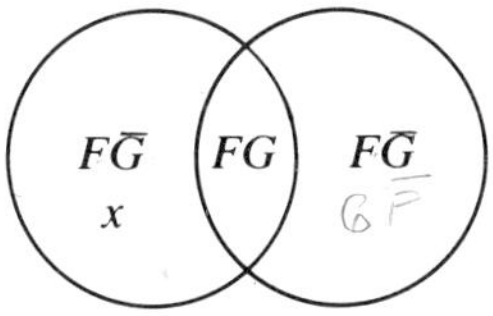

$F\bar{G}$ FG $F\bar{G}$
  x $G\bar{F}$

can't make inference about F̄G and FḠ

$F\bar{G}$ ≠ 0

The class of *F* and not *G* is not null.

Figure 7.5.   Particular negative

Table 7.1   Types of Categorical Statements

included in class of

A Universal-affirmative	*Fd* is *Gu*.	*Fd* < *Gu*	$F\bar{G}$ = 0	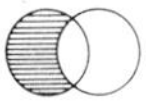 F⬭G
E Universal-negative	No *Fd* is *Gd*.	*Fd* ⊀ *Gd*	*FG* = 0	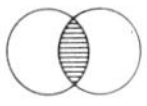 F◯G
I Particular-affirmative	*Fu* is *Gu*.	*Fu* < *Gu*	*FG* ≠ 0	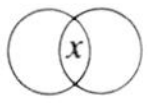 F(*x*)G
O Particular-negative	*Fu* is not *Gd*.	*Fu* ⊀ *Gd*	$F\bar{G}$ ≠ 0	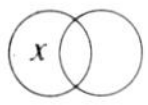 F(*x*)G

not included in class of

in the section of the diagram designated FG. A particular-negative categorical statement holds that the part of the circle designated F and not G ($F\bar{G}$) is not null; it has at least one member. This area also has an x marked within it.

Table 7.1 provides an analysis of the types of categorical statements.

EXERCISES

Give a complete analysis of each of the following categorical statements according to the form provided in Table 7.1.

1. Some research projects are interesting activities.

2. No anarchists are political conservatives.

3. All computers are instruments using formal languages.

4. Some fuels are not products easy to obtain.

5. Some textbooks are expensive works.

6. Some politicians are not advocates of compromise.

7. All humanitarians are humanists.

8. No diamonds are inexpensive jewels.

9. Miss Delta is not a pilot.

7.2 CATEGORICAL SYLLOGISMS: TERMS, PREMISES, AND RULES

1. Premises and Terms of a Categorical Syllogism

Arguments having two categorical statements as premises and a third categorical statement as a conclusion are categorical syllogisms. Logicians sometimes refer to the logic of categorical syllogisms as syllogistic logic or as Aristotelian logic.

The rules of the categorical syllogism specify the conditions for the validity of such arguments. And several of these rules require an analysis of the terms of a syllogism. A categorical syllogism has three and *only three* terms, and each term occurs twice in the syllogism. These terms are the major term, the minor term, and the middle term. Consider the following categorical syllogism.

All *physicians* are *college graduates*.

All *surgeons* are *physicians*.

Therefore, all *surgeons* are *college graduates*.

The *major term* of a categorical syllogism is the predicate term of the conclusion. The *minor term* of a categorical syllogism is the subject term of the conclusion. The *middle term* is the term common to each of the premises; it does not appear in the conclusion. In the above example, the major term is "college graduates," the minor term is "surgeons," and the middle term is "physicians."

The *major premise* for the syllogism is the premise having the major term. In the example above, the major premise is "All physicians are college graduates." The *minor premise* is the premise with the minor term. In the above example, the minor premise is "All surgeons are physicians." In ordinary usage, the premises and the conclusion may appear in any order. When we place them in logical order, however, we place the major premise first, the minor premise second, and the conclusion last.

Words such as "therefore," "hence," and "thus" introduce conclusions. Words such as "since," "as," "granted that," "given that," and "because" introduce premises. The premises count as evidence. To justify a conclusion we need to comply with the basic rules of the categorical syllogism.

EXERCISES

Identify the conclusion, the major term, the minor term, the middle term, the major premise, and the minor premise in each of the following categorical syllogisms.

1. (a) No dull sport is a fun thing.
   (b) All acts of skiing are fun things.
   (c) Thus, no act of skiing is a dull sport.

2. (a) Some fruits are not things good for health.
   (b) Thus, some foods are not things good for health.
   (c) All fruits are foods.

3. (a) Doris Jones is a well-trained M.D.,
   (b) Since Doris Jones is a good surgeon,
   (c) And all good surgeons are well-trained M.D.'s.

4. (a) All sunspots are occurrences with definite cycles.
   (b) Some sunspots are solar events with a life span of four days.

(c) Therefore, some solar events with a life span of four days are occurrences with definite cycles.

5. (a) All cases in which substances are heated are cases of accelerated molecular activity.
   (b) All instances of the burning of gas are cases in which substances are heated.
   (c) Thus, all instances of the burning of gas are cases of accelerated molecular activity.

6. (a) Since some advocates of the enjoyment of simple pleasures are romantic poets,
   (b) Hence, some advocates of the enjoyment of simple pleasures are not persons insensitive to the textures of natural qualities
   (c) Because no romantic poets are insensitive to the texture of natural qualities.

2.   The Rules of the Categorical Syllogism

For a categorical syllogism to be valid, it must conform to the following rules.

1. A valid categorical syllogism must have three and only three terms, each of which occurs twice with the same meaning in the syllogism.

2. A valid categorical syllogism must have the middle term distributed at least once.

3. A valid categorical syllogism must have every term that is distributed in the conclusion also distributed in the premises.

4. A valid categorical syllogism must have a negative conclusion if either premise is negative.

5. A valid categorical syllogism must have at least one affirmative premise.

6. A valid categorical syllogism cannot have a particular conclusion unless one of the premises also is particular.

The first rule requires a categorical syllogism to have three and only three terms. Some logicians would omit this rule. They claim that since it is implicit in the meaning of a categorical syllogism, it is not needed. We grant that their position has merit. But the rule focuses attention on the need to identify the terms of the syllogism to assure that each term occurs twice and that the meaning in each occurrence remains constant. The following invalid categorical syllogism shows the convenience of using this rule. (This argument also is a case of the informal fallacy of equivocation.)

Well-being is the end [purpose] of life.

The end [final outcome] of life is death.

Therefore, well-being is death.

The categorical syllogism makes possible a conclusion about the relation of class inclusion or of class exclusion between the minor term and the major term. The relation these terms have to the middle term provides the basis for the conclusion. If the meaning of a given term changes, or if the term fails to occur twice, then we have no basis for drawing a conclusion.

The second and third rules focus on the distribution of the terms. The second rule requires the middle term to be distributed at least once. Failure to meet this condition results in failure to provide grounds to find a necessary connection between the minor term and the major term. Consider the following invalid syllogism which we looked at in a previous chapter.

All Republicans are citizens of the United States.

All Democrats are citizens of the United States.

Therefore, all Democrats are Republicans.

If the middle term is not distributed, then the minor term can refer to one subclass designated by the middle term. And the major term can refer to a second subclass. No basis remains for relating the two terms. (A subclass refers to an identifiable class within a larger class. The class of all human beings is a subclass of the class of all animals.) A violation of this rule is called "fallacy of an undistributed middle term."

The third rule requires that any term distributed in the conclusion also occurs as a distributed term in the premise. This rule prevents a term in the conclusion from including all members of a class when this term includes only some members of the class in the premise. The following invalid syllogism exemplifies the need for this rule.

All students in this class are persons studying the syllogism.

All students in this class are persons preparing for a career.

Therefore, all persons preparing for a career are studying the syllogism.

"The fallacy of an illicit major" occurs when the faulty term in the violation of this rule is the major term. "The fallacy of an illicit minor" occurs if the faulty term in such cases is the minor term.

The fourth rule prevents the drawing of an affirmative conclusion from a negative premise. An affirmative conclusion states a relation of class inclusion between the subject and the predicate terms. However, with a negative premise involving class exclusion, we have no grounds in a categorical syllogism for deriving a conclusion about class inclusion. Consider the following invalid syllogism.

No humanitarian is a person who ignores human suffering.

All physicians are humanitarians.

Therefore, all physicians are persons who ignore human suffering.

The fifth rule prevents the derivation of any conclusion from two negative premises. The exclusion of part or all of the major and minor terms from the middle term does not make possible any conclusion about conditions which hold between the major and minor terms. The following invalid syllogism violates this rule.

No stones are sentient creatures.

No men are stones.

Therefore, no men are sentient creatures.

We can give good reasons to support a different conclusion, "All men are sentient creatures." But we have to justify our making such a conclusion on other grounds.

The sixth rule requires that a valid categorical syllogism cannot have a particular conclusion unless one of the premises also is particular. This rule is a convention based upon modern developments in logic. But traditional Aristotelian logic did not adhere to it. The need for such a convention is evident in the following invalid syllogism.

All professors with complete mastery of teaching techniques are highly popular with their students.

All professors with complete mastery of teaching techniques are perfect professors.

Therefore, some perfect professors are professors who are highly popular with their students.

The subject term of the conclusion is undistributed. Undistributed terms used as subjects of true categorical statements require that the class for which they are used have members. That is, the class cannot be empty. But the subject terms of the above premises are universal. Their subject terms are distributed. The classes for which we use distributed subject terms can be empty or null.

In the above case we have the fault of having a conclusion whose subject term requires some members in the class for which it is a term. But the distributed subject terms in the premises make no such requirement. The class of "professors with complete mastery of teaching techniques" can be empty. But the particular premise in the conclusion requires that the class of "perfect professors" have at least one member. The form of the above invalid syllogism would permit the faulty step of deriving a class required to have members from a class that could be empty. There may be no perfect professors.

Universal premises with a particular conclusion permit cases in which the premises can be true but the conclusion can be false. We cannot accept such a form as valid. We are following a decision principle of taking the lesser meaning of a statement rather than a possible larger meaning in order to avoid some mistakes. But we also shall be dealing with the requirement that we derive particular categorical statements only from other particular statements on other occasions in the following chapters.

EXERCISES

A. Determine the validity of the following syllogisms. State the rules violated in cases of invalidity.

1. All bats are night creatures.
   Some rodents are night creatures.
   Thus, some rodents are bats.
2. No mystics are beasts.
   Some beasts are brutes.
   Thus, some brutes are not mystics.
3. Some bosses are creeps.
   All creeps are clowns.
   Thus, some clowns are not bosses.
4. All jokers are wild cards.
   John is a joker.
   Thus, John is a wild card.
5. No cops are cowards.
   Jill is a cop.
   Thus, Jill is not a coward.
6. Some books are not worm-eaten things.
   No fruits are books.
   Thus, some fruits are not worm-eaten things.
7. All gnats are insects.
   Some gnats are not day creatures.
   Thus, some day creatures are not insects.
8. All ghosts are scary things.
   All ghosts are weird things.
   Thus, some weird things are scary things.
9. All hawks are birds with sharp claws.
   Some birds with good eyesight are hawks.
   Thus, some birds with good eyesight are birds with sharp claws.
10. All babies are learners.
    All babies are burpers.
    Thus, all burpers are learners.

B. In the following examples words like "hence," "thus," and "therefore" introduce conclusions. Words like "since," "because," and "and" introduce premises. There is need to identify some premises or conclusions by the context. Determine the validity of each syllogism. State any rule of the categorical syllogism that is violated in cases of invalidity.

1. All underdogs are persons having to fight harder. No popular heroes are underdogs. Therefore, no popular heroes are persons having to fight harder.

2. All land conservation is a practice in the national interest. All planting of forests is land conservation. Therefore, all planting of forests is a practice in the national interest.

3. No electronic industry is a business that is in a rut. Any business that is in a rut is an industry stunting its own growth. Hence, no industry stunting its own growth is an electronic industry.

4. All strange programs are risks and many creative programs are strange programs. Therefore, many creative programs are risks.

5. All activities exciting the imagination of people are actions conducive to progress. All explorations of frontiers are activities exciting to the imagination of people. Hence, all explorations of frontiers are actions conducive to progress.

6. Since some great writers are excellent students of history, Shakespeare is an excellent student of history, since Shakespeare is a great writer.

7. No statesmen are advocates of increasing internal tensions and some statesmen are not advocates of greater military spending. Therefore, some advocates of greater military spending are not advocates of increasing internal tensions.

8. Because all goblins are strange creatures, some goblins are creatures we do not trust, since all strange creatures are creatures that we do not trust.

9. Some things requiring planning are not wasteful of resources because no water-saving program is wasteful of resources and some water-saving programs are things requiring planning.

10. All budgets are things in need of review; thus, some things that take time are not things in need of review, because some budgets are things that take time.

7.3 CATEGORICAL SYLLOGISMS: FIGURES, MOODS, AND VENN DIAGRAMS

1. The Figures of Categorical Syllogisms

The proper ordering of categorical syllogisms requires that we state the major premise first, the minor premise second, and the conclusion last. The figure of a categorical syllogism refers to the position of the middle term in a proper ordering of the major and minor premises. Consider the following possible orderings of the middle term where M is a place holder for the middle term, P is a place holder for the major term, and S is a place holder for the minor term.

ΕΙΟ –
always
valid

one valid of figure
(argument each)

Syllogistic Logic   **131**

always
part...

Figures	I	II	III	IV
Major Premise	*M P*	*P M*	*M P*	*P M*
Minor Premise	*'S M*	*S M*	*M S*	*M S*
Conclusion	*S P*	*S P*	*S P*	*S P*

Four possible positions of the middle term occur. Each different position is a separate figure of the syllogism. In Figure I the middle term is the subject term in the major premise and the predicate term in the minor premise. In Figure II the middle term is the predicate term in both premises. In Figure III the middle term is the subject term in both premises. In Figure IV the middle term is the predicate term in the major premise and the subject term in the minor premise. The following example is an illustration of Figure I.

       M
No scientists are superstitious persons.

       M
Some teachers are scientists.

Therefore, some teachers are not superstitious persons.

Identifying the figure of a syllogism is helpful in the analysis of the validity of different forms in which different syllogisms occur. Many different combinations [$(4 \times 4 \times 4) = 64$] of **A**, **E**, **I**, and **O** categorical statements can occur in Figure I. But only four of these combinations result in valid syllogisms.

2.   The Mood of a Categorical Syllogism

We determine the mood of a categorical syllogism by the types of **A**, **E**, **I**, **O** statements found in properly ordered premises and the conclusion. Consider the types of categorical statements in the following syllogism in Figure II.

E   No tyrants are democratic rulers.

A   All liberal presidents are democratic rulers.

E   Therefore, no liberal presidents are tyrants.

Here the major premise is an **E** categorical statement. The minor premise is an **A** statement. And the conclusion is an **E** statement. The figure and mood of this syllogism is written II–EAE.

Determining the mood of a figure assists in the analysis of the form or structure of an argument. For example, any syllogism with particular and affirmative premises (**I** statements) is invalid. The fallacy of an undistributed middle term occurs. Any combination of **E** and **O** premises is invalid. The fallacy of two negative premises occurs. Likewise, any categorical syllogism with an **E** and **O** statement in a premise and an **A** or **I** statement in the conclusion is also invalid. The fallacy of a negative premise with an affirmative conclusion occurs.

EXERCISES

A. Write the figure and mood for each syllogism in Exercise A at the end of Section 7.2. (These syllogisms are arranged in proper order.)

B. Determine the validity of syllogisms having the forms indicated by the following figures and moods. State the name of any fallacy in cases of invalidity.

1.	I – **IEO**	6.	IV – **AIO**
2.	II – **AOO**	7.	I – **AEE**
3.	III – **IAI**	8.	IV – **EAO**
4.	IV – **AII**	9.	III – **EAE**
5.	II – **EOO**	10.	IV – **EAE**

C. Write the figure and mood for the following categorical syllogisms (after arranging them in proper order). Identify any invalid syllogism and indicate the fallacy in such cases.
1. Some apples are red fruits. Some apples are delicious-tasting food. Therefore, some red fruits are delicious-tasting food.
2. No computers are things that can feel. Some highly complex instruments are computers. Therefore, some highly complex instruments are not things that can feel.
3. All *ABA*s are *BCB*s. No *BCB*s are *CBC*s. Therefore, no *CBC*s are *ABA*s.
4. All marathon races are activities of endurance. Some track events are not marathon races. Therefore, some track events are not activities of endurance.
5. All successful hybrid wheat planters are smart marketers. Some smart marketers are not sellers at market troughs. Therefore, some sellers at market troughs are not successful hybrid wheat planters.
6. No *CAC*s are *BCB*s. Some *ACA*s are *BCB*s. Therefore, some *CAC*s are not *ACA*s.

3. The Use of Venn Diagrams

The use of Venn diagrams provides another way to determine the validity of categorical syllogisms. We construct such diagrams by drawing the circles for the Boolean analysis of each premise in the syllogism. We then impose these circles on a common set of three overlapping circles. We compare the markings made on the combined circles with the markings for the circles required only for the conclusion. A categorical syllogism is valid only if the overlapping circles drawn solely for the premises already have the complete markings required for the conclusion. A categorical syllogism is invalid if the overlapping circles drawn only for the premises do not have the complete markings needed for the conclusion. We can understand this procedure better by studying Figures 7.6–7.13, together with the following explanation.

Let us consider cases in which both premises are universal. We shall draw the Venn diagrams for the following syllogisms.

(1) All constitutionalists are persons respecting civil rights.
     All justices on the Supreme Court are constitutionalists.
     Hence, all justices on the Supreme Court are persons respecting civil rights.

(2) All conservatives are persons who respect the constitution.
     All liberals are persons who respect the constitution.
     Therefore, all liberals are conservatives.

The first syllogism in Figure I, Mood **AAA**, has the Boolean analysis of categorical statement as shown in Figure 7.6. We draw a common set of circles as in Figure 7.7. We draw the major premise and the minor premise on the common set of circles as in Figure 7.8. We compare the circles for the Boolean analysis of the conclusion with the common set of circles for both premises (Figure 7.9). The figure drawn only for the premises also contains the markings required in drawing the conclusion. Thus, the Venn diagram demonstrates that the conclusion is valid. The syllogism also conforms to the rules of the categorical syllogism. Showing that the syllogism meets the conditions essential for validity in a Venn diagram is an alternate way of proving validity.

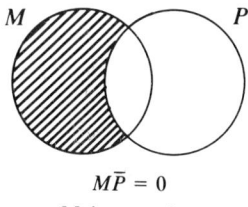

$M\bar{P} = 0$
Major premise

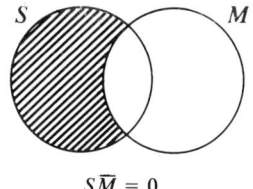

$S\bar{M} = 0$
Minor premise

$S\bar{P} = 0$
Conclusion

Figure 7.6

rules
1. Always draw circles for Universal arguments first.
2. If line goes thru center of section, put "x" on the line.

shaded parts are empty.

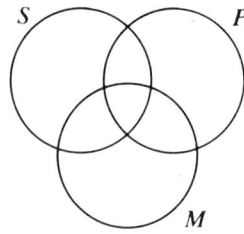

Figure 7.7

The premises and the conclusion for the second syllogism in Figure II, Mood **AAA**, has the analysis shown in Figure 7.10. The premises drawn on a common set of circles are shown in Figure 7.11. We compare the circles for both premises and for the conclusion in Figure 7.12. We see that the drawing of the premises did not fully draw the markings required by the conclusion. The markings required by the categorical statements in the premises do not show part of the class of S and not P, and specifically the class of $S\bar{P}M$ (Figure 7.13), to be null. But all of this class is marked out and shown to be null in the statement for the conclusion. Thus, we have shown this syllogism is invalid.

After students learn to draw the categorical statements used as premises on the common set of three circles, they can omit one step. We no longer need to draw separate overlapping circles for each statement in the syllogism. Rather we can use the common set of three overlapping circles for analysis of the premises and the conclusion. For the sake of convenience in analysis, let us always designate the circle on the left of the diagram as S, the circle on the right as P, and the lower circle as M.

In learning how to construct a Venn diagram for syllogisms with a

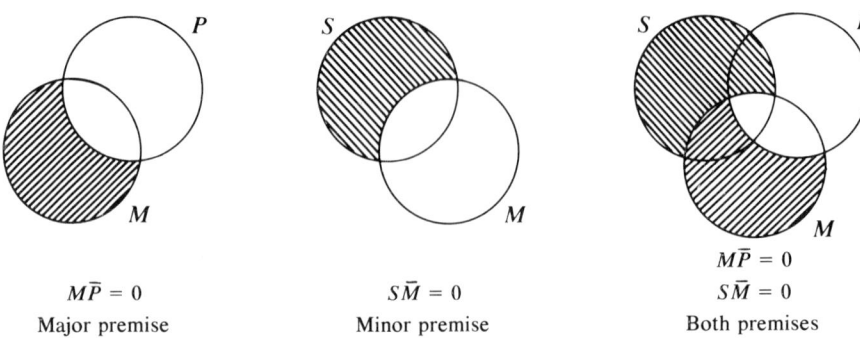

$M\bar{P} = 0$	$S\bar{M} = 0$	$M\bar{P} = 0$
		$S\bar{M} = 0$
Major premise	Minor premise	Both premises

Figure 7.8

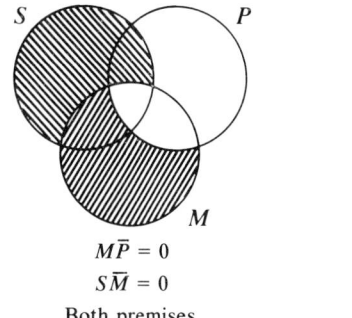

$M\bar{P} = 0$
$S\bar{M} = 0$
Both premises

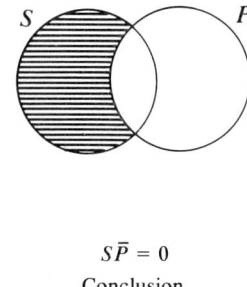

$S\bar{P} = 0$
Conclusion

Figure 7.9

particular premise, we follow the rules already given for the Venn diagram. But there is one basic difference. In this case we always use first the marking required by the universal premise. Let us consider the following syllogisms to illustrate how to impose an x for a particular premise in a Venn diagram.

(3) Some humanists are novelists.
All humanists are activists in the woman's liberation movement.
Hence, some activists in the woman's liberation movement are novelists.

(4) All employees are eligible for Social Security benefits.
Some stockholders are not employees.
Therefore, some stockholders are not eligible for Social Security benefits.

Particular categorical statements require the placing of an x in the designated class found in the circles.

But first we need to indicate the marking for the universal premise. We then can mark the x for any particular premise.

The first example above is an instance of Figure III, Mood **IAI**. We

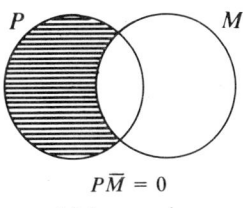

$P\bar{M} = 0$
Major premise

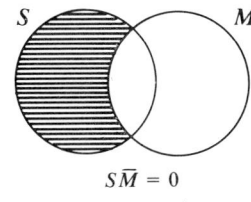

$S\bar{M} = 0$
Minor premise

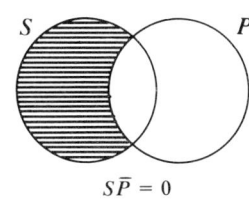

$S\bar{P} = 0$
Conclusion

Figure 7.10

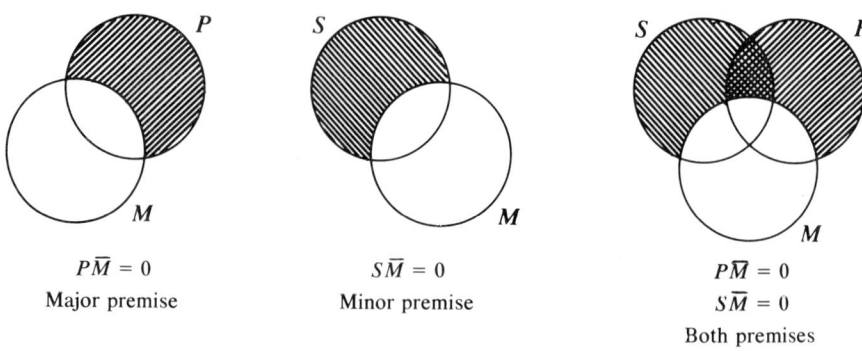

Figure 7.11

draw the Boolean markings for the categorical statements of each premise. And we then impose this drawing on the common set of circles as shown in Figure 7.14. First we draw the universal premise, which in this case also is the minor premise. We place the x to indicate that the class of MP is not null in the unmarked part of the class of MP. That is, we place it in the part of the class of MP that we have not shown to be null or empty. In drawing only the markings for the premises we also have drawn the marking required for the conclusion. And in this case the conclusion requires an x somewhere in the class of SP. In the above case we find that the x is in the area required by the conclusion. Thus, the Venn diagram shows that the conclusion is valid.

In the second example the syllogism is Figure I, Mood **AOO**. We draw the marking required for each statement in the syllogism. Then we first make the markings of the universal premise, which in this case also is the major premise, on the common set of circles. (See Figure 7.15.) However, a problem arises with regard to the placing of the x for the particular

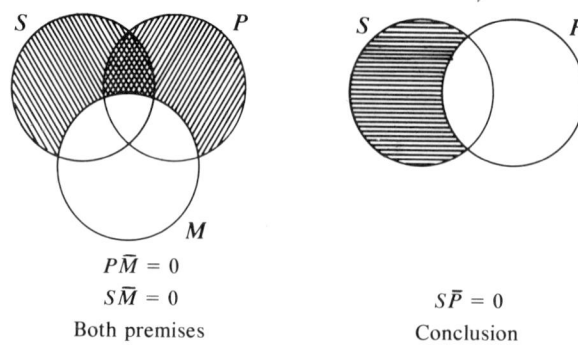

Figure 7.12

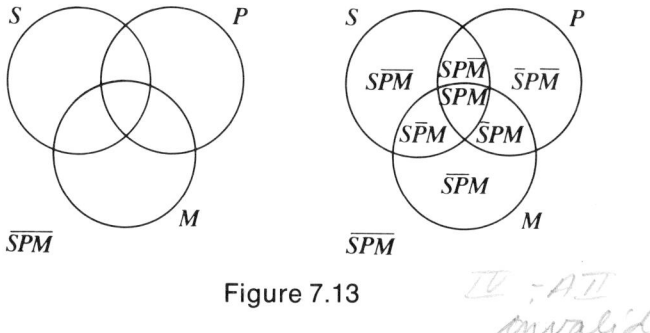

Figure 7.13

IV. -A.II.
invalid

premise. In the combined circles a line intersects the class of S and not M. Since it is possible for the members denoted by the x to be only in one of the two classes represented by the area of S and not M, we need to mark the x on the intersecting line. Note that the Venn diagram for this figure and mood has not drawn the conclusion which requires that the x be solely in a section of the class of S that is not P. It is possible for the members designated by the x to be wholly within the class of S and P. The marking

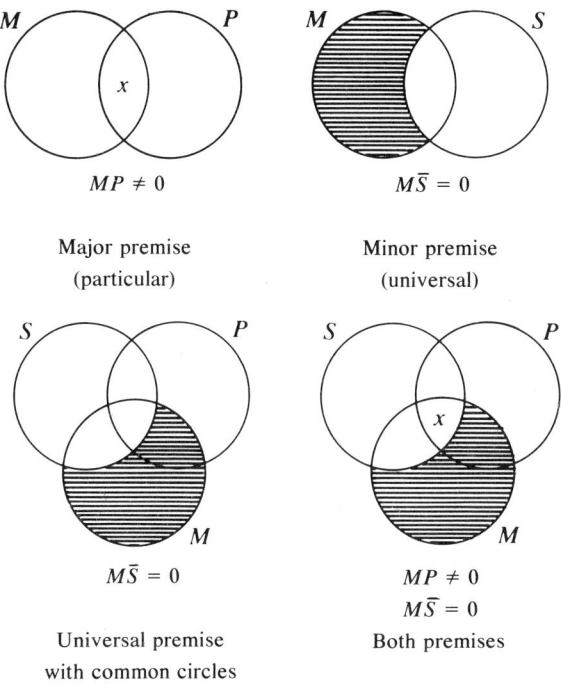

Figure 7.14

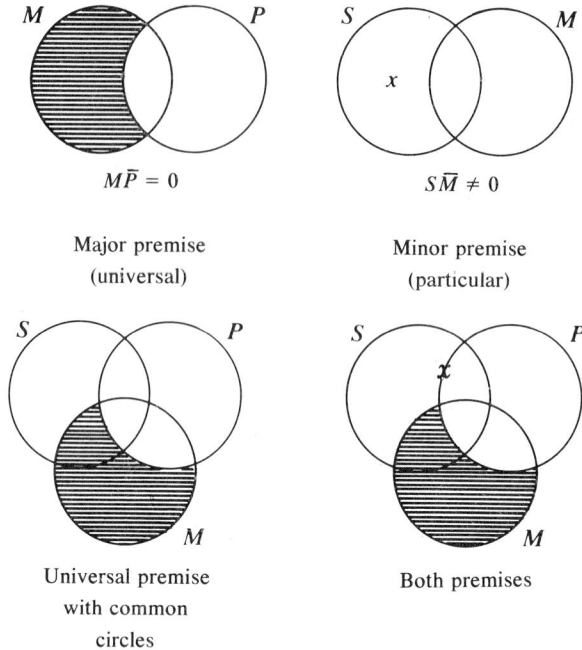

$M\bar{P} = 0$

Major premise
(universal)

$S\bar{M} \neq 0$

Minor premise
(particular)

Universal premise
with common
circles

Both premises

Figure 7.15

required by the conclusion did not occur in the marking of the classes indicated by the statements in the premises. And the syllogism is invalid.

We can summarize the steps in using a Venn diagram for a proof of validity in the following way.

1. We first mark for any universal premise (or premises) on the common set of circles.

2. We then mark for any particular premise (or premises) on the common set of circles. If a line intersects the class indicated by a particular premise, then we must place the x on the intersecting line.

3. We examine the diagram to see if we find the exact markings required by the conclusion merely by drawing the indicated markings for the premises. (For a conclusion with a particular premise to be valid in a Venn diagram, the x signifying class membership must fall clearly within the class designated by the conclusion and not merely on a line adjacent to the designated class. If both premises are universal and the conclusion is particular then an x does not appear in marking the classes for the premises. But the particular conclusion requires such an x. A Venn diagram shows that such a syllogism is invalid.)

EXERCISES

Draw the Venn diagrams for the following figures and moods. Indicate invalid forms by pointing out the reason according to the procedures of the Venn diagram.

1. Figure I, **AEE**
2. Figure II, **EAE**
3. Figure III, **AII**
4. Figure IV, **AII**
5. Figure I, **EAE**

6. Figure III, **AOO**
7. Figure II, **AEE**
8. Figure IV, **EAE**
9. Figure I, **EEE**
10. Figure IV, **OAO**

4.   Summary of Steps in the Analysis of Categorical Syllogisms

In ordinary language the premises and the conclusion of arguments can occur in random order. To analyze the arguments by the procedures discussed in this section, we need to order the premises so that the major premise is first, the minor premise is second, and the conclusion is last. We summarize the steps for arranging the argument in the standard form of categorical syllogisms in the following outline:

1. We express the premises and the conclusion in the form of standard categorical statements. The subject term appears first, the copula denoting class inclusion (or class exclusion with "no" or "not") occurs second, and the predicate term appears third.

2. We identify the conclusion of the syllogism. (Expressions such as "so," "hence," "thus," and "therefore" frequently introduce conclusions.)

3. We identify the major, minor, and middle terms. (The major term is the predicate term of the conclusion. The minor term is the subject term of the conclusion. The middle term is the term common to both premises.)

4. We identify the major premise and the minor premise. (The major premise is the premise with the major term and the minor premise is the premise with the minor term.)

5. We place in proper order the premises and the conclusion of the categorical syllogism—the major premise first, the minor premise second, and the conclusion last.

6. We analyze the structure of the syllogism by indicating its figure and mood, by use of Aristotelian forms, and by a Venn diagram.

7. We determine whether the syllogism is valid by use of the rules of the

categorical syllogism and by analysis of the Venn diagram. If the syllogism is invalid, we give the reason for invalidity by reference to a primary rule of the syllogism.[1]

EXERCISES

Give a complete analysis of the following syllogisms. Include proper ordering of premises, figure, mood, Aristotelian forms, Venn diagram, validity. If the syllogism is invalid, give the reason for invalidity by reference to the primary rules of the categorical syllogism and to the circles for the Venn diagram.

1. All actions subject to law are subject to a lawgiver. All movements of planets are actions subject to law. Therefore, all movements of planets are subject to a lawgiver.

2. All atoms are in movement. Some atoms are not subject to experimental control. Therefore, some things subject to experimental control are in movement.

3. No theories are moral commands. Thus, no categorical imperatives are theories, since all categorical imperatives are moral commands.

4. The universe is not infinite, since nothing infinite is an expanding sphere and the universe is an expanding sphere.

5. All control of behavior is control of volition. Some control of volition is a consequence of redirecting interests. Therefore, some consequence of redirecting interests is control of behavior.

6. Some theories of probability are rationalistic theories. All rationalistic theories are *a priori*. Therefore, some *a priori* theories are theories of probability.

7. Since George is a premed student, George is a person interested in biology. All premed students are persons interested in biology.

8. The urban renewal program is a form of social control. All forms of social control are instances of social determination. Therefore, the urban renewal program is an instance of social determination.

9. All dogs are quadrupeds. No upright animals are quadrupeds. Therefore, no dogs are upright animals.

10. All cases of justice are matters for the courts. Some cases of justice are cases of alleviation of poverty. Therefore, some cases of alleviation of poverty are matters for the courts.

---

[1] 8. (Optional) We can add an additional step. We may use abbreviations for the expressions used as terms in a categorical statement. This abbreviation can be a capital letter such as *B* or *N*. We can write "All boys are noisy persons" as "All *B*s are *N*s." In using such abbreviations we need to exercise care in the use of any signs of negations. We also need to remember that these capital letters are only abbreviations for the words in the original statement. They are not to be confused with *P*, *S*, and *M* which are place holders that stand for the major term, the minor term, and the middle term of any categorical syllogism.

11. Some trustworthy persons are talkative persons. All elderly persons are trust-worthy persons. Therefore, some talkative persons are elderly persons.

12. All parapsychologists are persons ~~optimistic about~~ ESP. No experimental psychologists are persons optimistic about ESP. Therefore, no experimental psychologists are parapsychologists.

13. No experiments are projects undertaken without tentative identification of relevant variables. All experiments are solutions proposed about an experimental question. Therefore, no projects undertaken without tentative identification of relevant variables are solutions proposed about an experimental question.

14. No experimentalist is an investigator indifferent to laboratory techniques. Some psychotherapists are not experimentalists. Therefore, some investigators indifferent to laboratory techniques are psychotherapists.

15. No gambling losses are expenses that ~~rise in inflation~~, since all fixed costs are expenses that rise in inflation and no gambling losses are fixed costs.

16. Because no conditioned reflex is innate and all conditioned reflexes are learned responses, nothing innate is a learned response.

17. All entomologists are biologists, because all persons who study insects scientifically are entomologists and some biologists are persons who study insects scientifically.

18. All air carriers are companies maintaining expensive ground schools. Therefore, all major air companies are companies maintaining expensive ground schools, because all major air companies are air carriers.

19. Some chess players are engineers. Mr. Smith is an engineer. Therefore, Mr. Smith is a chess player.

CHAPTER 8

CONSTRUCTING CATEGORICAL STATEMENTS AND SYLLOGISMS IN STANDARD FORM

8.1 EQUIVALENT FORMS FOR CATEGORICAL STATEMENTS

This chapter will continue the analysis of valid categorical syllogisms. It will demonstrate how to develop equivalent statements in arguments. Also, it will show how to translate sentences found in ordinary language into the form of standard categorical statements. Ways of making complete syllogisms will be developed in cases where omission of a premise or a conclusion occurs. The chapter also will discuss chain arguments and identify their correct forms. And it will show how we can derive the corollaries from the basic rules of syllogistic logic.

In this section we shall present different ways to write categorical statements in different equivalent forms. In some instances the use of an equivalent statement may provide a way to make valid a syllogism that otherwise would fail to meet the rules for a valid syllogism. Consider the following example:

> All populist appeals are movements directed to secure mass support.
>
> Some populist appeals are not nonpolitical endeavors.
>
> Therefore, some political endeavors are movements directed to secure mass support.

The above syllogism has four terms. The conclusion also is affirmative and a premise is negative. We can replace the minor premise with an equivalent form. The minor premise can be restated as: "Some populist appeals are political endeavors." The syllogism now has three and only three terms. And it does not have a negative premise with an affirmative conclusion. The translation of the minor premise in an equivalent form results in a valid syllogism.

An original statement is equivalent to a second statement if the same truth values hold for each statement. One may replace a statement by an equivalent statement anywhere in an argument.

Any statement in the logic we are using is either true or false in the same context. When we want to refer to the assigning of one and only one of these two properties, true or false, to a statement, we are talking about the truth value of the statement.

The three basic operations for deriving one equivalent categorical statement from another are obversion, conversion, and contraposition. But the replacement of one equivalent statement by another results in a valid syllogism only in some cases. For example, a categorical syllogism with three and only three terms, with affirmative premises, and with an undistributed middle term, cannot be made valid.

1.   Obversion

Obversion is a logical operation using negation.

1.   There is a change of the quality of the categorical statement. An affirmative statement becomes negative and vice versa.

2.   There is a negation of the predicate term by use of its complementary term.

3.   The subject term remains unchanged.

Previously we noted that a complementary term includes everything in the universe of discourse other than what the original term includes. The complementary term of "women" is "nonwomen," that is, "everything in the universe that is not a woman."

Obversion is applicable to all categorical statements. Consider the statement "All artists are creative persons." The obverse of this statement requires the negation of the statement as a whole and the use of the complementary predicate term. Its obverse is "No artists are noncreative persons."

The use of a complementary term does not present any major difficulties in working with the symbolic forms of statements. Thus, the obverse of "No S is P" is "All S is non-P." But ordinary language becomes stilted when we use it with this degree of precision. The obverse of the statement "No accountants are unskilled persons" is "All accountants are non-unskilled persons." But this is not the way we talk. In ordinary usage we say, "All accountants are skilled persons." Such ordinary usage overlooks both the class of "semiskilled persons" and the larger class of "everything that is not a skilled person." The use of categorical statements in ordinary discourse accommodates to the need for unstilted language. However, we need to recognize that errors in reasoning do emerge as a result of such accommodation. For example, let us assume that the predicate term of a statement is "rational behavior." The use of "irrational behavior" as its complementary term can suggest a more bizarre set of circumstances than may be expected by the term "nonrational behavior."

2. Conversion

In conversion there is an interchange of the subject and predicate terms of a statement. But one cannot increase the distribution of a term in such cases. The following conditions hold in conversion.

1. The predicate term becomes the subject term.

2. The subject term becomes the predicate term.

3. An undistributed term cannot be changed into a distributed term.

4. The quality (affirmative or negative) of the categorical statement remains the same.

Consider the converse of the statement "Some persons who achieve identification with their audience are persuasive speakers." The converse is "Some persuasive speakers are persons who achieve identification with their audience." A full converse is possible only for universal negative categorical statements and particular affirmative statements (the **E** and **I** forms).

There is only a partial conversion of a universal affirmative categorical statement (the **A** form). We cannot accept this form in syllogistic logic unless we make explicit the assumption that the classes expressed by the subject and predicate terms are not empty. The predicate term of an affirmative categorical statement is undistributed. Such a term must remain undistributed when it becomes the subject term in conversion. The conversion by limitation of the categorical statement "All members of the Supreme Court are lawyers" is "Some lawyers are members of the Supreme Court."

The fallacy of false conversion occurs when the original undistributed predicate term is changed into a distributed subject term in conversion. This fallacy occurs in the (false) conversion of the statement, "All major participants in the scandal of Watergate are lawyers," into the statement, "All lawyers are major participants in the scandal of Watergate." There is no conversion for the particular negative categorical statement (the **O** form). Let us consider the statement "Some persons indicted by grand juries are not persons found guilty by courts." We cannot convert this into the statement "Some persons found guilty by courts are not persons indicted by grand juries." In such an improper conversion the original undistributed subject term illicitly becomes a distributed predicate term. But negative categorical statements require the distribution of the predicate term.

3. Contraposition *interchanges & negates*

Contraposition requires an interchange of the subject terms and the predicate terms. And there also is use of the complementary terms of the original terms. The universal affirmative and the particular negative categorical statements (the **A** and **O** forms) have full contrapositives. The universal negative statement (**E** form) has only a partial contrapositive. (It is not accepted in syllogistic logic without making explicit the assumption that the subject term is not empty.) No contrapositive is possible for a particular affirmative statement (**I** form). There are three steps in deriving a contrapositive statement, as shown in the following example:

Original statement: All labor leaders are collective bargainists.

1. *Obverse of original statement:* No labor leaders are noncollective bargainists.

2. *Converse of step 1:* No noncollective bargainists are labor leaders.

3. *Obverse of step 2 (and the contraposition of the original statement):* All noncollective bargainists are nonlabor leaders.

The partial contrapositive of a universal negative statement comes about in the following way. "No *F* is *G*" becomes obverted to "All *F* is non-*G*." The converse of "All *F* is non-*G*" is only partial, "Some non-*G* is *F*." The obverse of "Some non-*G* is *F*" is "Some non-*G* is not non-*F*." When we attempt to derive a contrapositive for a particular affirmative statement (**I** form) we have difficulty in the second step. The obverse of "Some *F* is *G*" is "Some *F* is not non-*G*." But "Some *F* is not non-*G*" is a particular negative statement. It has no converse.

    Tables for Obversion, Conversion, and Contraposition.   Tables 8.1, 8.2, and 8.3 show the obversion, conversion, and contraposition, respectively, of the different types of categorical statements. The mark "−" placed before a term is read as *non* and signifies that reference is made to the denial of the original form of the term.

EXERCISES

Write the equivalent form indicated for each of the following categorical statements. Include the Aristotelian type of analysis for each statement.

1. Write the obverse of the following statements:
   (a) The use of the platoon system for football teams is a popular practice.
   (b) No relief pitcher is a regular starter.
   (c) Some catchers are slow athletes.
   (d) Some coaches are not lenient persons.

2. Write (where possible) the converse of the following statements:
   (a) All programs are things to be evaluated.
   (b) No waves are particles.
   (c) Some interference patterns are irregular patterns.
   (d) Some photographic plates are not rough objects.

3. Write (where possible) the contraposition of the following statements:
   (a) Some recessive characteristics are things transmitted to the young.

Table 8.1   Table for Obversion

A	$Fd < Gu$	All bets are risks.
	$Fd \not< -Gd$ Obverse	No bets are nonrisks.
E	$Fd \not< Gd$	No bets are risks.
	$Fd < -Gu$ Obverse	All bets are nonrisks.
I	$Fu < Gu$	Some bets are risks.
	$Fu \not< -Gd$ Obverse	Some bets are not nonrisks.
O	$Fu \not< Gd$	Some bets are not risks.
	$Fu < -Gu$ Obverse	Some bets are nonrisks.

Table 8.2   Table for Conversion

A	Fd < Gu		All judges are lawyers.
	*Gu < Fu	Partial converse	*Some lawyers are judges.
E	Fd ≮ Gd		No judges are lawyers.
	Gd ≮ Fd	Converse	No lawyers are judges.
I	Fu < Gu		Some judges are lawyers.
	Gu < Fu	Converse	Some lawyers are judges.
O	Fu ≮ Gd		(There is no converse for
	(none)		an **O** proposition.)

* Not valid in syllogistic logic without making assumptions explicit.

(b) All viruses are nucleoprotein.
(c) No gene is a thing capable of multiplying outside a cell.
(d) Some plants are not mutations.

8.2 CATEGORICAL STATEMENTS AND ORDINARY LANGUAGE

Many statements in ordinary language are not in proper form for use in categorical syllogisms. For their use in such syllogisms we have to express them in a standard form. In recasting these statements in categorical form we must make the subject and the predicate terms explicit. And we need to make precise the distribution of terms. We also must make definite the relation of class inclusion or class exclusion. To do this we use a form of the verb "to be" in the present tense.

There can be a variety of ways in which we can translate some statements in ordinary discourse. One way may be as good as another in some cases. But there still are other ways that are wrong. Included in the following ten recommendations are some of the basic ways we can follow in rewriting statements into proper categorical form.

Table 8.3   Table for Contraposition

A	Fd < Gu		All students are voters.
	-Gd < -Fu	Contrapositive	All nonvoters are nonstudents.
E	Fd ≮ Gd		No students are voters.
	*-Gu ≮ -Fd	Partial contrapositive	*Some nonvoters are not nonstudents.
I	Fu < Gu		(There is no contrapositive for an **I**
	(none)		statement.)
O	Fu ≮ Gd		Some students are not voters.
	-Gu ≮ -Fd	Contrapositive	Some nonvoters are not nonstudents.

* Not valid in syllogistic logic without making assumptions explicit.

1. There Is Need To Make Explicit the Distribution of the Subject Term.   Consider this statement:

Men are mortals.

We need to make explicit the distribution of the subject term by placing "All" or "Some" in front of "men." Such a decision must be made in light of the context. If there is serious doubt about which of the two meanings holds, the usual procedure is to use the more restricted quantifier ("some") rather than the universal quantifier ("all") for the statement. However, if one uses "some" with the subject term, the statement is particular. For the sentence to be true, there must be members in the class of the subject term. In the case of the statement, "Men are mortal," there is little room for serious doubt about the meaning of the sentence: "all men" customarily would be meant. And the sentence would be restated, "All men are mortal creatures."

In translating a given statement into standard categorical form, we need to recognize that we can express the meaning of many statements in more than one way. But once we decide on a given way of translating a term in a syllogism, we need to use that translation throughout that context. We shall let the letter O stand for the original statement and the letter T stand for the statement as translated in correct form.

Consider expressions like:

O: Many scholars are professors.

O: Most teachers are college graduates.

We translate such expressions as "many," "most," "almost everyone" for categorical statements by the word "some." The minimal meaning of "some" is "at least one." The introduction of "some" in these statements diminishes their original force. But this form makes clear that the subject term is undistributed and that the statement is particular. The categorical forms for the original statements are as follows:

T: Some scholars are professors.

T: Some teachers are college graduates.

2. There Is Need To Make Explicit the Notion of Class Inclusion or Class Exclusion by Use of the Verb Form of the Copula.   The main verb needs to have a form of the verb "to be" in the present tense. We must make definite the notion of class inclusion or exclusion of the subject term in the predicate term. Take the following statements and their translations:

O: Old generals fade away.

T: All old generals are persons who fade away.

O: Librarians read widely.

T: All librarians are persons who read widely.

3. *There Is Need To Make Explicit Both the Subject Term and the Predicate Term.* Consider the statements:

O: From many sources comes evidence of the invasion of Britain by William the Conqueror.

T: The invasion of Britain by William the Conqueror is an event attested by evidence from many sources.

The subject and predicate terms in the above case need to be made definite.

4. *There Is Need To Make Clear That the Predicate Term Is a Class Term.* Consider the following statements:

O: Students are curious.

O: Birds fly.

O: John's car hit a deer.

To form these sentences into categorical statements, we need to state the predicate term as a class term:

T: All students are curious persons.

T: All birds are creatures that fly.

T: John's car is a vehicle that hit a deer.

5. *There Is Need To Distinguish Clearly Universal Negative Statements from Particular Negative Statements.* Consider the statement:

O: All engineers are not scientists.

The expression "All . . . are not _____" is not clear. Is a statement using this form universal or particular? We must base such judgments on the context. If there is serious doubt remaining, we need to use the more limited meaning of the expression. The statement above may be rendered properly:

T: Some engineers are not scientists.

On the other hand, the context of the statement might indicate the need to translate the form "All . . . are not _____" into a universal negative statement. For example:

O: All freshmen are not permitted to enroll in graduate courses.

T: No freshmen are students permitted to enroll in graduate courses at institution x.

On tests ★ *6. There Is Need To Clarify the Meaning of Expressions Such as "Only" and "None But."* Consider the following examples:

O: Only good mathematicians are good theoretical physicists.

T: All good theoretical physicists are good mathematicians.

O: Only As are Bs.

T: All Bs are As.

O: None but As are Bs.

T: All Bs are As.

O: None but the courageous are victorious.

T: All victorious persons are courageous individuals.

In the above kinds of cases "only" or "none but" introduce the predicate term. But expressions using the form "the only" require further analysis. "The only" introduces the subject term of the categorical statement. Consider the statements:

O: The only clothes I have are out of date.

T: All my clothes are materials out of date.

O: Fingerprints are the only clue to the robbery.

T: All clues to the robbery are fingerprints.

An expression using the form "only some" requires both an **I** and an **O** proposition for the rendering of its complete meaning:

O: Only some hard-nosed guys win.

T: Some hard-nosed guys are persons who win. (And)

T: Some hard-nosed guys are persons who do not win.

Both forms of these statements need to be tested in determining the validity of a syllogism.

7. There Is Need To Clarify Exceptive Statements. These statements occur with the use of expressions such as "except," "but," and "all . . . except some."

Consider the following statement for analysis:

O: All freshmen except (but) honor students may leave.

The first statement clearly translates with the first meaning stated below and apparently also means but does not state explicitly the second translation below:

T_1: All freshmen who are not honor students are persons who may leave.

T_2 (suppressed): No freshmen who are honor students are students who may leave.

If such an expression occurs in a syllogism, we require the testing of the first meaning. If this form does not provide a valid syllogism, we can test the second form as an implicit premise with the notation that we are using a suppressed premise.

Consider the following translation for an original **E** type statement:

O: No students but (except) seniors are excused.

T_1: No nonsenior students are persons excused.

T_2 (suppressed): All senior students are persons excused.

We can test this last form by acknowledging that we are using a premise suppressed in the context.

We can have three translations to test in statements using the phrase ". . . except some _____" (or ". . . but some _____"):

O: No students except some seniors are persons excused.

T_1: No nonsenior students are persons excused.

T_2: Some senior students are persons excused.

T_3 (suppressed): Some senior students are not persons excused.

The clarification of exceptive statements may be summarized as follows:

(1) All As except Bs are Cs. *Restated as:*
    (a) All As that are non-Bs are Cs. (In all cases)
    (b) No Bs that are As are Cs. (Suppressed statement in some cases)

(2) No *A*s except *B*s are *C*s. *Restated as:*
  (a) No *A*s that are non-*B*s are *C*s. (In all cases)
  (b) All *A*s that are *B*s are *C*s. (Suppressed statement in some cases)

(3) All *A*s except some *B*s are *C*s. *Restated as:*
  (a) All *A*s that are non-*B*s are *C*s. (In all cases)
  (b) Some *A*s that are *B*s are not *C*s. (In all cases)
  (c) Some *A*s that are *B*s are *C*s. (Suppressed statement in some cases)

(4) No *A*s except some *B*s are *C*s. *Restated as:*
  (a) No *A*s that are non-*B*s are *C*s. (In all cases)
  (b) Some *A*s that are *B*s are *C*s. (In all cases)
  (c) Some *A*s that are *B*s are not *C*s. (Suppressed statement in some cases)

8. There Is Need To Translate Some Compound Statements into Categorical Statements. Such translations include some statements introduced by expressions like "when," "if," and "where." Expressions following "when" and "if" and not used with "only" introduce the subject term. But, "only when" and "only if" introduce the predicate term:

O: When he comes, I shall be ready.

T: The occasion of his coming is an occasion of my being ready.

O: Only if you put forth an extra effort can you win the game.

T: All occasions of your winning the game are circumstances in which you put forth an extra effort.

Statements using "unless" to introduce a clause are troublesome. Consider the statement:

O: John goes home on weekends unless a fraternity dance is held.

This expression clearly states, "If a fraternity dance is not held, then John goes home on weekends." It also appears to mean but does not explicitly state, "If a fraternity dance is held, then John does not go home on weekends." With this interpretation we can translate the original statement as follows:

*T*₁: All weekends on which a fraternity dance is not held are occasions on which John goes home.

The second form can be tested as an implicit premise:

*T*₂: All weekends on which a fraternity dance is held are occasions on which John does not go home. (Suppressed in some cases)

The following forms may assist in clarifying this use of "unless."

O: *A* unless *B*.

T_1: All non-*B*s are *A*s. (In all cases)

T_2: All *B*s are non-*A*s. (Suppressed statement in some cases)

9. There Is Need To Clarify Statements Using Notions of Time, Place, and Circumstances. Consider the statements:

O: There are boys playing in the streets.

O: There are several visitors arriving.

In such expressions, one adds references to time, place, occasion, or circumstances. Such references make the meaning of the sentence explicit and provide the form needed for a categorical statement. We can clarify these expressions as follows:

T: This time is included in the class of occasions in which boys are playing in the street.

T: This occasion is included in the class of circumstances in which several visitors are arriving.

10. There Is Need To Clarify Statements Using Other Forms of Ambiguity. Consider the statement:

O: Nothing is too good for you.

This statement could mean two different things:

T_1: You are included in the class of persons deserving the very best.

T_2: You are included in the class of persons deserving the very worst.

If the context itself is indeterminate, then both meanings of the premise need to be tested and each meaning applied to a syllogism and tested for validity.

Language indeed is much more varied than the logical forms into which we structure it for appraisal in the form of categorical statements. Yet, such translating is essential if we are to analyze the logical notions that language conveys by rigorous analysis in categorical syllogisms.

EXERCISES

A. Write the following statements in proper categorical form.
(1) Trucks are heavy.
(2) Youth dares where old men fear to plunge.
(3) Only the prepared survive.
(4) Old dogs do not learn new tricks.
(5) There is never a dull moment in Professor Smith's class.
(6) Times change.
(7) Many a former student wished he had studied more and played less.
(8) There are several books on the shelf.
(9) Puzzles intrigue Henry.
(10) The only survivors are small children.
(11) Only some students missed the exam.
(12) No students except seniors are invited to the meeting.
(13) You lose this hand unless you analyze the original bidding.
(14) Birds of a feather flock together.
(15) All seniors except those not graduating attended the banquet.
(16) Only if a thing has fins is it a fish.
(17) Goblins are invisible.
(18) I shall lose no time in returning this manuscript.
(19) No members except the executive committee left the room.
(20) Skeletons need not be brought out of the closet.
(21) Only some questions are difficult.
(22) If Tom sinks his putt, he wins the match.
(23) This experiment works unless contamination is present.
(24) No one would take that risk unless he is a fool.
(25) Cars washed any day except Monday.
(26) The students are not working all day.
(27) All college students are not pressed financially.
(28) All exercises except some requiring advanced math are easy.
(29) There are two visitors at the door.
(30) Charles missed the bus.

B. Write the following syllogisms in proper categorical form and in logical order. Make a complete analysis of each syllogism and determine its validity. State any rule that is violated in the invalid syllogisms.
(1) Jungle societies do not cultivate the arts, therefore societies concerned with only their own economic interests do not cultivate the arts, since such societies are jungle societies.
(2) If we risk losses in these circumstances, we may make money. And if we buy good bonds in these circumstances, we may make money. Thus, if we buy good bonds in these circumstances, we risk losses.
(3) No stop-and-frisk laws are practices that do not concern the courts. But only some stop-and-frisk laws are practices supported by police officers as a prevention against crime. Thus, some laws that are supported by police officers as a prevention against crime are practices that do concern the courts.

(4) Some particles repay the energy balance in nature; therefore, many things that repay the energy balance in nature are extremely short-lived, since many particles have very short lives.

(5) Since a wrong unprotested festers, radar traps will not fester, since they are not wrongs unprotested.

(6) All civilians except those active in the negotiations are evaluated, thus no civilians active in the negotiations are permitted to leave the country, because only evacuated persons are civilians permitted to leave the country.

(7) As all commonsense notions of time and space are uncritical and they do not fit into quantum-theory experiments, some notions that do not fit into quantum-theory experiments are uncritical.

(8) These are difficult times, since the only easy times were before the development of nuclear explosives and those days have gone forever.

(9) Racial troubles are not good for business, and community Smithville has conditions bad for business; therefore, community Smithville has racial troubles.

(10) All uncommitted nations form a neutral block in the United Nations, since none but the unaligned countries form a neutral block in the United Nations and the uncommitted nations alone do not align themselves with the East or West.

C. Give a complete analysis of the following syllogisms. Write them in logical form. Identify validity. If the syllogism is invalid, state the rule violated.

(1) Mr. Derby is a voter, since he is a citizen and only citizens are voters.

(2) No loans not approved by the credit department are granted; therefore, some loans approved by the credit department are not paid back, since only some loans that are granted are not paid back.

(3) Since some strikes are difficult to resolve, many situations that are difficult to resolve are not situations that work hardships on families of workers, since all strikes work hardships on families of workers.

(4) Any pain is to be avoided if possible and Johnny is a pain. Therefore, Johnny is to be avoided if possible.

(5) Some new issues occur during changing conditions. Therefore, this time is an occasion of new issues since this time is not an occasion of unchanging conditions.

(6) Anyone who does not have time on his side is other than the struggling masses, and the struggling masses cannot afford to ignore the need to improve slums. Therefore, the groups who have time on their side cannot afford to ignore the need to improve the slums.

(7) All except wise men make hasty decisions, therefore all statesmen are wise, since no statesmen make hasty decisions.

(8) Since no person who studies the stock market is a person who does not make errors, some bankers are persons who do not make errors since all bankers study the stock market.

(9) All mastery of the principles of reasoning requires work, since many good things require work and all mastery of the principles of reasoning is a good thing.

(10) The discovery of penicillin was a scientific accident, but scientific accidents

are made possible only where minds are trained. Therefore, the discovery of penicillin was made possible by minds that are trained.

(11) Men who seek money also seek power; therefore, men who seek money cannot ignore politics, since no one who seeks power can ignore politics.

(12) No events helping the offense are uncostly events, since no fumbles are uncostly events and no fumbles are events helping the offense.

(13) Nothing that is without nutritional value helps to develop strong bones. Therefore, all vitamins help to develop strong bones, since anything that does not have nutritional value is certainly something other than a vitamin.

(14) Only where there is order is political freedom able to flourish, but political freedom is not able to flourish in a totalitarian state. Therefore, there is no order in a totalitarian state.

(15) No muckrakers need to know when to stop raking the muck. Therefore, Mr. Charles does not need to know when to stop raking the muck, since he is not a muckraker.

(16) Anyone except players, coaches, and officials is permitted to wager on games. Therefore, players, coaches, and officials are not gamblers, since all gamblers are permitted to wager on games.

(17) No program approving of exposed lots for wrecked cars is worthy of support, since any program unworthy of support is other than a program of national beautification and a program of national beautification disapproves of exposed lots for wrecked cars.

(18) Some anemic persons are unhealthy. Therefore, some persons who do not take exercise are anemic, since none but persons who take exercise are healthy.

(19) Since Professor Donothing is a fossil and all fossils are remains of past life, Professor Donothing is a remains of past life.

(20) Advocates of unrest and discontent are following self-defeating programs, since no one who is not following a self-defeating program sows the seeds of his own undoing and only those who are not sowing the seeds of their own undoing are persons who are not advocates of unrest and discontent.

(21) Some reactions against excesses do not tend to become excesses themselves, since some reactions against excesses evoke excesses and all things that evoke excesses tend to become excesses.

(22) Since some uses of sound judgment are not a source of wealth and all wealth is a source of leisure, some uses of sound judgment are a source of leisure.

(23) Unless there is compromise there is no growth in cooperation, and only where there is growth in cooperation is there strength in interdependence. Therefore, there is strength in interdependence only where there are compromises.

(24) DMSO is not a drug whose use is authorized except under carefully controlled and limited conditions, since DMSO has extensive and unknown side effects and all drugs having extensive and unknown side effects are ones whose use is not authorized except under carefully controlled and limited conditions.

(25) Only some speculators make a profit. All speculators take risks. Therefore, some persons who take risks do not make a profit.

8.3 IMPLICIT STATEMENTS IN AN ARGUMENT

An argument may have a premise or a conclusion implicit in its context without an explicit expression of the statement of the suppressed premise or conclusion. An analysis of the argument requires that one make the suppressed statement explicit. An enthymeme, meaning "in the mind," is an argument with an implicit premise or conclusion. In a categorical syllogism, these suppressed statements can occur in one of four instances:

1.   The major premise can be suppressed.

2.   The minor premise can be suppressed.

3.   The conclusion can be suppressed.

4.   The minor premise and the conclusion can be suppressed.

The major premise is suppressed in the following enthymeme:

You diversify your investments. Therefore, you are a good investor.

The missing major premise can be:

All good investors are persons who diversify their investments.

However, if the implicit premise is expressed in this manner, the argument is invalid since it exemplifies the fallacy of an undistributed middle term. The above argument would be valid by stating the missing premise as "All persons who diversify their investments are good investors." However, there are sound economic reasons to hold that such a statement is false. If the statement were true, then sound investing would be a simple matter.

The minor premise is missing in the following argument:

All investors in low-grade bonds bearing high interest are taking risks.

Therefore, you are taking risks.

The conclusion is missing in the following enthymeme:

All financiers who restrict their investments to AAA bonds are conservative investors.

The Investment Firms of Smith and Jones are financiers who restrict their investments to AAA bonds.

If the minor premise and the conclusion are both missing in an enthymeme, we examine the context in which the major premise occurs. The suppressed minor premise and the conclusion are implicit in the following example. After an investor has lost heavily on speculative equities in a bear market, someone may remark:

> No enlightened investor takes an aggressive approach to purchasing equities in the earlier stages of a bear market.

The missing minor premise and the conclusion are as follows:

> Investor A is a person taking an aggressive approach to purchasing equities in the earlier stages of a bear market.
>
> Therefore, Investor A is not an enlightened investor.

EXERCISES

Write the appropriate premises or conclusion and determine the validity of the following enthymemes:

1. All good lawyers read fine print in contracts. Therefore, John reads fine print in contracts.

2. Background: Mr. Brown makes a foolish assertion in a conference. Later one of the participants remarks to another: "Any person making such a statement is uninformed."

3. All civil wars promote future internal division. Therefore, this war will promote future internal division.

4. All romanticists are idealistic. The "New Left" is idealistic.

5. Many folk-oriented songs are popular. Therefore, this song will be popular.

6. Picasso's works have strong imagery. Therefore, Picasso's works are superior works of art.

7. All persons sleeping have minds that are active. Therefore, persons who have died have minds that are active.

8. Some persons dreaming are persons with increases in blood pressure. Therefore, Mr. Blank is dreaming.

9. No careful driver "tailgates" another car. Therefore, Mr. Jones is not a careful driver.

10. No man with a poor credit rating can secure personal loans readily. Therefore, Mr. Smith can secure personal loans readily.

8.4 SORITES

Sorites are chain arguments which include several categorical syllogisms telescoped or condensed into a single argument. An example of a sorites is the following:

All students are restless persons.

All restless persons are excitable persons.

All excitable persons are activists.

All activists are persons committed to social change.

Hence, all students are persons committed to social change.

When the structure of a sorites has a proper form, it conforms to one of two kinds—the Aristotelian type or the Goclenian type. In a properly arranged Aristotelian sorites, the predicate term of each statement becomes the subject term of the succeeding premise. And the subject term of the original statement is also the subject term of the conclusion. The sorites presented at the beginning of this discussion is Aristotelian in form.

In a properly constructed Goclenian sorites, the subject term of an original statement becomes the predicate term of the second premise. And the succeeding terms introduced in the subject term become the predicate term of the immediately following premise. The predicate term in the conclusion is the predicate term in the first premise. The form for the Aristotelian and for the Goclenian sorites is illustrated as follows:

Aristotelian Form	*Goclenian Form*
All (or some) A is B	All (or no) B is A
All B is C	All C is B
All C is D	All D is C
All (or no) D is E	All (or some) E is D
Thus, ( ) A is E	Thus, ( ) E is A

In an Aristotelian or Goclenian sorites, only one premise can be negative and only one premise can be particular. In valid sorites, a particular premise occurs first in the Aristotelian form and last in the Goclenian form. A negative premise can occur only as the final premise in the Aristotelian form and as the first premise in the Goclenian form. In both forms of sorites, if any premise is particular then the conclusion must be particular. And if any premise is negative, then the conclusion must be negative.

In arranging sorites in proper form, we first identify the conclusion. In constructing an Aristotelian sorites the subject term of the conclusion becomes the subject term of the first premise. In writing a Goclenian sorites, the predicate term of the conclusion becomes the predicate term of the first premise. The term in the first premise that did not occur in the conclusion then becomes a term in the second premise.

Some sorites cannot be arranged in a valid and proper form. We need to restate these arguments by using separate categorical syllogisms. We begin with the first two premises and then make a conclusion. This conclusion then becomes a premise for a second syllogism. And the third premise of the sorites becomes a second premise in the second syllogism. We continue this procedure until the premises occur which do not permit our making a valid conclusion. We identify the fallacy occurring in the syllogism. We give this fallacy as the reason for the invalidity of the sorites. In arranging a sorites in proper form, we may need to use the operations of obversion, conversion, and contraposition.

We may find some incomplete sorites that do not have a stated conclusion. In such cases we need to determine what the conclusion is. We seek to identify the terms that occur only once in the premises. These terms are used to form a conclusion in the form of a categorical statement. A decision needs to be made in determining the subject term of the conclusion. We can test for the subject term of the conclusion as the term which is the subject term of an affirmative premise. However, additional testing may be needed. Consider the following example:

Originally given premises (with no conclusion stated)	Sorites reconstructed in proper Aristotelian form
(1) All D is R	Some L is D (Original #3)
(2) No R is non-N	All D is R (Original #1)
(3) Some L is D	All R is N (Obverse original #2)
(4) All non-S is non-N	All N is S (Contraposition #4)
Hence, ?	Hence, Some L is S.

By way of summary, we decide what structure (Aristotelian or Goclenian) we shall use to construct the sorites. If the premises cannot be placed in the proper order for that type of sorites, then the different statements in the sorites are to be broken down into separate syllogisms. We find and identify the fallacy occurring in one of the syllogisms. If a suppressed conclusion in a sorites occurs, then we use the terms that can occur only once in the premises to construct the conclusion.

EXERCISES

A. Analyze the following sorites. Write each in a proper Aristotelian or Goclenian form. If a sorites is invalid, reduce it to separate syllogisms and state the rule that is violated.

1. Television programs provide escape. All things that have unexpected side effects can be factors in producing social changes. All things providing escape play down human misery. All things that play down human misery have unexpected side effects. Therefore, some television programs can be factors in producing social changes.

2. No person who does not express stimulating ideas is an interesting conversationalist. All literary critics are well-informed on contemporary novels. Anyone well-grounded in the contemporary theater expresses stimulating ideas. Anyone who is not an interesting conversationalist is a person who is not well-informed on contemporary novels. Therefore, all literary critics are persons well-grounded in the contemporary theater.

3. No satisfied person is a disillusioned idealist. Any dissatisfied person is frustrated. No cynics are persons who are not disillusioned idealists. Anyone who is enthusiastic about the future is a person not frustrated. Therefore, no cynics are enthusiastic about the future.

4. Without inquiry facts are not secured. Intelligence requires insight. Good judgment requires facts. No insight occurs without good judgment. Therefore, intelligence requires inquiry.

5. Any programs that are not intellectually boring are programs not designed for mass audiences. Nothing that increases the appreciation for the arts is unworthy of support. No program that is intellectually boring increases appreciation for the arts. All TV serials are designed for mass audiences. Therefore, no TV serials are worth supporting.

6. All multibillion-dollar enterprises are industries that are the wave of the future. No industry that is the wave of the future is a source of poor investment in stocks. The data-processing industry is a multibillion-dollar enterprise. Some stocks that are subject to wide fluctuation in their value over a limited period of time are sources of poor investments in stock. Therefore, some data-processing industries are not subject to wide fluctuations in the value of stocks over a limited period of time.

B. Find the conclusion of the following sorites and determine the validity of the argument. To find the conclusion determine the two terms that occur only once in the premises; these terms will be the subject term and the predicate term of the conclusion. Give a complete analysis of the sorites. State it in proper Aristotelian or Goclenian form. If a sorites is invalid, break it down into syllogisms and state the rule of the syllogism that has been violated.

1. All situations requiring the asking of proper questions require persons skillful in formulating questions. All situations requiring persons with background knowledge also require persons who understand current problems in the area. Superior use of computers involves situations requiring the asking of proper questions. All situations requiring persons skillful in formulating questions also require persons with background knowledge. Therefore, . . .

2. Any problem that cannot be worked immediately is complex. Any problem that is easy to solve is simple. Sorites are chain arguments. Chain arguments are easy to solve. Therefore, . . .

3. Talent banks can ignore individual differences in computer selection. Any selection process that obscures superior leadership abilities cannot ignore

individual differences in computer selection. Any computer is a talent bank. No selection process that obscures superior leadership abilities is without need to be supplemented by other tested means of evaluating competence. Therefore, . . .

4. Elections not requiring information and judgment do not focus on issues. The need for an informed public with ability to analyze issues requires accurate reporting by newspapers and television during an election. Elections requiring both information and judgment are situations needing an informed public with an ability to analyze issues. Elections that do not focus on candidates focus on issues. Therefore, . . .

5. Instruments requiring the application of know-how and skill in devising proper learning situations also may be used in creating games that are exciting. Computers are instruments that can assist the student to learn by discovery. An instrument that is useless under proper programming conditions cannot assist the student to learn by discovery. No useful instrument under proper programming conditions fails to require the application of know-how and skills in devising a proper learning situation. Therefore, . . .

6. No opinion poll is a survey that is not designed to test public reaction to current questions. The use of any sample in a survey is reliable only if it is a random sample that has been properly collected and analyzed. Some surveys designed to test public reactions to current questions use samples that are reliable. All random samples that cannot be used as a reliable guide of current public opinion are random samples that have not been properly collected and analyzed. Therefore, . . .

7. Things that can be useful in the treatment of diseases and in economic development can help to improve health and provide time for the enjoyment of leisure. Things that can help to improve health and provide time for the enjoyment of leisure cannot assure the growth of the mind's creativity or the enjoyment of its fruits. Computers developed to transmit data by the use of satellites can be useful in the treatment of diseases and in promoting economic development. Therefore, . . .

8.5 SINGULAR UNIVERSAL CATEGORICAL STATEMENTS USED AS PREMISES

The convention we have been following permits universal categorical statements to be true and the class expressed by the subject term to be empty. This convention is the basis for the rule of the categorical syllogism requiring one particular premise in cases where the conclusion is particular.

In some contexts we have a singular universal statement that appears to hold clearly that the class of the subject term is not empty. Consider the context in which we would make the following statements: "That material is wool" and "John Smith is a sophomore." We appear to indicate definitely in these statements that the class of the subject terms is not null. That is, we are saying that "that material" and "John Smith" are members of a class with only one member. We are granting that there is at least one member of the class found in the subject term. On the basis of these considerations we can follow an alternative convention to the one noted above. This alternative convention makes allowance for the apparent intent of some singular-type universal statements to include a singular member in the class expressed by the subject term.

But the form of a singular universal statement is not sufficient to justify an interpretation that there are any members in the subject class. Consider a statement such as "This elf is a mischievous character." There does not appear to be any intention to claim that there is at least one member in the class of "this elf." Thus, if we hold that the class found in the subject term of any given universal singular categorical statement has at least one member, we cannot base our acceptance of the existence of such a member solely on the form of the statement itself. We have to justify our acceptance of the existence of such members in the context in which the statement occurs.

To use this convention which permits us to interpret a singular universal statement as having class membership we need to observe these restrictions:

1. The subject term of the minor affirmative premise uses a singular term. Singular terms can be proper names or pronouns like "I," "you," "she." Such singular terms also can be definite descriptions used with the definite article "the," with a personal pronoun, or with demonstrative expressions such as "this," "these," "that," and "those."

2. The subject term of both premises is the middle term of the syllogism; that is, the syllogism has the form of Figure III.

3. The context of the sentence provides a basis for justifying a decision attributing membership in the class expressed by the subject term of the minor premise.

When these restrictions are met, this convention permits the use of Moods **AAI** and **EAO** in Figure III. In using the circles for Boolean analysis in such cases, the minor premise is written and drawn first as an **A** premise and then as an **I** premise. (In the exercises in this book, the use of this convention will be limited to the examples in the exercises immediately following this discussion.)

EXERCISES

Determine the validity of the following syllogisms based upon the convention which permits certain cases of Figure III to be valid in Moods **AAI** and **EAO**.

1. James is a mathematician. James is a reporter. Therefore, some mathematicians are reporters.

2. Pythagoras is a historical figure who believes numbers are the key to the universe. Pythagoras is a wise man. Therefore, some wise men are historical figures who believe numbers are the key to the universe.

3. Some policemen are persons riding a motorscooter. Mr. Smith is a policeman. Therefore, Mr. Smith is a person riding a motorscooter.

4. Rudolph is a reindeer of Santa Claus. Rudolph is a reindeer with a red nose. Therefore, some reindeer with a red nose are reindeer of Santa Claus.

5. That house is a house that is for sale. That house is a house in need of repair. Therefore, some houses in need of repair are houses that are for sale.

8.6 COROLLARIES OF THE RULES TO CATEGORICAL SYLLOGISMS

In addition to the rules for the categorical syllogism already given, a number of corollaries hold. These corollaries apply in some cases to all categorical syllogisms, in other cases to one of the figures in categorical syllogisms. We derive these corollaries from the rules of the categorical syllogism. One way to attempt to prove a corollary is to make an effort to construct a categorical syllogism in violation of the stipulations made by the corollary. We examine the resultant forms of the syllogisms to see what violations of the rules of the syllogism occur. The giving of the conditions and reasons for invalidity constitutes an informal proof showing why these corollaries are correct.

The first corollary given below states, "No categorical syllogism is valid if the major premise is particular and the minor premise is negative." Let us find out what happens if we try to ignore this corollary.

> If the minor premise is negative, then the conclusion must be negative. Otherwise the fallacy of an affirmative conclusion with a negative premise occurs.

> If the conclusion is negative, the predicate term of the conclusion also must be distributed. This holds because the predicate term of any negative categorical statement is distributed. The predicate term of the conclusion also would need to be distributed in the major premise. But the corollary requires the major premise to be particular. And a particular affirmative major premise results in the fallacy of an illicit major.

> If the major premise is particular and negative the fallacy of two negative premises occurs.

Students can work out similar types of proofs for the other corollaries. The use of Aristotelian forms for categorical statements is useful in proving these corollaries. Among the corollaries that follow from the rules of the categorical syllogism are the following (we could give more):

1. No categorical syllogism is valid if the major premise is particular and the minor premise is negative.

2. No categorical syllogism is valid if both premises are affirmative and the conclusion is negative.

3. No categorical syllogism is valid if a conclusion is universal and a premise is particular.

4. No categorical syllogism is valid if both premises are particular.

5. A universal affirmative conclusion is possible only in Figure I.

6. The conclusion of all categorical syllogisms in Figure II is negative.

7. The conclusion of all categorical syllogisms in Figure III is particular.

8. The major premise in Figure IV is always universal if the conclusion is negative.

In this chapter we saw that we can use obversion, conversion, and contraposition to derive equivalent statements for categorical statements. These equivalent statements are useful to helping to put some syllogisms in a valid form. We analyzed ways for translating statements in ordinary discourse into standard categorical statements. We saw how to make explicit the meaning of unstated premises in an argument. We looked at ways to analyze and determine the validity of sorites. We also considered use of a special case of interpreting universal singular statements. And we looked at some corollaries to the rules of categorical syllogisms. In the next chapter we shall begin to look at other kinds of deductive arguments.

CHAPTER **9**

ARGUMENTS USING RELATIONAL TERMS AND MOLECULAR STATEMENTS

9.1 IMMEDIATE AND MEDIATE INFERENCE AND RELATIONAL TERMS

This chapter discusses additional kinds of inferences that are made possible by relations holding between terms, statements, and statement connectives. It distinguishes between immediate inference and mediate inference. The notions of reflexivity, symmetry, and transitivity will be analyzed. The different possible truth values which can hold between statements will be discussed. And the square of opposition will be used to exemplify how these truth values hold between different kinds of categorical statements.

The meaning of statement connectives and their use in arguments will be discussed in an elementary manner. The chapter concludes with an analysis of the valid argument forms of the dilemma, together with the three accepted procedures for attacking the dilemma. We present in a more technical manner the meaning and use of statement connectives in arguments in a subsequent chapter.

The previous chapters on deductive logic present arguments that use both immediate inference and mediate inference. In immediate inference only one premise or a simple statement provides the evidence for the conclusion. An example of immediate inference is the way we form the obverse of a statement. Let us assume the following statement is true: "All elected public officials are persons who are expected to avoid conflict of interest ties." We can form the obverse of this statement directly, without the need for other evidence or other steps in drawing the conclusion. That is, it also is true that "No elected public officials are persons who are not expected to avoid conflict of interest ties." Given as true the statement, "John made the same grade on the test as George," it is also true that "George made the same grade on the test as John." Again we derive the truth of the second statement directly (and immediately) from the evidence given by the original statement. These examples illustrate cases of immediate inference.

In mediate inference one uses more than one premise or simple statement as steps in providing evidence to derive a conclusion. The relation holding between the statements provided as evidence makes possible an inference which we state as the conclusion. Consider the following example:

New York City is larger than Chicago.

Chicago is larger than El Paso.

Therefore, New York City is larger than El Paso.

We derive the conclusion in this example of mediate inference from two statements provided as evidence. Categorical syllogisms also are examples of mediate inference.

The use of the notion of relations that hold between statements or their elements makes possible a significantly broader range of arguments than we can have merely by using the categorical syllogisms. "Included in the class of" and "excluded from the class of" express only a few of many other relations we use in making inferences. Let R mean any relational term and the letters x, y, z, stand for the terms related. The symbols xRy signify that x has the relation R to y. If s stands for Smith and j for Jones and C

for the relation "is a more capable student than," the meaning of the symbols sCj would be "Smith is a more capable student than Jones." (In a more technical treatment we would adopt a different way of symbolizing this relation.)

Mediate and immediate inference depend on the proper interpretation and use of the meanings found in relational expressions. We can advance and evaluate arguments using such expressions as "is equal to," "is greater than," "is a cousin of," "is a member of the class of," "is clearer than," "is less likely to fumble than," and "is more likely to overreact." A relation expressed by the letter R can relate another term x to itself or to a second term y. It also can relate the term y to x or to a third term z. Such a series could proceed indefinitely in cases such as 1 is less than 2, 2 is less than 3, and 3 is less than 4.

In our discussion of relational expressions we are making an assumption of relevance between the relation expressed by the relational term and the individuals or classes which we claim to have the indicated relation. That is, we are using the notion of a field of a relation. The set of objects that can be related by a given relation is the field of that relation.

If we are dealing with the relation "is a brother of" the field of this relation is the set of objects to which the relation is applicable. We do not apply the relation "is the same age as" to numbers. Numbers are not a part of the set of objects to which the relation "is the same age as" applies. Some logicians hold that an expression like "The number 10 is the same age as the number 10" is not meaningful. Others hold that it is trivially false. We are using the notion of a field of a relation in order to simplify the use of relations in arguments.

We shall discuss three different contexts in which relational expressions occur. In these contexts we use the notions of reflexivity, symmetry, and transitivity.

Reflexivity uses only one individual (or class) and one property. In reflexivity we want to know the truth value of a statement having the form xRx. If j stands for Jones and W stands for the relation "is wiser than," we want to identify what we know about the truth value of jWj. That is, we want to be able to know the truth value of the statement "Jones is wiser than Jones."

Three kinds of reflexivity are possible. A relation can be reflexive, irreflexive, or nonreflexive. A relation is reflexive if it must apply to the individual, or class expressed by the related term. If a reflexive relation holds, then any statement having the form xRx is true. If the letter I stands for the relation "is identical with" and the letter c stands for "my only car," then we know that the statement cIc is true. That is, the statement "My only car is identical with my only car," is true.

Other examples of reflexive relations are "is equal to," "is not less than," "is not older than," and "is the same as."

A relation is irreflexive if it cannot hold for an individual or class expressed by the related term. In an irreflexive relation we know that any statement having the form xRx is false. And we know that it is false by understanding the meaning of the relational expression. The relation expressed by "is older than" is irreflexive. We know that the statement "Professor Lewis is older than Professor Lewis" is false. And we know this merely because of what "is older than" means.

A relation is nonreflexive if it may or may not apply to a given individual or class. The relation expressed by the form xRx may hold or it may not hold. Some statements making use of the nonreflexive relations and whose truth or falsity cannot be determined by the meaning of a relational expression are "Jones is hostile toward himself," "Mrs. Smith is pleased with herself," and "Mr. Able is not critical of himself."

The notion of symmetry applies to a stated relation between two individuals or classes. Assume we are given any two individuals or classes represented by the letters x and y and the relation R. And we are told that a statement with the form xRy is true. We need to identify the truth value of a statement with the form yRx on the basis of the meaning of the relation R. Assume we know that the statement, "John is a cousin of Mary," is true. We need to identify the truth or falsity of the statement "Mary is a cousin of John." And we want to determine the truth value of this statement solely by the meaning of the relational expression "is a cousin of."

A relation is symmetrical if the relation of one individual or class to a second requires that the second individual or class has the same relation to the first. If we know that xRy holds, then we also know that yRx must hold. Assume that we know this statement is true: "Ann has the same parents as Tom." We also know this statement is true: "Tom has the same parents as Ann." We know this is true by knowing the meaning expressed by the relation "has the same parents as." Other expressions which indicate a symmetrical relation are "is a spouse of," "is a relative of," and "is unequal to."

A relation is asymmetrical if the relation of one individual or class to a second requires that the second individual or class cannot have the same relation to the first. In this case if we know that xRy holds, then we also know that yRx cannot hold. If lead is heavier than water, then water cannot be heavier than lead. We know this because the relation "is heavier than" is asymmetrical. Other examples of asymmetrical relational expressions are "is older than," "is greater than," and "is a better physics student than."

A relation is nonsymmetrical if the relation of one individual or class to a second does not provide a basis to determine the relation of the second individual or class to the first. Let us assume that we know a statement of the form xRy is true. If a relation is nonsymmetrical, we do not know whether a statement of the form yRx is true. If Susan is an admirer of her coach, her coach may or may not be an admirer of Susan. Other examples of nonsymmetrical relations are "is the nearest neighbor of," and "is not less than."

In notions of transitivity we use mediate inference. Relations of transitivity hold between three or more individuals or classes. We are given as true two statements with the form xRy and yRz. We then need to determine what we know about the truth value of the statement expressed by the form xRz solely on the basis of the meaning of the relation R.

A relation is transitive if it meets these conditions. We know that one individual or class has a stated relation to a second. We also know that the second individual or class has the same relation to a third. If a relation is transitive, then we know that the first individual or class must have that relation to the third individual or class. In a transitive relation if statements with the form xRy and yRz hold, then xRz also must hold. If Mary is a better math student than John, and John is a better math student than George, then Mary is a better math student than George. Other expressions in which a transitive relation holds are "is a descendent of," "is a person more experienced in politics than," and "exercises better judgment in financial matters than."

A relation is intransitive if statements expressed by the form xRy and yRz hold but xRz cannot hold. A given individual or class has a given relation to a second. And the second individual or class has the same relation to a third. We are then able to determine that the first individual or class cannot have that relation to the third. Let us assume that John is the son of Henry and Henry is the son of Mike. We then can determine that John cannot be the son of Mike solely on the basis of the meaning of the expression "is a son of." Other examples of expressions in which intransitive relations hold are "is the closest friend of" and "is greater by one half than."

A relation is nontransitive if the following conditions hold. We know that a statement with the form xRy and yRz are true. But we are unable to determine whether a statement with the form xRz is true or is false solely by knowing the meaning of the relational expression that is used. We are given as true the statement, "Jane is a friend of Janet and Janet is a friend of Kathy." By restricting our source of knowledge to the meaning of the expression, "is a friend of," we are not able to determine whether the following statement is true: "Jane is a friend of Kathy." Other examples of expressions in which nontransitive relations hold are "is a cousin of," "is unequal to," and "is a member of the class of."[1]

---

[1] It sometimes is claimed that the relation expressed by the relational term "is included in the class of" is transitive. This view is not the case in a rigorous sense. In an affirmative categorical statement with a distributed subject term, "is included in the class of" expresses a transitive relation. If the subject term of an affirmative categorical statement is undistributed, "are included in the class of" expresses a nontransitive relation. But it does express a symmetrical relation. With a distributed subject term (that is, with an E categorical statement) "is excluded from the class of" expresses a symmetrical relation. It also expresses a nontransitive relation.

Relational expressions make possible a more extensive range of inferences than does the use of the traditional categorical syllogism. In order to make inferences by use of relational expressions, we may need to specify the context in which the statement is made. The relation expressed as "on the right of" could appear to be asymmetrical. However, if two persons are facing in opposite directions, each of them would be on the right of the other. We can refer to logical errors occurring as a result of the misuse of the indicated types of relations as the fallacy of misusing an x relational expression. (In this case x is a place holder for the name of the indicated relation.) Consider the argument: "Since Smith is a member of the basketball team at Yule College and the basketball team at Yule College is a member of the West Central Conference, Smith is a member of the West Central Conference." The error in reasoning in this instance would be called "the fallacy of misusing a nontransitive relational expression."

Many disputes in ordinary life as well as in technical philosophy result from lack of precision in the meaning of some relational expressions. Some imprecision in these disputes can be attributed to changes of time and circumstances. But such disputes also turn on the meaning the indicated relations have in a given context. Consider the relational expression "the same as" in the following statements and indicate some disputes that can arise:

You are not the same person as you were yesterday.

This is not the same team as it was a month ago although the players, coaches, and plays that were used a month ago continue to be used.

This is not the same stream as I stepped in moments ago.

EXERCISES

A. Identify the type of relation exemplified in each of the following expressions. Include reflexivity, symmetry, and transitivity.
1. Greater than
2. Brother of
3. A cousin of
4. Not less than
5. An enemy of
6. East of
7. A secret admirer of
8. A sibling of
9. A descendent of
10. The same as
11. The disappointed admirer of
12. On the left of

13. A better student in logic than
14. The nearest neighbor of
15. Twice as heavy as

B. Identify the invalid arguments in the following examples and state the reason for their invalidity.

1. If John runs as fast as Tom and Tom runs as fast as George, then John runs as fast as George.

2. If Smith is a political supporter of Jones and Jones is a political supporter of Doe, then Smith is a political supporter of Doe.

3. If Mary has different classes than Margie, and Margie has different classes than Kathie, then Mary has different classes than Kathie.

4. If tomorrow is no colder than today, and today is no colder than yesterday, then tomorrow will be no colder than yesterday.

5. Jim is a rival of Joe. Therefore, Joe is a rival of Jim.

6. Ann is the nearest of kin to Mary. And Mary is the nearest of kin to Sue. Thus, Ann is not the nearest of kin to Sue.

7. Frank is related by marriage to Rob. Rob is related by marriage to Bill. Thus, Frank is not related by marriage to Bill.

8. Joan is no more aggressive than Jane. Jane is no more aggressive than Alice. Thus, Joan is no more aggressive than Alice.

9.2 RELATIONS BETWEEN STATEMENTS BASED ON THEIR TRUTH VALUES

There are seven possible relations of truth values between statements. Six of these permit some form of immediate inference about the truth or falsity of a second statement if we know the truth value of a first statement. These seven relations are the following:

1. Independence

Statements are independent in truth values if the truth or falsity of any one statement does not permit us to determine the truth or falsity of the other statement. Consider the truth-value relation between these two statements:

Washington was the first President of the United States.

President Lincoln was assassinated.

We can know the truth or falsity of one of these statements. But we have no logical basis for making a conclusion regarding the truth or falsity of the second statement.

2. Equivalence

Two statements are equivalent if in any case in which one statement is true, the other also is true, and if in any case one is false, the other also is false. If we know one of these statements is true, we can determine directly that the second is true. If we know one of these statements is false, we can determine directly that the second is false. Consider the statements:

All democracies are forms of government that permit dissent.

All governments that do not permit dissent are nondemocracies.

These statements are equivalent. (The following statements also are equivalent: "No complaints are trivial concerns" and "All complaints are nontrivial concerns.")

3. Contradiction

One statement is the contradiction of another by meeting these two conditions. The truth of either statement requires the falsity of the second. And the falsity of either statement requires the truth of the second. Both statements cannot be true, and both statements cannot be false. One statement must be true, the other false. The statements in each of the following sets are contradictory:

All physicians are surgeons.
Some physicians are not surgeons.

No engineers are scientists.
Some engineers are scientists.

All philosophy students are logic students.
Some philosophy students are not logic students.

4. Contrariety

The relation of contrariety between two statements holds if both statements cannot be true, but both can be false. If one statement is true, one can conclude immediately that the other statement is false. If one statement is known to be false, no inference can be made about the truth or falsity of the second. Each of the following sets of statements is an example of contrariety:

All library books are in open stacks.
No library books are in open stacks.

All premed students are majors in chemistry.
No premed students are majors in chemistry.

All lawyers are students of the Constitution.
No lawyers are students of the Constitution.

In the foregoing examples of contrariety as well as in subsequent examples through the discussion of superalteration, the problem of membership in classes of the subject terms of categorical statements is not taken into account. That is, we shall assume that the class expressed by the subject term in our examples has a member. It is not an empty class.

5. Subcontrariety

Two statements are subcontraries if at least one statement is true and both statements cannot be false. If one subcontrary is false, the other subcontrary must be true. If one subcontrary is true, the truth or falsity of the other is undetermined. Each of the following is a set of subcontrary statements:

Some animals are mammals.
Some animals are not mammals.

Some TV programs are educational.
Some TV programs are not educational.

Some logic assignments are easy.
Some logic assignments are not easy.

6. Subalternation

Two statements are subalternates if the falsity of the first requires also the falsity of the second. However, if the first statement is true, no conclusion can be made about the truth or falsity of the second. In this relationship, the order of the statements cannot be reversed. Consider the examples:

Some milk cows are Longhorns.
All milk cows are Longhorns.

Some presidents are statesmen.
All presidents are statesmen.

If the first statement is false, then the second statement also must be false. If the first statement is true, one cannot derive from it the truth of the second.

7.   Superalternation

Two statements are in a relation of superalternation by meeting these two conditions: the truth of the first requires the truth of the second; and the falsity of the first does not provide a basis to derive the truth or the falsity of the second. The order of the statements is not reversible. The first statement in each of the following sets is a superalternate of the second statement:

> All athletes are strong persons.
> Some athletes are strong persons.
>
> All deep-sea diving is dangerous.
> Some deep-sea diving is dangerous.

Superalternation is particularly vulnerable to the issue of class membership in the class expressed by the subject term in examples using categorical statements.

9.3 TRUTH RELATIONS OF CATEGORICAL STATEMENTS AND THE SQUARE OF OPPOSITION

1.   The Traditional Square of Opposition

One can show the relation of contradiction, contrariety, subcontrariety, subalternation, and superalternation on the traditional square of opposition. In this case we assume membership in the classes of the subject term of categorical statements (Figure 9.1).

All adults are students.   No adults are students.

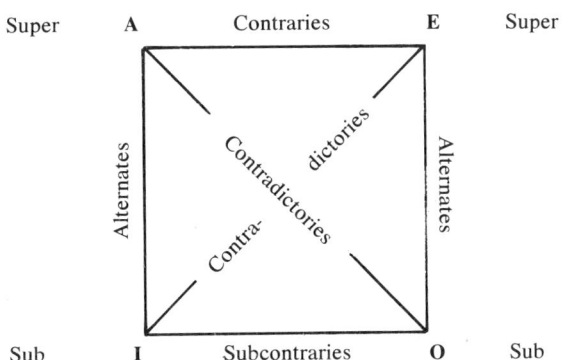

Figure 9.1   The traditional square of opposition

2.   Contradictories: **A** and **O**; **E** and **I**

If the **A** form, "All adults are students," is true, then the **O** form is false.

If the **A** form is false, then the **O** form is true.

If the **O** form is true, the **A** form is false.

If the **O** form is false, then the **A** form is true.

The **E** form of the statement, "No adults are students," and the **I** form, "Some adults are students," also have opposite truth values in every case.

3.   Contraries

If the **A** form, "All adults are students," is true, the **E** form, "No adults are students," is false.

If the **A** form is false, the **E** form is undetermined.

If the **E** form is true, the **A** form is false.

If the **E** form is false, the **A** form is undetermined.

4.   Subcontraries

If the **I** form, "Some adults are students," is true, the **O** form is undetermined.

If the **I** form is false, the **O** form is true.

If the **O** form is true, the **I** form is undetermined.

If the **O** form is false, the **I** form is true.

5.   Subalternates

If the **I** form, "Some adults are students," is true, the **A** form, "All men are students," is undetermined.

If the **I** form is false, the **A** form is false.

If the **O** form is true, the **E** form is undetermined.

If the **O** form is false, the **E** form is false.

6.   Superalternates

If the **A** form, "All adults are students," is true, the **I** form is true.

If the **A** form is false, the **I** form is undetermined.

If the **E** form is true, the **O** form is true.

If the **E** form is false, the **O** form is undetermined.

7. The Principle of Existential Import and the Square of Opposition

Let us take up an issue which keeps bobbing up. This is the question of what to do with classes that can be empty or null.

We follow the convention in the rules of the categorical syllogism that the form of true universal categorical statements does not require any members in the class expressed by the subject term. But true particular categorical statements do require members in the class expressed by the subject term. That is, such a class cannot be empty.

Existential import is the property of a statement in which there exists at least one member in the class expressed by the subject term. The convention we are using holds that the form of true particular categorical statements requires that their subject terms have members. But the form of true universal categorical statements does not require that their subject terms have members. That is, true particular categorical statements must have existential import. But true universal categorical statements need not have existential import.

When we apply the principle of existential import to the traditional square of opposition, the square flattens out. We continue to use the notions of contrariety, subcontrariety, superalternation, and subalternation. But the traditional square of opposition no longer serves as a basic model for illustrating these relations. Only the contradictory relations between the **A** and **O** statements and between the **E** and **I** statements continue to hold. Let us explore further what happens when we use the principle of existential import on the traditional square of opposition.

If one uses the principle of existential import, the **A** and the **E** forms on the square of opposition both can be true and the relation of contrariety does not hold between them. For example, if there does not exist any form of life on the planet Mercury, then both of the following statements could be true: "All forms of life on the planet Mercury are primitive" and "No form of life on the planet Mercury is primitive." This is more obvious if we interpret the statements in an equivalent form by use of a conditional statement: "If forms of life are found on the planet Mercury, they are primitive" and "If forms of life are found on the planet Mercury, they are not primitive."

We base the above interpretation, as well as those which follow in this section, on a convention. This is the convention that requires us to interpret an **A** statement, "All F is G," in the form, "If anything is F, then it also is G." We interpret the **E** statement as "If anything is F, then it is not G." Statements using these forms are false only if the part introduced by "if" is true and the part introduced by "then" is false.

This convention also requires us to interpret an **I** statement, "Some F

is G," as "There is something that is F and that something is G." We interpret an **O** statement, "Some F is not G" as "There is something that is F and that something is not G." Statements using these forms are true only if each separate part which is joined by "and" also is true.

Likewise, in using the principle of existential import, statements having the **I** and the **O** forms as expressed on the square of opposition can both be false. Consider the examples, "Some forms of life on the planet Mercury are primitive" and "Some forms of life on the planet Mercury are not primitive." Again, we may make the relevant truth values more obvious by writing these statements in the form of conjunctive sentences: "There is a form of life on the planet Mercury and that form of life is primitive." "There is a form of life on the planet Mercury and that form of life is not primitive." Each of these statements is false if the first conjunct, "There is a form of life on the planet Mercury," is false.

The relations of subalternation and superalternation do not hold on the square of opposition when the principle of existential import is applied. A statement with an **I** form may be false and the corresponding statement with an **A** form may be true. The **O** statement may be false and the **E** statement true. If, for example, the **I** statement, "Some goblins are grotesque," is false, the **A** statement, "All goblins are grotesque," can be true. Likewise, the **O** form, "Some goblins are not grotesque," can be false, and the **E** form, "No goblins are grotesque," can be true. The possible truth values of these statements are more obvious if they are rendered in comparable statements. If the statement "There is something that is a goblin and that something is grotesque" is false, the statement "If anything is a goblin, it is grotesque" can be true.

In this section we have examined the truth relations between categorical statements and the traditional square of opposition. We also have seen that these relations change when we apply existential import to categorical statements. In the next section we shall begin a study of other types of arguments that can use the truth relations between statements as a basis for justifying arguments using compound statements.

EXERCISES

A. If the first statement is true in each of the following sets of statements, state the truth values of the other statements in the set. Assume the truth values between categorical statements hold on the traditional square of opposition. (In working out the last three problems it will be helpful to use Aristotelian symbols for categorical statements in constructing as many equivalent statements of the original statement as you can. These equivalent forms are useful in helping to determine the relation of the original statement to each of the other statements.)
1. Some labor leaders are political activists.
    (a) Some labor leaders are not political activists.

(b) No labor leaders are political activists.
(c) All labor leaders are political activists.
2. All plays are entertaining.
   (a) Some plays are entertaining.
   (b) Some plays are not entertaining.
   (c) No plays are entertaining.
3. No logic problems are difficult.
   (a) Some logic problems are difficult.
   (b) All logic problems are difficult.
   (c) Some logic problems are not difficult.
4. The fifth symphony is Beethoven's best work.
   (a) The sixth symphony is Beethoven's best work.
   (b) The fourth symphony is not Beethoven's best work.
5. All bankers are capitalists.
   (a) Some bankers are not noncapitalists.
   (b) No bankers are capitalists.
   (c) All capitalists are nonbankers.
   (d) Some noncapitalists are not nonbankers.
   (e) All noncapitalists are nonbankers.   true contraposition of original
   (f) Some capitalists are bankers.
   (g) Some bankers are not capitalists.
   (h) All capitalists are bankers.
   (i) No noncapitalists are bankers.
6. No crows are green.
   (a) Some green things are crows.
   (b) All crows are nongreen.
   (c) Some green things are not crows.
   (d) No green things are crows.
   (e) All crows are red.
   (f) All green things are noncrows.
   (g) All noncrows are green things.
   (h) Some nongreen things are crows.
   (i) Some noncrows are green.
7. No carriages are blue.
   (a) Some carriages are blue.
   (b) No noncarriage is nonblue.
   (c) Some noncarriages are not nonblue.
   (d) No blue objects are carriages.
   (e) Some blue objects are not carriages.
   (f) All blue objects are carriages.
   (g) Some carriages are pink.
   (h) All carriages are nonblue.
   (i) Some blue objects are not noncarriages.
   (j) All blue objects are noncarriages.

B. If the original statement is true, determine the truth value of the succeeding statement in the following examples. But in this exercise apply the principle of existential import.

1. All perfect students are well-rounded.
   (a) Some perfect students are not well-rounded.
   (b) No perfect students are well-rounded.
   (c) Some perfect students are well-rounded.
2. All poltergeists are noisy.
   (a) No poltergeists are noisy.
   (b) Some poltergeists are not noisy.
   (c) Some poltergeists are noisy.
   (d) Some nonnoisy things are not nonpoltergeists.
   (e) All poltergeists are nonnoisy.
   (f) All nonnoisy things are nonpoltergeists.
   (g) Some nonnoisy things are poltergeists.
   (h) No nonnoisy things are poltergeists.
   (i) Some poltergeists are nonnoisy.
   (j) All nonpoltergeists are nonnoisy.
3. Some babies are hungry.
   (a) All hungry creatures are nonbabies.
   (b) Some babies are not nonhungry.
   (c) No babies are hungry.
   (d) No nonhungry creatures are babies.
   (e) Some babies are not hungry.
   (f) Some hungry creatures are babies.
   (g) Some nonhungry creatures are not nonbabies.
   (h) All nonhungry creatures are nonbabies.
   (i) Some hungry creatures are nonbabies.
   (j) All babies are hungry.

Stop here for test

9.4 THE USE OF COMPOUND STATEMENTS IN BASIC ARGUMENTS

In this section we shall develop some basic argument forms that use compound statements. Valid forms of these arguments will be explained, by reference to notions like contrariety, subcontrariety, superalternation, and subalternation.

A compound statement has two or more simple statements as elements. Let us assume we have the following two simple statements: "The test is easy." "The test is short." We can make a compound statement by saying "The test is easy and the test is short." Other examples of compound statements are "If the test is fair, Betty makes a good grade." "Either John overslept or he is delayed." We also can refer to compound statements as molecular statements.

We need to help our analysis get off the ground by agreeing on the use of some symbols. We shall let the small letters p, q, r, and s serve as place holders for any statement. Such place holders are stand-ins for any statement we make. We shall use such place holders to analyze the form of an argument.

We shall use capital letters like A, C, M, and T as abbreviations for a statement that has a specific content. These capital letters have only a single unit of meaning in a given context. Let us consider the sentence "If April is rainy, then May has many flowers." This statement can be abbreviated, "If A, then M." We can show the statement form of the above statement or of any statement having that form as "If p, then q."

In this section we shall use four symbols to connect component statements of compound statements. The horseshoe, "⊃," signifies the notion of "if . . . then _____." The wedge, "V," signifies the notion of "either . . . or _____." The dot, "·," signifies the notion of ". . . and _____." We also shall use the symbol for the tilde, "~," to deny a statement which can be either simple or compound.

We are on safer grounds if we limit the use of these connectives to statements in the indicative mood. We are not claiming that all uses of expressions such as "if," "then," "or," have the meaning which we are assigning them in this section. We are assigning them a minimal meaning to deal with the logical relations they express and the operations they perform in some arguments.

Let us examine in greater detail the way we use the tilde, "~." One of its uses is to deny a simple statement. We can deny the statement "A" by writing "$\sim A$." We can write the compound statement "A and not B" as "$A \cdot \sim B$." We can deny a compound statement by placing parentheses (or brackets) around the complete statement and then placing the tilde, "~," in front of the parentheses (or brackets). The compound statement, "It is not the case both that A and that B," can be written as $\sim(A \cdot B)$. For convenience we sometimes read "$\sim A$" as "not A." But the more exact rendering is "It is not the case that A." When we use the tilde, "~," another statement is present and the resultant statement is compound.

A conjunctive statement joins two statements with the connective "and." The statements joined by the "and" in such sentences are conjuncts. We can write the conjunctive statement "Jan is short and Mary is tall" as "$J \cdot M$." Two true statements can be joined by "and." The resultant statement is a true conjunctive statement. Thus if we have the separate true statements "J" and "M" we can get the true conjunctive statement "$J \cdot M$." We can separate the conjuncts of a true conjunctive statement. These resultant statements are true. Thus, if "$J \cdot M$" is true, "J" is true. And "M" also is true.

1. Simple Conditional Arguments

Basic Arguments Having One Conditional Statement as a Premise. Conditional statements use the connective "if . . . , then _____." The sentence that completes the "if . . ." is the antecedent. The sentence that completes the "then _____." is the consequent.

In a conditional statement that is true, the antecedent has the contextual truth relation of a superalternate to the consequent. That is, if the antecedent is true, then the consequent is true. But if the antecedent is false, the truth value of the consequent is undetermined. One way of constructing a valid argument with a conditional statement as a premise is for the statement used as a second premise to affirm the antecedent. And the statement appearing as a conclusion affirms the consequent. The traditional name given to this argument form is *modus ponens* (manner of affirming).

An example of an argument with this argument form is the following:

If the tank is empty, the engine fails to start.

The tank is empty.

Thus, the engine fails to start.

We can indicate the form of the above argument in either of two ways:

If p, then q $p \supset q$

p p

Thus, q $\therefore q$

With a conditional statement that is true, the consequent has a contextual truth relation of a subalternate to the antecedent. That is, if the consequent is false, then the antecedent is false. But if the consequent is true, the truth value of the antecedent remains unknown. We can construct a valid argument using one conditional statement as a premise. A second premise then denies the consequent. And the statement used as a conclusion denies the antecedent. The traditional name for this kind of argument is *modus tollens* (manner of denying). An argument using this form is the following:

If the dog barks, the burglar flees.

The burglar does not flee.

Thus, the dog does not bark.

Either of the following schemes exemplify the form of this kind of argument:

If p, then q $p \supset q$

Not q $\sim q$

Thus, not p $\therefore \sim p$

There are two fallacies that occur with some frequency in the use of a single conditional statement as a premise. In one of these fallacies a second premise denies the antecedent. And the statement used as a conclusion denies the consequent. This error is the fallacy of denying the antecedent. In the second fallacy a second premise affirms the consequent. The statement used for the conclusion affirms the antecedent. This error is the fallacy of affirming the consequent. Consider the following examples of these two fallacies:

> If the dog barks, the burglar flees.
>
> The dog does not bark. (Denying the antecedent)
>
> Thus, the burglar does not flee. (Invalid)

> If the tank is empty, the engine fails to start.
>
> The engine fails to start. (Affirming the consequent)
>
> Thus, the tank is empty. (Invalid)

2. Disjunctive Arguments

A disjunctive statement uses the connective "either . . . or _____." The sentences introduced by "either" and by "or" are disjuncts. In a true disjunctive statement the disjuncts have a contextual relation of subcontraries to each other. That is, if one disjunct is false, then the other disjunct is true. But if one disjunct is true, we do not know the truth value of the other disjunct.

The following disjunctive argument is valid:

> Either there are new initiatives or there is a lack of progress.
>
> There are not new initiatives.
>
> Thus, there is a lack of progress.

Valid disjunctive arguments use one of the following two argument forms.

Either p or q	Either p or q
Not p	Not q
Thus, q	Thus, p

Either of the following two argument forms are invalid:

Either p or q	Either p or q
p	q
Thus, not q (Invalid)	Thus, not p (Invalid)

The above interpretation uses the weaker meaning of "either . . . or
_____." There are contexts when "either . . . or _____" has an added
meaning. In such contexts its complete meaning is "either . . . or _____
and either not . . . or not _____." In the latter case there is the use of the
stronger sense of this connective. In that instance the disjuncts are contextually contradictory. In this work we shall limit our interpretation of instances using "either . . . or _____" to its weaker sense where the disjuncts are presented as subcontraries.

3.   Denial-of-Conjunction Arguments

A denial-of-conjunction statement has the form "It is not the case both
that . . . and that _____." A simpler but less precise way of expressing
this form is "Not both . . . and _____." An example of a denial-of-conjunction statement is "It is not the case both that you keep your cake and
that you eat your cake."

The two component statements in a denial-of-conjunction sentence are
contraries in their truth relation to each other. That is, if the denial-of-
conjunction statement is true, then at least one of its simpler statements is
false. But each of these simpler statements also can be false. A denial-of-
conjunction statement simply asserts that each of its component statements
cannot be true in the same context. The two component statements that
comprise a denial-of-conjunction statement are conjunctive contraries.

In a valid denial-of-conjunction argument, one premise is a denial-of-
conjunction statement. A second premise affirms a conjunctive contrary.
And the conclusion denies the other conjunctive contrary. The following
argument is valid:

It is not the case both that Beta completes his reading assignments this afternoon and that he plays golf all afternoon.

Beta completes his reading assignment this afternoon.

Thus, he does not play golf all afternoon.

The above argument has the following form:

It is not the case both that p and that q $\sim(p \cdot q)$

p p

Thus, not q $\therefore \sim q$

Assume that the first premise in the above argument is true. We have
the fallacy of denying a conjunctive contrary with either of the following
continuations of the above argument: "Beta does not complete his reading

assignment this afternoon. Thus, he plays golf all afternoon.'' (Invalid)
''Beta does not play golf all afternoon. Thus, he completes his reading
assignment.'' (Invalid)

The following arguments forms are invalid.

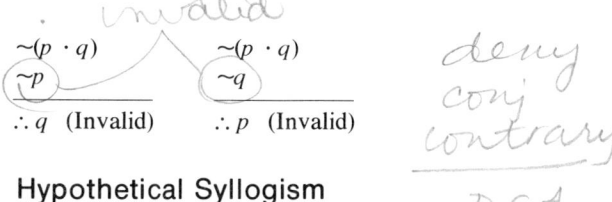

~(p · q)   ~(p · q)
~p   ~q
∴ q (Invalid)   ∴ p (Invalid)

deny
conj
contrary

D C A

4. Hypothetical Syllogism

In a valid hypothetical syllogism there is the use of two conditional
statements as premises and of a third conditional statement as a conclusion.
The two premises have a component statement in common. This component
statement is the consequent in the first premise and the antecedent in the
second premise. The conclusion has the antecedent in the first premise as
its antecedent. It has the consequent in the second premise as its consequent.

An example of a valid hypothetical syllogism is as follows:

If Smith makes the free throw, we win the game.

If we win the game, we win the conference title.

Thus, if Smith makes the free throw, we win the conference title.

The following schemes present the form of a valid hypothetical syllogism.

If p, then q	$p \supset q$
If q, then r	$q \supset r$
Thus, if p, then r	$\therefore p \supset r$

We can get a valid derived hypothetical syllogism with a conclusion
that interchanges and denies the component statements of a conclusion of
a valid hypothetical syllogism. For example, in the previous syllogism one
can use the original premises and validly derive the conclusion:

Thus, if we do not win the conference title, then Smith does not make the free
throw.

Either of the following schemes is a valid form for a derived hypothetical syllogism.

If p, then q	$p \supset q$
If q, then r	$q \supset r$
Thus, if not r, then not p	$\therefore \sim r \supset \sim p$

Any one of the following forms is an invalid hypothetical syllogism. (There are others.)

$p \supset q$
$r \supset q$
$\therefore p \supset r$ (Invalid)

$p \supset q$
$p \supset r$
$\therefore q \supset r$ (Invalid)

$p \supset q$
$q \supset r$
$\therefore r \supset p$ (Invalid)

$p \supset q$
$q \supset r$
$\therefore \sim p \supset \sim r$ (Invalid)

We can translate the premises and the conclusion of a hypothetical syllogism into the form of categorical statements. A valid hypothetical syllogism translates as a valid categorical syllogism, and an invalid hypothetical syllogism translates as an invalid categorical syllogism.

In the next chapter, we shall use truth tables to develop the meaning of compound statements and their use in arguments. But first we need to analyze the forms of the dilemma, which will be done in the next section.

5. Summary: Valid Argument Forms Using Compound Statements

1. Conditional arguments

	Modus Ponens	Modus Tollens				
Valid	$p \supset q$ p $\therefore q$	$p \supset q$ $\sim q$ $\therefore \sim p$	Invalid	$p \supset q$ q $\therefore p$	$p \supset q$ $\sim p$ $\therefore \sim q$

2. Disjunctive arguments

Valid	$p \lor q$ $\sim p$ $\therefore q$	$p \lor q$ $\sim q$ $\therefore p$	Invalid	$p \lor q$ p $\therefore \sim q$	$p \lor q$ q $\therefore \sim p$

3. Denial-of-conjunction arguments

Valid	$\sim(p \cdot q)$ p $\therefore \sim q$	$\sim(p \cdot q)$ q $\therefore \sim p$	Invalid	$\sim(p \cdot q)$ $\sim p$ $\therefore q$	$\sim(p \cdot q)$ $\sim q$ $\therefore p$

4. Hypothetical syllogism

	Tradi-tional	Derived			
Valid	$p \supset q$ $q \supset r$ $\therefore p \supset r$	$p \supset q$ $q \supset r$ $\therefore \sim r \supset \sim p$	Invalid	$p \supset q$ $q \supset r$ $\therefore r \supset p$	$p \supset q$ $p \supset r$ $\therefore r \supset V$
			Invalid	$p \supset q$ $q \supset r$ $\therefore \sim p \supset \sim r$	$p \supset q$ $r \supset q$ $\therefore p \supset r$

5. Conjunctive arguments

Valid	$p \cdot q$ $\therefore p$	$p \cdot q$ $\therefore q$	p, q $\therefore p \cdot q$

EXERCISES

always assume commutation

Determine the validity of each of the following arguments. Identify the fallacy in any argument that is invalid.

1. Either we develop faster supersonic jets or we lose out in competition. We lose out in competition. Therefore, we do not develop faster supersonic jets.

2. If the gas is nitrogen, it is colorless and tasteless. The gas is colorless and tasteless. Therefore, it is nitrogen.

3. If the corruption is not corrected, the government will fall. The government will not fall. Therefore, the corruption is corrected.

4. Either conflict is inevitable or peaceful solutions can be found. Conflict is not inevitable. Therefore, peaceful solutions can be found.

5. Not both can the government increase taxes and the cost of living be reduced. The cost of living is not reduced. Therefore, the government increases taxes.

6. The module landed safely on Mars. The mission was a success. Therefore, the module landed safely on Mars and the mission was a success.

7. If the weather prediction is reliable, then a storm develops. If a storm develops, then we need to protect new plants. Thus, if we do not need to protect new plants, then the weather prediction is not reliable.

8. Not both can the blooms develop and the plants not be sprayed against red spider mites. The blooms do not develop. Therefore, they are not sprayed against red spider mites.

9. If the exploiters do not refrain from cutting the trees to make syrup from the sap, the forest will be destroyed. The exploiters do refrain from cutting the trees to make syrup from the sap. Therefore, the forest will not be destroyed.

10. Either the student is a poor reader or he is distracted easily. The student is a poor reader. Therefore, he is not distracted easily.

11. If the fares are reduced, then the market will develop. If the market develops, then more persons have employment. Thus, if the fares are reduced, more persons have employment.

12. Not both can this be a crayfish and not be a crustacean. This is not a crustacean. Therefore, it is not a crayfish.

13. It is not the case both that the conference is successful and that the tensions increase. Tensions increase. Therefore, the conference is not successful.

14. If rapid changes occur, social stability is threatened. Social stability is threatened. Therefore, rapid changes occur.

15. Either the Incas had no written language, or they left records of a written language. They left no records of a written language. Therefore, they had no written language.

16. If the market drops, Smith will borrow more money. The market does not drop. Therefore, Smith does not borrow more money.

17. If you understand the use of compound statement connectives, you can work these problems. If you can work these problems, then you can have tonight free. Thus, if you have tonight free, then you understand the use of compound statement connectives.

18. Not both can the board be abolished and the complaints be considered fairly. The complaints are considered fairly. Therefore, the board is not abolished.

19. Either there is educational innovation or there is educational stagnation. There is educational innovation. Therefore, there is not educational stagnation.

20. If the actress is cast properly, then she will be a success. If she is cast properly, then she will become popular. Therefore, if she is a success, then she will become popular.

21. If conservation is not practiced, the fields will turn into deserts. The fields will not turn into deserts. Therefore, conservation is practiced.

22. Either the destruction of their native habitat by drainage and development will cease or alligators will not survive. Alligators will survive. Therefore, the destruction of their native habitat will cease.

9.5 THE DILEMMA

1. Valid Forms for Dilemmas

A dilemma makes an argument which presents alternate choices or courses of action. A given consequent is stated to follow on the basis of the choice that is made. Frequently the consequences expected from the alternatives are undesirable. But there also can be other cases in which the alternatives presented are favorable. Consider the following arguments set forth in the form of a dilemma:

> (1) If the Fed follows policies to reduce inflation, then it establishes policies that increase the rate of unemployment and if the Fed establishes policies designed to establish full employment, then it establishes inflationary policies.
> Either the Fed follows policies that reduce the rate of inflation or it establishes policies designed to assure full employment.
> Therefore, the Fed establishes policies that increase the rate of unemployment or it establishes inflationary policies.

> (2) If real estate continues to appreciate, then your purchase of this house will provide you with a good investment and if real estate fails to increase in value, then your purchase of this house will assure you of the security of owning your own home.
> Either real estate continues to appreciate in value or real estate fails to increase in value.
> Therefore, either your purchase of this house will provide you with a good investment or your purchase of this house will assure you of the security of owning your own home.

The dilemma makes use of conditional, disjunctive, conjunctive, and (in some cases) simple statements. The major premise sets forth two conditional statements. These premises are connected to make a longer conjunctive statement. The minor premise also takes the form of a disjunctive statement. It designates a set of alternative choices given in the major premise. The conclusion states the other alternatives which follow from the alternatives chosen in the minor premise.

We classify traditional dilemmas as simple or complex depending on whether the major premise uses three or four simple statements. We also classify them as constructive or as destructive. In a constructive dilemma the minor premise affirms the antecedents of the conditional statements set forth in the major premise. In a destructive dilemma the minor premise denies the consequents set forth in the conditional statements in the major premise. These four variants of the dilemma are exemplified in Table 9.1. If a dilemma is valid, then either it is in one of the forms in this table or it can be restated in one of the above forms. For example, if the minor premise in a complex constructive dilemma had the form "either r or p" then this

Table 9.1.   Table of Forms for Valid Dilemmas

	Constructive	Destructive
Simple	If p, then q, and if r, then q. Either p or r. Therefore, q.	If p, then q, and if p, then r. Either not q or not r. Therefore, not p.
	(Constructive)	(Destructive)
Complex	If p, then q, and if r, then s. Either p or r. Therefore, either q or s.	If p, then q, and if r, then s. Either not q or not s. Thus, either not p or not r.

form could be reexpressed in the equivalent form "either p or r." And the dilemma would be in the proper form. The dilemma would be invalid if the minor premise in a complex form is expressed as "either not p or not r" or as "either q or s." The fallacy of denying the antecedents in a complex dilemma would occur in the first instance. And the fallacy of affirming the consequents in a complex dilemma occurs in the second instance.

2.   Rebuttals of Dilemmas

Rebuttals of a dilemma take three forms: (1) attacking it by going through the horns, (2) attacking it by taking it by the horns, (3) attacking it by proposing a counterdilemma.

(1) Attack by Going Through the Horns.   The attack on a dilemma by going through the horns consists in adding another disjunct to the minor premise. In such a case the argument is no longer valid. However, in practical use another disjunct may be added to the conclusion to show that another alternative is possible as a consequence of the statement added to the minor premise. The form of the minor premise in attacking a complex constructive dilemma by going through the horns is "Either p or r or t." In the first example given previously the minor premise could state:

> Either the Fed follows policies that reduce the rate of inflation or it establishes policies designed to assure full employment or it follows a monetary policy that keeps the rate of inflation at a minimal level consistent with the support of a low unemployment level.

If the disjuncts in the minor premise express exclusive alternatives, it is difficult to provide a satisfactory argument by going through the horns. In some cases a division can be made in one of the disjuncts to form a third alternative.

We can divide a disjunctive minor premise such as "Either we study or we do not," by stating "Either we study for an extended period of time or we study for a limited period of time or we do not study."

(2) Attack by Taking the Dilemma by the Horns.   In attacking a dilemma by the horns, we call into question the truth of one of the conditional statements in the major premise. We deny a conditional statement by bracketing the statement and placing a "not" in front of the brackets. The denial of "If p, then q" is "not [if p, then q]" which can be stated more simply as "p and not q." Let us determine the denial of the statement "If the Fed establishes policies designed to establish full employment, then it establishes inflationary policies." The denial is "The Fed establishes policies designed to establish full employment and it does not establish inflationary policies." The denial of one of the conditional statements in a major premise of a dilemma makes the form of the argument invalid. In most cases we attack only one of the horns of the dilemma.

(3) Attack by Proposing a Counterdilemma.   In the proposal of a counterdilemma, we alter the major premise and we interchange and deny the consequents of the conditional statements. The minor premise remains the same. But we interchange and deny the disjuncts in the conclusion.

Original form:	Counterdilemma:
$(p \supset q) \cdot (r \supset s)$	$(p \supset \sim s) \cdot (r \supset \sim q)$
$p \lor r$	$p \lor r$
$\therefore\ q \lor s$	$\therefore\ \sim s \lor \sim q$

The classical illustration of the counterdilemma concerns a teacher who desired that the court order his former student to pay him for logic lessons. The student originally had agreed to pay the teacher for the lessons after winning his first case in court. But he had not taken any cases to court and did not plan to do so. The teacher, who had the "burden of proof," proposed the following argument:

> If the court decides in favor of the teacher, the student must pay for the lessons because of the decision of the court, and if the court decides in favor of the student, the student must pay for the lessons because of his original agreement.

> Either the court decides in favor of the teacher or it decides in favor of the student.

> Therefore, either the student must pay for the lessons because of the decision of the court, or he must pay because of his original agreement.

The student proposed as a rebuttal a counterdilemma:

> If the court decides in favor of the teacher, the student does not have to pay for his lessons because of the original agreement, and if the court decides in favor of the student, the student does not have to pay because of the decision of the court.

> Either the court decides in favor of the teacher or it decides in favor of the student.

> Therefore, either the student does not have to pay for his lessons because of the original agreement or he does not have to pay because of the decision of the court.

A counterdilemma has definite limitations as a sound procedure in rebutting an original dilemma. It is a rebuttal in a strict sense only if the conclusion of the counterdilemma denies the conclusion of the original dilemma. However, such a denial rarely occurs. When it does happen, there is reason to question the consistency of the original premises stated in conditional form. The conclusion of the counterdilemma in such cases helps to focus on this original inconsistency.

A counterdilemma does present another side to the proposed predicament. In this situation it is not technically a rebuttal but it emphasizes the other (usually more favorable) viewpoint. Consider the following pessimistic conclusion:

> If we permit freedom of ideas, we are threatened with an attack on our security; and if we restrain the free expression of ideas, we are confronted with an attack upon our basic rights.

> Either we permit freedom of ideas or we restrain their free expression.

> Therefore, either we are threatened with an attack on our security or we are confronted with an attack on our basic rights.

The use of the form of the counterdilemma makes possible a more optimistic conclusion:

> If we permit freedom of ideas, we are not confronted with an attack on our basic rights; and if we restrain the free expression of ideas, we are not threatened with an attack on our security.

> Either we permit freedom of ideas or we restrain their free expression.

> Therefore, either we are not confronted with an attack upon our basic rights or we are not threatened with an attack on our security.

The more optimistic conclusion of the counterdilemma does not rebut in a theoretical sense the conclusion of the original dilemma. Both conclusions hold without any inconsistency. However, in popular speech the counter-dilemma might subjectively persuade the listener toward putting aside the original dilemma. We can rebut the original dilemma by taking the first conjunct of the major premise by the horns. This rebuttal would take the form:

> We permit freedom of ideas and we are not threatened with an attack on our security.

We also could rebut the original dilemma by making a division in the minor premise and going through the horns.

Some dilemmas do not have an effective rebuttal. This is most likely to occur in the following situation: (1) the alternatives presented in the premise with the disjunctive form of "either . . . or" are exhaustive; (2) the premises expressed in conditional form represent genuine entailments so that the consequents are the case given the truth of the antecedent; and (3) no counterdilemma is proper.

This chapter developed additional types of arguments based on the use of relations expressed by relational terms. It looked at some forms of immediate inference. The truth relations holding between statements were examined and these relations were illustrated on the traditional square of opposition. In this chapter we also analyzed the use of arguments using compound statements. The chapter concluded with an analysis of the dilemma. In the next chapter we shall develop a more rigorous procedure to analyze arguments, using compound statements.

3. Summary: Forms of Rebuttal of a Dilemma (With a Constructive Complex Dilemma as a Model)

Original Dilemma:

(1) $(p \supset q) \cdot (r \supset s)$
(2) $p \vee r$
_____
(3) $\therefore q \vee s$

1. Attack by going through the horns:

(2) $p \vee r \vee t$ *add alternative to minor premise*
_____
(3) $\therefore q \vee s \, (\vee \, w)$

2. Attack by taking it by the horns:

(1) $(p \cdot \sim q) \cdot (r \supset s)$ or
(1) $(p \supset q) \cdot (r \cdot \sim s)$ or
(1) $(p \cdot \sim q) \cdot (r \cdot \sim s)$

3. Attack by counterdilemma:

$$(1) \ (p \supset \ \sim s) \cdot (r \supset \ \sim q)$$
$$p \vee r$$
$$\overline{}$$
$$\therefore \sim s \vee \sim q$$

EXERCISES

Analyze the following dilemmas for validity. Use symbols to show the different types of possible rebuttals and state in words the key premise in a rebuttal that might be used in each of the valid dilemmas.

1. If sufficient time is given to preparation of the defense, then preparation of the offense is neglected, and if adequate preparation for the offense is made, the defense is neglected. Either sufficient time is given to the preparation of the defense, or adequate preparation for the offense is made. Therefore, either the preparation for the offense is neglected, or preparation for the defense is neglected.

2. If taxes rise, then the cost of living rises, and if inflation continues, the cost of living rises. Either taxes rise or inflation continues. Therefore, the cost of living rises.

3. If the bonds are approved, the needed civic improvements can be made, and if the bond issue does not carry, then conditions essential for growth will not be attained. Either the bonds are approved or the bond issue does not carry. Therefore, either the needed civic improvements can be made or conditions essential for growth will not be attained.

4. If you compete and win, you have the satisfaction of victory, and if you compete and lose, you have gained valuable experience. Either you compete and win or you compete and lose. Therefore, you have the satisfaction of victory or you have gained valuable experience.

5. If the problem is solved, its answer is accepted, and if its statement is not correct, a new statement has to be formulated. Either the problem is solved or a new statement has to be formulated. Therefore, either its answer is accepted or its statement is not correct.

6. If the crime is admitted, then a prison sentence will be given, and if the case is tried, the defendant will be found guilty. Either the prison sentence will not be given or the defendant will not be found guilty. Therefore, either the crime is not admitted or the case is not tried.

7. If you know the material, you need not read outside material to make a good grade, and if you do not understand the material, outside reading is useless. Either you do not know the material or you do understand it. Therefore, either you need not read outside material to make good grades or outside reading is useless.

8. If freedom of speech is permitted, then extremist groups can advocate undemocratic practices, and if freedom of speech is curtailed, then democratic institutions are threatened. Either freedom of speech is permitted or it is curtailed. Therefore, either extremist groups can advocate undemocratic practices or democratic institutions are threatened.

9. If wages are permitted to rise, inflation will result in increased costs of goods, and if wages are frozen, popular unrest will result in a change in the elected representatives to Congress. Either inflation will result in increased costs of goods or popular unrest will result in a change in the elected representatives to Congress. Thus, either wages are permitted to rise or wages are frozen.

10. If I lead the six of hearts and the bidder plays his ace of hearts, he makes his bid; and if I lead my low trump and the bidder plays his high trump, he makes his bid. Either I lead the six of hearts and the bidder plays his ace of hearts, or I lead my low trump and the bidder plays his high trump. Therefore, he makes his bid. (Can this dilemma be rebutted if each player has only two cards?)

CHAPTER **10**

TRUTH TABLES AND THE LOGIC OF TRUTH FUNCTIONS

10.1 TRUTH TABLES AND TRUTH VALUES

This chapter develops the use of truth tables to determine the validity of arguments. The truth table will also be used here to define statement connectives and to determine contradictory or equivalent relations between two or more statements.

This chapter does not presuppose that a student is familiar with Chapters 7, 8, and 9. But a reading of section 9.4 would be helpful as a background for this material.[1]

---

[1] There is need to restate some basic notions found in Section 9.4 for those who have not read that material. In analyzing statements we have need to use some abbreviations. We can use capital letters, such as A, D, L, Q, and R, as abbreviations for any statements. An abbreviation for the statement "Lead is heavy" is L. We can abbreviate a sentence having two statements as elements with two capital letters. For example, one can abbreviate the sentence "If lead is heavy, then it sinks in water" as "if L, then S."

Capital letters used as abbreviations always have a fixed value in a given context. They are constants for statements. Once we give such a letter a specific meaning, that meaning remains "constant" throughout that context. And one should not use these capital letters as abbreviations for statements with other meanings in that context.

We can use small letters beginning with p as a form for any statement. The statement "If lead is heavy, then it sinks in water" has the statement form "if p, then q." Any statement having the same structure as the above sentence also has the statement form "if p, then q." These small letters such as p, q, r, and s are place holders. They are stand-ins for any statement

In constructing truth tables we use the postulate of a two-valued logic. And the truth value of any statement has as its limits the values of true or of false. Such a postulate is in keeping with the "laws of thought."

The "laws of thought" are the principle of identity, the principle of excluded middle, and the principle of contradiction. The *principle of identity* holds that the truth value of a given statement (in a given context) remains constant. That is, the truth value of a statement does not shift within a given context. The *principle of excluded middle* restricts the truth value of a given statement to one of two values. Either the statement is true or it is false in a given context. The *principle of contradiction* holds that the truth value of any given statement cannot have both the value of true and the value of false.

The truth value of any one statement has as its limits the alternatives expressed in the following table; p is a place holder for any statement in which T stands for the value of true and F for the value of false.

p
T
F

If we consider the truth value of both p and not p, the following table results:

p	not p
T	F
F	T

In a truth table there is an orderly arrangement of all possible combinations of the values of T and of F for a set of simple statements. One assigns values to other statements having as components simple statements that are connected by logical operators like "if . . . , then _____." Let us look at a truth table which defines the dot "·"—the logical connective used for "and"—to join two statements or statement forms.

p	q	$p \cdot q$
T	T	T
T	F	F
F	T	F
F	F	F

---

that can replace them. The statement form, "either p or q" holds the place for an indefinite number of statements having that form. Examples of such statements are "Either more money is invested or production is cut back," and "Either M or P."

We refer to the vertical order of Ts or Fs in a truth table as a column. The order of Ts and Fs on any one horizontal entry is a row. The column under q in the above table is TFTF. The third row of Ts and Fs reads FTF.

In drawing a truth table we list all simple statements that occur in an argument as the initial entry on the top line of a truth table. (In the above case we write p, q.) We shall want to show all possible combinations of T and of F between these simple (or atomic) statements. We can draw a vertical line after the last atomic statement in this first series of entries. We must assign values to all other statements listed at the top of the truth table (and to the right of the line we have just drawn). Such other statements consist of the premises, the conclusion, and in some cases whatever other statements are needed to assign truth values to the premises and the conclusion. In the case of the previous truth table there is need to assign a value to $p \cdot q$. And we do this by looking at the truth values assigned to the atomic statements p and q. The molecular statement $p \cdot q$ is to the right of the indicated line and we assign a value to that statement on the basis of the rule for operating the dot, "·". This rule requires that one assign the value of T in the column under this connective only when both of its component statements have the value T on any given row. If at least one atomic statement has the value of F, then we write an F under $p \cdot q$ on the row where that atomic statement is F. In the truth table we are analyzing, there is a T on row 1 since both components have T. There is an F on rows 2, 3, and 4 since at least one of the components has the value of F.

The previous truth table provides us with a definition of the truth-functional connective "and." (A connective is truth functional if it provides a rule for assigning truth values to the simple statements it connects in a compound statement. We shall discuss this matter later in greater detail.) There will be other comments about constructing truth tables after students have had experience in constructing simple ones. In the next section we shall construct definitions of other logical connectives.

10.2 TRUTH-TABLE DEFINITIONS OF LOGICAL CONNECTIVES

In the last section we saw how to construct a truth table. And in discussing this technique the truth table definition of the dot, "·," was also presented. In this section we shall provide truth table definitions of other logical connectives.

The sign for denial is "~"—called a tilde. The definition of this sign is as follows:

p	$\sim p$
T	F
F	T

The use of the "~" before any statement denies that statement. And we assign the opposite truth value to its denial. Thus, if p is T, then its denial, $\sim p$, is F. We interpret the meaning of the "~" as "It is not the case that." But we sometimes shorten this in a statement like $\sim p$ to "not p," which in a strict sense is an abbreviation for the longer expression, "It is not the case that p." The form $\sim(p \cdot q)$ is expressed as "It is not the case both that p and that q." Note the use of parentheses in the form $\sim(p \cdot q)$. The parentheses show that we are treating everything enclosed within them as a unit of analysis until we remove such parentheses.

We should take note that the use of "not" has a technical and precise meaning in the logic of truth functions. Consider the statement, "It is snowing." We can negate the statement by saying, "It is not snowing." We deny the statement by holding, "It is not the case that it is snowing." There are instances, particularly in more advanced studies, to hold rigorously to these differences. But for our purposes we are making some accommodation to ordinary usage. In some cases we shall refer to the form $\sim(p \cdot q)$ as "the denial of p and q," or "the negation of p and q," or "It is false that p and that q," or "not both p and q." But the meaning we shall hold in all cases for such translations is the notion, "It is not the case both that p and that q."

The wedge symbol "v" is used for the connective "either . . . or _____." Its truth table function is as follows:

p	q	$p \lor q$
T	T	T
T	F	T
F	T	T
F	F	F

The statement $p \lor q$ is true in all cases where p is true or q is true (including cases where both are true). The statement form $p \lor q$ is expressed as "either p or q." The atomic statements in a disjunctive statement are called disjuncts. The above definition of the wedge interprets the meaning of "either . . . or _____" as an inclusive disjunction which holds that the truth value of the disjunctive statement is true in all cases in which at least one disjunct is true. (The other disjunct can be true or false.) Some expressions using "either . . . or _____" express exclusive disjunction. In these exclusive disjunctive statements, one disjunct must be true and the other must be false. We can use the form $(p \lor q) \cdot (\sim p \lor \sim q)$ to express exclusive disjunction. But the use of arguments and argument forms using "either . . . or _____" in this work will be interpreted as restricted to inclusive disjunction. We are following the convention of using the weaker meaning of an expression.

The horseshoe symbol "⊃" is used for the connective "if . . . , then

_____." It operates as follows:

p	q	$p \supset q$
T	T	T
T	F	F
F	T	T
F	F	T

We also can call the above table the definition of the truth-functional conditional "⊃," or the definition of the material conditional. The material conditional requires that any statement having the form $p \supset q$ is true in every instance except where p has the value of T and q has the value of F.

The element in a conditional introduced by "if" is the antecedent. The element introduced by "then" is the consequent. Expressions introduced by "only if" need to be restructured to make their meaning explicit. We restructure the statement form, "only if p, then q" to read "if q, then p." The meanings of the connectives "if . . . then _____" are more varied than can be expressed by material conditionals. We are following the convention of using a restricted meaning of a connective such as "if . . . then _____." Some uses of "if . . . then _____" require further analysis.[2]

The meaning of the material conditional is difficult to grasp intuitively since it requires any material conditional statement to be true in all cases where its antecedent is false. For example, let us assume that the statement, "Today is Friday," is false. The material conditional statement, "If today is Friday, then we go to the theater," is true. The material conditional carries no additional meaning in regard to its truth value than the meaning expressed by the statement form $\sim(p \cdot \sim q)$. In the case of the previous example, the conditional statement signifies only that "It is not the case both that today is Friday and that we not go to the theater." After you have

[2] The material conditional is applicable in a strict sense to statements in the indicative mood. We refer to a conditional statement whose antecedent is known to be false and whose consequent (usually) is in the subjective mood as a contrary-to-fact conditional. An example of this form of statement is, "If the stock market crash of 1929 had not occurred, then we would not have had the Great Depression which brought about the New Deal." The material conditional does not apply to statements whose elements taken separately do not have truth values assignable to them. Consider the general conditional, "If anything is a horse, then it is a quadruped." In this context the separate elements of the conditional, "anything is a horse" and "it is a quadruped," do not have the value of true or of false. The elements of general conditionals can be representative of a group or cluster of individual statements, each of which can be true or false. Such statements as "Greyboy is a horse," and "Greyboy is a quadruped," can have the value of true or false. Other types of conditionals that could be discussed include logical, definitional, causal, decisional, and evaluative. Some uses of "if" and of "then" do not express a conditional. Consider these examples. "There is a good TV program on Channel 6 if you want to see it." "You can telephone home if you are concerned." "George reviewed his assignments, then he took the exam."

Exclusive or — one true, other false
contingent sense

had more experience with the handling of material conditional statements, reasons for interpreting its meaning in the above way will be better understood.

We use the sign "≡" for the material biconditional or material equivalence. The "≡" has the meaning of ". . . if and only if _____." It has the following truth-table definition.

p	q	$p \equiv q$
T	T	T
T	F	F
F	T	F
F	F	T

[handwritten annotations: true when these have same truth value; false when diff. truth value; equivalent]

An alternate manner of defining the material biconditional, which gives the same results, is $(p \supset q) \cdot (q \supset p)$.

p	q	$p \supset q$	$q \supset p$	$(p \supset q) \cdot (q \supset p)$
T	T	T	T	T
T	F	F	T	F
F	T	T	F	F
F	F	T	T	T

[handwritten annotation: equivalent stmts]

The statement form $(p \supset q) \cdot (q \supset p)$ is a conjunctive form and is true only if both conjuncts, $(p \supset q)$ and $(q \supset p)$, are true. The usual manner of expressing a material biconditional statement is "p if and only if q," or "If p, then q, and if q, then p."

We have given the truth-table definitions of the logical operators "·," "V," "⊃," "≡," and "~." These operators do a job based on their truth function as specified by the truth table. We refer to the type of logic that combines the simple use of these logical operators and of statement forms that use them as truth-functional logic. Some logicians also refer to this kind of logic as propositional logic.

We have been talking about truth functions. We have been using truth-functional connectives such as "if . . . then _____" and "either . . . or _____." We also have been using truth-functional compound statements like "Mary is a student and she is a sophomore." To say that a connective is truth-functional is to hold that the connective, as defined by a rule, determines how we are to assign truth values to a compound statement when we assign truth values to each of its component statements. To say that a compound statement is truth-functional is to hold that one determines the truth of such a statement exclusively by the truth values assigned to its separate statements and by the rule for the use of its truth-functional connective.

Take the statement form $p \supset q$. The value of true or of false given to the statement $p \supset q$ depends on the logical meaning assigned to "$\supset$" and on the truth values assigned to p and to q. That is, the connective "$\supset$" "functions to determine" the truth value of $p \supset q$ solely on the basis of the truth value given to p and to q.

We are studying arguments in this chapter that make use of truth-functional compound statements. And many compound statements are not truth-functional. Examples of compound statements that are not strictly truth-functional are the following: "The coach anticipates that his next opponent will try some new plays." "We went to the ski resort *and then* we went skiing." In a strict sense we do not have a way to determine the truth or falsity of the above compound statements by the definitions we have given for the logical connectives we are using. The use of "and then" introduces an element of time or succession that the strict use of "and," as defined by the dot "$\cdot$," does not have. But we frequently attempt to translate such compound statements into other statements and to analyze them by techniques of arguments using truth-functional statements. However, in some such cases we can introduce errors into an argument.

The unraveling of many technical issues related to the notion of truth functions is beyond the scope of this work. We have seen that when we use the notion of truth function, we are talking at least about a special class of compound statements or their logical connectives. And we determine the truth value assigned to such statements by the truth value held by their simpler statements and by the rule for the use of the logical connective that brings together these components.

In truth-functional logic the connective "if . . . then _____" carries a heavier burden than in ordinary discourse. We can translate connectives like "when," and "where," that we use to introduce adverbial clauses, as an "if-then" connective. We translate connectives like "but" as "and" when we use it to join two other statements. We also restrict the meaning which logical connectives have in a more stringent manner than the meaning they may have in ordinary discourse.

10.3 THE SCOPE OF LOGICAL CONNECTIVES

Punctuation

We need to know the range covered by any logical connective in a statement. The notion of scope is used to make clear what components of a statement fall within the range of operation of any given connective.

The scope of a logical connective refers to the elements in a statement that are covered by a connective's use. The scope of the operator "$\sim$" in $\sim(p \cdot q)$ is everything included in the parentheses following the "$\sim$." But the scope of the "$\sim$" in the following case, $\sim(p \cdot q) \vee r$, remains the same as in the above case. That is, it covers only $\sim(p \cdot q)$.

The scope or range of applying such connectives as "~," "·," "v," "⊃," and "≡," needs to be made precise in order to avoid ambiguity. Parentheses, brackets, and braces are used in order to avoid such ambiguity. Consider the following statement:

> If either the international situation significantly deteriorates or the federal monetary policies result in exorbitant interest rates, then the conservatives will win the election.

By designating the elements in the form of this statement as p, q, and r, and writing the connectives as they occur in the sentence, the following notations can be made:

$$p \vee q \supset r$$

abstract

This series of symbols allows for the meanings "Either p or if q, then r," and "If either p or q, then r." The original statement has the latter form. Parentheses are needed to make explicit in the above form the scope of the disjunctive connective "V" and the material conditional connective "⊃." The original statement form is correctly expressed as $(p \vee q) \supset r$.

The statement form $\sim p \cdot q$ is a conjunctive statement meaning "not p and q." But the statement form $\sim(p \cdot q)$ has a different meaning. This form denies the conjunction of p and q. It holds that it is not the case both that p is true and that q is true.

Brackets and braces are used to make the scope of connectives explicit in more complex statement forms. We express the statement form $[(p \cdot q) \vee r] \supset \sim(s \cdot t)$ as "If either both that p and q or that r, then it is not the case both that s and that t." In analyzing statement connectives it is preferable to begin by identifying the connectives with the broader scope. Then we determine the scope of the connectives with a more restricted range.

We apply parentheses, brackets, and braces in a similar manner to statements and to statement forms. Consider the following statement.

> If either Alex defaults or Bill is ill, then both Carl advances and Don will play the next set. (A, B, C, D)

concrete

The abbreviation of the above statement is $(A \vee B) \supset (C \cdot D)$. Its statement form is: $(p \vee q) \supset (r \cdot s)$.

We also assign truth values to a statement on a truth table in the same way that we write its corresponding statement form. The statement $A \supset B$ has the same truth values as the statement form $p \supset q$. The values given to A correspond to those given to p. The values given to B correspond to q. And the values given to $A \supset B$ are the same as those given to $p \supset q$.

Consider the following:

A	B	A ⊃ B
T	T	T
T	F	F
F	T	T
F	F	T

We also can manipulate a statement in an argument in the way that we can manipulate its corresponding statement form.

In the next section we shall look at ways of using the truth table to characterize a statement's relation to itself or to other statements.

EXERCISES

A. Symbolize the following complex statements by using the indicated letters for the elementary statements and by using parentheses and brackets to make clear the scope of the connectives.
1. If interest rates fall, the price of bonds rise. (I, B)
2. Either they will be on time or they stopped for lunch. (T, S)
3. The lobby is strong and the pressure is great. (S, P)
4. If John wins the match, then he wins the tourney. (M, T)
5. Either wages hold steady or prices increase. (W, I)
6. It is not the case both that the President's program has the support of Congress and that his party loses more seats in Congress. (S, L)
7. It is not the case both that we accept the offer and that we not accept the asking price. (O, A)
8. Either the unrest continues or if different interests are satisfied, then the discontent will lessen. (U, I, D)
9. We make a bid and if our bid is low, then we get the job. (M, L, J)
10. If either Jefferson's recommendations are followed or Lincoln's are followed, then democratic procedures will be practiced and civil rights will be respected. (J, L, D, R)
11. If we leave early and we have no difficulty, then if we arrive on time, we shall finish the job. (L, D, T, F)
12. Either the rate of inflation is reduced and the percent of unemployed is decreased, or if a national election is held, then the party in power will not be reelected. (I, P, N, R)
13. If either Smith wins or Jones wins, then the finals will be tough and the match will be hard fought. (S, J, T, M)
14. If we develop our abilities, then we can have a wider range of opportunities and if we fail to increase our skills, then our choices become more limited. (D, R, F, C)
15. If it is not the case both that Congress adjourns early and that the bill is passed, then either we find stronger support, or we shall suffer defeat. (C, B, F, D)

16. If it is the case that if all human actions are determined by prior events and all causes of action are the consequence of events beyond our control, the individual cannot behave in a manner other than he does, then either a greater effort is needed to provide opportunities to improve the standard of living conditions in inner cities or individuals living in inner cities will become more aggressive in their behavior and they will be more hostile in their attitudes. (*D, C, B, O, A, H*)

B. Write the appropriate truth values on a truth table for the following statements.
   1. *C* V *D*
   2. *A·D*
   3. *C* ≡ *F*
   4. ~(*A* ⊃ *B*)
   5. ~(*K·L*)
   6. (*C* ⊃ *D*)·(*D* ⊃ *C*)
   7. ~(*M* V *N*)

C. Identify the logical connective having the major operation in each of the following statement forms. Indicate the scope of each connective in these forms.
   1. (*p* V *q*) ⊃ *r*
   2. (*p·q*) V (*r* ⊃ *s*)
   3. [*p* V (*q·r*)] ⊃ ~*s*
   4. [(*p* ⊃ *q*) V *r*]·~*s*
   5. [(*p·q*) V (*p·r*)] V (*s* ⊃ *t*)
   6. [(*p·q*) V *r*] ≡ [(*p* V *r*)·(*q* V *r*)]
   7. {[(*p* ⊃ *q*)·(*r* ⊃ *s*)]·(*p* V *r*)} ⊃ (*q* V *s*)
   8. {[(~*p* V *q*)·(~*r* V *s*)]·~(~*p*·~*r*)} ⊃ (*s* V *q*)

major operation with usually followed will usually largest bracket

10.4 TRUTH TABLES AND SOME TRUTH RELATIONS OF STATEMENTS

Statements That Are Tautologous, Contradictory, or Contingent

In this section we shall use the truth tables to analyze some truth relations of a statement to itself and to other statements.

The logical forms of some statements require that these statements are true. The forms of other statements require that these statements are false. The forms of another set of statements permit them to be true or false.

A statement whose logical form yields only instances of true statements is *tautologous*.[3] Consider the forms *p* V ~*p* and ~(*p·~p*).

"trivially" true

---

[3] Although all of the equivalent forms (*p* · *p*)/∴*p* and (*p* v *p*)/∴*p* are sometimes called "tautologies" (Taut.), they are not tautologies as we define the term here. Rather, they are tautologous in the sense of "repetition" or "redundancy." The following sentence is a tautologous expression in the latter sense: "The essential essentials are prepared."

p	$\sim p$	$p\cdot\sim p$	$p \lor \sim p$	$\sim(p\cdot\sim p)$
T	F	F	T	T
F	T	F	T	T

The columns under the forms $p \lor \sim p$ and $\sim(p\cdot\sim p)$ yield only true values. Thus, any statement having this form is true on logical grounds alone.

internally true / contradictory A statement whose logical form yields only instances of a false statement is *contradictory*. Consider the possible truth values for the form $p\cdot\sim p$ in the truth table above. The truth value for each possible occurrence is false. Thus, any statement having this form is false on logical grounds alone.

A statement whose logical form yields instances that may be either true or false is *contingent*. Examine the forms p, q, $p \lor q$, $p\cdot q$, $p \supset q$ given in previous uses of the truth table. We cannot determine the truth or falsity of instances of these forms on logical grounds only. Rather, their truth or falsity is contingent upon the material content of statements using these forms.

The Determination of Contradictory or Equivalent Relations between Two or More Statements

Two statements are *contradictory* if their logical forms yield opposite truth values in each row of the truth table. Consider the relation of $p\cdot q$ and $\sim(p\cdot q)$ or of $p \lor q$ and $\sim p\cdot\sim q$.

p	q	$\sim p$	$\sim q$	$p\cdot q$	$\sim(p\cdot q)$	$p \lor q$	$\sim p\cdot\sim q$
T	T	F	F	T	F	T	F
T	F	F	T	F	T	T	F
F	T	T	F	F	T	T	F
F	F	T	T	F	T	F	T

In each row where $p\cdot q$ is true, $\sim(p\cdot q)$ is false. And where one is false, the other is true. In each case where $p \lor q$ is true, $\sim p\cdot\sim q$ is false. Since the designated forms have opposite truth values in every case, they are contradictory statement forms.

Two statements are *equivalent* if they have identical truth values in all cases. Consider the forms $p \supset q$, $\sim p \lor q$, $\sim(p\cdot\sim q)$ and $\sim q \supset \sim p$ in the following table:

p	q	$\sim p$	$\sim q$	$p\cdot\sim q$	$p \supset q$	$\sim p \lor q$	$\sim(p\cdot\sim q)$	$\sim q \supset \sim p$
T	T	F	F	F	T	T	T	T
T	F	F	T	T	F	F	F	F
F	T	T	F	F	T	T	T	T
F	F	T	T	F	T	T	T	T

In each case the indicated forms have identical truth values; in the rows in which one is true, the others are true, and in the row in which one is false, the others are false. Thus, these statement forms are equivalent. Equivalent forms may replace each other wherever they occur, either as statement forms or as elements in statement forms.

EXERCISES

A. Identify each of the following statement forms as tautologous, contradictory, or contingent by truth-table analysis.
  1. $p \supset p$ *taut*
  2. $\sim(p \vee \sim p)$ *contra*
  3. $\sim q \supset \sim p$
  4. $p \supset (p \supset \sim q)$
  5. $(p \cdot q) \cdot (\sim q \vee \sim p)$ *contra*
  6. $(p \vee q) \vee (\sim p \cdot \sim q)$ *taut*

B. Use a truth table to write the different possible truth values of the following statement forms. Identify the statement forms that are equivalent to the first form, $p \vee q$, and identify the statements that are contradictions of this form.
  1. $p \vee q$
  2. $\sim q \supset p$ *equiv*
  3. $\sim p \cdot \sim q$
  4. $\sim(\sim p \supset q)$
  5. $\sim(\sim q \cdot \sim p)$ *equiv*
  6. $\sim p \cdot \sim(\sim p \supset q)$ *contradictory*

10.5 ARGUMENT FORMS AND THE TRUTH TABLE

   In this section there is a discussion of the way we construct truth tables to analyze arguments and to determine their validity.

   An argument form is valid if no instance can occur in which the conclusion is false and the premises are true. An argument form is invalid if at least one instance can occur in which the premises are true and the conclusion is false. Consider the argument form of *modus ponens*, $p \supset q$, p, / $\therefore q$.

p	q	$p \supset q$	p	$/\therefore q$
T	T	T	T	T
T	F	F	T	F
F	T	T	F	T
F	F	T	F	F

In the analysis of this argument form on the truth table, the conclusion, q, is false in the second row and one premise, $p \supset q$, is false. The conclusion also is false in the fourth row. Again one of the premises, p, is false. There is no case (that is, no row) in which the conclusion is false and the premises are true. This demonstrates that the argument form is valid. In no case is it possible both for the conclusion to be false and the premises to be true.

Consider the invalid argument form $p \vee q$, p, $/\therefore \sim q$.

p	q	$\sim q$	$p \vee q$	p	$/\therefore \sim q$	
T	T	F	T	T	Ⓕ	(Invalid)
T	F	T	T	T	T	
F	T	F	T	F	F	
F	F	T	F	F	T	

In the first row the conclusion, $\sim q$, is false, and the premises, $p \vee q$ and p, are true. Since this argument form has at least one instance in which the conclusion can be false and the premises true, it is invalid.

Let us review some of the techniques for constructing a truth table and add some suggestions for writing more complex tables for testing the validity of arguments. To illustrate this discussion look at Table 10.1, which is a truth table for a complex constructive dilemma. We write the values T or

Table 10.1   Truth Table for a Constructive Complex Dilemma

p	q	r	s	$p \supset q$	$r \supset s$	$(p \supset q) \cdot (r \supset s)$	$p \vee r$	$/\therefore q \vee s$
T	T	T	T	T	T	T	T	T
T	T	T	F	T	F	F	T	T
T	T	F	T	T	T	T	T	T
T	T	F	F	T	T	T	T	T
T	F	T	T	F	T	F	T	T
T	F	T	F	F	F	F	T	F
T	F	F	T	F	T	F	T	T
T	F	F	F	F	T	F	T	F
F	T	T	T	T	T	T	T	T
F	T	T	F	T	F	F	T	T
F	T	F	T	T	T	T	F	T
F	T	F	F	T	T	T	F	T
F	F	T	T	T	T	T	T	T
F	F	T	F	T	F	F	T	F
F	F	F	T	T	T	T	F	T
F	F	F	F	T	T	T	F	F

F under the indicated form by referring to the values originally assigned to the atomic statement forms (in the present case p, q, r, and s) in the columns appearing in the first part of the truth table. It is helpful to use a vertical line to separate the original assigned values of possible truth relations between the atomic statement forms (p, q, r, and s) and the remaining part of the truth table. Likewise, it is helpful to use a vertical line to separate the conclusion from other portions of the truth table. We need to write the forms for the premises adjacent to the conclusion. This makes it easier to compare the truth values of the premises and of the conclusion by placing the forms for these entries next to each other.

If additional forms are needed to assist in the determination of the truth values of the premises or of the conclusion, it is preferable to separate these forms from the premises by drawing a vertical line. Thus, for the sake of convenience vertical lines can be drawn in the truth table: (1) after the listing of the truth values of the original elementary statement forms; (2) after the forms helpful in the analysis of the truth values of the premises or the conclusion; and (3) before the conclusion. It also is helpful to draw horizontal lines under the original statements that we analyze, and under every fourth row in the proof (to facilitate reading the rows).

The number of rows in a truth table is determined by the number of atomic statements occurring in the argument. If two elementary statements are used, the number of rows is 2 × 2 or 4. If three atomic statements are used, the number of rows needed is 2^3 or 2 × 2 × 2 or 8. If four simple statements are used, as in the present case the number of rows needed is 2^4 or 16, and so on. If sixteen rows are needed, we assign the value of T to the first eight rows (or the initial one-half of the rows) under the first atomic statement. And we assign the value of F to the last eight rows (or the remaining one-half of the rows). Under the second simple statement we assign the value of T to the first set of four rows and the third set of four rows. We then assign the value of F to the second and fourth sets of rows. In each succeeding case the number of consecutive rows with the value of T is one half the number in the sequence of the preceding column. The column under the last simple statement will alternate T and F on each successive row.

In analyzing the truth table for the validity of the argument form for the constructive complex dilemma, we find that it has $(p \supset q)\cdot(r \supset s)$ and $p \vee r$ as premises. Its conclusion is $q \vee s$ (see Table 10.1). The conclusion has the value of F in the sixth, eighth, fourteenth, and sixteenth rows. In each of these cases at least one premise is false. Since there is no instance in which the conclusion has a value of F without at least one premise in the same row having a value of F, the argument form is valid.

An argument is valid if its corresponding argument form is valid. In arguments we write the truth values for the capital letters used as abbreviations for statements directly under these capital letters. For example, we can analyze the argument $\sim A \lor B$, A, $/\therefore B$ as follows:

A	B	$\sim A$	$\sim A \lor B$	A	$/\therefore B$
T	T	F	T	T	T
T	F	F	F	T	F
F	T	T	T	F	T
F	F	T	T	F	F

In the next section we shall look at ways to use shortcut methods in using truth tables to determine validity.

EXERCISES

A. Determine the validity of the following argument forms by the use of the truth table.

1. $p \supset q$
   $p \supset r$
   _____
   $\therefore q \supset r$

2. $(p \supset q) \cdot (p \supset r)$
   $\sim p \lor \sim r$
   _____
   $\therefore \sim q$

3. $p \supset (q \cdot r)$
   $\sim q \lor \sim r$
   _____
   $\therefore \sim p$

4. $(p \lor q) \supset (r \lor s)$
   $\sim q \cdot \sim s$
   _____
   $\therefore p \supset r$

5. $\sim (p \cdot \sim q)$
   $q \lor \sim r$
   $\sim r$
   _____
   $\therefore p$

6. $(p \supset q) \cdot (r \supset s)$
   $\sim s \lor \sim q$
   p
   _____
   $\therefore \sim r$

B. Determine the validity of the following arguments by the use of the truth tables.

1. $A \lor B$
   $\sim A$
   ___
   $\therefore B$

2. $\sim (A \cdot B)$
   A
   ___
   $\therefore \sim B$

3. $\sim (A \lor B)$
   $\sim A \supset C$
   ___
   $\therefore C$

4. $C \supset (D \lor E)$
   C
   ___
   $\therefore D$

5. $\sim F \lor G$
   $G \supset H$
   ___
   $\therefore \sim H \supset \sim F$

6. $\sim (H \cdot I)$
   $I \lor J$
   ___
   $\therefore H \supset J$

10.6 SHORTCUT METHODS OF USING TRUTH TABLES IN CONSTRUCTING PROOFS

The use of truth tables in proving the validity or invalidity of argument forms can require extensive and time-consuming techniques. Shortcut methods can be used. Shortcut methods of using truth tables to prove validity are as conclusive as the construction of complete truth tables. But in proving an argument valid, the practical use of this method decreases as the number of simple statements increases. In the next chapter, we shall discuss an alternative method of proving valid arguments by the use of extended proofs. The shortcut method for proving invalidity uses a technique for proving invalidity similar to complete truth tables, but there is need to construct only one row of the truth table.

Proving Valid Arguments by a Shortcut Use of the Truth Table

An argument form is valid if there is no instance in which the conclusion is false and all the premises are true. We can devise a shortcut method of using the truth table to provide valid arguments by examining only those rows on a table in which the conclusion is false. Consider the table given previously for the form of the constructive dilemma. The shortcut method focuses only on those rows in which truth values of the initial set of atomic statements require that the conclusion have the value of false. Truth values for the premises are found for these rows. At least one F needs to occur as the value for a premise in each row in which the conclusion also has an F in order for the argument to be valid. The F found under a premise can be circled to indicate that at least one premise has the value of F. This shorter version of the truth table is sufficient to prove validity.

As another example let us consider a shortcut method of proving the argument form for the hypothetical syllogism, $p \supset q$, $q \supset r$, $\therefore p \supset r$, is valid (Table 10.2). This table establishes that in every case that the conclusion has the value of F at least one premise also has the value of F. The tests for validity have been met.

Proving Invalidity by a Cross-Section of the Truth Table

In proving an argument invalid by a cross-section of the truth table we want to show that one row of a truth table has a false conclusion when each of the premises on that row are true. We use the following steps to draw this cross-section:

1. Write the initial line occurring at the top of the truth table. This line has the atomic statements found in the argument, any forms needed to assist in determining the truth values of premises or of the conclusion, the premises, and the conclusion.

2. Write the value of F under the conclusion and the value of T under the premises.

Table 10.2   Shortcut Truth Table for Illustrating Proof of Validity

p	q	r	$p \supset q$	$q \supset r$	$/\therefore p \supset r$
T	T	T			
T	T	F	T	Ⓕ	F
T	F	T			
T	F	F	Ⓕ	T	F
F	T	T			
F	T	F			
F	F	T			
F	F	F			

3. Write the truth values that must hold for each of the atomic statements occurring in the conclusion which has the assigned truth value of F.

4. Write the truth values for the remaining atomic sentences such that each premise can be true. (Usually the truth values for the atomic statements in some premises are easier to determine than others.) We then proceed, sometimes by trial and error, to work out truth values for the remaining atomic statements in the argument.

We shall consider two examples of invalid arguments by use of cross-sections of truth tables.

$$A \lor B$$

$$B \supset C$$

$$C$$

$$\therefore A$$

We write the atomic statements in the argument, the premises, and the conclusion on a single line. We proceed to write F under the statement for the conclusion and T under the statements for the premises. Our cross-section now appears as follows:

A B C		$A \lor B$	$B \supset C$	C	$\therefore A$
		T	T	T	F

We now look for truth values for the atomic statements A, B, and C, that will make the premises true and the conclusion false. We enter the value of F under A in the first part of the cross-section. The conclusion requires this value. We enter the value of T also under C in the first part. The third premise requires this value. We look at the other premises to determine what truth values we can assign to any other atomic statements so that each premise will have the value of T. We must enter a value of T for the statement B in the first premise. For the premise to have the value of T, one of the disjuncts must be true. And the first disjunct A already has the value of F.

We now have truth values assigned to each atomic statement in the argument. And we have the following cross-section of the truth table:

A B C		$A \lor B$	$B \supset C$	C	$\therefore A$
F T T		T	T	T	F

We check our work to see if the truth value assigned to each atomic statement yields the value of T for each premise and the value of F for the conclusion. These truth values check out. We have a proof that the argument is invalid.

We shall consider the following more complex argument:

$$A \supset B$$

$$\sim(B \lor C)$$

$$\sim(C \cdot \sim D)$$

$$D$$

$$\overline{}$$

$$\therefore A$$

In drawing the cross-section, we write the initial line occurring at the top of a truth table. Then we write the value of F under the conclusion and the value of T under the premises. Our cross section now appears as follows:

A	B	C	D	~D	B V C	C·~D	A ⊃ B	~(B V C)	~(C·~D)	D	∴A
							T	T	T	T	F

We proceed to try to find the value of T or F for the atomic statement placed in the first part of the cross-section. We enter F under the statement A and T under D. The conclusion and the fourth premise require these values.

We search for clues to find the truth values for the remaining two atomic statements. We note that if $\sim(B \lor C)$ has the value of T, then $B \lor C$ must have the value of F. But this requires that the statement B have the value of F and that the statement C have the value of F. We check the other premise, $\sim(C \cdot \sim D)$ to make sure that the truth values now assigned to each of its atomic statements yield a value of T. We find that this premise does have the value of T. And we have the following cross-section of a truth table which shows that the argument is invalid:

A	B	C	D	~D	B V C	C·~D	A ⊃ B	~(B V C)	~(C·~D)	D	∴A
F	F	F	T	F	F	F	T	T	T	T	F

In some cases of writing a cross-section of a truth table to prove invalidity, we can construct more than one row in which the premises are true and the conclusion is false. In such cases we need to draw only one of these rows. In this case any one of the rows satisfies the condition for proving the argument is invalid.

In this chapter we have seen how the use of truth tables provides a basis for defining basic logical notions. Their use enables us to test the validity of many arguments. In the next chapter we shall look at alternate ways to construct proofs for arguments.

EXERCISES

A. Determine the validity of the following arguments by use of the truth table. The shortcut method of using the truth table may be used.

1. (1) $A \supset B$
   (2) B
   $\overline{\quad\quad}$
   $\therefore A$

2. (1) $A \supset (B \vee C)$
   (2) $\sim B \cdot \sim C$
   $\overline{\quad\quad}$
   $\therefore \sim A$

3. (1) $D \supset E$
   (2) $E \supset F$
   $\overline{\quad\quad}$
   $\therefore F \supset D$

4. (1) $(G \supset H) \vee I$
   (2) $\sim(H \vee I)$
   $\overline{\quad\quad}$
   $\therefore G$

5. (1) $(A \supset B) \cdot (C \supset B)$
   (2) $A \vee C$
   $\overline{\quad\quad}$
   $\therefore B$

6. (1) $(A \supset B) \cdot (A \supset C)$
   (2) $\sim(B \vee C)$
   $\overline{\quad\quad}$
   $\therefore \sim A$

7. (1) $L \cdot (O \vee R)$
   (2) $(L \cdot R) \supset H$
   $\overline{\quad\quad}$
   $\therefore H$

8. (1) $(A \vee B) \cdot (C \vee D)$
   (2) $\sim A \vee D$
   $\overline{\quad\quad}$
   $\therefore \sim A \vee C$

9. (1) $(A \supset B) \cdot (C \vee D)$
   (2) $\sim(\sim A \cdot \sim C)$
   $\overline{\quad\quad}$
   $\therefore B \vee D$

10. (1) $E \supset (F \supset G)$
    (2) $G \vee H$
    (3) $\sim(E \cdot \sim F) \cdot E$
    $\overline{\quad\quad}$
    $\therefore H$

B. Write the following arguments with the indicated abbreviations for each atomic statement. Determine their validity by use of the truth table. Shortcut methods may be used.

1. It is not the case both that Smith be elected and that he not campaign vigorously. (*E, C*) If he campaigns vigorously, then he must spend considerable money on TV announcements. (*S*) He will not spend considerable money on TV announcements. Therefore, Smith will not be elected.

2. If either we depend on memory or we depend on the testimony of others, then we can be mistaken. (*D, T, C*) We depend on memory. Therefore, we can be mistaken.

3. If the weather prediction is correct, then we shall have rain at the game. (*P, R*) If we do not have rain at the game, the stands will fill up. (*S*) The weather prediction is not correct. Thus, the stands will fill up.

4. Either introspection is subject to error or it is subject to doubt. (*E, D*) If it is subject to error, then it does not provide us with complete certainty and if it is subject to doubt, it does not provide us with complete certainty. (*C*) Therefore, introspection does not provide us with complete certainty.

5. Either a machine is conscious or it merely follows programs that are fed into it and it is not the case both that a machine is conscious and that it merely follows programs that are fed into it. (*C, P*) A machine follows programs that are fed into it. If a machine is not conscious, then it is the product of intelligence. (*I*) Therefore, a machine is the product of intelligence.

6. Either Tom is mistaken or George is telling the truth. (*T, G*) If George is telling the truth, then either James is ill or Bill is out of town. (*J, B*) Tom is mistaken and James is not ill. Thus, Bill is out of town.

7. James is in class and either he is wearing a coat or he is wearing a sweater. (*J, C, S*) If he is in class, then he forgot his glasses. (*F*) It is not the case both that he forgot his glasses and that he is wearing a sweater. Therefore, he is wearing a coat.

8. If this argument is sound, then it is valid, and if this argument is correct, it is sound. (*S, V, C*) This argument is not correct. Therefore, this argument is not valid.

9. Either tensions are easing and a peace treaty will be signed or tensions are easing and some progress will be made. (*E, P, R*) A peace treaty will not be signed and if tensions are easing then new compromises are made. (*C*) Thus, new compromises are made.

10. Our political leaders are persons with self-interest and either they use their political office for self-interest or political restraints are placed upon their expression of self-interest. (*L, O, R*) If it is the case that if our political leaders are persons with self-interest, political restraints are placed upon their expression of self-interest, then we can hope for less corruption in government. (*H*) Therefore, we can hope for less corruption in government.

CHAPTER 11

EXTENDED PROOFS

11.1 EXTENDED ARGUMENTS AND ARGUMENT FORMS

Truth tables provide a precise way to define logical operators. They also make possible an accurate manner of determining the validity of an argument. But they can be cumbersome in dealing with arguments with a number of atomic statements.

This chapter develops an alternative way of writing proofs for valid arguments. We use extended proofs, which depend on basic argument forms and on equivalent statements. One can construct tables for these forms, which we use by showing they hold on truth tables. This chapter also develops the technique of constructing conditional proofs and indirect proofs.

The following argument requires a truth table with thirty-two rows:

$$(1) \quad A \supset (B \lor C)$$
$$(2) \quad (B \lor C) \supset D$$
$$(3) \quad \sim(D \cdot E)$$
$$(4) \quad A$$
$$\therefore \sim E$$

By use of the basic argument forms given for writing extended proofs we can save work by writing three steps and having a proof of this argument.

We can justify the basic forms we use in constructing extended arguments by referring to truth tables. And we continue to hold that an argument is valid if it has a valid argument form.

Let us review the difference between an argument and an argument form. Consider the following argument.

If we invest in real estate, we take risks. (*I, R*)

We invest in real estate.

Therefore, we take risks.

Letting the letter *I* serve as the abbreviation for the statement "We invest in real estate," and the letter *R* be the abbreviation for the statement "We take risks," we can express the argument and the argument form as follows:

(1)

Argument	Argument Form
$I \supset R$	$p \supset q$
I	p
$\therefore R$	$\therefore q$

This argument has the argument form of *modus ponens*, which is one of the basic forms we shall be using in writing extended proofs. The argument form of *modus ponens* is valid. Thus, the above argument also is valid.

Extended proofs use a step-by-step combination of valid argument forms and equivalent statement forms to construct proofs of arguments. In the use of argument forms, the small letters, p, q, r, . . . , refer to the *major elements* in a statement covered by the connective under the analysis. For example, we find the argument form of *modus ponens*, $p \supset q$, p, $\therefore q$ in both of the following arguments:

(2) $K \supset L$ (3) $A \supset [(B \lor C) \cdot D]$

$\underline{K}$ $\underline{A}$

$\therefore L$ $\therefore (B \lor C) \cdot D$

We also find use of the equivalent form of contraposition, $(p \supset q) \equiv (\sim q \supset \sim p)$, in each of the following statement equivalences:

(4) $(A \supset B) \equiv (\sim B \supset \sim A)$

(5) $[(E \lor F) \supset (G \cdot H)] \equiv [\sim (G \cdot H) \supset \sim (E \lor F)]$

We also can use equivalent statement forms to apply only to a part within a longer statement. But we shall discuss this matter in another context.

The accompanying table (Table 11.1) presents the basic argument forms, together with their names and abbreviations, that we use in extended proofs. We can show these forms are valid by use of truth-table analysis. A second table presented later gives the forms for equivalent statements.

We use these basic argument forms to construct formal proofs. A formal proof of an argument is a statement or series of statements serving as premises with an added statement or series of statements derived from the premises by use of basic argument forms and equivalent statement forms to justify a conclusion. A formal proof of an extended argument has the following elements:

1. It has a statement or a series of statements given as premises.

2. It has a statement or a series of statements entered as steps in the proof.

3. It has a justification for each step entered in the proof. Each step in the proof requires the use of a basic argument form or of a statement equivalence.
    a. In justifying a step in the proof by use of an argument form, the argument form must replace a complete line occurring previously as a premise or as a step in the proof. That is, we cannot apply an argument form only to a part of a line in a step of the proof.
    b. We can replace an equivalent statement form by another equivalent statement form anywhere it is convenient to do so in the steps of the proof. That is, we can apply an equivalent statement form to only a part of a line in writing a proof, or we can apply it to the complete line.

4. It has a conclusion justified by the premises, and statements derived from these premises, in entries made in each step of the proof.

The following examples illustrate the way we construct proofs for extended arguments. But for the time being we are using only proofs that use basic argument forms. Consider the following argument:

If John is a graduate, he is eligible for the job. (*G, E*)

John is a graduate.

If John is eligible for the job, he will apply for it. (*A*)

Therefore, he will apply for the job.

Table 11.1   Table of Basic Argument Forms for Extended Proofs

1. *Modus ponens* (MP):

$$p \supset q$$
$$p$$
$$\therefore q$$

2. Addition (Add.):

$$p$$
$$\therefore p \lor q$$

3. Simplification (Simp.):

$$p \cdot q$$
$$\therefore p$$

4. Conjunction (Conj.):

$$p$$
$$q$$
$$\therefore p \cdot q$$

5. Hypothetical syllogism (HS):

$$p \supset q$$
$$q \supset r$$
$$\therefore p \supset r$$

6. *Modus tollens* (MT):

$$p \supset q$$
$$\sim q$$
$$\therefore \sim p$$

7. Disjunctive argument (DA):

$$p \lor q$$
$$\sim p$$
$$\therefore q$$

8. Denial-of-conjunction argument (DCA):

$$\sim (p \cdot q)$$
$$p$$
$$\therefore \sim q$$

9. Constructive complex dilemma (CCD):

$$(p \supset q) \cdot (r \supset s)$$
$$p \lor r$$
$$\therefore q \lor s$$

10. Absorption (Abs.):

$$p \supset q$$
$$\therefore p \supset (p \cdot q)$$

Using abbreviations we have the following argument:

$$G \supset E$$

$$G$$

$$\underline{E \supset A}$$

$$\therefore A$$

We want to construct an extended proof for this argument. But where do we begin in writing a proof? We focus on the statement given as the conclusion. We locate the statements that are a part of the conclusion in the premises. We try to determine the steps that we can take by use of argument forms (and of equivalent statement forms) to derive the statement in the conclusion from the statements given as premises. In the example we are considering we write the proof as follows:

Column I	Column II	Column III
(1) $G \supset E$		
(2) G		
(3) $E \supset A$		
$\therefore A$		
(4) E	(1), (2) $p \supset q, p, /\therefore q$	(1), (2) MP
(5) A	(3), (4) $p \supset q, p, /\therefore q$	(3), (4) MP

In the above case, A is the statement appearing in the conclusion. We identify A in the premises. It occurs as the consequent of the statement $E \supset A$ in the third premise. If we can affirm atomic statement E, then we can affirm A (by *modus ponens*). The atomic statement E occurs in the statement $G \supset E$ in the first premise. We can affirm E if we can affirm the atomic statement G. The statement in the second premise affirms G. The use of *modus ponens* provides the basis for affirming E. We can use *modus ponens* again with the statements $E \supset A$ and E. Thus, we derive A. And we have a proof for our conclusion.

Further analysis of the above proof shows that Column I sets forth the premises and the steps used in deriving the conclusion. Column II refers to the argument forms (or to the equivalences) used to derive each specific entry in the proof [(4) and (5) above] from previous steps in the proof. Column III refers to the name of the argument form (or statement equivalences) used to derive the step in Column I from previous steps or premises in the proof. The numbers in Columns II and III refer to the line numbers in Column I, to show which previous entries in the proof we use for deriving the argument forms (or equivalences) in Column II and Column III.

Consider the following argument together with its proof:

Either Mary will cut class or she does not go to town. (C, G)

Not both can she see her boyfriend and cut class. (S)

Mary sees her boyfriend.

Therefore, she does not go to town.

Column I	Column II	Column III
(1) $C \lor \sim G$		
(2) $\sim(S \cdot C)$		
(3) S		
$\therefore \sim G$		
(4) $\sim C$	(2), (3) $\sim(p \cdot q), p, /\therefore \sim q$	(2), (3) DCA
(5) $\sim G$	(1), (4) $p \lor q, \sim p, /\therefore q$	(1), (4) DA

Let us look at another example:

Column I	Column II	Column III
(1) $(A \supset B) \cdot (C \supset D)$		
(2) $A \lor C$		
(3) $(B \lor D) \supset \sim(E \cdot \sim F)$		
(4) $(E \cdot \sim F) \lor (G \cdot H)$		
$\therefore G$		
(5) $B \lor D$	(1), (2) $(p \supset q) \cdot (r \supset s), p \lor r, /\therefore q \lor s$	(1), (2) CCD
(6) $\sim(E \cdot \sim F)$	(3), (5) $p \supset q, p, /\therefore q$	(3), (5) MP
(7) $G \cdot H$	(4), (6) $p \lor q, \sim p, /\therefore q$	(4), (6) DA
(8) G	(7) $p \cdot q, /\therefore p$	(7) Simp.

EXERCISES

A. Complete Column II and Column III in the following arguments:

Column I	Column II	Column III
1. (1) $A \supset B$		
(2) $\sim B \lor C$		
(3) A		
$\therefore C$		
(4) B		*1,3 MP*
(5) C		*2,4 DA*

Column I	Column II	Column III

2. (1) $B \lor C$
    (2) $C \supset (D \lor E)$
    (3) $\sim B$
    (4) $\underline{\sim D}$
    $\therefore E$
    (5) C
    (6) $D \lor E$
    (7) E

Column I	Column II	Column III

3. (1) $(E \supset F) \cdot (G \supset H)$
    (2) $E \lor G$
    (3) $\underline{(F \lor H) \supset K}$
    $\therefore K$
    (4) $F \lor H$
    (5) K

Column III:
1,2 CCP
3,4 MP

Column I	Column II	Column III

4. (1) $A \supset B$
    (2) $B \supset C$
    (3) $\underline{[A \supset (A \cdot C)] \supset D}$
    $\therefore D$
    (4) $A \supset C$
    (5) $A \supset (A \cdot C)$
    (6) D

Column I	Column II	Column III

5. (1) $G \cdot H$
    (2) $\sim (G \cdot I)$
    (3) $\underline{(\sim I \lor J) \supset K}$
    $\therefore K$
    (4) G
    (5) $\sim I$
    (6) $\sim I \lor J$
    (7) K

Column III:
1) Simp
4,2) DCA
5) Add
3,6) MP

	Column I	Column II	Column III

6.   (1) $A \supset B$
     (2) $\sim B$
     (3) $C \vee D$
     (4) $[\sim A \cdot (C \vee D)] \supset E$
     (5) $(E \vee F) \supset G$
       $\therefore G$
     (6) $\sim A$
     (7) $\sim A \cdot (C \vee D)$
     (8) E
     (9) $E \vee F$
   (10) G

B. Complete Column III in the following set. Completion of Column II is optional.

Column I	Column II	Column III

1.   (1) $B \vee A$
     (2) $B \supset C$
     (3) $\sim C$
       $\therefore A$ *2,3 MT*
     (4) $\sim B$ *1,4 DA*
     (5) A

Column I	Column II	Column III

2.   (1) $C \supset D$
     (2) $D \supset E$
     (3) $\sim E$
       $\therefore \sim C$
     (4) $C \supset E$
     (5) $\sim C$

Column I	Column II	Column III

3.   (1) $\sim (E \cdot F)$
     (2) $F \vee G$
     (3) E
       $\therefore G$ *1,3 DC A*
     (4) $\sim F$ *2,4 DA*
     (5) G

Column I	Column II	Column III

4.   (1) $(A \vee B) \supset C$
     (2) $D \supset A$
     (3) D
       $\therefore C$
     (4) A
     (5) $A \vee B$
     (6) C

	Column I	Column II	Column III
5.	(1) $(A \cdot B) \supset C$		
	(2) $A \supset B$		
	(3) A		$2, 3$ MP
	$\therefore C$		$3, 4$ Conj
	(4) B		$1, 5$ MP
	(5) $A \cdot B$		
	(6) C		

	Column I	Column II	Column III
6.	(1) $(A \lor B) \supset C$		
	(2) $D \lor A$		
	(3) $\sim D$		
	$\therefore C$		
	(4) A		
	(5) $A \lor B$		
	(6) C		

	Column I	Column II	Column III
7.	(1) $(C \supset D) \cdot (E \supset F)$		
	(2) $\sim G \lor (C \lor E)$		$2, 3$ DA
	(3) G		$1, 4$ CCD
	$\therefore D \lor F$		
	(4) $C \lor E$		
	(5) $D \lor F$		

	Column I	Column II	Column III
8.	(1) $\sim (A \cdot B)$		
	(2) $B \lor (C \supset D)$		
	(3) A		
	$\therefore C \supset (C \cdot D)$		
	(4) $\sim B$		
	(5) $C \supset D$		
	(6) $C \supset (C \cdot D)$		

11.2 EXTENDED ARGUMENTS AND STATEMENT EQUIVALENCES

The use of statement equivalences greatly increases the number of arguments for which we can write extended proofs. We have seen that two statements are equivalent if they have identical truth values on a truth table. In writing extended proofs we use the rule of replacement. The rule of replacement holds that one equivalent statement can be replaced by another one in any new entry in a proof. We can replace one statement by its equivalent form within a line of a proof, or one statement can replace another on a complete line of the proof. An equivalent statement form for $p \vee q$ is $q \vee p$. Assume we are given the statement $(D \vee E) \supset F$ in a line of a proof. We can change the order of atomic statements by replacing an equivalent form for $(D \vee E)$ by $(E \vee D)$. The original statement now reads $(E \vee D) \supset F$. Let us consider another example. We also can replace $H \vee (F \cdot G)$ by the equivalent statement $(F \cdot G) \vee H$. We may need to make such replacements in order to have a valid disjunctive argument in writing a proof with our basic argument forms.

In the table which follows we have a list of statement equivalences for use in extended proofs. (See Table 11.2.)

The following example illustrates the use of statement equivalences in an extended proof:

Not both can an element be plutonium and not be transuranium. (P, T)

Either an element is not transuranium or it has atomic number 94. (N)

Therefore, if it is plutonium, it has atomic number 94.

Column I	Column II	Column III
(1) $\sim(P \cdot \sim T)$		
(2) $\sim T \vee N$		
$\therefore P \supset N$		
(3) $P \supset T$	(1) $(p \supset q) \equiv \sim(p \cdot \sim q)$	(1) DeC
(4) $T \supset N$	(2) $(p \supset q) \equiv (\sim p \vee q)$	(2) MC
(5) $P \supset N$	(3), (4) $p \supset q, q \supset r, /\therefore p \supset r$	(3), (4) HS

Line (3), Column II, shows that $P \supset T$ replaces $\sim(P \cdot \sim T)$ as an equivalent. In line (4), $T \supset N$ replaces $\sim T \vee N$ in line (2) as its equivalent. Line (5) shows that the conclusion is derived from lines (3) and (4) by the use of a hypothetical syllogism.

In constructing rigorous proofs using these statement equivalent forms, we give only one form for a disjunctive argument and only one form for a denial-of-conjunction argument. We can use commutation and then the disjunctive argument form to prove some disjunctive arguments to be valid. Our argument forms permit the denial of the first disjunct and then the affirmation of the second. If we have the statement $A \vee B$ in one line of the proof, and the statement $\sim B$ in another line, we need to commute $A \vee B$ to $B \vee A$. We then have entries to which we can apply a disjunctive argument form. We sometimes use commutation in order to use the argument form of simplification, or to change the order of an atomic statement in a denial-of-conjunction statement.

We also need to use the principle of double negation rather than merely

Table 11.2   Table of Statement Equivalences for Use in
Extended Proofs

1. Material conditional (MC):

$$(p \supset q) \equiv (\sim p \lor q)$$

2. De Morgan's law (DeM): *triple negation*

$$(p \lor q) \equiv \sim(\sim p \cdot \sim q)$$

$$(p \cdot q) \equiv \sim(\sim p \lor \sim q)$$

3. De Morgan's law and material conditional (DeC):

$$(p \supset q) \equiv \sim(p \cdot \sim q)$$

$$\sim(p \supset q) \equiv (p \cdot \sim q)$$

4. Contraposition (Contrap.):

$$(p \supset q) \equiv (\sim q \supset \sim p)$$

5. Commutation (Comm.):

$$(p \lor q) \equiv (q \lor p)$$

$$(p \cdot q) \equiv (q \cdot p)$$

6. Material biconditional (or material equivalence) (MBC):

$$(p \equiv q) \equiv [(p \supset q) \cdot (q \supset p)]$$

$$(p \equiv q) \equiv [(p \cdot q) \lor (\sim p \cdot \sim q)]$$

7. Double negation (DN):

$$p \equiv \sim\sim p$$

8. Repetition (Rep.):

$$(p \lor p) \equiv p$$

$$(p \cdot p) \equiv p$$

9. Distribution (Dist.):

$$[p \lor (q \cdot r)] \equiv [(p \lor q) \cdot (p \lor r)]$$

$$[p \cdot (q \lor r)] \equiv [(p \cdot q) \lor (p \cdot r)]$$

10. Association (Assoc.):

$$[p \lor (q \lor r)] \equiv [(p \lor q) \lor r]$$

$$[p \cdot (q \cdot r)] \equiv [(p \cdot q) \cdot r]$$

11. Exportation (Exp.):

$$[p \supset (q \supset r)] \equiv [(p \cdot q) \supset r]$$

assume it. In a strict sense, the denial of a negated statement is another statement with two marks of negation preceding it. We deny the statement $\sim A$ by $\sim\sim A$. Double negation permits us to derive A from $\sim\sim A$, or $\sim\sim A$ from A.

Let us consider some other extended proofs which require the use of the rule of replacement:

Column I	Column II	Column III
(1) $B \supset C$		
(2) $(\sim C \lor D)\cdot\sim D$		
(3) $\sim(\sim B\cdot E)$		
$\therefore \sim E$		
(4) $\sim C \lor D$	(2) $p\cdot q, /\therefore p$	(2) Simp.
(5) $\sim D\cdot(\sim C \lor D)$	(2) $(p\cdot q) \equiv (q\cdot p)$	(2) Comm.
(6) $D \lor \sim C$	(4) $(p \lor q) \equiv (q \lor p)$	(4) Comm.
(7) $\sim D$	(5) $p\cdot q, /\therefore p$	(5) Simp.
(8) $\sim C$	(6), (7) $p \lor q, \sim p, /\therefore q$	(6), (7) DA
(9) $\sim B$	(1), (8) $p \supset q, \sim q, /\therefore \sim p$	(1), (8) MT
(10) $\sim E$	(3), (9) $\sim(p\cdot q), p, /\therefore \sim q$	(3), (9) DCA

Either reports of consumer studies are correct or both the energy crisis is serious and the reports of oil exporters are unreliable. (R, S, E)

If the reports of consumer studies are correct, then the energy crisis is serious and if the reports of oil exporters are unreliable, a crisis of confidence is widespread. (F)

A crisis of confidence is not widespread and the need for controls on gas consumption is not exaggerated. (N)

Therefore, the energy crisis is serious.

Column I	Column II	Column III
(1) $R \lor (S\cdot E)$		
(2) $(R \supset S)\cdot(E \supset F)$		
(3) $\sim F\cdot\sim N$		
$\therefore S$		
(4) $(R \lor S)\cdot(R \lor E)$	(1) $[p \lor (q\cdot r)] \equiv [(p \lor q)\cdot(p \lor r)]$	(1) Dist.
(5) $(R \lor E)\cdot(R \lor S)$	(4) $(p\cdot q) \equiv (q\cdot p)$	(4) Comm.
(6) $R \lor E$	(5) $p\cdot q /\therefore p$	(5) Simp.
(7) $S \lor F$	(2), (6) $(p \supset q)\cdot(r \supset s), p \lor r, /\therefore q \lor s$	(2), (6) CCD
(8) $\sim F$	(3) $p\cdot q /\therefore p$	(3) Simp.
(9) $F \lor S$	(7) $(p \lor q) \equiv (q \lor p)$	(7) Comm.
(10) S	(9), (8) $(p \lor q), \sim p /\therefore q$	(9), (8) DA

Other ways of writing the above proof can be followed.

If an argument has an inconsistency within its premises, we can prove any conclusion by using addition. Although the argument is valid, it cannot be sound. All of the premises in such an argument cannot be true. Consider the following argument:

If the movie has a haunting melodic theme, it will be popular. (H, P)

The movie has a haunting melodic theme and it is not popular.

Therefore, the movie will be a great success. (S)

Column I	Column II	Column III
(1) $H \supset P$		
(2) $H \cdot \sim P$		
$\therefore S$		
(3) H	(2) $p \cdot q / \therefore p$	(2) Simp.
(4) P	(1), (3) $p \supset q, p / \therefore q$	(1), (3) MP
(5) $\sim P \cdot H$	(2) $(p \cdot q) \equiv (q \cdot p)$	(2) Comm.
(6) $\sim P$	(5) $p \cdot q / \therefore p$	(5) Simp.
(7) $P \lor S$	(4) $p / \therefore p \lor q$	(4) Add.
(8) S	(7), (6) $p \lor q, \sim p / \therefore q$	(7), (6) DA

The use of addition also is useful in writing other kinds of proofs. The argument form of addition makes possible our adding another disjunct to any statement that occurs in any line of a proof. Suppose we have the statement A on one line of a proof and the statement $(A \lor B) \supset C$ on another line of that proof. Since we can add any disjunct to a statement given as true we can use addition and have the statement $A \lor B$. This gives us the statement needed for completion of a *modus ponens* argument to get C.

After students have learned to use the basic argument forms and the statement equivalences, they can omit the writing of these forms as recommended for Column II.

We can prove the last six argument forms listed as basic argument forms by use of statement equivalence and of the first four argument forms, which are *modus ponens*, addition, simplification, and conjunction. (The forms for the hypothetical syllogism and absorption can be proven easily by use of conditional proofs, which are discussed later.) Consider the following case of the complex constructive dilemma that occurs when we permit the hypothetical syllogism to be included with these other four forms:

Column I	Column III
(1) $(p \supset q) \cdot (r \supset s)$	
(2) $p \lor r$	
$\therefore q \lor s$	
(3) $p \supset q$	(1) Simp.

(4) $(r \supset s) \cdot (p \supset q)$	(1) Comm.
(5) $r \supset s$	(4) Simp.
(6) $\sim q \supset \sim p$	(3) Contrap.
(7) $\sim p \supset r$	(2) MC
(8) $\sim q \supset r$	(6), (7) HS
(9) $\sim q \supset s$	(8), (5) HS
(10) $q \lor s$	(9) MC

The derived argument forms are not needed in the strictest sense. But we include them for convenience in reducing the number of steps used in an extended proof.

(If students have not read Section 9.6 on the dilemma, they might do so at this time.)

Suggestions for Writing Extended Proofs

In writing extended proofs, several suggestions are helpful in determining how we can proceed. These suggestions are made in outline form for convenience in reference:

1. Check for accuracy in the writing of each statement and statement connective in the argument.

2. Identify the conclusion and note its atomic statements.

3. Find in the premises the atomic statements which also occur in the conclusion. (But remember that addition permits the introduction of new statements in the proof by a step forming a disjunctive statement with any previous line of the proof.)

4. Seek to identify those statements which would enable one to establish other statements needed to prove terminal steps of proof.

5. Try to develop a plan of proof prior to writing the proof.

6. Apply the argument forms and the equivalent forms properly.
    (1) A line on an argument form corresponds to a line on the proof. Each line on an argument form must be applied to a complete line in a premise or a step in the proof.
    (2) Equivalent forms can be replaced anywhere they occur. They can be used to replace any element or combination of elements within a line of the premises or within a step in the proof.

7. If no plan of procedure becomes apparent consider:
    (1) Testing for invalidity.

(2) Using conditional or indirect proofs (which are discussed in the next section).

(3) The use of different steps of combining or separating terms such as addition, distribution, or association.

(4) Seeking different ways of writing equivalent forms with connectives for conjunctive, disjunctive, and conditional statements.

8. Shortcuts (applicable by agreement):

(1) Elimination of the column (II) containing the specific argument forms or the equivalent forms that are used in a step of the proof.

(2) Multiple changes involving the same kind of equivalent form on one line of the proof. (For example, $(p \cdot q) \vee (r \cdot s)$ could be changed to $(q \cdot p) \vee (s \cdot r)$ by writing "Comm. -2".)

(3) Reduction of use of double negation in cases involving negation of negated elements. (For example, the negation of $\sim p$ can be given as p rather than as $\sim\sim p$.)

(4) Joint use of a disjunctive argument form or a denial-of-conjunction argument form (DA or DCA) and of commutation (Comm.). For example, consider $\sim(A \cdot B)$ and B as separate lines in a proof. $\sim A$ can be derived directly with the notation "Comm. and DCA".

EXERCISES

A. Complete Column II and Column III in the following exercises.

		Column I	Column II	Column III
1.	(1)	$\sim A \vee B$		
	(2)	$\sim(B \cdot \sim C)$		
		$\therefore A \supset C$		*1 m C*
	(3)	$A \supset B$		*2 Dec*
	(4)	$B \supset C$		*3,4 HS*
	(5)	$A \supset C$		

		Column I	Column II	Column III
2.	(1)	$(A \vee B) \vee C$		
	(2)	$\sim A$		
	(3)	$(B \vee C) \supset (D \cdot E)$		
		$\therefore E$		
	(4)	$A \vee (B \vee C)$		
	(5)	$B \vee C$		
	(6)	$D \cdot E$		
	(7)	$E \cdot D$		
	(8)	E		

	Column I	Column II	Column III
3.	(1) $(A \cdot B) \supset C$		
	(2) $\sim C \lor D$		
	(3) $\sim D$		
	$\therefore \sim A \lor \sim B$		
	(4) $C \supset D$		
	(5) $(A \cdot B) \supset D$		
	(6) $\sim (A \cdot B)$		
	(7) $\sim A \lor \sim B$		

2 mc
1,4 HS
5,3 MT
6 Dem

	Column I	Column II	Column III
4.	(1) $(\sim A \lor B) \supset C$		
	(2) $\sim A$		
	(3) $\sim C \lor (D \supset E)$		
	$\therefore D \supset (D \cdot E)$		
	(4) $\sim A \lor B$		
	(5) C		
	(6) $D \supset E$		
	(7) $D \supset (D \cdot E)$		

	Column I	Column II	Column III
5.	(1) $\sim (A \cdot B)$		
	(2) $\sim B \supset (C \cdot D)$		
	(3) $A \cdot \sim D$		
	$\therefore F$		
	(4) A		
	(5) $\sim D \cdot A$		
	(6) $\sim D$		
	(7) $\sim B$		
	(8) $C \cdot D$		
	(9) $D \cdot C$		
	(10) D		
	(11) $D \lor F$		
	(12) F		

internal contradiction

	Column I	Column II	Column III
6.	(1) $(H \lor K) \supset L$		
	(2) $\sim (L \cdot \sim M)$		
	(3) $\sim M$		
	(4) $\sim H \supset N$		
	$\therefore N$		
	(5) $L \supset M$		
	(6) $(H \lor K) \supset M$		
	(7) $\sim (H \lor K)$		
	(8) $\sim H \cdot \sim K$		
	(9) $\sim H$		
	(10) N		

	Column I	Column II	Column III
7. (1)	$A \supset (B \supset C)$		
(2)	$C \supset (D \lor E)$		
(3)	$\sim[D \lor \sim(A \cdot B)]$		
	$\therefore E$		
(4)	$(A \cdot B) \supset C$		
(5)	$(A \cdot B) \supset (D \lor E)$		
(6)	$\sim\sim[\sim D \cdot \sim\sim(A \cdot B)]$		
(7)	$\sim D \cdot \sim\sim(A \cdot B)$		
(8)	$\sim D \cdot (A \cdot B)$		
(9)	$\sim D$		
(10)	$(A \cdot B) \cdot \sim D$		
(11)	$A \cdot B$		
(12)	$D \lor E$		
(13)	E		

	Column I	Column II	Column III
8. (1)	$E \lor (F \cdot G)$		
(2)	$(E \lor F) \supset H$		
	$\therefore H$		
(3)	$(E \lor F) \cdot (E \lor G)$		
(4)	$E \lor F$		
(5)	H		

	Column I	Column II	Column III
9. (1)	$\sim A \lor (B \supset C)$		
(2)	$\sim(C \cdot \sim D)$		
(3)	$(\sim D \lor A) \cdot (\sim D \lor B)$		
	$\therefore D \equiv (A \cdot B)$		
(4)	$A \supset (B \supset C)$		
(5)	$(A \cdot B) \supset C$		
(6)	$C \supset D$		
(7)	$(A \cdot B) \supset D$		
(8)	$\sim D \lor (A \cdot B)$		
(9)	$D \supset (A \cdot B)$		
(10)	$[D \supset (A \cdot B)] \cdot [(A \cdot B) \supset D]$		
(11)	$D \equiv (A \cdot B)$		

B. Write in Column III the name of the argument form or equivalence form taken in each step. You may omit Column II.

	Column I	Column III
1. (1)	$A \supset B$	
(2)	$\sim B \lor D$	
	$\therefore A \supset D$	
(3)	$B \supset D$	2 *MC*
(4)	$A \supset D$	1,3 *HS*

Column I   Column III

2. (1) $\sim(C\cdot\sim D)$
   (2) $\sim D \vee E$

   $\therefore \sim E \supset \sim C$
   (3) $C \supset D$
   (4) $D \supset E$
   (5) $C \supset E$
   (6) $\sim E \supset \sim C$

Column I   Column III

3. (1) $(E \vee F) \supset (G\cdot H)$
   (2) $F \vee E$
   (3) $H \supset I$

   $\therefore I$
   (4) $E \vee F$
   (5) $G\cdot H$
   (6) $H\cdot G$
   (7) H
   (8) I

2 Comm
1,4 MP
5 Comm
6 Simp
3,7 MP

Column I   Column III

4. (1) $A \equiv B$
   (2) $B \supset C$

   $\therefore(\sim A \vee C)\cdot(\sim B \vee A)$
   (3) $(A \supset B)\cdot(B \supset A)$
   (4) $(B \supset A)\cdot(A \supset B)$
   (5) $B \supset A$
   (6) $A \supset B$
   (7) $A \supset C$
   (8) $\sim B \vee A$
   (9) $\sim A \vee C$
   (10) $(\sim A \vee C)\cdot(\sim B \vee A)$

Column I   Column III

5. (1) $(\sim A \vee B)\cdot(\sim A \vee C)$
   (2) $[\sim A \vee (B\cdot C)] \supset D$

   $\therefore D$
   (3) $\sim A \vee (B\cdot C)$
   (4) D

1 Dist
2,3 MP

Column I   Column III

6. (1) $A \supset (B \supset C)$
   (2) $C \supset [D\cdot(E \vee F)]$

   $\therefore(A\cdot B) \supset [(D\cdot E) \vee (D\cdot F)]$
   (3) $(A\cdot B) \supset C$
   (4) $(A\cdot B) \supset [D\cdot(E \vee F)]$
   (5) $(A\cdot B) \supset [(D\cdot E) \vee (D\cdot F)]$

Column I   Column III

7. (1) $A \supset B$
   (2) $(\sim A \supset C)\cdot(B \supset D)$
   (3) $(C \lor D) \supset (\sim E \lor F)$
   $\therefore E \supset (E\cdot F)$
   (4) $\sim A \lor B$
   (5) $C \lor D$
   (6) $\sim E \lor F$
   (7) $E \supset F$
   (8) $E \supset (E\cdot F)$

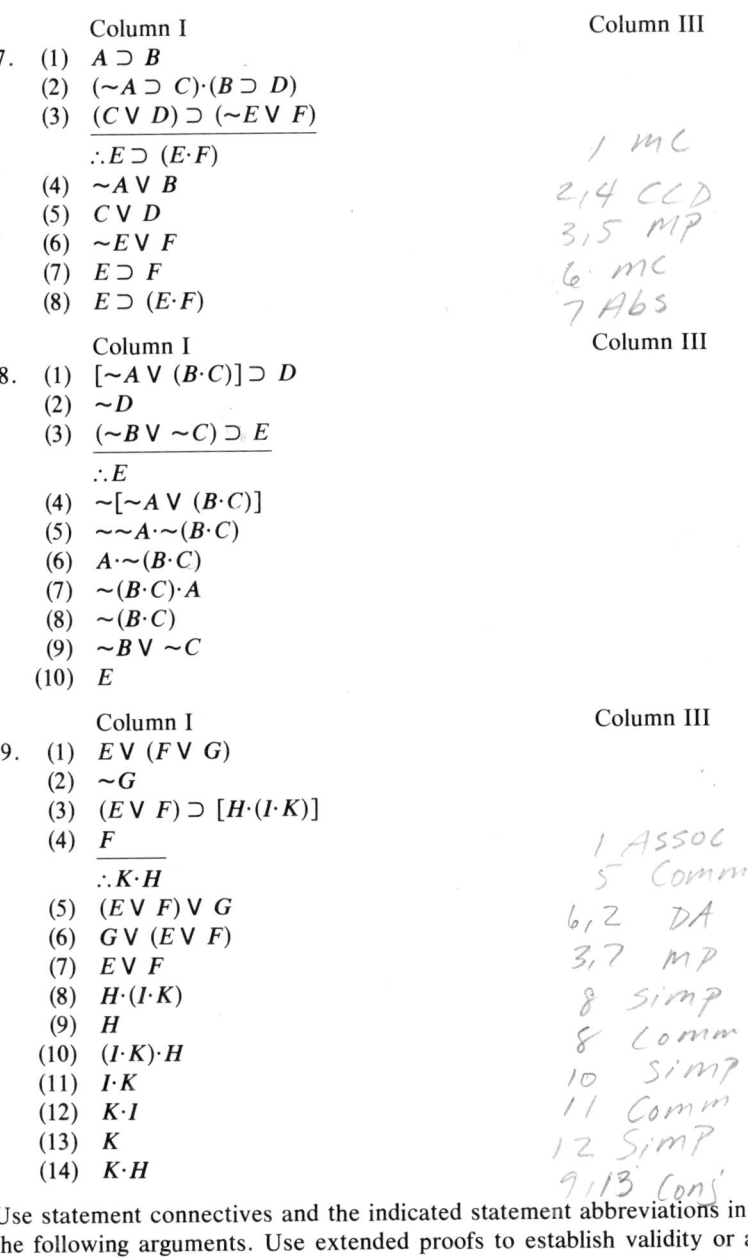

1 mc
2,4 CCD
3,5 MP
6. mc
7 Abs

Column I   Column III

8. (1) $[\sim A \lor (B\cdot C)] \supset D$
   (2) $\sim D$
   (3) $(\sim B \lor \sim C) \supset E$
   $\therefore E$
   (4) $\sim[\sim A \lor (B\cdot C)]$
   (5) $\sim\sim A\cdot\sim(B\cdot C)$
   (6) $A\cdot\sim(B\cdot C)$
   (7) $\sim(B\cdot C)\cdot A$
   (8) $\sim(B\cdot C)$
   (9) $\sim B \lor \sim C$
   (10) E

Column I   Column III

9. (1) $E \lor (F \lor G)$
   (2) $\sim G$
   (3) $(E \lor F) \supset [H\cdot(I\cdot K)]$
   (4) F
   $\therefore K\cdot H$
   (5) $(E \lor F) \lor G$
   (6) $G \lor (E \lor F)$
   (7) $E \lor F$
   (8) $H\cdot(I\cdot K)$
   (9) H
   (10) $(I\cdot K)\cdot H$
   (11) $I\cdot K$
   (12) $K\cdot I$
   (13) K
   (14) $K\cdot H$

1 Assoc
5 Comm
6,2 DA
3,7 MP
8 Simp
8 Comm
10 Simp
11 Comm
12 Simp
9,13 Conj

C. Use statement connectives and the indicated statement abbreviations in writing the following arguments. Use extended proofs to establish validity or a cross-section of the truth table to prove invalidity. (Review suggestions for writing extended proofs. You can use some of the shortcuts permitted in these suggestions.)

1. If Susan is either ill or sleepy, then she is in her room. (I, S, R) Not both

can she be in her room and be in the drugstore. (*D*) She is in the drugstore. Therefore, she is not ill.

2. Either there is not free interchange of information or the advancement of science is helped. (*I, A*) Not both can the advancement of science be helped and censorship of scientific publications be practiced. (*C*) There is free interchange of information. Therefore, the censorship of scientific publications is not practiced.

3. If the scientist is honest, then he will make true statements and will indicate evidence that is difficult to account for by his views. (*H, T, I*) If he makes true statements and he indicates evidence that is difficult to account for by his views, then he supports thoroughness of inquiry. (*S*) The scientist is honest. Therefore, he supports thoroughness of inquiry.

4. Not both can research methods be sound and not provide some basis for verification. (*S, V*) If research methods are sound, then appeals to guesses will not be made. (*G*) Appeals to guesses are not made. Therefore, research methods provide some basis for verification.

5. If our defense is not good, then we shall lose more games than we win. (*D, G*) If either we are in top shape or our defense is good, then we are sharp in our execution of plays. (*S, E*) We are not sharp in our execution of plays. Therefore, we shall lose more games than we win or we shall need a lot of luck. (*N*)

6. If the Yankees have strong pitching, they win the series. (*P, W*) If the Yankees have strong pitching and they win the series, then they have good hitting. (*H*) The Yankees have strong pitching and they do not have good hitting. Therefore, the Mets win the series. (*M*)

7. Kant is a philosopher and Hume's view of the mind is too restricted. (*K, H*) If either Kant is a philosopher or Newton is a philosopher, then either our knowledge is limited to the phenomenal world or we can know Plato's world of forms. (*N, L, F*) Therefore, either our knowledge is limited to the phenomenal world and Hume's view of the mind is too restricted or we can know Plato's world of forms and Hume's view of the mind is too restricted.

8. If and only if an acceptable theory is supported by evidence can it be tested. (*E, T*) If there are not found reasons to hold to an acceptable theory, then it is not supported by evidence. (*R*) It is not the case both that an acceptable theory is not supported by evidence and that unfavorable evidence is not ignored in scientific investigation. (*I*) Unfavorable evidence is not ignored in scientific investigation. Therefore, an acceptable theory can be tested and there are found reasons to hold to an acceptable theory.

9. Either we go to the coast for our vacation or we shall invite friends to join us, and either we go to the mountains or we shall rest quietly in the cabin for two weeks. (*C, I, M, R*) If we go to the coast for our vacation, we shall not go to the mountains. Therefore, if we do not invite friends to join us, we shall rest quietly in the cabin for two weeks.

10. If an overdose of irradiated ergosterol has been given these adult rats, then either widespread metastatic calcification occurs in their cardiovascular system or it occurs in other organs of their bodies. (*E, C, O*) If no symptoms of calcification occur, then widespread metastatic calcification has not occurred in their cardiovascular system and it has not occurred in other organs

of their bodies. (*S*) No symptoms of calcification occur. Either an overdose of irradiated ergosterol has been given these adult rats or a vitamin C preparation was given them. (*V*) Therefore, a vitamin C preparation was given to them.

11. Either Smith wins the award or, if Jones' work was recognized as superior and his discovery was regarded as highly significant, then Jones wins the award. (*S, W, D, J*) Smith does not win the award. Therefore, if Jones' work was regarded as highly superior, then either his discovery was not regarded as highly significant or Jones wins the award.

12. If both the forms are understood and the problem is not solved, then the statements are vague. (*F, P, V*) It is not the case either that the forms are understood or that the work is complete. (*C*) If the work is complete, then the answers are correct. (*A*) Either the problem is not solved or the answers are correct. Therefore, the statements are vague.

13. If death has been rediscovered as an important philosophical problem, then existential philosophers have contributed to awakening interest in this problem and international conflicts have contributed to awakening interest in questions regarding death. (*D, E, C*) Not both have existential philosophers contributed to awakening interest in this problem, and Heidegger not be recognized for his discussions regarding dread and death. (*H*) Death has been rediscovered as an important philosophical problem. Therefore, Heidegger is recognized for his discussions regarding dread and death, and international conflicts have contributed to awakening interests in questions regarding death.

14. If the report is correct and the contract is good, then the deal goes through. (*R, C, D*) If it is the case that if the contract is good, the deal goes through, then we go to Vienna. (*V*) We do not go to Vienna. Either it is the case either that the report is correct or that the deal goes through, or we make money. (*M*) Thus, either the deal goes through or we make money.

15. Either John is innocent or both Beth is telling the truth and James is not telling the truth. (*J, B, A*) If either John is innocent or Beth is telling the truth, then the prosecution has a weak case. (*P*) Either it is the case that either the prosecution does not have a weak case or that the defense attorney will expose the cover-up, or John is innocent. (*D*) Thus, either John is innocent or both the defense attorney will expose the cover-up and James is not telling the truth.

D. Review the exercise at the end of Section 9.5.

11.3 CONDITIONAL PROOFS AND INDIRECT PROOFS

Another way to establish the validity of an extended argument is the use of conditional proofs. Such proofs are relevant to cases in which the conclusion has the form of a conditional statement or can be replaced by a conditional statement.

Consider the following argument:

Not both can some sedimentary rocks be weakly magnetized and this factor be irrelevant to the original formation of these rocks. (W, F)

If this factor is not irrelevant to the original formation of these rocks, then the magnetism in sedimentary rocks provides evidence for determining the direction of the earth's magnetic field at the time of the formation of these rocks. (D)

Either the magnetism in sedimentary rocks does not provide evidence for determining the direction of the earth's magnetic field at the time of the formation of these rocks, or there is strong evidence to support the hypothesis of a continental drift. (H)

Therefore, if some sedimentary rocks are weakly magnetized, then there is strong evidence to support the hypothesis of a continental drift.

A validation of this argument using the form of a conditional proof begins with an added premise as an assumption:

(1) $\sim(W \cdot F)$
(2) $\sim F \supset D$
(3) $\sim D \vee H$
———————————
   $\therefore W \supset H$

(4) W	AP	(Added premise)
(5) $\sim F$	(1), (4)	DCA
(6) D	(2), (5)	MP
(7) $\sim\sim D$	(6)	DN
(8) H	(3), (7)	DA
(9) $W \supset H$	(4)–(8)	CP (Conditional proof)

The conclusion, $W \supset H$, is in the form of a conditional statement. The first step in the proof states the antecedent of this conditional as an added premise. We indicate the conditional nature of this premise and the steps dependent upon its addition by indentation and two right-angle markings. We label the added (and conditional) premise with the abbreviation AP, indicating an added or assumed premise. The entries of forms of proof within this indented section refer to forms that logically follow from the added or assumed premise taken together with the original premises. Thus, in the case above, if W as the added premise is true, then $\sim F$ is also true, as is D and H. The final step in the conclusion shows that, by the use of this conditional proof, it must be the case that if the premises are true, then $W \supset H$ also is true. Given the premises, $W \supset H$ is a necessary conclusion. This type of validation is optional and is useful in simplifying some forms of proof.

Another form of proof is the *reductio ad absurdum*, or indirect proof. This kind of proof establishes that the negation of the conclusion requires a contradiction to occur within the set of statements used as premises. Therefore, in order to avoid this absurdity (of establishing by denial of the conclusion that a statement occurring in the premise has to be assigned values that are both true and false), this argument shows that the conclusion must be true.

The proof begins by the denial of the conclusion. Consider the following argument:

If the intelligence information is correct, then tension within minority groups is building up in this metropolitan area. (I, T)

If tension within minority groups is building up in this metropolitan area, then greater effort to achieve conditions lessening tensions needs to be made. (A)

Either peaceful settlement of issues is attained or greater effort to achieve conditions lessening tensions is not being made. (P)

The intelligence information is correct.

Therefore, peaceful settlement of issues is attained.

(1)	$I \supset T$		
(2)	$T \supset A$		
(3)	$P \lor \sim A$		
(4)	I		

	$\therefore P$		
(5)	$\sim P$	**AP**	
(6)	$\sim A$	(3), (5)	DA
(7)	$\sim T$	(2), (6)	MT
(8)	$\sim I$	(1), (7)	MT
(9)	$I \cdot \sim I$	(4), (8)	Conj.
(10)	P	(5)–(9)	**IP** (Indirect proof)

internal contradiction

The proof above shows that if the conclusion P is assumed to be false $(\sim P)$, then I must be false $(\sim I)$. However, the premises require I to be true. Therefore, the added *reductio* premise, $\sim P$, must be false. The assumption of the truth of $\sim P$ introduces a contradiction in the premises and the resulting argument is shown to be absurd.

In an indirect proof one adds the denial of the conclusion as a *reductio* premise and marks this premise and any other statement derived by its use by two right-angle markings and indentation in the proof. An indirect proof is acceptable only if it shows that a conclusion derived by the added (or *reductio*) premise introduces a contradiction in the argument.

The example above shows that if the *reductio* premise is accepted, the following contradiction develops in the argument:

(5) Peaceful settlement of issues is not attained.

(6) Greater effort to achieve conditions lessening tension is not to be made.

(7) Greater racial tension is not being built up in large cities.

(8) The intelligence information is not correct.

(9) The intelligence information is correct and the intelligence information is not correct.

The adding of the *reductio* premise in the fifth entry leads to the contradiction in the ninth step. Hence, the added *reductio* premise must be false.

The indirect proof is a variant of the conditional proof. An alternative way of writing the indirect proof also exemplifies its use as a form of conditional proof. This alternative procedure also is the form for writing an indirect proof preferred by some logicians. This form uses addition after establishing a contradiction by use of the assumption made in the initial step of the indirect proof. Compare the following valid alternative proof with the one already given:

(1)	$I \supset T$		
(2)	$T \supset A$		
(3)	$P \lor {\sim}A$		
(4)	I		
	$\therefore P$		
(5)	${\sim}P$		AP
(6)	${\sim}A$	(3), (5)	DA
(7)	${\sim}T$	(2), (6)	MT
(8)	${\sim}I$	(1), (7)	MT
(9)	$I \lor P$	(4)	Add.
(10)	P	(9), (8)	DA
(11)	${\sim}P \supset P$	(5)–(10)	IP
(12)	$P \lor P$	(11)	MC
(13)	P	(12)	Rep.

Conditional and indirect proofs can provide a manner of beginning a proof, where there is difficulty in deciding the steps needed to write an extended proof by the more traditional method. They also provide a simpler manner of writing some proofs, and can be useful in justifying a step needed within a proof. (In such cases, the proof can begin prior to the introduction of these procedures and extend beyond them.)

EXERCISES

A. Construct conditional or indirect proofs for the following arguments.

_1. (1) $D \supset E$
   (2) $E \supset F$
   (3) $F \supset G$
       $\therefore D \supset G$

2. (1) $\sim A \vee B$
   (2) $\sim(B \cdot \sim C)$
   (3) $\sim C$
       $\therefore \sim A$

_3. (1) $\sim A \vee B$
   (2) $\sim(B \cdot \sim C)$
   (3) $\sim D \supset \sim C$
       $\therefore A \supset D$

4. (1) $(\sim A \vee B) \cdot (\sim A \vee C)$
   (2) $\sim B \vee \sim C$
   (3) $\sim A \supset (D \cdot \sim E)$
   (4) $(\sim D \vee E) \vee F$
       $\therefore F$

—5. (1) $(\sim A \vee \sim C) \vee B$
   (2) $\sim C \supset D$
   (3) $E \vee \sim D$
   (4) $\sim E \cdot A$
       $\therefore B$

6. (1) $A \cdot (B \supset C)$
   (2) $C \supset D$
   (3) $\sim(\sim B \cdot A)$
   (4) $\sim D \vee (\sim E \vee F)$
       $\therefore E \supset F$

_7. Either more taxes are not asked or there will be controversy. (T, C) Not both can there be controversy and there not be congressional hearings. (H) If there are congressional hearings, then there will be greater voter discontent. (D) Therefore, if there is not greater voter discontent, then the taxes will not be asked.

8. Not both will there be strong opposition to the legislation and there not be a fight on the floor. (O, F) If there is a floor fight, then there will be executive pressure and party division will occur. (P, D) Party division will not occur. Either there will be strong opposition to the legislation or stronger Social Security benefits will be made available. (S) Therefore, stronger Social Security benefits will be made available.

9. Either the strike is not successful or wages will rise. (*S, R*) If wages do rise, then there will be an increase in the cost of producing automobiles. (*C*) Not both can there be an increase in the cost of producing automobiles and the price of automobiles not increase. (*P*) If the price of automobiles increases, then the cost-of-living index will rise. (*I*) Therefore, if the strike is successful, the cost-of-living index will rise.

10. If either a public announcement is made about opening bids or kickbacks are not made, then the prices paid for goods and services are noted in public documents. (*A, K, D*) The prices paid for goods and services are not noted in public documents. If kickbacks are made and a public announcement is not made about opening bids, then a public investigation is held. (*I*) Therefore, a public investigation is held.

B. Use statement connectives and the indicated statement abbreviations in writing the following arguments. Use extended proofs to establish validity or a cross-section of the truth table to prove invalidity.

1. Either a job is not interesting or it is challenging. (*I, C*) Not both is a job challenging and it fails to provide an opportunity for developing abilities. (*O*) Therefore, if a job fails to provide an opportunity for developing abilities, it is not interesting.

2. If greater benefits are made possible, then both payments are higher and the sense of security is stronger. (*B, P, S*) Greater benefits are made possible. Either the sense of security is not stronger or less fear of catastrophic illness occurs. (*F*) Therefore, less fear of catastrophic illness occurs.

3. If an actor does not have an agent, then he has to negotiate contracts for himself. (*A, N*) It is not the case both that an actor has to negotiate contracts for himself and that he not need to secure satisfactory provisions in the contract. (*P*) If an actor needs to secure satisfactory provisions in the contract, then he needs to be satisfied with his working arrangements. (*W*) Therefore, if he does not have an agent, he needs to be satisfied with his working arrangements.

4. If the domestic difficulties continue, then either troublesome issues do not come to the surface or the account of their intensity is unreliable. (*D, T, A*) Either the account of their intensity is reliable, or the troubles of the president are exaggerated. (*E*) The domestic difficulties continue and troublesome issues do come to the surface. Therefore, the troubles of the president are exaggerated.

5. If inflation is curtailed, then income taxes are increased and interest rates are reduced. (*I, T, R*) If widespread unemployment threatens, then interest rates are not reduced. (*U*) If income taxes are increased, then increased dissatisfaction among voters will spread and widespread unemployment threatens. (*D*) Income taxes are increased. Therefore, inflation is not curtailed.

6. Not both can Epictetus go back to the traditions of Zeno and not be concerned about apathy on occasions of tension. (*Z, A*) If Epictetus is concerned about apathy on occasions of tension, then he taught that man should be the master and not the victim of circumstances. (*M*) Either Epictetus was a Stoic philosopher, or he did not teach that man should be the master and not the

victim of circumstances. (S) Not both was he a Stoic philosopher and not a Roman slave. (R) He goes back to the tradition of Zeno. Therefore, he was a Roman slave.

7. If the plant is not built, then if we have more workers without jobs, then more families will suffer. (P, W, F) More families will not suffer. If either the plant is built or we do not have more workers without jobs, then other businesses will grow. (G) Thus, other businesses will grow.

8. Either we get ahead or we have to play catch up. (A, C) Either we get ahead or we make mistakes. (M) If either we get ahead or both we have to play catch up and we make mistakes, then it will be a rough game. (R) Therefore, it will be a rough game.

9. Either John arrives or it is the case that Steve is ill and that both the car does not work and bad weather is expected. (J, S, C, W) John does not arrive. Either the car works, or it is not the case either that we can go to the beaches or that we can go to the mountains. (B, M) Thus, we cannot go to the mountains.

10. If Aristotle formulated the rules of the categorical syllogism, then the categorical syllogism is a very old form of argument. (A, O) Not both do other arguments supplement the categorical syllogism and the categorical syllogism be a very old form of argument. (S) If other arguments do supplement the categorical syllogism, then modern logic needs to be studied. (M) Therefore, if Aristotle formulated the rules of the categorical syllogism, then modern logic needs to be studied.

11. If there is a healthy interaction between the arts and the sciences, then both fields are enriched. (H, E) If there is no opportunity for a healthy interaction between the arts and the sciences, then both fields are impoverished. (O, I) Either there is a healthy interaction between the arts and the sciences or there is no opportunity for healthy interaction between them. If either both fields are enriched or both fields are impoverished, then there is need for efforts of mutual appreciation of the accomplishments of the other. (A) Therefore, there is need for efforts of mutual appreciation of the accomplishments of the other.

12. Not both can an action be rational and not anticipate a desired result. (A, D) Not both can a desired result be anticipated and it not satisfy some interest or it not meet some need. (I, N) If a result meets some need and satisfies some interest, then adequate motivation is needed for encouraging the action. (M) Therefore, if adequate motivation is not needed for encouraging the action, the action is not rational.

13. If Judge Smith's decision is arbitrary or if it is uninformed, then the decision can be appealed successfully. (A, U, S) If the decision can be appealed successfully, then if both competent attorneys appeal the case and they exercise good judgment, the decision will be reversed. (C, E, R) The decision will not be reversed. Competent attorneys appeal the case and they exercise good judgment. Therefore, Judge Smith's decision is not arbitrary and it is not uninformed.

14. If the support of the prime minister does not fade away, then either he has the strong support of labor or he has the strong support of industry. (F, L, I) If either the prime minister supports policies essential for strengthening

economic conditions or he supports conditions essential for strengthening foreign policy, then his support does not fade away. (*E, C*) He supports policies essential for strengthening economic conditions. Therefore, it is not the case both that he does not have the strong support of labor and that he does not have the strong support of industry.

15. If the price is right, then the quality is good and the price is competitive. (*R, G, C*) If either the quality is good or the price is competitive, then the package is a good buy. (*B*) Thus, if the package is a good buy, then the price is right.

16. Either Mary returns to school, or both Jane goes home and Sue takes up flying. (*M, J, S*) If either Mary returns to school or Sue takes up flying, then Doris gets a new job. (*D*) Therefore, either Doris gets a new job and Mary returns to school or Doris gets a new job and Jane goes home.

17. If either Russia's split with Communist China continues or Communist China continues her policy of seeking to expand her sphere of influence, then Russia's security will be threatened. (*S, E, T*) If Russia's security is threatened, then if Communist China continues her policy of seeking to expand her sphere of influence, China will not refrain from further nuclear experiments. (*N*) Russia's split with Communist China continues and Communist China continues her policy of seeking to expand her sphere of influence. Therefore, China will not refrain from further nuclear experiments.

18. If and only if higher education becomes less concerned with research will it provide the optimum learning situations in freshman and sophomore courses. (*R, L*) If higher education provides the optimum learning situations in freshman and sophomore courses, then innovations in the curriculum will be accelerated. (*I*) It is not the case both that there is no major breakthrough in the relation of faculties to students and that innovations in the curriculum will be accelerated. (*B*) There is no major breakthrough in the relation of faculties to students. Therefore, higher education does not become less concerned with research.

19. Either the governor is not aware of the primary interests of the voters or, if he is interested in winning the election, then he needs to pay more attention to the polls. (*A, W, P*) If either the governor is not interested in winning the election or he needs to pay more attention to the polls, then he needs to be more critical of his advisors. (*C*) Either he does not need to be more critical of his advisors or he needs to bring in persons with newer ideas. (*N*) The governor is aware of the primary interests of voters. Therefore, he needs to bring in persons with newer ideas.

20. Either the injections were harmless or their side effects were not obvious immediately. (*H, O*) If their side effects were not obvious immediately, then either counteracting agents were present or the dose was small. (*C, S*) If either counteracting agents were present or the dose was small, then there are no visible symptoms of disturbance. (*D*) There are no visible symptoms of disturbance. Therefore, the injections were harmless.

21. Either it is true that either we have followed the proper procedure for peace or peace is not assured by making agreements, or else peace does not require greater economic productivity in less-developed nations. (*F, A, E*) If the threats of war continue, it is the case both that we have not followed the

proper procedures for peace and that peace requires more economic productivity in less-developed nations. (*T*) It is the case both that either peace is not assured by making agreements or peace does not require more economic productivity in less-developed nations and that threats of war continue. Therefore, peace is not assured by making agreements.

CHAPTER 12

QUANTIFICATION LOGIC

Integrates all logics (previously studied in this book) into one system.
Deals w/ indicative mood only

12.1 QUANTIFIED STATEMENTS

Preceding chapters discussed arguments using simple and compound statements. In this chapter such statements are broken down into more elementary units. We shall seek to unify arguments using such statements into a more inclusive system. We shall analyze ways of writing and manipulating quantifiers. And we shall develop rules for using quantified expressions in writing proofs. This material requires further refinement for more complex problems in the subject area. A detailed treatment of logic using quantifiers falls beyond the scope of this discussion.

Universal and Existential Quantifiers

In the section on the logic of truth functions, we dealt with complete statements and saw how we can write proofs using such statements. In this chapter we shall examine ways of breaking down statements into more basic elements. This will make possible an analysis of the internal structure of such statements.

Consider the following argument from the standpoint of the logic of truth functions:

All humans are rational.

All students are humans.

Thus, all students are rational.

It has the form

$$H$$
$$S$$
$$\therefore R$$

We have an invalid form in the strict logic of truth functions, but the argument is valid when other procedures are used. By having a means of analyzing the internal structure of such statements, we can develop an argument form showing that the above argument is valid in a logic that both uses truth functions and is more inclusive than the logic of truth functions.

In much of this chapter we shall be dealing with statements that are categorical or that can be rewritten as categorical statements. We have distinguished in Chapter 7 four different kinds of categorical statements:

A All humans are mortal.

E No humans are mortal.

I Some humans are mortal.

O Some humans are not mortal.

In syllogistic logic there are two basic quantifiers, "all" and "some." In quantification logic we have similar quantifiers. But for universal quantification we use such expressions as "for anything in the universe" or "for everything in the universe." To express existential quantification we use words like "there is something" or "there exists at least one thing."

The symbol used for universal quantification is (x). It signifies "for any x."

The symbol used for existential quantification is $(\exists x)$. It signifies "there is an x."

Let us look at the way we construct statements using the symbols (x) and $(\exists x)$. In the following set one can render the first statement in any of the other ways found in the set:

All miners are exploiters.

Everything is such that if it is a miner, then it is an exploiter.

Everything x is such that if x is a miner, then x is an exploiter.

(x) (x is a miner $\supset$ x is an exploiter)

(x) $(Mx \supset Ex)$ [$Mx = x$ is a miner; $Ex = x$ is an exploiter]

Consider another statement:

Some workers are miners.

There are other ways of saying the same thing:

> There is at least one thing such that that thing is a worker and that thing is a miner.

> There is an x such that that x is a worker and that x is a miner.

> $(\exists x)(Wx \cdot Mx)$ [$Wx = x$ is a worker]

In each of the above sets of statements we reached a quantified sentence that expressed a precise meaning of the original sentence in that set. We can use these quantified sentences as premises to construct the following argument:

$$(x)(Mx \supset Ex)$$
$$\underline{(\exists x)(Wx \cdot Mx)}$$
$$\therefore (\exists x)(Wx \cdot Ex)$$

We are interested in showing a way to construct proofs for arguments using quantified statements like those above.

Individuals and Properties

In the logic of quantification, we use the notions of individuals and properties. We can attribute a property such as "tall" to the individual "John." And we can say "John is tall." By using the abbreviation j for "John" and T for "tall" we can also abbreviate the above sentence as Tj. In such cases the property abbreviation, a capital letter, comes first. The abbreviation for the individual is a lowercase letter to the right of the letter for the property. Other examples of such abbreviations are: "Sue is clever," Cs, and "Beth is artistic," Ab.

But we use the notion of individual in a much broader sense than the above illustrations might suggest. An individual can be any specific object whether animate or inanimate. An individual can be a specific rabbit, a specific building, a specific mountain, or a specific nail.

In the logic of quantification, we designate the name of individuals by using lowercase letters from a through t. These letters also are constants for individuals. In a given context they have a fixed value. We use capital letters such as A, M, S, and V as abbreviations for properties. These letters also are property constants and in a given context they signify a given property. In the abbreviations given previously (Tj, Cs, and Ab), T, C, and A are property constants, j, s, and b are individual (or name) constants.

There is a heavy burden placed upon the notion of properties in the logic of quantification. Since there is use of predicates to attribute properties to individuals, we frequently call this kind of logic "predicate logic."

Place Holders

We also need to use place holders in predicate logic. In a previous example we used the form, $(x)(Mx \supset Ex)$. In this sentence the x following both the M and the E is a place holder. The x is a stand-in for any individual that we can substitute for "it." That is, the x stands for any individual such as Smith, Jones, . . . , and John Doe, who has the property of being a miner.

We also use capital letters, beginning with F, as place holders for properties. But we have to identify these place holders by the context in which they occur. There are contexts in which they are assigned other values. In the following example F and G have use as place holders (or as variables) for properties. $(x)(Mx \supset Ex)$ has the quantified statement form $(x)(Fx \supset Gx)$.

One-Place Predicates and Multiple-Place Predicates

We need to distinguish one-place predicates from multiple-place predicates. Some properties like "tall" or "artistic" can characterize a single individual. Thus we can say "Joe is tall" or "Mary is artistic." We can write these statements as Tj or Am. The constants for names, j and m, have one place after the properties abbreviated by T and by A. That is, in the above examples T is a one-place predicate and so is A.

Other properties characterize two individuals or the same individual twice. Some relational properties like "is older than" or "loves" are examples. We can abbreviate the sentence "Frank loves Sue" as Lfs. The property abbreviated as L has two individuals, f and s, that have places on its right side.

Other properties require three or more predicates. We can write the sentence, "St. Louis is between Chicago and Memphis," with the abbreviation $Bscm$.

We shall be interested in this chapter primarily with one-place predicates which are also called "monadic predicates." But in dealing with multiple-place predicates there is particular need to expand the material that we use in this chapter.

Scope of Quantifiers

In predicate logic there is continued use of parentheses, brackets, and braces to avoid ambiguity in the writing of a quantified sentence. In addition to the kind of job parentheses and other such markings have in the logic of truth functions, they provide a means to make explicit those parts of an expression to which a quantifier applies. Consider the following examples:

$(x)(x$ is organic v x is inorganic)

$(x)(x$ is organic) v $(x)(x$ is inorganic)

The first sentence holds that "For everything x, either that x is organic or that x is inorganic." That is, "everything either is organic or is inorganic." The second statement reads "Either for everything x, x is organic or for everything x, x is inorganic." That is, "Either everything is organic or everything is inorganic." The placing of the parentheses makes a difference in what the sentence signifies.

The scope of a quantifier is the elements that it governs in any given expression. A quantifier covers the entire set of parentheses (or brackets or braces) beginning immediately after the quantifier (or set of quantifiers). But such parentheses can have a tilde, "$\sim$," in front of them. In the following sentence forms, the quantifier (x) governs only the form $(Fx \supset Gx)$:

$(x)(Fx \supset Gx)$

$(x)(Fx \supset Gx)\cdot(y)Hy$

If there are no parentheses (or similar markings) following a quantifier, then the quantifier governs only the single unified expression (together with a "$\sim$" in some cases) that immediately follows it. In the following cases the quantifier governs only the form Fx or the form $\sim Hx$:

$(x)Fx$ V Gy $(x)\sim Hx$ V Gy

If there are multiple quantifiers occurring next to each other, then any quantifier on the left includes the remaining quantifiers in its scope. In the form $(x)(\exists y)Fxy$, the quantifier (x) includes $(\exists y)$ in its scope. But in the form $(x)(Fx \supset Gx)\cdot(y)(Hy \supset Iy)$, the (y) is not in the scope of (x).

Bound Variables and Free Variables

We shall begin using the more traditional notion of variable in the same way that we have been using the notion of place holder. Some variables are bound and others are free. The difference between a bound variable and a free variable depends upon whether the quantifier for a given variable covers that variable in the expression in which that variable appears. A bound variable is one whose quantifier includes it within its scope. A free variable is one that in a given context does not fall within the scope of a quantifier appropriate for it. An expression having a free variable is an open sentence. In the following instances x is used as a free variable. These expressions are also open sentences:

x is a friend.

x is square and x is small.

If x is a dance, then x is an art.

A variable such as x in an open sentence has the meaning of an indefinite "it," as in "It is a friend" or "It is an ace." In these cases the "it" covers an unspecified object or set of objects, as in the expression "_____ is a friend." Open sentences are not true or false in themselves. But such sentences can become true or false either by quantifying them or by providing an instance of them. The statement used previously, $(x)(Mx \supset Ex)$, either is true or false. It quantifies the previously open sentence $(Mx \supset Ex)$. Likewise, the statement "If Joe Z. Smith is a miner, then he is an exploiter" is true or is false. Statements like $(x)(Mx \supset Ex)$ or "If Tom Z. Jones is a miner, then he is an exploiter" are closed sentences. A closed sentence has no free variables.

It is essential to be able to identify bound variables and free variables in order to use the rules of predicate logic. There are instances when some operations can be carried out only if a variable is bound in an expression. There are other cases in which we can perform other operations only if a variable is free.

Writing Statements in Quantification Logic

The use of quantification logic makes possible the use of many different sentence constructions. By analyzing the examples that follow one can get an insight into the way we can quantify statements. We shall begin by showing how we can write in quantified logic the form of categorical statements in the following table:

A	All F is G.	$(x)(Fx \supset Gx)$
E	No F is G.	$(x)(Fx \supset {\sim}Gx)$
I	Some F is G.	$(\exists x)(Fx \cdot Gx)$
O	Some F is not G.	$(\exists x)(Fx \cdot {\sim}Gx)$

Let us consider some examples of the kinds of sentences we shall be using. In some of these examples we provide two sentences that one can write with the same quantified sentence:

(1) All humans are mortals.
  Every human is mortal.
  $(x)(x \text{ is human} \supset x \text{ is mortal})$
  $(x)(Hx \supset Mx)$

(2) No students are dull persons.
Nothing that is a student is dull.
$(x)(x$ is a student $\supset$ x is not a dull person)
$(x)(Sx \supset \sim Px)$

(3) Some ores are iron.
There are some ores that are iron.
$(\exists x)(x$ is an ore $\cdot x$ is iron)
$(\exists x)(Ox \cdot Ix)$

(4) Some metals are not expensive.
There is something that is a metal and that something is not expensive.
$(\exists x)(x$ is a metal $\cdot x$ is not expensive)
$(\exists x)(Mx \cdot \sim Ex)$

(5) Everything is round.[1] (Rx)
$(x)x$ is round
$(x)Rx$

(6) Something is square. (Sx)
$(\exists x)x$ is square
$(\exists x)Sx$

(7) Someone likes someone (or other).
$(\exists x)(\exists y)x$ likes y
$(\exists x)(\exists y)Lxy$

(8) Everyone loves someone (or other). $(Px = x$ is a person)
$(x)(\exists y)x$ loves y
$(x)(\exists y)Lxy$ or $(x)[Px \supset (\exists y)(Py \cdot Lxy)]$

(9) Someone loves everyone.
$(\exists x)(y)x$ loves y
$(\exists x)(y)Lxy$

(10) Everyone loves everyone.
$(x)(y)x$ loves y
$(x)(y)Lxy$

(11) Some grapes are either purple or green. (Gx, Px, Rx)
$(\exists x)[Gx \cdot (Px \lor Rx)]$

(12) Every guard is fast and strong. (Gx, Fx, Sx)
$(x)[Gx \supset (Fx \cdot Sx)]$

---

[1] "Each one," "everyone," and "anyone" traditionally are interpreted as requiring universal quantifiers in an affirmative context. "Not each one," "not everyone," and "not all" are interpreted as requiring existential quantifiers. "Not any," like "none," requires a universal quantifier. "Someone" may mean "anyone" in some sentences or "at least one" in other sentences. If it refers to "anyone," a universal quantifier is used. If it means "at least one," an existential quantifier is used. Examples in this book are limited to the meaning of "at least one."

(13) If all players carry out their assignment, then some receivers catch passes.
(Lx, Ax, Ry, Sy)
$(x)(Lx \supset Ax) \supset (\exists y)(Ry \cdot Sy)$

(14) Either some students are sharp or some teachers are good instructors.
(Dx, Hx, Ty, Iy)
$(\exists x)(Dx \cdot Hx) \lor (\exists y)(Ty \cdot Iy)$

(15) Some tackles are stronger than some guards. (Tx, Gy, S)
$(\exists x)(\exists y)[(Tx \cdot Gy) \cdot Sxy]$

(16) If all students are learners, then they are alert. (Sx, Lx, Ax)
$(x)[(Sx \supset Lx) \supset (Sx \supset Ax)]$

(17) Wood is lighter than water. (L, Wx, Ty)
$(x)(y)[(Wx \cdot Ty) \supset Lxy]$

As a general rule, in writing quantified statements a universal quantifier is used to quantify an open sentence having a horseshoe as the primary connective. An existential quantifier is used to quantify an open sentence having a dot as the primary connective.

A quantifier should include any variable over which it ranges in a sentence. Use of personal pronouns to refer to previous parts of a sentence provides a basis for having one quantifier to range both over the original variable and over the variable for the pronoun that refers back to it. Thus, we write the sentence, "If all roses are red, then they are pretty," as $(x)[(Rx \supset Dx) \supset (Rx \supset Px)]$.

In introducing a variable, the context needs to provide some basis for determining the set of objects to which the variable applies. Such a set of objects is the domain of that variable. One domain may be living things, another may be numbers, and a third may be statements. Unless there is some implicit restriction of the domain of discourse, there is the presumption that the domain is the universe. But frequently such an implicit restriction is present. In saying "Someone loves someone," we usually would be talking about the domain of persons.

From the previous examples we can note some additional changes we are making in writing the symbols for statements in the logic of quantification:

1. One writes a universal categorical statement as a conditional statement.

2. One writes a particular categorical statement as a conjunctive statement.

3. One can symbolize many statements that can be translated into standard categorical statements without restating the sentence in a standard categorical pattern.

4. One writes the variables for a relational expression, such as ". . . x is greater than y_____," as *Gxy* rather than as *xRy*.

We have seen that in writing names of individuals we use constants. Let us look at some other examples of writing names:

(1) Mary is a teacher.
     Tm

(2) Smith is not old.
     ~*Os*

(3) If Jane is alert, then she answers the question.
     Aj ⊃ Qj

(4) Carl is older than Dan.
     Ocd

(5) If Carol is older than Debbie and Debbie is older than Eva, then Carol is older than Eva.
     (Ocd·Ode) ⊃ Oce

The use of "not" requires special attention in the logic of quantification. In some cases we need to provide an accurate translation of a sentence prior to writing any symbols for "not." We discussed such translation problems in Chapter 8 and again in Chapter 10. Consider the expression "none but" in the sentence, "None but the guilty are penalized." This sentence is translated as "All persons who are penalized are guilty." And it would be written *(x)(Px ⊃ Gx)* or *(x)[(Px·Nx) ⊃ Gx]*.

In the logic of truth functions, we have interpreted the strict meaning of the "~" as "it is not the case that." And it retains this meaning in the logic of quantification. In order to avoid some possible repetition let us follow the convention of permitting the expression "it is false that" also to serve as a translation of the "~" when it occurs before a quantifier.

There are occasions when we want to deny a quantified sentence. If one quantifier binds or has within its scope all remaining elements in a sentence, then we deny that sentence by placing a "~" before the quantifier. But if a single quantifier does not bind the sentence that one is denying, then one brackets the complete sentence and places the "~" before the brackets. The denial of *(x)(Fx ⊃ Gx) ⊃ (∃y)(Hy·Iy)* is *~[(x)(Fx ⊃ Gy) ⊃ (∃y)(Hy·Iy)]*. Let us consider the following examples where the abbreviations are obvious:

(1) No students are ill.
     (x)(Sx ⊃ ~Ix)

(2) It is false that no students are ill.
     ~*(x)(Sx ⊃ ~Ix)*

(3) Some apples are not green.
     $(\exists x)(Ax\cdot\sim Gx)$

(4) It is false that some apples are not green.
     $\sim(\exists x)(Ax\cdot\sim Gx)$

(5) It is false that all teachers are geniuses.
     $\sim(x)(Tx \supset Gx)$ or $\sim(y)(Ty \supset Gy)$

(6) It is not the case both that no students are ill and that it is false that all teachers are geniuses.
     $\sim[(x)(Sx \supset \sim Ix)\cdot\mathrel{\sim}(y)(Ty \supset Gy)]$

(7) Not everyone likes everyone. (P = person)
     $(\exists x)(y) \sim Lxy$ or $(\exists x)[Px \supset (y)(Py \supset \sim Lxy)]$

Manipulating Quantifiers

There are occasions when we want to remove a ''~'' when it is placed before a quantifier. We also may want to restate an existential quantified statement in an equivalent form as a universal quantified statement, or vice versa. And we reach these objectives by quantifier negation. In going from a universal quantified statement to an existential quantified statement the $(\exists x)$ replaces the (x) and one places the ''~'' on each flank of the $(\exists x)$. That is, we can replace (x) by $\sim(\exists x)\sim$ and the rest of the statement remains the same. A justification for this move is as follows:

1. Take the statement form $(x)(Fx \supset Gx)$.

2. Its contradiction is $(\exists x)(Fx\cdot\sim Gx)$.

3. We can also contradict the statement form in (2) by placing a ''~'' in front of the quantifier, giving us $\sim(\exists x)(Fx\cdot\sim Gx)$.

4. The use of DeMorgan's law and of the Material Conditional enables us to write (3) as $\sim(\exists x) \sim (Fx \supset Gx)$.

5. The statement forms in both (1) and (4) are contradictions of the statement form in (2). Thus, the statement forms in (1) and (4) are equivalent. And the difference between these written statement forms is that found between (x) and $\sim(\exists x)\sim$.

A similar procedure can show that we can derive an equivalent universal quantified statement from an existential quantified one by exchanging the quantifiers and adding a ''~'' to each side of the derived quantifier. That is, from $(\exists x)Fx$ we can derive the equivalent form $\sim(x)\sim Fx$.

Expansion of Quantified Statements

We can expand quantified statements. We do this by instantiating. Using names of individuals to instantiate, the universal quantified statement $(x)(Mx \supset Ex)$, expands in the following manner:

$$(Ma \supset Ea) \cdot (Mb \supset Eb) \cdot (Mc \supset Ec) \cdot \ldots \cdot (Mn \supset En)$$

There is need to note that with a universal quantified statement the expansion uses the dot, "·," as the connective between the instantiated statements.

Using individual names to instantiate, the existential quantified statement $(\exists x)(Wx \cdot Ex)$ expands in the following way:

$$(Wa \cdot Ea) \lor (Wb \cdot Eb) \lor (Wc \cdot Ec) \lor \ldots \lor (Wn \cdot En)$$

It is essential to note that in expanding an existential quantified statement, the expansion uses the "∨" as the connective between the instantiated statements. And all that is being claimed in expanding a true statement of this kind is that at least one of these disjuncts is true.

In practice it is impractical to complete such expansions beyond a few instantiations. This expansion technique has importance in proving invalidity. But it obviously becomes cumbersome in dealing with proofs of validity, and there are more convenient ways to deal with instantiation. And we shall discuss a way to do this in the next section.

EXERCISES

A. Write the following statements in proper symbols for the logic of quantification.
1. Some women are good speakers. (Wx, Sx)
2. Some oranges are not ripe. (Ox, Rx)
3. All cars are heavy. (Cx, Hx)
4. No books are things on the desk. (Bx, Tx)
5. Some players are strong or fast. (Px, Sx, Tx)
6. Either some teams are poor or some coaches are not good. (Tx, Px, Cy, Gy)
7. It is false that all men are dishonest. (Mx, Dx)
8. John is a graduate. (G, j)
9. Anyone reading the novel is persistent. (Rx, Px)
10. If Joe has interest in the sale, then Tom will buy the car. (Ij, Bt)
11. If all the grain is ripe, then some machines go to the fields. (Gx, Rx, My, Fy)
12. Lead is heavier than water. (H, Lx, Wy)

13. Either all students are late sleepers, or some classes are held at 8 A.M. (Tx, Lx, Cy, Hy)
14. If today is colder than yesterday, and tomorrow is colder than today, then tomorrow will be colder than yesterday. (C, Dx, Yy, Mz)
15. Someone doing this exercise is a premed student. (Dx, Px)
16. It is false that no issues are serious. (Ix, Sx)
17. Either all exercises are difficult or if some problems are easy, then some students do their homework quickly. (Ex, Dx, Py, Ay, Sz, Hz)
18. Someone is happy. (Hx)
19. Everyone admires someone. (Axy)
20. Someone admires everyone. (Axy)

B. State the following sentences in ordinary English.

$Hx = x$ is human
$Rx = x$ is rational
$Lx = x$ is a language user or $Ly = y$ is a language user
$Tx = x$ is a teacher or $Ty = y$ is a teacher
$Fx = x$ is a friend of
$Sx = x$ "is the spouse of"
$m =$ Mary
$s =$ Sue
$j =$ Joe

1. $(x)(Hx \supset Rx)$
2. $(\exists x)(Lx \cdot Rx)$
3. $\sim(x)(Hx \supset \sim Rx)$
4. $(\exists x)(Lx \cdot \sim Hx)$
5. Fjs
6. $\sim Fsm$
7. Fmj
8. $Sjm \supset Smj$
9. $\sim Ssj \supset \sim Sjs$
10. $Ssj \supset \sim Smj$
11. $\sim Sjs \supset Sjm$
12. $(x)(Hx \supset Rx) \cdot (y)(Ty \supset Ly)$
13. $(x)[(Tx \supset Rx) \cdot (Tx \supset Lx)]$

C. In the following sentences or sentence forms, identify the (1) bound variables, (2) free variables, (3) property constants (capital letters other than F, G, H in this case), (4) property variables (F, G, H in this case), (5) open sentences, and (6) closed sentences.

1. $(x)(Bx \supset Cx)$
2. $Fy \supset Gy$
3. $(\exists x)Lx \lor My$
4. $Lx \lor My$
5. $(x)(y)Nxy$
6. $(y)Nzy$
7. $(x)[Fx \supset (Gx \lor Hx)]$
8. $Fy \supset (Gy \lor Hy)$

12.2 RULES OF INFERENCE IN QUANTIFICATION LOGIC

In quantification logic we want to construct proofs to show that an argument is valid. But we have not yet developed a method to use the rules of inference found in truth-functional logic directly on the internal structure of a quantified statement. We need to break down a quantified expression in order to use these rules effectively. Consider the following argument:

All bees are insects.

All insects are fliers.

Thus, all bees are fliers.

By using quantified statements we can reexpress the argument:

$$(x)(Bx \supset Ix)$$
$$(x)(Ix \supset Lx)$$
$$\therefore (x)(Bx \supset Lx)$$

In order to proceed with an argument in quantification logic, we need some way to break down the quantified statements in the last argument. We can do this by providing instances of Ix, Lx, and Bx. Then we can break these premises down as follows:

$By \supset Iy$

$Iy \supset Ly$

By use of the form for a hypothetical syllogism we can derive the open sentence $By \supset Ly$, which makes possible our inferring the conclusion we want. But there is need to justify the way in which we derive this open sentence. In this section we shall develop rules of inference for the logic of quantification.

Rules of Inference of Truth-Functional Logic. In quantification logic we carry over the basic rules of inference of the logic of truth functions. But we cannot use these basic rules of inference to deal with the internal structure of a quantified statement.

The Rule of Replacement. In truth-functional logic any two statements or statement forms that are logically equivalent may replace each other whenever they occur in a proof. This principle also applies to statements and statement forms in quantification logic. It specifically includes quantified expressions. That is, unlike the use of basic argument forms which only apply to a quantified expression as a unit, one can replace one equivalent form by another within a quantified expression. By using DeMorgan's law we can write the equivalent form of $(x)(Fx \lor Gx)$ as $(x) \sim (\sim Fx \cdot \sim Gx)$. This rule of replacement also applies to any new equivalent forms developed in this chapter.

The Rule of Quantifier Equivalence (QE). A universally quantified expression is equivalent to an existentially quantified expression if it is the same in all respects to the other expression, except in the sign of denial or in its absence both before and after the quantifier. Any one of the following lines shows equivalent forms of quantifiers and counts as a rule for the use of QE:

$$
\begin{array}{ll}
(1) & (x)Fx \equiv \sim(\exists x) \sim Fx \\
(2) & \sim(x)Fx \equiv (\exists x) \sim Fx \\
(3) & (x) \sim Fx \equiv \sim(\exists x)Fx \\
(4) & \sim(x) \sim Fx \equiv (\exists x)Fx
\end{array}
$$

The following example shows the way one can use the Rule of Quantifier Equivalence in writing proofs:

It is not the case that some stocks are not risks.

It is not the case that some risks are not exciting.

Therefore, all stocks are exciting.

$$
\begin{array}{lll}
(1) & \sim(\exists x)(Sx \cdot \sim Rx) & \\
(2) & \underline{\sim(\exists x)(Rx \cdot \sim Ex)} & \\
& \therefore (x)(Sx \supset Ex) & \\
(3) & (x) \sim (Sx \cdot \sim Rx) & (1) \text{ QE} \\
(4) & (x)(Sx \supset Rx) & (3) \text{ DeC} \\
(5) & (x) \sim (Rx \cdot \sim Ex) & (2) \text{ QE} \\
(6) & (x)(Rx \supset Ex) & (5) \text{ DeC} \\
(7) & \ldots &
\end{array}
$$

In the above example we eliminate a denial sign before the quantifier by using the Rule of Quantifier Equivalence (QE). We usually can eliminate a denial sign immediately after the quantifier by the use of DeMorgan's law together with the definition of the Material Conditional (DeC).

The Rule of Universal Instantiation (UI). We have seen that in breaking down a quantified expression, one can provide instances of that expression. In providing instances of a quantified expression we instantiate it. There are two kinds of instantiations one can make. One can instantiate by providing an individual name appropriate for a given quantified expression. Let

P be the abbreviation for "past presidents of the United States" and *S* be the abbreviation for "statesmen." And we have the quantified statement $(x)(Px \supset Sx)$. We can instantiate this statement by dropping the quantifier (x) and by substituting the name of a former president for the *x* within the expression $(Px \supset Sx)$. By letting *l*, *a*, and *j* be abbreviations for Abraham Lincoln, John Adams, and Andrew Jackson, we can instantiate the quantified statement $(x)(Px \supset Sx)$ in any of the following ways:

$Pl \supset Sl$

$Pa \supset Sa$

$Pj \supset Sj$

It is essential to recognize that use of small letters like *a*, *j*, and *l* (up to the letter *t*) are names of individuals. For example, in the above case they are constants that name specific individuals such as Adams, Jackson, and Lincoln.

There is a second way we can instantiate the above quantified statement. We can use a variable such as *y* that does not occur previously in the premises. We can let this variable signify "any arbitrarily selected individual that is an instance of the original quantified expression." One can instantiate the statement, $(x)(Px \supset Sx)$, with the open sentence $Py \supset Sy$.

In order to develop rules for instantiation and generalization, it is useful to develop a special set of symbols. We are working toward instantiating a sentence like $(x)(Mx \supset Nx)$ with an open sentence like $My \supset Ny$.

We shall use the Greek letter phi, ϕ, together with a u or a w. ϕu represents any open sentence in which there is at least one u that is a free variable. ϕw also represents an open sentence with a w as a free variable. The u and the w can represent any one of the set of letters from *u* to *z* that we have set aside to use as individual variables. For example, ϕu can represent the open sentence $Mu \supset Nu$ or the open sentence $Mx \supset Nx$. ϕw also can represent open sentences such as $Kw \supset Lw$ or $Ky \supset Ly$. But in order to do a job needed for this occasion we also shall let w represent a constant in this limited context.

There are occasions when we shall want to quantify the open sentence represented by ϕu and we write (u)ϕu. The u variables in (u)ϕu are obviously bound. But without the quantifier (u), the u variables in ϕu are free. For example, if (u)ϕu represents the closed sentence, $(x)(Bx \supset Cx)$, the variables in $(x)(Bx \supset Cx)$ are bound. But if we remove the quantifier, the variables in $Bx \supset Cx$ are free. Many of our rules for instantiating and generalizing will focus on those cases in ϕu and ϕw where the u variables and the w variables are free.

In general, the *Rule of Universal Instantiation* holds that from a universal statement we can derive any of its instances. We can state the rule as follows:

$$\text{UI:} \quad \frac{(u)\,\phi u}{\therefore \phi w}$$

w is any individual variable or constant that replaces all instances of u variables free in ϕu.

If w is an individual variable, then it represents any arbitrarily selected individual that is an instance of the original quantified expression.

Let us use UI in working with a previous example with the following argument:

(1) $(x)(Bx \supset Ix)$
(2) $(x)(Ix \supset Lx)$
$\therefore (x)(Bx \supset Lx)$

We can proceed to instantiate these premises and begin writing its proof as follows:

(3) $By \supset Iy$	(1) UI
(4) $Iy \supset Ly$	(2) UI
(5) $By \supset Ly$	(3), (4) HS
(6) . . .	

In some arguments a singular name, such as "Jones," occurs in a premise. Consider the statement, "Jones is president." One can abbreviate this as Pj. We can use this statement as a premise in the following argument and proof:

All presidents are citizens.
Jones is president.

Thus, Jones is a citizen.

(1) $(x)(Px \supset Cx)$	
(2) Pj	
$\therefore Cj$	
(3) $Pj \supset Cj$	(1) UI
(4) Cj	(3), (2) MP

In the above example the entry in line (3) provides an instance in which line (1) holds. And in line (3) there is instantiation by naming a specific individual rather than by use of the notion of any arbitrarily selected individual. The use of the open sentence, $Py \supset Cy$, to instantiate in line (3) would not have led to fruitful results.

The rule for UI (and for EI) requires that if there is an instantiation of any variable such as u in ϕu by a w in ϕw in a line of a proof, then every occurrence of the free variable u must be instantiated with w. (That is, every u variable free in ϕu has to become a w occurring in ϕw.) This rule prohibits the use of UI (and EI) in the following manner:

(1) $(x)(Fx \supset Gx)$

    $\vdots$

(3) $Fy \supset Gx$ (1) UI   (Wrong)

The rule for UI also provides that in any use of UI, the quantifier that one is dropping in (u)ϕu has to cover the complete line of the proof. This provision prohibits the use of UI (and EI) on lines like the following:

$(x)(Fx \lor Gx) \supset (z)Hz$
$\sim(x)(Fx \supset Gx)$

In both examples the quantifier does not cover the complete line of the proof. (In the second example the quantifier does not cover the "$\sim$.")

The rule for UI (and EI) also requires that all of the elements in ϕu require a corresponding element in ϕw.

This rule prohibits moves like the following:

(1) $(x)[(Fx \supset Gx) \lor Hz]$
(2) $Fy \supset Gy$ (1) UI   (Wrong)

The Rule of Existential Instantiation (EI).   The rule of existential instantiation holds that for any existential statement one can derive an instance of it, provided that the variable used in instantiation does not occur free previously in the proof. We can express this rule by the general form:

$$\text{EI:} \quad \frac{(\exists u)\phi u}{\therefore \phi w}$$

w is an individual variable (and never a constant).

w replaces all instances of u free in ϕu.

w cannot occur free in any prior line of the proof.

One finds an example of the use of EI in an incomplete proof of the following argument:

All blades are sharp. (*Bx, Sx*)

Some steel things are blades. (*Tx*)

Thus, something sharp is steel.

(1) $(x)(Bx \supset Sx)$
(2) $(\exists x)(Tx \cdot Bx)$

$\therefore (\exists x)(Sx \cdot Tx)$

(3) $Ty \cdot By$	(2) EI
(4) $By \supset Sy$	(1) UI
(5) Ty	(3) Simp.
(6) $By \cdot Ty$	(3) Comm.
(7) By	(6) Simp.
(8) Sy	(4), (7) MP
(9) $Sy \cdot Ty$	(5), (8) Conj.
(10) $\ldots$	

The following argument is invalid:

Some advisors are wise.

Some advisors are stupid.

Thus, someone stupid is wise.

(1) $(\exists x)(Ax \cdot Wx)$
(2) $(\exists x)(Ax \cdot Sx)$

$\therefore (\exists x)(Sx \cdot Wx)$ (Invalid)

(3) $Ay \cdot Wy$	(1) EI	
(4) $Ay \cdot Sy$	(2) EI	(Wrong)

In step (4) there is use of y to instantiate. But this violates the rule of existential instantiation, since y occurs in step (3) and cannot be used to instantiate in another line of the proof. To instantiate line (2) we need to use another variable, such as z, that does not appear in a previous line of the proof.

In EI we use only the letters used for individual variables, such as y or z. Although we refer to these letters as variables, in a strict sense they are ambiguous names and they are used similar to the way that we use "John Doe." The reason we are not using constants like a and b in existential instantiation is that these constants are used only for individuals (in this system). And any given individual, such as Bob Hope, may not be an appropriate instance of the expression that we are instantiating.

The following argument also is invalid since we are using the same variable, with EI on two different lines of the proof:

Something is round.
Something is square.

Thus, something round is square. (Invalid)

(1) $(\exists x)Rx$
(2) $(\exists x)Sx$

$\therefore (\exists x)(Rx \cdot Sx)$ (Invalid)

(3) Ry	(1) EI
(4) Sy	(2) EI (Wrong)
(5) $Ry \cdot Sy$	(3), (4) Conj.

It is possible to prove many arguments in quantification logic by the use of UI, EI, and QE, together with conditional or indirect proofs. Consider the following examples:

(1) $(x)(Fx \supset Gx)$	
(2) $(x)(Gx \supset Hx)$	
$\therefore (x)(Fx \supset Hx)$	
(3) $\sim(x)(Fx \supset Hx)$	AP
(4) $(\exists x) \sim (Fx \supset Hx)$	(3) QE
(5) $(\exists x)(Fx \cdot \sim Hx)$	(4) DeC
(6) $Fy \cdot \sim Hy$	(5) EI
(7) $Fy \supset Gy$	(1) UI
(8) $Gy \supset Hy$	(2) UI
(9) $Fy \supset Hy$	(7), (8) HS
(10) $\sim Hy$	(6) Comm. & Simp.
(11) $\sim Fy$	(9), (10) MT
(12) Fy	(6) Simp.
(13) $Fy \cdot \sim Fy$	(11), (12) Conj.
(14) $(x)(Fx \supset Hx)$	(3)–(13) IP

An example of a proof using a two-place predicate is the following:

(1) $(\exists x)(y)(Lxy)$	
$\therefore (\exists x)(\exists y)Lxy$	
(2) $\sim(\exists x)(\exists y)Lxy$	(1) AP
(3) $(x) \sim (\exists y)Lxy$	(2) QE
(4) $(x)(y) \sim Lxy$	(3) QE
(5) $(y)Lzy$	(1) EI
(6) $(y) \sim Lzy$	(4) UI
(7) $\sim Lzw$	(6) UI
(8) Lzw	(5) UI
(9) $Lzw \cdot \sim Lzw$	(8), (7) Conj.
(10) $(\exists x)(\exists y)Lxy$	(2)–(9) IP

Rule of Existential Generalization (EG).   The rule of existential generalization holds (in part) that from an open sentence, one can derive the existential quantification of that sentence.

The rule for EG has the form:

$$\text{EG:} \quad \frac{\phi w}{(\exists u)\phi u}$$

u is a free variable that does not occur free in ϕw.

There must be a comparable free w (or a constant) in ϕw for each u free in ϕu.

ϕw represents any sentence or sentence form in which either a constant, or at least one but not necessarily all free occurrences of w in ϕw, is replaced by u in ϕu.

We need to recognize that the above rule requires the assumption that there is at least one individual in the universe of discourse. This assumption permits us to make the following kind of derivation:

(1) $(x)(Fx \supset Gx)$
    $\therefore (\exists x)(Fx \supset Gx)$
(2) $Fy \supset Gy$ (1) UI
(3) $(\exists x)(Fx \supset Gx)$ (2) EG

Any statement having the form $(\exists x)(Fx \supset Gx)$ is very weak. It holds only that there is something such that if that something is F, then that something also is G. This stated assumption does not permit the following derivation:

(1) $(x)(Fx \supset Gx)$
    $\therefore (\exists x)(Fx \cdot Gx)$ (Invalid)

By instantiating (1) we derive only (2) $Fy \supset Gy$. But we have no way of deriving $Fy \cdot Gy$ solely from $Fy \supset Gy$. Thus, this assumption does not make possible our deriving an I categorical statement directly from an A statement.

EG makes possible the completion of a proof discussed earlier:

(1) $(x)(Mx \supset Ex)$
(2) $(\exists x)(Wx \cdot Mx)$
    $\therefore (\exists x)(Wx \cdot Ex)$
(3) $Wy \cdot My$ (2) EI
(4) $My \supset Ey$ (1) UI
(5) Wy (3) Simp.
(6) My (3) Comm. & Simp.
(7) Ey (4),(6) MP
(8) $Wy \cdot Ey$ (5),(7) Conj.
(9) $(\exists x)(Wx \cdot Ex)$ (8) EG

EG also makes possible for us to derive the statement, "Something is tall," from the premise, "Joe is tall."

$Tj \, / \therefore (\exists x)Tx$
(1) Tj Premise
(2) $(\exists x)Tx$ (1) EG

In any use of **EG** (or **UG** discussed later), there is need for the scope of the quantifier to include the complete line of a proof. Consider the following examples:

$Fzw \cdot Gzw$
_____
$\therefore (\exists y)(Fzy \cdot Gzy)$ **EG**   (Right)

$(Fy \cdot Gy) \cdot Hy$
_____
$\therefore (\exists x)(Fx \cdot Gx) \cdot Hy$ **EG**   (Wrong)

The rule for **EG** (and for **UG**) also blocks these moves.

$(\exists y)(Myz)$
_____
$\therefore (\exists y)(\exists y)(Myy)$ **EG**   (Wrong)

$(\exists y)(Fyz \lor Gyz)$
_____
$\therefore (\exists y)(Fyy \lor Gyy)$ **EG**   (Wrong)

Bxz
_____
$\therefore (\exists x)Bxx$ **EG**   (Wrong)

To avoid these moves, the rule is so stated that if there are two different variables such as y and z on any line, then a single quantifier, such as $(\exists x)$ [or (x)], cannot be used to bind both variables. That is, we want to avoid catching both the y and z variables above by the same quantifier such as $(\exists y)$. This is the significance of the following rule: In **EG** (and **UG**), the u in ϕu must be a free variable that does not occur free in ϕw.

A similar error is found in the following example (T = talks to):

(1) $(x)(\exists y)Txy$ Premise
(2) $(\exists y)Tzy$ (1) UI
(3) Tzw (2) EI
(4) $(\exists z)Tzz$ (3) EG   (Wrong)

In the above case, from "Everyone talks to someone," we have derived "Someone talks to himself," which does not follow from the premise.

In **EG** and in **UG**, we also need to block the following move:

$Fz \cdot (Gw \cdot Hzw)$
_____
$\therefore (\exists x)[Fx \cdot (Gx \cdot Hxx)]$ **EG**   (Wrong)

There is a failure to have for each u variable free in ϕu a comparable w variable free in ϕw.

Rule of Universal Generalization (UG). The rule of universal generalization in a simple but incomplete form holds that one can derive a universal quantified statement from any of its instances. In a more technical way, UG holds that from any arbitrary selected instance of a universally quantified statement, we can derive the universal quantification of that statement subject to needed restrictions. One primary restriction is that the free variable to be generalized cannot be introduced in a proof as a free variable in an assumed premise, and then generalized both when it is derived from the assumed premise *and* when it remains within the scope of that premise. A second restriction is that the free variable to be generalized cannot be derived from a line in the proof introduced by the use of EI. A third restriction is that a u free in ϕu replaces each w free in ϕw.

The general form for Universal Generalization is the following:

$$\text{UG:}\quad \frac{\phi\text{w}}{\therefore(\text{u})\phi\text{u}}$$

w is always an individual variable.

u is a free variable that does not occur in ϕw and a u free in ϕu replaces each occurrence of w free in ϕw. (For each u free in ϕu there must be a comparable w free in ϕw.)

w is not a free variable on a line derived in the proof by the use of EI.

w is not introduced as a free variable in an assumed premise and then generalized (with UG) when (a) it is derived from the assumed premise *and* (b) it remains within the scope of that premise.

UG makes possible the completion of the following proofs:

(1)	$(x)(Fx \supset Gx)$	
(2)	$(x)(Gx \supset Hx)$	
	$\therefore(x)(Fx \supset Hx)$	
(3)	$Fy \supset Gy$	(1) UI
(4)	$Gy \supset Hy$	(2) UI
(5)	$Fy \supset Hy$	(3), (4) HS
(6)	$(x)(Fx \supset Hx)$	(5) UG

(1)	$(x)(y)Fxy$	
	$\therefore(x)(\exists y)Fxy$	
(2)	$(y)Fzy$	(1) UI
(3)	Fzw	(2) UI
(4)	$(\exists y)Fzy$	(3) EG
(5)	$(x)(\exists y)Fxy$	(4) UG

In the use of UG there is a restriction against capturing one variable by another similar to the one discussed in EG. And the general rule is that u in ϕu cannot occur as a variable free in ϕw. Likewise, in the use of UG, u replaces each occurrence of w free in ϕw and for each u free in ϕu, there must be a comparable w free in ϕw.

The rule for **UG** blocks the following:

(1) $(x)(Fx \supset Gx)$
(2) $(\exists x)(Fx \cdot Hx)$
_____
     $\therefore (x)(Gx \cdot Hx)$ (Invalid)
(3) $Fy \cdot Hy$ (2) EI
(4) $Fy \supset Gy$ (1) UI
(5) Fy (3) Simp.
(6) Gy (4), (5) MP
(7) $Hy \cdot Fy$ (3) Comm.
(8) Hy (7) Simp.
(9) $Gy \cdot Hy$ (6), (8) Conj.
(10) $(x)(Gx \cdot Hx)$ (9) UG   (Wrong)

In the above proof there is an incorrect use of **UG** in step (10). In step (3) EI introduces the variable y in the proof. And the rule prohibits a subsequent use of **UG** on the variable introduced by EI.

We want to block the following move where $(x)(\exists y)Txy$ signifies "Everyone talks to someone":

(1) $(x)(\exists y)Txy$ Premise
(2) $(\exists y)Tzy$ (1) UI
(3) Tzw (2) EI
(4) $(x)Tzx$ (3) UG   (Wrong)
(5) $(\exists y)(x)Tyx$ (4) EG   (Invalid argument)

The conclusion of the invalid argument holds that "Someone talks to everyone" and this obviously does not follow from the premise. The error is in line (4). And to prevent this kind of error we need a new restriction. This restriction holds that one cannot use **UG** on a free variable, such as w above, when that variable is on any line derived by EI in the proof. In the above example z is free when we use EI in line (3). This condition prevents the use of **UG** in step (4).

The rule for **UG** blocks the following kind of move:

$Fy \supset Gy$
_____
$\therefore (x)(Fx \supset Gy)$ (Erroneous)

To avoid this error we have the following provision: For any use of **UG**, if a given variable, such as y, is generalized on any line of a proof, then all occurrences of that variable on that line have to be generalized.

Another obvious provision in the rules for **UG** is that one cannot use **UG** on a constant. This restriction prevents us from making the following move where "*Mt*" abbreviates the statement, "Tim is a millionaire":

Mt
$$\therefore (x)Mx \quad \text{(Invalid)}$$

The rule for **UG** also blocks the following kind of move. Let $\sim(x)Ax$ be the abbreviation for the statement, "It is not the case that everything is alive":

(1) $\sim(x)Ax$ Premise
(2) Ay AP
(3) $(x)Ax$ (2) UG   (Wrong)
(4) $(x)Ax\cdot\sim(x)Ax$ (3), (1) Conj.
(5) $\sim Ay$ (2)–(4) IP
(6) $(x)\sim Ax$ (5) UG   (Invalid argument)

The above conclusion reads, "Nothing is alive," which obviously does not follow from the original premise. In step (3) there was the incorrect use of **UG** on a free variable introduced in an assumed premise. This generalization is derived from a free variable in step (3) while it remains within the scope of the assumed premise that introduces that variable.

The following example shows a correct use of **UG** after a variable introduced in a premise is no longer within the scope of that assumption:

All Saturday night specials are dangerous.

Thus, anyone that makes Saturday night specials makes dangerous things.

(1) $(x)(Sx \supset Dx)$
$$\therefore (y)[(\exists x)(Sx\cdot Myx) \supset (\exists x)(Dx\cdot Myx)]$$
(2) $(\exists x)(Sx\cdot Mwx)$ AP
(3) $Sz\cdot Mwz$ (2) EI
(4) Sz (3) Simp.
(5) Mwz (3) Comm. & Simp.
(6) $Sz \supset Dz$ (1) UI
(7) Dz (6), (4) MP
(8) $Dz\cdot Mwz$ (7), (5) Conj.
(9) $(\exists x)(Dx\cdot Mwx)$ (8) EG
(10) $(\exists x)(Sx\cdot Mwx) \supset (\exists x)(Dx\cdot Mwx)$ (2)–(9) CP
(11) $(y)[(\exists x)(Sx\cdot Myx) \supset (\exists x)(Dx\cdot Myx)]$ (10) UG

In summarizing the uses of **UI**, **EI**, **UG**, and **EG** the following provisions hold, together with the additional rules set forth in the statement of the *Simplified Rules in the Logic of Quantification*:

In any use of these inferences there must be both a use of the complete line of a proof, and the quantifier that is dropped or added must cover the complete line of the proof in ϕu.

In EG and UG the new variable added to ϕu cannot already be a variable free in ϕw.

In any use of EI and UG for each case of an original variable free in ϕu or in ϕw, there must be a comparable variable free in ϕw or ϕu. The same principle holds for UI, except that in ϕw the comparable w can be a constant.[2]

Simplified Rules in the Logic of Quantification

The following simplified rules hold for uses of one place predicates in quantification logic:

1. Universal Instantiation (UI):

$$\frac{(u)\phi u}{\therefore \phi w}$$

2. Existential Instantiation (EI):

$$\frac{(\exists u)\phi u}{\therefore \phi w}$$

w cannot be used previously in the proof.

3. Universal Generalization (UG):

$$\frac{\phi w}{\therefore (u)\phi u}$$

w cannot be a variable free on a line derived by the use of EI.
w cannot be introduced as a variable free in an assumed premise and generalized in the scope of that premise.
u cannot occur as a variable free in ϕw.

4. Existential Generalization (EG):

$$\frac{\phi w}{\therefore (\exists u)\phi u}$$

u cannot occur as a variable free in ϕw.

5. Quantifier Equivalence (QE):

$$\sim(u)\phi u \equiv (\exists u) \sim \phi u$$
$$\sim(\exists u)\phi u \equiv (u) \sim \phi u$$

---

[2] This rule requires that in EI the newly introduced w variable be free in ϕw and that in UG the newly introduced u variable also be free in ϕu. The same principle holds for UI and EG except for the possible use of individual constants in ϕw.

Likewise, the above rule requires that in any use of EI and UG, if there is a replacement of one variable in ϕw (for EI) or in ϕu (for UG), then all occurrences of that variable have to be changed into the variable added in the derived line. The same principle holds for UI, except the w in ϕw can be a constant.

In the use of EG there must be a replacement of at least one free variable or constant in ϕw by a different variable free in ϕu.

EXERCISES

A. Identify the errors in the following proposed "derivations."

1. (1) $(x)(Lx \supset Mx)$ Premise
   (2) $(\exists x)(Mx \cdot Nx)$ Premise
   (3) $Ly \supset My$ (1) UI
   (4) $My \cdot Ny$ (2) EI

2. (1) $(x)(Lx \supset Px)$ Premise
   (2) $(\exists x)(Rx \cdot Lx)$ Premise
   (3) $Ry \cdot Ly$ (2) EI
   (4) $Ly \supset Py$ (1) UI
   (5) Ry (3) Simp.
   (6) Ly (3) Comm. & Simp.
   (7) Py (4), (6) MP
   (8) $Ry \cdot Py$ (5), (7) Conj.
   (9) $(x)(Rx \cdot Px)$ (8) UG

3. (1) $(x)Mx$ Premise
   (2) Py AP
   (3) $(x)Px$ (2) UG
   (4) $Py \supset (x)Px$ (2)–(3) CP
   (5) $(z)[Pz \supset (x)Px]$ (4) UG

4. (1) $(x)(Ax \supset Bx)$ Premise
   (2) $Ay \supset Bx$ (1) UI

5. (1) $(x)Cx \supset (Dy \supset Ty)$ Premise
   (2) $Cz \supset (Dy \supset Ty)$ (1) UI

6. (1) $\sim(\exists x)(Fx \cdot Gx)$ Premise
   (2) $\sim(Fy \cdot Gy)$ (1) EI

7. (1) $Mj \supset Nj$ Premise
   (2) $(x)(Mx \supset Nx)$ (1) UG

B. Write proofs for the following arguments.

1. (1) $(x)(Fx \supset Gx)$
   (2) $(x)Fx$
   $\therefore (x)Gx$

2. (1) $(\exists x)(Fx \cdot Gx)$
   (2) $(x)(Gx \supset Hx)$
   $\therefore (\exists x)(Fx \cdot Hx)$

3. (1) $(x)(Ax \supset Bx)$
   (2) $(x)(Bx \supset Cx)$
   $\therefore (x)(\sim Cx \supset \sim Ax)$

4. (1) $(x)[Cx \supset (Dx \lor Ex)]$
   (2) $(\exists x)(Cx \cdot \sim Dx)$
   $\therefore (\exists x)(Cx \cdot Ex)$

5. (1) $(x)[Kx \supset (Lx \cdot \sim Mx)]$
   (2) $(\exists x)(Kx \cdot Nx)$

   $\therefore (\exists x)(Kx \cdot \sim Mx)$

6. (1) $(x)[(Lx \cdot Mx) \supset Nx]$
   (2) $(x)[(Mx \supset Nx) \supset Ox]$

   $\therefore (x)(Lx \supset Ox)$

7. (1) $(x)[(Px \cdot Qx) \supset (Rx \supset Sx)]$
   (2) $(\exists x)(Rx \cdot \sim Sx)$

   $\therefore (\exists x) \sim (Px \cdot Qx)$

8. (1) $(x)[(Px \lor Qx) \supset (Rx \lor Sx)]$
   (2) $(\exists x)(Px \cdot \sim Rx)$

   $\therefore (\exists x)(Px \cdot Sx)$

9. (1) $\sim(\exists x)(Ax \cdot \sim Bx)$
   (2) $(x)[(Ax \supset Bx) \supset Cx]$

   $\therefore (x)Cx$

10. (1) $\sim(x)(Px \supset Qx)$
    (2) $(x)[(Rx \cdot Sx) \supset Qx]$
    (3) $(x)[(Px \lor Tx) \supset Rx]$

    $\therefore (\exists x) \sim Sx$

11. (1) All models are attractive. (Mx, Ax)
    (2) Some models are active in civil rights movements. (Cx)
    (3) All attractive persons are envied persons. (Ex)
    Thus, some persons active in civil rights movements are envied persons.

12. (1) Any actions increasing taxes are actions lowering purchasing power. (Ty, Lx)
    (2) Any actions lowering purchasing power are unpopular with voters. (Ux)
    (3) All actions unpopular with voters are actions threatening political careers. (Px)
    (4) Some actions increasing taxes are a result of new demands for federal spending. (Sx)
    Thus, some actions threatening political careers are a result of new demands for federal spending.

13. (1) Meaninglessness is boredom. (Mx, Bx)
    (2) Boredom is frustration. (Fx)
    (3) Frustration is despair. (Dx)
    (4) Despair is anxiety. (Ax)
    Therefore, meaninglessness is anxiety.

14. (1) Any violence is either dangerous or foolhardy. (Vx, Dx, Fx)
    (2) Anything that is either dangerous or foolhardy is risky. (Rx)
    Thus, if anything is advisable, then if it is violent it is risky. (Ax)

C. Identify the errors in the following proposed "derivations."

1. (1) $(x)(\exists y)Oxy$ Premise
   (2) $(\exists y)Ozy$ (1) UI
   (3) Ozw (2) EI
   (4) $(x)Ozx$ (3) UG
   (5) $(\exists y)(x)Oyx$ (4) EG

2. (1) $(y)(Ozy)$ Premise
   (2) $(x)(Oxx)$ (1) UG

3. (1) $(y)(Ozy)$ Premise
   (2) $(y)(Oyy)$ (1) UG

4. (1) $(\exists x)(y)Oxy$ Premise
   (2) $(y)Ozy$ (1) EI
   (3) Ozz (2) UI
   (4) $(x)Oxx$ (3) UG

D. Write proofs for the following arguments.

1. (1) $(\exists x)(y)Oxy$
        $\therefore (\exists x)(\exists y)Oxy$

2. (1) $(\exists x)(y)Oxy$
        $\therefore (\exists x)Oxx$

3. (1) $(x)(y)(Txy \supset \sim Tyx)$
   (2) Tge
        $\therefore \sim Teg$

4. (1) $(x)(y)(Sxy \supset Syx)$
   (2) $\sim Sba$
        $\therefore \sim Sab$

5. (1) $(x)(y)(z)[(Sxy \cdot Syz) \supset Sxz]$
   (2) $Sab \cdot Sbc$
        $\therefore Sac$

6. Everyone respects everyone. (Rxy) Thus, someone respects himself.

7. No one haunts anyone. (Hxy) Thus, John does not haunt himself. (j)

8. When anyone hurts Joe, then someone needs to help Joe. (j) $\{(x)[Hxj \supset (\exists y)Lyj)]\}$ George hurt Joe. (g) Thus, someone needs to help Joe.

9. Becky is older than Linda and Linda is older than Alan. Thus, Becky is older than Alan. (O, b, l, a) (Use as a second premise $(x)(y)(z)[(Oxy \cdot Oyz) \supset Oxz]$.)

10. James is the son of Tom and Tom is the son of Bill. Thus, James is not the son of Bill. (S, j, t, b) (Use as a second premise $(x)(y)(z)[(Sxy \cdot Syz) \supset \sim Sxz]$.)

11. All good things are fun things. Thus, all producers of good things are producers of fun things. Conclusion: $(y)[(\exists x)(Gx \cdot Pyx) \supset (\exists x)(Fx \cdot Pyx)]$.

12.3 TECHNIQUES IN WORKING WITH ARGUMENTS USING QUANTIFIERS

Proof of Invalidity

In the logic of quantification we can prove an argument is invalid by showing that the argument form can yield a conclusion that is false with premises that are true. In some cases such proofs are as simple as we find them in the logic of truth functions. But in other cases we find more serious difficulties.

One kind of proof of invalidity in the logic of quantification uses a cross-section of the truth table. Its primary use is for arguments having statements with one-place predicates, such as we find in the statement form $(x)(Fx \supset Gx)$. It is impractical to use this method with many arguments having statements with multiple-place predicates, such as $(x)(y)Fxy$ or $(x)(y)(z)Fxyz$.

In writing proofs of invalidity in quantification logic we can use the procedure of expanding a quantified statement. We have seen that in expanding a universal quantified statement such as $(x)(Fx \supset Gx)$, we can write $(Fa \supset Ga) \cdot (Fb \supset Gb) \cdot (Fc \supset Gc) \cdot \ldots \cdot (Fn \supset Gn)$. A universal quantified statement obviously includes each instantiation of it. And for such statements to be true, each instantiation also must be true. One uses a "$\cdot$" to connect this series of conditional statements to each other.

We expand an existential quantified statement such as $(\exists x)(Fx \cdot Gx)$ by using disjuncts. And the resulting expansion is $(Fa \cdot Ga) \lor (Fb \cdot Gb) \lor (Fc \cdot Gc) \lor \ldots \lor (Fn \cdot Gn)$. For a statement having the form $(\exists x)(Fx \cdot Gx)$ to be true, only one of its expanded disjuncts has to be true.

We begin our proof of invalidity by testing for a universe with only one individual. Let us consider the following argument which obviously is invalid:

All dogs are mammals.

All cats are mammals.

Thus, all cats are dogs.

In quantification logic this has the form:

$(x)(Dx \supset Mx)$
$(x)(Cx \supset Mx)$
___
$\therefore (x)(Cx \supset Dx)$

We instantiate the premises and the conclusion by substituting an individual name, such as a, for each occurrence of the variable x in the argument.

The argument now appears as follows:

$Da \supset Ma$
$Ca \supset Ma$
$\therefore Ca \supset Da$

We then draw a cross-section of the truth table and test for invalidity. The cross-section has the following pattern:

Da	Ma	Ca	$Da \supset Ma$	$Ca \supset Ma$	$/\therefore Ca \supset Da$
F	T	T	T	T	F

Some argument forms in quantification logic require that one use a universe of discourse of two (or more) individuals to instantiate to prove invalidity. Consider the following invalid argument and its form:

All problems are interesting.

Some problems are easy.

Thus, all easy things are interesting.

$(x)(Px \supset Ix)$
$(\exists x)(Px \cdot Ex)$
$\therefore (x)(Ex \supset Ix)$

If we use only one individual that we designate as an instance of the premises and the conclusion of the argument, we do not find a way to prove the argument is invalid:

	Pa	Ia	Ea	$Pa \supset Ia$	$Pa \cdot Ea$	$/\therefore Ea \supset Ia$
	T	F	T	F	T	F
or	F	F	T	T	F	F

If we use a universe of two individuals, a and b, then we find a way to show the above argument is invalid. The cross-section of the truth table now has the following pattern:

	Pa	Pb	Ia	Ib	Ea	Eb	$(Pa \cdot Ea) \lor$ $(Pb \cdot Eb)$	$(Pa \supset Ia) \cdot$ $(Pb \supset Ib)$	$/\therefore (Ea \supset Ia) \cdot$ $(Eb \supset Ib)$	
(Row 1)	T	F	T	F	T	T	T	T	F	
(Row 2)							T	F T	T	F

Row 1 shows values that hold for a case in which the premises can be true and the conclusion is false. We add Row 2 to help us check on the truth values assigned in Row 1 to each compound form we introduce in the premises and in the conclusion.

In some complex arguments, we would need to use more than two constants, such as *a*, *b*, and *c*, to prove an argument is invalid. But we shall not consider such cases in this work.

If we have a "~" before a quantifier, we have to use QE to remove the quantifier from that position. Then we may want to use a form of DeMorgan's law to remove a "~" before a set of parentheses. Consider the following invalid argument:

It is false that no birds are song birds.

Some red birds are berry-eaters.

Thus, some berry-eaters are song birds.

(1) $\sim(x)(Rx \supset \sim Sx)$
(2) $(\exists x)(Rx \cdot Ex)$
      $\therefore (\exists x)(Ex \cdot Sx)$
(3) $(\exists x) \sim (Rx \supset \sim Sx)$ (1)   QE
(4) $(\exists x)(Rx \cdot Sx)$ (5)   DeC

Ra	Rb	Ea	Eb	Sa	Sb	$(Ra \cdot Ea) \lor$ $(Rb \cdot Eb)$		$(Ra \cdot Sa) \lor$ $(Rb \cdot Sb)$		$\therefore (Ea \cdot Sa) \lor$ $(Eb \cdot Sb)$	
T	T	T	F	F	T	T		T		F	
						T	F	F	T	F	F

The cross-section shows that the form of the argument is invalid.

If we have a universe with no members (or a class that is null), then we can show invalidity in the following way.

Consider an argument with the premises "All goblins are happy" and the conclusion "Something is happy." Assume that the expression "all goblins" represents a universe of discourse without any individuals. We can give the value of T to the universal quantified statements in which "all goblins" occurs in a premise. And we can give the value of F to the existential statement that occurs as the conclusion. We now have the following cross-section of the truth table:

G	H	$G \supset H$	$\therefore G$
F	T	T	F
F	F	T	F

If we have a universe of discourse of only one individual, then the following argument holds on intuitive grounds:

All stones are tough. (Sx, Tx)

All stones are sharp. (Hx)

Thus, some sharp things are tough.

If there is only one individual in the universe of discourse and if that individual is a stone, then the above argument has to hold. But if there are at least two individuals (and one of them may not be a stone), the above argument is invalid. The following cross-sections of the truth table prove its invalidity:

$(x)(Sx \supset Tx)$
$(x)(Sx \supset Hx)$
$\therefore (\exists x)(Hx \cdot Tx)$

	Sa	Ta	Ha	$Sa \supset Ta$	$Sa \supset Ha$	$/\therefore Ha \cdot Ta$
	F	T	F	T	T	F
or	F	F	T	T	T	F
or	F	F	F	T	T	F

In seeking to prove invalidity in arguments with multiple-place predicates, we must make extensive use of counterexamples. But such counterexamples need to apply to the domain of discourse relevant to that context. (A universe of discourse can include everything. Or it can include only humans or numbers or some other set of objects.)

A counterexample used for purposes of showing invalidity also needs to be invalid. For example, if someone proposed to derive $(\exists x)(y)Fxy$ from the premise $(x)(\exists y)Fxy$, we can propose that we use a universe of discourse of numbers. In such a universe the original premise holds that for any number x there is another number y that is greater. But the conclusion requires that there is a number x, such that for any number that number x is greater. And this requires that there is a number that is greater than itself, a conclusion that is obviously absurd.

Arguments and Relations

Many arguments use relational expressions such as "... is older than _____" and "... is greater than _____." In such cases we need to use an added premise that makes explicit the properties held by such relations. We can use quantified statements to express the precise meanings of the properties of such relational expressions. The following set of statement forms makes explicit the way these relational properties hold. And these statement forms have use as premises introduced in proofs using relational expressions.

1. Transitive relation:
   $$(x)(y)(z)[(Fxy \cdot Fyz) \supset Fxz]$$
   Examples: "is larger than," "is younger than."

2. Intransitive relation:
   $$(x)(y)(z)[(Fxy \cdot Fyz) \supset \sim Fxz]$$
   Examples: "is the mother of," "is greater by one-half than."

3. Symmetrical relation:
   $$(x)(y)(Fxy \supset Fyx)$$
   Examples: "is equal to," "is married to."

4. Asymmetrical relation:
   $$(x)(y)(Fxy \supset \sim Fyx)$$
   Examples: "is the father of," "is heavier than."

5. Reflexive relation:
   $$(x)(y)[Fxy \supset (Fxx \cdot Fyy)]$$
   Examples: "is the same as," "is equal to."

6. Totally reflexive relation:
   $$(x)Fxx$$
   Example: "is identical to."

7. Irreflexive relation:
   $$(x)(y)[Fxy \supset (\sim Fxx \cdot \sim Fyy)]$$
   Examples: "is less than," "is the grandfather of."

We can write the proof for the following argument by using the form for the appropriate relational notion as a premise:

Lisa is the sister of Ann and Ann is the sister of Beth.

Thus, Lisa is the sister of Beth.

(1) $(x)(y)(z)[(Sxy \cdot Syz) \supset Sxz]$ Assumed Relational Premise
(2) $Sla \cdot Sab$
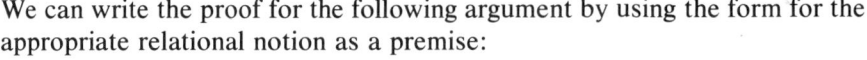
∴Slb
(3) $(y)(z)[(Sly \cdot Syz) \supset Slz]$ (1) UI
(4) $(z)[(Sla \cdot Saz) \supset Slz]$ (3) UI
(5) $(Sla \cdot Sab) \supset Slb$ (4) UI
(6) Slb (5), (2) MP

Shifting Quantifiers

There are various ways in which we can manipulate quantifiers. If we are dealing with one-place predicates, then some of the manipulations that we can make are the following:

Shifting Scope of a Quantifier with One-Place Predicates

1. $(x)(Fx \cdot Gx) \equiv [(x)Fx \cdot (x)Gx]$
2. $(\exists x)(Fx \lor Gx) \equiv [(\exists x)Fx \lor (\exists x)Gx]$
3. $(x)(Fx \supset Gx) \supset [(x)Fx \supset (x)Gx]$
4. $[(\exists x)Fx \supset (\exists x)Gx] \supset (\exists x)(Fx \supset Gx)$
5. $[(x)Fx \lor (x)Gx] \supset (x)(Fx \lor Gx)$
6. $(\exists x)(Fx \cdot Gx) \supset [(\exists x)Fx \cdot (\exists x)Gx]$

One can show the above manipulations hold by proofs.[3]

There is need to have a quantifier cover a complete line in writing some proofs. The following shifts in scope of a quantifier are correct and provable. Let P represent any sentence or sentence form that does not have x as a free variable.

Shifting Scope of Quantifiers to Cover a Complete Line

1. $[(x)Fx \cdot P] \equiv (x)(Fx \cdot P)$
2. $[(\exists x)Fx \cdot P] \equiv (\exists x)(Fx \cdot P)$
3. $[(x)Fx \lor P] \equiv (x)(Fx \lor P)$
4. $[(\exists x)Fx \lor P] \equiv (\exists x)(Fx \lor P)$
5. $[P \supset (x)Fx] \equiv (x)(P \supset Fx)$
6. $[P \supset (\exists x)Fx] \equiv (\exists x)(P \supset Fx)$

Developing Strategies for Proofs

In writing proofs in quantification logic, we need to focus continually on the conclusion and to trace back a possible way of writing a proof. Practice in recognizing forms and in manipulating them is essential.

---

[3] There is an analysis of some of these logical truths in the exercises that follow. Consider the derivation of $(\exists x)Fx \cdot (\exists x)Gx$ from $(\exists x)(Fx \cdot Gx)$.

(1)	$(\exists x)(Fx \cdot Gx)$		AP
(2)	$Fy \cdot Gy$	(1)	EI
(3)	Fy	(2)	Simp.
(4)	Gy	(2)	Comm. & Simp.
(5)	$(\exists x)Fx$	(3)	EG
(6)	$(\exists x)Gx$	(4)	EG
(7)	$(\exists x)Fx \cdot (\exists x)Gx$	(5), (6)	Conj.
(8)	$(\exists x)(Fx \cdot Gx) \supset [(\exists x)Fx \cdot (\exists x)Gx]$	(1)-(7)	CP

There are other suggestions helpful in working out a strategy to write a proof:

1. Check for accuracy in the way one has written the statements in quantified form.

2. Consider some way to use a conditional proof.

3. See if some shifting of quantifiers within a line of the proof will provide a way to use a conditional proof.

4. Look for ways to use equivalent forms, including the use of QE to derive expressions that can provide a way to complete a proof.

5. Consider a use of UI or EI to derive a line that will enable one to carry forward a proof.

6. Consider using IP either if it offers obvious promise of completing a proof or if no other strategy for writing a proof appears.

To illustrate the above suggestions consider writing a proof for the following derivation:

$(x)(Fx \lor P)$
$\therefore (x)Fx \lor P$

One can use IP and have the following proof:

(1)	$(x)(Fx \lor P)$		Premise
	$\therefore (x)Fx \lor P$		
(2)	$\sim[(x)Fx \lor P]$		AP
(3)	$\sim(x)Fx \cdot \sim P$	(2)	DeM
(4)	$\sim(x)Fx$	(3)	Simp.
(5)	$\sim P$	(3)	Comm. & Simp.
(6)	$(\exists x) \sim Fx$	(4)	QE
(7)	$\sim Fy$	(6)	EI
(8)	$Fy \lor P$	(1)	UI
(9)	P	(8), (7)	DA
(10)	$P \cdot \sim P$	(9), (5)	Conj.
(11)	$(x)Fx \lor P$	(2)–(10)	IP

There also is a way to use CP to secure the above derivation:

(1)	$(x)(Fx \lor P)$		Premise
	$\therefore (x)Fx \lor P$		
(2)	$\sim P$		AP
(3)	$Fy \lor P$	(1)	UI
(4)	$P \lor Fy$	(3)	Comm.
(5)	Fy	(4), (2)	DA
(6)	$(x)Fx$	(5)	UG

(7) $\sim P \supset (x)Fx$	(2)–(6) CP
(8) $P \lor (x)Fx$	(7) MC
(9) $(x)Fx \lor P$	(8) Comm.

There are some arguments in which one needs to provide a missing premise. We saw this was essential in working with arguments using relational expressions such as "is older than." The following kind of argument also requires that one make a missing premise explicit in order to prove that the argument is valid:

All bird watchers are nature lovers.

Thus, some nature lovers are either specialists in bird songs or in bird habitats.

(1)	$(x)(Bx \supset Nx)$	
(2)	$\underline{(\exists x)[Bx \cdot (Sx \lor Hx)]}$	Suppressed premise
	$\therefore (\exists x)[Nx \cdot (Sx \lor Hx)]$	
(3)	$By \cdot (Sy \lor Hy)$	(2) EI
(4)	$By \supset Ny$	(1) UI
(5)	By	(3) Simp.
(6)	$Sy \lor Hy$	(3) Comm. & Simp.
(7)	Ny	(4), (5) MP
(8)	$Ny \cdot (Sy \lor Hy)$	(7), (6) Conj.
(9)	$(\exists x)[Nx \cdot (Sx \lor Hx)]$	(8) EG

We have seen that some arguments use premises or conclusions without a quantifier whose scope covers the complete line of a proof. But there is a quantifier covering each part of the line. Consider the expression, "If all miners return to work, then some factories can resume production." We can write this as $(x)(Mx \supset Rx) \supset (\exists y)(Fy \cdot Py)$. We can prove many of these arguments by manipulation of quantifiers discussed previously in this section. We also can prove many of them primarily by use of the rules for QE, together with an occasional use of UI or EI on one variable. In these cases we continue to use the basic rules of inference in working with a quantified statement as a unit. But we still cannot use the basic rules of inference internally within quantified sentences with bound variables. We can, however, use equivalent forms anywhere in an argument.

In these kinds of proof we make frequent use of quantification equivalence (QE). (And we could extend the list of forms for QE.) We need to remember that we deny a quantified expression by placing the sign of negation on the outside flank of the initial quantifier that covers a complete expression.[4]

---

[4] Let us review and extend our examples about the use of QE. We deny $(x)(Fx \supset Gx)$ by $\sim(x)(Fx \supset Gx)$. But we deny a complete expression having two separate quantifiers whose scope is limited to only part of the expression by placing brackets around the complete expression. Then we place the sign of denial before the first bracket. Consider the denial of

If we use argument forms to work with quantified expressions as a unit together with equivalent forms, then we can write the following kinds of proofs.

If some drugs are dangerous, then it is false that some prescriptions are not risks. (Dx, Gx, Py, Ky)

If all prescriptions are risks, then some regulations are needed. (Rz, Nz)

Therefore, if some drugs are dangerous, some regulations are needed.

(1) $(\exists x)(Dx \cdot Gx) \supset \sim(\exists y)(Py \cdot \sim Ky)$
(2) $(y)(Py \supset Ky) \supset (\exists z)(Rz \cdot Nz)$
―――――――――――――――――
$\therefore (\exists x)(Dx \cdot Gx) \supset (\exists z)(Rz \cdot Nz)$

(3) $(\exists x)(Dx \cdot Gx) \supset (y) \sim (Py \cdot \sim Ky)$ (1)   QE
(4) $(\exists x)(Dx \cdot Gx) \supset (y)(Py \supset Ky)$ (3)   DeC
(5) $(\exists x)(Dx \cdot Gx) \supset (\exists z)(Rz \cdot Nz)$ (4), (2)   HS

Every diplomat is trained and cautious.

If every diplomat is trained and cautious, then all negotiations are difficult.

If all negotiations are difficult, then some progress is slow.

Therefore, it is false that no progress is slow.

(1) $(x)[Dx \supset (Tx \cdot Cx)]$
(2) $(x)[Dx \supset (Tx \cdot Cx)] \supset (y)(Ny \supset Fy)$
(3) $(y)(Ny \supset Fy) \supset (\exists z)(Pz \cdot Sz)$
―――――――――――――――――
$\therefore \sim(z)(Pz \supset \sim Sz)$

(4) $(y)(Ny \supset Fy)$ (2), (1)   MP
(5) $(\exists z)(Pz \cdot Sz)$ (3), (4)   MP
(6) $\sim(z) \sim (Pz \cdot Sz)$ (5)   QE
(7) $\sim(z)(Pz \supset \sim Sz)$ (6)   DeC

In the above kinds of arguments, we can show invalidity by arguing with counterexamples. Or we can use proofs of invalidity developed earlier in this chapter for expressions whose variables are bound by only one quantifier.

In writing proofs for the above kinds of expressions we may need to use translation techniques developed in Section 8.2. In writing the contradictions of statements, we also may need to refer to the square of opposition in Section 9.3.

―――――――――――――――――

the complete expression $(x)(Fx \supset Gx) \supset (y)(My \supset Iy)$. It is $\sim[(x)(Fx \supset Gx) \supset (y)(Hy \supset Iy)]$. The expression "It is false both that all students are wealthy and that no students are secure" can be written "$\sim(x)[(Sx \supset Wx) \cdot (Sx \supset \sim Cx)]$." The expression "It is false both that all students are wealthy and that all teachers are underpaid" can be written "$\sim[(x)(Sx \supset Wx) \cdot (y)(Ty \supset Uy)]$."

With this discussion of the logic of quantification we complete our presentation of deductive logic. Let us remember that for a more advanced treatment of the logic of quantification, we need a more precise development of procedures for translation of ordinary language into a proper quantified form. Likewise, we need to consider the development of additional rules, such as those for identity.

In the next part of this work we shall talk about the use of inductive logic in science and in critical common sense.

EXERCISES

A. Prove the validity or invalidity of the following arguments. Write proofs in each case.

1. $(x)(Mx \supset Nx)$
   $(x)(Nx \supset Px)$

   $\therefore (x)(Px \supset Mx)$

2. $(x)(Px \supset Qx)$
   $(x)(Rx \supset Qx)$

   $\therefore (x)(Px \supset Rx)$

3. $\sim(x)(Kx \supset Lx)$
   $(x)(Lx \supset Mx)$

   $\therefore (x)(Kx \supset \sim Mx)$

4. $(x)(Mx \supset Nx)$
   $(x)(Nx \supset Ox)$
   $(x)(Px \supset Ox)$
   $(\exists x)(Mx \cdot Rx)$

   $\therefore (\exists x)(Px \cdot Rx)$

5. $(x)(Px \supset Qx)$
   $(\exists x)(Px \cdot Rx)$

   $\therefore (\exists x)(Rx \cdot Qx)$

6. $(\exists x)(Kx \cdot Lx)$
   $(x)(Lx \supset Mx)$
   $(x)(Kx \supset Nx)$

   $\therefore (\exists x)(Mx \cdot Nx)$

7. $(x)(Gx \supset Hx)$
   $(\exists x)(Gx \cdot Ix)$
   $(x)[(Ix \cdot Hx) \supset (Kx \cdot Lx)]$

   $\therefore (\exists x)(Kx \cdot Lx)$

8. All pla 'ers are strong. (Px, Sx) All players are athletes. (Ax) Therefore, all athletes are strong.

9. All reviews are brief. (*Rx*, *Bx*) All brief things are readable. (*Ex*) Some readable things are boring. (*Ox*) Therefore, some reviews are boring.

10. All Egyptians are Arabs. (*Ex*, *Ax*) Some Moslems are Egyptians. (*Mx*) Therefore, all Moslems are Arabs.

11. All sailors are travelers. (*Sx*, *Tx*) All travelers are knowledgeable. (*Kx*) All knowledgeable persons are enlightened. (*Ex*) Therefore, all sailors are enlightened.

B. Prove the validity or invalidity of the following arguments.

1. (1) $(x)[Ax \supset (Bx \cdot Cx)]$
   (2) $(x)[(Bx \cdot Cx) \supset Dx]$

   $\therefore (x)(\sim Ax \supset \sim Dx)$

2. (1) $(\exists x)(Dx \cdot \sim Ex)$
   (2) $(x)(Fx \supset Ex)$

   $\therefore (\exists x)(Dx \cdot \sim Fx)$

3. (1) $(x)(Hx \supset Ix)$
   (2) $(x)(Ix \supset Jx)$
   (3) $(x)(Jx \supset Kx)$

   $\therefore \sim (\exists x)(\sim Kx \cdot Hx)$

4. (1) $(x)[Ax \supset (Bx \lor Cx)]$
   (2) $(x)[\sim (Bx \lor Cx) \lor (y)Dyx]$

   $\therefore (x)[Ax \supset (y)Dyx]$

5. (1) $(x)[(Ax \cdot Bx) \supset (Cx \cdot Dx)]$
   (2) $(\exists x)[(\sim Dx \lor Ex) \cdot \sim Ex]$

   $\therefore (\exists x)(\sim Ax \lor \sim Bx)$

6. (1) $(x)(Cx \supset Dx) \supset (y)(Ey \supset Fy)$
   (2) $(\exists y)(Ey \cdot \sim Fy) \lor (z)(Hz \supset Iz)$
   (3) $(\exists z)(Hz \cdot \sim Iz)$

   $\therefore (\exists x)(Cx \cdot \sim Dx)$

7. Anyone buying the stock is either uninformed or incautious. (*Bx*, *Ux*, *Ix*) There is someone who is buying the stock and who is unable to suffer losses. (*Sx*) Therefore, there is someone who is unable to suffer losses and who is uninformed.

8. Some problems are easy. Some problems are not interesting. Therefore some easy things are not interesting. (*Px*, *Ex*, *Ix*)

9. Any Cadillac is faster than a Volkswagen. (*F*, *c*, *l*) Any Volkswagen is faster than a Jeep. (*j*) Therefore, any Cadillac is faster than a Jeep.

10. Any furniture in this room is clean. (*Fx*, *Cx*) Therefore, any chairs or tables in this room are clean. (*Hx*, *Tx*)

11. John is a physicist. (*P*, *j*) Some physicists are mathematicians. (*Mx*) All physicists are scientists. (*Sx*) Therefore, John is a scientist and John is a mathematician.

12. Either George drives or James drives. (*D*, *g*, *j*) Anyone who drives is

licensed. (*Lx*) Anyone who is licensed is not inexperienced. (*Ix*) If James is not inexperienced, then George does not drive. James drives. Therefore, George does not drive.

13. Either some operations are risks or some reports are exaggerated. (*Ox*, *Rx*, *Py*, *Ey*) If some reports are exaggerated, then every (news) release is questionable. (*Nz*, *Qz*) Therefore, if no operations are risks, then every (news) release is questionable.

14. If every bird watcher is a conservationist, then some forests are protected. (*Wx*, *Cx*, *Fy*, *Py*) If it is false that no forests are protected, then some game laws are respected. (*Lz*, *Rz*) Therefore, if every bird watcher is a conservationist, then it is false that no game laws are respected.

15. If some conflicts are in support of self-determination, then some conflicts are justifiable. (*Cx*, *Sx*, *Jx*) If some conflicts are in support of self-determination, then some conflicts are not successful deterrents. (*Dx*) Therefore, if all conflicts are successful deterrents, then some conflicts are justifiable.

16. If some participants are supporters of self-determination, then some justifications are credible. (*Px*, *Sx*, *Jy*, *Cy*) If every conflict is imperialistic, then no justifications are credible. (*Nz*, *Iz*) Either every conflict is imperialistic or some aggressions are threats to peace. (*Aw*, *Tw*) Therefore, if no aggressions are threats to peace, then no participants are supporters of self-determination.

17. If some television sets are radioactive, some x-rays are damaging. (*Sx*, *Rx*, *Xy*, *Dy*) Either no x-rays are damaging or some precautions are recommended. (*Pz*, *Mz*) It is not the case both that some precautions are recommended and that no supervision is essential. (*Vw*, *Ew*) Therefore, if no supervision is essential, then no television set is radioactive.

C. Prove the following derivations.

1. $(\exists x)(Fx \cdot Gx)$

    $\therefore (\exists x)Fx \cdot (\exists x)Gx$

2. $(\exists x)(Fx \lor Gx)$

    $\therefore (\exists x)Fx \lor (\exists x)Gx$

3. $(x)(Fx \cdot Gx)$

    $\therefore (x)Fx \cdot (x)Gx$

4. $(x)Fx \cdot (x)Gx$

    $\therefore (x)(Fx \cdot Gx)$

5. $(x)(Fx \cdot P)$

    $\therefore (x)Fx \cdot P$

6. $(x)Fx \cdot P$

    $\therefore (x)(Fx \cdot P)$

7. $(x)(P \supset Fx)$

    $\therefore P \supset (x)Fx$

8. $\dfrac{P \supset (x)Fx}{\therefore (x)(P \supset Fx)}$

9. $\dfrac{(x)Fx \vee P}{\therefore (x)(Fx \vee P)}$

10. $\dfrac{(\exists x)Fx}{\therefore \sim(x) \sim Fx}$ (Do not use QE)

11. $\dfrac{(x)Fx}{\therefore \sim(\exists x) \sim Fx}$ (Do not use QE)

Something to Do

A. Use editorials as a basis for writing five arguments. And prove the validity or invalidity of these arguments.

B. Write proofs for the even-numbered categorical syllogisms at the end of Section 8.2.

C. Write proofs for the first group of sorites at the end of Section 8.4.

PART III

INDUCTIVE LOGIC

induction + enumeration
 probable inference
 all premises true, conclusion can be
 false, high probability conclusion is true
 leading into a conclusion
deduction - necessary inference

 In all cases argument form valid,
   conclusion false, one premise must
   be false

CHAPTER 13

INDUCTION AND ANALOGY

13.1 SCIENCE, COMMON SENSE, AND INDUCTION

In the third part of this work we shall look at the method of induction as it has use in critical common sense and in science. The different types of induction will be described, as well as the way in which inductive hypotheses are formed and tested. We shall consider the use of arguments in moral evaluation and in policy formation. We conclude this division by analyzing ways to challenge and to construct arguments.

This chapter will examine some different kinds of inductive arguments. An inductive argument is a form of reasoning that leads into a conclusion. In a strong inductive argument we regard the falsity of the conclusion as highly unlikely. But we also recognize that the form of an inductive argument permits that a conclusion can be false even though all statements providing evidence are true.

In inductive logic we appraise an argument as strong or weak. "Strong" and "weak" permit degrees of strength or of weakness. Two inductive arguments can have the same form; one can be strong and the other weak. But some forms of inductive arguments provide stronger arguments than others.

Our knowledge of a subject area and our experience in working with problems in that area contribute to our advancing a strong inductive argument about matters in that field.

We use inductive procedures in attempting to solve many problems in our everyday experience. We can attempt to start the motor of a car and find that the motor does not turn over. We turn on the light switch and there is no light. We attempt to turn on the car radio and again nothing happens; neither will the horn sound. We induce, or lead into, the conclusion that something is wrong with the electric circuit of the car. The trouble can be in the cable connection at the battery, a loose wire, a blown-out fuse, a bad switch, or some other problem. But we have been led into the conclusion that the electrical system is not working properly. We are making an induction.

In the above case, we continue to want to start the car and we search for clues to test. We begin to focus on more specific solutions that we can test. Perhaps the battery cable connection has corroded. We remove the cable and clean the connection. We anticipate that after doing this, maybe we can then start the car. But if the motor still does not turn over and there is still no current in the lights, radio, or horn, we reject this solution. And we try another solution, such as a blown-out fuse or a faulty ground wire for the battery. We have been testing some possible inductions.

Let us consider another example of induction. But in this case, we shall assume that we are interested in accounting for how people relate to other persons. And we recognize that the same persons sometimes are friendly and helpful in some situations and that on other occasions they are neither friendly nor helpful. There are many different possible ways of explaining such conditions. We shall consider the way that one class of female introductory psychology students in a northwestern university became involved in studying this problem.

The teacher of the class designed an experiment to help study the relation of stress to behavior. Students were divided into two groups. Group 1 was to complete twenty-six shopping tasks within a half hour in a shopping center. Group 2 was to complete twice as many tasks within the same time. These two groups were subdivided. Group 1a and group 2a were to complete their tasks during periods of crowded shopping conditions. But groups 1b and 2b were to complete their tasks during periods of low concentration of people in the mall.

Each student was to begin her tasks at different times. After completing her tasks, the student was to meet with an interviewer in a dimly lighted and deserted hallway in the mall. Upon arriving at the hallway, the student found a planted person who claimed to be searching for a lost contact lens. One design of the study was to determine how many students from each of the groups would assist in searching for the lens.

No one from group 2a, with the greater number of shopping tasks to complete during crowded conditions, stopped to help look for the lens. About one third of the students from groups 1a and 2b helped to look for the lens. But 80 percent of the students from group 1b, who completed fewer tasks during uncrowded conditions, helped to look for the lens.[1]

The above study shows that under some conditions, dispositions to be friendly or helpful can vary with the degree of stress that a person undergoes. But our interest in the study is in its inductive procedures. The designer of the experiment wanted to test a hypothesis. The teacher identified a set of conditions under which the hypothesis could be tested, brought about those conditions, kept an accurate record of what happened, made an analysis of the data, and derived justifiable conclusions.

The context in which inductive arguments develop in the natural and social sciences differs from the context in which arguments in formal sciences like mathematics and symbolic logic unfold. The natural and social sciences advance their knowledge claims, in part, through evidence and arguments based upon experience. Mathematics and symbolic logic develop formal systems. These systems develop out of a set of primitive notions, a set of postulates, and a set of operational procedures. They deal with an abstract world of concepts, numbers, relations, properties, sets, and the like. And the justification for accepting views advanced in these formal sciences relies on consistency within the system rather than on appealing to experience.

In our discussion of science in this chapter and the following ones we shall be talking about the natural and social sciences rather than formal sciences. But we recognize that both mathematics and symbolic logic have significant influence on the way these other sciences develop their arguments and advance their conclusions.

In traditional schemes there are three levels on which scientists work. On the first level are tacticians or practitioners. They use the findings of *practice* other scientists to get a specific job done—to cure patients, build roads, construct engines, design airplanes, or send rockets into outer space.

On the second level are the applied scientists, whose purpose is to advance scientific knowledge at intermediate levels with a primary view to developing technical knowledge that others can put to practical use. They seek to develop disease-preventing vaccines that others can administer to patients. Or, they develop metals that others will use on rockets that reenter the Earth's atmosphere. Or, they devise ways to separate petrochemicals from petroleum and to break these materials down so that others can use them to make fibers.

On the third level, some scientists work at basic research. They have as their primary goal the development of general laws and theories and the *research* advancement of knowledge for its own sake. They set forth such laws as

[1] *Science News*, Vol. 112, No. 11 (September 10, 1977), p. 170.

heredity, the germ theory of disease, the theory of relativity, the atomic theory of matter, or the theory of continental drift.

We should not draw too sharp a line between these levels on which scientists work. Any given scientist may be working on more than one of these levels. And many research projects, such as cancer research, require the cooperation of scientists working on all three levels.

But the fact that we have these three levels makes difficult sweeping generalizations about the common features of scientific work. The physician treating a patient has an interest in the patient's recovery. But the medical researcher in the laboratory is interested in knowing what the effect of a new drug on mice will be rather than in the physical well-being of the mice.

Some basic notions used in scientific work have different meanings at different levels. The notion of cause may have one meaning for someone working in basic science. Its meaning can become broader as we move to other levels. Likewise, a model we may use to interpret the way scientists work may shift not only from one level to another but also as we move from one subject area to another in scientific work. A part of the art of the medical practitioner relates to the bedside manner of the physician. And a model to account for the work of a physician would be other than the model for a medical researcher working in a laboratory.

Usually a discussion of the logic of induction as it relates to the methods of science uses the level of basic research as a primary model. But we shall extend our discussion to include inductive procedures used on the other two levels and in critical common sense as well.

We need to recognize that we use induction both in science and in critical common sense. But basic science differs in many ways from the level on which we operate in critical common sense. Along with others, Ernest Nagel has pointed out what some of the differences are.[2] Common-sense notions often are imprecise and even inconsistent. Selection of one principle rather than another to guide action frequently is arbitrary. The range of situations covered by a commonsense principle often remains unknown and in using such principles we frequently apply them to cases where they do not fit. The use of commonsense notions often is restricted to matters of immediate concern. Such notions also may be meshed with customs that blind us to alternative and better ways of resolving some issues. But we do not want to write off critical common sense, as this is an area in which many of our day-to-day decisions and actions take place. And use of fitting inductive procedures in critical common sense can help in enlarging the scope and effectiveness of our actions on this level.

A basic goal of scientists in basic research is to develop hypotheses, laws, and theories. They are interested in accounting for facts through the

[2] Ernest Nagel, "The Nature and Aim of Science," in Sidney Morgenbesser, ed., *Philosophy of Science Today* (New York: Basic Books, 1967), p. 5.

development of hypotheses, and they use facts as a means of testing their hypotheses. The laws and theories they develop will in turn enable them to predict the occurrence of other facts and conditions and to develop other hypotheses, laws, and theories.

Hypotheses, laws, and theories develop in a cultural and historical context. But scientists in basic research have an interest in developing laws and theories that have universal scope. Let us consider an example.[3] Some scientists are interested in factors related to aging as a universal process. However, to study aging they have to begin within a limited context. One scientist advanced the hypothesis that a process known as free radical reaction may be a source of accelerating the aging of animals. He was aware that an inhibitor of such free radical reaction is vitamin E. In an experiment, he found that the giving of vitamin E to some animals extended their life 30 percent over their life expectancy.

Interest in the above issue continues. How can one account for the acceleration of aging by free radical reaction? There was testing of the hypothesis that such free radical reaction may result in a decline in the immune system of an animal. A test for this hypothesis was to give vitamin E to aging animals to see if it affected their immune systems. In a subsequent experiment, the researchers found that the giving of vitamin E to old mice helped to preserve their immune systems, in comparison to other old mice that did not receive doses of this vitamin. It is anticipated that laws or theories built up through this type of experimentation can apply not only to the original types of experimental subjects, but to other kinds of animals wherever they are found.

It is difficult to state what such expressions as "hypothesis," "law," and "theory" mean when they occur in a context of scientific writing. They have various uses. But we shall use them in the following way. A hypothesis *proposed solution* is a statement of a tentative principle that sets forth a rule to account for a given class of events or conditions in a given context. A law is a well-confirmed hypothesis that is consistent with other laws that together form a system of interrelated principles. A theory is a principle that unifies a set *system of laws* of laws in a system. Theories also have abstract entities like mass, force, energy, species, that in themselves are not the source of direct observation. In addition, theories form a series of orders, or levels, in which some theories extend over others.

Let us consider another example. Since 300 B.C. the disease of rabies has been recognized. Since 1804 it has been known that the disease can be transmitted to humans through the bite of an infected animal. In 1886 Pasteur established the hypothesis that the causal agent of the disease, a virus, is present in the brain of infected animal carriers. He also established another hypothesis that by mixing infected brain tissue with other materials

---

[3] *Science News*, Vol. 110, No. 15 (October 9, 1976), p. 232.

Science —

it would be possible to develop an effective vaccine against rabies. He developed his hypothesis on the basis of a general theory that specific infective agents were the causal agents of specific diseases. The set of conditions, in which a given infective agent causes a specific disease such as rabies or smallpox, constitutes a law relative to the transmission of such a disease.

There are standards which scientists expect to be met in carrying out research. Basic in such standards are objectivity, accuracy, and completeness. These standards relate to the context in which scientific knowledge advances. They also serve to further cooperation among the members of the scientific community.

Objectivity means that the record of observations, descriptions, and tests is of the kind that other qualified scientists in similar circumstances can verify. Claims to secret cures or to evidence not available for examination by other qualified scientists make a procedure a pseudoscientific approach. If a company advances a claim that a specific antibiotic attacks and destroys a given kind of bacterium under specified conditions in a given laboratory, then we expect that similar results will occur under similar conditions in other laboratories. But objectivity does not require that a given problem be approached with a blank mind, if such is possible. We do not observe, describe, and test conditions in an intellectual vacuum. Qualified observers bring to their work a background of knowledge, experience, and beliefs about the relevance of certain kinds of facts to other kinds of information. Yet we also expect researchers to be alert to new ways of relating facts and hypotheses to each other and to correct and enlarge their views to account for a broader range of experience.

Accuracy of findings requires precise and exact recording of data and of the conditions under which such data are found. There is need to use the best practical tools available to make measurements. Both the accuracy of any measurements and the recording of any data must be double-checked. Findings should be presented by use of formulas, ratios, percentages, charts, graphs, or tables that are accurate in what they represent. Interpretations of findings need to be distinguished from the findings themselves. Yet we recognize that, in proposing any set of findings, some interpretation is present. For example, in the context in which we make findings we also use some notion of relevance as a guide to identify what we accept as a finding.

Completeness in recording of findings requires taking note of all relevant facts in the context in which the research is carried out. To be complete, the data reported need to cover as wide a range as is essential to support the conclusion that one expects to derive from the data. Specifically, completeness requires the inclusion in a report of any significant data that one finds in a study and that may count against a position that is being set forth. Completeness does not require an exhaustive listing of irrelevant materials, but is relative to the context of the experiment. A scientist focuses on a set of conditions with the aim of identifying those facts that will be clues in making hypotheses and in testing hypotheses already made. In such contexts the recording of data should be selective rather than rambling.

13.2 INDUCTION BY ENUMERATION AND BY ANALOGY

Inductive arguments use premises to enumerate particular instances of a property, event, or a condition of objects found in a general class. They derive a conclusion that this property, event, or condition also holds for the unobserved objects in the same general class. Such conclusions can take the form of a uniform generalization, a statistical generalization, or a singular statement. In this section we shall look at inductions using enumerated instances either to lead into uniform or statistical generalizations or to lead into singular statements found in analogies.

ratio holds

certain class
certain

Induction by Enumeration

We seek to justify some uniform generalizations on the basis of enumerating instances of some elements found in a common set of objects or of similar events. Let us consider some examples of this procedure. On repeated occasions we find that under a given set of conditions, a ball always rolls downhill when it is not obstructed by other objects. And from these particular instances we conclude that under similar conditions any other similar ball will roll downhill. We find that under a given set of conditions, rainwater collected in a barrel with an opening in the top will flow out of a hose connected to the bottom of a barrel to the height of the water level in the barrel. And we conclude that under similar conditions water will flow out of a hose connected to the bottom of a barrel up to the height of the water level in the barrel. We find that a copper tube at room temperature will expand each time it is heated. And we conclude that under similar conditions the copper tube will always expand. Or we observe that dolphins that accompany boats breathe when they surface. As we always find that they do this, we conclude that all dolphins breathe when they surface.

A model for inductions by enumeration leading into uniform generalizations is the following:

 # instances important in statistical

Fa is G.

Fb is G.

Fc is G.

$\vdots$

Fn is G.

Thus, all Fs are Gs.

As an example of the above model we can find that raven *a*, raven *b*, and raven *c* in the cornfield are black. We also note that other ravens in the field and in the trees at the edge of the field are black. All the ravens we have seen are black. And we have no grounds for believing that some ravens are not black. Thus, all ravens are black.

If we examine all the members of a group for a given property and find that every member has that property, the enumeration of instances is exhaustive. Aristotle called such a procedure perfect induction. But many logicians would hold that such an enumeration is not an example of induction. Rather it is a descriptive summary of a finding and no inference is made. Making an induction to a uniform generalization requires that we make a leap from finding that some objects of a given class have a stated property to the conclusion that all objects of that class have the stated property.

Statistical generalizations are also justified by enumeration. We seek to justify statistical generalizations by finding ratios or percentages that hold between some elements found in a representative sample of a population. Then we derive a conclusion that the ratios found to hold in the sample will also hold for the population. Let us use the following model for this kind of generalization:

P percent of *F*s in a representative sample are *G*s.

Thus, *P* percent of all *F*s are *G*s.

Let us consider an example. Persons whose spleens have been surgically removed or who have sickle-cell anemia appear to be highly vulnerable to infection by bacteria of the coccal strains, and particularly to one type of pneumonia. There were 500,000 cases of this type of pneumonia each year in the United States during the middle 1970s. And there were approximately 25,000 deaths. Medical researchers on the West Coast developed a new pneumococcus vaccine. After conducting thousands of tests in the United States and South Africa they concluded that the vaccine was 80 percent effective in preventing the occurrence of this kind of pneumonia.[4] By projecting these findings into the future, they could propose that 80 percent of all persons receiving this vaccine will also develop an immunity to this kind of pneumonia.

We shall make a more extensive analysis of statistical generalization in a later chapter.

Modern science has not found the method of simple enumeration, in isolation, a satisfactory manner of proceeding with a large part of its research. As an alternative to mere enumeration, modern science has empha-

---

[4] Robert Austrian, "Pneumococcal Infection and Pneumococcal Vaccine," *New England Journal of Medicine,* Vol. 297, No. 17 (October 27, 1977), pp. 338-339.

sized the development of hypotheses which in turn are tested through experiments. This way of deriving inductive conclusions lends itself more readily to the establishment of laws and theories, which in turn can be interrelated and formed into a system. The need to distinguish such a procedure from mere enumeration has led various students of methods used in science to propose names other than induction for the method that science follows. Such students prefer such names as the experimental method or the hypothetico-deductive method.[5] We shall discuss procedures found in these methods in the following two chapters.

Basically these methods contrive a situation in which particulars play a part in confirming a hypothesis. But they specify what these particulars are and they seek to have them cover as wide a range of differing circumstances as possible. There also is an expectancy that these hypotheses, laws, and theories will have an internal consistency and that they will fit into a system. They also seek to specify other particulars, which if they occur would count as reasons for not accepting a hypothesis.

Inductions by Analogy

Inductions by analogy identify two sets of objects that have a set of known elements in common. They then derive the conclusion that an additional element known to characterize one set of objects also will characterize a second set. A simple form of induction by analogy would be our going to a restaurant on several occasions and finding that it had good food on each occasion. At a later time we want a meal with good food. And we derive the conclusion that since the food has been good at the restaurant on previous occasions that the food will be good on a new occasion.

Obviously the method of analogy has some difficulties. There is need to build in many safeguards to prevent our making numerous errors in judgment.

An argument by analogy takes either of the following forms:

Fs are Gs.

F and H each have property P.

Thus, H also is G.

Fa, $(Fb, Fc, Fd \ldots)$ are Gs.

Thus, another specified instance of F also is G.

---

[5] See, for example, Karl R. Popper, *The Logic of Scientific Discovery* (New York: Harper & Row, 1965); Ernest Nagel, *The Structure of Science* (New York: Harcourt Brace Jovanovich, 1961); Carl G. Hempel, *Aspects of Scientific Explanation* (New York: Free Press, 1965).

Consider the following example. Rocks photographed on Earth that show a given size, shape, and texture (F) are of volcanic (G) origin. Rocks photographed on Mars by Viking 2 show similar sizes, shapes, and texture. Thus, the rocks photographed by Viking 2 probably are of volcanic origin.

Analogies have many uses other than for making arguments. In their simplest form analogies point out that a characteristic of one object also can characterize another object. Consider the following examples. "A bureaucracy is like an organism. Each part needs to function well in order to carry out the mission of the bureaucracy." "An analysis is like a microscope. It brings to light small elements that otherwise would go undetected." "A bad boy is like a bad apple. It takes only one to spoil a barrel."

Some analogies have use in illustrating a point or in clarifying an issue. Some physicists have compared the movements of particles of atoms to the movement of planets about the sun. "An atom is like a solar system. Both the atom and the solar system have fast-moving parts orbiting around a central nucleus."

Many parables and metaphors used in illustrating a religious view or principle take the form of an analogy. "Wisdom excels folly as light excels darkness" (Ecclesiastes 2:13). "Every tree is known by the fruit it bears; you do not pick figs from thorn bushes or gather grapes from bramble bushes" (John 6:44).

Many analogies have use as clues for solving a problem or developing a strategy. If we say that plants have plumbing systems, then we can explain how fluids flow upwards in some plants. Water flows upwards in a pipe from a well by the pressure of suction having a pump as one of its sources. We may look for some kind of flowing action in a plant. And we find that the evaporation of the moisture on the leaves of the plant by the light of the sun provides, in part, for a suction that creates a pressure to help draw the fluids upward in a plant.

Some market analysts compare the strategy of investing in common stocks to trying to row a boat near the shore of a sea with strong tides. Progress in rowing the boat is a lot quicker and easier when one goes in the direction the tide is moving. And, they claim, greater progress is made in investing in common stocks by following the direction of the major long trend of the market.

Some analogies can be used as means of showing that another argument or analogy is a poor one. Someone could claim that all politicians are corrupt because a few are known to be corrupt. We can point out that this is like arguing that all politicians are persons who would make good presidents because a few are known to have abilities that would enable them to be good presidents.

There is need to recognize that analogies used to illustrate a point or to develop a strategy can be pressed too far. We can compare a quiet period in a dispute to a lull before a storm. But it is possible to control a dispute in a manner not possible with a storm.

Evaluating Analogies

There are several standards that we can use in evaluating the strength or weakness of an argument based on analogy or on simple enumeration.

Number of Instances *(Add (More Cases) +*

It is customary to hold that an analogy becomes stronger as further instances confirm its claims. For example, we find two ancient coins (1) having the same kind of metal and (2) having similar kinds of inscriptive work. The first coin has an added inscription that enables us to place its date at approximately 75–50 B.C. By analogy we conclude that the second coin is about the same age as the first. The analogy is strengthened if we find similar coins with these first two properties, whose inscriptions also enable us to place their date at 75–50 B.C.

Relevance of Properties *(Do they affect the whole argument) May or may not strengthen argument*

An analogy is stronger, as expected, when we know that the properties used in the analogy have some connection to each other and that they customarily are found together in a given kind of object. For example, Russian and Chinese geologists, along with geologists from the United States, are studying the use of a gas, radon, as a means of predicting earthquakes. This radioactive gas is a product of the uranium residue in decaying rock formations. In periods prior to earthquakes there tends to be an expanding of rocks with a release of radon which enters into ground-water.[6] Thus, the finding of an increase in the radon content of underground water has been a basis for the claim of an argument by analogy that there will be an increase in underground turbulence in that given geological area. For our purpose we need to note that the increased amount of radon found in underground water has relevance to and customarily occurs with the properties it finds holding in the analogy.

Differing Contexts and Conditions *(Variety in Premises)+*

An argument by analogy becomes stronger when there is a wide variety of situations in which the objects used in the analogy are known to have the compared properties. For example, one method of looking for uranium

[6] *Science News*, Vol. 110, No. 5 (July 31, 1976), p. 71.

More likenesses

Fishers

deposits near the surface of the Earth is through the use of Geiger counters. But as deposits lie deeper beneath the surface, or certain types of rock formations appear, the detecting value of the Geiger counter decreases. In these cases a core in the surface of the earth can be dug and examined for trace metals. The finding by chemical analysis of a combination of favorable trace metals can increase the expectancy that uranium is present in that geological site. Continued success of the use of this method in widely varying geological sites would strengthen arguments based on the use of this analogy.

4 Restraint in the Claims Made in an Analogy

Arguments by analogy or by enumeration become stronger when there is use of appropriate restraint in advancing a conclusion. For example, in a study made at a Canadian hospital of both 100 children and three adults who were subject to convulsions, there was a finding that these patients had a significant deficiency of magnesium. Two mothers of children in the study also showed low levels of magnesium. The researchers also found that the taking of magnesium by these patients helped to control the spells of convulsions.[7] Other studies have shown that female rats with a magnesium deficiency tend to have offspring that cannot coordinate voluntary muscle movement.

In the above case those making the report exercised restraint in their conclusion. They pointed out that there was a need for further study of the relation of magnesium deficiency to convulsions. But they did claim that they found solid evidence for holding that in some cases of convulsions, particularly those associated with epilepsy, the deficiency of magnesium can be a factor in accounting for the convulsion. And they held that the taking of magnesium can be helpful in the treatment of such cases.

5 Avoiding Significant Differences
— (Disanalogy between premises & conclusion)

A significant disanalogy weakens an analogy or an inference based on enumeration. A disanalogy occurs when there is some significant difference between the objects used in an analogy. This difference can provide grounds for expecting that the conclusion of the argument is in error.

The *Journal of the American Medical Association* reports the case of a man who went to a psychiatric institute thirty times over a period of five years with a specific set of symptoms which attending physicians associated with schizophrenia. The patient had auditory hallucinations, ran screaming down the street, and in some cases he would run in the nude. He would mutter, groan, grunt, grin, blow, scrape, rock, and roll. On each occasion

---

[7] *Science News*, Vol. 112, No. 11 (September 10, 1977), p. 171.

Relative strength of Conc.
How great are your claims in the conc. relative
to the premises. Conc. should be modest.

Look for evidence beyond analogy.

he was given a drug for the treatment of schizophrenia and after spending three hours recovering in the institute and an additional five days for observation, the patient would be released. But further examinations showed that the patient also had other kinds of symptoms and that his illness was a mild form of epilepsy. He was not mentally ill. After a change of his treatment to an antiseizure drug, the patient was able to perform his usual tasks normally with only one seizure in six months.[8] The failure to identify the significant difference in the case had resulted in the patient's being treated for five years for the wrong disease.

EXERCISES

A. Which of the following analogies are descriptive (or illustrative) and which are argumentative? Appraise the argumentative analogies on the basis of the criteria set forth in this chapter.

1. "Let me cite another case, one in which an experimenter produces an observation and voluntarily brings it to birth. The case is, so to speak, included in the preceding case; but it differs from it in this, that, instead of waiting for an observation to present itself by chance in fortuitous circumstance, we produce it by experiment. Returning to Bacon's comparison, we might say that an experimenter, in this instance, is like a hunter who, instead of waiting quietly for game, tries to make it rise, by beating up the locality where he assumes it is."[9]

2. If it is permissible to deceive to prevent the enemy from knowing the position of our troops, if it is accepted that a physician may deceive a patient in order to keep alive her will to live as a means of increasing the probability of her recovery, if it is accepted that lawyers may deceive a jury by concealing evidence that might be prejudicial to their client being tried for first-degree murder, it is permissible for a college student to deceive his teacher about his ability in a subject by paying a superior student to write his term essay for a course.

3. Computers are like brains. Both confront problems to be solved, both have procedures for dealing with problems, and both propose solutions to problems in the manner in which they have been conditioned.

4. The proton is like an onion in having layers with radii of different magnitude.

5. This western movie is like the last one I saw. In both cases, the hero was being framed by the leader of an unscrupulous gang that was trying to run the town; in both cases the hero was in love with a girl who was victimized by the leader of the gang; and in both cases the hero was accused of a crime committed by the leader of the gang. In the former case the hero killed the leader of the gang in a street gunfight. Therefore, the hero will kill the leader of the gang in a street gunfight in the present movie.

---

[8] Victor R. Adebimpe, "Complex Partial Seizures Simulating Schizophrenia," *Journal of the American Medical Association*, Vol. 237, No. 13 (March 28, 1977), pp. 1339–1341.

[9] Claude Bernard, *An Introduction to the Study of Experimental Medicine*, trans. by H. C. Greene (New York: Dover Publications, 1957), p. 157.

6. The person who robbed the store was about six feet tall, with blond hair, blue eyes, and a limp. He was neatly dressed in a dark suit. The defendant also is about six feet tall with blond hair, blue eyes, and a limp. He was in the neighborhood, neatly dressed in a dark suit, immediately prior to the robbery. Therefore, the defendant is the person who robbed the store.

7. A good ruler is like a good captain. He steers his ship-of-state safely through troubled waters.

8. "I wonder at the attitude of some advertisers. Their expertise enables them to recognize unlawful practices of competitors immediately. But they choose to fight their own battles—for to report the matter to FTC would be like running to mother to snitch on a brother. The FTC is a law enforcement agency and it is your responsibility to report unlawful advertising to the Commission—just as you report crimes to the police."[10]

9. "In the question period later, he was asked if lawyers are more concerned in fair trial or in getting their clients freed. Mr. Belli fielded that with an analogy to the man who obtains a lawyer to defend and free his son. Which lawyer are you going to get to get your son off? he asked, adding: 'Behind every so-called crooked lawyer there is a crooked layman.'"[11]

10. "There is little doubt left that the floors of the oceans behave like gigantic conveyor belts, transporting the continents on their backs slowly but inexorably from place to place."[12]

11. "The soul is like a vase filled with water; while the semblances of things fall like rays upon its surface. If the water is moved, the ray will seem to be moved likewise, though it is in reality without motion. When, therefore, anyone is seized with a giddiness in his head, it is not the arts and virtues that are bewildered, but the mind in which they lie; when this recovers its composure, so will they likewise." (Epictetus, C.A.D. 60)

12. "The true method of discovery is like the flight of an aeroplane. It starts from the ground of a particular observation; it makes a flight in the thin air of imaginative generalization; and it lands for renewed observation rendered acute by rational interpretation."[13]

B. In the cases below, determine whether the original argument is strengthened, weakened, or not affected by each of the statements that follow. Give a reason for your answer. Each statement following the argument is to be considered as separate from the others.

1. On the last three occasions that we have eaten dinner at Restaurant Delta, we have had excellent food. Therefore, we should have excellent food if we eat dinner there tonight.

---

[10] Paul Rand Dixon, Former Chairman, Federal Trade Commission, quoted in *Editor & Publisher*, Vol. 99, Pt. 1 (March 12, 1966), p. 18.

[11] Robert U. Brown, "Shop Talk at Thirty," *Editor & Publisher*, Vol. 100, Pt. 3 (September 23, 1967), p. 60.

[12] Peter Stubbs, "The Mechanism of Continental Drift," *New Scientist*, Vol. 32, No. 525 (December 15, 1966), p. 616.

[13] Alfred North Whitehead, *Process and Reality* (New York: Macmillan, 1929), p. 7.

ω (1) There is a new chef.

NA(2) There is a new manager who claims that the policies of the previous management will continue.

NA(3) There has been an increase in the cost of a meal.

S (4) The restaurant has become more crowded.

S (5) You have eaten at the restaurant on ten previous occasions and the food was always good.

NA(6) You have previously ordered lamb chops, but on this occasion you plan to order fish.

2. You plan to drive 400 miles and have only nine hours in which to make a trip, with an additional two hours for eating or resting. And you claim that you can make this trip safely in nine hours driving time since you have made this trip on three previous occasions in the past and on each occasion there was no difficulty in completing the trip within that time.

ω (1) It is the beginning of a holiday weekend and the other trips have been made during the middle of the week.

ω (2) The other trips were made during good weather, and it is predicted that you will have bad weather.

NA (3) You are making the trip during the summer and the other trips also have been made during the summer. And you have made them in different kinds of weather common to that region in the summer.

S (4) During the other trips you have been the only driver. On this occasion there is an experienced and safe driver who has safely driven this road on several trips. This driver will be sharing some of the driving with you.

NA ω (5) During the other trips you have driven the same car. And on this trip you are still driving the same car. But you have driven fifteen thousand miles since the previous trip. And there have been no checkups, inspections or repairs on the mechanical condition of your car.

3. On three previous occasions you have made investments through a broker at a reliable firm and on each occasion your broker has been able to help you make conservative investments that have a net total return of 7 percent per year. Most of these investments have been made in high-quality bonds and good common stocks yielding good dividends. And you hold that since you have had a total net return average of 7 percent per year on your investments in recent years, you want to receive as good a total net return during the coming year on this year's new investment as in previous years. (For purposes of this illustration we shall not consider commission costs which would need to be averaged out over the period of the investment.)

ω (1) Your broker is away and you buy gold stocks, which, you are told, have reached their highest price per share in three years.

S (2) You invest one-half in U.S. Government bonds which are yielding 7 1/ percent a year and one-half in high-grade corporate bonds which yield percent.

S (3) Your last major investment was five years ago. High-grade corporate bonds such as the ones you have been buying have risen to 8 1/4 percent. And you buy high-grade corporate bonds.

ω (4) You buy without an investment counselor's advise some common stock in a newly formed company on the basis of a tip you receive from a friend that the stock may double in price over the next year.

(5) You buy without consulting anyone Tri Gamma common stocks on the basis that a share of this stock has lost 50 percent of its value over the past year and that it should come back.

CHAPTER 14

TESTING HYPOTHESES AND DECISIONS

14.1 ELEMENTS IN DECISION MAKING

In this chapter we discuss how we go about making trustworthy decisions and good hypotheses. We find that in each case what is basic is the ability to identify the context in which a decision or hypothesis occurs, to know what to test for, to know how to carry out the test, and to be able to recognize the significance of such tests.

In everyday life we make decisions or advance claims in some context. And we proceed to make tests to determine whether a decision is a good one or whether a conclusion is an acceptable one. For example, we want to buy a pants suit or a suit of clothes. We want the suit for casual occasions—to wear to work, to visit friends, and to informal meetings. We carry into this decision-making process a set of assumptions and beliefs which have as their basis our past experience. We have some general beliefs about what types of material will wear well, what types of lines and seams indicate good work, what stores or brands are likely to have good products at reasonable prices. And we have some knowledge about the way we can go about testing for good work and quality materials.

In making a decision about what suit to buy, we have to make our conditions more explicit. We go shopping and we find a specific suit that we like and that is within our accepted price range. We look at its lines and colors to see if it is "in style." We examine the material. Is it cotton, wool, nylon, polyester, or something else? Is the material a tight or a loose weave? Is the material heavy or light weight? We crumple the fabric in our hands. Will it show wrinkles easily? We look at the seams on the inside of the jacket. Are they well made? Is there extra material around the seams in the event there is need for later alterations? We examine any design in the jacket fabric. Do the appropriate lines match at the seams? Does the design on one side of the jacket match that on the other side both in front and in back, as well as around outside pockets? We try on the suit. Does it fit properly or does it bulge in the wrong places?

In the above example we also would want to consider other conditions, which, if they held, could result in our not buying the suit. For example, given today's prices, is the suit worth its price? Would we likely do better at another store?

For many decisions, we also have to take into account the cultural and historical context in which they are made. What set of social habits, attitudes, and life-styles are we dealing with? What past events appear to be influencing the present course of events and what expectations regarding the future do present trends indicate? What changes can be brought about in the present to help insure a future that we regard as desirable?

In making a sound decision we tend to take into account at least four kinds of factors. They are set forth in the scheme below, where T stands for a decision that we might make. S stands for the context in which we make the decision. F stands for the conditions that we want the decision to satisfy. And G stands for other conditions that would count against our making a particular decision. This scheme is as follows:

If T and S, then F and not G.

If we expand the scheme and place numbers to stand for the different specific elements that we consider in making a considered decision, then we would have the following scheme:

If T and S_1, S_2, S_3, then F_1, F_2, F_3, and not G_1, not G_2.

Let us assume that we are considering an offer of a job after completing school. The "T" in the above scheme would represent a decision favorable to taking a given job. The different "Ss" represent the context of beliefs we have and the assumptions we make relative to the kind of job we want. The "Fs" would represent the specific conditions we want the job to meet as a basis for accepting it. And the "not Gs" represent other conditions, which if they are found, would strengthen our interest in taking the job. That is, a "G" represents a condition we want to avoid and "not G" is a condition we want to be present. But we also need to remember that the parties offering us the job use a similar scheme, and their "Fs" have to do with a set of qualifications that they expect the candidate to have. The "Gs" are conditions they hope to avoid and the "not Gs" are conditions they want to find.

In the above case we test for the Fs and the not Gs. We could find that within the opportunities available, some of these conditions would have to be set aside. But we do need to make a decision. The decision may or may not turn out to be a happy one. The reason for a wrong decision may be in the assumptions and beliefs that we hold. We may not have identified the appropriate conditions and we may not have made the proper tests. But by having conditions to be tested, we have some guidelines to help us make a decision within our set of beliefs about what we want to do.

Testing for good decisions is not a recent thing. In primitive societies, simple tests can be made to determine good sites for villages or good food for eating. Even lower animals appear to go through processes similar to testing. Dogs or cats may smell food before eating it. A horse may appear to test for safe footing before he crosses a stream. Robins appear to test for worms by placing their heads against the ground.

In some respects we can say that human beings are the species who use beliefs to make tests through the use of highly developed tools and symbols. Advances in science and technology occur as we develop sophisticated tools (like computers), symbolic systems (like mathematics), and as we confirm laws (such as those in genetics to improve grain yields in agriculture).

In inductive procedures used in science there is a testing for the consequences of a hypothesis in a manner similar to the way we test for critical commonsense decisions. But there also are significant differences. The laws developed and used in science are subject to rigorous confirmation. In such cases there is usually greater control over critical factors in the laboratory testing procedures. Greater precision characterizes the taking of measurements. Also, scientists need to make public the evidence found, the methods used, and the conclusions reached in testing hypotheses. This high degree of control and precision and the publishing of data are generally not part of commonsense procedures.

14.2 STEPS IN DEVELOPING HYPOTHESES

In this section we shall examine steps in developing hypotheses. We need to form hypotheses, identify ways of testing them, carry out such tests, and evaluate their results.

1.   Forming a Hypothesis for Testing

Scientists approach their work in a context that includes training and experience in dealing with issues in their subject area, as well as beliefs about laws or regularities used to predict and explain what happens in such areas. They also recognize acceptable ways of identifying relevant issues, facts, and methods for carrying out an investigation that will yield trustworthy results. But the clue to their work is their use of hypotheses.

Hypotheses help to guide research on a specific problem. The forming of a hypothesis can help in making important discoveries in science, even though one eventually rejects the original hypothesis. Claude Bernard writes about the usefulness of one of his rejected hypotheses:

> The result was therefore precisely the reverse of what my hypothesis, deduced from theory, had led me to expect; thereupon I did as I always do, that is to say, I at once abandoned theories and hypotheses, to observe and study the facts themselves, so as to define the experimental conditions as precisely as possible. . . . This example like the preceding ones, proves that in experiments we may meet with results different from what theories and hypotheses lead us to expect. But . . . without the original guiding hypothesis, the experimental fact which contradicted it would never have been perceived. . . . The hypothesis had prepared my mind for seeing things in a certain direction.[1]

Let us consider an example of the above use of a hypothesis. In 1852, Claude Bernard was experimenting in his Paris laboratory on the effect of severing cervical sympathetic nerves of rabbits. His original hypothesis was that this severing would lower body temperature. But this did not happen in his experiment. Rather the body temperatures of the experimental rabbits became higher. Further research led him to make the hypothesis that nerves have a critical function in regulating the flow of blood in the arteries. The confirmation of this hypothesis was one of the most important advances in knowledge about the flow of blood in the arteries after Harvey's initial discovery of such circulation. (This relation of nerves to the heart muscle still appears to be a major factor related to a patient's reaction to heart transplants.)

In forming hypotheses on elementary levels our interests, training, and ongoing activities serve to focus our attention on a problem and in some cases on a proposed solution to it. And we begin to consider using the proposed solution as a hypothesis to be tested. For example, two researchers at a western university were interested in finding out what students remembered best from classroom lectures. In carrying out their research on this topic, they set forth the hypothesis that students have better ver-

---

[1] Claude Bernard, *An Introduction to the Study of Experimental Medicine,* trans. by H. C. Greene (New York: Dover Publications, 1957), pp. 169–170.

batim memory of anecdotes and jokes told as asides by their teachers than they have of specific topics or of details related to those topics. In the researchers' investigation, this hypothesis was significantly supported by their findings.[2] And the hypothesis will be tested by others. These findings do not support the view that the best way to teach is by using anecdotes. But they do support the view that some of them can be helpful to illustrate a point being covered in a lecture.

There does not appear to be a formula for assuring creative work in making a breakthrough in developing novel and fruitful hypotheses in science. In many cases an investigator will have an imaginative insight into how to solve a problem. This insight sometimes follows an investigator noticing that something different or unexpected happens. And she begins to wonder how to account for it. Many initial insights lead into blind alleys, but others turn out to be highly productive. After having what appears to be a novel insight into solving a problem, the researcher's basic task is to find ways to test the insight as a hypothesis.

In the history of science, there are numerous examples of such novel insights. We shall mention two of them. In 1928, Alexander Fleming was examining some bacteria cultures in his laboratory in London. His research focused on the way the bacteria multiplied and remained true to their original type. A culture left on a window ledge for several days appeared to be contaminated. Should it be thrown out? In the culture there was a mold colony about a half inch in diameter. But between the mold colony and the colonies of bacteria there was a gap in which the bacteria did not grow. Fleming's interest became directed toward finding an explanation for the reason that this bacteria did not grow in the area immediately around the mold. Fleming was not the first to observe this kind of gap in such cultures. But he developed an insight that the mold itself could have elements that would explain why there were no bacteria immediately around it. This insight led to his discovery of *Penicillium.* Yet it took the imaginative work of other researchers to develop and establish the added hypothesis that this type of mold could become a highly useful agent in destroying disease-causing bacteria in human beings.

In 1895, Roentgen was experimenting with electrical discharges at a university in Bavaria. After placing a black cardboard over a vacuum tube carrying electrical discharges, he noticed something unusual. There were some fluorescent salts more than ten feet from the tube and they glowed in a completely darkened room. How could one explain this glowing? He began his inquiry by forming the hypothesis that "the cause of the fluorescence proceeds from the discharge apparatus and not from any other points

---

[2] Walter Kintsch and Elizabeth Bates, "Recognition Memory for Statements from a Classroom Lecture," *Journal of Experimental Psychology: Human Learning and Memory,* Vol. 3, No. 2 (March, 1977), pp. 150–159.

in the conducting circuit.''[3] He confirmed this hypothesis and developed others. One of these was that he was dealing with a ray with elements not found in other rays known at that time. This newly discovered ray he called an x-ray. He developed the hypothesis that this x-ray was different from ultraviolet light and that its elements enabled it to penetrate other objects. Another of his hypotheses was that other properties like the density and thickness of an object helped to determine the degree of transparency found in such objects upon their exposure to these x-rays.

2. Identifying Testable Consequences of a Hypothesis

If scientists are to test a hypothesis, they need to know specifically what it is that they are to test. They expect that a good hypothesis will provide some clues about what can be tested either to confirm or to dis-confirm it. The clues that one looks for in testing a hypothesis are those observable events or conditions that one would expect to follow if the hypothesis is true. One also can seek to identify those conditions or events which, if they occur, would result in rejecting the hypothesis.

One of the more interesting geological views is the theory of continental drift. The German meteorologist Alfred Wegener proposed this view more than fifty years ago. It holds that some 300 million years ago, the continents formed a solid land mass. Some of the continents proceeded to drift away from this original mass. This theory is widely held today. But our present interest is in another hypothesis related to this broader theory. There are continuing differences regarding some details about how some of these land masses originally fit together. We want to see how developing tests for hypotheses relate to one of these controversies.

In current discussions of the continental-drift theory, there are differences of views about the original position which the island of Madagascar had in relation to the southeastern coast of Africa and to the land mass that became South America. Some geologists are placing Madagascar further south than others did previously. Various tests to confirm this hypothesis are being proposed.

In the above case, if we hold that Madagascar had a more southwesterly position, then we would expect to find such conditions as the following. The basalt deposits found on Madagascar match similar deposits on the southern coasts of Africa. The more northern region of Kenya would show evidence of Madagascar's earlier location near there. (But it is claimed that deep-sea sediments point to an earlier exposure to the ocean for the Kenya

---

[3] G. F. Barker, ed., *Roentgen Rays* (New York: Harper, 1899). Excerpts from this report by Roentgen can be found in Morris H. Shamos, *Great Experiments in Physics* (New York: Holt, Rinehart and Winston, 1959), pp. 201–209.

region than apparently would be the case if Madagascar had been there.) Marine deposits in the rocks of Madagascar would be similar to those of southern Africa. There also would be a similar aligning of some geological strata and faults. The movement of Madagascar would be consistent with the movement of other bodies in the area, including the land mass that became India (which moved northeast). The magnetism in the rocks on the deep sea bottom in the area also would support the more southerly position for Madagascar.[4]

In the above case the hypothesis set forth has some consequences. In order to confirm the hypothesis, there is need to identify these consequences in order to test them.

Sometimes scientists set out an elaborate procedure for testing consequences of a given type of problem. For example, the rules followed in identifying the specific microorganism which is the causal agent of a given disease call for carrying out a series of tests. These tests relate to determining if the expected consequences hold for a given hypothesis. These rules, or postulates, developed by Robert Koch, and set forth here in simplified form, require that the following conditions be met in testing such hypotheses:

1. Tests have to show that the specific agent is present in the infected host in every examined case of the disease.

2. The specific agent has to be isolated from the infected host and then grown in a pure culture that does not contain any other microorganisms.

3. The specific agent grown in this culture has to be injected into an appropriate host and the given disease must develop in that host.

4. The specific agent has to be isolated from the latest experimental host, grown in another pure culture, and shown to be of the same kind as the agent isolated and grown in the original culture.

The above conditions cover a number of possible hypotheses dealing with causal agents of disease. In any given experiment it would be essential to test for each of the expected consequences under strict laboratory conditions. And one would need to show that each condition holds.

Another example of identifying testable consequences occurs in Roentgen's experiments with x-rays. But in this case Roentgen used them as a basis for rejecting a hypothesis. In order to test whether these x-rays were ultraviolet light, he formed a tentative hypothesis that they were ultraviolet

---

[4] For a discussion of the continental drift theory, see *Continents Adrift*, readings from *Scientific American* with an introduction by J. Tuzo Wilson (San Francisco: W. H. Freeman and Company, 1972). There also is a brief discussion of this view in *Science News*, Vol. 111, No. 24 (June 11, 1977), p. 372.

light and then tested the consequences of what one would expect if such a hypothesis were true:

"If the x-rays are ultraviolet light, this light must have the following properties:"

1. "On passing from air into" such bodies as water, salt, glass, and zinc, the light "suffers no noticeable refraction."

2. It is not "regularly reflected to any appreciable extent" by the above types of bodies.

3. None of the ordinary methods of polarizing a light ray apply in this case.

4. The property that most influences the absorption of the light in such bodies is the density of the body.[5]

Because Roentgen found that the x-rays did not meet all of these conditions, he rejected the hypothesis that they were ultraviolet rays. But let us focus on his method. He proposes a set of conditions which need to be met in order to confirm his hypothesis. He tests for these conditions. These conditions are not met and he rejects this hypothesis.

3. Testing a Hypothesis to Determine Whether Its Anticipated Consequences Hold

Critical to the use of the experimental method is testing for what one expects to find if a hypothesis is true. Testing procedures can be simple or complex. A simple test can determine if a given solution is an acid. We place a piece of litmus paper in a solution. If the solution is acid, the litmus paper turns red; if it is alkaline, the paper turns blue. We have other tests but they are not as dependable as the litmus paper. For example, if a solution is acid, its taste is sharp and biting as in the case of vinegar.[6]

Testing the consequences of a complex hypothesis may require designing an appropriate instrument that can aid in making critical tests for the experiments. In reporting on an experiment, scientists seek to describe accurately the instruments and techniques they use in testing the consequences of their hypotheses. The original reports of many classical experiments had diagrams and explanations of the basic equipment used in car-

---

[5] Roentgen, in Shamos, *Great Experiments in Physics,* p. 206.

[6] We need to become aware of a problem that will require more attention in a later discussion. When we confirm a consequence in testing a hypothesis, we are also affirming the consequent from the point of view of deductive logic. In deductive logic we have a formal fallacy of affirming the consequent in the form "if p then q, and q, therefore p." But since we are studying the procedures of inductive logic, we hold only that conclusions in inductive logic are probably true. It is possible for us to make mistakes, so we say that we confirm the hypothesis rather than prove it. But this is not the end of this issue.

rying out the experiments. A critical factor in the design of such experimental tools is determining what it is that they actually test. It needs to be shown that they are testing for those conditions or events which they are designed to test for in the experiment. Scientists want to guard against the possibility that some unknown factor that is not the object of the test and that happens merely because of the kind of instrument used in the test is responsible for the results found in the testing.

There are many examples of testing the consequences of hypotheses in medical research. In seeking some effective treatment for rheumatoid arthritis, a researcher in a northwestern university was aware that patients with this ailment tend to have less zinc in their blood than persons not having rheumatoid arthritis. He developed the hypothesis that administering zinc sulfate to these patients would aid in reducing some of the severity of their discomfort. If the zinc sulfate was to be a helpful treatment, then one would expect that patients given this compound would have less stiffness and swelling in their joints and less tenderness in the surrounding tissue.

The researcher conducted an experiment on twenty-four patients who were being treated for this condition. For a period of twelve weeks, some of the patients in the double-blind experiment took zinc sulfate three times each day while another group took dummy pills. The patients taking the zinc sulfate reported less soreness of joints and less morning stiffness than the patients taking the placebos. They also reported less tenderness and a greater sense of making some headway in coping with the disease. Then, all the patients were given the zinc sulfate during a second twelve-week period. All showed improvement in their condition.

In the above experiment the researcher concluded that there was need to extend the study of this type of treatment for this kind of arthritis. The tests provided grounds for holding that the zinc deficiency in the fluids surrounding the arthritic joints appeared to have some relation either to the beginning of the disease or to its intensifying.[7]

Another example of a critical (indirect) test for the consequences of a hypothesis is Isaac Newton's effort to provide evidence for his views about gravitation. He proposed to account for the monthly revolutions of the Moon by using calculations required only by his hypothesis. But the first time he tested his hypothesis, his predictions did not conform to the movements of the Moon. He set aside the theory for twenty years. Then a French expedition made new and corrected estimates about the circumference of the Earth. Using this new information, Newton revised his calculations about the movement of the Moon. He found that his revised calculations conformed to such movements. This he accepted as a confirming instance of his hypothesis of the attraction of masses to each other.

[7] Peter A. Simkin, "Oral Zinc Sulfate in Rheumatoid Arthritis," *Lancet*, Vol. II for 1976, No. 7985 (September 11, 1976), pp. 339–345.

4. Acceptance or Rejection of the Hypothesis

Once the proposed consequences of a hypothesis are tested, we expect a decision about the significance of the test in relation to the hypothesis under review. Is the hypothesis rejected or is it accepted? For example, scientists from both Denmark and the United States sought to test a hypothesis that an extra Y chromosome in some human males led to more aggressive behavior on their part. The study took place in Denmark where the kinds of records needed for such a study were more available. The following knowledge was available to these researchers. The normal female chromosome pattern is XX and the normal male pattern is XY. A human cell typically has forty-six chromosomes while a chromosome normally has about 900 genes. A small percentage of human males have a chromosome pattern of XXY, and another small percentage have XYY. There is a higher frequency of XYY patterns in tall men. Some previous studies suggested that the XYY chromosome variation results in a higher level of aggression and of criminal acts by men having this pattern. The researchers knew that in some cases where there is an atypical chromosome pattern, there are other atypical physical conditions.

In the above study there was an initial selection of 30,000 men who were born between 1944 and 1947. The researchers were interested in finding men with XYY patterns. They selected 4,558 tall men as a sample for further analysis. For each thousand men in this sample, they found that there was a ratio of 2.9 having the XYY chromosome pattern and 3.9 having the XXY pattern.

They set forth the following hypotheses to be tested. (1) The aggression hypothesis: the XYYs tend to be more aggressive and they will commit more aggressive crimes than human males with the XY pattern. (2) The intellectual dysfunction hypothesis: the XYYs will show a greater tendency to intelligence dysfunction and that this condition together with other factors can result in a higher tendency to commit crimes. And (3) the height hypothesis: height may tend to intensify acts of aggression.

The researchers did not find that height intensified acts of aggression. Neither could they link aggression either to the extra X chromosome or to the extra Y chromosome. They did discover that there tends to be some lag in intellectual development in the group with the extra Y chromosomes. In addition, they found that any tendencies to commit crimes correlated with comparable intelligence and education levels of persons with the XY pattern. But they rejected the view that the Y chromosome controls the capacity for intellectual development.[8] This kind of research continues.

Our interest in the above study centers in the fact that these researchers

---

[8] Herman A. Witkin, Sarnoff A. Mednick, and others, "Criminality in XYY and XXY Men," *Science,* Vol 193, No. 4235 (August 13, 1976), pp. 547–555.

developed and made extensive tests of the hypotheses and then proceeded to accept, modify, or reject them. Such researchers also may recommend further testing with or without modifications either of their hypotheses or of their research design. They also may propose alternative hypotheses for additional experimental work. But the fact that such researchers make one or more recommendations does not assure that the scientific community will accept their views. Their peers will review such reports. Others may find it desirable to make independent testings of the hypotheses for themselves. Or, they may review the data carefully to determine if other interpretation and conclusions can be supported by the findings.

We need to remember that experimental hypotheses are confirmed or not confirmed, verified or not verified—but usually we would not say they are proven. We more appropriately use the term "formal proof" in mathematics and formal logic. In saying that one confirms a hypothesis, we are pointing out that we have strong evidence in its support after having followed sound testing procedures. But we continue to recognize that future experiments may show the need to correct or to modify such hypotheses. By holding that we confirm or verify hypotheses rather than prove them we are not proposing any kind of secondary status for them. We are suggesting that the type of methods and the nature of subject matter in the experimental sciences makes appropriate the use of the notion of confirming or of not confirming, of rejecting or of not rejecting, the hypotheses tested.

We expect that a hypothesis will enable us to solve any given problem that gave rise to our interest in testing it. But a given hypothesis may solve the problem that gave rise to its being formed and still be faulty. For example, near the end of the nineteenth century, the Danish veterinarian Schmidt developed a hypothesis that milk fever in cows was a result of a degeneration of a given type of cells in the cow's udder. He found that injection of potassium iodide together with small amounts of air was an effective cure for the disease. And he claimed that the iodide was the curing agent. Later others found that the injection of the air without the iodide brought about the same results.[9]

In confirming hypotheses through testing, we continue to work with the type of scheme we recommended for making decisions. That is, in our scheme we advance a hypothesis in a context which includes a set of assumptions, beliefs, and recognized methods of identifying and analyzing evidence. We also identify the consequences of what we expect to happen if the hypothesis is to be accepted. And we check to determine if there are reasons for our rejecting the hypothesis. We make the indicated tests and evaluate the results. If the anticipated consequences hold and there is no

[9] W. I. B. Beveridge, *The Art of Scientific Investigation* (New York: Vintage Books, 1957), p. 59.

justifiable basis for rejecting the hypothesis, we accept, at least for the time being, the hypothesis as confirmed.

In this section we have looked at ways to develop and test hypotheses. In the next section we shall look at standards for evaluating hypotheses.

14.3   EVALUATING HYPOTHESES AND DECISIONS

1.   Evaluating Sound Hypotheses and Good Decisions

In this section we shall review the standards that sound hypotheses and good decisions are expected to meet. We shall also look at some troublesome problems relating to the testing of hypotheses.

Evaluating hypotheses can occur throughout an experiment or a decision-making process. We may raise the question, "Is this hypothesis actually worthy of our serious consideration?" The use of standards may assist in choosing those hypotheses offering greater promise and in rejecting less promising ones. We should not, however, regard such standards as inflexible. In the initial stages of making decisions or forming hypotheses, no set of criteria can assure that we shall make the best decisions or that we shall ultimately accept the hypotheses. In making good decisions and in forming sound hypotheses, our past experience, our training, and our knowledge can be decisive factors.

Directing Attention to Relevant and Interesting Matters.   A good hypothesis serves as a useful guide to focusing our attention on things we need to look for and do in resolving a problem. In the initial stages of an inquiry, we may need to be concerned not only with the truth of an idea. We also want to determine whether exploring the consequences of the idea would be interesting and fruitful. Hypotheses help us to find new facts and discover new ways of doing things.

Finding Things to Test.   As we have seen, if a hypothesis or proposed decision is a good one, we expect to find ways of making tests to justify our accepting or rejecting it.

Searching for Simplicity and Economy.   Why do things the hard way when there is an easier way? Why take risks in doing a job if we can do the same job without risk? The notion of simplicity is relative. Simplicity with its economy of effort has to do with our taking only those steps and holding only to those assumptions (unknown factors) that are essential for doing a job. Simplicity also suggests that in having to choose between two equally promising ways of trying to get the same results, we should economize by taking the way that is most direct and requires the least effort. If more unknown factors are relative to one choice than to another, then why not try first the choice with the fewest number of unknown factors or risks? Other things being equal, the fewer the assumptions that a hypothesis has, the greater the likelihood that unknown factors will not contaminate our findings. We are not claiming that in every case the simplest hypothesis is the best one—that would be absurd. We also want the best hypothesis and the best decision. Striving for simplicity and economy helps to achieve these goals.

Locking into Known Successes.   Our hypotheses or decisions need to tie in with things that have worked well in the past. We hope for novelty and applaud creativity. And we anticipate finding ways of doing some things better than they have been done. But our rejection of past solutions needs to be selective. Some ways of doing jobs and of reaching some conclusions have been well tested.

In science we expect a good hypothesis both to support and to be supported by other hypotheses. That is we expect good hypotheses in science to corroborate each other. In seeking to have their hypotheses interlock into a system, scientists try to avoid hypotheses that are merely *ad hoc*. An *ad hoc* hypothesis accounts only for one type of event or for one set of facts. For example, some flying saucer buffs are sometimes asked why there is no detection of their so-called flying saucers by radar. They may reply, "But flying saucers are made of metal that radar does not detect." This solution may be ingenious, but it is also *ad hoc*. It does not lead to other fruitful hypotheses. Nor does it fit into a system related to what we know about metals or radar.

Kepler's hypothesis about the elliptical orbit of planets provided a base for Newton to launch his theory of gravitation. Newton's theory of gravitation locked in with Kepler's hypothesis and also provided a base for correcting Kepler's views. In challenging a well-founded scientific hypothesis, the challenger has the burden to prove that such a hypothesis is incorrect. In such cases it takes more than noise and isolated bits of data. It requires evidence, experiment, and usually the establishing of a hypothesis that accounts for everything the earlier one did and a bit more as well.

Getting the Job Done.   In making a hypothesis or in considering a decision, we are looking for something that promises the kinds of results we want. The idea we choose to act on needs to be at least as promising as other ideas. We hope it offers more promise. Clearly this is not the only basis on which we make choices, because we need to consider other matters relevant to how we choose the most promising idea. We also operate under some restraints. We might find it easier to get conclusive results about the curative effect of some drugs by using such drugs immediately on patients in hospitals. But we want to know more about such drugs and their side effects before we begin to risk the health, sanity, and even the lives of other persons.

We may need to recognize that in some cases we are trying to do the wrong job. In the history of science Kepler tried to show that a somewhat mystical notion had scientific support: he proposed to show that there was a mathematical harmony in the movement of heavenly bodies. His hypothesis required planets to move in epicycles (with some deviations). Using other theories developed by Tycho Brahe, he made the calculations required by his view. But he found that by accepting an error of up to eight minutes in Brahe's views, he could claim support for his views about the harmonies of the heavenly bodies. He decided to give up the original job since the data suggested that trying to do another job might be more successful. This time he reached his goal—he showed that the planets follow an elliptical orbit.

2.   Some Problems in Testing Hypotheses and Decisions

It is time to pause and look at what we have been talking about. Are there not some serious problems with the method we have been discussing? Is it not possible that we still can make mistakes? Clearly there are troublesome problems, and mistakes can be made. We shall look at four such problems: the practice of affirming the consequent of a conditional statement, the problem of not always rejecting the hypothesis once we find the consequent of a conditional statement denied, the issue of the principle of induction, and the problem of relevance.

These issues are a part of the context of the structure of the scheme in which we seek to reach conclusions through an inductive process. We have advanced this scheme as follows:

If T and S, then F and not G.

We also know both that F_1, F_2, F_3, . . . and F_n can hold by the tests we make and that we do find instances of not G_1 and not G_2. And it still is possible for T and S not to hold. In deductive logic we would have the formal fallacy of affirming the consequent. How do we justify this procedure?

By use of the above method we do have some protection against premature acceptance of a hypothesis by seeking the statement of conditions, which if they hold, would justify its rejection. If the hypothesis T and those assumptions and beliefs, S_1 and S_2, that we hold in making the hypothesis are well founded, then condition G_1 will not be present. But if we find condition G_1, we also have found a reason to reject the hypothesis in the context in which it appears. We should not dismiss lightly the safeguards which such a procedure afford us. We want some positive reasons for accepting a hypothesis, and we seek to find those reasons in testing for F_1, F_2, and F_3.

There are other safeguards to protect against error of judgment. We pointed out some of these safeguards in the previous discussion of standards for evaluating sound hypotheses and good decisions. An added safeguard is the insistence that the tests and the methods used in making them are made public to give others the opportunity to look at the evidence and to repeat the tests.

Any justifying of the acceptance of a hypothesis by testing its consequence depends on the relevance of the tested factors to the claims made by the hypothesis. We shall see later that the establishing of such relevance is not an easy matter.

We still have some difficulties. They point to the need for caution in the use of the method, and in allowing for future corrections of hypotheses and, where possible, of decisions. But some decisions are irreversible and we have to live with their outcomes. Perhaps at the time of making some decisions we would do well to allow for hedging against the uncertainties of the future. That is, we can make some decisions in such ways that in carrying them out, we have some ways of modifying them, together with the results which flow from them.

Another apparent difficulty in accepting this method of confirming hypotheses also relates to a formal problem in logic. If F_1 is the consequence of a hypothesis in this method and not F_1 turns up, we do not immediately reject the hypothesis T or the context, S, in which T is proposed. For example, in this case we would not accept the following argument as sound: "If Newton's theory of gravitation is true, then he needs to make accurate predictions in his (first) efforts to predict the movements of the Moon by the use of his hypothesis. But he does not (at first) make accurate predictions about the movements of the Moon merely by the use of his hypothesis. Therefore, his hypothesis is in error." In the above case it turns out that it was not Newton's original hypothesis, but the context in which it was made that was faulty. After revising the context to allow for a more accurate measurement of the Earth's circumference, he was able to use his hypothesis to predict accurately the movement of the Moon.

There are other reasons for not rushing to find a hypothesis in error on the basis of initial findings that fail to show their anticipated results. The error could be in holding that a given test is a proper one for the hypothesis. Some errors may occur in carrying out the mechanical aspects of an experiment. And there is contamination in the testing results. An unobserved factor may intervene to account for a failure of a test. Human error in some form may account for the failure to follow precisely the specified testing method. It may take time to get the flaws out of the experimental design. And one may need more time and effort to search for and correct errors that may be present in the experiment. Or some other error may be present in the context, S, and what the experiment is rejecting is the context, S, rather than the hypothesis. However, we need to recognize that a hypothesis is not accepted until there are definite and positive reasons for doing so.

In practical decisions, our risks tend to increase as the anticipated consequences of the evidence on which we base our decisions are not confirmed. Of course, the risks we take may be even greater if we fail to make any tests of such consequences at all.

A third issue in dealing with this method of confirming hypotheses is the justification of the principle of induction. There is a gap between what the evidence appears to strictly justify and the conclusion derived from it. How do we know that the unknown past is similar to the known past? And how do we justify believing that the future will resemble the known past? (David Hume raised this difficult question in the eighteenth century.)

Many philosophers who have discussed this issue at length propose various solutions. We do not find any of these solutions entirely satisfactory. Nor do we know of one that is.

One solution proposes that we justify filling this gap on the basis of past experience. We can point to past instances where we filled the gap and predicted and controlled what happened, and there was success. But since our past experience is highly limited, there is a projection of hypotheses toward the future of which we have no experience. So at least in principle it could be different from the past.

A second solution is that we assume the principle of the uniformity of nature. But this also appears to assume the point in dispute. How do we know that nature is uniform? Do we assume that it is?

A third solution is that ultimately we have to have some point of beginning, which is the inductive procedure. We cannot go beyond this procedure without going in a circle. This position may be correct in showing that there has to be a point of beginning. But it is less convincing in holding that that point has to be the principle of induction.

A fourth position holds that this principle of induction permits the correcting of views, which, indeed, it does. But why should we not want this to be a part of any method that we adopt?

The position we recommend is that of looking at the context in which we carry on inductive procedures. In this context we project a continuing uniformity in the kinds of things that we have found uniform in the past. If we continue to find such uniformity, we take note of that. But if we fail to find such uniformity, then we have to recheck on our data and procedures. We may find that there are some things to which the method is not adapted. In the meanwhile we find that the method does enable us to predict and explain some of the things that interest us. This is not a justification of the principle of induction in any technical sense. It does offer a proposal that we continue to use this method until we find something better to help us organize and understand the knowledge we gain about the world.

A fourth critical difficulty in justifying the method of testing discussed in this chapter is relevance. What basis do we have for claiming that the tests we perform have some relevance to the testing of a hypothesis or of a decision that we are making? One reason the problem is so difficult is that any proposed answer tends to assume the issue that is in need of proof. That is, we have to assume that we know what relevance is in order to discuss what is relevant to discussing relevance. But relevance is the point at issue. We shall not claim that we can provide a wholly satisfying answer to this problem. But we shall discuss some features of the problem.

Carl G. Hempel sharpened the issue of relevance in his argument that the use of anything in the universe can provide for a type of confirming instance of a hypothesis such as "All ravens are black." He points out that an equivalent form of this statement is "All nonblack things are nonravens." He also claims that any statement that confirms an equivalent statement confirms the original statement. Thus, to find anything that is black also counts for that thing being a raven. Likewise, if one finds anything that is nonblack, it also counts as evidence that the thing is a nonraven. The class of "all black things" and the class of "all nonblack things" exhausts the universe, leaving us with the possibility that everything counts as a confirming instance of the hypotheses. Nothing could count against it. But we should see this problem in the way that Hempel presents it. He does not claim that different kinds of positive evidence confirm to the same degree or carry the same weight in the testing of a hypothesis.[10] But this paradox points to the need to establish some relevance between what a hypothesis holds and what one accepts as a confirming instance as well as a disconfirming instance of a hypothesis.

In seeking to provide some justification for our use of relevance, we look for the context in which we use this notion. Let us assume that we are looking for some causal connection between the conditions required by the hypothesis and the tests used to confirm the hypothesis. If a hypothesis requires a relative increase in the growth of a plant by the use of a given amount of nitrogen, then we add the nitrogen around the plant to see what happens. But the mere fact that such a test works out does not prove the relevance of such factors in all cases. For example, it has been reported that in a study of kindergarten children in a given area, there was a high correlation between the number of bathtubs in a house and a high performance level of achievement (as measured by the test) for the children living in such houses. But to account for the achievement level by the number of bathtubs in a house does not appear to be directly relevant to high achieve-

---

[10] *Aspects of Scientific Explanation* (New York: Free Press, 1965), pp. 35, 48.

ment levels. If the number of bathtubs in a house could result in such achievement, then we could go around and put more bathtubs in houses rather than spend so much money on school construction! We recognize that the number of bathtubs may be indicative of something about the children's background—perhaps family affluence. The relevance we are searching for may be at this point.

In justifying some notions of relevance, we also appeal to our ability to make accurate predictions. But the ability to make accurate predictions also can be tied in with the notion of causal relations. When scientists test a hypothesis, in some respects they are making a prediction that a given event will occur. And, in part, what they are predicting is that a given event or condition will occur as a result of their testing. If a hypothesis states that sound travels at a given speed, we predict that it will do so in a given case. Then we measure its speed in that case.

We also make commonsense predictions and hold the results we predict relevant to our justifying the decision we make. For example, Alice is baking some cupcakes and wants to know if they are done. To test for doneness, she can insert a toothpick in a cupcake to see whether any dough sticks to it. If it has no dough on it, she takes the cupcakes out of the oven. She makes the prediction that the cupcakes will have a firm texture.

But predicting does not solve the problem of relevance. In some cases we may want to hold that two things have some relevance to each other, but we are unable to make predictions. Persons highly informed about common stocks and the relevance of different factors to the action of the stock market frequently make the wrong predictions about the direction it will move. There is even a contrary opinion view. This holds that a strong indication of the direction the market will take is contrary to any strong consensus developed about the market's direction by the experts in market forecasting.

In some cases we may be able to make predictions, but the matter of relevance is the point at issue. We may be able to use the number of bathtubs in a house to predict the performance level of a group of children in a given population. But the point at issue could be the relevance, if any, that the number of bathtubs in a house has to the achievement level of children.

We might propose that we limit the notion of relevance to those cases which are "beyond a reasonable doubt." But we immediately note that "beyond a reasonable doubt" has a subjective ring that we may prefer to avoid. Let us explore it further.

Let us look at the use of circumstantial evidence in courts of law where "beyond a reasonable doubt" has a legal meaning. Let us assume that a grand jury indicts Mr. Jones on the charges of armed robbery; he is accused of having robbed a drive-in grocery store. The case is being tried. The applicable laws and judicial procedures are a part of the context in which the court determines the guilt of the accused. If circumstantial evidence is the basis for the charges, then we have a part of the argument form we have been using in this chapter. If Jones committed the crime, then circumstances F_1, F_2, F_3, and F_4 are present. It is shown that these circumstances are the case. But this only shows that Jones' circumstances were such that he might have committed the crime. These circumstances might also apply to many other persons.[11]

Although only circumstantial evidence is present in some convictions, the prosecution has to convince the members of the jury "beyond a reasonable doubt" that the defendant is guilty of acting as charged. To try to establish a case "beyond a reasonable doubt," the prosecution attempts to show that the relevance of the circumstantial evidence as a whole to actions taken by the accused is so interwoven that in a legal sense the members of the jury no longer have any reasonable doubt about the guilt of the accused. But juries have rendered bad verdicts.

In science, after there is confirmation of a hypothesis, one submits the evidence to a qualified body of peers. A review of the evidence occurs. Other qualified persons may repeat the tests. And the scientific community tends to adopt a position about the relevance of the evidence and the claims made about it. We strongly support this procedure. But peer judgment also can be in error.

The significance of the peer judgment in such cases is in the safeguards it provides in evaluating the relevance of the evidence as well as the methods followed. "Beyond a reasonable doubt" no longer applies to only one investigator. Rather it now includes the findings of a qualified group of scientific peers.

Peer judgment also has some relevance in making decisions. At times we seek feedback from persons experienced in the field to which a judgment applies. The quality of counsel in such cases varies widely. For such counsel to be comparable to peer judgment in accepting a scientific hypothesis, it would need to consist of a group of persons highly experienced and informed in the field to which the decision applies.

It also is possible to appeal to past experience as a basis for our being able to know whether something is relevant in a given case. We apparently have had some success with knowing what is relevant in the past. We have confirmed hypotheses and have applied these hypotheses to the world about us. By the use of such hypotheses, we have succeeded in making our environment more responsive to satisfying our interests. We see significant progress made in science, technology, and other areas of human interest.

---

[11] Courts of law give much stronger weight to direct evidence. A witness, Smith, might say in a variation of the above case: "I saw Jones in a car in the neighborhood ten minutes before the robbery [circumstantial evidence]. And I also saw Jones in the drive-in grocery pointing a gun at the cashier and I saw him grab the money, put it in a sack, and leave [direct evidence]."

But this type of argument tends to dodge the issue of relevance. It simply assumes we have known what relevance is as a condition for our having succeeded when we used this assumption.

We have seen that efforts to resolve the issue of relevance tend to assume what they need to prove. It is recommended that we recognize the specific contexts in which an issue of relevance arises. We can intertwine the reasons we have been using into a cable, to use an analogy from Charles S. Peirce. We make the proposal to appeal to predictions, qualified peer judgment, and past experience to determine what counts as relevant in that case.[12] We also raise the following issue: On the basis of these considerations and of the context in which we make a given hypothesis, what conditions would count in its support and what conditions could count against it? In the meanwhile, let us use the knowledge and methods which science and critical common sense have provided, while we hope for further correction and growth in our knowledge and in our decision-making abilities.

In this chapter we have discussed some stages in testing sound decisions and some steps for testing hypotheses. We have looked at some issues related to our seeking to justify our knowledge by making such tests. In the next chapter we shall discuss the forming of causal hypotheses.

EXERCISES

A. In the following examples state the primary hypothesis that is tested. State also any tests that are made in evaluating the strength of the hypothesis. Do you have suggestions about additional methods that could be used in testing these hypotheses?

   1. In further tests on x-rays Roentgen proposed to test the hypothesis that his heretofore undetected x-ray was able to penetrate and to pass through bodies. He proceeded to test the consequences of this hypothesis. If such a penetrating ray is present, then it could penetrate both a sheet of paper and paper bound together in a book. It also could penetrate a deck of cards, tin foil, blocks of wood, aluminum, hard rubber, and a human hand. His tests showed that these consequences held.
   2. Roentgen made the hypothesis that the degree to which the x-ray penetrated an object varies with some of the properties found in the object. Again he proceeded to test its consequences. He tested glass that contained lead and glass without lead and found the glass with lead was less transparent. He also sought to test for the penetration of the x-ray in such metals as copper, silver, and gold. His tests show that a fluorescence was present behind the plates of these metals, as his hypothesis required, provided the plates were

---

[12] The above suggestion is a proposal. But even then some may claim that it is a form of begging the question. However, as a proposal it invites a counterproposal. It suggests a willingness to examine other proposals on resolving this issue. And it recognizes that a proposal does not prove anything.

not too thick. He also tested a fairly thin sheet of lead (1.5 mm thick). His tests showed that this lead was "practically opaque." Since his anticipated consequences held, he accepted his hypothesis as confirmed.

3. Researchers at a university medical center on the East Coast made a study of some possible relationships between tendencies for blood clots to form in rats and the presence of male hormones in these rats. They believed that with a greater tendency for blood clotting in an animal, there also is a greater incidence of heart attacks.

In the study they induced a clotting of the blood, or thrombus, on a major stomach artery of rats. Young male rats developed thrombus twice as large as young female rats. And their death rate was twice as high. With aging there was a narrowing of the difference both in the size of the thrombus and in the death rate between the male rats and the females. These circumstances parallel conditions found in humans.

In further experiments they injected the male hormone, testosterone, into both male and female rats. In a second group they injected the female hormone, estrogen, into other male and female rats. And for a third and control group they did not inject any hormones. Then they induced the thrombi in the rats in the three groups. The death rate in both the male and female rats receiving the male hormone was four times as high as for the rats in the third control group. But the death rates in the male and female rats treated with the female hormone were comparable to those in the third and control group. Likewise, the size of the thrombos became much larger with the group given the male hormone than for those in the other groups.

They also found that when they induced a thrombus in rats and then injected some with the male hormone and others with an anti-male hormone, antitestosterone, the following ratios held. In the rats receiving only the male hormone the death rate was 62.5 percent of the males and 34.3 percent of the females. In the rats receiving both the male hormone and the anti-male hormone, the death rate was 33.3 percent among the males and 16.7 percent among the females.[13]

4. A study was made at a hospital in England of the effect on a person when a sweet drink such as tonic mixed with alcohol is taken on an empty stomach. The taking of pure glucose (a sugar) on an empty stomach results in changes in behavior and mood. The degree of such changes varies directly with the amount of glucose taken. The taking of a sweet drink with alcohol on an empty stomach releases large amounts of glucose into the system.

In the above study there was a test with ten healthy subjects. On one occasion the subjects had 50 g of gin (about three drinks) mixed with tonic having 60 g of sucrose (a sugar). On a second occasion they drank another 50 g of gin mixed with a Slimline tonic having only 5 g of sucrose. And on a third occasion they drank only tonic having 60 g of sucrose. Within one hour after taking the gin and high-sucrose tonic, there was a sharp rise in both the blood sugar and sense of levity. There was a sense of levity without

[13] Anelia Uzunova, Estelle Ramey, and Peter W. Ramwell, "Effect of Testosterone, Sex, and Age on Experimentally Induced Arterial Thrombosis," *Nature*, Vol. 261, No. 5562 (June 24, 1976), pp. 212–213.

the high rise of blood sugar with the gin and low-sucrose tonic. But within the next two hours there was a sharp decrease in the amount of blood sugar in all subjects taking the alcohol with the high-sucrose tonic. There also was a sense of depression, of grief reactions, and of sleepiness in some subjects. The taking either of the tonic without the gin or of only low-sucrose tonic with the gin did not result in the severe low blood sugar or in the degree of depression or of sleepiness found when the larger amounts of tonic were drunk. There was no sense of levity when they drank only the tonic.[14]

5. Pasteur cultured chicken cholera microbacilli in a broth heated at 37°C. Inoculation of chickens with the microbacilli resulted in the death of the chickens. He left on vacation. And on his return he inoculated other chickens with the original microbacilli. He found that this last group of chickens was not seriously affected by this injection. But he also found that by injecting the attenuated bacilli successively through several chickens within a brief period he could restore their virulence.[15]

6. Over a period of eight years, researchers in Australia used male Wistar rats in eight of nine different studies to analyze the relation of the growth of the size of the brain to the rats' living environment. One group of rats would be isolated for a period ranging from eighteen to 120 days. They stayed in small walled units with mesh floors and ceilings. The other group was tested for similar time periods. But these rats were in groups of six to twelve animals. This latter group had large cages and new playthings daily.

     At the end of each test period the researchers killed the rats and weighed the components of their anterior brain. There was a significant difference between the brain development of the isolated rats and of the other rats. The explanation provided for this difference was that there was an adequate amount of sensory stimulation for the rats living together. But there was deficiency of such stimulation and a retarded development of groups of neurons in the isolated rats.[16]

7. When marine protozoa, called the red tide, invade the shells of clams, they produce a toxin which with sufficient strength can destroy the commercial value of the clams. In the Northeast, marine biologists found some clams infected with the toxin of the red tide. After arranging the clams in a concentrated area, they bubbled ozone into the seawater where the clams were. Their purpose was to seek to break up the concentration of the toxin in the clams. The researchers took samples of the toxin from the clams and injected these samples into mice. They found the rate of toxin in the treated clams was 50 percent less than it had been. This lowered amount of toxin was within the amount permitted for commercial use of the clams.[17]

8. A study was conducted at university centers in the Midwest on the relation

[14] Stephen J. D. O'Keefe and Vincent Marks, "Lunchtime Gin and Tonic. A Cause of Retroactive Hypoglycemia," *Lancet*, Vol. 1 for 1977, No. 8025 (June 18, 1977), pp. 1286–1288.

[15] Rene Taton, ed., *Science in the Nineteenth Century*, trans. by A. J. Pomerons (New York: Basic Books, 1965), pp. 394–395.

[16] R. A. Cummings, R. N. Walsh, and others, "A Developmental Theory of Environmental Enrichment," *Science*, Vol. 197, No. 4303 (August 12, 1977), pp. 692–694.

[17] *Science News*, Vol. 112, No. 13 (September 24, 1977), p. 201.

of environmental factors to the scores made on I.Q. tests. Both heredity and environment appear to have relevance in predicting the level of performance on such tests. This study sought to analyze the difference between the social and economic status of a family and the family environment itself in predicting I.Q. scores. They conducted a series of tests with 105 three-year-old children. Some of the children were from black families and others were from white families. The researchers found that the combining of intellectual stimulation and of emotional support within the family provided a more reliable base for predicting performance of the children on the I.Q. tests than was possible by the use of the social and economic status of their families.[18]

9. There is a yearly death rate of 12 percent of kidney patients taking a dialysis treatment. Some of the deaths occur after patients fail to take the dialysis treatment according to instructions. Investigators sought to identify potentially high-risk patients. They found that any combination of three out of four factors placed a patient in a high-risk category. These factors are: a strong rejection of dependency, strong tendencies to anger or excitability, proneness to anxiety and depression, and poor control over impulses.[19]

10. Different parts of the brain specialize in different functions. Researchers have found that in 99 percent of right-handed people, there is a specialization in the left hemisphere of the brain for language development and right hemisphere for spatial relations and imagery. The same hemispheres of the brain have similar functions for 60 percent of left-handed people. But in the other 40 percent, language development occurs in the right hemisphere and spatial relation in the left.

Two psychologists at an eastern university wondered if there was some relation between the writing habits found with some frequency in left-handed persons and the hemisphere of the brain that specializes in language. Most right-handed people whose language specialization is in the left hemisphere of the brain write with the palm of their hands below the line on which they are writing. But many left-handed persons write with the palm of their hands above this line. These psychologists advanced the hypothesis that this inverted way of writing would be found primarily in persons whose writing hands and whose brain hemisphere for specializing in language behavior were on the same side. They found that when there was a crisscrossing (such as left to right) from the side of the brain hemisphere specializing in language to the other side for the writing hand, persons wrote with the palm of their hand below the writing line. But that when the writing hand and the side of the hemisphere of the brain specializing in language use were on the same side of the body, there was a strong tendency to write in hooked position with the palm of the hand above the writing line.

The basis of this conclusion was a study of seventy-three students— right- and left-handed males and females, some of whom wrote in an inverted position and others who wrote in the usual way. They found that the twenty-

[18] Robert H. Bradley, Bettye M. Caldwell, and Richard Evans, "Home Environment, Social Status and Mental Test Performance," *Journal of Education Psychology*, Vol. 69, No. 6 (December, 1977), pp. 697–701.
[19] *Science News*, Vol. 110, No. 19 (November 6, 1976), p. 296.

four left-handed persons who wrote in an inverted style did not have the criss-crossing pattern. In these cases the left hemisphere of their brains specialized in language functions and the right side in spatial dimensions and imagery. But there was no apparent tendency for left-handed persons, with language specializations in their right hemisphere, to write in this inverted fashion. Comparable results were found with the right-handed persons who wrote with an inverted style.[20]

11. In the confirmation of Einstein's theory of relativity, a basic problem was that within the customary accuracy of observation most of its anticipated consequences were similar to those of Newton's theory of gravitation. However, three consequences were proposed to distinguish the predictive ability of the two views. One consequence was that the deflection of a ray of light by the sun would be twice as great as was anticipated by Newton's theory. The second was that it would be possible to account for the precession (in seconds of arc per century) in the orbit of the planet Mercury in a more accurate manner. The third was that an atom would vibrate less rapidly in a gravitational field. To test the first consequence, the image of a star barely on the outside of the sun was photographed in 1919 in Brazil and in the Gulf of Guiana. It was found that the apparent displacement of the star was in accord with the anticipation of Einstein's theory. In the case of the discrepancy of 42 seconds of arc per century in the orbit of the planet Mercury, Einstein's view improved on the Newtonian view by calculating a change of 43 seconds of arc. The confirmation of the third consequence was more difficult, but barely perceptible differences were found in studies of the spectrum of the sun.[21]

B. Something to do.

Formulate a generalization that has been held or that might be held about the following cases. Identify some consequences that you would expect to find if these generalizations are to be accepted. How would you test for these consequences?

1. A significant generalization related to some area of your interest.
2. A generalization related to a current case to be tried in a court of law.
3. A generalization related to the political future of a contemporary politician.
4. A generalization related to the development of a particular social tension in a large city in your general geographical area.
5. A generalization related to a college or university athletic team that is "a favorite" to win a conference title for the coming season.

---

[20] Jerre Levy and Marylou Reid, "Variations in Writing Posture and Cerebral Organization," *Science,* Vol. 194, No. 4262 (October 15, 1976), pp. 338–339.

[21] Sir William Cecil Dampier, *A History of Science*, 4th ed. (New York: Macmillan, 1949), pp. 408–409.

CHAPTER 15

CAUSAL
RELATIONS

15.1 EXPLANATIONS AND CAUSAL RELATIONS

An interest in why things happen as they do is basic to science as well as to everyday life. In this chapter we shall look at one way of providing explanations by use of causal relations.

We often want to know why some conditions hold or why something happens. Why does the rate of automobile insurance go up? Why did the energy crisis occur? Why did the municipal workers strike? Why do we have inflation? Why do medical costs continue to rise faster than other costs? Why is John absent from class? Why should a person accused of a felony not be required to testify against himself? Why are rents so high? Why are more red blood corpuscles needed at very high altitudes? Why are the orbits of planets more like an oval rather than a circle? Why is the sum of angles of a triangle equal to 180 degrees? Responses to such queries provide different kinds of explanations.

Explanations do not occur in a vacuum. We propose them in a social context. In providing an explanation, we are responding to some interest which we or others have. In response to many requests for an explanation, we tend to select one factor out of a number that may be relevant. We likely will give a response that will serve to satisfy both ourselves and the party seeking it. We may satisfy one party by saying that we need more red blood corpuscles at higher altitudes in order to breathe better. We may tell another party that at higher altitudes the amount of oxygen in the air is less than at lower altitudes. Since red blood corpuscles are carriers of oxygen there is need for more of them in the bloodstream at higher altitudes to keep bodily functions normal. A biologist may want a more technical explanation. To explain why a given car wreck occurred, a psychologist might seek one explanation, an attorney a second, a road engineer a third, a sociologist a fourth, and a physicist still another.

There are various kinds of explanations. In a general sense they are responses to a question beginning with "why." Some philosophers like Carl Hempel, Ernest Nagel, and Karl Popper have proposed two basic types of scientific explanations—deductive and probabilistic. A deductive explanation can have the following scheme:

Explicans: 1. A statement of a general law or laws.

2. A statement of conditions holding that the requirements of the above laws are met in a particular case.

Explicandum: 3. A singular statement that a given condition or event holds on the basis that the conditions for meeting a general law have been met.

In the above case one might state that water freezes at 32° Fahrenheit. And it is now 31°. Thus, surface water on overpasses is freezing.

Probabilistic explanations have premises which hold that with a given set of conditions, a given kind of event happens at a stated frequency and that such conditions are present in a given case. Thus, one can expect that the likelihood for a given event to happen in this case will be at the frequency usually holding for this kind of event. An illustration of this type of explanation is as follows:

1. The probability of a resident of the United States having a blood type with a Rh negative factor is 15 percent.

2. The students in this logic class are residents of the United States.

3. Thus, the probability that any student in this logic class has a blood type with a Rh negative factor is 15 percent.

It has been claimed that the above kinds of explanations can be misleading. They appear to be arguments, but it is not their purpose to prove that a conclusion is true. Rather they serve to explain why something is the case rather than to prove that something is the case.

Some explanations use the notion of purpose. And purposive explanations can be of two kinds. These are explanations based on functions and on motives. We can explain why cars have wheels by accounting for the function wheels have in the movement of the car. We can explain why labor union members pushed for higher fringe benefits in a collective bargaining agreement by reference to their motives or reasons for wanting these added salary supplements.

There also can be other types of explanations. We may want to explain what the principle of identity is in defining zero. We may want to explain why a middle term in a categorical syllogism has to be distributed at least once. We may seek to account for belief that human beings have been in North America for 25,000 years by reference to findings of carved animal bones that are that old. We may seek to give a genetic account for the Boston Tea Party. In this case we would refer to the social and political conditions in the Colonies during the 1770s. We also would talk about the British policies toward the colonists and about the colonists' response to those policies. We also might attempt to explain some matters about a religious institution by reference to the kinds of traditions, value systems, and governance structure that it has followed in the past.

The idea that all explanations are causal in character, although widely accepted at one time, is no longer the general view. Such a position cannot account for explanations of generalizations by other generalizations. And it does not provide for explanations by reference to noncausal or quasi-causal reasons in formal science and in common sense. One generalization does not cause another, nor does a formal rule or principle cause another. Yet the older view persists, emphasizing the significance of causal explanations in science.

A major use of hypotheses in science is to develop causal explanations for events. With the developing of these hypotheses we can understand and in some cases predict and control the way some things happen as they do. Thus, we can understand and predict tides by using the laws of motion and of the attraction of masses to each other and by knowing the orbits of the Earth and the Moon, and the relation of these bodies to each other.

In basic science, several notions appear to be associated with the interpretation of causal relations. David Hume pointed out some of these relations:

1. A given kind of cause in similar circumstances always has the same kind of effect.

2. A given kind of effect always recurs in the presence of similar kinds of causal connections in relevantly similar circumstances.

3. A given kind of cause is always prior to (or simultaneous with) its kind of effect.

4. A given kind of cause has some connection with its effect, such that there are grounds other than merely a temporal sequence of events for interpreting a cause-and-effect relation.

5. The cause and effect are not jointly the effect or the symptoms of a prior
   cause.

In this stricter interpretation of causal relations there is present a set
of conditions that frequently remain unstated and that relate to the notion
of the total cause. In medical science there is a search for a common cause
for a given kind of disease. But in many cases there tends to be other
conditions that must be present. For example, the infective agent for swine
influenza is a specific virus. But this virus can invade a human body without
that person developing influenza. Other conditions such as the age, general
health, and immune system have relevance to what happens in such cases.

On the other hand, in every case of swine influenza there is present in
the body of the infected person a given kind of virus. Whenever there is
this kind of effect, there is a similar kind of cause. We want to hold that the
infective virus attacks the body of the host prior to the host's developing
the disease. We also know of some connection between the infective agent
and the victim's becoming ill. Numerous diseases result from a virus infection. And the connection that we find between the initial exposure to the
virus and the disease is other than merely one of a temporal sequence.
Likewise, in the case of influenza, there may be a reddening and soreness
of the throat prior to the feeling of aches in bones and nausea. But we
would want to hold that these are joint effects or symptoms of a common
cause. That is, the reddening of the throat is not the cause of the aches and
nausea. Rather the cause of the aches and nausea is the infection that also
is the source of the sore throat.

There are other kinds of influenza such as the Russian or Hong Kong
or Asian varieties. But each of these has a different kind of virus and each
represents different kinds of effects caused by different infective agents.
Knowledge that different infective agents are present makes possible the
preparation of a vaccine that protects against infection by the different
viruses.

The view that the same kind of cause has the same kind of effect and
the same kind of effect has the same kind of cause requires that we break
down the notion of an effect to highly specific kinds of cases. If we are
dealing with the cause of death or the cause of aggressiveness, then we
need to break such effects down into different kinds of death or of aggression
in order to discuss the specific causes in any given case.

There are other meanings of the notion of causal relations. One meaning
holds that a cause is either an essential condition or a sufficient condition
for a given kind of event. An essential condition is a state of affairs that
must be present for a given kind of event to occur. But such a condition
may be present and the given event does not occur. An essential condition
for lighting a match is the presence of oxygen. But the oxygen can be
present without a match being lit. An essential condition for driving an

automobile on a trip is the presence of gasoline in the car's tank. But the gasoline may be in the tank without our taking a trip. An essential condition for students completing college work is their attainment of a certain level of intellectual development and ability. Yet it is possible for students to attain this level of development and ability without completing their college work.

Many times when we are planning to prevent something from happening we seek to manipulate essential conditions. If we do not want someone to drive our car, we try to prevent such a person from gaining access to the ignition switch of the car. Thus, we do not leave our keys around where some associate may use them to start the car. Or, we keep the car locked as a means of trying to prevent its being stolen. If we want to prevent the spoiling of food, we put it in the refrigerator to slow down the growth rate of bacteria.

A sufficient condition is a happening in whose presence another given event always takes place, provided the essential conditions for that event are also present. We usually think of a sufficient condition as a kind of event that has a triggering action. A sufficient condition for lighting a match is striking it, provided there is oxygen present. A sufficient condition for having a picture and sound on the television set is closing its circuit by turning on the switch, provided the set is in working order. A sufficient condition for burping a baby may be a patting on the back, provided the baby is in a position where the air can be belched out easily.

One problem with sufficient conditions is that this notion can lead to accepting a plurality of causes. In basic science there usually is a preference to avoid this position. In a given illness a physician may treat a bacterial infection in several ways; with each kind of treatment the patient may throw off the infection. In such cases at least two approaches are possible. One may seek to find a common factor in the different kinds of reactions to the medical treatment. Or, in some cases one may claim there is a different kind of effect with a different kind of cause.

A stronger notion of cause develops when we combine essential and sufficient conditions. We then can define a cause as the combining of any essential and sufficient conditions in whose presence a given kind of event always occurs. In this case we do not restrict the cause of an event either to the essential condition alone or to the sufficient condition alone. In this context, the cause of lighting the match is heating its surface by striking it in the presence of oxygen.

Sometimes we also speak about a contributing condition. A contributing condition is a state of affairs which increases the likelihood that a given kind of event will occur, but in itself is neither essential nor sufficient to bring about a given event. A condition such as "being run down" may lower one's immunity system to increase the likelihood of catching a common cold. We might have a common cold without "being run down." And we might have the condition of "being run down" without catching the common cold.

Statistical correlations supported by careful experiment or other rigorous types of inquiry provide a basis for another view of causal relations. In a statistical study we may find a significant degree of correlation between two factors such as income and formal education. In some cases we may want to hold that one of these factors has a causal relation to the second. In correlating the amount of yearly income of a group of persons with their level of formal education, we can call their yearly income a "function" of their formal education. If we say that x is a function of y in such instances, then y may have resemblances to a cause and x may have resemblances to an effect. If we find a high correlation between lung cancer and heavy cigarette smoking, we say that the lung cancer is a function of heavy cigarette smoking. And we may want to hold that the heavy cigarette smoking is causally related to the development of the lung cancer in a given group.

The causal relations discussed in such statistical data relate to the performance of a whole class of persons and not to a given person singled out in the class. It would be erroneous to conclude only on the basis of the statistical data above that a named person who is a heavy smoker will have lung cancer. It would be satisfactory to claim that lung cancer would be significantly more likely to occur in a person who is a member of a group identified as being heavy cigarette smokers than in a person who does not smoke.

The above data are comparable to tables compiled by insurance companies, which show the frequency of the occurrence of certain factors and some correlations between them. These tables make possible a more accurate prediction of the behavior of a group of persons, including the degree to which a given set of factors will be scattered in the group. They do not provide assurance that a given person in the group will conform to the statistical norm for the group. A man with a life expectancy of an additional forty years may die within a week or a year or he may live sixty years.

Interpreted on the basis of statistical correlations, the notion of a causal relation provides a basis for manipulating conditions in a large group. If we manipulate one set of conditions, then we anticipate that another set of conditions will follow. Thus, if an engineering school raises its entrance standards for admission to its program, its administrators may expect, within limits, a higher level of academic performance by newly admitted students.

We have seen that in its strictest use a cause is an event which in similar circumstances always has the same given effect and that a given effect always has the same cause. But we also want to use the notion of a causal relation in a broader context than such a view permits. Another view holds that a causal relation is an essential and a sufficient condition from which a given effect always follows. A third view is that a causal relation holds between two relevant factors such that if x is a function of y then y may have a causal relation to x. The notion of some relevance of an attributed cause to its effect is present in any causal relation. In the next section we shall look at some inductive methods that help us identify causal relations.

15.2 MILL'S METHODS FOR IDENTIFYING CAUSAL RELATIONS

In this section there is a discussion of inductive methods to help identify causal relations. These are the methods of agreement, of difference, of the joint methods of agreement and difference, of concomitant variations, and of residues.

In modern scientific inquiry, the use of inductive methods for identifying causal relation is basic in many forms of research. John Stuart Mill, a nineteenth-century British philosopher, discusses five of these methods. Logicians refer to them as "Mill's methods of experimental inquiry." But Mill did not originate any of the methods, nor was he the first to identify and discuss them. The positive use of these methods focuses on identifying a causal relation. Their negative use helps to establish that a given event or condition either has no causal relation to another event or that it is not the sole cause of the latter.

Let us look at Mill's methods of determining causal relations.

The Method of Agreement *instances w/ one common factor that have same outcome*

Mill makes the following statement about the method of agreement:

> If two or more instances of the phenomenon under investigation have only one circumstance in common, the circumstance in which alone all the instances agree is the cause (or effect) of the given phenomenon.

If some students in a dormitory have food poisoning, we would inquire about the food eaten by all of those who are ill. If a tunafish salad is the only food common in each case of illness, then there are strong reasons for identifying this salad as the source of the food poisoning.

In a negative way the method of agreement can help to show that one factor does not have a significant relation to a second as a possible cause. In the example above we might have believed at first that rice pudding had a causal relation to the food poisoning. But we find several persons with food poisoning who did not eat the rice pudding. The effect occurred without this factor. Therefore, we reject the view that the rice pudding is the probable cause of the food poisoning.

We can use the following diagram to show the design of the method of agreement. (Capital letters from *F* to *M* stand for factors identified as possibly relevant to the occurrence of a given kind of effect. And *E* stands for a given kind of effect.)

Case 1   *F G H I*   followed by an instance of *E*

Case 2   *G H   K*   followed by an instance of *E*

Case 3   *G   I K L* followed by an instance of *E*

Thus, factor *G* may have a causal relation to an instance of *E*.

In the strict use of the method of agreement, we may need to manipulate factors other than the factor being tested. A strict demonstration of a causal relation by this method proposes to show that "All cases of *F* are followed by cases of *G*" and "All cases of *G* follow cases of *F* and only cases of *F*." The first form is easier to establish than the second.

In the method of agreement (as well as in other methods discussed later), the factor tested as the cause is usually more complex than the single factor identified. For example, we find after repeated testing the water boils at the temperature of 212° F. The claim that water boils because it reaches this temperature ignores the relevant factor of atmospheric pressure. An adequate statement of cause in this case needs to specify the pressure at which water boils at 212° F. For such reasons, many writers prefer to speak of *causal relations,* or of causal connections of events, rather than merely the cause of an event.

The Method of Difference *2 instances, all factors common but or diff outcome*

Mill makes the following statement about the method of difference:

Only 2 instances

If an instance in which the phenomenon under investigation occurs, and an instance in which it does not occur, have every circumstance in common save one, that one occurring only in the former; the circumstance in which alone the two instances differ is the effect, or the cause, or an indispensable part of the cause, of the phenomenon.

In using the method of difference, we seek to determine the relation of one manipulated factor to a set of constant conditions. This manipulated factor has a causal relation to the given event if the two following situations hold. In one case the given event always occurs in the presence both of the manipulated factor and the set of constant conditions. In the second case the set of constant conditions is present but the given event never occurs in the absence of this manipulated factor. This method is highly useful in laboratories where one can strictly control relevant conditions.

Pasteur sought to show that a vaccine with which he was experimenting prevented anthrax. After assuring that other relevant conditions were similar, he gave his anthrax vaccine to one group of animals and withheld it from a second group. To test the difference this vaccine made, he then gave all animals in both groups virulent anthrax bacilli. This was an added but a controlled condition. Later he examined both groups of animals. The animals who had the vaccine were healthy. All animals without the vaccine were either dead or showed signs of infection. The critical difference in this experiment was the vaccine. He showed that the vaccine was a causal factor in the continuing health of animals that one would otherwise expect to have an anthrax infection.

If we are checking for a food allergy, we first identify a group of foods to which a subject is not allergic. We then can test other foods one at a time. We may find that the allergy appears after the subject eats strawberries, but not when he does not. So we decide that strawberries are the source of the allergy.

The following diagram shows the model for the method of difference:

Case 1   *F G H I*   followed by an instance of *E*

Case 2   *F G H*   not followed by an instance of *E*

Thus, factor *I* is probably the cause of *E*.

Used in a negative way, the method of difference helps to show that a given factor has no significant causal relation to a specific event. For example, there were reports that an extract from apricot pits called Laetrile could help in the cure of cancer. The design of experiments to test the proposed cure required the use of animals with cancer. After selecting animals with cancer, researchers divided them into two groups. They kept conditions for both groups similar except that they gave the apricot pit extract to one group and they withheld it from the other. After a reasonable time the researchers examined the cancer tissues in both groups of animals. They were unable to find any significant difference between the growth rate of cancer tissue in the two groups. By using the method of difference, they concluded that there was no experimental evidence that the extract was an effective cure for cancer. The reports on these experiments did not put an end to the public controversy about the extract. But it did provide a basis for the claim that available scientific research could not find any grounds for accepting this extract as a cure for cancer.

In everyday life we may not be able to exercise the rigorous controls that can be used in laboratories. But we still may want to adapt the method of difference in seeking causal relations. In such cases we need to exercise great care to guard against the possibility of unidentified factors adversely affecting the results of our work.

The Joint Method of Agreement and Difference

We can use both the method of agreement and the method of difference in working on some issues of causal relations. Mill makes the following statement about the use of the joint method of agreement and difference:

A+ Least 3

> If two or more instances in which the phenomenon occurs have only one circumstance in common, while two or more instances in which it does not occur have nothing in common save the absence of that circumstance, the circumstance in which alone the two sets of instances differ is the effect, or the cause, or an indispensable part of the cause, of the phenomenon.

Consider the following possible case. In a particular study, persons who have malaria have one common antecedent factor: a female *Anopheles* mosquito bit them prior to their becoming ill. Subsequently a control group and an experimental group are placed in conditions that are similar in every respect save one. Female *Anopheles* mosquitoes previously exposed to malaria patients bite the members of the experimental group. But such mosquitoes do not bite members of the control group. The bitten persons subsequently develop malaria, but no member of the second group develops malaria. Here the joint method for determining a cause has been used. In the first instance we identify the common factor in the cases of malaria. In the second instance this common factor is introduced in the experimental group but withheld from a control group. In this experiment the effect accompanies only those cases where the difference (bite of the female *Anopheles* mosquito in recent contact with malaria patients) is present.

The joint method of agreement and difference strengthens any conclusion found by the use of only one of these methods.

The Method of Concomitant Variations   *ratio*

The method of concomitant variations focuses on two factors that vary in some ratio with each other. Mill made the following statement about this method:

> Whatever phenomenon varies in any manner whenever another phenomenon varies in some particular manner, is either a cause or an effect of that phenomenon, or is connected with it through some fact of causation.

The variations may occur in direct proportion to each of the factors studied or in inverse proportion to them. For example, we might find that within given limits, the more fertilizer placed on a field of maize, the greater the yield of the maize. The two variables (the fertilizer and the yield of the maize) vary directly with each other. We would hold that the yield of the maize is a function of the amount of fertilizer used. The higher up a mountain we take a barometer, the lower its reading of the air pressure becomes. The variation here is inverse. In both of the above cases a concomitant variation between the concerned factors suggests a causal relation.

The Method of Residues

Mill makes the following statement about the method of residues:

Subduct from any phenomenon such part as is known by previous inductions to be the effect of certain antecedents, and the residue of the phenomenon is the effect of the remaining antecedents.

Let us assume we know the value of four factors in a compound and we find these four factors joined with a fifth one. The value of the fifth factor is "the residue." The value of this added factor is what is left over from the known values of the other four factors.

A classic illustration of the use of the method of residues is the discovery of the planet Neptune. In the mid-nineteenth century, astronomers working separately noted that they were unable to account for the orbit of the planet Uranus on the basis of known celestial objects. After determining the value of the gravitational pull on Uranus by the known celestial objects, they decided that an unidentified planet likely accounted for this unexplained movement of Uranus. After making careful observation of the area where they expected this unidentified planet to be, they found it and named it Neptune. In a similar way, the discovery of the planet Pluto occurred in this century.

Another traditional example of the use of the method of residues is the work of the Curies with pitchblende. They found the radioactivity of pitchblende to be much higher than that of its known components. The Curies developed the hypothesis that an unknown element in the pitchblende accounted for this great variation from the radioactivity of its known elements. This hypothesis led to their discovery of radium, which then accounted for the otherwise unexplained radioactivity.

A negative use of the method of residues is the classical experiment of the Flemish physician Jean-Baptiste van Helmot in the seventeenth century. He wanted to account for the source of the weight of a willow tree. He placed a five-pound willow tree in an earthenware pot filled with two hundred pounds of oven-dried soil. He covered the top of the pot and watered the tree with rainwater. At the end of five years he dried the soil and separated it from the tree. He found that the soil weighed only two ounces less than when he placed it in the pot. But the tree weighed 165 pounds—a gain of 160 pounds. What was the source of the added weight? The method he used showed that the added weight of the tree was not to be accounted for by the reduction of the weight of the soil in which it grew.

The soil might account for two ounces of the 160 pounds, but some additional factor must account for this residue. Subsequent experiments have shown that a primary source for this added weight in such trees is the carbon in carbon dioxide, the hydrogen, and the oxygen which the trees absorb from the environment.

The method of residues has been particularly useful in some areas of scientific research, including astronomy and physics.

In reviewing these methods of determining causal relation, we have seen that using them rigorously is essential. In the next section we shall look at some difficulties that arise in seeking to apply these methods.

Evaluation of Mill's Methods

The experimental methods discussed by Mill for the determining of causal relations do not apply in the same manner or in the same degree to all subject matters. Their misuse can occur readily. In the method of agreement, the factor found to be in agreement can be trivial or unrelated to the effect. The observation of common factors also can be too limited. If a given effect has many common antecedents, there can be some difficulty in separating causal from noncausal factors. And an unidentified factor may be the causal one. If contaminated tap water is the source of dysentery, the dysentery might be spread even though the victims did not drink tap water. Vegetables washed in the water or ice made from it might be an unidentified source. When we test by this method, using a number of varied cases helps assure accurate results.

Various difficulties may arise in the use of the method of difference. When two factors vary with each other, the cause-and-effect relationship is not always in one direction. These two factors may be a part of a wider syndrome of events, in which various factors relate to a causal explanation of what happens. Higher prices may accompany wage increases. Are they due to wage increases, or are wage increases due to higher prices? Or, are these merely a function of a wider syndrome with prices and wages determined by other economic conditions such as money supply and demand for goods and services? In applying the method of difference, there can be difficulty in keeping all variables constant except the one that is the object of the experiment.

The joint method of agreement and difference provides a stronger means of establishing a case for causally connected events than does either of these methods used separately. It is questionable that it should be classified as a separate method. It has some of the weaknesses of the methods it combines. These include the difficulties of precisely determining the common relevant factors and of adequately designing the experimental procedure to test for the difference.

Several problems also occur in the use of the method of concomitant variations. The control of the relevant factors may present difficulties. The range of some factors may obscure a significant degree of difference in the reaction of subgroups. If we correlate the factor "high school graduate" with the factor "superior performance in college work," the first factor would not distinguish high school graduates with good records from those with poor records. For some purposes it would be preferable to reduce the range of the first factor to "high school graduates in the upper 25 percent of their class."

The concomitant variations between both factors may be relevant only to a limited range of the effect studied. The use of commercial fertilizer up to a point increases the growth of plants; but its use beyond a given amount can harm their growth. The concomitant variations in some processes may require a joint use of several factors rather than the one isolated for study. An investor might note that over a period of time, the worth of stock in electronic companies varies directly with government contracts in electronics. He might assume that new government contracts would increase the price of the stock. After buying some stock in such companies, he may find the value of the stock diminishes even though the number of government contracts with these firms increases. The factor appearing to account for the rise of the price of the stock was not the only significant one. Likewise, other variations might be due to chance or to coincidence.

Mill viewed the method of residues as a special variation of the method of difference. He held it to be more of a method using mathematics and deduction than a strict experimental method. But it was possible to use it as a means of identifying causal relations. He also viewed this method as designed to deal with cases similar to those treated by the method of difference, but not adapted to that method.

Each of these methods for determining causal relations has its limitations. Abuses also can occur. But each one can lend supporting evidence for cause-and-effect relations. They can provide a basis for holding on tested grounds that a causal hypothesis is reliable. We can eliminate some unsound explanations with the negative use of appropriate methods. Their effective use usually requires knowledge and skill in dealing with the subject matter as well as imagination and insight into the problem at hand. Such use also may depend on finding a technique to develop research tools appropriate to carrying out the needed testing.

EXERCISES

Discuss the methods used for establishing explanatory hypotheses in the following examples. How significant is the evidence?

1. Louis Pasteur poured liquid from the same container into two flasks. He left one flask open. The second flask was constructed to minimize any possibility that air would reach the liquid. After several days he found that "microscopic

beings began to develop in the first flask." In the second flask, however, microscopic beings did not develop.

2. Pasteur continued his experiment with germs in liquids by exposing flasks in the streets of Paris, in his laboratory, in the open fields, and in the Alps. His reasoning was based on the premise that the greater the dust content of the air, the greater would be the bacterial growth in the flask. His subsequent investigations demonstrated that the growth of the bacteria in the flasks varied directly with the amount of dust in the air. He found this to support his thesis that the bacteria occurring in the liquids had as their source the particles of dust that were deposited in the liquids.

3. In the study of the cause of yellow fever, researchers needed to "test" the generalization that the waste products of the body do have a causal relation to someone becoming infected with the disease. In testing this hypothesis, persons wore and slept with the clothing and bedding used by others who had the disease. The persons using such clothing did not become ill with yellow fever. The use of such clothing "made no difference." And the view that such factors had a causal relation to infection with yellow fever was rejected.

4. Under controlled conditions researchers tested groups of desert iguanas. They found a means of artifically keeping the temperature of infected desert iguanas at their usual body temperature. In a study of various groups of desert iguanas, there was an average death rate of 0 to 33 percent among infected iguanas whose temperature was allowed to rise during the infection. But there was a death rate of 75 percent in the infected iguanas whose temperature was kept artifically at their usual body temperature. Thus, the rise in temperature of an infected desert iguana helps to keep the iguana alive and to enable it to recover from the infection.[1]

5. Scientists have identified heredity, diet, smoking, and stress as factors increasing the likelihood of heart disease. Some Norwegian scientists screened 10,000 fellow Norwegians who had heart attacks between 1971 and 1975. They found 78 persons who had had heart attacks and who also had a living identical twin sibling. The twin had not suffered a heart attack. They undertook an intensive study of the social environment, life-styles, and physical conditions of these twins. In an initial report on about one-half of the group, they found that the primary difference between those who had had heart attacks and the twins who had not suffered one was the degree of stress in the life-style of the heart victims.[2]

6. There is a way to test for stress through the levels of body chemicals such as catecholamines. Researchers measured the level of this body chemical and found that there was a lowering of stress after trained practicioners engaged in a period of "transcendental meditation." But could this lowering of stress be attributed to the meditation?

A research project studied the stress level in two groups. One group had extensive training in transcendental meditation and the second group had none.

---

[1] *Science News*, Vol. 110, No. 4 (July 24, 1976), p. 55.
[2] *Science News*, Vol. 112, No. 11 (September 10, 1977), p. 166.

Researchers measured stress levels in both groups before, during, and after a period of 20 to 30 minutes of meditation or of resting. The persons in the group that meditated reported a successful period of meditation. And the control group sat quietly with eyes closed, but without any of the special techniques of the meditating group. The tests found that there was no significant difference in the body chemical measuring stress for those engaging in meditation and for those who merely rested. The conclusion reached was that any decrease in the level of stress as measured by blood samples could be accounted for by the act of resting rather than by the additional factor of meditation.[3]

7. When he was a boy, Edward Jenner heard of a local belief in Gloucestershire that persons who had contracted cowpox appeared to be immune from smallpox. The local physicians tended to discount this theory as an old wives' tale, and Jenner did not investigate it in detail until after he had practiced medicine a number of years. Jenner took material from a pustule of a milkmaid who had cowpox and injected it into the body of James Phipps. Jenner then showed that Phipps appeared to be immune to smallpox. This vaccination, which occurred in 1796, may not have been the first, but it was the first to be widely publicized. In a later discussion of his research, Jenner showed that some twenty-three persons appeared to be immune from smallpox, and each of these had had either cowpox or a vaccination.

8. An English biochemist, Frederick Gowland Hopkins (1861-1947), became interested in the relation between proteins and amino acids, particularly as these were related to health. Protein had been shown to be essential for living organisms, but in some cases some forms of protein were lacking in the feature essential to preserve life. Different kinds of amino acids had been found in protein. Hopkins discovered in 1900 a new amino acid, tryptophan, and he devised a chemical test to indicate its presence. Zein, a protein derived from corn, did not respond to this test. He concluded that it was lacking in tryptophan. Although zein was a protein, it would not sustain life if it were the only protein in the diet.[4]

9. Claude Bernard devised a test of the prevailing view that organic compounds were not synthesized but only broken down by animals—a hypothesis in accord with the view that plants rather than animals synthesized organic compounds. Bernard examined the blood leaving the liver of a dog that had been fed a diet heavy with sugar. He found what he expected: the blood had a high sugar content. However, Bernard was not content to leave the matter at this point. His experimental method required that he examine a dog fed a meal without sugar; and when he did so, he found a high concentration of sugar in the dog's hepatic blood. Bernard rejected the hypothesis that he was testing. And he formulated and later established a hypothesis about the activity of the liver in producing sugar in the blood.[5]

[3] *Science News,* Vol. 109, No. 25 (June 19, 1976), p. 390.
[4] Isaac Asimov, *A Short History of Biology* (Garden City, N.Y.: National History Press, 1964), p. 109.
[5] W. I. B. Beveridge, *The Art of Scientific Investigation* (New York: Vintage Books, 1957), p. 216.

10. Researchers sought to test a pneumococcus vaccine for a given type of pneumonia to which persons without spleens or with sickle-cell anemia are particularly vulnerable. This vaccine has been 80 percent effective in places where it has been tested in North America and in South America. These researchers gave the vaccine to seventy-seven children without spleens or with sickle-cell anemia. They carefully watched a matched control group of 106 children in comparable physical condition. None of the immunized children developed pneumonia. But ten children in the control group developed pneumonia and two of them died.[6]

11. In a report published in the March 29, 1977, issue of *Studies in Family Planning*, there is an analysis of the difference in the rate of heart attack among women between the ages of forty and forty-four who both smoke and take an oral contraceptive and those who do not. The report states that the death rate from heart attacks in Great Britain and the United States for women in the above age group who neither smoke nor use the pill is 7.4 per 100,000. The death rate is 10.7 per 100,000 for those who use the pill but who do not smoke. The death rate is 15.9 per 100,000 for those who smoke but do not use the pill. And the death rate is 62 per 100,000 for those who both smoke and use the pill. They also found a higher incidence of death by heart attack for women who were in the thirty-to-thirty-four age group or in the thirty-five-to-thirty-nine age group and who both smoked and used the pill.[7]

12. In a southwestern university, there was a three-year study made on persons who had experienced light heart strokes. In an analysis of 178 cases, 12 percent were discovered to have had additional strokes during a period when they were taking two aspirins a day. But in a control group that took dummy nonaspirin pills, 42 percent had additional heart strokes. Continuing research in other centers also supports these results. This research suggests that two aspirin a day may help to reduce by about 50 percent the expected number of additional strokes in patients who have had light strokes.[8]

15.3 CAUSAL FALLACIES

In using the notion of cause, several fallacies occur with some frequency. Some of these we have already noted.

✓ Post Hoc Fallacy

One event may precede a second one without having a causal relation to the latter event. The post hoc causal fallacy occurs if the only grounds

---

[6] Robert Austrian, "Pneumococcal Infection and Pneumococcal Vaccine," *New England Journal of Medicine*, Vol. 297, No. 17 (October 27, 1977), pp. 938–939. (There is also another article in this issue developing this experiment in greater detail.)

[7] *Science News*, Vol. 111, No. 15 (April 9, 1977), p. 233. This report has as its basis the article cited above.

[8] *Science News*, Vol. 113, No. 5 (February 4, 1978), p.72.

for holding to a causal relation is merely that one event follows another with the prior event accepted as the cause of the second. Some accidents may occur after we break a mirror. But it does not follow that the cause of the accident is the breaking of the mirror.

Misleading Correlations

One factor may vary directly or inversely with another factor without a causal relation holding between the two. The price of potatoes in Idaho and the success of the New York Yankees baseball team in winning games may vary directly with each other. But it does not follow that there is any connection between the price of Idaho potatoes and the success of the Yankee team. If we find two factors whose occurrence appears to vary in a constant ratio, we may want to examine the situation further. But we want independent reasons showing some functional relation between the two factors before we accept the view that a causal relation is present.

Joint Effects of a Prior Cause

We can confuse the joint effects of a prior cause with a cause-and-effect relationship. A person may have both a rash and a high fever. But each may be the effect of another cause, such as an infection.

Reversal of Cause and Effect

We also can mistakenly identify which factor is the cause and which is the effect. That is, we confuse the effect by labeling it the cause. This error is the fallacy of reversal of cause and effect. In popular talk, we refer to this as putting the cart before the horse. Let us assume that John and his father have a bitter dispute and John moves to another city. And someone says, "The cause of the break-up in the family was John's leaving home." A reversal of cause and effect can be present. If we want to use "cause" in this context, it would be more correct to say, "The cause of John's leaving home was a breakdown in his relation with his father."

Oversimplifying Conditions Treated as Causes

Another causal fallacy is the oversimplifying of conditions treated as causes. For example, someone might say that a superior job of recruiting was the cause for the winning of the football conference title by a state university. Such superior recruiting certainly may be an expected condition for being a contender for the title. But many other factors enter into winning a football title in addition to recruiting.

Misuse of Common Factors

The misuse of common factors in a causal explanation is another fallacy. This error may follow from the neglect of common relevant factors or from an emphasis on common irrelevant factors. A traditional example of this fallacy is the inebriate who sought to determine the cause of his getting drunk. He found periods of intoxication followed drinking gin and soda, vodka and soda, bourbon and soda, and scotch and soda. And he decided that the cause of the inebriation was the soda.

Confusions of Reasons and Causes

The confusion of reasons and causes is another type of causal fallacy. We may use the word "because" to refer either to a causal relation or to provide evidence in support of an argument. For example, we might say, "The fire occurred because of a short in the wiring of the house." This use of "because" signifies a causal relation. We also might say, "Professor James Smith knows modern mathematics because he is a physicist and all physicists know modern mathematics." Here the word "because" introduces evidence in support of a conclusion. It does not provide a causal explanation for the events related to Professor Smith's knowledge of modern mathematics. It would not be correct to say that the cause of Professor Smith's knowledge of mathematics is his being a physicist.

In this chapter we have emphasized that a causal explanation is crucial in the development of science. Use of causal laws enables us to explain, to predict, and in some cases to control what happens. In reviewing the different methods used in determining causes, we found that we can identify common factors, establish a critical difference, find two factors that vary with each other, or look at residues. But we also saw that the use of these methods can be abused. In the next chapter we shall analyze what we mean when we say that statements we make about causal relations are probable rather than certain. We also shall look at various ways of determining the probability of events.

EXERCISES

Identify the causal fallacies in the following examples.

1. If you had not been late for work, you would not have been at the intersection at the time of the accident. Therefore, the accident was your fault, since it was caused by your leaving late for work.

2. New England and the Middle Atlantic states became major industrial centers because there were large deposits of coal and iron readily available.

3. Smith struck out after he lost his temper. Therefore, he struck out because he lost his temper.

4. The river is beginning to rise because the water is becoming muddy.

5. Since there have been higher interest rates after the last five declines in the price of common stocks, the cause of the higher interest rates is the decline in the price of common stocks.

6. The patient's pain was relieved on three occasions. On the first occasion he took aspirin and water; on the second he took Bufferin and water; and on the third he took Excedrin and water. Therefore, the pain was relieved because he drank water.

7. The cause of his industriousness is his working long hours.

8. The cause of the intoxicated person's stumbling was his double vision.

9. The high grade was made after Mary arrived late for the test. Therefore, the high grade was made because she was late for the test.

10. There has been a tendency for an inverse correlation to hold between the price trend of gold and the price trend of common stocks in the United States market. One might propose a cause-and-effect relation. This view appears simplistic. But apparently there is some kind of connection. The connection may be that the price of gold and the price of common stocks are reacting to a set of economic conditions and that they react in opposite directions to those conditions. But what kind of fallacy results if someone makes the following argument? The cause of the decline in the price of common stocks is that the price of gold is going up.

CHAPTER 16

PROBABILITY

In this chapter there is a simplified discussion of notions of probability. First we shall look at the notion of probability as it applies to statements about matters of fact. Then we shall consider some issues related to determining the probability of events.

In prior sections of this work, we claimed that in a strict sense, statements about matters of fact are probable rather than cognitively certain. In this section we explain what this position means. We shall try to justify this claim by a brief discussion of the ways we go about knowing things.

16.1 PROBABILITY AND STATEMENTS

Many of our everyday decisions are based on generalizations about past experience. Frequently a determining factor in a decision is the state of affairs we hope to see come about in the future. If we want to buy a new TV set, we may inquire about dealers and brands. We find that dealer Smith has given good prices to other students, that he stands behind his warranties, and that other dealers respect his business activities. We generalize that dealer Smith is a reliable person with whom to do business. We find that brand Beta has an excellent picture and good sound, that its parts wear well, and that it is easily repaired. We decide that for the price we want to pay, brand Beta likely will serve as well as any other model in quality of color and sound, and in durability and upkeep. So we buy brand Beta from dealer Smith. Generalizations and future expectancies, even though some of them may turn out to be wrong, have played a decisive role in our decision making.

How do we go about determining the degree of confidence we can place in our generalizations? This question is vague. There are many kinds of generalizations. The way we go about making them varies widely. And we have to consider them in the context in which they occur. On a common-sense basis we can raise a number of issues about them. Do we have enough data to justify our making a generalization? What kind of generalization does the evidence warrant? How reliable is this evidence? Are the kinds of future situations to which we are projecting the generalization significantly similar to the sources which gave rise to the generalization? Are new factors likely to enter into the case to bring about a state of affairs other than what we expect? What risks are we taking if our projections turn out wrong? In response to each of these questions, we are dealing with probabilities. But these probabilities are of different kinds.

One notion of probability relates to the way in which we hold that a statement is warranted. Statements about facts are more accurately appraised by notions such as "probable" and "improbable" rather than "certain" or "necessary." By using "probable" rather than "certain" in referring to well-founded statements about matters of fact, we are emphasizing several things. In a positive way we are asserting something about the future. New knowledge and evidence may provide grounds for our revising our beliefs about the matter at hand. We also may be pointing out something about the past. We have found good evidence for holding to and advancing these knowledge claims. We also can hold that views with claims that logically conflict with those we are advancing in a given context are faulty. In a negative way we are recognizing that some of the data on which we base our beliefs may be other than what we now hold them to be. We do not want to be pushed into a position in which we cannot correct errors or interpretations of experience. However, we also are pointing out that, given the evidence, we believe it is improbable that the statement we are asserting is false.

The three traditional ways of knowing statements about matters of fact are experience, reason, and intuition. Each of these ways of knowing yields statements that we appraise as probable rather than absolutely certain. In its narrow sense, experience refers to the knowledge we attain through the use of our five senses of touch, taste, sight, smell, and hearing. We are aware that we can develop the sensitivity of each of these senses. And we also can make and use instruments that can improve the accuracy of measuring the objects, qualities, and relations that we perceive. But if we use our senses in any attempt to show that the knowledge gained by their use is reliable, then we assume in part the point at issue. That is, we would assume some degree of reliability of our senses in making a case for their reliability. Furthermore, we are aware that in some cases our senses appear not to be reliable and that in other cases we are mistaken in our reports about what we do sense. In reporting what we experience, we interpret and introduce new grounds for error. But this is not an argument against experience as a source of knowledge. We would hold that experience is basic both in our knowledge and in our generalizations about matters of fact. Rather this argument seeks to justify the view that we interpret statements about matters of fact to be probable rather than absolutely certain. The critical point in justifying our knowledge claims is the evidence we use to justify statements. We accept as reliable those statements about a state of affairs that have relevant and sufficient evidence to back them up.

We can interpret experience in a broader sense to include the generalizations we have formed from what we have observed or learned in the past. We have seen that such generalizations can help us to deal effectively with some issues or to respond to some situations. But these generalizations depend, in part, on probable statements we have accepted about matters of fact. They also can include mistaken interpretations. In seeking the best generalizations as guides to future action, we still want to be able to improve them. We accept them as probable and seek to hold those best supported by evidence.

In the case of those statements about matters of fact supported by reason, we have seen that reason can give us good forms for making arguments. But it does not give us the original content for the statements about matters of fact which we use as evidence in these arguments. We have grounds for accepting conclusions derived as true only if the premises used in the reasoning process are true. And we have to derive this content of factual premises ultimately from sources other than reasoning. If those sources yield only statements that are probable, then the conclusion of an argument based on such evidence is probable. We are not faulting the use of reason, but we are recognizing the kind of jobs that it can and cannot do.

Intuition as a way of knowing usually refers to an immediate insight or cognitive grasping of the relations or conditions holding about a situation. Its philosophical use does not refer to hunches, guesses, or premonitions about present or future situations. Some writers claim that an intuitive element is present when a person recognizes that an object of perception pertains to a given group. (For example, "The object on the table is a glass.") Some philosophers claim that intuitive elements are present in recognizing logical relations or in our awareness of moral and aesthetic values. Some writers also claim that an intuitive element is present in scientific discoveries. But our purpose is not to determine the accuracy of such views about intuition. Rather we want to determine whether we can be cognitively certain about the truth of matter-of-fact statements justified by appeal to intuition. We find that intuitive claims differ among persons and that we cannot resolve many disputes merely by appeal to intuition. In addition, we want intuitive claims to have other kinds of evidence to support them. In the cases of matter-of-fact statements, we would expect this support to be based on experience. So we are thrown back on well-founded statements that are probable rather than certain.

We are confronted with similar conditions when we use authority as a secondary way of knowing. If, ultimately, we examine the grounds the authority has for advancing such knowledge claims, we find such claims based on experience, reason, and intuition. Again we have statements based on matters of fact that are probable.

To help clarify what we mean by holding that statements about matters of fact are probable, let us analyze the logical meaning of words like "certain" and "necessary." There are many different meanings of the word "certain." Many of these are accepted in ordinary discourse without much difficulty. But in a critical discourse we need to distinguish these different meanings and to determine how we are using the word. Consider the following statements:

1. I am certain that John is honest.

2. I am certain that I see a book on the table.

3. I am certain that in a component of radium, 50 percent of the radium atoms will disintegrate in a period of 1,660 years.

4. I am certain that all triangles have three angles.

In each of these statements, we can give reasons to justify our claim. But we may not be speaking about cognitive certainty in all cases. The type of certainty expressed in the statement, "John is honest," is subjective. We may have heard John make honest statements when he was under stress. A person making such a claim apparently is asserting that in a state of affairs in which John might be dishonest, he is confident that John would be honest.

The second assertion, which states, "I see a book on the table," represents a *commonsense* notion of certainty. Yet anyone making this statement might conceivably be mistaken. One can make a strong case, however, for insisting that a given statement has a much higher degree of probability than possible alternative statements relative to a given state of affairs. This type of commonsense notion of certainty is an expression of confidence in our being able to give good and sufficient reasons for our assertions about a state of affairs. But this use of certainty continues to have a subjective element.[1]

[1] Some philosophers have argued for the possibility of first-person reports about one's private experiences that have the properties of certainty and indubitability.

The third statement, "I feel certain that in a component of radium, 50 percent of the radium atoms will disintegrate in a period of 1,660 years," represents a consistency notion of certainty. The grounds for making the statement are in a coherent system of beliefs. It supports other statements within the system and they support it. Experimental evidence also supports the statement. But we may find the system to have errors or deficiencies. We have seen that scientists prefer to leave a system open for correction by further observations and experiments. Even if we insist that this statement has strong justifying evidence to support our holding to it, there remains a significant gap between "strong, justifying evidence" and "absolute certainty."

The fourth statement, "I am certain that all triangles have three angles," contains an assertion that is true in any conceivable set of circumstances. A part of the meaning of the word "triangle" is "to have three angles." We can determine the truth or falsity of the statement merely by analyzing the linguistic meaning of its component parts. The type of certainty asserted here is *analytic*. Given the meaning of its components, the assertion must be true. Analytic certainty is possible only if the denial of a statement results in an internal contradiction within the statement. To deny that all triangles have three angles would exemplify such a contradiction. In contrast, statements about matters of fact are contingent. We can deny such statements without making a statement with an internal contradiction.

To summarize, we hold that statements about matters of fact are probable rather than certain. In a rigorous and theoretical sense, "certainty" signifies that we hold to the impossibility of an assertion's being false. We distinguish analytic certainty from subjective certainty. In the latter case there may be complete confidence in the truth of an assertion or belief. But the possibility remains that the assertion or belief is in error. Rigorous theoretical certainty is possible only in statements that are logically true. In such cases, it is impossible for the statement itself to be false, given the meaning of its component parts.

Like the word "certain," "necessary" has a variety of meanings in different contexts. Many statements using "necessary" have a condition that is left unstated. Consider the statement, "It is necessary to go to the grocery store." What is implicit here is that if certain food items are to be secured, then going to the grocery store is a condition for securing them. It might be asserted, "It is necessary to pass calculus before taking an advanced course in physics." Again, a condition is implicit. If a student is to take an advanced physics course, then a condition for his enrolling in the course is having a final passing grade in calculus. Consider the statement, "It is necessary for 50 percent of the radium atoms of a component of radium to disintegrate within a period of 1,660 years." Although a claim might be made that this is a case in which some specified physical conditions are necessary, the above statement contains implicit conditions. Such conditions are evident in the following restatement of the sentence: "If the present statistical laws are dependable and if they continue to hold in the future, then the most reliable predictions would indicate that 50 percent of the radium atoms will disintegrate in 1,660 years."

A strict use of "necessary" occurs in the following statement: "It is necessary that a square contain four and only four right angles." "Necessary" here has an analytic basis. Unless the plane figure has four and only four angles and unless each angle is a right angle, it is not possible for this figure to be a square. The same kind of condition holds in the statement, "It is necessary that all bachelors are unmarried men." If an adult male is married, he is not a bachelor. It is not the case both that the components of the statement have their usual meaning and that the statement is false.

If a statement is logically necessary, then its denial would constitute a contradiction. Statements that are logically necessary also are logically certain when they are known.

In a logically necessary statement, we are asserting something about the way the component parts of the statement must fit together. In a logically certain statement we are expressing our awareness that these component parts must fit together.

In saying that well-founded statements about matters of fact are probable, we are denying that such statements are either logically necessary or logically certain. In such cases we cannot determine the truth or falsity of the statements merely by analyzing the meaning of their component parts. Such matter-of-fact statements are also contingent. And their truth or falsity depends upon what we assert about a given state of affairs and what holds with regard to that state of affairs.

We also use the notion of probability to refer to hypotheses in the empirical sciences. In confirming such hypotheses we depend on our senses and we use matter-of-fact assertions. They are more critically formed than our generalizations based on common sense, and we may accord them a higher level of credibility. To hold that a hypothesis in the experimental sciences is reasonable is to assert that if it is a part of a system of beliefs, there are strong reasons for keeping it within this system. And if it is not a part of such a system of beliefs, there are strong reasons for including it in such a system.

In discussing the probability of statements about matters of fact we are referring to the degree of confidence that is warranted in their reliability as testable by evidence, such as first-hand experience based on observation. In talking about the probability of hypotheses, we are referring to the degree of confidence that is warranted in their reliability as testable by standards appropriate to them. (We have discussed such standards in the chapter on hypotheses.) The probability of commonsense generalizations refers to the degree of confidence that the evidence in their support warrants and in the likelihood of their serving as good guides for decision making.

In ordinary discourse, words like "certain," "necessary," and "probable" have other uses than the strictly logical ones we have emphasized in this section. We are not proposing that in such discourse these words be limited to a more rigorous logical meaning. But we need to recognize the subjective element present in advancing such statements. We also need to associate the notion of the probability of statements with the need for having sound and relevant evidence in making assertions and in forming generalizations. Critical common sense can be a good guide in making sound decisions. But in logic as well as in science we have to meet additional standards in supporting the statements we accept, the methods we use, and the generalizations we advance.

In summary, we have seen that we justify generalizations and other statements about matters of fact by appeal to experience, reason, intuition, and authorities. But ultimately, we depend on experience. Experience can provide us with knowledge claims that we accept critically on the basis of evidence. In saying that statements about matters of fact are probable, we are leaving the door open for new evidence. And we are recognizing that we may want to change some of our present views about the way things are.

16.2 PROBABILITY AND EVENTS

If we could know about certain kinds of future events and conditions, we could use such knowledge to advance our interests. What will be the cost of building a new house five years hence? What will the interest rate be a year from now? Which stocks will gain the most during the next year? What basketball team will be the conference champion next year? In each of these cases we are dealing with events. Qualified analysts could make informed estimates about such matters. And they would use theories of probability in developing their opinions.

In this section we discuss the probability of events. But we shall not attempt to deal with such complex questions as those raised above. We state probabilities about events with values ranging from zero to one. If the probability for the occurrence of a given event is zero, then we are saying that there are no chances for that event to occur within the system in which we are working. The probability of drawing five aces from an ordinary deck of playing cards (one that is not rigged) is zero. The probability of throwing heads or tails on a coin in every case in which at least one of these events occurs is one. It is customary to claim that probabilities either of zero or of one for a given event to occur are a result of a logical relation that holds in the given case. In the above examples, there is a statement with a contradiction in the case with the probability of zero: "A normal deck of playing cards has five aces and a normal deck of playing cards does not have five aces." There is a statement which must be true in the case of the probability of one: "Either the event heads occurs or the event not heads (tails) occurs" (given the assumptions of the problem as stated).

There are two traditional methods for determining the probability that a given event will occur: These are (1) empirical, or *a posteriori*, probability and (2) mathematical, or *a priori*, probability. In working with some problems we can use both methods.

If we want to determine the probability of tossing heads on a coin, we can proceed in two ways. We can flip the coin, keep a record of what event (heads or tails) occurs and then determine the relative frequency in which heads occurs in tossing the coin. This method is *a posteriori* in that we use previous experience to determine the probability of the kind of event under discussion by finding out the relative frequency in which the stated event occurs. A second method is *a priori* in character. We determine the probability of the event prior to any experience of flipping the coin. This method relies on mathematical considerations not dependent on past events. In mathematical probability, we are expressing the degree of rational confidence that we believe to be jusitified in holding that a given kind of event will occur in a specified ratio in a specific context.

The way to calculate empirical probability is to determine the frequency that a specified event occurs in relation to other relevant events occurring in such contexts. How would one determine the probability that the next car approaching a given stop sign will come to a complete stop? One would need to build a probability table recording observations of cars that stop and cars that do not stop at this sign. Let us assume that 5,000 cars passed this sign and 4,763 stopped. With other conditions remaining constant, the empirical probability that the next car approaching the sign would stop would be 4,763/5,000 or .95. The probability of the car not stopping would be 237/5,000 or.05.

The basic formula for determining empirical probability is to divide the number of times the specified event occurs by the total number of occurrences of the kinds of events under review. In the latter case we include both the favorable and unfavorable events. In writing this formula as:

$$p = \frac{s}{t}$$

p refers to the probability of occurrence of the specified event, s refers to the occurrence of the specified event, and t refers to the total number of events of that general class. That is, t refers to the specified event plus the other relevant unspecified ones occurring in that context. If, in tosses of a given coin, "heads" occurs on 493 occasions in 1,000 tosses, then the empirical probability for the occurrence of "heads" will be 493/1,000 or .493.

In some cases, a special circumstance may be relevant to determining the empirical probability of an event. A given baseball player may have a batting average of .303. Irrespective of other conditions, the empirical probability of his hitting safely his next time at bat is 303/1,000. But he is hitting .353 against right-handed pitching and .253 against left-handed pitching. On this occasion he is batting against a left-handed pitcher. Disregarding other conditions, the empirical probability of his getting a safe hit rather than making an out is .253.

We determine mathematical probability by calculating the chance that a specified event, in relation to the total number of relevant events of that class, will occur. When the specified event is "heads" in the flipping of a coin, the mathematical chance of the event's occurring is 1/2. Two possible events may occur, namely heads or tails. Only one of these, heads, is the specified event. (It is assumed that either heads or tails is an equally probable event.) The formula for determining this kind of probability again is $p = s/t$, with s again signifying "the specified event" and t meaning "the total number of events possible, and equally probable." The application of this formula in specific cases can be quite difficult.

Several troublesome problems can occur in the use of mathematical probability. In a given situation, several different events may occur, but the chance of a given event occurring may be greater or less than the mathematical probability accorded it. That is, these events may not be equally probable. A roulette table, for example, can have a mechanical defect. In such cases the indicator stops less frequently at some positions and more frequently at others than the mathematical probabilities indicate. Experienced gamblers are aware that one can load dice, stack decks, or rig machines. Applied to such cases, the normal mathematical probability calculations about events are faulty because the relevant events are not equally probable.

There are many cases not adapted to the strict use of mathematical probability. That is, one cannot apply independently of experience the formula for determining the chances of the occurrence of specific kinds of events. Consider the following kinds of cases. What is the probability of rain tomorrow? What is the probability of an adult male developing lung cancer if he continues to smoke two packs of cigarettes a day? What is the probability of a student with a 3.5 grade point average getting into a good law school? If a safety man fields a punt, two events are possible—he can keep hold of the ball or he can fumble it. But these events do not appear to be equally probable in any given case. Determining the chances for one of these events to occur requires reference to previous cases under comparable conditions which include moisture and temperature.

Another problem with mathematical probability is more theoretical in character and may be phrased as a question. What is the justification for believing that events will conform to a number system that is built up independently of any specific reference to the events themselves? If the proposed answer points to a tendency of a given class of events to occur with a frequency indicated by their mathematical probability, one justifies accepting the proposed mathematical probability by appeal to past experience rather than only on mathematical considerations. Such justification is not merely in terms of a mathematical system itself, but rather in terms of practice. If we make such an argument, we appeal to a postulate found also in the relative frequency notion of empirical probability. This postulate is that future or unobserved relevant events of this class will occur in the same ratio as the observed and tabulated events. If such a postulate is made, it has to do with the way things happen and not merely with the formal notions about mathematics.

Empirical theories of probability also have their difficulties. A given body of data about the occurrence of events in a given class may have a distortion based upon special conditions present when the observed events occur. Likewise, data based on relative frequency provide a ratio that one expects to hold in the long run. But the primary use of probability tables built on such data in any given case may be for a short run, or even for one case. For a given fielded punt, the receiver either fumbles the ball or he does not. Relative frequency theories appear to be of greater help in determining the strategy for the receiving team to follow than in helping us to determine whether the punt receiver will or will not lose possession of the football on any given catch.

Use of mathematical probability has the decided advantage of providing a critical basis for calculating probabilities in some cases where an immediate decision is needed. Its use may not require the expense and delay incurred in building up a table for determining empirical probabilities. Expectancies based on mathematical probabilities are more rationally justifiable and appear to come about with a significantly greater frequency than those based upon hunches or guesses.

Use of mathematical probabilities may provide a means of finding flaws in the way some operations develop. When using mathematical and empirical probability, if there is a significant discrepancy about the probability values of a given class of event, we look for reasons to account for the discrepancies. The error may be in the construction either of the mathematical probabilities or of the empirical ones. But we may also need to examine the conditions under which these events occur. The design for an experiment may be a bad one. The mechanism related to the occurrence of a given event may be faulty. An unidentified factor may be operative and may account for the difference between the expected mathematical values and actual empirical values.

In both theoretical and applied research, the construction of accurate probability tables can require hundreds of hours of research time. But computers can be of great assistance in helping to record and analyze the data and in constructing charts based on such data.

16.3 CALCULATIONS OF MATHEMATICAL PROBABILITIES

The determination of the mathematical probability of many events may require complex mathematical procedures. But simpler procedures can be helpful in resolving many elementary problems. Consider an ordinary die with six sides, each side bearing a dot or dots representing a different number from one through six. What is the probability on a given throw of casting a six on the die? What is the probability of throwing a six consecutively on any two casts? What is the probability of not casting a six on the die on a single throw?

We have seen that the general formula determining probabilities is that the probability of a specified event equals the number of the specified events divided by the total number of possible events, or $p = s/t$. In the case of casting a six, we determine the probability by dividing the number of specified events that can occur, which in this case is one, by the total number of events that can occur, which in this case is six, or 1/6.

How would one determine the probability of throwing either a five or a six on a die? Notice that the word "or" appears in the expression "a 5 or a 6." In a probability statement "or" usually indicates interdependent events. The appearance of either one of the events satisfies the conditions for the specified event. Where events of this kind are interdependent, addition is proper: "With 'or' one adds." The probability of the six is 1/6; the probability of the 5 is 1/6; the probability of the five or the six is 1/6 plus 1/6 or 2/6. The probability of throwing a one or a two or a three or a four or a five or a six on a die is:

$$1/6 + 1/6 + 1/6 + 1/6 + 1/6 + 1/6$$

that is, the probability is one. In this set of events, any possible event occurring would be included as one of the specified events.

Consider the probability of casting a six both on the first and second throws of the die. Notice that the word "and" is used. In a probability statement "and" usually refers to independent events. What happens on the first event has no bearing whatsoever on what happens on the second event. To determine the probability of independent events we multiply: "With 'and' one multiplies." The probability of the first event is multiplied by the probability of the second event. The probability of the occurrence of a six as the specified event on the first throw is 1/6. The probability of its occurrence as the specified event on the second throw is 1/6. The probability of these specified events occurring on any two consecutive throws is $1/6 \times 1/6$ or a probability of 1/36.

What is the probability of throwing the die and not casting a six? Notice that the "not" occurs in the statement of the problem. In such cases "not" may indicate a need to subtract the probability of the unfavorable event from one: "With 'not' one subtracts." In the present example, the unfavorable event is casting the number six. The probability of the occurrence of the unfavorable event is 1/6. The probability of a favorable event or of not casting a six is 1 − 1/6, or 5/6. (There also are other ways to work this problem.)

What is the probability of tossing three coins and throwing heads on at least one of the coins? If this problem is restated with the use of "not," its solution is more apparent. "What is the probability of tossing three coins and not having three tails?" The unfavorable event is three tails. The probability of this unfavorable event, or of three tails, is $1/2 \times 1/2 \times 1/2$, or 1/8. By subtracting the probability of the unfavorable event from one, we obtain the probability of a favorable event. The probability of not tossing three tails, or of tossing three coins and having one head on at least one of the coins, is 1 − 1/8 or 7/8.

What would be the probability of throwing a pair of dice and having the sum of the numbers of both dice be 2, 3, or 12? The number 2 occurs only if a 1 occurs on each die. The probability of one dot on each die is $1/6 \times 1/6$ or 1/36. Likewise, the probability of a 12 is 1/36. The sum of 3 can be cast if we get a 1 on die A and a 2 on die B or a 2 on die A and a 1 on die B. The probability of casting a 3 is 1/36 + 1/36 or 2/36. By adding these separate probabilities, we find that the probability of throwing a 2, 3, or 12 is 1/36 + 1/36 + 2/36 = 4/36, or 1/9.

What is the probability of casting a 7 or an 11 on a pair of dice? There are two ways of casting an 11: 6—5 or 5—6. There are six ways of casting a 7: 1—6, 6—1, 2—5, 5—2, 3—4, or 4—3. The probability of casting an 11 is 2/36. The probability of casting a 7 is 6/36. The probability of casting an 11 or a 7 is 2/36 + 6/36 or 8/36.

What is the probability of not casting either a 7 or an 11 or a 2 or a 3 or a 12? The probability of the unfavorable event, or of the 2, 3, 7, 11, or 12, is 1/36 + 2/36 + 6/36 + 2/36 + 1/36, or 12/36. The probability of the unfavorable event subtracted from one, 1 − 12/36 or 24/36, is the probability of the favorable event or of not throwing any of the indicated numbers.

In some cases we need to pay careful attention to the conditions which hold in the example in order to determine the probability of events. If one is talking about the use of playing cards as an example, then the probabilities found for drawing a specified card depend on whether one keeps a drawn card or replaces it in the deck. The probability of drawing an ace four times consecutively from a deck of 52 playing cards is $4/52 \times 3/51 \times 2/50 \times 1/49$ if we keep the cards. It is $4/52 \times 4/52 \times 4/52 \times 4/52$ if we put each card back into the deck after it is drawn.

Let us look at another example. Four women have won prizes at a party and they draw lots to see which of four prizes each one wins. Each of them wants a different prize. What is the probability that the last person to draw will get the prize she wants, if each of the first three persons draws the lot for the prize that she wants? The probability is 1. If each of the first three persons has drawn the prize she wants, only one lot will be left for the last person to draw. And it is the lot for the prize wanted.

Mathematical probabilities are sometimes misused in making gambling calculations. Some persons believe that if they have had a series of gambling losses, the odds turn in their favor to increase their chances of winning on a succeeding play. But in such cases the mathematical probabilities remain the same. And obviously the empirical probabilities have not increased. If a party has lost four consecutive tosses of a coin, he can double up on the next toss by betting the amount of money he has lost on the four previous tosses. But his mathematical chances of winning remain 1/2 on the next toss of the coin. With regard to the practice of "doubling up," a report states that the late billionaire H. L. Hunt gave the following advice to a son about a basic principle of playing poker:

> It's all right to gamble, but don't ever try to get even. You lose what you can afford to and then leave the table. But you can lose it all trying to play double and catch up.[2]

In this section we have looked at two different ways to determine probabilities about events. In empirical probability we determine the relative frequency that a given event has occurred in relation to other relevant events in a specified context. In mathematical probability we determine the rational expectation for a given kind of event in a context in which other similar and relevant events are equally possible. For any limited sequence of events there is no assurance that either the mathematical or the empirical probabilities will be in line with a given relative frequency or a rational expectation. But in making decisions about the future, our anticipation of the probabilities of the occurrence of designated events under specified conditions may provide us with as reasonable a guide as we can find. In the next section we shall discuss some special cases using probability estimates.

EXERCISES

Determine the mathematical probability of each event described.

1. There are 100 beans in a jar; 30 are red, 25 are brown, 20 are yellow, 15 are green, and 10 are purple. Each bean is replaced after each draw.
   (a) What is the probability of drawing a brown bean on any given draw?
   (b) What is the probability of drawing a yellow bean on two consecutive draws?
   (c) What is the probability of drawing in order a red bean, a yellow bean, and a purple bean?

[2]*Wall Street Journal*, July 14, 1977, p. 12.

(d) What is the probability on any draw of not picking a yellow bean or a green bean?

2. There are six sides on a die with the sides numbered 1 through 6. A pair of dice are cast.
   (a) What is the probability of casting a 6?
   (b) What is the probability of casting an 8 or a 9?
   (c) What is the probability of casting a 4, 5, 6, 8, 9, or 10?
   (d) What is the probability of not casting a 7?

3. There are 52 cards in a deck, with 13 cards in each suit. The cards are not replaced in the deck after they are drawn. Write the fractions and the mathematical operations needed to determine the following probabilities.
   (a) What is the probability of drawing five cards of the same suit?
   (b) If the king, queen, jack, and ten of spades are held in a hand, what is the probability of drawing an ace or a nine of spades?
   (c) If the ten, nine, eight, and six of hearts are held in a hand, what is the probability of drawing the seven of hearts?
   (d) If the jack of spades and the six of hearts are held, what is the probability of drawing a card that will make the sum of the cards held 21 or less, if each card counts according to its own number, with face cards counting 10 and aces counting 1 or 11?

4. There are numbers 1 through 20 spaced at equal intervals on each of three wheels. Each wheel stops on a different pointer, and a pointer indicates any one of the twenty numbers on each wheel. Each wheel is spun separately until a pointer indicates a number.
   (a) What is the probability of having the pointers indicate the number 20 on each wheel?
   (b) What is the probability of having the pointers indicate the same number on each of the three wheels?
   (c) If the pointers on the first and second wheels indicate the number 10, what is the probability of having the pointer on the third wheel not indicate the number 10?

5. Four men agree to rent four cars. Each draws a key at random from a box containing only the four keys for the four cars, and each goes to a different car to determine whether he has the proper key.
   (a) What is the probability that the tallest man has the right key?
   (b) What is the probability that each man goes successively to the car that his key fits?

16.4 PROBABILITY AND WEIGHTED ESTIMATES

In this section we shall look at some special cases where statements refer to probabilities. But various factors appear to have a causal relation to a given outcome. Some of these factors may be more important than others for a given outcome to occur. And in many instances one either cannot control the causal factors or one can use only limited controls. These special cases include predicting the weather, forecasting the state of the economy six months hence, and gambling on sporting events. To what degree are we warranted in having confidence in probability estimates in such cases? Are we to regard such estimates as worthy of critical acceptance?

Forecasting is a big business. Those who have a knack of doing it well can find good positions. We have forecasts about the economy, about politics, real estate, stock markets, and sporting events. We have forecasts about population explosions, energy supplies and consumption, and military capabilities. In many of these forecasts we find that estimates occur in some form of percentages. They may state that the probability of rain tomorrow is 20 percent, that the probability of a production slowdown in six months is 60 percent, or that the probability of Slim Chance winning the Kentucky Derby is 20 percent (that is, the odds are 5 to 1).

In determining what credibility we are to give such statements, we have to raise questions about the evidence given to justify them. We find that on these grounds we can reject some proposed forecasts out of hand. We know that the position of the moon has relevance for predicting actions of the tide. But we fail to see that the fullness of the moon has any relevance to forecasting the performance of the economy or the action of the stock market.

In the case of predicting the weather, forecasters gather information about the movements of air masses and their moisture content and temperatures. They also find out about high- and low-pressure areas and other factors relevant to movements of frontal systems. They have a large body of public and verified data showing what happened under different sets of conditions. We expect a wider margin of error in predicting short or intermediate weather conditions than in predicting other kinds of events in a laboratory under controlled conditions. Many different factors enter into predicting weather. Forecasters may not know what some of the conditions are at any given time. And there may be some unidentified causal relations that have a bearing on the turn the weather takes. At the same time, competent weather forecasters can give reasons acceptable to qualified inquirers for the predictions which they make. We also can check on their performance. Allowing for error margins, we have good grounds to accept some forecasts as reputable probability estimates about future weather conditions.

Let us look briefly at economic forecasting. In a complex economy such as ours, the large number of different factors and the weight to be given these factors contribute to making probability estimates about future economic conditions quite hazardous. Some such estimates also have a way of introducing changes into the economy. And such changes require revised estimates about future economic activities. Economists frequently qualify their forecasts by stating the assumptions under which they expect their predictions to hold. A report states that one president became tired of his chief economic advisers telling him that "on the one hand, if this condition develops, the economy will move in one direction and on the other hand, if that condition develops, the economy will move in another direction." The president remarked, "What I need is a good economic adviser with one hand." We also have some grounds for questioning some economic forecasting that appears to be tied closely with the future economic concerns of a vested-interest group.

Good economists can distinguish between well-founded probability estimates about the future state of the economy from poorly founded ones. And they can provide public and tested evidence to other qualified persons to justify some of their projections. Allowing again for a margin of error, we have good grounds for accepting some economic projections as well-founded probability estimates about future conditions under the assumptions set forth in the projections.

Weighted probability estimates also occur in gambling operations. Before we examine such statements, we need to look at some of the conditions under which large-scale gambling operates. Among other considerations, they give their own profits a high priority. Gambling houses and bookies expect to develop a table of probabilities that will enable them to gain a significant profit on the percentage of all monies bet. (Some games such as traditional dice do not lend themselves to the setting up of the degree of profit preferred by such houses. Others, like roulette and slot machines, do. Casinos tend to make their money on dice by side bets when they stack the odds in their favor.)

Gambling houses also seek to develop a clientele sufficiently large or affluent to assure a high volume of bets. (And in many instances they expect to make additional profits from other operations, such as food and lodging.) In some cases, gambling houses also may rely on what they call "gambling psychology." Some players may tend "to overextend their luck" when they are ahead. And others may attempt to begin "doubling up" when they are behind. Although probability tables on these facts can be built up to some degree, they appear to be more difficult to use than the probability tables for specific gambling games. Gambling houses also can employ highly skilled personnel to handle games where skill is a factor. They can require their operators to play the odds strictly.

Such houses also develop policies for internal use. Some of these policies, like using only the dice or cards provided by the house, have as their purpose the prevention of cheating against the house. Others, like setting a limit on the amount of money that can be wagered on any one play, limit the degree of the house's risk on any one play.

There is no reason why we cannot accept as well-founded a probability table set up by standard mathematical procedures on the likelihood of winning or losing on some games like dice. But some gambling houses have house rules to prevent the working out of empirical probability tables by customers on some games like roulette. They may change the tables periodically.

What shall we say about probability statements relative to sporting events like football games and racing? In predicting winning and losing teams over a football season, a good sportswriter who keeps up with team performances may have a record of .750 at the end of a season (usually with the help of eliminating tie games from the percentages.)

In taking bets on football games, bookies may give spreads. Northern State U. may be given three points over Eastern U. But factors other than the past performances of the two football teams enter into the making of these spreads. Let us not forget that the bookies expect to gain a percentage of the total money bet. If we want to regard such spreads or odds as probability estimates, we need to determine what the estimate refers to. The estimate refers to the expectation that the bookmakers can make their anticipated margin of profit on the total money wagered regardless of which team wins any given contest. Spreads or odds can rise or fall due to the amount of money that is being wagered on a given team.

This discussion makes several assumptions which in some specific cases would not hold. One assumption is that the odds makers have some fairly reliable way of evaluating the relative strength of teams based on past performances and present conditions such as injuries. Other assumptions are that they know how to use such tables to their own interests and that there is no rigging of the game. But even with these assumptions we cannot accept their statements about spreads or odds as well-founded probability statements about the outcome of such games or races. We have seen that other factors, such as the amount of money wagered on a given team or horse, influence the spread or the odds that are given. Furthermore, given the nature of their operation, bookmakers do not tend to provide any way for the public to evaluate the manner in which they make their estimates about spreads. We can have confidence in the view that successful bookies will seek to operate their business in such a way that they can meet large overhead expenses and make a profit. We are not suggesting that all bookmaking is as coldly calculated as the kind discussed in this section. But successful, large-scale bookmakers or casino operators need to have more than luck going for them. And one of the things they want on their side is a probability table in which the odds are stacked in their favor.

In this chapter we considered various issues related to probability. We examined reasons for holding that the notion of probability rather than certainty best characterizes our knowledge claims about matters of fact. The difference between the empirical probability of events and their mathematical probability was compared, and we looked at the simplest ways of calculating such probabilities. We also found that public and well-founded evidence may provide grounds for our accepting some probability estimates about events whose causal factors are highly complex. But we discovered reasons to reject some of these claims whose evidence either was not public or well-founded.

CHAPTER 17

STATISTICS
AND RELIABLE
GENERALIZATIONS

17.1 THE SCOPE OF STATISTICS

This chapter[1] analyzes some features about the reliability of data based on statistical research. To do this we need to know something about the gathering and analysis of statistical data, the way one makes sound statistical arguments, and the kinds of common errors that can occur in making these arguments. Our discussion of this topic is elementary.

In statistics one develops and uses critical methods to analyze large batches of information collected about members of a given population. The goal is to summarize characteristics about the population or to generalize about differences and relationships in the population. For example, there may be interest in knowing the distribution of the property "political party preference" (a variable) in a given population of voters. A survey of such a population can show the percentages of Democrats, Republicans, third-party members, and Independents.

---

[1] I wish to thank Barbara E. (Sally) Kilgore, a teacher of statistics and chairperson of a department of sociology, for assistance in revising a draft of this chapter. Statisticians and logicians do not always speak the same language. In this chapter some accommodation occurs in the way both groups use language. The results will probably not satisfy purists in either field.

One may add other variables, such as age, to be studied in such surveys. Having determined the distribution of "political party preference" and of "age" we can compare the distribution found in these two variables (properties) within the given population. One may choose to carry out such a survey by enlarging the number of variables. One may choose to add family income, occupation, religious preference, and formal education. With the determining of the distribution of these properties, we can compare how one property varies in relation to another in the population surveyed. We can see how voters with a given political party preference group vary with different age groups and with different family income groups. That is, we can identify party preference by age and by family income.

It also is possible to include in the survey still another set of variables having to do with specific political issues. These may cover views about human rights, a guaranteed minimal annual income, enforced retirement ages, environmental laws, and price controls. Further analyses can be made of the distribution of these properties in the population and of the relations found to hold between these properties.

We have introduced the word "variable." In a statistical study, a variable refers to any given identifiable property whose value differs among members in a population. Such characteristics as "opinion on human rights," "views on price controls," "age of respondent," or "annual family income" may be variables in a statistical survey.

Competence to gather and interpret statistical data requires extensive training and practice. There are good as well as poor ways to carry out research using statistical methods. Likewise, there are sound ways as well as poor ways to seek to justify conclusions of statistical arguments.

The misuse of statistical data is widespread. It occurs in many advertisements as well as in many news media reports. Political candidates and vested interest groups often cite biased statistical data to support their claims. For example, a drug maker reports the findings of a survey taken of persons with sinus congestion. It claims that 40 percent of persons using the company's remedy experience significant relief within two hours. And an additional 40 percent report significant relief within twenty-four hours. But the report fails to tell us about the statistical methods used. (How was the sample taken? Was a control group used?) What conclusions are justified about the healing power of the remedy? To evaluate statistical evidence we have to know something about good and bad ways of using statistics.

Generalizations based on statistical data occur in many current research reports. Progress in such sciences as nuclear physics, biology, medicine, economics, psychology, sociology, and political science depends, in part, upon proper statistical analysis. The making and justifying of decisions about national defense, energy policies, urban programs, transportation systems, education, marketing, investments, and television programming use arguments based on statistical data. And the use of computers facilitates the use of statistical data on a scale vastly greater than anything we have known in the past.

In this work, our primary interest in discussing statistics is to find out how one justifies statistical arguments and to see what degree of confidence one can place in their reliability.

A statistical argument holds that a given variable has a specified distribution in a given population. Or, it holds that a given variable occurs with a given frequency in relation to another variable in a given population.

17.2 SOME PURPOSES OF STATISTICAL SURVEYS

In this section we shall look briefly at some reasons for making statistical studies. These reasons include the gathering of information and the use of such information to make decisions and to influence the actions of others. Frequently we find many of these purposes present in one survey. But if the purpose of the survey is something other than to gather information, there is particular need to determine if other interests bias the findings of the study itself.

1. The Gathering of Information

Studying statistical information is a major way of increasing our knowledge. The kinds of things about which we may want information vary with our needs and interests. We may want to know about certain conditions found in our society. For example, what is the median income for workers on the West Coast? How does the cost of living in New York City compare with the cost of living in Seattle? How do illness and death rates compare between able-bodied persons who retire early and persons who continue to be employed until seventy or later? What are the political party preferences of persons eighteen to twenty-five today as compared with five years ago?

We may want to identify differences between certain subgroups in a population. One can analyze the weight and height of children to find norms of growth for different ages. Achievement tests are used as indicators of relative intellectual development as measured by specified norms.

Statistical studies also can help in evaluating the relative reliability of different measuring devices. One can compare the grades of graduating college seniors both to their precollege national board exams scores and to their high school records. By analyzing the correlations of these factors, one can specify which of these measuring devices is a superior predictor of college performance. (Correlation measures quantify the extent to which two variables occur together in some pattern in a given population.)

Statistical correlation measures can point to possible causal relations. For example, researchers found significant correlations between frequent smoking of cigarettes high in tar or nicotine and lung cancer. Is there a causal relation? Some medical reports show a positive correlation between persons under sixty-five with high cholesterol counts and persons with given types of heart attacks. They find a low correlation between persons with moderate cholesterol counts and persons who have these types of heart problems. Do these correlations point to a causal relation?

2.   The Use of Information in Decision Making

A second purpose of statistical surveys is to help in decision making. A whole system of management, sometimes called systems analysis, bases its decision-making procedures to a significant degree on the findings of statistical analyses. The purchasing of replacement equipment may depend on a projection of maintenance costs of old equipment against the projected cost and added uses of new equipment. The building of a new plant or the selling of an existing one may depend upon the anticipated per unit cost of producing a product and the anticipated market demand for that product.

Statistical data collected by the federal government has a determinative role in identifying areas eligible for certain types of federal funding. Unemployment rates, minority composition, and condition of housing are examples of statistical data used to determine the eligibility of cities for federal funding. Cities use statistical data to plan mass transportation systems or to plan new school construction.

We also use statistical analyses to help us make every day types of decisions. If we want to buy a TV set, we may look at consumer surveys. We want to compare the initial costs of given types of TV sets with the record of their quality and upkeep. If we are making a decision about what vocation to enter, we may look at the results of job market surveys. There we can identify vocations with high median incomes and with high levels of anticipated job opportunities. We also want to relate such findings to our own interests and abilities.

3.   The Use of Information in Influencing Actions

Another use of statistical data is to influence the actions of others. All kinds of action groups as well as counteraction groups use such data for these purposes. Claims found in such contexts need careful scrutiny.

To illustrate a case in which statistical data serve as a basis to influence the actions of people, let us assume that a Mr. Smith is running for Congress. Smith is politically astute and a man of some integrity. He also has a strong desire to win. He wants to operate within the law and to follow democratic principles. He also plans to serve the common interests of his constituents and to advance those causes to which he has a personal commitment. His astuteness leads him to recognize that he needs to secure both adequate financial backing and the support of influencial party members. He also needs to appeal to the interests of identifiable voter groups sharing a common interest and to take a stand on some issues of broad popular concern. How can he use information provided by statistical studies to help him get elected?

For one thing, he can survey the electorate to find out the current states of affairs regarding his candidacy and his voter concerns. What issues are viable? What issues do not create much interest? How do different groups respond on certain issues? And how strong are their feelings either in favor of a proposed outcome on an issue or against it? He may find that his strength is weaker among retired people, labor groups, and youth (under age twenty-five) than it is with business groups, middle-income groups, and rural voters. Among retired persons there is a strong interest in increasing Social Security benefits; among labor groups there is a strong interest in higher wages and job security; and among younger persons there is a strong interest in job opportunities and lower education costs. He can proceed to emphasize issues which appear to have greater appeal to the voter groups in which his relative strength is lower. But he must seek to do this without alienating voters already leaning his way or other groups supporting his campaign. He may decide that some issues are so divisive that, although he will address the issue, he actually straddles the fence.

As Smith's campaign progresses he continues to analyze statistical surveys made on the progress of his campaign and adapts strategies that will bring him more votes. Of course, the statistical surveys are not his only source of information about the attitudes of his electorate. He meets with his constituents, talks with them, corresponds with them, has public answer sessions with them, and interacts with reporters in press interviews. But even in these situations he is aware of what his statistical analyses have shown. In actual practice, what he learns through his surveys and his public contacts provides a way for him to check on the reliability he should accord these information sources and to respond to inquiries about his position on specific issues.

Politicians are not the only ones who use the findings of statistical surveys to further their political goals. Almost anyone seeking to influence the actions of other groups in our society uses such information as well. Salesmen use statistics to increase their sales. Recruiters use them to increase their effectiveness. Organizers use them to increase their following. Promoters use them to gain support for their interests. Activists use them to persuade others and to gain followers for their cause.

In this section we have discussed some uses made of statistical data. But we expect any good statistical survey to meet the objective standards of a survey designed only for information purposes. In the following sections we shall be looking at some more technical issues in the analysis of statistical arguments.

17.3 STATISTICAL ANALYSIS AND THE RESEARCH DESIGN

To achieve sound statistical findings one must follow some very specific procedures. Such procedures cover all stages of the research. The scheme used in classifying data, the method used to select subjects, and the instruments used to measure them affect the soundness of statistical findings. We shall.discuss the first two of these factors in this section.

1. Procedures of Sound Classification

Clarity and precision in categorizing groups or their characteristics are essential in statistical analysis. The problem arises at two points in the research design. Given a certain population of interest for a survey, one must be able to determine clearly who is and who is not a member of that population. Given certain characteristics for analysis in a survey, one must be able to determine how to identify them.

If we want to survey community attitudes toward a proposed expressway, we have to determine how we are to decide whether a given person is a member of that community. Is the criterion to be legal residence? Is to be where one works? Is it where one owns real estate? Is it where one shops? Or is it some combination of these? We may want to see how different variables affect opinions on these issues. What opinion do college students, business owners, laborers, and other subgroups have on these issues? Clearly, we need some orderly way to break down the way we go about classifying the subgroups we want to study. Let us look at some of the principles we need to use in classifying a group and a variable found in that group.

Purpose for Classifying. The principle of classification needs to be determined by the purpose for which it is used. If one undertakes a study of the length of residence of persons living in a neighborhood, a determinative factor for classifying groups might be the ownership of the residence. Is the residence owned or rented? If the purpose of a survey is to study conditions relevant to marginal housing conditions in a given urban area, the determinative factor might be the general physical condition of the residence. If a survey is to study factors related to integration of different racial groups in a neighborhood, a determinative factor would be the ethnic group or groups found in different residences.

Use of Only One Principle for Classifying. Only one principle should be used in making a series of subclasses for a given class. One might propose to classify a group of professors in a given university campus. The determinative factor here can be the professors' age, their health, their scholarly attainments, their teaching efficiency, their interest in counseling students, their political attitudes, or the areas of their specialization. The following classification of professors violates the principle: professors, associate professors, assistant professors, instructors, good lecturers, good researchers.

Distinguishing All Relevant Classes. The principle of classification needs to distinguish all classes relevant to the purpose of the study. Principles for classifying need to be able to include all subgroups relevant to a survey. The following example represents a case of too few classes. A student proposed three classifications for students in the junior high school: the athletes, the delinquents, and those who are neither athletes nor delinquents. The languages spoken in the Western Hemisphere might be classified as follows: English, Spanish, Portuguese, and others. This final class would group together those who speak French, those who speak a native dialect, such as Navajo or Guaraní, and those immigrants who speak German or Italian. For such a survey this miscellaneous class would be too large and too varied.

Avoiding Unessential Classes. A principle of classification should provide only for those classes that are needed. That is, it should not permit a needless duplication of classes. In deciding on the degree of breakdown of classes, one should consider both the possible divisions of the subject area and the purpose of the classification. If a general study is to be made of the library holdings of a given university, the breaking down of the holdings into major subject areas might be entirely sufficient for some purposes. If a study is made of the works in chemistry, additional classes representing different fields in the subject area would be essential. The use of all classes found in the analysis of the works in chemistry also in the general study of the library holdings needlessly multiplies classes.

2.   Selection of Subjects: The Sampling Procedure

The way one selects subjects for a survey has a great bearing on the reliability of statistical findings. Very rarely can one survey entire populations. The use of probability theory in analyzing statistical data requires random selection of subjects. Here we shall discuss common methods of selecting subjects.

1. Random Sampling. The kind of sample taken by statisticians is a *random sample*. The word "random" here has a technical meaning. It requires that two conditions be met: (1) the method of choosing a member of the sample gives every member of the population studied an equal chance of being included in the sample; (2) the method used in such cases assures that the choice of any given member of the sample has no predictive effect on the next choice. We expect a rigorous use of random methods of selection to provide a representative sample of a population.

SIMPLE RANDOM SAMPLE.   The method used to determine the members of a simple random sample may vary. One way of selecting a random sample is to give a different number to represent each member of the total population studied. The number of each member appears on a separate object, such as a small ball. All balls are placed in a lottery wheel. The wheel is turned. A ball is drawn and its number recorded. The wheel is turned after the drawing of each ball until one acquires the sample size needed for the study. (If the population is small, each object drawn should be replaced before the wheel is turned and another object drawn.) For example, someone wants to survey the opinions of students in a given university about their views on the energy crisis. One assigns a different number to represent each student and records the numbers on separate slips of paper. All the slips are placed in a lottery wheel. If five hundred students are to be included in the sample, then, with proper shufflings of the slips, there is a drawing of the five hundred numbers needed for the sample. There are other ways to select the random sample. But it is a random sample only if at the time of each selection, each student has an equal chance of being chosen as a member of the sample and each drawing has no predictable effect on subsequent drawings.

PROPORTIONAL STRATIFIED RANDOM SAMPLING.   To decrease sampling errors, some researchers use a highly technical procedure called a proportional stratified random sample. One breaks down, or stratifies, the population according to relevant 'differences in the total population. (This assumes that there is some known basis for determining the proportionate membership and relevant characteristics in each group.) Then, one takes a random sample from each of the different strata. The number of individuals chosen for each stratum depends on the numerical proportion of that stratum to the total population. The developing of relevant criteria for the stratification of samples and the determining of any subgroups within such strata can become highly complex. Many national polls use this procedure. Experience and training are prerequisites to making sound surveys in such cases.

Stratified sampling is also used to compare subgroups that may constitute a small portion of the population. A simple random sample would produce too small a number of some groups for proper comparison. Thus, if we wanted to compare blacks, Anglos, and Spanish-speaking residents of a given large city, we would stratify the population along this variable and randomly select an equal number from each category.

2. Nonrandom Sampling. Many researchers seek to approximate the results of random samples through the use of easier, but nonrandom, methods of selecting subjects. The most common of these methods are systematic sampling and quota sampling.

SYSTEMATIC SAMPLING. Systematic sampling selects every n^{th} object in a population. Suppose we are auditing the books of a small office supply store. Using a systematic sample we take every thirtieth sales slip from the order of their consecutive appearance on the sales slips of the store and review it for errors. It is likely that the "thirtieth sale" is made at similar times in the day. Errors in calculation are not randomly distributed throughout the day. But rather they may occur at regular intervals during each day when the clerks are tired or extremely busy. Thus, our sample may have too many of these errors. In other cases our sample would have too few errors. A substantial bias in the estimate of error can result. Systematic sampling is most problematic when there is no random mixing of objects prior to selecting the sample.

QUOTA SAMPLING. Marketing groups frequently seek to approximate some features of a proportional stratified random sample by the use of quota sampling. In quota sampling one collects a given number of subjects with characteristics assumed to be relevant to the survey. Those quotas are designed to compile a representative group of the population. A requirement for the interviewers can be that they interview a given number of blacks and of Anglos, a given number of people between the ages of twenty and twenty-five, twenty-six and thirty-five, and so on. Bias usually occurs in the interviewers' selection of people. They generally find it easier to select receptive and available subjects. Done repeatedly, this selection method can produce a sample quite unrepresentative of the general population.

In this section we have looked at some features of research design for statistical analysis. In the next section we shall look at some distinctions useful in helping us to understand the way statisticians carry out their work.

17.4 SOME BASIC STATISTICAL DISTINCTIONS

In this section we shall distinguish between descriptive and inferential statistics. And we shall discuss the meaning of such notions as a population, a parameter, a statistic, and levels of measurement.

Descriptive Statistics and Inferential Statistics

Statisticians distinguish two approaches in analyzing data: descriptive and inferential. Descriptive statistics are methods used to summarize large batches of data (information). Graphs, charts, percentiles, and averages exemplify methods for summarizing information. Inferential statistics combine the use of tests and manipulations with probability theory to infer (generalize) something about a total population. For example, one can take a random sample of voters and, from the data provided from the sample, find a basis for "inferring" (predicting) how the entire population will vote. The process of testing formal hypotheses, which we will discuss later in the chapter, uses inferential statistics.

Random selection of subjects is essential for use of inferential statistics. Statistical inferences based on nonrandom samples are highly questionable.

Statistical Populations

The word "population," as used in statistics, has a related but more inclusive meaning than in ordinary language. In the latter case it usually refers to the number of people in a specific geographical area. In statistics, "population" refers to specifiable groups or aggregates of any measurable kind of entity, event, or process. Such populations can consist of all members of any one of such groups as the following: freshman students in community colleges, eligible voters, professional athletes, electric ovens, or freshwater fishing lures.

Parameters and Statistics

Statisticians use the terms parameter and statistic to identify what part of the population—all or some—one uses to calculate a summary measure. A parameter refers to summary measures whose calculations use the total population. A statistic is a summary measure whose calculations use a sample of the population. The mathematical operations required to determine the value of a parameter and a statistic are similar. But the different labels alert one to the data base used—that is, whether it is from a total population or from a sample. Generally, statisticians use sample statistics to estimate population parameters.

Levels of Measurements

Statisticians have to make distinctions about the types of variables on which they are trying to summarize data. One can summarize some types of data only with specific statistical tools. This limitation is similar to those found in using carpenter tools. There is little need to claim that a hammer is an effective tool for inserting a screw into a piece of wood. The problem is similar in statistics.

A basic factor in determining the statistical tool for analysis of data is the level of measurement for a given variable. A level of measurement refers to the relationship holding between different groups (categories) relevant to a variable.

There are four different levels of measurement: the nominal scale, the ordinal scale, the interval scale, and the ratio scale. In the *nominal* scale there is a distinction of categories based on the notions of sameness or of difference. A different number designates each category. Such numbers do not designate any progression. One may find the faculties in a college distinguished as: (1) humanities, (2) natural sciences, (3) social sciences, (4) fine arts, (5) vocational. Any one teacher would be either in the same class with another teacher or in a different class from another teacher. That is, nominal scales can identify sameness and difference.

An *ordinal* scale provides for the assigning of an order or rank in the scales as well as identifying sameness or difference. That is, with the ordinal scale the categories represent the presence of more or of less of some quality found in a subject. For example, in a 1000-meter track event, one runner will finish first, another second, and another third. The runner who finishes second may have been behind the first place winner only by a pace, but have been fifty paces ahead of the next runner. The rankings—first, second, and third—merely place participants in order. Some run with more speed than others, but how much more is not specified. Ordinal variables show a ranking. But there is no indication of equal distance between the points on the scale.

Certain confusions can arise with ordinal level data. For instance, percentile rankings can represent very little or a great deal of difference among people. It is possible for a person to score in the 50th percentile on a test, and yet be only a few score points away from one scoring in the 80th percentile. Although this may happen infrequently, it is important to remember that percentile ranks only place people in order; they do not indicate how much more or less of a characteristic one person has than another.

An *interval* scale distinguishes categories as having more or less of something, but in addition the differences are measurable. There is an identifiable and equal distance (or interval) between the categories used to measure the variable. An example of an interval scale is a Fahrenheit thermometer. Some statements about comparisons made on such scales are proper while others are not. Let us assume that the (Fahrenheit) temperature at a given place is 40° on April first, 60 ° on May first, and 80° on June first. It is not proper to say that June first is twice as hot as April first. It would be proper to state that the temperature on May first was half the difference between the temperature on April first and June first. Thus, the interval scale makes possible a comparison of intervals as well as sameness or difference and greater than or less than.

A *ratio* scale has all of the characteristics outlined above, but in addition it has an absolute zero. That is, the zero represents the absence of the variable. Measurements in terms of feet, pounds, and quarts are ratio scales.

The numbers used in a ratio scale represent the interval from a point of origin or of zero. Statements such as "twice as much as" and "four times greater than" apply to a ratio scale. Using this scale it is proper to state that 80 pounds is twice as heavy as 40 pounds. On a ratio scale one also can speak about sameness or difference, about greater than or less than, and about comparison of intervals.

Statisticians do not always insist that in every case one restrict an analysis to the measures provided by a given scale. But they insist that one acknowledge any variation in such cases. They also require that one identify any unwarranted conclusions that might be made in such cases as well as any information superimposed on the data. But even in these cases, one must avoid the fault of an unwarranted shifting of the proper use of a given scale. For example, let us grant that the type of scale used in measuring IQs is an interval scale. The statement, "a person with an IQ of 130 is twice as intelligent as a person with an IQ of 65," is in error. This makes an improper use of an interval scale as a ratio scale.

In this section we have distinguished between descriptive statistics and inferential statistics. We also have examined the notions of a parameter and a statistic. In the next section we shall look at measures of central tendencies.

17.5 MEASURES OF A CENTRAL TENDENCY OR AVERAGES: A METHOD FOR SUMMARIZING INFORMATION

In this section we seek to clarify some elementary concepts about measures of a central tendency. We examine such notions as the arithmetic mean, the median, and the mode as general types of central tendencies.

Measures of a central tendency indicate where the observed scores tend to cluster in a distribution. There is a selection of one number or value as most representative of all the values or scores.

In ordinary discourse we frequently talk about averages. But what is an average? What do we mean when we call a student "average"? Is it when the student has a grade that falls about where the "arithmetic average" is for all students in that class? Or, is it when a student's grade falls halfway between the scores of those having higher scores and those having lower scores? Or, is it when a student's grade is the score that occurs with greatest frequency in relation to other such scores in the student body? Or, is it some combination of the above? Or, does it signify something other than these meanings? To avoid such ambiguities, statisticians prefer to use the notion of a central tendency rather than average.

The three most common types of such measures are the arithmetic mean, the median, and the mode. The arithmetic mean, often called the arithmetic average, is the one used most frequently. (It also provides a basis for more sophisticated procedures in statistics.) One finds the *arithmetic mean* by adding the sum of scores and dividing this total by the number of scores entered. This method is familiar to many students as the procedure many instructors use in averaging grades. For example, consider the following possible test scores obtained by a group of students: 40, 50, 55, 60, 65, 70, 70, 75, 80, 80, 80, 80, 85, 95, 95. The total number of students is 15. The sum of all scores is 1,080. Dividing this by the total number of scores, 15, the arithmetic mean is 72. One should use this measure only with interval and ratio level data.

The *median* is the midway value in an ordered list of scores. At this point the number of scores having a lesser value is equal to the number of scores having a greater value. In the above case, the eighth score stands in this relation, with a value of 75. Seven scores are lower than this and seven scores are higher; thus, the median of these scores is 75. One may use this measure with ordinal, interval, and ratio level data.

The *mode* is the value of the entry occurring with greatest frequency in the table. The entry occurring with greatest frequency in the scores above is 80. Thus, the mode is 80. One may use the mode for all levels of measurements, but it is the only measure of central tendency available for nominal level data.

Another way of stating the last two definitions is that the median is the point occurring midway in the distribution of the indicated measures. The mode is the score occurring with greatest frequency in those measures.

None of these three ways of computing central tendencies presents a balanced perspective in every case. The exclusive use of any one of them in a given sample can grossly distort the information about a given population. Let us consider the following case. One might report that the average (mean) per capita yearly income for a small, oil-producing country in the Middle East is $15,000. This may provide the basis for believing that most of the inhabitants in that country have good incomes. But a very few of the people may be getting most of the income. Viewed in another perspective, the median per capita income in that country is less than $400 a year. The second figure provides for a completely different view of the yearly income of most of these inhabitants.

The relation found between the mean, the median, and the mode in any given distribution indicates whether or not the data form a normal distribution.

In analyzing central tendencies, we need to pay careful attention to the point of reference used in the statistical study. In this context, by "point of reference" we mean the total population covered by the central tendency. A frequent source of difference between one set of statistical data and a second is that the two surveys employ different points of reference. That is, they refer to two different populations. For example, in a wage dispute at a small plant with twenty-five employees, the management may release a statement to the press stating that the average salary at the plant is 40 percent higher than comparable figures released by the employees' union. Why this difference? It has to do with the point of reference used in determining these amounts. The data used by the management include the much higher salaries of the president, the manager, and two assistant managers. The data used by the labor union include the salaries only of the employees who do not have any supervisory job. Vested interest groups tend to stack the population they use in a survey to best suit the view which they want the findings of a survey to support.

In some cases it is desirable to weigh the arithmetic mean. This provides for correcting some distortion that otherwise would appear in the analysis of a central tendency.

In this section we have seen that statisticians need a more precise word than "average" to talk about central tendencies. In the next section we shall look at one method statisticians use to evaluate some of their findings.

17.6 FORMAL HYPOTHESIS TESTING AND SIGNIFICANCE LEVELS

This section discusses one way statisticians evaluate findings about information taken from random samples. This way uses a null hypothesis and a significance test. Since the procedure of making such tests is highly technical, we shall talk only about what such tests do and why they are important.

In the analysis of statistical data, a hypothesis is a statement about some observable and measurable things that one wants to test. The purpose of such tests is to find out about: (1) differences between two or more groups (populations), or (2) relationships between two or more variables.

Suppose we have interest in the effects of a new pain-killing drug. We randomly select arthritic patients for an experiment. A tablet containing the new drug will be given to an experimental group. But we provide a plain tablet without the drug to a control group. We use a randomly assigned double-blind experiment in which neither the patient nor the doctor knows who receives the tablet with the drug. And we test for the results of the treatment two hours after administering the drugs.

As a matter of chance, we might expect some differences in the outcomes for the control group and for the experimental group. Even though we follow strict procedures we can expect some difference between estimates based on different random samples taken from the same population. We need to determine the likelihood that we can account for our findings by chance rather than by actual differences found in the population studied. A critical issue here is the point where we reject the view that chance accounts for the differences, and accept the alternative hypothesis that these differences actually characterize the populations represented by the samples.

Using probability theory, statisticians can calculate the likelihood that they can account for differences found in their analyses of a sample on the basis of chance. And they frequently structure their investigation of this likelihood on a procedure called formal hypothesis testing.

In formal hypothesis testing, a statistician generally advances two hypotheses, the null hypothesis and the alternative hypothesis. The null hypothesis states that there is no difference between the groups studied— that chance can account for any observed differences or relationship that one finds in the sample. The alternate hypothesis states that the observed differences are actual differences found in the sample. The null hypothesis is the only hypothesis for which there is a statistical test.

In the example discussed above, the null hypothesis would hold that there is no difference between persons who received the pain-killing drug and those who received the tablet without the drug, with respect to the amount of pain present two hours after administering it. The alternative hypothesis would state that there is a difference between the two groups, or that less pain is present in one group than the other.

In using the null hypothesis, statisticians use a test to determine the probability that the initial findings (about a difference or a relationship) in the study can be accounted for by chance. This test provides the basis for justifying either the rejecting or the accepting of the null hypothesis.

There always is some probability that any finding can be chance. A statistician has to decide prior to conducting a test for a null hypothesis how small the probability of chance occurrence must be to justify rejecting any given null hypothesis.

A statistician selects a point such as .01, where the probability of chance appears to be low enough to justify rejecting safely a given null hypothesis. If one does not find this point reached, then there is not a rejection of the null hypothesis.

The point selected as a basis for rejecting a null hypothesis is the significance level. But this point varies with different types of subject areas and statistical analyses. This significance level is seldom greater than .05 or less than .001. The significance level for some surveys in the social sciences can be as high as .05. But the physical and medical sciences tend to select smaller probabilities, around .001. An observed significance level of .01 can be very strong for a survey dealing with social issues, but it would be very weak for a sample used in a laboratory experiment in physics or medicine. In the former case of the social sciences, the null hypothesis would be rejected. But in the latter case the null hypothesis would not be rejected.

News media sometime report about "a significant difference between group x and group y" in summaries about research findings. But such

reports can be highly ambiguous. Given the wide range over which significance levels vary from one type of research to another, the reader has little
information on which to evaluate the importance of the finding in such
contexts.

Perhaps this problem of ambiguity helps to account for the use of a
different approach by some statisticians. They claim that a preselection of
a point at which to reject a null hypothesis is arbitrary and may be uninformative. They likewise consider somewhat arbitrary the rejecting or accepting of a null hypothesis by use of this preselection point. They do
expect the reporting of the exact probability that chance can account for
any observed difference or relationships in the findings. Reviewers of a
report accumulate evidence from many other reports in a given subject
area. They can decide for themselves whether the evidence warrants holding
that the observed difference is due to chance on the one hand or to actual
conditions characterizing the sample on the other.

There are other reasons to find somewhat unsatisfactory some current
uses of null hypotheses as the primary model for statistical investigation.
Some statisticians find rather uninformative the mere rejecting of the view
that chance can readily account for observed differences or relationships.
One can compare such use of the notion of chance to telling someone who
is looking for an unfamiliar object in a warehouse that the sought for object
is not a cube. What such a person wants to know are such things as the
size, shape, and color of the object rather than merely what shape the object
is not. That is, there is need for a model which will provide statisticians
with information about what does account for an observed difference or
relationship rather than what does not account for such matters. In seeking
to develop such a model some statisticians are placing increased emphasis
on testing mathematical models whose purpose is to actually describe the
data.

To illustrate the above view, let us consider the following case. Suppose
one believes that persons with past medical injuries are more likely to have
future medical injuries than persons who have not had these kinds of injuries. The traditional null hypothesis test provides essentially for one of two
possible conclusions. Either chance does account for the different injury
rates observed in the two groups or chance does not account for them. In
this case, one is accepting or rejecting the model of "chance." In contrast,
a mathematical modeling approach tries to find a model that fits the observed data without restricting such data to the kinds of testing and analysis
that the model of chance can fit. The issues focus, in part, on whether some
model other than chance better accounts for the data. Or, if the chance
model cannot account for a pattern, is there another model that can account
for it?

In the above case of medical injuries, one can test a mathematical
model of contagion to determine if, indeed, past injuries have some predi-

catable relation to future injuries. The use of mathematical models in contrast to the model of chance has increasing acceptance in dealing with some statistical approaches in the social sciences. It offers promise of finding more satisfactory explanations of some social phenomena than procedures based on the notion of chance.

Decisions based on the findings of formal hypothesis testing cover a wide range of interests. Such decisions may relate to the drugs we take, to the job opportunities we have, to the goods we consume, and to whether the Internal Revenue Service carries out investigations of unusual tax returns.

In this section we have looked at the use of null hypotheses and of some alternatives to the use of this approach. In the next section we shall review some errors that may occur in statistical analyses.

17.7 ERRORS IN THE USE OF STATISTICAL ANALYSES

Abuses of the principles of statistics provide some basis for the misleading cliché that one can prove anything by statistics. Such abuses or errors can occur at all stages of a statistical report. This section reviews some of the abuses and errors found most often in reports citing statistical data. The examples used in this section relate primarily to studies found in areas of interest to the social sciences. But these types of errors also occur in other types of statistical studies.

Errors in Planning a Statistical Analysis

A number of errors may occur in the planning stage of a statistical survey. These may be present in an improper statement of the hypothesis. It may have the wrong focus. It may be too broad or too vague. The concepts used may be improper or imprecise in the way they are formulated. The manner in which one classifies for different groups or identifies different properties may be faulty. The sponsoring agency may want a given result and may introduce a bias in the survey design. The personnel chosen to carry out the survey may have poor training. Differences in the method used to gather data may introduce biases into the survey. Provisions for some answers to questions may be too restricted.

Technical Errors in Gathering Data

Investigators introduce bias in gathering data in many ways. They can fail to secure a random sample or to obtain reliable responses. They can make wrong use of measuring devices. Bias can be introduced if they collect data on the basis of easy and convenient access to sources. Consider this case. A random sample is made for a survey to determine women's attitudes about abortion. An interviewer goes to the home of a Mrs. Jones, who is one of the persons chosen for a random sample. But Mrs. Jones is not home. Would it be all right to go next door to interview another woman who is home? The making of such a substitution introduces bias into the sample. It could introduce bias against the representation in the sample of women who work or who are busy in community activities.

A variety of technical errors may occur in the recording of data. There may be guessing for answers whose meanings, as recorded on the original data sheet, are not clear. One item could be checked and then partially erased, leaving the respondent's intention in doubt. One may misinterpret abbreviations made on an interview schedule. Coding of data for computers may be improper. And other mechanical errors of recording may occur. All of the potential sources of error need to be kept to a minimum by reviewing the work at each stage.

Errors in the Interpretation of Statistical Data

Many errors may occur in the interpretation of statistical data. One may misinterpret or misuse an average. One may distort evidence by failure to make proper cross-references. The manner of making some measurements can result in a claim for greater precision in a generalization than the evidence justifies. It is also possible to extend a trend line for a period longer than the statistical data warrant.

Correlations are often misinterpreted. They may suggest, but they do not necessarily demonstrate, causal relationships. A higher relative percentage of high school students studying advanced math go to college than those who do not take such courses; but the studying of advanced math has not been shown to be the cause of their going to college. Plans to go to college may have been a factor in their taking advanced math.

One of the more frequent misuses of statistical analyses is the attempt to apply the norms of a large group to a restricted and small subgroup found within the larger group. For example, a survey may find that among college students, one out of four has used some form of illegal drugs. It does not follow from this that in a group of twelve students, three have used such drugs.

Hasty generalization constitutes another form of unwarranted inference based on improper use of statistical data. A hasty generalization infers a general principle from too few cases. Hasty generalization occurs if broad or sweeping generalizations are made from a random sample too small to justify such conclusions.

There also are many technical errors that may occur in analyzing and interpreting statistical data. Reference to some of these appear elsewhere in this chapter.

Deliberate Errors in the Recording and Interpretation of Statistics

A deliberate manipulation of data obviously distorts the findings of a survey. Extremist groups frequently make such distortions to gain support for their views. They may put spurious data in the sample. They may falsify the record about the data found. Or, they may omit data conflicting with the position supported by the report.

Another form of distortion of findings occurs in some uses of charts and graphs. Even if the other parts of the statistical analysis are accurate, one can minimize significant differences by using cubes on a chart rather than lines or squares. Or one can maximize minor differences by presenting them as lines rather than cubes. Linear graphs can misrepresent distribution if they do not begin at zero. Competent statisticians indicate a definite break in their graphs, such as use of a wavy line if there is any omission between zero and the units presented on the chart.

The many kinds of error possible in the use of statistics increase the need for careful appraisals of data and of the conclusions derived from them. Only persons technically trained in the use of statistics can detect many of the errors occurring in surveys. But laymen can also detect some of these errors, particularly if they are simple or gross.

This chapter has developed topics related to using statistical reports to appraise the reliability of arguments. We have seen that good statistical analysis requires the ability to use statistical tools and to follow reliable statistical procedures.

EXERCISES

A. Propose an evaluation of the conclusions derived in the following examples. Give reasons for your evaluation.
  1. A teacher gives a social attitudes test to a large introductory class. He accompanies a volunteer group consisting of one-third of the class to slum areas, and then retests this group for social attitudes. He found a difference between the norms of this group and those for the larger class, and he concluded that a supervised visit to slum areas made a significant difference in the attitude of students.
  2. An organization of conservative veterans wants to report on the public's opinion on various government activities. It selects and surveys every tenth house in a West Coast community. Dressed in uniform, the members ask an adult present in the house to state whether they ''approve'' or ''disapprove'' of items worded as follows:
    (1) Less government and more private initiative
    (2) Unfair government competition with private business

(3) A sound dollar

(4) Federal intervention in education

(5) Federal domination of medical practice

(6) Forced federal mediation of free enterprise–labor disputes

(7) Foreign giveaway programs

(8) Honest elections

(9) Tax-paid rent subsidies

(10) Gag rule in Senate

3. A study of the effectiveness of a new approach to teaching logic is proposed. A class of seventy students is divided into two groups. The experimental group consists of volunteers who are willing to try out the new approach. A review of the results shows that the experimental group has a better knowledge of the material studied than the control group.

4. A reporter seeks to determine some of the major sources of tension in a slum area. One afternoon and evening he interviews twenty persons in four different bars in the neighborhood. To conform to the population characteristics of the area, one-half of the group is black, one-half white. In response to a question regarding the source of the tensions, 42 percent claim that unemployment is a major cause, 40 percent mention police brutality, and 18 percent mention poor housing. That evening on television, the reporter summarizes his findings by stating that "residents of this community consider unemployment as the major cause of tension."

5. A news release announces that three out of four citizens in an area are for Governor Beta, since three out of four signs held by persons attending a rally carry pro-Beta slogans such as "Cleveland Is Beta Country" rather than slogans such as "Beta Must Go!"

6. A survey is made to determine the amount of outside study done by members of a class in freshman English. The thirty-five students in each of five classes report orally to the graduate assistant. The reports show that a weekly average ranging from two to twelve hours is spent in outside study. The graduate assistant averages the figures and reports that freshmen spend an average of 5.672 hours each week studying freshman English.

B. State the null hypothesis and the alternative hypotheses you would use in the following cases.

1. Suppose you believe that there is a difference between cities where the locally elected officials announce that they will try to change federal school integration policies and cities where elected officials do not make such announcements. Specifically, you believe that more violence against integration of schools occurs where locally elected officials make such announcements.

2. Suppose you are doing marketing research for a national chain of supermarkets. You notice that the sales for one of their most profitable items—children's toys—varies considerably from store to store. You have reason to believe that the number of toys sold varies according to their placement in the store: (1) dispersed throughout the store, (2) collected in one aisle, or (3) concentrated at the checkout counters.

C. At a given store the length of service of the employees is as shown below.

Number of years	Number of employees
26	1
23	1
19	2
16	1
14	2
10	1
7	3
3	2
2	5
1	3

Determine the arithmetic mean, the mode, and the median for the length of service of these employees.

CHAPTER 18

ARGUMENTS AND MORAL ISSUES

18.1 ARGUMENTS AND MORALS

In previous chapters we have discussed arguments as they relate to the social and physical sciences and to commonsense decisions. In this chapter we shall turn to the use of arguments as they relate to moral issues.[1] To do this we shall review some of the arguments related to major issues in ethics.

In a broad sense social morality refers to the type of actions, common habits and customs subject to group approval or disapproval on the basis of beliefs held by such a group relative to its preserving its social identity and advancing its well-being. Societies appear to disapprove of incest, in part because they find such a practice is destructive of its interest in having physically able children. Some societies may approve of letting older persons die by shaking them out of palm trees because of a need to keep an adequate food supply for those who are younger and more useful.

Any given social morality may not be an enlightened morality. Practices some societies approve are undermining of their interests, social identity, and well-being. The critical point in describing social morality is that a society regards some practices as supporting its well-being and others as

---

[1] Since there is a discussion of how to construct arguments in Chapter 20, some students may find it helpful to read Chapter 20 prior to reading Chapters 18 and 19.

injurious to its interests. And it may be indifferent to practices which it does not believe affect its vital interests.

In a philosophic sense, morality refers to human conduct related to reducing conflicting interests in a way consistent with justice, and to attaining the enlightened interest and well-being of all persons. "Enlightened" in this instance means well-informed, rationally conceived, and reasonable in the actions it expects. A moral issue is one that relates to achieving such enlightened interests. Likewise, a moral issue may be about an action believed to be destructive of such social or personal well-being.

We make value judgments about moral issues. "Your cheating on the test is wrong." "Your telling the truth is right." "Job discrimination on the basis of ethnic background or sex of worker is wrong." Historically, one meaning of philosophical ethics is that it is a critical analysis of rational ways to justify moral judgments about human conduct judged as good or bad, right or wrong, obligatory or not obligatory. Such ethics focus on the reasons given for making moral judgments and for justifying moral arguments, rather than on actually making moral judgments about specific moral issues. That is, they deal with the kinds of issues that we need to clarify and resolve in order to make rational moral judgments. Practical or applied ethics deal with proposals for resolving specific moral cases. In current discussion we find applied ethics included as a part of normative ethics. In this section our interest is not applied ethics. But we shall have some interest in the use of arguments made in resolving disputes about issues in applied ethics.

Current philosophers frequently use the term metaethics to cover the subject matter treated historically as ethics. But in some cases a more restricted use occurs than in the previous definition of ethics. In its more restricted sense, metaethics is an analysis of the meaning of the language of morals and of the logic, methods, and standards used in advancing strong moral arguments. In this chapter we are concerned primarily with logical issues in ethics interpreted both in the broader historical and philosophical meanings of ethics and in the more restricted sense of metaethics. However, we shall need to review some of the basic positions taken in some of the major systems of ethics in Western culture.

In analyzing moral arguments we find various sources used to justify some of the evidence and claims made in such arguments. Our interest is in the critical use of these sources such as the following.

Commonsense Data.   We can observe what people believe to be morally right or wrong and what they believe to be morally good or bad. What do they mean by "moral duty" or "moral good"? We also can inquire about their reasons for supporting such views.

Cultural Anthropology.   Cultural anthropologists and sociologists point out how views regarding moral conduct develop in different societies. They take note of the kinds of actions that come to be approved or disapproved in such societies. And they may look for cultural reasons to explain beliefs about behavior regarded as morally good or morally bad in these cases.

Model Cases.   We also can study model cases in which people single out instances of moral conduct that is highly praiseworthy or blameworthy. Some people praise the type of moral conduct demonstrated by persons like Mahatma Ghandi or Martin Luther King, Jr. Others find censurable the actions of Hitler and Stalin. Why do we find some people's conduct to be highly praiseworthy but others to be wicked?

Proposals of Moralists.   Some persons have gained recognition teaching about morality. What types of conduct have they found to be good and what types to be wicked? How do they justify their beliefs?

Religious Views.   The religious traditions in which many persons participate condition their views about moral right and wrong. Such traditions have helped to mold the general moral sentiments and practices in a given culture, and have been modified by them.

History of Ethics.   A study of the history of ethics helps to show how philosophers have analyzed their views about the meaning of expressions used in moral discourse. We also find proposals about the nature of the good life for human beings and about how they can best attain well-being. We are particularly interested in the reasons given in support of such proposals.

Critical Reflection.   We can critically reflect on the meaning we give to moral expressions and the way we engage in moral reasoning. What do we appear to be saying when we hold that an act is right or wicked or obligatory?

Key words used in moral discourse also have other uses that do not refer to a moral situation. We talk about a good car as a car that runs well with a minimum amount of repair. We refer to a good house as one that is superior in its construction and utility, relative to other houses in its class. We talk about a good carpenter as one who is skillful at his trade. We talk about a good example as one that clarifies an issue in a discussion. We talk about a good day as one that is pleasant and satisfying. We also can refer to a bad car, a bad house, a poor carpenter, a bad example, or a bad day.

We also refer to a right tool as one we need to do a given job. We talk about the right call of a football play as one that gains needed yardage. We refer to a right mix of persons on a committee to indicate a varied background of experience or wide base of support from different interest groups. We can talk about the right answer as the one supported by the evidence. We can talk about the right dress as one that is proper for the occasion. We also can talk about a wrong tool, a wrong call, a wrong mix, a wrong answer, or the wrong dress. But it would be unusual for us to talk about a wicked tool, a wicked call, or a wicked mix.

We also talk about obligations that are legal, political, or financial. Meeting such obligations can be conditions for our enjoying certain services or opportunities. We also use "ought" in a conditional way. We can say, "I ought to go to the post office." And we mean, "My going to the post office is essential if I want to pick up my mail."

But we also use these words in a moral sense and we shall be exploring these uses as we proceed.

In this section we have distinguished between morality and ethics. We looked at some sources used to provide evidence in making moral claims. We have seen that key words used in moral arguments also have uses in broader contexts. In the next section we shall examine some of the principle ways in which philosophers have sought to organize their views in dealing with moral arguments.

18.2 SYSTEMS OF ETHICS

1. Subjective Views

In this section we shall review some of the major views developed to justify claims made in moral arguments. We discuss ethical systems based on subjectivism, cultural relativism, duties, utilitarianism, and self-realization.

In its most elementary sense, a subjective view of ethics refers to a position that interprets moral judgments as a matter of individual taste or preference. The morally right is what one prefers. As tastes for paintings, food, and clothing can vary, so do preferences about what we accept as right and wrong. We sometimes refer to such a view as ethical relativism.

In a more developed sense, some subjective views of ethics stress the emotive meaning of moral evaluations. Such expressions of emotion can represent our commitment to one set of actions rather than to another. We can be saying: "This is the kind of attitude that I approve. You would do well to consider approving it as well." We also can claim in such views that moral judgments are not subject to being true or false. For example, the statement, "Mugging is wrong," in this view expresses an attitude. It would not be accurate to say that the statement is true. Neither would it be false in this view. But we can give reasons in support of our holding the attitudes we express about such acts as mugging. Such reasons keep our moral judgments from being arbitrary. And they provide a basis for our commending these attitudes and dispositions to others.

A difficulty with the elementary subjective view is that we do have rational disputes about choices based on taste. We regard some actions as expressions of good taste and others as expressions of bad taste. Some preferences we regard as well-grounded and others as foolish. It appears odd that we cannot find some objective ground for saying that an act is morally right. Some acts do help to resolve conflicting interests; some do contribute to social well-being; other actions do increase human happiness. It appears strange that we would want to hold that inflicting needless suffering on others is not morally wrong and that it is not morally wrong in some objective sense.

Sensitivity to the claims of the elementary subjective view can provide a type of caution against our proposing to seek some bland uniformity in moral choices without regard to individual differences in persons. In making moral judgments such individual differences need to be taken into account.

A difficulty with the view that our moral judgments are merely expressions of emotion or of our attitudes and dispositions is similar to our problems with the more elementary subjective view. We do not merely express attitudes and dispositions when we refer to some actions as wicked. We want to say that brutality to children and the slaying of hostages are wicked, not merely because of our feelings. Rather they are wicked because of identifiable reasons. Our dispositions and attitudes, like our conscience, can be too restrictive a guide. They can be oversensitive to some moral issues, insensitive to others, and misdirected still in other cases. But we can commend some features in this view. Our attitudes and dispostions do appear to have some relevance to our moral decisions. We do well to seek specific reasons for our moral judgments. We cannot assume that moral judgments are subject to the same types of standards for judging their truth or falsity as hold in other types of arguments. And we certainly need to try to clarify the meaning of our moral expressions.

2. Cultural Relativism

We have noted that social morality refers to human actions associated with the interests and well-being of a society, subject to the approval or disapproval of that society. Statements about group approval are descriptive—they are true or false depending upon what they hold to be the case and what the situation is. If we propose that social morality provides the basis for making correct judgments about what is right and wrong, then we are proposing an ethical theory known as cultural relativism. We are saying that group approval or disapproval provides the needed standard for making moral evaluations. Such approval or disapproval determines our moral ob-ligations—helps us to identify what in a moral sense we ought to make happen or to prevent from happening. Cultural relativism holds that what is morally good, morally right, and morally obligatory depends on the approval of the society in which any given action occurs. The "done thing" also is the "ought-to-be-done thing."

But such a view strikes us as odd. We would appear to be saying that mass slayings of persons within a society for ethnic, religious, or political reasons is morally right, provided such societies approve of such actions. We also would be saying that acts of mercy, kindness, and caring would be morally wrong provided such societies disapprove of such actions. Rather than justifying moral judgments by standards rationally set forth after weigh-ing alternative views, such a position justifies moral judgments by appealing to a general consensus. The failure of this view to capture what we mean by the morally right is evident by the apparent meaning of the question, "Is what a society approves morally right?" We also appear to hold that we can and do make moral judgments from within a society about its moral judgments. That is, we say that some consensus views about a moral issue are wrong and that others are right. We would hold that a consensus view which approves of torture of political prisoners is wrong and that those who torture political prisoners are wicked in doing so. Discrimination against other persons on the basis of race was not morally right as long as it had the approval by our society. Nor did it become morally wrong only after a consensus developed that it was morally wrong. There appear to be rational grounds for holding that it was morally wrong even at the time it found social approval. We have good reasons to question the view that what is morally right or wrong is merely a matter of social convenience.

Yet some claims found in cultural relativism appear to be relevant to a rational analysis of moral issues. Different kinds of social situations do provide a context for a different ordering of our priorities in making moral judgments. Even courts of law recognize that applying some laws without regard to circumstances imposes unfair hardships. They hold that exten-uating circumstances are relevant to determining the legal guilt of the ac-cused. A position that does not allow for some flexibility in applying moral rules in different contexts has serious deficiencies.

3. Duties and the Morally Right

Duty theories give priority to the notion of right and duty over the notion of the morally good, as a basis for making moral judgments. We need to distinguish between a duty that is a claim on moral behavior and a duty that we regard as an obligation in a specific context. We shall refer to the former as a duty claim and to the latter as a duty obligation. A duty claim is a moral rule that has relevance for a person in making moral decisions.

We express duty claims by moral rules such as the following. "Tell the truth," and "Do not lie." "Respect the property of others," and "Do not steal." "Do not depend on outside help in writing your exam," and "Do not cheat." "Keep your promises," and "Do not go back on your word."

A duty obligation is a moral rule that we hold as having priority, as binding, and as requiring us to try to make certain things happen or not happen in a given situation. In the absence of a conflict between one duty claim and another, this view of ethics would require that we tell the truth if truth-telling is relevant to a given moral situation. But if conflict arises, for example, between truth-telling and not contributing to the injury of another party by a person intending mugging, the duty not to contribute to the injury of another party would be our duty obligation.

In other situations we would hold that our duty obligation is truth-telling. It has prior claim on our actions rather than nonparticipation in injury to another party. For example, consider a formal inquiry into charges of an alleged gross abuse of authority relative to unfairness in grading on the part of a grader or a teacher. We have been eyewitnesses to some of the events cited as evidence to support the allegations. We are called to testify about these matters at a formal inquiry. Truth-telling in such a situation can be the duty obligation even though we are aware that such testimony can contribute to the injury of the accused party.

A critical logical issue is how we go about making decisions about our duty obligations. Proposals that we merely intuit our duty obligations do not provide us with a sufficient rational grounding for decisions. Proposals that we make such decisions on the basis of the greatest good or the greatest happiness, shift from a standard of duty and right to a standard of obligation and good based on consequences. We note this problem in passing, but we shall need to give it more serious consideration in a later section.

Some duty claims use rules that apply to a wider range of situations than others. If a moral rule tends to apply to all or almost all situations, we can refer to this moral rule as a moral principle. We find several such principles mentioned in the history of ethics. One such principle would be a moral rule not to inflict needless suffering on other persons. Another would be that one should act so as to seek to minimize social conflict in a way that is consistent with requirements for justice. A third moral principle would be that one should act so as always to treat other persons as ends and never only as means. A fourth would be that one should act so as to be the master and not the victim of circumstances.

Some moral principles are formal. That is, they do not depend on any material circumstances to determine their merit. And they are universalizable without exceptions. One such principle would be that we should act on the basis of a maxim that always can be universalized. It applies to all moral choices and applies to any moral situation that can arise. But the difficulty with such formal principles is that the kinds of moral rules derived from them tend to be too inflexible. For example, from the above formal principle we could derive the more specific rules regarding truth-telling, property-respecting, and promise-keeping. We appear to be left without guidance in cases of conflict regarding more specific rules derived from our formal principle. For example, we may have to choose either not to keep a promise or not to tell the truth in a given situation. To hold that such conflicts are only apparent appears to ignore some of the more difficult types of moral decisions that we face.

We have noted several difficulties with a view of ethics based on duties. How do we justify the moral rules which we regard as relevant to a duty claim on our actions? How do we rationally justify acting on one duty claim when acting on it precludes our acting on another in a given context? And how do we justify a choice of a duty claim as binding in a given context even though a decision to act in another manner can appear to bring about a greater amount of good? In some cases the use of a duty rule can appear to lead to arbitrary and capricious actions. We shall return to these questions. But we hold that duty rules do provide the basis for justifying some actions as duty obligations.

The use of duty rules does, however, have some advantages. Duty rules can have the weight of the collective experience of a social group in their favor. They can supply a basis for acting when we have examined a context and still remain in doubt regarding the kind of moral decision we should make. They can provide some immediate guidance when we lack time or opportunity to make a thorough review of factors relevant to a moral decision.

4.   Utilitarianism

Utilitarianism is one of several ethical theories that hold that consequences determine what is morally right. Some ethical theories hold to an act view of consequences, others hold to a rule view of consequences, and still others tend to shift from one to the other. An act view of consequences holds that we determine a morally right action by the results which we can reasonably expect to follow from a specific response in a given situation. A rule view of consequences holds that we determine what is morally right by rules that usually maximize what we hold the good to be. But ethical theories that emphasize consequences are not in agreement about what the good is that we are to maximize.

Hedonistic utilitarianism holds that the good we are to optimize is happiness. And it identifies happiness with pleasure. The morally good is what produces the greatest happiness for the greatest number. Act utilitarianism holds that the morally right act is that act which results in the greatest happiness for the greatest number. In such a case, truth-telling is morally right and obligatory, provided it is that act most conducive to the greatest happiness for the greatest number in a given context. Rule hedonistic utilitarianism holds that we determine the morally right and obligatory by those rules we use to make possible the greatest happiness for the greatest number. In this case, truth-telling is morally right provided it is a rule whose use consistently supports the greatest happiness for the greatest number.

Some critics of hedonistic utilitarianism have held that this view in some way fails to recognize human dignity and cannot provide enlightened moral guidance for human choices. But some criticisms of utilitarianism fail to take into account that a consistent following of this view would represent a level of moral behavior that is much more humane than we are accustomed to seeing. We also want to hold with this view—that happiness is a part of the good life for man.

We would differ, however, with the claim that we can define good merely as happiness. G. E. Moore, a major British moral philosopher during the first half of this century raises the open-question argument about any view that both defines good by reference to some consequence and then identifies that consequence with a specific property. It makes sense to ask the question, "But is that specified property always good?" In the case of hedonistic utilitarianism we can ask, "Is happiness always good?" We need to note that by the time some advocates of the greatest happiness principle complete their analysis of what they mean, they probably fare better in their response to some critics than they frequently are given credit for doing. But Moore's objection points out with good reason that the notion of good as happiness does not appear to capture the meaning of what we mean by good. These two questions appear to be different: Is something morally good? Is something conducive to the greatest happiness?

If we attempt to distinguish between types of pleasure and regard some pleasure as better than others, we find another difficulty with this view of utilitarianism. How do we justify distinguishing between pleasures? If we use some standard such as self-enrichment to justify such a distinction, then we appear to move outside the greatest happiness principle to another view, to determine what the morally good is.

Act hedonistic utilitarians can find difficulty in justifying as right a specific act that one normally would regard as morally wrong on the grounds that the doing of this act works for the greatest happiness for the greatest number. We would find it odd to hold that inflicting needless injury on one person is good if it is conducive to the greatest happiness of a large number of persons. We also are aware that some wicked deeds have been done by appealing to the notions of the greatest good. (Even political assassinations can be lurking around the corner.) Act utilitarians can claim that some critics misinterpret their views. But the ease with which these views can be misused raises some questions about their clarity or adequacy.

Rule utilitarians can find difficulty in justifying which rule to follow in cases where several moral rules can apply. Different actions follow from the different rules that are relevant. Rule utilitarians can be pressed back to an act utilitarianism or pushed outside utilitarianism to find a decision-making procedure for ordering the priority of their rules.

G. E. Moore supports a view known as ideal utilitarianism. In his view, the good is a moral and nonnatural property that we cannot define. We intuit the good and reflect about it. The morally right act is that act which will provide the greatest good for the greatest number. Even if we have some intuitive basis to determine the good in a given case, we need to be able to provide some rational basis to support claims based on such a process. And we need reasons in settling moral disputes and justifying one action in preference to another. It appears rather easy to come up with intuitions of the good that coincide only with our limited self-interests.

5.   The Ethics of Self-Realization

Self-realization is another ethical view that emphasizes consequences. And the consequence it holds up for us is the development of the self. But views regarding what constitutes self-realization vary widely. Self-development usually emphasizes growth of some distinctively human aspect of the self. For example, one aspect might be the use and maturing of our rational abilities. Or, it might be developing the social aspects of the self with emphasis upon our relations with other persons and upon our contributions to service-related institutions. It also can be, at least in the construction we are placing on this notion, the developing of an authentic self. Most self-realization views hold that the good is that which develops our intellectual, moral, spiritual, and aesthetic capacities. And the morally good is that which is conducive to our achieving our maximum capacities as human beings.

A difficulty with this theory is that it is vague. We have many capacities that we can develop. Do we want to accept as good the development of every capacity that we have? And if we propose a harmonious developing of these capacities, we can raise questions about whether every kind of harmony is good. The development of some of our capacities restricts our ability to cultivate others. One may become a fair musician or a superior athelete, but not both. On what basis are we to choose the direction of such development? We are thrown back on the kind of person we want to become. We appear to have wrapped ourselves up in our own development, when most moral actions appear to concern our relation to other persons. If our concern becomes directed primarily toward the developing of other persons, we may be presuming that we know the direction in which someone else needs to develop. And we might unfortunately begin to impose our views on such a person because we believe we know what her good is. But a self-realization view does not require this course of action.

Our realizing some of our own self-interests can conflict with others realizing a given value for themselves. We may be able to develop our capacities of political leadership only by thwarting the interests of others who are aspiring to the same positions we want. Many may feel called but only a few may be chosen.

Some self-realization theories have many commendable features. Concern about how we make our choices does relate to the growth of our intellectual abilities and aesthetic sensitivities. An ordering of the policies and practices of our political and economic institutions to facilitate the developing of human rights and the opportunity to live with dignity is worthy of our strongest support. In some self-realization theories, emphasis on the development of a morally good character and of morally good habits appears to have merit.

Some views that we are including with self-realization ethical theories emphasize self-authenticity as the moral good. An authentic self accepts responsibility for his actions. Freedom to choose carries with it the responsibility for determining what kind of person one becomes by the choices that one makes. To be inauthentic is to let others make such choices for us or to let events drift and take their course through the customs and pressures operating in a situation. Authenticity requires that we be honest with ourselves. We need to order our choices on the basis of the kind of person we believe we ought to become. The choices a person is making are determining the kind of self she is becoming. Authenticity also requires a type of self-esteem which enters into our decisions. A person must aspire to authenticity and must want to keep giving expression to it in order to keep on being authentic. Sometimes we have to pursue this authenticity with feelings of dread, despair, and loneliness. In this view we need to recognize that in our choices we, in some sense, are also willing that all people make such choices.

We may want to hold that authenticity is a good, but that it is not the only good. This view tends to place such a burden on persons making choices that we can neglect the social and institutional dimensions of our conduct. Some interpretations of this view can be vague and border on the irrational. Persons holding this view can become so preoccupied with their own authenticity that they fail to share their interests with others or to care about the suffering of others.

We can share with those who hold to this view the need to develop into a person who prizes being honest with himself, taking responsibility for his actions, and having self-esteem. We also can take seriously the idea that in making moral decisions, we need to recognize that in some sense we are willing that others in similar circumstances make a similar kind of choice. We may choose not to accept the view that despair and loneliness have to be our lot. But we can recognize that moral choices can evoke in us a sense of awesome responsibility that accompanies our freedom to make happen those situations that we choose to bring into being.

In this section we have reviewed some of the alternative positions taken by philosophers in attempting to find some base from which one can discuss moral issues. We have looked at subjective and cultural relativism. We examined positions based on duty claims and on maximizing pleasure. We also considered views that emphasize the realization of the self.

18.3 A PLURALISTIC AND CONTEXTUAL APPROACH TO ETHICAL ISSUES

1.   A Context View of Duty Claims and Duty Obligations

In the previous section we examined arguments used in various ethical views. In this section we shall look at some arguments in support of a pluralistic and contextual approach to ethical issues.

In this discussion, the kind of approach that we recommend for consideration will be grounded in the context in which we make moral decisions. Various factors enter into the decision about what we believe to be morally obligatory. The duty claims on our conduct need to be considered. We need to weigh the consequences of our choices. In addition, we need to test the formal consideration of making universal the rule on which we are acting for relevantly similar situations. But the ordering of our duty claims is our point of departure.

We begin to learn about duty claims by living in a community which recognizes duty claims on our conduct. We reflect about these duty claims, appraise their apparent reasonableness, and consider the consequences both of their being accepted as duty claims and of their being rejected on account of the kinds of moral order for which they make. We inquire about their fittingness to serve as universal duty claims in relevantly similar contexts. And we consider their general consistency with the other duty claims that we are willing to accept. But we require only a general consistency in principle. We recognize that in a given context the following of one duty claim can preclude our acting on another.

We also raise further questions about duty claims. Do they make for the kind of moral order that other informed and morally sensitive persons can reasonably accept? Do they make for the kind of moral order that we believe would be more humane and fairer than another ordering of duty claims? Do they make for the kind of person that we can respect? Do they make for a resolution of social conflict consistent with the requirements for justice? Do they make for attaining the enlightened interest and well-being of all persons, consistent with our reasonable expectations about safeguarding human rights?

We have seen that some duty claims relate to promise-keeping, truth-telling, and not inflicting injury. Other duty claims relate to respecting the rights of others, dealing honestly with others, and fulfilling our commitments.

In some cases, the context in which we make moral decisions can be relatively simple, and a given duty claim appears to apply in governing our action. Our decision to make something happen is based on a moral reason. But frequently the context in which we make a moral decision has some degree of complexity. That is, we find that more than one duty claim can govern our decision. Or, the result of basing an act on a duty claim can bring about a situation we regard as unfair. This raises the issue of determining a duty obligation and the action it requires.

We do not propose to advance a simple formula for determining a duty obligation for all cases. Such formulas can become so vague as to be essentially useless, or they can tend to dry up our moral sensitivity if we attempt to apply them in a mechanical fashion. What we can do in determining a duty obligation is to analyze the context in which the need for a given moral decision arises. We can decide on the obligation in a manner comparable to the way recommended earlier in this section for identifying our duty claims. We can use an appeal to consequences and at the same time have some distrust of such appeals in considering our duty obligations.

But why should we distrust appeals to consequences? The results that we reasonably can expect in a given context can be subject to some ambiguity. Consequences unfold indefinitely from a given act. What kind of consequences—the greatest happiness, self-realization, not causing needless suffering, or some other results? Some acts appear to be inherently wrong, even though we might anticipate that the consequences of the wrong act would be a greater amount and distribution of good results than what we expect to result from doing the right act. For example, to propose to deny someone a fair trial on the grounds that the consequences of such a trial would bring about a wide range of discord and unhappiness in a community appears on its face to be inherently wrong. In some cases, an appeal to consequences appears to be a veiled effort to find a socially respectable means of seeking our own limited self-interest under the guise of promoting the interest of the larger public. Lacking good faith, we can seek to justify any act by appeal to results—a tactic limited only by our degree of cleverness. We are not, however, proposing reasons to reject an appeal to consequences. But such considerations justify our making careful scrutiny of appeals to consequences.

A person in good faith who appeals to consequences is looking toward the future; this is the strength of such an appeal. It can help to alert us to other duty claims that may be relevant to the resolution of an issue. And it can help to overcome some of the narrow considerations that result from too limited a focus on one rule or principle that we are considering as a resolution of a restricted situation. A review of consequences also can help provide insight into the degree to which one duty claim is more fitting than another in a given situation.

As a general expectancy, we want duty obligations and appeals to consequences to support each other. If they fail to do so, we usually need to examine further the context of the choice before us. The kind of decision we make points to the kind of moral order we want to prevail in our society. This provision for moral order may be a key consideration in our setting the priorities of duty claims. That is, we can accept to select one duty claim as binding on the basis that such a rule in this context supports the kind of moral order that we believe is the best for our society. But we have to provide good reasons in support of such views. We should also distrust recommendations that are arbitrary or capricious. If we cannot justify our decision by good reasons, then there are grounds for doubting that such a decision is sound and morally good.

2.   Acts as Morally Right and as Morally Obligatory

How shall we view morally right acts, morally good acts, and moral obligations? A morally right act gives expression to a duty claim that is equal in priority to any other in a rational ordering of duty claims on our conduct. In some cases, a morally right act also gives expression to a duty claim whose use is less destructive of the enlightened interests of a society than other courses of action. A morally wrong act tends to affect adversely the enlightened interest of a society.

A morally right act is obligatory if it has the highest priority in a rational ordering of duty claims on our conduct. An act becomes contextually obligatory if it is a morally right act chosen in a context that requires us to act on a duty claim.

Morally good acts are those human actions chosen for moral reasons, which result in supporting or attaining the enlightened interest of a society. Morally bad acts are those human actions whose consequences are more destructive of the enlightened interest of a society than other actions that can be taken in that context. An act can be morally good without being morally right for that context. For example, in a given context one has two duty claims. One fulfills a promise to attend a meeting for the purpose of obtaining better night lighting for the neighborhood, so the number of muggings in that area will be reduced. The other duty claim is to assist a neighbor who has been severely beaten in a mugging and needs help. Either of these duty claims is a morally good act. But only one of these, possibly the rendering of immediate aid, would be the morally right act in this occasion. Attending the meeting would be the morally wrong act. To act on the duty claim with lesser priority does some social good, but at the same time, the doer neglects to render immediate and desperately needed aid to a neighbor. However, we need to recognize that reasonable men can differ on such ordering of priorities of duty claims.

Many statements made about duty claims and duty obligations can be judged as true or false, as can many statements made in a discussion of moral issues. Moral judgments are not only recommendations that we can judge as happy or unhappy or as wise or foolish. We also can judge many such statements as true or false by placing them in the context in which they occur. Such a context includes the way we justify the ordering of the priorities of duty claims relevant to a moral judgment, and the way in which we construct our duty claims.

A change in the context in which duty claims occur can mean a similar change in our ordering of priorities. We have seen that given a conflict between two duty claims—to tell the truth or to keep promises—our duty obligation in one context may be to tell the truth and in another to keep our promises.

We are not suggesting here either a morality of convenience or a morality of relativism. There is a difference between a duty claim and a duty obligation and we cannot proceed blindly to apply duty claims in some abstract way. Individual differences are a part of the context in which moral decisions are made. But setting the priority of a duty claim in a given context also rationally requires that we grant this duty claim priority in other contexts with similar relevance. We shall further explore the issue of moral statements as true or false in looking at the traditional problem of the "ought" and the "is."

3. The "Ought" and the "Is"

In moral deliberation we give reasons for saying that one action or kind of action is right and another is wrong. Many of these reasons are factual, that is, they describe events or states of affairs. On the basis of these kinds of reasons, we have no immediate basis for jumping to the conclusion that "X ought to do thus and so." The matter of how we can derive an "ought" in the conclusion of a moral argument is a matter of controversy among logicians. But if the "ought" occurs in the conclusion, it needs to occur either explicitly or as an understood premise. If the "ought" appears only implicitly as a premise, then we have to make it explicit in reconstructing a moral argument. Consider the following argument:

You promised to give us your political support if this legislative bill is contested.

This legislative bill is contested.

Therefore, you ought to give us your political support.

On its face, this argument is invalid. Something is missing—an explicit "ought" statement as a premise and another statement that links the "ought' statement more concretely to the argument. Reconstructed, we have the argument in the following context:

> If this bill is contested, you promised to give us your political support.
>
> This bill is contested.
>
> If you promise to give us your political support, then you have an obligation to keep your promise.
>
> If you have an obligation to keep your promise, then you ought to give us your political support.
>
> Thus, you ought to give us your political support.

Let us consider another argument that on its face is invalid:

> This legislative bill is contested.
>
> This legislative bill corrects inequities in the income tax laws.
>
> Therefore, you ought to give us your political support.

We can reconstruct the context of this argument by including its understood missing premises as follows:

> This legislative bill is contested.
>
> This legislative bill corrects inequities in the income tax laws.
>
> If this legislative bill is contested and it corrects inequities in the income tax laws, then you can assist in correcting such inequities by giving us your political support.
>
> If you can assist in correcting such inequities, then you have an obligation to seek to correct such inequities.
>
> If you have an obligation to seek to correct such inequities, then you ought to give us your political support.
>
> Thus, you ought to give us your political support.

There are other proposals for deriving the "ought" in the above cases. We justify introducing assumed premises in the above case on the nature of the context of moral reasoning and on the acceptance of duty obligations in determining morally right conduct. We can propose objections to the above examples. But we are showing one way among others of justifying an "ought" in the conclusion of a moral argument. And we are holding that some such procedure is essential for justifying the "ought" in the conclusion.

Someone can raise another objection about the conclusion in the above argument. The expression, "You ought to give us your political support," can be a directive use of language. And one can argue that we evaluate directive use of language by such expressions as justifiable or not justifiable. But in such cases the conclusion is not a statement that is true or false. In this case, the "ought" expression would not fall within the scope of the kind of logic we are using in discussing arguments.

We can agree that the conclusion can have the form of a recommendation. But we also want to hold that in its larger context, it represents another language use—a statement that we can regard either as true or false. We derive a conclusion in the last argument from statements that can be judged as true or false in the premises. The "ought" is a part of a true or false statement in the premises, and it remains a true or false statement in the conclusion. We are not deriving an "ought" from an "is" in the above case. But we are saying that a part of the meaning of the "ought" in the above case is a context which includes the notion of "having an obligation." And "having an obligation" is a part of a statement that either is true or is false.

4.   Freedom of Action

Immanuel Kant and others have pointed out that to claim that we "ought" to do something requires that we be free to do what we ought to do. In this limited space, we cannot provide an extensive discussion of human freedom in moral action. But we can outline what would appear to be some reasonable expectations for responsible moral freedom. To have human freedom in moral action, we expect the following conditions to be present:

1.   The moral agent must be able to act voluntarily and without coercion in choosing between alternative courses of action.

2.   The moral agent needs to have the ability or power to carry out the indicated act.

3.   The moral agent needs to be able to set himself to initiate the action chosen and to have reasonable expectancies of making headway in carrying out the intended action.

We usually expect a fourth condition for responsible human freedom: that the moral agents need to be able to work toward the enlarging of alternatives on which they can act in relevantly similar cases in the future.

It is difficult to make moral freedom consistent with a view of hard mechanistic determinism. In such a view every human action is a part of a network or a chain of events in which each link is a result only of what has already occurred in the preceding links. Evidence for such a position, particularly as this relates to human behavior, does not have the conclusive scientific support that some of its advocates claim. Hard mechanistic determinism appears to require the universality of causality and the uniformity of nature that are postulates used by some scientists in their analysis of data and construction of laws about the universe. But we have no way of knowing that these postulates actually are also principles either that characterize all events in the universe or that characterize all human acts. We are not objecting to the making of such postulates, provided it is recognized that they are postulates and that they are made for a specific and limited purpose.

Some persons hold that a proposed indeterminancy principle in nature can account for human freedom. But we cannot support a view of human freedom merely by the claim that some events in nature occur merely by chance. If an event does occur merely by chance, then chance would account only for a certain kind of randomness in nature. Something that randomly occurs does not provide a basis for supporting responsible human freedom.

Two of the remaining alternatives in this traditional division are soft determinism and self-determinism. But each of these views has its difficulties. Soft determinism holds that an agent is free provided she has the power to carry out the act she chooses. And if the agent has such power, then she is responsible for what she does. Yet a set of antecedent conditions determines the agent's choice, which continues to be part of a determined sequence of events.

According to self-determinism, an agent can act on the basis of reasons by which he analyzes alternative courses of action. The agent uses his knowledge, insight, and past experience to decide the course of action taken. Self-determinism acknowledges causal connections in human actions. But it also holds that some decisions to act are best understood as initiating activities of an agent rather than as unavoidable links in a sequence of events. Self-determinism has the unresolved problem of a self-caused cause. The discussion continues and the issues are unresolved.

Perhaps the above difficulties result from the context in which the discussion about freedom occurs. And by seeking to deal with the issue in another context, we can have some basis for holding to responsible human freedom. Such a view redirects emphasis from causal theories that cover all human behavior to an intelligible understanding of rational human behavior viewed in the context in which some human actions occur.

We do have rational grounds for making some claims that provide some justification for believing in responsible human freedom. In analyzing human choices we need to focus on the reasons an agent gives for his actions.

Some features of human actions do not appear to be understood merely by use of the traditional kinds of explanations used in science. Actions of human agents include several distinctive features. Agents frequently have the ability to enlarge alternatives for making their choices. These choices are made on the basis of considerations about the future. Agents also can make something happen, which is a consumating phase of their act of choosing. In the action chosen, agents can express what we mean by responsible human freedom.

In this section we have sought to place a moral decision in context. We have claimed that a moral argument has to make some of that context explicit. By making such a claim we also seek to justify our acceptance of moral statements as true or false, of using an "ought" in a moral argument, and of responsible human freedom.

18.4 CHARACTER VIRTUES

In this section we shall look at some traditional human virtues. Some moral arguments use statements about such virtues as evidence in seeking to establish a conclusion.

Some historical writers on ethics place more emphasis on habits and virtues than do contemporary writers. They argue with some justification that some personal habits have a relation to moral behavior. We are more likely to make the right moral choices when making such choices has become a habit of character. We shall look at some of these character virtues.

In historical ethics, a virtue refers to an excellence of character developed through habit, particularly the habit of exercising rational control over desires. These virtues are habits of character of morally good and mature persons. Some character virtues found in such persons may include the following.

1. Enlightened Self-Regard

Enlightened self-regard is expressed in statements like the following: "You should love your neighbor as yourself." "Do unto others as you want them to do unto you." We practice enlightened self-regard when we support social conditions in which other persons are as free to pursue their interests as we would like to be. Enlightened self-regard means that we support the developing of social institutions that are fair and sensitive to the needs of other persons. It means that we try to develop our rational capacities and our good judgment in practical affairs. It also relates to the development of our economic well-being and of our abilities to enjoy a decent livelihood and a satisfying means of employment. Self-regard includes an attentiveness to conditions which support personal happiness and health. It also takes account of developing an enjoyable personal life through establishing family ties and personal associates with whom one finds personal enrichment.

Enlightened self-regard helps to develop temperance, the exercise of moderation in our pleasures and other activities. As a classical Greek virtue, it finds expression in the writing of Aristotle as desiring "the right thing in the right way at the right time." In an extended sense it can include the exercise of restraint both in the case we make for those causes we support and in the case we make against some views with which we differ. But the exercise of temperance does not require the bland notion that temperance covers any kind of activity. The virtue of moderation does not support acts that are morally wrong, such as cruelty or prejudicial discrimination against minority groups.

2. Courage

Another classic Greek virtue, courage, is the active support of what we believe on reasonable grounds to be good in the face of some threat of harm to our self-interests. Aristotle regarded it as a mean between the extremes of rashness and cowardice. He stated, "Courage is the observance of the mean in relation to things that inspire confidence or fear." Moreover, "It is confident and endures because it is noble to do so or base not to do so." "To fly from trouble," Aristotle claims, is a fault.

An enlightened expression of courage requires the developing of practical widsom—the habit of exercising good judgment in choosing the effective means to achieve worthy goals. It differs from cleverness, which is an ability to achieve goals without regard to their being worthy. It differs from an impractical moralism, which may have worthy goals, but which so clutters the path to their attainment that it makes more difficult their fulfillment either by ourselves or by others. The exercise of practical wisdom does not follow the lines of mere expediency. There are occasions when stands on issues need to be taken for moral reasons, even if chances of reaching such goals are remote.

3. Enlightened Sensitivity

Enlightened sensitivity is a habit of conditioning ourselves to respond to and to support those features in our surroundings that we find worthy of appreciation. It has aesthetic, cognitive, and social dimensions. It can include our responding to the artistic creations of man's imagination and skill. It finds expression in appreciation for superior expression of art forms such as literature, architecture, painting, music, sculpture, acting, and ballet. In its broadest sense, it covers our responding to the beauty of many fascinating features of our universe including the starry heavens, the mountains, prairies, streams, wildlife, and even the minute structures seen through a microscope. It also can include our capacity to respond in awe and reverence to the sense of mystery we find in the universe, in living things, and within ourselves.

We give evidence of enlightened sensitivity when we develop an appreciation for knowledge and for the forms in which such knowledge finds expression.

We also practice enlightened sensitivity when we show sociability which includes a disposition to relate to other persons in a manner that is responsive to their interests and concerns. It covers the ability to enter into friendships and to treasure friends as persons rather than merely as instruments to satisfy our own interests or goals. Sociability does not require that we avoid conflict situations. Our willingness to be assertive in our relation with others can be a condition for our being able to appreciate them as persons and for them to respect us.

4. Authenticity

Authenticity is a habit of character in which we exercise honesty with ourselves and in relation to others. It includes an acceptance of our responsibility for fulfilling obligations and the practice of the kind of behavior worthy of our own respect and the respect of others. It requires a commitment to what we have reasonable grounds to believe is right, such as fairness in dealing with others, the opportunity to enjoy with others equal political rights, equal treatment under the law, and equal opportunity to seek redress for grievances.

Authenticity also finds expression in our anticipations of ongoing participation in those activities we find satisfying. It includes our continuing commitment both to achieving social conditions in which others can share in a broader participation in cultural values and to a fairer distribution in the fruits of the earth and of industry and labor. We can direct our energies so that the kinds of reasonable concerns for which we have lived will find new expression as the future unfolds.

18.5 METHODS OF RESOLVING DISPUTES ON MORAL ISSUES

We have seen that a moral issue relates to any human action about which we make duty claims, assert duty obligations, or find to be morally good or bad. But we have differences about what conclusion we should reach on various moral issues. In this section we shall examine further some ways to make moral arguments and resolve moral disputes.

In some cases, a reasonable resolution of moral disputes is difficult because the parties in the dispute find themselves in a closed position. That is, they are not open to consider new positions or to weigh new evidence. Their minds are made up and they appear to be immune to rational persuasion to positions other than those they hold. We can attribute their taking such positions to various factors.

1.   Some Restraining Factors in Reaching Agreement in Moral Arguments

Emotional Involvement.   Some people have a strong emotional attachment to a view held about a moral issue. This attachment to one set of beliefs appears to be so strong that they reject out of hand any argument, no matter how rational, that supports a position other than their own.

Institutional Commitments.   Some people have a relation to institutions that strongly reinforces the acceptance of a given ordering of priorities on some moral issues. In discussing a moral issue in these cases, we can be covering a whole range of economic, political, religious, or professional commitments. A change in view on some moral issues may require a change in a person's institutional relations. Yet some institutions do change their positions in the way they respond to moral issues. It may happen that rational argument penetrates beneath such institutional ties. We sometimes change our institutional relations as a result of the positions an institution adopts about moral issues. In some cases, pressures from within institutions can be a factor in bringing about changes in institutional positions on moral issues.

Peer Group Identity.   We are members of peer groups and we may aspire to belong to others. To gain or to hold acceptance and status in such groups, we find ourselves under subtle and not-so-subtle pressures to support the views on moral issues that such peer groups approve. In these cases we appear to be under a restraint of peer group identity to reject some views on a given moral issue and to be assertive in favor of other moral issues.

Personal Interests.   Our self-interests in the outcome of some issues can prompt us to interpret moral issues so as to protect these interests. Our views on such issues are likely to change only as we develop a different perspective about our self-interests or as we are able, at least temporarily, to rise above self-interest.

Future Expectancies.   In striving to attain certain goals or objectives, we may accept some moral issues as supportive of these goals and reject other issues as hurting the chances of attaining them. Some of our views on moral issues may change with our expectancies about the future. But this process can work both ways. Our expectancies about the future also may change with some of our views on moral issues. Rational argument can make a difference in some of these cases but not in others.

Such factors as those mentioned above do not prohibit some moral disputes from being resolved. But they can signify that some moral beliefs or positions can be so deeply entrenched that finding a practical acceptance of a view we are advancing on rational grounds has serious nonrational obstacles to overcome. We should point out that the above factors are dynamic rather than static. An enlightened discussion of moral issues can bring about some change in attitudes toward issues. Over a period of time, It can also result in people changing their views about moral positions they now hold.

2.   Resolving Disputes on Moral Issues

The following steps are one method of resolving disputes on moral issues in a rational manner, to the degree that they can be resolved in this way. These steps also are relevant to our making decisions on moral issues when a moral choice is offered.

(1) Identifying Relevant Facts.   Identifying the facts relevant to the settlement of moral disputes is not always an easy matter. Differing sets of statistics may be brought out in support of different views. The relevance of certain types of data also can be subject to controversy. There can be differing interpretations of what a factual situation is. We also need to clarify any verbal dispute that can appear as a factual dispute.

(2) Identifying Differing Duty Claims and Social Goods Relevant to the Dispute.   In trying to resolve a dispute, parties can differ on what duty claims on actions or what social goods are relevant. Agreement on what these claims or goods are and what relative strength they carry can be of use in reaching a decision.

(3) Identifying the Alternative Courses of Action.   We need to identify the different courses of action that are feasible in a given case. In some cases, we may find an intermediate position between two proposed courses of action that appear to be mutually exclusive. In other cases, we may find new alternatives of actions that we have not considered. We also can identify those actions that can be taken jointly. One course of action might be proposed with a back-up recommendation for initiating another set of actions if the original choice turns out to be unfeasible or undesirable.

(4) Ordering of Priorities.   We need to determine whether we believe that a given duty claim has a priority on our actions to such a degree that we should proceed to act on it. We may find that different claims on conduct have relatively equal merit. Or the possible good coming from one course of action might significantly outweigh the slight priority that we might give to another claim on our action, simply on the basis that in other contexts the latter claim usually would be stronger. In some instances we may have to argue in favor of the principle that the lesser evil is the desirable course of action. We can be confronted with hard choices such au having a leg amputated or significantly risking a much shorter life expectancy.

(5) Testing for Universalizing the Decision.   We want to consider whether the parties in the dispute are willing to apply the rule they have chosen to any other relevantly similar contexts. In some instances we may not be able to press the matter this far. One party in a dispute may want to plead for more experience or for a case-by-case approach. We may grant the need for more experience and for subsequent corrections of our present judgment. But we can still press for a position that even "given the present state of our knowlege and understanding" we have a need to act. Our decision can be for tentatively agreeing to universalize the duty claim on our action in relatively similar contexts.

(6) Testing for Personal Equations.   We want to know if in making this kind of decision, we can continue to have our own self-respect and to anticipate the respect of other persons knowledgeable and sensitive to the issues in the case. We also would want to determine if our decision (rather than some other duty claim on our action) would make for the kind of world that is more sensitive to moral issues and more concerned with an equitable distribution of enjoyable goods.

(7) Reviewing the Evidence and Arguments.   Even after having studied the methods discussed in this section, we may still not have resolved our dispute. We can review the evidence with the other party and seek to awaken greater sensitivity to the issues. We, as well as the other party, may be mistaken in our views. We may find a resolution, or we may continue to differ. Morally good and sensitive men skilled in moral arguments can and do differ. But the agent responsible for making a choice has to decide what course of action he will take. Choosing to delay a decision can be a moral choice that has moral consequences. Our choice helps to determine the kind of persons we are becoming and the kind of world that we prefer to live in.

In this section we have seen that the restraining factors in the context of an argument may make some moral disputes difficult to resolve. In making moral arguments, we can identify relevant facts, duty claims, and social goods relevant to a moral issue. Alternative actions can be identified and priorities can be set for duty claims. We also can test for the universalizing of the rule and for personal equations. A further review of the evidence and arguments may be needed.

In this chapter we have considered the use of arguments in moral decisions. We have looked at some arguments in support of different ethical systems. A contextual approach to ethical issues was developed and some character virtues were considered. We looked at some steps we can take in resolving disputes over moral issues. In the next chapter we shall consider the use of arguments in some decisions about policy.

SOME THINGS TO DO

1. Analyze the different kinds of duty claims that can be relevant to the consideration of various controverted moral issues (such as euthanasia or abortion).

2. Show how a moral argument could develop in a context in which the following issues are present.
   (1) A person experiences a conflict between keeping a promise to hold a matter confidential and telling the truth (or some other duty claim).
   (2) Someone finds himself in a conflict between helping a friend who has done something injudicious and in providing information requested by law enforcement officers that could be socially and professionally harmful to this friend.

CHAPTER 19

ARGUMENTS AND POLICIES

19.1 ARGUMENTS AND GENERAL POLICY FORMATION

This chapter looks at the use of arguments as they can relate to making policies. The use of arguments in developing general policies and in bureaucratic settings will be discussed. We shall also consider arguments as they relate to more specific plans of actions. Finally we shall look at arguments related to public policies and the common good.

A basic feature of our society is the degree to which different groups seek to achieve their goals through organized activity. We carry out such organized activity by forming institutions. What such institutions do tends to affect in many ways the lives and fortunes of all members of our society.

The policies of an organization consist of the general principles by which it governs overall operations and such specific principles it uses to carry out plans to reach its overall goals. These principles serve as guidelines to provide direction for decision making and action.

In some respects, organized groups use a policy in the way that scientific experimenters use a hypothesis. A primary purpose of both policy and hypothesis is to help look for certain results and to carry forward projects to see if those results can be reached. If the policy or the hypothesis does not help us reach the anticipated results, we may change it so as to obtain our results in another way. But their original uses may have been instrumental in identifying factors that helped in producing a better policy or a better hypothesis.

In some respects a policy also is like a habit. An organized group has a response prepared for certain situations. Use of the policy may avoid the need for detailed consideration of each decision that needs to be taken. It also provides for some uniformities in responses. Interacting groups can anticipate these responses and can plan their actions so that the outcomes of such actions become more predictable.

There are several levels of policymaking. Institutions have policies about how policies themselves originate. Some policies cover the entire operations of an institution and others relate to a specific area of activity. And there also may be policies for carrying out specific plans of action. (One might try to identify such policy levels in an institution such as a college or university.[1])

[1] Colleges and universities have charters. These give responsibility for developing the general institutional policies to a group such as a board of governors. This board then may develop policies about how it will develop policies on the basis of the requirements of the charter, relevant laws, institutional goals, and other agreements into which they enter.

The board then establishes general operating policies that cover some features of the whole university or university system. In many instances, the policies it adopts are issued as being recommended by the administration and an appropriate faculty body.

Arguments on this level tend to be justified by reference to the charter or constitution of the institution, the relevant federal and state laws, and the best ways of meeting the institution's goals. That is, such charters, laws, or goals serve as evidence to justify the policies developed.

The board of governors makes or approves the appointment of the primary administrative officers of the system. These groups in turn have a responsibility for seeing that policies relevant to the administrative operations of the institution as a whole are developed and carried out. In many cases, such policies as they adopt are subject to the approval of the board of governors. Likewise, they may act on general policies recommended by appropriate faculty or student groups.

Colleges or universities may proceed to make general policies that include the following areas:

governance	student placement
admissions	course loads
libraries	grading procedures
degree programs	grievances
finance	student life
faculty standards	endowments
research	government relations
continuing education	athletic programs

Arguments and disputes can develop in forming policies in any of these areas. And the charter of the institution, its general policies, educational goals, and standards of accrediting agencies are sources of evidence for advancing arguments.

Colleges and universities (or systems of such institutions) develop entities for achieving different goals set for the institution. We shall not detail the composition of such groups. But they can include different academic units, research units, students, the physical plant and its operation, to name a few. These groups in turn develop more specific policies for carrying out their operations.

We could also point to other policymaking levels within each of the above bodies. But let us hope we have achieved our purpose in showing how different policy levels develop and how such policies can affect the whole institutional life.

Institutions also have procedures, regulations, and rules to assist in carrying out their policies.[2]

When we look at government operations we find policies operating on a broad scale. The federal government develops policies in such areas as the following:

foreign relation policies	educational policies
national security policies	civil service policies
trade policies	welfare policies
fiscal policies	tax policies
monetary policies	national resources policies
energy policies	environmental protection policies
national health policies	freedom of information policies
transportation policies	internal security policies
labor policies	international intelligence policies
agriculture policies	urban planning policies

In discussing the use of arguments in making decisions about policies we might consider some of the types of issues about which such decisions are made. Let us look at the following types of issues as examples where arguments about policies help to decide how an issue is settled:

1. The national economy appears to be caught between the pincers of having to live with an unacceptable rate of unemployment for its labor force or an unacceptable rate of inflation. What policies, if any, can be followed to minimize both the rate of unemployment and the rate of inflation?

2. We expect industries to meet certain standards for the control of pollution both in their own industrial activity and in the products which they manufacture. Each higher level of quality control of pollution appears to require a higher level of cost to the industry and ultimately to the consumer. What policies regarding pollution controls best serve the long-range national interests?

3. Our foreign policy appears to vacillate between our national interest in human rights and the degree of emphasis we want to place on alliances with friendly nations to try to assure our common security. What type of policy should we adopt in cases where the emphasis on one goal appears detrimental to achieving the other goal?

---

[2] A procedure is an operational guideline that specifies a series of acts for carrying out a policy or a plan. For example, a university administration may develop a procedure or series of steps it follows in making faculty appointments or in admitting students.

Regulations constitute a body of rules that usually govern a specific activity of an institution. Universities may develop general rules about parking or about use of a room in a student union building by a student group. Rules usually specify acts that institutional members are to do or to refrain from doing.

4. A major urban area has a need to expand its sources of electricity at an annual growth rate of 6.5 percent. What policies, if any, can it adopt to help assure that these needs can be met?

5. American corporations doing business abroad find themselves competing for business in these foreign countries. And their business activity abroad also appears vital for our having a needed balance of payments and an acceptable economy. To what extent should we expect these corporations to adopt policies that conform to standards of business ethics required of companies doing business exclusively in this country? And to what extent should we adopt policies to permit these corporations to accommodate to competitive business practices accepted in the areas where they are operating?

We also can refer to policies in a more restricted sense than we find in the above examples. A teacher may establish policies for students taking exams. A coach may have policies regarding eligibility for players to participate on a team. A contractor may set forth policies about safety regulations on a job site. An editor may establish policies about publication of letters to the editor. A group in a car pool may establish policies about the rotation of persons who use their cars and what practices will be followed when members of the car pool do not appear at the designated places at agreed-on times. But we shall not focus our attention on these more restricted kinds of policies.

EXERCISE

Discuss the way policies for colleges or universities are formulated and justified and how they are used in arguments. (See footnote 1.)

19.2 ARGUMENTS AND GENERAL POLICIES OF INSTITUTIONS

Arguments can help to justify positions taken by interested parties about the general policies of institutions. And reasonable persons expect the reasons used in such arguments to relate to the charter of an institution and to the context in which the institution pursues its mission.

1. Consistency of a General Policy with the Institution's Charter

Charters and constitutions provide a primary basis for justifying the policies and actions of an institution. In a legal sense, an institution may be required to justify its policies and actions by reference to such documents. Some institutions also can provide charters to another group to exercise some rights or privileges that the granting body has authority to confer. A challenge to the institution's authority to follow some policies or to take some actions may occur. And these charges may require arguments to show that the institution is acting within the rights and privileges accorded to it by its charter and constitution.

Let us consider an example. A particular government agency may have the task of preventing the polluting of rivers and streams by industrial and urban waste. The agency adopts a policy which calls for it to have jurisdiction over any kinds of waste that might enter into rivers or streams affected by pollutants from industries and cities. It then seeks to specify that only given kinds of soil cultivation will be permitted within one mile of rivers or streams subject to its regulatory authority. But many people object. And such objections may be on several levels. One may claim that the agency has exceeded its own authority granted by its charter, in this case the law creating the agency. Another may challenge the substance of the law itself, by claiming that the provisions of the law do not fall within the powers granted to the lawmaking body by its charter or the constitution governing its actions.

2.   Consistency of a General Policy with Requirements Established by Law

We expect general policies to be consistent with duly authorized laws relevant to the operations of an institution. For example, we expect a corporation building a nuclear power plant to meet legal standards for the disposal of its waste materials. In specific cases, arguments develop about whether a given nuclear power plant does or does not take steps needed to assure that it will comply with these laws. But in a broader context, arguments develop about the maze of conflicting and even inoperative regulations which different regulating agencies may impose on the institutions they deal with. Arguments are used to determine what policies have priority in a given case. Arguments also may develop about the jurisdiction of different regulating agencies.

3.   Relevance of a General Policy to Institutional Goals

We justify some arguments about general policies by appeal to the goals of an institution. Arguments can seek to show that a given policy is not consistent with such goals, or that a general policy needs to be adopted to help attain a goal.

Some groups appear deliberately to misrepresent their goals. Front groups follow this practice. They may announce as their objective the meeting of some basic social need such as the delivery of health care. And they follow lobbying practices designed to protect or promote the vested interests of a restricted group in the health care field. We do not suggest that such parties do not have the right to protect and advance such interests. What we are pointing out is that one can argue that there is a striking difference between the stated policies and objectives of such institutions and their actual procedures and practices.

One expects an institution's policies to be as effective in helping it to reach its basic goals as any other set of policies that might be adopted in those circumstances. Let us assume that the goal of an institution is to deliver health care to underprivileged groups in a community. It may adopt a policy which requires a person to pay a monthly fee in order to be eligible to receive its services. But this requirement may be counterproductive. That is, those most in need of the health care services may turn out to be the ones who do not pay such fees..

4. Fairness of General Policies

Arguments may have as their basis a claim about the fairness of a general policy. What people regard as fair can vary. But by fairness we are referring to the treatment of those affected by a general policy in similar ways under similar circumstances in a manner conducive to meeting the goals of an institution. Arguments about fairness may claim that some general policies either unduly favor some groups, or they impose undue hardships on others. Admissions policies of a public college that use the same standards for all applicants may or may not be fair. It may not be sufficient that one applies the policies in the same way in all cases. The policies themselves could be unfair. Policies of such an institution also may be invidious if they introduce unusual admission requirements for some students over and above what they require of others.

5. Consistency of General Policies

Arguments may claim that a new general policy needs to be adopted to enable an institution to carry out other policies it already has. Or, they may claim that a general policy needs to be changed in order to make consistent the policies of an institution. In such cases, there may be arguments about how to interpret a general policy and who makes the interpretation. For example, how is one to interpret a policy of nondiscrimination on the basis of sex in employment and promotion? And whose interpretation of such a policy is the one to be followed by the institution? Should one hold to a given ratio based on the total number of persons of both sexes who are qualified for a given type of work in that district? Or, should one base such a ratio, in part, on the number of persons of each sex who seek to employ their skills in that particular job in that region? Or, should the sex of applicants not be regarded as a relevant factor in making job offers, with such offers being based on the highest level of demonstrated skill as outlined in the job description? Are the standards for determining levels of skill biased in favor of one sex? Are those who judge skill levels biased either knowingly or unknowingly, in the way they evaluate skills? And who gets the job if the qualifications of several people appear to be equal? The problems and proposed solutions to them could continue.

Arguments also may develop about the priority of one general policy over another when an organization can follow only one of several policies in a given case. We have foreign policies that support the general policies of respect for human rights, the working toward peace through disarmament, and the strengthening of ties with our allies. But what policy takes priority in any given case in the event that the policies are mutually exclusive?

Arguments about interpretation of general policies may originate from within or without an institution. But usually an institution itself will have some policy about who is entitled to receive an official response for an interpretation of its policies, and what conditions need to be met in order for such a request to be acted upon.

In this section we have looked at some uses of arguments in the forming of general policies. In the next section we shall consider the use of some arguments in bureaucracies.

19.3 ARGUMENTS IN BUREAUCRATIC SETTINGS

In this section we shall look at the way some arguments about policies find use in bureaucratic settings. We shall discuss some arguments that point out how some bureaucracies become immune to arguments coming from outside them. But we also shall see that bureaucracies do an essential job both in helping to form policies and in carrying them out.

A bureaucracy is a group of people who have as their primary job the directing and overseeing at intermediate and higher levels the way in which an organized group carries out its policies. It, in turn, has some form of top-level administration or policy-making body over it. We are using "bureaucracy" in a neutral sense. Included in such groups are people who work in government as well as in private corporate groups. We find bureaucracies in organizations of consumers, foundations, labor unions, religious bodies, educational institutions, industry, finance, and government. Political orders may be democratic, totalitarian, or dictatorial. Economic orders may have tendencies supporting capitalism, socialism, or communism. But they all have bureaucracies.

We find these bureaucracies using their offices to gain power in various ways. One of these ways is to gain power over other bureaucracies. But bureaucracies have power of different types. The power of one may be primarily economic and the power of another may be enforcing regulations through imposing detailed paperwork.

We need to recognize that many bureaucracies are well run. They provide services needed by the consumers. And, many bureaucrats have interest in satisfying those needs that their agency is set up to meet. In many cases they are responsive to arguments. In making such arguments we seek to relate an objective to a responsibility of the bureaucracy to meet a specific type of need. That is, we want to show that the conditions are present for a bureaucracy to move toward satisfying a given need that we point out.

But there are some cases in which bureaucracies do not appear to be responsive to arguments. Let us focus on some of the reasons for having difficulty in securing action on good arguments used in some bureaucratic settings.

1. Some Difficulties in Making Arguments in Some Bureaucratic Settings

We are directing these comments more toward how some bureaucracies respond rather than to a stereotyped model that would tend to cover each bureaucracy or any people working in it. Neither are we making a case for the futility of making arguments with people in bureaucracies. But we are recognizing that in some cases we have tasks other than the types that arguments can do when we deal with bureaucrats.

Positions as Advocates.   It is the job of bureaucrats to represent and advocate the policies, interests, and views of the group they represent. Their own interests, their future, their status, and their power within their group may depend, in part, upon how well they represent such interests. Because it is their position to interpret or advocate given policies, bureaucrats tend to have worked out fixed responses to arguments critical of their policies. This is the case particularly when such criticism originates from outside the bureaucracy itself. At the same time they may not be in a position to openly accept an argument that a policy or directive is in need of change. Likewise, in many cases they simply may be carrying out a policy which they have no power to change.

Developing of Self-Interest Groups within a Bureaucracy.   Persons linked with a bureaucracy may identify their self-interests with the success of the bureaucracy. They may see their own futures intermeshed with the fate of their agency. Their self-interests support their making the power of their bureaucracy stronger. Their arguments and decisions may relate not only to the merits of a proposal or of an argument. But they also may relate to the way in which such positions would help or hurt the growth of the bureaucracy itself.

Large bureaucracies usually break down into different self-interest groups. Various factors enter into the way different alignments develop. Some alignments may form on the basis of how different bureaucrats interpret the primary mission of the bureaucracy and the ways they believe such missions should be carried out. Another alignment may form on the way priorities should be given for using the bureaucracy's personnel and other resources. Other alignments may follow other patterns. Some members of a bureaucracy may prefer to work rather strictly within the traditions formed by past operations. Others may seek more innovations and new ways to give expression to their mission. Some bureaucrats may see a weakness or power vacuum in a related agency and seek to increase the area of their own control and operations.

Individuals can base their alignments to the interest groups within the bureaucracy by following what they believe to be the best way to achieve its goal. But others may make alignments by choosing the group which they believe will have the greatest influence and power within the bureaucracy. And in some bureaucracies, power alignments may not develop. Responses of individuals to arguments about the policies of the organization can reflect their views on what alignment within the bureaucracy will most likely favor such a response.

Semiautonomous Workings of Some Bureaucracies. Some members of bureaucracies tend to take a proprietary attitude toward the agency for which they work. They respond to arguments or advance arguments on the basis of how well their expressed views will enable them to strengthen this proprietary position. They may react to those responsible for overseeing the work of the bureaucracy as a group to be pacified or tolerated. In many cases, the bureaucracy prepares the position papers for responses by the overseeing group. They also may develop the guidelines for carrying out the proposals which they also have prepared. Bureaucrats carry out many arguments within the organization itself. But with the development of a position paper, they tend to respond to arguments on the basis of the position they have worked out within the organization. Some of the arguments in these position papers may be well-thought-out. Others, depending in part on the kind of bureaucracy with which one is dealing, may be prepared as propaganda.

Some bureaucracies become remarkably insulated from outside arguments, influences, and democratic pressures. The external group responsible for overseeing the work of the bureaucracy may adopt changes in policies and programs. And it may make provisions for the bureaucracy to carry these out. In some cases, these new policies and programs are not in line with the dominant views of the bureaucrats. And the bureaucracy can continue to follow its older procedures and find ways to undermine and circumvent the newer guidelines. The overseeing group can find itself again having to go through the motions of arguments about policies and guidelines on which it had made a prior decision. The making of arguments in some such cases can appear to be a fruitless effort. But not all bureaucracies work this way.

In many cases bureaucracies develop standard responses to specific types of arguments, inquiries, or situations. Responses to exceptional cases or to new sets of circumstances tend to be dealt with only as routine cases. In some cases, bureaucrats claim that some other agency has responsibility in a particular area. One can spend several days, weeks, or months going in circles only to end up at the original agency.

Presenting some members of a bureaucracy with an argument about a decision can be comparable to putting the same issue to a computer. A programmed response comes out. In some instances, such responses can be satisfactory. But in other cases, novelties are present or the factors relevant to a policy decision can require a different weighting than they customarily have. Making such exceptions or allowing variations to established policies may be possible only at the top. And the top may be relatively inaccessible. The best arguments may be brushed aside. A sense of futility—of walking a treadmill—can develop.

Bureaucratic Cultivation of Friends.   In some contexts bureaucracies can influence the way arguments develop in their overseeing group, particularly if such an overseeing group also includes laypersons not very familiar with the details of bureaucratic operation. Such an overseeing group might be a lay committee that supervises the work of a state agency, such as public welfare or education. Or, it might be a lay group chosen to oversee the way investments of a pension fund are made by a large fraternal body. In many cases the approval and support of members of such overseeing groups is essential to get some projects off the ground. Their recommendations can carry great weight in determining the way in which an organized group spends its resources and energies and develops its policies.

Bureaucrats may be in a position to reward persons who seek to use the resources of the agency. Likewise, they may be able to frustrate the efforts of others who attack or fail to support their positions. Persons who direct arguments against the positions of some bureaucrats may find their projects without funds or resources to carry them out. The merits of some arguments advanced in favor of given projects can result in their acceptance by some bureaucracies. But in other cases favoritism to known supporters may be the determining factor in the decisions these bureaucrats make. These supporters in turn can assist the "in group" to maintain their control and influence in the bureaucracy.

2. Use of Arguments in Helping to Build Efficient Bureaucracies

Arguments have roles to play within bureaucracies in the development of their policies. We need to recognize that some bureaucracies are more efficient than others.

Uses of Arguments in Carrying Out Policies and in Bringing About Changes within the Bureaucracy.   Arguments may be used, as we have seen, in developing policies and in carrying out policies within a bureaucracy. Likewise, bureaucracies can and do change in some of the positions they hold. While there may be various pressures bearing on such changes, bureaucrats do need to show some results. And they may need to be sensitive to the interests of those whom they represent. Good arguments can help identify needs that bureaucracies can meet and ways of meeting those needs.

In a viable burcaucracy, members may develop different views about policies that can be adopted and about others that may be in need of change. Different persons within the bureaucracy see issues from the background of their individual viewpoints and interests. And they receive different types of feedback from the different segments of the constituents whom they serve and of the public with whom they interact. Conflicts based primarily on the best way to meet the organization's goals can develop. The different views expressed within a bureaucracy can represent a wide spectrum of the kinds of arguments that one finds in groups outside the bureaucracy. In the process of developing and refining these arguments, bureaucrats are exposed to the stronger arguments and counterarguments about the best ways to develop and carry out their policies.

Viable interaction can take place in an exchange of views between bureaucrats and their overseeing group, particularly if the overseeing group is knowledgeable and alert to what is happening with regard to the organization and its carrying out of its mission. Arguments again develop about the more promising policy positions to adopt and ways to carry them out. In some cases, by the time a position paper emerges, it represents a thoroughly examined position that the corporate group may take in meeting its institutional goals. An alert and efficient bureaucracy does more than help to maintain its strength within a corporate group by the services it performs. Through its arguments and responses to the pressures within the organization, it can develop ways to enable the corporate group to best meet its goals.

Getting Bureaucracies to Act by Directing the Arguments at the Right Parties.   One needs to direct arguments related to some bureaucracies at groups or persons who are ultimately responsible for the policies and actions followed by these bureaucracies. Some government agencies follow policies, and perform or avoid certain activities, according to guidelines strictly determined by law. Such agencies are expected to express a neutral position with regard to legislation. Laws may provide that they refrain from advocacy of changes in the law. Arguments in such cases need to be directed, not towards such agencies themselves, but to the legal bodies which set up these regulations and policies, and to the public responsible for electing such lawmakers.

But some agencies have their own way of evoking arguments to help bring about changes in policies which they may want or may not like. In some cases they may use what appears to be arbitrary enforcement of their regulations. That is, they appear to be somewhat selective of their victims. And some victims to whom they choose to apply the extreme interpretation of a regulation can protest with pressures that can help bring about some changes. Such protesting can focus attention on some provision of the policy or law that some bureaucrat wants changed.

In other cases such agencies appear to develop to the extreme some provisions of a policy or law. They may want existing controls strengthened or they may want some provisions removed. For example, they may be testing a given product for harmful side effects. And the agency produces a stimulus five hundred times as great as one will find in life conditions. These agencies can then publish findings that such stimulants also have produced harmful side effects on a given subject or material under laboratory conditions. They may have as their ultimate goal getting more funding for their work. Or, they may have as their goal, not the ban of the substance tested, but another set of more reasonable guidelines for the way they work.

In some cases, agencies also appear to give a distorted description about a state of affairs covered by their supervision. The data which they gather on some issues related to their supervision can focus on irrelevant and tangential matters. And they can fail to gather the data that is relevant to a policy they want to keep or to a proposed policy they do not want to have. That is, they may fail to ask the kinds of questions needed to be answered in order to make decisions about a given type of policy. Such tactics, as we have seen, sometimes provide data for not adopting a policy under consideration. Or, they may be directed toward changing a policy already on the books.

Uses of Arguments in Developing Efficiency within a Bureaucracy. Arguments develop within bureaucracies to bring about a greater efficiency in those agencies. Good management in corporate endeavors depends greatly upon the ability to have a group of top managers who can develop bureaucracies that function well. We can evaluate the bureaucratic structure of different large corporate groups as one measure of determining how well we expect that corporate body to function. We also can compare different political and economic systems by looking at their bureaucracies. That is, we can evaluate different kinds of delivery systems, in part, by how well the types of bureaucracies they create do their job in reaching the goals which the systems are designed to meet.

One argument, if it were true, would appear to make it difficult, if not improbable, for bureaucracies to operate efficiently. This argument perhaps may be stated here in too simple a form. It holds that members of a bureaucracy move forward in an agency until they reach one level higher than the level at which they are capable of effective performance. Or one can express this view in the form known as The Peter Principle: "In a Hierarchy Every Employee Tends to Rise to His Level of Incompetence."[3] The previous job level represents the step on the bureaucratic ladder which completely utilizes such a person's abilities. Sometimes we find the argument that one reaches two levels, rather than one, of operating beyond one's performance level. And we may see so many examples where such performance appears to occur, that we may be inclined to accept the view. But let us consider some arguments against it.

Why should everyone want to get to the top of the ladder? A person may not want the pressures and strains that come with such jobs. He may prefer to have more leisure and to pursue hobbies and interests that the added demands on time would not permit. Or, she may find other things more enjoyable than job status and power.

Why may it not be the case that a person can function in some situations better at a higher level than at a lower level? But one may never have an opportunity to demonstrate this ability. Perhaps some high-level jobs require different types of abilities than those at lower levels. At some high-level jobs, an ability to have an overview, to relate to other persons, to have a knack for recognizing ability in others, or to carry out large-scale projects, may have greater importance than the ability to carry out the kind of detailed work required in some lower-ranked bureaucratic jobs.

Is merit always the reason someone moves up in an agency? In some cases, family, money, or political friends appear to lend a pushing hand. But efficient people who are passed by may remain in those positions. Are they operating at a level beyond their capacity?

Other arguments can be made. Perhaps one's spouse has a good job and prefers not to move to another location if one's moving up the ladder also requires moving the family residence. Moreover, some people do get to the top. But is everyone who operates at the top performing at one or two levels beyond his ability? And if someone never gets there does that mean he was incapable of operating there? Perhaps we know he did not have such ability since he did not reach the top, because if he had such abilities he would have reached the top! [Circular reasoning]

---

[3] Lawrence F. Peter and Raymond Hull, *The Peter Principle* (New York: Morrow, 1969), p. 25.

In this section we have seen that arguments used in bureaucratic settings have a significant function to play in policy reviews and policy decisions. Arguments also serve as an external restraint on the way bureaucracies use their power and authority. We need to recognize that in some cases a bureaucracy is more responsive to internal or external pressures than to rational arguments.

19.4 ARGUMENTS ON POLICIES LEADING TO PLANS OF ACTION

In this section we shall look at how arguments can relate to the development of a plan of action. General policies and procedures of organized groups provide a framework for the development of more specific plans of action to carry out their mission. In making arguments about the developing and carrying out of plans of action, a number of factors are relevant to the arguments advanced and decisions made.

1.   Creating a Knowledge Base from Which to Develop a Plan of Action

In making plans to carry out an action, an organized group has a specific objective in mind. It seeks to determine what this objective is and the best way to attain it.

Identifying the Conditions for Reaching a Goal.   In working toward a specific goal, an organized group needs to specify what such a goal is. It needs to know how to tell when the goal is reached. It can draw up a list of stated conditions which it wants to meet. It may want these conditions to be as explicit as possible. This is comparable to someone who wants to build a house and draws up a list of specific things she wants to have in the house when it is built. She advises the architect about these before he designs the house.

Finding Specific Details Relevant to Reaching a Goal.   We need to base our arguments about reaching our objective on sound information. The specific facts relevant to forming and carrying out any plan of action need to be gathered, organized, and analyzed. The accuracy of such factual materials needs to be appraised. Any further developing of a plan of action depends on the completeness and accuracy of the knowledge base from which we work. Let us consider a case in which plans of action need to be made for a large urban area to increase its source of electric power. One needs to determine answers to various questions. How much electrical energy will be needed for anticipated expansion needs? What are the different sources available? How dependable is the supply of these sources? What projections can be made about changes in the type of energy users and the amount of energy needs such changes will bring about? Would breakthroughs in technology be likely to create a shift in the kinds and amount of energy that is needed? We then would proceed to use such data in making plans for the size and type of plant required to meet these energy needs.

Searching for Any Social, Legal, and Environmental Restraints Relevant to a Goal.   In developing arguments about plans of action, we need to consider any restraints on carrying them out. Some such plans may not be feasible. Or they may need alteration on account of social, legal, and environmental restraints under which they would have to operate. In the case of an energy delivery system, we would need to know the relevant laws about safety, pollution control, zoning, and waste disposal. What changes in such matters can we expect to occur? What advantages or limitations do geographical or geological factors have in considering the relative merits of different possible energy systems? What would be the proposed effect of any given type of energy system on the dislocation of persons? What effect would it have on the operation of social institutions like schools, hospitals, or public service agencies? What other energy sources are available for tie-ins in the event of a breakdown in the entire planned energy system or in a part of it?

2.   Determining the Plan of Action to Follow

We need to develop arguments in considering the merit and limitations of feasible plans of action that we can take to attain a specific objective.

Identifying Feasible Plans of Action to Meet Stated Objectives.   In preparing arguments about plans of action, we need to identify the different kinds of plans that might be feasible in a given situation. But we need to recognize that in talking about feasible plans of action, we also have to take into account not only such matters as costs and efficiency. We also have to consider the fecundity of the operation. Will it also help to generate additional goods and services? Will it help to generate more jobs? Will it help to stimulate the development of cultural interests? Likewise, we have to consider the response of groups affected by the proposed plan of action. Will their response be such that the plan will have a greater likelihood of success? If they oppose such plans, in what way will their opposition be expressed and what weight will it carry? What will be the long-range effects of such opposition on attaining the sought-for goals?

In the case of providing a delivery system of electrical energy in the immediate future, we might ask which of the plans offers more promise on its face. But we would need to go beyond this. Could features of some plans be combined with others to achieve greater efficiency? If costs relative to expected income run too high, is there some way of cutting back now and making additions when revenue appears great enough to justify the higher costs?

Investigating Responses to Future Commitments.   When we choose a plan of action, we are making ongoing commitments about other actions that we may have to take in the future. We need to know what such commitments might be and the kind of responses we could adapt in meeting such commitments. And in some cases, we may be unable to reverse the direction of events that follow from our actions. We also may be locking ourselves into a position which would prevent us from moving toward some goal in the future, even though we might prefer to achieve that goal at that time. In the case of the electrical energy system, we can raise several questions. What will be the drop-out effect of this plan on other phases of our social, cultural, and institutional life? In the case of the use of nuclear energy, we have some irreversible effects to consider. There may also be some other kinds of irreversible effects on possible industrial development if our sources of fuel oil and natural gas run out. But we shall turn over the arguments about the use of nuclear energy and the extent of oil and gas reserves to those who know more about it, at least for the purposes of this discussion.

Developing Quality Controls.   In making arguments about plans of action, we need to direct our attention also to the quality control of the product we are turning out. We need to know if we can take steps to assure that this desired level of quality will continue. Will we continue to be able to get the quality of materials needed for the project? Will there continue to be the supply of trained and technical help needed to maintain the desired level of quality? Can the delivery system assure efficiency on the basis of per unit cost required to produce and deliver its product to its market for the period of its expected use? In the case of the electrical energy plant, we would need to make sure that the proper voltages, frequencies, and current could be produced. And we would want to have a constant flow of electricity available for use during peak, as well as other, periods.

Determining a Plan of Action Most Likely to Achieve the Results Needed.   An agency has to reach a decision. It has to choose which plan of action will help it to achieve its goal. But having chosen a basic plan of action, an agency has to consider how it can bring about the result for which the plan of action was designed. It will want to choose those legitimate means that will most likely assure that those plans can be carried out.

Setting such plans in motion will require the selecting of a corporate group with the know-how and resources to carry out the project. But the experience of a corporate group in carrying out a given type of project is not the only thing an agency needs to consider. In our society, an agency also tends to look at those social and political factors which may have some relevance to completing the project. In such cases, it may be essential to identify those agencies or individuals that are in a position to assist a project to reach its stated goals. It may be desirable to show such agencies or individuals why the plan of action is needed, and in what way it contributes to the social good of the community.

In this section we have looked at some kinds of arguments that an agency might need to consider in carrying out a specific plan of action. In the next section we shall examine some overall value considerations that are relevant to arguments about policy decisions.

19.5 ARGUMENTS ABOUT POLICY AND THE COMMON GOOD

In this section we shall review some basic features for directing arguments in making and evaluating policies for the common good.

1.   Policies and Making Right Decisions

In making public arguments about public policy, we can emphasize those practices found to characterize enlightened decision making. We have seen that in sound decision making, we look for such features as simplicity and economy, a locking-in with tested experience, and an ability to carry out the job that needs to be done. (We discussed some of these matters in Section 14.3.)

2.   Policies and the Opportunity to Achieve Individual Goals

Arguments about policies can be supportive of enlarged opportunities for developing individual freedom, initiative, responsibilities, and creative achievements. (Section 18.4 presents some goals that may be of interest to some people.)

3.   Policies and the Opportunity to Achieve Social Goods

We can use arguments that encourage developing the quality of life enjoyed by a community, not to a low common denominator, but to as high a level as possible.

Some of these social goods that can provide guidelines in public policy making in our social order include the following:

Respect for human dignity, freedom, and rights.

Rule by duly constituted laws.

Equality of persons under laws that are a part of an impartially administered system of justice.

Determination of political leadership and public policy by democratic and open processes based upon a duly authorized constitution.

Opportunity of persons, who, through their own choices and initiative, can find it possible to achieve well-being and to pursue happiness.

Encouragement of the development of the arts and other cultural activities.

Opportunity of persons and groups to own and develop property consistent with duly constituted laws.

Adequate production of goods and services:
>   by using standards of quality, of quantity, and of balance to help determine the flow of such production;
>   by carrying out such production to create and preserve an acceptable physical environment;
>   by providing incentives to seek to assure innovations that increase efficiency and create new jobs.

Equitable distribution of goods and services that supports:
>   participating in the creation of goods and providing services;
>   recognizing quality of work and contribution to social needs;
>   providing opportunities for receiving essential goods and services for those who, because of special circumstances, are particularly in need of such support;
>   finding means for assisting those who, due to economic dislocation, have an opportunity to retrain, to relocate, and to seek and find employment to increase their participation in providing goods and services.

Responsibility of those engaged in the marketing of goods and services:
>   to fairly represent such goods and services, and
>   to engage in fair competitive pricing practices.

Providing international cooperation that
>   helps to strengthen the prospects for a just and lasting peace, and
>   participates in programs in such nations that need and request assistance in:
>>   ways to improve their own economic development, and
>>   ways to enhance their own cultural achievements.

In this chapter we have looked at some uses of arguments in making and evaluating policies.

SOME THINGS TO DO

A. Assume you are a member of a professional, vocational, or trade organization (you name it). Make arguments about three different policies or plans of action that you want your organization to take. Some proposals you can consider are the following:
1. You want to increase the political strength of the organization in influencing the development of state and national laws in its area of interest and in dealing with government agencies.
2. You want to seek greater assurances that persons engaged in your profession or vocation in your region have qualifications needed to do their work in a satisfactory manner.
3. You want to conduct a community relations program so that the larger community understands what kind of service your group is providing, and what conditions your group regards as essential to carrying out efficiently its professional work.

B. Assume you are a member of a student congress. What arguments would you advance to have the congress take steps to achieve three different goals (which you name)? Some courses of action might be the following.
1. Initiate a volunteer program for tutoring students making low grades.
2. Initiate a program in which the student body would seek to have a fairer set of parking regulations.
3. Initiate a program in which the students would have fuller participation in institutional regulations that affect them.

C. Assume you are the member of an administration of a college or university (that you name).
1. How would you justify a policy (that you name) related to the entrance requirements of the institution?
2. How would you justify a proposed change in a program for a given academic degree (that you name)?
3. How would you justify a proposal that the adult education program of the institution be expanded to give a larger number of persons an opportunity to benefit from the services of the institution?

CHAPTER **20**

CONTROVERTING AND MAKING ARGUMENTS

20.1 CONTROVERTING ARGUMENTS

In this chapter we shall examine different ways to controvert arguments. We also shall look at how we can prepare arguments. In this section we review various ways of objecting to arguments.

The person advancing an argument has the burden of proof. She is making a claim. This claim is that the evidence presented in the argument justifies the conclusion. To have the burden of proof, then, is to have the responsibility of justifying the claim one makes in advancing an argument by adequate evidence.

To controvert an argument, we have to show that in some way an argument's evidence does not justify its conclusion. And this difference between having the burden of proof and having only to show that an argument does not justify its claim is very important. To controvert an argument, we do not have to prove that a view different from the original conclusion is true. We have to show only that the original conclusion advanced does not follow from the evidence given in its support. But one may choose to controvert an argument by showing that a different conclusion justified by another argument applies to the given case. Sometimes in practical situations it is desirable to try to do this. But the reasons for doing so are the dynamics of the context in which the argument occurs.

Let us look at some common ways to controvert arguments. We should note that there may be several ways to challenge any given argument.

1.   Indicating a Formal or an Informal Fallacy

We can controvert any argument that violates a formal principle of logic. But we need to recognize that the criteria we apply to an argument should be relevant to the kind of argument it is. It is not sufficient to show that an inductive argument violates a rule of deductive logic. We have seen that we do not dismiss an inductive argument on the grounds that in a formal sense the fallacy of affirming the consequent occurs in it. But we also have to examine the structure of the argument itself. We do not accept an argument as inductive merely on the basis that someone gives it an inductive label.

In ordinary discourse we may find it desirable to point out a flaw in an argument by use of a similar argument form which has a clearly absurd claim. For example, consider the following invalid argument. "All Communists support a reduction in the size of the U.S. armed services. Professor Beta believes in reducing the size of the U.S. armed services. Therefore, Professor Beta is a Communist." One could respond to this type of argument by pointing out, "That's like saying, 'All Communists believe in developing natural resources, and the head of the Republican Party believes in the developing of natural resources; therefore, the head of the Republican Party is a Communist.'"

We also can point out informal fallacies in an argument. For example, someone might claim, "All men have free will because you cannot prove they do not." A response might be, "That makes as much sense as to say, 'The actions of all men are determined by causes outside their control because you cannot prove they are not.'" The context in which the argument occurs could help us to decide whether it is desirable to give the fallacy its more technical name [the appeal to ignorance (or *Argumentum ad Ignorantiam*) in the present case].

2.   Rejecting a Premise

Claiming That a Premise Is False.   We can challenge an argument by showing that a premise is false. We can point to other statements which are true and show that if these statements are true, then the premise cannot be true.

Claiming That One Premise Is Not Consistent with Another Premise.   We can attempt to show that an argument uses two premises and that both of these premises cannot be true. For example, a given argument might seek to show that Congress needs to fight inflation by use of wage and price controls. One can controvert this argument by showing that in the given context in which the argument occurs, there is an assumption of a lower federal deficit next year. But in another part of the argument, there is the assumption of a higher federal deficit. However, if one advances an argument using several conditional statements, this way to controvert an argument may not be proper. Thus, the following premises can be proper for some arguments: "If the federal deficit is lower next year, then we need these controls. And if the federal deficit is higher next year, we need these same controls."

Claiming That One Premise Is Not Consistent with a Prior Position. On some occasions, one may challenge a premise on the grounds that it is not consistent with a speaker's prior position. One uses the "ghost of the past" to haunt the speaker. For example, in running for election to Congress, Joe Z. Beta promises to support laws increasing the amount of aid given college students from lower income families. After his election he opposes such aid. He argues that money for increased funding for such aid would require giving up funding for dams in his district. He can be accused of not being consistent with a prior position and commitment.

We need to use care in attacking an argument this way. Sometimes there are good reasons to change a point of view. Some uses of this method of challenging an argument may not lie in attacking the other argument so much as in trying to show bad faith. It is reasonable to expect a speaker to make consistent statements on any given occasion. Yet we would expect to change our views when new facts and more experience justify our doing so.

Claiming a Lack of Consistency within One Premise or within the Argument as a Whole. We have a difficulty in dealing with some types of statements which, if they are true, appear to require the opposite of what they are claiming. Some statements which have such problems are like the following: "All generalizations are false." "A Cretan says, 'All statements made by Cretans are lies.'" These types of statements require special care. Bertrand Russell has claimed that such statements may not refer back to themselves and for this reason may not be self-refuting. He claims that such statements themselves refer to a state of affairs on a first order of statements. The statement itself belongs to a second order of statements. In such a case, tests for consistency are relevant to statements occurring in the first order of statements, but not between a statement in the first order and another statement in the second order. However, Russell's views on this issue remain in dispute.

Some arguments appear to lack consistency between what the premises assert and what the conclusion holds. Consider the following type of claim: "We cannot know anything because we know that our senses are not reliable." If one accepts the evidence for the conclusion, then it would appear that the conclusion itself cannot be true. That is, the premise asserts that we can know something. And the conclusion denies this.

3.   Finding Fault with Concepts Used in Arguments

We can fault some arguments by the misuse of concept schemes found in the argument. But if we want to criticize the concepts used in an argument, it is not enough simply to point to other concepts that we find preferable. This way of attacking an argument has to show that the use of the concepts is deficient in some basic respect that introduces bias into the argument. For example, we can question the result of some surveys that provide only for "yes" or "no" answers to broad questions. We might find confusing a "yes" or "no" answer to the following question: "Do you support the present policies of the United States toward the Third World?" We need to have more choices than the ones we have in this question, and we are in need of choices with sharper distinctions. We also find that some persons who take an extreme position on public issues tend to use concepts that exclude our taking a middle ground in such cases. If we do not accept their extreme view, then they would have us in the camp of the opposing extreme view.

Finding Fault with Fuzzy Meanings.   Although we could treat fuzzy meaning as a type of informal fallacy, we shall deal with it separately. This fault can occur with great frequency in public controversy. The meaning of some words may be so vague that although people may applaud when they are used, we have no clear idea of how they apply to specific situations. Some politicians appear to gain strong support by making such statements as the following. "Let's throw the rascals out." "We need to get the economy rolling." "We need to find ways that make our foreign policies respected abroad." In many cases the speaker is trying to redirect attitudes and to influence the way people vote.

How do we respond to an argument whose actual meaning we cannot determine? Of course, we can point out the lack of clarity in what is said. We also can try to find out what the speaker means in clearer terms. A problem is that the speaker probably has deliberately planned to be fuzzy in what he says. If we can break down such slogans into more specific ideas, then we are in better position to make arguments in response to those given by the speaker.

Making Needed Distinctions.   On several occasions we have pointed out the need to be able to make sharp distinctions in order to know how to respond to arguments. But on some occasions a speaker uses the making of distinctions as a tactic to confuse an audience and to evade issues. A rule sometimes followed by speakers in a public discussion runs somewhat as follows. "If you find yourself in a tight corner in a discussion and you do not see an easy way to respond, begin to make distinctions. Divide and redivide the issues and then find some meaning that will make some point brought up by the other side appear either trivial or absurd."

But we should not sell short the need to be able to make needed distinctions in finding ways to reject some arguments. For example, we might be dealing with the questions, "Do we have democratic institutions at the national level of government?" We can divide the question: (1) Do we use the principle of "one man—one vote" deciding in each case what federal policies we have and how these policies are to be administered? (This would be a difficult principle to follow even for a small town.) (2) Do we use the principle of government under a constitution, in which the citizens have equal legal access to the protection of laws, and equal opportunity to participate in electing both the legislators who make the laws and the president who is responsible for administering them? The above question could be further divided by raising questions about "equal opportunity." The dividing of some questions becomes essential in challenging some arguments. We may show that an argument applies only to one division of a question, and that the other divisions are more basic. We also may claim that the basic issue in the question is not covered by the argument.

4.   Challenging Methods Used in Getting Evidence

Challenging Use of Faulty Sources.   We can attack an argument by showing the use of faulty sources in gaining the evidence given to support the conclusion. We may show that a view attributed to a writer actually is a spurious passage in the work. We may point out that a secondary source used in an argument misstates a position taken from a primary source. In some cases, it is relevant to point out that a given writer was not in position to know about the matters which he claims to be true. There are careful tests used in some court proceedings about the use of some sources as testimony before a jury. For example, a judge may "strike from the record" testimony based on "hearsay," that is, testimony that the witness has heard others talk about, but which comes to her secondhand. The court usually requires that the witness limit such testimony only to what she actually saw or heard.

Appeals to Defects in Method Used to Get Evidence.   One can controvert an argument by showing that the method used to get the data was faulty. A lawyer may attempt to show that the device used to measure the speed of a car was not accurate at the time an officer used it. We may want to attack the findings of a survey on the grounds that bias entered into the way it was made. For example, one might try to show that persons who move into a fully integrated housing project are likely to develop fewer racial biases than those who do not move into such areas. But one may find such a conclusion either in a sound argument or in a faulty one. It would be in a faulty survey if the sample consisted merely of comparing the attitudes of a community where the housing was actually integrated with another one where it was not. It is possible in this case that one of the reasons why some people wanted to move into the fully integrated housing area was that they already held to different racial attitudes than those found in the larger community. Such surveys would not be testing properly for changes in attitudes that occurred after such persons had become members of such communities. The method used to make the survey would bias its findings.

Appeal to a Faulty Model.   Some arguments can be used by attacking the kind of model used to present them. For example, many industries use the notion of "per unit costs" in determining the efficiency of their operations. They may compare such "per unit costs" with other companies in their type of industries as well as with the record of their own past operations. Some people may want to apply this model to higher education in the same way it is used in industry. We do not dispute that it may have some value in these cases, but one can abuse such a model. Per unit costs in required classes likely will be lower than in electives. Likewise, lab equipment, which is a factor in determining per unit cost, may be very high for physics and low in the humanities. In some areas such as music or art, one may need to have individual instruction or small classes. And per unit costs go up. Thus, the business model can make unfair comparisons in these cases.

Let us consider another misuse of a model. In some cases, institutions, or at least their management, tend to identify their position with that of a political party. They expect others managing that institution to go along with their views. And they may reinforce this position by subtle systems of rewards and penalties. In the past, some persons have sought to apply such a model to universities. They might argue that as officers of their institutions, faculty members had some kind of obligation to support the political views of those at the top of the administration. Or, at least they should not enter into public controversy in opposition to such views. One can argue against such a view by pointing out that such a model is not appropriate for universities. To fulfill their mission, universities require an environment which supports the freedom of inquiry and criticism, and the free exchange of ideas. These conditions require that faculty members be able both to "pursue the truth" as they see it and to enjoy their rights as citizens, including their right to take a stand on public and controversial issues.

pragmatism
workability
technical mvmt type of something

5. Examining the Outcome of Applying the Conclusion of an Argument

Appeal to No Outcome of Any Significance. A basic maxim of pragmatism is that where there is a difference between two concepts or views, one needs to show what different visible effects result from the use of those concepts or views. "Where there is a difference (in views) there must be a difference (in results)." In dealing with arguments, this appeal to results has various uses. For one thing, it may be used to show that some arguments are not relevant to the situation they address. That is, one might show that acting on the conclusion of a given argument would not make any difference in the situation. This is an appeal to the argument's lack of practical relevance. Arguments relative to tax reform frequently use this kind of tactic. Someone might argue that by increasing the taxes on higher income groups, who are already heavily taxed, the total revenue of the government also would increase. Someone else argues that such a tax increase takes money away from production, decreases the number of jobs, and thereby results in a decrease of tax revenues from other sources. And the total revenue of the government would not increase and might decrease. Usually this type of argument occurs in a context with other highly developed arguments.

Appeal to an Outcome Different than the Consequences Assumed in an Agrument. We can claim that an argument uses false assumptions about the result of following its recommended course of action. We sometimes accuse a person making this kind of argument—of "throwing the baby out with the bathwater." Let us look at some examples. A newspaper business manager might propose to raise the costs of advertising to increase earnings. Someone else might claim in that context that an increase in such rates would decrease the revenue from advertising, since it would cut down on the amount of advertising in the paper. A director of a city bus system might argue that the company could increase its profits by reducing the number of trips made each day by the buses. Fuel and personnel costs could be cut. Someone else might argue that riders would then seek other means of travel and that the bus system would lose more money by not providing needed services. A city tax office might propose to raise property taxes to increase city revenue. Someone else might argue that such increased taxes can encourage greater movement to the suburbs by many persons in a position to pay the higher taxes. Many of the persons remaining within the city would be unable to pay the increased taxes and keep up the property. The property then would deteriorate and lose much of its tax value.

6. Advancing an Alternative Conclusion

Appeal to a Counterargument. A counterargument uses the evidence given in the original argument that one seeks to reject. But it uses such

Significance of difference in 2 views diff in words - must be diff in consequences

evidence to reach a different conclusion that may be more restrictive than the original. The outcome of acting on the conclusion may be more to our liking. For example, a student might claim that he is dropping out of school in order to get a job and make some money to help his family. We could reply in some contexts that he could make more money and be of greater help to his family in the long run by staying in school and completing his work.

Another argument might be advanced to support a view that the government should increase interest rates through use of its monetary policies. Reasons given for such a view could vary. We might claim that the demand for consumer goods exceeds their supply. Installment debts are rapidly rising. The government has entered into a program of increased spending. Industry is accelerating its plant expansion and the building of new plants. A counterargument to the above view might claim, "You are killing the goose that lays the golden egg." In some contexts we would grant the above premises, but the conclusion would be different. We might argue that the pressure on interest rates comes from excessive spending by the government. The money it is using to increase government programs is being taken out of production, which is the primary source of jobs and future tax revenue. What is needed, the counterargument would hold, is to decrease government spending rather than to increase the interest rates. Supply could catch up with demand, and job security would provide some means of assuring that the installment debts would be paid.

Appeal to a Different Argument.   Sometimes we want to use evidence other than that used in the argument we are attacking. We also expect to reach a different conclusion. This method of attacking an argument usually will claim that those presenting the original argument did not take into account all of the relevant facts of the case. Some controversies related to the conflicts between government agencies and private groups take this form. The early stages of the controversy about the effect of cigarette smoking exemplifies this method of attacking an argument. One interest group offers a set of statistics to support its views. In these statistics, there was no significant correlation between the cigarette smoking and lung cancer. But government groups came up with another set of statistical findings that supported the claim that smoking has a causal relation to the developing of cancer in some cases.

Another example of using a different argument to controvert an original one is the classical argument about the properties of light. Isaac Newton advanced the position that light moves like particles. He argued that if light moves like waves, it spreads around a corner. After failing to find evidence for such a spread (which others found later), he held that light travels in a straight line. Huygens and others supported the view that light moves more like a wave. If light is a particle, he argued, then the particle needs to show the effect of some kind of colliding or bouncing when two light beams cross each other. Since the crossing of two light rays showed no such effect, Huygens held that a wave theory explains more clearly the way light moves than the particle theory does. This controversy has continued.

Appeal to the Greater Simplicity of an Alternative Argument. We have seen in Section 14.3 that an argument of greater simplicity is to be preferred in many cases over one that uses more steps or assumptions. Sometimes one refers to this appeal to simplicity as the principle of parsimony, or the principle of Occam's razor. William of Occam stated this principle as follows: "[Explanatory] entities are not to be multiplied beyond necessity."

Consider a classical example of discarding of a notion about phlogiston. Some chemists assumed this was a substance consumed during a fire, which accounted for the burning of a fire. But tests failed to support such a notion. Some scientists compared the weight of ashes with the weight of the original material and found no difference in the weights. If there is any substance such as phlogiston, then the weight of an object prior to its being burned should be heavier than its remaining ashes. But there was no such difference. Experimental bases to support the view were lacking. Simpler explanations were available. And the notion of phlogiston ceased to be used. We might note that this illustration also can apply to our challenging an argument on the basis that the argument made no difference in the outcome of accepting a conclusion.

7. Appealing to Irrational Positions Found within an Argument

Appealing to an internal inconsistency has been a classic way to challenge an argument. In a previous discussion of this section, we pointed out that one basis for refuting an argument was by pointing to inconsistencies in it. If it turns out that the inconsistencies hold and that a contradiction internal to the argument also develops, then a logically absurd position is present.

Appeals to the Absurdity of an Argument. We shall consider two types of absurdities—logical and commonsense. If logical absurdity is present, the argument cannot be sound. Two contradictory premises cannot both be true. If commonsense absurdity is present, then we have to look further. Common sense can be wrong.

In cross-examining witnesses, many attorneys seek to discredit their testimony by showing that there are contradictions within the testimony of one witness or between the testimony of one witness and that of a more credible one. That is, they are seeking to break down the argument of the opposition by pointing to these contradictions.

In a logical absurdity, we have two statements in the same general context. One has the form P is true; the other has the form P is false. For example, consider the statements, "I was in a bar on North Street at the time of the robbery of the gas station," and "I was not in the bar on North Street at the time of that robbery." However, we do not find most contradictions so readily. Usually they develop in the course of an argument by implicit meanings found in two different sections of the argument. Thus, in the above case a witness may have testified that he was in the indicated bar. But in cross-examination he also admits that one hour prior to the robbery he was in a location thirty miles from the bar. And it is also shown that the witness did not have sufficient time to get to the bar on North Street by the time he claimed to have been there.

Appeals to commonsense notions of absurdity take the following form:

That argument is to be rejected.

Its acceptance requires the acceptance of an obviously absurd view.

We reject such an absurd view.

Therefore, we reject your argument.

An absurd view, in this case, is some statement about states of affairs that one believes to be false on its face. It is held to be patently false. It is in opposition to "beliefs that cannot be reasonably doubted." But appeals to "beliefs that cannot be reasonably doubted" do not always appear to be well-grounded. Many of the major advances in scientific inquiry came about in opposition to common-consensus beliefs about the world in which we live. The belief that the world was flat prevailed for centuries. When Columbus wanted to argue that it was round, many rejected his views as absurd. But may there not be some beliefs that are absurd on their face?

We find a classic example of an appeal to the absurdity of a belief in responses to Zeno's denial of the possibility of motion. The belief that an arrow moved in flight, he stated, was an error. At any given time an arrow is either where it is or where it is not. To suggest that it moves where it is not does not make sense. And if an arrow is where it is, then it is not moving. He also presented other arguments in his efforts to show that the notion of motion is an illusion. These paradoxes of Zeno motivated extended controversy. One basis for rejecting his views was that his position was so contrary to common sense that it was absurd. This appeal to absurdity did not provide a theoretical refutation to the view. Rather it sought a practical justification for its rejection. (Some claim that a conclusive theoretical refutation of this view did not occur until the development of calculus or of the later theory of relativity.)

Let us consider another problem frequently discussed in modern philosophy. Solipsism is the view that the self essentially is a bundle of its own sensations and that nothing other than the self and its sensations can be known to exist. This view is skeptical about any knowledge of the presence of an external world, other bodies, and other minds. It is commonly held that if one can show that a philosophical position requires acceptance of solipsism, then one has sufficient basis to reject that position on the basis of its absurdity. From a purely theoretical point of view, solipsism remains a possible answer to the question, "What can be known to exist?" Other reasons can be advanced to deal with this issue. Yet the appeal to the absurdity of the view continues as a basic justifying reason for the rejection of solipsism.

The rejecting of an argument by appeal to its absurdity also occurs in social and political theory. Many political theorists hold that any theory of government requiring the view of anarchism is absurd and to be rejected on this basis.

An attack on an argument by a commonsense appeal to its absurdity has a stronger subjective than logical weight. The fact that a view differs from other views based on common sense is not, in itself, a fault. There may be good reasons for calling into question some commonsense notions. The appeal to the absurdity of a view on the basis of commonsense notions may, however, be the most effective way of attacking an argument at a given stage of knowledge.

Appeal to Circularity.   We can appeal to the circularity of an argument as a basis for rejecting it. We have seen that a circular argument first uses premises to justify a conclusion. It then seeks to use this conclusion to establish the truth of the premises. Many arguments proposing to show the superiority of capitalism over socialism or of socialism over capitalism are circular. Contrast these statements: "A socialistic economy is preferable to a capitalistic one, since it is based upon sharing of economic goods according to economic needs. Why is it preferable to base an economy upon the sharing of economic goods according to economic needs? Because this is the principle of a socialistic economy, and a socialistic economy is the type that is better." Consider an argument on the opposite side: "A free enterprise system is desirable because it is a part of a capitalistic economy. But why is a capitalistic economy preferable? A capitalistic economy is preferable because it makes possible a free enterprise system."

Appeal to an Infinite Regress.   An argument appeals to an infinite regress when its form requires a second reason for a first reason, a third reason for the second. And the series can proceed indefinitely with no rational way to end. It becomes impossible to examine the original reason for the argument. There is no original ground supporting the final reason given in the series. That is, the evidential reasons offered to support the conclusion require an infinite regress. And an infinite regress is irrational.

Consider the argument in the Platonic dialogue *Parmenides*. Parmenides seeks to establish that Socrates' view of forms requires the notion of an infinite regress. Socrates appears to recognize that if his view requires an infinite regress, this would provide a sufficient basis for its rejection. Socrates acknowledges a form for largeness. And he says that large objects in some way participate in this form for largeness. But Parmenides argues that this view of forms requires a third form of largeness to relate a given large form to the form of largeness. He further suggests that the form that related the particular form of a large object to the form of largeness would, in turn, itself need a form, and so on *ad infinitum*. If an argument such as Parmenides accuses Socrates of advancing has such an infinite regress, rationality is not achieved. There is a multiplying of reasons with no way of stopping the regression.

Philosophers such as John Passmore[1] distinguish between a vicious and a harmless infinite regress. A *harmless infinite regress* merely presents an indefinite series within which it is possible to begin an explanation anywhere. There is no need to regress to a proposed beginning of the series. Let us consider this example. In a given laboratory experiment, two parts of hydrogen and one part of oxygen mixed within certain ranges of temperature and pressure will become water. Such an event could be a part of an indefinite or possibly infinite series of events. But the experiment does not require that such prior causal factors be considered. This is an infinite or indefinite series that is "harmless." We can explain an event by reference to other events without explaining the causes of these additional events.

Let us consider another example. We can account for the flight of a rocket to Mars, in part, by reference to various conditions. We can refer to the kinds of materials and design used in constructing the rocket as well as to the initial conditions of the thrust of the rocket and to the position of Mars in relation to the Earth and other bodies in the solar system. We also can refer to the "law of gravity" and to the theory of relativity. But we do not have to explain each of these matters in terms of a prior series of events. We can seek more information. But the explanation of the event in question does not require such an elaborate pursuit which, if pressed far enough, would be beyond our ability to carry out.

A *vicious infinite regress* characterizes reasons rather than facts or events. One offers evidence in the form of a reason. The support for this reason is another one supposedly of higher order. But this new reason in turn rests upon a comparable reason of still higher order. One never attains a limit beyond which such appeals need not be pushed. We find an example of a vicious infinite regress in the following attempt to justify induction. "The principle of induction can be established by appeal to a higher principle of induction. But how is this latter principle justified? It is established

[1] *Philosophical Reasoning* (New York: Charles Scribner's Sons, 1961).

by an appeal to a still higher principle of induction. And how is this still higher principle justified?''

Avoidance of a vicious infinite regress does not require that all reasons given in an argument be proved by other reasons, which in turn are established by other reasons indefinitely. If such an approach were pushed far enough, the result more likely would be circular reasoning rather than an infinite regress. However, we avoid an infinite regress as well as circular reasoning by appealing to a general set of principles that are justifiable, as Whitehead points out, on the basis of such considerations as their coherency, consistency, applicability, adequacy, and corrigibility. We seek to justify such principles not by appeal to an additional or higher set of principles but by their intelligibility and utility. Since they are corrigible, they can be the subject of further inquiry. Until someone advances better alternatives, they provide a context for the justification of beliefs. This suggestion about ways to avoid a vicious infinite regress is not an appeal to a kind of world view, such as Whitehead develops. Rather it permits a more modest kind of justification based on rigorous inquiry and consistency within the context of a limited range of experience. Within such a range, rationality, intelligibility, and usefulness remain significant factors. We use them to justify a general set of principles on whose basis we develop a context for understanding our experience and how to develop and analyze arguments.

Sometimes in an argument, an effort is made to avoid a vicious infinite regress by an appeal to a privileged assumption, such as ''Man's freedom of choice is self-evident.'' In such cases the question can always be raised, ''But is it self-evident?''

The various ways to controvert arguments are subject to abuse. Disputes can become tedious, and doubly so when they stray from the central issues. But many arguments are more than trivial quibbling.

EXERCISES

Using a form adapted to ordinary language, propose a controverting argument for each of the following arguments and identify the controverting argument by type.

1. We cannot accept the view of "one man, one vote," because it violates the principle of states' rights and it also helps demagogues gain greater political power.

2. Our foreign aid policy is an example of the folly of extravagance. Its principal results consist in keeping socialistic governments from going bankrupt and in making possible their bureaucratic control over the lives of their citizens.

3. Shakespeare could not have written the plays attributed to him. He lacked the educational background necessary for writing such significant works, and he did

not have the opportunity to acquire the kind of political and psychological insight reflected in the works attributed to him.

4. "In the mind there is no absolute or free will. But the mind is determined to wish this or that by a cause which also has been determined by another cause, and this last by another cause, and so on to infinity." (Baruch de Spinoza, 1632–1677)

5. You can't teach an old dog new tricks and you can't expect a man who has spent years in public office to have any new proposals for public policies.

6. The placing of Cuba in the hands of the Communists was a consequence of the deliberate planning of the federal government. Not only did they suspend in 1958 the sending of arms to the rightful government of Cuba but they used every tactic possible to place arms in the hands of the opposition to the official government.

7. There is no question but that the economy is headed for a period of radical inflation. Workers constantly demand higher salaries without regard to increasing their own productivity. The government introduces artificial controls on the economy to prevent a lowering of prices. The only change in prices it permits is an upward change. The increased trend toward installment purchases has the net effect of a sharp increase in the availability of consumer goods in the absence of immediate resources for paying for what is used, thereby pushing prices even higher.

8. A class consciousness prevails among those who control the power structure of the American scene. Political, economic, industrial, military, and bureaucratic leaders are acutely conscious of their own status. They associate with others having comparable status and form social barriers to avoid becoming involved with persons who do not share in their status situation. The class requires that its members recognize and respect its own self-image. Those who share in this class consciousness are the leaders of government, business, industry, and the military.

9. Religion is the opiate of the people, because it takes their minds off the sources of their exploitation and the means of combating it. But how do we know that it takes their minds off the source of their exploitation and the means of combating it? We know this simply because religion is the opiate of the people.

10. The opinion poll on the attitude of all students in this university toward the school president is reliable, since the views of over one hundred students who attended the demonstration were taken as the sample.

11. If qualities like a green and a red color are splotches on a canvas that require a connecting link, then what unites the connecting link with the qualities? If another connecting link unites the connecting link to the qualities, then an additional connecting link would be required to connect the connecting link connecting the connecting link to the qualities.

12. Corporation taxes should be raised, even though the economy is sluggish, in order to prevent a greater deficit in the federal budget.

13. If the government has followed a sound fiscal policy, then inflation is not a threat and credit is not tightened. If inflation is not a threat, then the amount of the gross national product is increased. If the amount of the gross national product is increased, then the government has followed a sound fiscal policy and credit is not tightened. The amount of the gross national product is increased. Therefore, credit is not tightened.

14. Like a biological organism, the organism of the state develops through various stages. Once a state develops into a state that is wholly rational, it will be able to dominate subrational expressions of the state and to control the ends of human endeavor for the benefit of mankind.

15. Man has the power of choice because he can will to act. He can will to act because he has the power of choice.

16. We have combined a liberal political vocabulary with a conservative political behavior. More radical elements on the left and on the right engage in verbal vitriolics, but the conservative mood under the slogan of a ''middle-of-the-road policy'' effectively controls the political life of the country. Changes that occur in the executive, legislative, and judicial branches of the government are justified by appeal to the action, the policies, the statements, and the decisions of predecessors in government. The past acts as a magician's hat. It provides a source for what the actors on the public scene wish to pull out of it. By having to bind the present to the past, those responsible for determining public policy are assured of the preservation of a conservative mood.

17. An agent is free to do an act because he can choose to do an act. He is free to choose to do an act because he is free to choose to choose to do an act.

18. Expenditure of large sums of money for public works in times of high unemployment should not be practiced, since it interferes with the law of supply and demand.

19. College students should not be given an opportunity to determine those rules and regulations under which they are governed in college. A college is a center of learning, and if students become involved in determining policies affecting student life, they will neglect their academic work and thus miss the major purpose for which they are attending school.

20. Daylight Saving Time is opposed by most of the residents of this state. A major newspaper asked its readers to write letters to the editor indicating either preference for Daylight Saving Time or opposition to it, and the vast majority of letters received indicated opposition to this practice.

20.2 MAKING ARGUMENTS

In this section we shall look briefly at how to plan, draft, and review a complex argument. We have seen in Section 6.3 some conditions which we expect good arguments to meet.

In simple arguments we find something about which we want to make a conclusion. We look at the evidence. And we relate the evidence to a conclusion. We organize the evidence and seek to justify a tentative conclusion. In glancing at a newspaper we can find such statements as the following. "Rocket on way to outer space has trouble with camera." "Talks on Middle East not going well." "Star quarterback out for season." We can readily relate these statements to some interest and have arguments beginning as follows. "If the rocket is to achieve its mission, then its photographic equipment must function properly." "Not both can we have an outstanding season and the star quarterback be injured." "Either the talks on the Middle East need to make reasonable progress, or tensions will build up in that area."

We have interest in this section in looking at how we can go about writing a complex argument. This is the kind of argument that a student might develop in a theme or a writer might use in an article. And we shall see how one can extend such arguments to more complex cases. Such arguments attempt to prove one thing. But while proving that general conclusion, one may need to establish several other things in the process.

There are various models we can use in making complex deductive and inductive arguments. Let us consider the following model for a complex deductive argument. In this model T stands for the conclusion, or thesis, of an argument, and F, G, H, and not I for primary premises of the argument:[2]

> If F, G, H, and not I hold, then T.
>
> F, G, H, and not I hold.
>
> Hence T.

Let us also consider a model which a complex inductive argument can take. But please note these assumptions which go along with this model. The factors F, G, H, and I are relevant to showing that hypothesis T holds, and together they provide a sufficient basis for accepting hypothesis T. The factors J and K are relevant and critical to showing that if either of them holds, the conclusion T is rejected:

> If the hypothesis T and its underlying assumption S hold, then F, G, H, and I hold.

---

[2] In the above scheme for a complex deductive argument we are assuming the context. If we add the notion of context (S) to a complex deductive argument, we have the following form:

> If (F and not J) and S, then T.
> [Thus, if F and not J, then if S then T. (Exportation)]
> F and not J.
> Thus, if S then T.

This latter form provides added support to the view that our knowledge of matters of fact is conditioned on the context in which it is held. Likewise, it is obvious that any knowledge claim based on deduction has a dependence on the deductive system in which it occurs.

If hypothesis *T* and its underlying assumption *S* hold, then not *J* and not *K* hold.

F, G, H, and *I* hold.

Hence, hypothesis *T* probably holds.

Conditions not *J* and not *K* do hold.

Hence, hypothesis *T* is not rejected.

We have seen elsewhere that a valid deductive argument provides a conclusion that is necessarily true if its premises are true. And a good inductive argument provides us with a conclusion that is probably true if the evidence is relevant and sufficient for making the claim of the argument. But in both induction and deduction, we want the evidence to be well-founded. For any argument to be sound its essential premises must be true.

In developing sound deductive or strong inductive arguments, we are critically dependent upon having relevant and sufficient evidence to make a claim.

By sufficient evidence in this context, we refer, in part, to the breadth of the evidence we present in a complex argument. That is, in a complex argument there is a need to present as many different kinds of cases as are required to justify the conclusion. But in any given instance there may be some question as to whether such evidence is sufficient. Peer judgment among qualified and experienced persons about what is sufficient in any given context can provide some guidance. We also can propose a negative test. "Let us examine the argument for ways in which one might controvert it. If we can find a successful way of controverting it due to a fault in the lack of breadth of the evidence we present, then the evidence is not sufficient!" However, we should note that sufficient conditions to make a claim also refer to factors other than the breadth of the evidence. It also can refer to the truth of the premises and to the validity of an argument.

Let us show how we could proceed to carry out a complex argument using the complex deductive model.

1. Planning an Argument

We have seen that we make arguments in response to some interest or to meet some need. We narrow these interests down to focus on a specific issue. And then we develop plans for an argument to show that a given conclusion holds.

Let us consider some factors relevant to our making such plans for a complex argument. To illustrate our suggestions, let us assume that someone has an interest in Abraham Lincoln. After wide reading, she wants to make an argument that Lincoln is the foremost president the country has had. (Generally this is too broad a topic on which to write a paper.)

Use of Past Experience.   We draw upon our past experience to help us analyze problems and ways to go about resolving them. Such experience can help us to determine what kind of goal we might choose. It also can help us to know the best routes to take, what signs to look for, and the traps that may be in the way. In some respects, education is, in part, a storing up of the experience of the past through the use of symbols. But we still have to learn some things, even about arguments, the hard way. But at times our past experience also can condition us in the wrong way. We come to expect some things but not others. And our sense of what to expect can be distorted. Some of the things we believe to be true may turn out to be false and to mislead us in making decisions. That is, our past experience can also blind us to some evidence and to some possible conclusions, which, if we found them, would be correct.

In our study of the argument about Lincoln, one's training in the use of primary sources and in the evaluation of historical materials and one's knowledge of how to make arguments can be of some help.

Clarifying Basic Concepts.   In making an argument, we need to make certain that our basic concepts are clear. Once we make these basic notions clear we have a better idea of what will count as evidence either in support of any argument we are developing or in opposition to it.

In working with the problem on Lincoln, a key notion is "greatest president." And included in a notion of greatest president would be someone who shows outstanding leadership in carrying out his oath of office to preserve, protect, and defend the Constitution.

Gaining and Analyzing Information.   In making arguments we need facts and ideas. In basic research we need to go to the primary and original sources. We should use secondary sources with care and not with the purpose of proving a primary issue in our argument. We also need to check on the accuracy of information. We need some system to organize our information along specific topics. We may want to review our way of organizing such materials once we have a clearer idea of the kind of arguments we shall be using.

As our information builds up, we analyze it for developing trends. We also need to be alert for statements that appear not to be consistent with other statements. Sooner or later we have to make judgments about the weight to give conflicting sources. And we may find such conflicting statements in the same source. We also may need to give an explanation for this difference in our arguments.

Sketching a Plan for a Tentative Argument.   As we begin to see the direction in which our data are pointing, we can begin to sketch a tentative complex argument. We begin to get a wider view of the issues, and some lines of arguments toward some conclusions begin to shape up. We can write down the tentative conclusion toward which we may decide to work. We need to begin trying to identify two sets of conditions. One set is those conditions which, if they hold, will help to justify the conclusion toward which we are working. The second set is to identify those conditions which, if they hold, would discredit such a conclusion. We also would do well to discuss what we have found with someone with experience in working in the area of our study. We also can get their reactions to our plan of procedure.

Filling Out Information Gaps.   Our sketching a tentative argument has probably shown that our research is incomplete. We will need to fill in the information gaps. We also may consider other lines of arguments that may be useful.

2.   Drafting a Complex Argument

Focusing on a General Conclusion.   We are attempting to reach a goal. And that goal is the making of a sound argument that establishes a general conclusion. We may decide that our tentative conclusion is in need of revision. Such a view also may be reached at later stages in developing the argument. But we now need to be as explicit as possible to form the conclusion toward which we shall be working. This tentative conclusion serves as a guide to our work.

Usually an argument focuses on a single conclusion about a single issue. But in developing an argument we may reach a number of other conclusions needed to provide evidence for our major conclusion. This major conclusion becomes the thesis of our major argument.

With regard to our illustration about Lincoln, we could consider narrowing our conclusion to a more limited scope. It would be preferable, for example, in writing a history paper to try to work with a more restricted thesis. For example, we might want to try to prove that Lincoln's plans for reconstruction were designed to bring about as early an economic recovery for the South as could be attained.

Statement of Those Premises or Conditions Which Are Sufficient to Prove the General Conclusion.   We need to state those primary premises which, if they hold, will enable us to prove the general conclusion. These premises are the statement of the conditions which we plan to establish in the argument. And if these conditions are met, we can combine them in an argument to prove our conclusion. We also will need evidence to show that our primary premises are true.

Let us go back and develop our illustration about Lincoln in greater detail. The general conclusion toward which we are working is that Lincoln is the foremost president the country has had. What conditions would we need to show that this conclusion is well-founded? Let us propose the following conditions which we then need to establish. (a) He fulfilled in a superior way his constitutional obligations as president. (b) He provided through his leadership the foundations needed at that time for subsequent national growth. (c) He directed his policies and actions with reasonable success toward meeting the total national interests given the conditions of his term in office. (d) He made many critical decisions that were in the long-range interest of the country. (e) On balance, the way in which he met conditions (a) through (d) measure up to a better performance level than that of any other president.

On the other hand if any of the following conditions hold we would expect our proposed conclusion to be rejected. (f) He was responsible for widespread corruption in government. (g) He was responsible for numerous policies that were injurious to the long-range national interest. (h) He was responsible for widespread inefficiency in the government.

We would begin to work on these arguments in some order. What evidence do we need to show that each of these is true in the series (a) through (e) and is false in the series (f) through (h)? We may want to wait until we are dealing with a given premise to specify the conditions which, if shown to be true, would in turn justify that premise. But let us look at the first premise we want to establish. (a) Lincoln fulfilled in a superior way his constitutional obligations as president. How do we go about showing this to be true? We could point out such things as the following. (1) Lincoln showed superior leadership by helping to preserve the Constitution, by insisting on its application to all states and citizens of those states who were a part of the union at a time when this was a primary issue before the nation. (2) He showed superior leadership in protecting the principles of the Constitution by extending the rights of the Constitution to groups that had been deprived of enjoying the provisions set forth in it. (3) He defended it by superior leadership in times of internal crises from those who sought to release themselves from its provisions. And the list could go on. And in some cases we may have to offer additional arguments in the event a dispute might develop about a particular premise.

Carrying Out the General Argument.   We proceed to carry out the arguments whose premises needed to be established to prove the general conclusion. We may find it desirable to make further revision in what we believe counts as evidence as we carry out these arguments.

In the case of the argument about Lincoln, we would proceed to try to establish the primary premises (a) through (e).

Bringing the Argument Together to Justify the Conclusion.   We restate what conditions need to be established to justify the conclusion and show that we have established these conditions. Then we state our conclusion as we have established it.

In the case of our general model we would show that Lincoln met the conditions (a) through (e). In developing (e) we usually would not need to compare the performance of Lincoln with each former president, but only with those presidents who might be regarded as outstanding.

Answering Objections.   Other persons may have different views to those with which we began. We need to have anticipated those objections which are most relevant and crucial to our argument. We now proceed to deal with those. In our model we would want to show that Lincoln did not meet any of the conditions specified as (f), (g), and (h). These arguments would proceed in a manner similar to those shown for (a) through (e). That is, we would set forth the conditions for (f), (g), and (h) to hold. But in this case we would need to show that the conditions for (f), (g), and (h) did not hold. If we have justified our steps, then we point out that we do not have any basis for rejecting our conclusion and that the conclusion stands.

Summarizing Our Argument.   We can summarize the primary premises we use to justify the conclusion and the responses made to the objections for the conclusion we have reached. And our draft is now complete.

3.   Reviewing the Argument and Preparing the Final Draft

In reviewing an argument we need to check on the quality of work we have done. We also want to see if we can find ways to improve the argument.

Accuracy of Evidence.   We need to check on the accuracy of the evidence we have used in the argument, also on the accuracy of the references. This check on accuracy of references needs to be repeated in the final draft.

Clarity of Language.   We want to go over the draft and try to improve both the clarity of our language and the style in which the argument is written. In most cases we would want to write several drafts prior to making the argument public.

Structure of Arguments.   We want to review the structure of the general argument together with those arguments used in support of our primary arguments. We may find it desirable to add other arguments or to take away some that we have made. There is no need to add arguments beyond what is essential and sufficient to establish our general claim.

Securing the Reactions of Other Persons.   We can find the views of others helpful in noting things in the argument we did not intend. They also may make suggestions about improving arguments or adding better ones.

Preparing the Final Draft.   We are now in position to write the final draft, which also needs to be reviewed prior to our making it public. We may be in better position to evaluate our own work if there is a lapse of some days between completing of our initial draft of a complex argument and the final revision we make of a draft.

We could provide other forms for a complex deductive argument. For example, let A refer to the set of premises that constitute the positive evidence, B refer to the set of premises which would discredit the conclusion, and T to the conclusion (or thesis) of an argument. And we have the deductive form:

If A and not B, then T.

A and not B.

Thus, T.

In this section we have discussed briefly some basic steps in preparing an argument. These steps include planning, drafting, and reviewing the argument.

SOME THINGS TO DO

A. Read some editorials and letters to editors in national journals or in major newspapers like *The New York Times, The Washington Post,* or *The Wall Street Journal.* Analyze and evaluate some of the arguments found in the editorials or letters.

B. Analyze some arguments found in professional journals and in some critical decisions of the Supreme Court or other legal bodies.

C. Sketch an argument that you would make in dealing with some of the following topics. Develop one of these arguments at some length.
   1. The team most likely to win a conference title (e.g. football, basketball) in your geographic area.
   2. A change that you believe is desirable in some agency policy (school or government).
   3. A support of some agency policy that you believe is worthy of keeping in its present form.
   4. A way of dealing with some community issue (housing, crime, recreation) that you believe would help to bring about a better state of affairs.

5. A currently discussed issue in the social, behavioral, or physical sciences to show what you believe to be the best resolution of some issue. (For example, what do intelligence or aptitude tests measure or what use should they have in determining admissions policies of schools?)
6. A way of dealing with the energy crisis that will meet the energy needs of the country.

BIBLIOGRAPHY

Alston, William P. *Philosophy of Language*. Englewood Cliffs, N.J.: Prentice-Hall, 1964.

Austin, J. L. *How to Do Things with Words*. New York: Oxford University Press, 1965.

Barker, Stephen F. *The Elements of Logic*. 2nd ed. New York: McGraw-Hill, 1974.

Cohen, Morris R., and Ernest Nagel. *An Introduction to Logic*. New York: Harcourt, 1962.

Copi, Irving M. *Introduction to Logic*. 5th ed. New York: Macmillan, 1978.

Hempel, Carl. *Philosophy of Natural Science*. Englewood Cliffs, N.J.: Prentice-Hall, 1966.

Kahane, Howard. *Logic and Philosophy*. 3rd ed. Belmont, Calif.: Wadsworth, 1978.

Nagel, Ernest. *The Structure of Science*. New York: Harcourt, 1961.

Popper, Karl. *The Logic of Scientific Discovery*. New York: Harper & Row, 1965.

Quine, W. V. *Methods of Logic*. 3rd ed. New York: Holt, Rinehart and Winston, 1972.

ANSWERS TO SELECTED EXERCISES

EXERCISES ON PP. 19–20

A.

2. Ambiguity of Significance
4. Composition
6. Accident
8. Equivocation
10. Division

12. Equivocation
14. Amphiboly
16. Division
18. Composition
20. Complex Question

B.

2. "well"
4. "right"

6. "those who wait" and "best things"
8. "profitable"

EXERCISES ON PP. 29–33*

2. Appeal to Ignorance
4. Appeal to Authority—Consensus

6. Argumentative Leap
8. Begging the Question

* Other answers also can be acceptable.

10. Appeal to Force
12. Missing the Point at Issue
14. Appeal to Authority—Misplaced
16. Argumentum ad Hominem—
    Circumstantial
18. Argumentum ad Hominem—
    Circumstantial (Tu Quoque)
20. Accident
22. Complex Question
24. Ambiguity of Significance
26. Argumentum ad Hominem—
    Abusive
28. Composition
30. Ambiguity of Significance
32. Begging the Question
34. Accent
36. Appeal to Force
38. Composition

40. Begging the Question
42. Accident or Equivocation
44. Accident
46. Missing the Point at Issue
48. Composition
50. Appeal to Force
52. Complex Question
54. Appeal to Ignorance
56. Equivocation
58. Complex Question—Leading
60. Appeal to the Gallery
62. Ignorance
64. Equivocation and Division
66. Argumentum ad Hominem—
    Circumstantial
68. Begging the Question
70. Appeal to the Galleries (and
    Missing the Point at Issue)

EXERCISES ON P. 36

2. "Poliomyelitis," "polio"
4. "one," "five," "ten"

EXERCISES ON PP. 45–46

A.

2. Book, textbook, logic textbook, symbolic logic textbook.
4. Social organization, political system, constitutional government, constitutional
   monarchy, British constitutional monarchy.

B.

Full extension: (2) dog; (3) goals; (4) roses; (5) things.
Partial extension: (1) students, persons; (3) prizes; (4) shrubs, varieties; (5) rules.

C.

Denotation—Point to objects for which you can use these words for 1-5.
   6. U.S. Senate
   8. The professional staff of a federal or state agency, such as the _____ Edu-
      cation Agency

10. Your walking on the right side of a sidewalk
Connotations—Different persons will make different lists.
   2. Object with a surface for sitting
   4. Smooth surface suitable for writing on a wall
   6. Popularly elected governing body
   8. Group of persons employed by a corporate body
   10. Repetition by a person of similar kinds of acts in similar circumstances

EXERCISES ON P. 50

2. "Conservative student"—one that has economic views that strongly support free enterprise, or one that holds to traditional moral values.
4. "Rights"—entitlements based on the national constitution, or claims based on a universal declaration of human rights of the United Nations. (Likewise, "oppressed" can be ambiguous.)
6. "Good teacher"—one who presents material in a manner that the students readily learn, or one whose requirements are minimal and who tells interesting stories in class.
8. "Nothing"—you always want more than you get, or you have an excellent sense of quality, or you do not deserve anything.
10. "All . . . do not"—some who sow do not reap, or no one who sows reaps.

EXERCISES ON PP. 69–70

A.

Please note that several different sets of conditions can be given for each expression.
2. Sister-in-law: a woman who is a sibling of one's spouse.
4. Physician: a person, trained in medicine, practices some form of healing of illnesses of human beings.
6. Politician: a person, active in an organization concerned with governance, has significant influence in determining the way a governing body exercises its powers, use of both elective and appointive processes as a means of exercising powers.
8. Human rights: a set of moral and social entitlements, applicable to human beings everywhere, based on respect for human dignity and worth, commended as practices for political bodies to extend or guarantee to all persons living within their jurisdiction.

B.

2. Rejecting an invitation, encouraging a new invitation, informing.
4. Complaining, accusing, influencing actions.

C.

2. Teacher: giving class term and identifying property, stating conditions for use, describing a situation, pointing, use of similar words.
4. Defendant: conditions for use, giving class term and identifying properties, describing, pointing, typical case.

D.

2. Faulty mixing of elements
4. Missing elements

EXERCISES ON P. 77

A.

2. Influencing
4. Performing
6. Conforming (evaluative, informing?)
8. Informing (influencing?)
10. Evaluative
12. Evaluating (emotive, informing, influencing)
14. Emotive

B.

Views can differ on the following classifications:
2. Usually neutral: "scroll," "vocal cords," "freckle"
   Usually emotive: "stupid," "pusillanimous," "lonely," "crook," "cheese eater"
   Others can be emotive in some contexts.
4. Emotive in most cases

EXERCISES ON PP. 90–91

A.

2. Clear and neutral language, persuasive definition.
4. Fails to state essential characteristics.
6. Fails to state essential characteristics, too narrow, persuasive definition.
8. Circular.
10. Not clear and neutral language, persuasive definition.
12. Not clear and neutral language, fails to state essential characteristics.
14. Circular as stated in this context.
16. Not clear (what I call life).

B.

2. It advances a definition in part by classifying; historical definition.
4. These examples have some features of connotative definitions, but they are not clear in this context. (Historical definition)

EXERCISES ON PP. 97–98

A.

Example 2 is an argument. The conclusion is the following:
  2. We cannot go to the lab.

B.

Deductive Argument: 6
Inductive Arguments: 2, 4, 8

EXERCISES ON PP. 101–102

The counterarguments in these answers are all invalid. Many other examples could be given.
2. Some humans are environmentalists. All pollution advocates are humans. Therefore, some pollution advocates are environmentalists.
4. No student is a person who has won a Nobel prize. All students are persons that are alive. Thus, no person who is alive is a person who has won a Nobel prize.
6. All poisons are things that are liquids, solids, or gases. All poisons are dangerous things. Thus, all things that are liquids, solids, or gases are dangerous things.

EXERCISES ON PP. 105–106

2. No matter what we do, our lot as human beings is to be tossed backward and forward between pain and boredom.
4. If a rational being can determine itself to an actual willing, then it stands in a reciprocal relation to something external.

EXERCISES ON PP. 111–114

A.

2. Verbal dispute.
   (1) "Go around."

(2) (a) "Go around" means to walk a path about the tree so that the one describes an area that includes within it the area in which the squirrel is residing. (*D*)

(b) "Go around" means to pass successively from the one part of a squirrel, such as head (or stomach) to the opposite side (such as the tail) and complete the circle being described about the squirrel back to the head. (*H*)

(3) (a) The hunter did *D*.   (4) (a) *D* is true.

(b) The hunter did *H*.   (b) *H* is false.

4. There is no dispute; Jones is making an evaluation, Smith is making a factual claim.

6. There is some difference in their evaluation of the present conditions and what they expect these conditions to lead to in the future. But the context does not provide a ground for determining how great this difference is. If such an argument is pressed further, there likely will develop a difference on what is believed to be relevant evidence.

8. There is no dispute. These positions can be consistent with each other.

10. Factual dispute.

B.

2. There are two lawyers. Let us call the first man *A*, the second man *B*, and the third man *C*.

   A has to claim to be a lawyer. (If *A* is a lawyer who makes only true statements, he claims to be a lawyer. And if *A* is a crook who makes only false statements, he claims to be a lawyer. Either he is a lawyer or a crook. Therefore, he claims to be a lawyer.) *B* tells the truth. And if *B* tells the truth, he is a lawyer. Therefore, *B* is a lawyer. (*B* states that *A* said he was a lawyer and that is what *A* said.) If *C* lies, then he is a crook and *A* is a lawyer. If *C* tells the truth, then *C* is a lawyer and *A* is a crook. Either *C* tells the truth or *C* lies. Therefore, either *A* is a lawyer, or *C* is a lawyer. *B* and either *A* or *C* are lawyers. But either *A* or *C* is not a lawyer. Therefore, there are two lawyers.

4. Jones knows that he must have an even number. If there must be two even numbers, then only one number of the three can be odd. If Smith or Brown sees an odd number on Jones, then Smith or Brown knows that he must have an even number. Smith or Brown does not see an odd number on Jones, therefore Jones does not have an odd number. And Jones can know that he has an even number.

6. The pilot will pass fifteen planes. He passes a plane every half-hour up to and including the time when $7\frac{1}{2}$ hours have expired.

8. (1) Marty is the tallest member of the group and is a physician.

   (2) Louis is an attorney since he is the shortest of the group and the nearest neighbor of Marty, who is a physician.

   (3) Herbert is the dentist. The physician and attorney have been eliminated

previously. Herbert is not the engineer since Herbert is married, and he is not the architect since he has a swimming pool and the architect does not have a swimming pool.
(4) Kelly is the architect since the physician, the attorney, and the dentist have been eliminated, and he is not the engineer since he plays golf with the engineer.
(5) John is the engineer.

EXERCISES ON PP. 119–120

2. Universal, affirmative
4. Particular, negative

6. Universal, affirmative
8. Universal, affirmative

EXERCISES ON PP. 123–124*

2. E, Universal-negative, No Fd is Gd, $Fd \not< Gd$, $FG = 0$.
4. O, Particular-negative, Some Fu is not Gd, $Fu \not< Gd$, $F\bar{G} \neq 0$.
6. O, Particular-negative, Some Fu is not Gd, $Fu \not< Gd$, $F\bar{G} \neq 0$.
8. E, Universal-negative, No Fd is Gd, $Fd \not< Gd$, $FG = 0$.

EXERCISES ON PP. 125–126

2. Conclusion, (b); Major term, "things good for health"; Minor term, "foods"; Middle term, "fruits"; Major premise (a); Minor premise (c).
4. Conclusion, (c); Major term, "occurrences with definite cycles"; Minor term, "solar events with a life span of four days"; Middle term, "sunspots"; Major premise (a); Minor premise (b).
6. Conclusion, (b); Major term, "persons insensitive to the textures of natural qualities"; Minor term, "advocates of the enjoyments of simple pleasures"; Middle term, "romantic poets"; Major premise (c); Minor premise (a).

EXERCISES ON PP. 129–130

A.

2. Valid.
4. Invalid. A categorical syllogism must have three and only three terms. ("Joker" has different meanings in each use in the premises.)

* See Table 7.1 for the Boolean circles.

6. Invalid. No conclusion can be drawn if both premises are negative.
8. Invalid. If the conclusion is particular, then one premise must be particular.
10. Invalid. There is need for any term distributed in the conclusion to be distributed in the premises.

B.

2. Valid.
4. Valid.
6. Invalid: Fallacy of undistributed middle term.
8. Invalid: Fallacy of a particular conclusion without a particular premise.
10. Invalid: Fallacy of a negative conclusion with affirmative premises.

EXERCISES ON P. 132

A.

2. IV—EIO
4. four terms

6.   I—OEO
8.   III—AAI
10.   III—AAA

B.

2.   II—AOO   Valid.
4.   IV—AII   Invalid: Undistributed middle term.
6.   IV—AIO   Invalid: Negative conclusion with affirmative premises (and undistributed middle term).
8.   IV—EAO   Invalid: Particular conclusion with universal premises.
10.   IV—EAE   ~~Valid.~~ Invalid: Illicit minor

C.

2. Proper order in original syllogism. Fig. I, EIO, valid.
4. Proper order in original syllogism. Fig. I, AOO, invalid, fallacy of illicit major.
6. Proper order: Some *ACA*s are *BCB*s. No *CAC*s are *BCB*s. Therefore, some *CAC*s are not *ACA*s. Fig. II, IEO, invalid, fallacy of illicit major.

EXERCISES ON P. 139

2. S ⊗ P Valid.
         M

4.   *S* ⬤ *P*
     M

Invalid. The conclusion requires that the class of *SP* is not null. The *x* needs to be in the class of *SP* and not on a line.

6.   *S* ⬤ *P*
     M

Invalid. The conclusion requires that an *x* be found somewhere in the class of *S* and not *P*. But there is no *x* in that class.

8.   *S* ⬤ *P*
     M

Invalid. The conclusion requires the class of *SP* to be null.

10. *S* ⬤ *P*
     M

Invalid. The conclusion requires the class of *S*$\bar{P}$ to be not null.

EXERCISES ON PP. 140–141

2. Major term: (Things) in movement
   Minor term: Things subject to
   experimental control
   Middle term: Atoms

   III – AOI
   $Md < Pu$ $M\bar{P} = 0$
   $Mu \not< Sd$ $M\bar{S} \neq 0$
   $Su < Pu$ $SP \neq 0$

   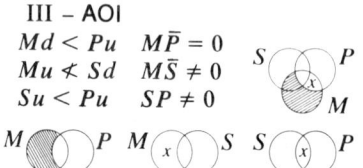

   Invalid: Fallacy of affirmative
   conclusion with negative premise.
   (See Rule 4)

4. Major term: Infinite (object)
   Minor term: The universe
   Middle term: Expanding sphere

   II – EAE
   $Pd \not< Md$ $PM = 0$
   $Sd < Mu$ $S\bar{M} = 0$
   $Sd \not< Pd$ $SP = 0$

   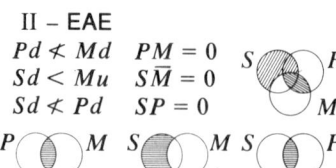

   Valid

6. Major term: Theories of probability
   Minor term: *A priori* theories
   Middle term: Rationalistic theories

   IV – IAI
   $Pu < Mu$ $PM \neq 0$
   $Md < Su$ $M\bar{S} = 0$
   $Su < Pu$ $SP \neq 0$

   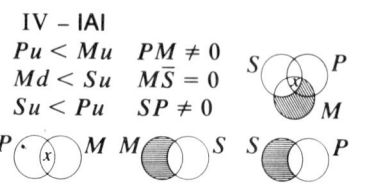

   Valid

8. Major term: Instance of social
   determination
   Minor term: Urban renewal
   program
   Middle term: Form of social control

   I – AAA
   $Md < Pu$ $M\bar{P} = 0$
   $Sd < Mu$ $\bar{S}\bar{M} = 0$
   $Sd < Pu$ $S\bar{P} = 0$

   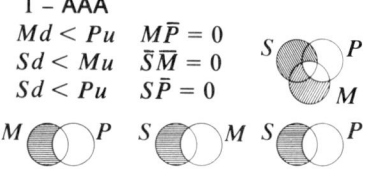

   Valid

10. This can be a four-term fallacy and invalid. With three terms it is valid.
Major term: Matters for the courts
Minor term: Cases of alleviation of poverty
Middle term: Cases of justice

III – **All**

$Md < Pu$ $M\bar{P} = 0$
$Mu < Su$ $MS \neq 0$
$Su < Pu$ $SP \neq 0$

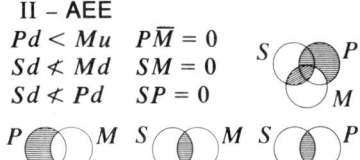

Valid

12. Major term: Parapsychologists
Minor term: Experimental psychologists
Middle term: Persons optimistic about ESP

II – **AEE**

$Pd < Mu$ $P\bar{M} = 0$
$Sd \not< Md$ $SM = 0$
$Sd \not< Pd$ $SP = 0$

Valid

14. Major term: Psychotherapist
Minor term: Investigators indifferent to laboratory techniques
Middle term: Experimentalists

IV – **OEI**

$Pu \not< Md$ $P\bar{M} \neq 0$
$Md \not< Sd$ $MS = 0$
$Su < Pu$ $SP \neq 0$

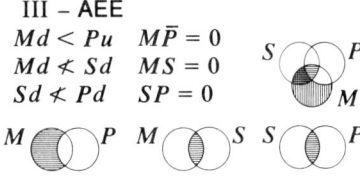

Invalid: Fallacy of two negative premises. (See Rule 5)

16. Major term: "Learned response"
Minor term: "Innate (thing)"
Middle term: "Conditioned reflexes"

III – **AEE**

$Md < Pu$ $M\bar{P} = 0$
$Md \not< Sd$ $MS = 0$
$Sd \not< Pd$ $SP = 0$

Invalid: Fallacy of illicit major term. (See Rule 3)

18. Major term: "Companies maintaining expensive ground schools"
Minor term: "Major air companies"
Middle term: "Air carriers"

I – **AAA**

$Md < Pu$ $M\bar{P} = 0$
$Sd < Mu$ $S\bar{M} = 0$
$Sd < Pu$ $S\bar{P} = 0$

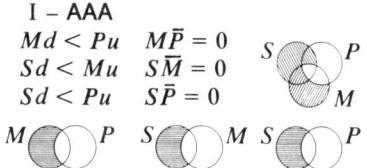

Valid

EXERCISES ON PP. 146–147

(*F* refers to the original subject term and *G* to the original predicate term.)

2. (a) (Partial) Some things to be evaluated are programs.* $Gu < Fu$
   (b) No particles are waves. $Gd \not< Fd$

* Not valid in syllogistic logic without making assumptions explicit.

(c) Some irregular patterns are interference patterns. $Gu < Fu$
(d) No converse of an O categorical statement.

EXERCISES ON PP. 154–156

A.

2. All occasions of old men fearing to plunge are circumstances of youth daring.
4. No old dogs are creatures learning new tricks.
6. All times are occasions of change.
8. Some books are objects on the shelf.
10. All survivors are small children.
12. No nonseniors are students invited to the meeting. (And in some cases—All seniors are students invited to the meeting.)
14. All birds of a feather are creatures that flock together.
16. All fish are creatures with fins.
18. This statement is ambiguous; two meanings would need to be tested: This manuscript is an object that I shall return immediately. This manuscript is an object that I shall return at some convenient future time.
20. No skeletons are objects that need to be brought out of the closet.

22. The occasion of Tom sinking his putt at this time is an occasion of his winning the match.
24. All nonfools are persons who would not take that risk. (In some cases— All fools are persons who would take that risk.)
26. This statement is ambiguous; several meanings might be tested; This occasion is a time in which the students work a part of a day. This is an occasion in which the students do not work part of a day. No days are occasions in which the students work throughout the day.
28. All exercises not requiring advanced math are easy. Some exercises that require advanced math are not easy. (In some cases—Some exercises that require advanced math are easy exercises.)
30. This occasion is a circumstance of Charles missing the bus.

B.

2. All times of our risking losses in these circumstances are occasions that we may make money.
    All times of our buying good bonds in these circumstances are occasions that we may make money.
    ∴ All times of our buying good bonds in these circumstances are times that we take risks.

II – AAA
$Pd < Mu$ $P\overline{M} = 0$
$Sd < Mu$ $S\overline{M} = 0$
$Sd < Pu$ $S\overline{P} = 0$

Invalid: Undistributed middle term

4. Some particles are things with very short lives.
   Some particles are things that repay the energy balance in nature.
   ∴ Some things that repay the energy balance in nature are things with very short lives.

   III – III
   $Mu < Pu$ $MP \neq 0$ S P M
   $Mu < Su$ $MS \neq 0$
   $Su < Pu$ $SP \neq 0$
   Invalid: Undistributed middle term

6. All civilians permitted to leave the country are persons evacuated.
   No civilians active in the negotiations are persons evacuated.
   ∴ No civilians active in the negotiations are persons permitted to leave the country.

   II – AEE
   $Pd < Mu$ $P\bar{M} = 0$ S P M
   $Sd \nless Md$ $SM = 0$
   $Sd \nless Pd$ $SP = 0$
   Valid

8. All times subsequent to the development of nuclear explosives are difficult times.
   These times are times subsequent to the development of nuclear explosives.
   ∴ These times are difficult times.

   I – AAA
   $Md < Pu$ $M\bar{P} = 0$ S P M
   $Sd < Mu$ $S\bar{M} = 0$
   $Sd < Pu$ $S\bar{P} = 0$
   Valid

10. All countries forming a neutral block in the United Nations are unaligned nations.
    All unaligned nations are uncommitted nations.
    ∴ All uncommitted nations are countries forming a neutral block in the United Nations.

    IV – AAA
    $Pd < Mu$ $P\bar{M} = 0$ S P M
    $Md < Su$ $M\bar{S} = 0$
    $Sd < Pu$ $S\bar{P} = 0$
    Invalid: Illicit minor term

C.

2. Some loans granted by the credit department are loans that are not paid back.
   All loans granted by the credit department are loans approved by the credit department.
   ∴ Some loans approved by the credit department are loans that are not paid back.

   III – IAI
   $Mu < Pu$ $MP \neq 0$ S P M
   $Md < Su$ $M\bar{S} = 0$
   $Su < Pu$ $SP \neq 0$
   Valid

4. All pain is a circumstance to be avoided in all possible cases.
   Johnny is a pain.
   ∴ Johnny is a circumstance to be avoided in all possible cases.

   Invalid: Fallacy of four terms. (Otherwise the syllogism would be Figure I, Mood AAA.)

6. All cases of the struggling masses are groups who cannot afford to ignore the need to improve the slums.
   All cases of the struggling masses are groups who have time on their side.
   ∴ All groups who have time on

their side are groups who cannot afford to ignore the need to improve the slums.

III – AAA

$Md < Pu \quad M\bar{P} = 0$
$Md < Su \quad M\bar{S} = 0$
$Sd < Pu \quad S\bar{P} = 0$

Invalid: Illicit minor term

8. No persons who study the stock market are persons who do not make errors.
   All bankers are persons who study the stock market.
   ∴ Some bankers are persons who do not make errors.

   I – EAI

   $Md \nless Pd \quad MP = 0$
   $Sd < Mu \quad S\bar{M} = 0$
   $Su < Pu \quad SP \neq 0$

   Invalid: Affirmative conclusion with negative premise and particular conclusion with universal premises

10. All scientific accidents are things made possible by trained minds.
    The discovery of penicillin is a scientific accident.
    ∴ The discovery of penicillin is something made possible by trained minds.

    I – AAA

    $Md < Pu \quad M\bar{P} = 0$
    $Sd < Mu \quad S\bar{M} = 0$
    $Sd < Pu \quad S\bar{P} = 0$

    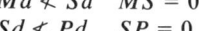

    Valid

12. No fumbles are uncostly events.
    No fumbles are events helping the offense.
    ∴ No events helping the offense are uncostly events.

    III – EEE

    $Md \nless Pd \quad MP = 0$
    $Md \nless Sd \quad MS = 0$
    $Sd \nless Pd \quad SP = 0$

    Invalid: Fallacy of two negative premises.

14. No flourishing of political freedom is a situation found in totalitarian states.
    All flourishing of political freedom is a circumstance characterized by order.
    ∴ No circumstance characterized by order is a situation found in totalitarian states.

    III – EAE

    $Md \nless Pd \quad MP = 0$
    $Md < Su \quad M\bar{S} = 0$
    $Sd \nless Pd \quad SP = 0$

    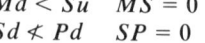

    Invalid: Illicit minor term

16. All gamblers are persons permitted to wager on games.
    No players, coaches, and officials are persons permitted to wager on games.
    ∴ No players, coaches, and officials are gamblers.

    II – AEE

    $Pd < Mu \quad P\bar{M} = 0$
    $Sd \nless Md \quad SM = 0$
    $Sd \nless Pd \quad SP = 0$

    Valid

18. Some anemic persons are unhealthy.
    All persons who do not take exercises are unhealthy persons.
    ∴ Some persons who do not take exercises are anemic.

    II – IAI

    $Pu < Mu \quad PM \neq 0$
    $Sd < Mu \quad S\bar{M} = 0$
    $Su < Pu \quad SP \neq 0$

    Invalid: Undistributed middle term

20. All persons sowing the seeds of their own undoing are persons who are following a self-defeating program.
    All persons who are sowing the seeds of their own undoing are persons who are advocates of unrest and discontent.

∴ All advocates of unrest and discontent are persons following a self-defeating program.

III – **AAA**

$Md < Pu$ $M\bar{P} = 0$

$Md < Su$ $M\bar{S} = 0$

$Sd < Pu$ $S\bar{P} = 0$

Invalid: Illicit minor term

22. All sources of wealth are sources of leisure.

Some uses of sound judgment are not a source of wealth.

∴ Some uses of sound judgment are sources of leisure.

I – **AOI**

$Md < Pu$ $M\bar{P} = 0$

$Su \not< Md$ $S\bar{M} \neq 0$

$Su < Pu$ $SP \neq 0$

Invalid: Affirmative conclusion with a negative premise

24. No drugs having extensive and unknown side effects are drugs whose use is authorized except under carefully controlled and limited conditions.

DMSO is a drug having extensive and unknown side effects.

∴ DMSO is not a drug whose use is authorized except under carefully controlled and limited conditions.

I – **EAE**

$Md \not< Pd$ $MP = 0$

$Sd < Mu$ $S\bar{M} = 0$

$Sd \not< Pd$ $SP = 0$

Valid

Other analyses of some of the above syllogisms are possible.

EXERCISES ON P. 158

2. Minor premise: Mr. Brown is a person making such a statement.
   Conclusion: Mr. Brown is uninformed.
   Valid

4. Conclusion: The "New Left" is romanticist.
   Invalid: Undistributed middle term

6. Major premise: Two possibilities—All (art) works with strong imagery are superior. (Valid)
   All superior works of art are works with strong imagery. (Invalid: Undistributed middle term)

8. Minor premise: Mr. Blank is a person with increases in blood pressure.
   Invalid: Undistributed middle term

10. Minor premise: Mr. Smith is not a man with a poor credit rating.
    Invalid: Two negative premises

EXERCISES ON PP. 160–162

A.

2. (Proposed) Aristotelian form:
   All literary critics are persons

   well-informed on contemporary novels.

All persons well-informed on contemporary novels are interesting conversationalists.
All interesting conversationalists are persons expressing stimulating ideas.
All persons well-grounded in the contemporary theater are persons expressing stimulating ideas.
∴ All literary critics are persons well-grounded in the contemporary theater.

$Ad < Bu$
$Bd < Cu$
$Cd < Du$
$Ed < Du$
∴ $Ad < Du$

Invalid: Undistributed middle term in the third syllogism. (See analysis below)

(1) $Bd < Cu$ (2) $Cd < Du$
    $Ad < Bu$ $Ad < Cu$
    ∴$Ad < Cu$ ∴$Ad < Du$

(3) $Ed < Du$
    $Ad < Du$
    ∴$Ad < Cu$

Invalid: Undistributed middle term

4. Aristotelian form:
All cases of intelligence are cases requiring insight.
All cases requiring insight are cases requiring good judgment.
All cases requiring good judgment are cases requiring facts.
All cases requiring facts are cases requiring inquiry.
∴ All cases of intelligence are cases requiring inquiry.

$Ad < Bu$
$Bd < Cu$
$Cd < Du$
$Dd < Eu$
∴ $Ad < Eu$
Valid

6. (Proposed) Aristotelian form:
The data-processing industry is a multibillion-dollar enterprise.
All multibillion-dollar enterprises are industries of the wave of the future.
All industries that are the wave of the future are sources of good investment in stocks.
Some stocks that are subjected to wide fluctuation in their value over a limited period of time are not sources of good investments in stocks.
∴ Some data-processing industries are not subject to wide variations in the value of stocks over a limited period of time.

$Ad < Bu$
$Bd < Cu$
$Cd < Du$
$Eu \not< Dd$
∴ $Au \not< Ed$

Invalid: Illicit major term in third syllogism

(1) $Bd < Cu$
    $Ad < Bu$
    ∴$Ad < Cu$

(2) $Cd < Du$
    $Ad < Cu$
    ∴$Ad < Du$

(3) $Eu \not< Dd$
    $Ad < Du$
    ∴$Au \not< Ed$

Invalid: Illicit major term

B.

2. Goclenian form:
All simple problems are problems that can be worked immediately.
All problems easy to solve are simple problems.

All chain arguments are problems easy to solve.
All sorites are chain arguments.
∴ All sorites are problems that can be worked immediately.

$Bd < Au$
$Cd < Bu$
$Dd < Cu$
$Ed < Du$
$\therefore Ed < Au$
Valid

4. Aristotelian form:
All elections not requiring
accurate reporting by newspapers
and television are cases not
needing an informed public with
the ability to analyze issues.
All cases not needing an informed
public with an ability to analyze
issues are cases without elections
requiring both information and
judgment.
All cases without elections
requiring both information and
judgment are elections that do
not focus on issues.
All elections that do not focus on
issues are elections that focus on
candidates.
$\therefore$ All elections not requiring
accurate reporting by newspapers
and television are elections that
focus on candidates.

$Ad < Bu$
$Bd < Cu$
$Cd < Du$
$Dd < Eu$
$\therefore Ad < Eu$
Valid

6. (Proposed) Aristotelian form:
All opinion polls are surveys
designed to test public reactions
to current questions.
Some surveys designed to test
public reactions to current
questions are surveys using
samples that are reliable.
All surveys using samples that
are reliable are random samples
that have been properly collected
and analyzed.
All random samples that have
been properly collected and
analyzed are reliable guides of
current public opinion.
$\therefore$ All opinion polls are reliable
guides of current public opinion.

$Ad < Bu$
$Bu < Cu$
$Cd < Bu$
$Dd < Eu$
$\therefore Au < Eu$
Invalid: Undistributed middle
term in the first syllogism
(1) $Bu < Cu$
   $Ad < Bu$
   $\therefore Ad < Cu$
Invalid: Undistributed middle
term

EXERCISES ON PP. 163–164

2. Valid
4. Invalid

EXERCISES ON PP. 171–172

A.

2. irreflexive, nonsymmetrical, transitive

4. reflexive, nonsymmetrical, transitive

6. irreflexive, asymmetrical, transitive (on a nonglobal basis)
8. irreflexive, symmetrical, transitive
10. reflexive, symmetrical, transitive
12. irreflexive, nonsymmetrical, nontransitive (Two persons may be facing different directions.)
14. irreflexive, nonsymmetrical, intransitive

B.

2. invalid—fallacy of misusing a nontransitive relation
4. valid
6. valid
8. valid

EXERCISES ON PP. 178–180

Let T refer to true, F refer to false, and U to undetermined.

A

2. (a) T
   (b) F
   (c) F
4. (a) F
   (b) T

6. (a) F
   (b) T
   (c) T
   (d) T
   (e) U
   (f) T
   (g) U
   (h) T
   (i) T

B.

2. (a) U
   (b) F
   (c) U
   (d) F
   (e) U

   (f) T
   (g) F
   (h) T
   (i) F
   (j) U

EXERCISES ON PP. 187–188

2. Invalid—fallacy of affirming consequent
4. Valid

6. Valid
8. Invalid—fallacy of denying a conjunctive contrary
10. Invalid—fallacy of affirming a disjunct
12. Valid
14. Invalid—fallacy of affirming a consequent
16. Invalid—fallacy of denying an antecedent
18. Valid
20. Invalid—fallacy of an illicit hypothetical syllogism
22. Valid

EXERCISES ON PP. 194–195

2. (a) $(p \supset q) \cdot (r \supset q)$
    $p \lor r$
    $\therefore q$ (Valid)
   (b) $(p \cdot \sim q) \cdot (r \supset q)$ (by horns)
    $p \lor r \lor t$ (through horns)
    $(p \supset \sim q) \cdot (r \supset \sim q)$ (counterdilemma)
   (c) Either taxes rise or inflation continues or credit is tightened.
4. (a) $(p \supset q) \cdot (r \supset s)$
    $p \lor r$
    $\therefore q \lor s$ (Valid)
   (b) $(p \cdot \sim q) \cdot (r \supset s)$ (by horns)
    $p \lor r \lor t$ (through horns)
    $(p \supset \sim s) \cdot (r \supset \sim q)$ (counterdilemma)
   (c) If you compete and win, you have the satisfaction of victory, and you compete and lose, and you have not gained valuable experience.
6. (a) $(p \supset q) \cdot (r \supset s)$
    $\sim q \lor \sim s$
    $\therefore \sim p \lor \sim r$ (Valid)
   (b) $(p \cdot \sim q) \cdot (r \supset s)$ (by horns)
    $\sim q \lor \sim s \lor \sim t$ (through horns)
    $(p \supset \sim s) \cdot (r \supset \sim q)$ (counterdilemma)
   (c) If the crime is admitted, then a prison sentence will be given, and the case is tried, and the defendant is not found guilty.
8. (a) Same analysis as 4(a) above.
   (b) Same analysis as 4(b) above.
   (c) Freedom of speech is permitted and extremist groups can advocate undemocratic practices, and if freedom of speech is curtailed, then democratic institutions are threatened.
10. (a) $(p \supset q) \cdot (r \supset q)$
    $p \lor r$
    $\therefore q$
   (b), (c) There is no way of rebutting this dilemma.

EXERCISES ON PP. 204–205

A.

2. $T \lor S$

4. $M \supset T$

6. $\sim(S \cdot L)$

8. $U \lor (I \supset D)$

10. $(J \lor L) \supset (D \cdot R)$

12. $(I \cdot P) \lor (N \supset \sim R)$

14. $(D \supset R) \cdot (F \supset C)$

16. $[(D \cdot C) \supset \sim B] \supset [O \lor (A \cdot H)]$

B.

2.

A	D	A·D
T	T	T
T	F	F
F	T	F
F	F	F

4.

A	B	A ⊃ B	~(A ⊃ B)
T	T	T	F
T	F	F	T
F	T	T	F
F	F	T	F

6.

C	D	C ⊃ D	D ⊃ C	(C ⊃ D)·(D ⊃ C)
T	T	T	T	T
T	F	F	T	F
F	T	T	F	F
F	F	T	T	T

C.

2. The "v" is the major connective.
   Its scope is the complete line.
   The scope of the "·" is $p \cdot q$.
   The scope of the "⊃" is $r \supset s$.
4. The "·" is the major connective.
   Its scope is the complete line.
   The scope of the "v" is $(p \supset q) \lor r$.
   The scope of the "~" is s.
   The scope of the "⊃" is $p \supset q$.
6. The "≡" is the major connective.
   Its scope is the complete line.
   The scope of the first "v" is $(p \cdot q) \lor r$.
   The scope of the second "·" is $(p \lor r) \cdot (q \lor r)$.
   The scope of the first "·" is $p \cdot q$.
   The scope of the second "v" is $p \lor r$.
   The scope of the third "v" is $q \lor r$.
8. The "⊃" is the major connective.
   Its scope is the complete line.
   The scope of the second "·" is $[(\sim p \lor q) \cdot (\sim r \lor s)] \cdot \sim (\sim p \cdot \sim r)$.
   The scope of the third "v" is $s \lor q$.

The scope of the first "·" is $(\sim p \vee q)\cdot(\sim r \vee s)$.
The scope of the third "$\sim$" is $\sim(\sim p\cdot\sim r)$.
The scope of the third "·" is $(\sim p\cdot\sim r)$.
The scope of the first "v" is $\sim p \vee q$.
The scope of the second "v" is $\sim r \vee s$.
The scope of each remaining "$\sim$" is the atomic sentence form that immediately follows it.

EXERCISES ON P. 207

A.

2. Contradictory

p	$\sim p$	$p \vee \sim p$	$\sim(p \vee \sim p)$
T	F	T	F
F	T	T	F

4. Contingent

p	q	$\sim q$	$p \supset \sim q$	$p \supset (p \supset \sim q)$
T	T	F	F	F
T	F	T	T	T
F	T	F	T	T
F	F	T	T	T

6. Tautologous

p	q	$\sim p$	$\sim q$	$p \vee q$	$\sim p\cdot\sim q$	$(p \vee q) \vee (\sim p\cdot\sim q)$
T	T	F	F	T	F	T
T	F	F	T	T	F	T
F	T	T	F	T	F	T
F	F	T	T	F	T	T

B.

p	q	$\sim p$	$\sim q$	$\sim p \supset q$	$p \vee q$	(2) $\sim q \supset p$	(4) $\sim(\sim p \supset q)$	(6) $\sim p\cdot\sim(\sim p\supset q)$
T	T	F	F	T	T	T	F	F
T	F	F	T	T	T	T	F	F
F	T	T	F	T	T	T	F	F
F	F	T	T	F	F	F	T	T

2. Equivalent (to $p \vee q$)
4. Contradiction

6. Contradiction

EXERCISES ON PP. 210–211

A.

2. Invalid

p	q	r	$\sim p$	$\sim r$	$p \supset q$	$p \supset r$	$(p \supset q) \cdot (p \supset r)$	$\sim p \vee \sim r$	$/ \therefore \sim q$	
T	T	T	F	F	T	T	T	F	F	
T	T	F	F	T	T	F	F	T	F	
T	F	T	F	F	F	T	F	F	T	
T	F	F	F	T	F	F	F	T	T	
F	T	T	T	F	T	T	T	T	Ⓕ	(Invalid)
F	T	F	T	T	T	T	T	T	Ⓕ	(Invalid)
F	F	T	T	F	T	T	T	T	T	
F	F	F	T	T	T	T	T	T	T	

4. Valid

p	q	r	s	$\sim q$	$\sim s$	$p \vee q$	$r \vee s$	$(p \vee q) \supset (r \vee s)$	$\sim q \cdot \sim s$	$/ \therefore p \supset r$
T	T	T	T	F	F	T	T	T	F	T
T	T	T	F	F	T	T	T	T	F	T
I	T	F	T	F	F	T	T	T	F	F
T	T	F	F	F	T	T	F	F	F	F
T	F	T	T	T	F	T	T	T	F	T
T	F	T	F	T	T	T	T	T	T	T
T	F	F	T	T	F	T	T	T	F	F
T	F	F	F	T	T	T	F	F	T	F
F	T	T	T	F	F	T	T	T	F	T
F	T	T	F	F	T	T	T	T	F	T
F	T	F	T	F	F	T	T	T	F	T
F	T	F	F	F	T	T	F	F	F	T
F	F	T	T	T	F	F	T	T	F	T
F	F	T	F	T	T	F	T	T	T	T
F	F	F	T	T	F	F	T	T	F	T
F	F	F	F	T	T	F	F	T	T	T

6. Valid

p	q	r	s	~s	~q	p ⊃ q	r ⊃ s	(p ⊃ q)·(r ⊃ s)	~s v ~q	p	/∴ ~r
T	T	T	T	F	F	T	T	T	F	T	F
T	T	T	F	T	F	T	F	F	T	T	F
T	T	F	T	F	F	T	T	T	F	T	T
T	T	F	F	T	F	T	T	T	T	T	T
T	F	T	T	F	T	F	T	F	T	T	F
T	F	T	F	T	T	F	F	F	T	T	F
T	F	F	T	F	T	F	T	F	T	T	T
T	F	F	F	T	T	F	T	F	T	T	T
F	T	T	T	F	F	T	T	T	F	F	F
F	T	T	F	T	F	T	F	F	T	F	F
F	T	F	T	F	F	T	T	T	F	F	T
F	T	F	F	T	F	T	T	T	T	F	T
F	F	T	T	F	T	T	T	T	T	F	F
F	F	T	F	T	T	T	F	F	T	F	F
F	F	F	T	F	T	T	T	T	T	F	T
F	F	F	F	T	T	T	T	T	T	F	T

B.

2. Valid

A	B	A·B	~(A·B)	A	/∴ ~B
T	T	T	F	T	F
T	F	F	T	T	T
F	T	F	T	F	F
F	F	F	T	F	T

4. Invalid

C	D	E	D v E	C ⊃ (D v E)	C	/∴ D
T	T	T	T	T	T	T
T	T	F	T	T	T	T
T	F	T	T	T	T	Ⓕ (Invalid)
T	F	F	F	F	T	F
F	T	T	T	T	F	T
F	T	F	T	T	F	T
F	F	T	T	T	F	F
F	F	F	F	T	F	F

6. Valid

H	I	J	H·I	~(H·I)	I V J	/∴ H ⊃ J
T	T	T	T	F	T	T
T	T	F	T	F	T	F
T	F	T	F	T	T	T
T	F	F	F	T	F	F
F	T	T	F	T	T	T
F	T	F	F	T	T	T
F	F	T	F	T	T	T
F	F	F	F	T	F	T

EXERCISES ON PP. 215–216

In writing the truth tables for valid argument forms we are writing only those rows where the conclusion is false.

A.

2. Valid

A	B	C	~B	~C	B V C	A ⊃ (B V C)	~B·~C	/∴ ~A
T	T	T	F	F	T	T	Ⓕ	F
T	T	F	F	T	T	T	Ⓕ	F
T	F	T	T	F	T	T	Ⓕ	F
T	F	F	T	T	F	Ⓕ	T	F
F	T	T						
F	T	F						
F	F	T						
F	F	F						

4. Invalid

G	H	I	G ⊃ H	H V I	(G ⊃ H) V I	~(H V I)	/∴ G
F	F	F	T	F	T	T	F

6. Valid

A	B	C	A ⊃ B	A ⊃ C	B V C	(A ⊃ B)·(A ⊃ C)	~(B V C)	/∴ ~A
T	T	T	T	T	T	T	Ⓕ	F
T	T	F	T	F	T	Ⓕ	Ⓕ	F
T	F	T	F	T	T	Ⓕ	Ⓕ	F
T	F	F	F	F	F	Ⓕ	T	F
F	T	T						
F	T	F						
F	F	T						
F	F	F						

8. Invalid

A	B	C	D	~A	A∨B	C∨D	(A∨B)·(C∨D)	~A∨D	/∴~A∨C
T	T	F	T	F	T	T	T	T	F
or T	F	F	T						

10. Invalid

E	F	G	H	~F	F⊃G	E·~F	E⊃(F⊃G)	G∨H	~(E·~F)·E	/∴H
T	T	T	F	F	T	F	T	T	T	F

B.

2. Valid

D	T	C	D∨T	(D∨T)⊃C	D	/∴C
T	T	T				
T	T	F	T	(F)	T	F
T	F	T				
T	F	F	T	(F)	T	F
F	T	T				
F	T	F	T	(F)	(F)	F
F	F	T				
F	F	F	F	T	(F)	F

4. Valid

E	D	C	~C	E⊃~C	D⊃~C	E∨D	(E⊃~C)·(D⊃~C)	/∴~C
T	T	T	F	F	F	T	(F)	F
T	T	F	T					
T	F	T	F	F	T	T	(F)	F
T	F	F	T					
F	T	T	F	T	F	T	(F)	F
F	T	F	T					
F	F	T	F	T	T	(F)	T	F
F	F	F	T					

6. Invalid

T	G	J	B	~J	J∨B	T∨G	G⊃(J∨B)	T·~J	/∴B
T	F	F	F	T	F	T	T	T	F

8. Invalid

S	V	C	S⊃V	C⊃S	(S⊃V)·(C⊃S)	~C	/∴~V
F	T	F	T	T	T	T	F

10. Invalid

L	O	R	H	O∨R	L⊃R	L·(O∨R)	(L⊃R)⊃H	/∴H
T	T	F	F	T	F	T	T	F

EXERCISES ON PP. 222–225

A.

	Column I	Column II	Column III
2. (1)	$B \vee C$		
(2)	$C \supset (D \vee E)$		
(3)	$\sim B$		
(4)	$\sim D$		
	$\therefore E$		
(5)	C	(1), (3) $p \vee q, \sim p / \therefore q$	(1), (3) DA
(6)	$D \vee E$	(2), (5) $p \supset q, p / \therefore q$	(2), (5) MP
(7)	E	(6), (4) $p \vee q, \sim p / \therefore q$	(6), (4) DA

	Column I	Column II	Column III
4. (1)	$A \supset B$		
(2)	$B \supset C$		
(3)	$[A \supset (A \cdot C)] \supset D$		
	$\therefore D$		
(4)	$A \supset C$	(1), (2) $p \supset q, q \supset r / \therefore p \supset r$	(1), (2) HS
(5)	$A \supset (A \cdot C)$	(4) $p \supset q / \therefore p \supset (p \cdot q)$	(4) Abs.
(6)	D	(3), (5) $p \supset q, p / \therefore q$	(3), (5) MP

	Column I	Column II	Column III
6. (1)	$A \supset B$		
(2)	$\sim B$		
(3)	$C \vee D$		
(4)	$[\sim A \cdot (C \vee D)] \supset E$		
(5)	$(E \vee F) \supset G$		
	$\therefore G$		
(6)	$\sim A$	(1), (2) $p \supset q, \sim q / \therefore \sim p$	(1), (2) MT
(7)	$\sim A \cdot (C \vee D)$	(3), (6) $p, q / \therefore p \cdot q$	(3), (6) Conj
(8)	E	(4), (7) $p \supset q, p / \therefore q$	(4), (7) MP
(9)	$E \vee F$	(8) $p / \therefore p \vee q$	(8) Add.
(10)	G	(5), (9) $p \supset q, p / \therefore q$	(5), (9) MP

B.

	Column I	Column III
2. (1)	$C \supset D$	
(2)	$D \supset E$	
(3)	$\sim E$	
	$\therefore \sim C$	
(4)	$C \supset E$	(1), (2) HS
(5)	$\sim C$	(4), (3) MT

	Column I		Column III
4.	(1) $(A \lor B) \supset C$		
	(2) $D \supset A$		
	(3) D		
	$\therefore C$		
	(4) A	(2), (3)	MP
	(5) $A \lor B$	(4)	Add.
	(6) C	(1), (5)	MP

	Column I		Column III
6.	(1) $(A \lor B) \supset C$		
	(2) $D \lor A$		
	(3) $\sim D$		
	$\therefore C$		
	(4) A	(2), (3)	DA
	(5) $A \lor B$	(4)	Add.
	(6) C	(1), (5)	MP

	Column I		Column III
8.	(1) $\sim(A \cdot B)$		
	(2) $B \lor (C \supset D)$		
	(3) A		
	$\therefore C \supset (C \cdot D)$		
	(4) $\sim B$	(1), (3)	DCA
	(5) $C \supset D$	(2), (4)	DA
	(6) $C \supset (C \cdot D)$	(5)	Abs.

EXERCISES ON PP. 231–237

A.

2.	Column I	Column II	Column III
	(1) $(A \lor B) \lor C$		
	(2) $\sim A$		
	(3) $(B \lor C) \supset (D \cdot E)$		
	$\therefore E$		
	(4) $A \lor (B \lor C)$	(1) $p \lor (q \lor r) \equiv (p \lor q) \lor r$	(1) Assoc.
	(5) $B \lor C$	(4), (2) $p \lor q, \sim p \ /\therefore q$	(4), (2) DA
	(6) $D \cdot E$	(3), (5) $p \supset q, p \ /\therefore q$	(3), (5) MP
	(7) $E \cdot D$	(6) $(p \cdot q) \equiv (q \cdot p)$	(6) Comm.
	(8) E	(7) $p \cdot q \ /\therefore p$	(7) Simp.

4. Column I   Column II   Column III
  (1) $(\sim A \lor B) \supset C$
  (2) $\sim A$
  (3) $\sim C \lor (D \supset E)$
  _____
  $\therefore D \supset (D \cdot E)$
  (4) $\sim A \lor B$ (2) $p \: / \therefore p \lor q$ (2) Add.
  (5) C (1), (4) $p \supset q, p \: / \therefore q$ (1), (4) MP
  (6) $D \supset E$ (3), (5) $p \lor q, \sim p \: / \therefore q$ (3), (5) DA
  (7) $D \supset (D \cdot E)$ (6) $p \supset q \: / \therefore p \supset (p \cdot q)$ (6) Abs.

6. Column I   Column II   Column III
  (1) $(H \lor K) \supset L$
  (2) $\sim(L \cdot \sim M)$
  (3) $\sim M$
  (4) $\sim H \supset N$
  _____
  $\therefore N$
  (5) $L \supset M$ (2) $(p \supset q) \equiv \sim(p \cdot \sim q)$ (2) DeC
  (6) $(H \lor K) \supset M$ (1), (5) $p \supset q, q \supset r \: / \therefore p \supset r$ (1), (5) HS
  (7) $\sim(H \lor K)$ (6), (3) $p \supset q, \sim q \: / \therefore \sim p$ (6), (3) MT
  (8) $\sim H \cdot \sim K$ (7) $(p \lor q) \equiv \sim(\sim p \cdot \sim q)$ (7) DeM
  (9) $\sim H$ (8) $p \cdot q \: / \therefore p$ (8) Simp.
  (10) N (4), (9) $p \supset q, p \: / \therefore q$ (4), (9) MP

8. Column I   Column II   Column III
  (1) $E \lor (F \cdot G)$
  (2) $(E \lor F) \supset H$
  _____
  $\therefore H$
  (3) $(E \lor F) \cdot (E \lor G)$ (1) $[p \lor (q \cdot r)] \equiv [(p \lor q) \cdot (p \lor r)]$ (1) Dist.
  (4) $E \lor F$ (3) $p \cdot q \: / \therefore p$ (3) Simp.
  (5) H (2), (4) $p \supset q, p \: / \therefore q$ (2), (4) MP

B.

  Column I   Column III
2. (1) $\sim(C \cdot \sim D)$
   (2) $\sim D \lor E$
   _____
   $\therefore \sim E \supset \sim C$
   (3) $C \supset D$ (1) DeC
   (4) $D \supset E$ (2) MC
   (5) $C \supset E$ (3), (4) HS
   (6) $\sim E \supset \sim C$ (5) Contrap.

Column I		Column III	
4.	(1) $A \equiv B$		
	(2) $B \supset C$		
	$\therefore (\sim A \lor C) \cdot (\sim B \lor A)$		
	(3) $(A \supset B) \cdot (B \supset A)$	(1)	MBC
	(4) $(B \supset A) \cdot (A \supset B)$	(3)	Comm.
	(5) $B \supset A$	(4)	Simp.
	(6) $A \supset B$	(3)	Simp.
	(7) $A \supset C$	(6), (2)	HS
	(8) $\sim B \lor A$	(5)	MC
	(9) $\sim A \lor C$	(7)	MC
	(10) $(\sim A \lor C) \cdot (\sim B \lor A)$	(9), (8)	Conj.

Column I		Column III	
6.	(1) $A \supset (B \supset C)$		
	(2) $C \supset [D \cdot (E \lor F)]$		
	$\therefore (A \cdot B) \supset [(D \cdot E) \lor (D \cdot F)]$		
	(3) $(A \cdot B) \supset C$	(1)	Exp.
	(4) $(A \cdot B) \supset [D \cdot (E \lor F)]$	(2), (3)	HS
	(5) $(A \cdot B) \supset [(D \cdot E) \lor (D \cdot F)]$	(4)	Dist.

Column I		Column III	
8.	(1) $[\sim A \lor (B \cdot C)] \supset D$		
	(2) $\sim D$		
	(3) $(\sim B \lor \sim C) \supset E$		
	$\therefore E$		
	(4) $\sim [\sim A \lor (B \cdot C)]$	(1), (2)	MT
	(5) $\sim \sim A \cdot \sim (B \cdot C)$	(4)	DeM
	(6) $A \cdot \sim (B \cdot C)$	(5)	DN
	(7) $\sim (B \cdot C) \cdot A$	(6)	Comm.
	(8) $\sim (B \cdot C)$	(7)	Simp.
	(9) $\sim B \lor \sim C$	(8)	DeM
	(10) E	(3), (9)	MP

C.

2.	(1) $\sim I \lor A$		
	(2) $\sim (A \cdot C)$		
	(3) I		
	$\therefore \sim C$		
	(4) A	(1), (3)	DA
	(5) $\sim C$	(2), (4)	DCA

4. Invalid

S	V	G	~V	S·~V	~(S·~V)	S ⊃ ~G	~G	/∴V
F	F	F	T	F	T	T	T	F

6. (1) $P \supset W$
   (2) $(P \cdot W) \supset H$
   (3) $P \cdot {\sim}H$
   ___
   ∴M
   (4) P (3)   Simp.
   (5) ${\sim}H \cdot P$ (3)   Comm.
   (6) ${\sim}H$ (5)   Simp.
   (7) W (1), (4)   MP
   (8) ${\sim}(P \cdot W)$ (2), (6)   MT
   (9) ${\sim}W$ (8), (4)   DCA
   (10) $W \lor M$ (7)   Add.
   (11) M (10), (9)   DA
        (Inconsistent Premises)

8. (1) $E \equiv T$
   (2) ${\sim}R \supset {\sim}E$
   (3) ${\sim}({\sim}E \cdot {\sim}I)$
   (4) ${\sim}I$
   ___
   ∴T·R
   (5) ${\sim}({\sim}I \cdot {\sim}E)$ (3)   Comm.
   (6) ${\sim}{\sim}E$ (5), (4)   DCA
   (7) E (6)   DN
   (8) $(E \supset T) \cdot (T \supset E)$ (1)   MBC
   (9) $E \supset T$ (8)   Simp.
   (10) T (9), (7)   MP
   (11) ${\sim}{\sim}R$ (2), (6)   MT
   (12) R (11)   DN
   (13) $T \cdot R$ (10), (12)   Conj.

10. (1) $E \supset (C \lor O)$
    (2) ${\sim}S \supset ({\sim}C \cdot {\sim}O)$
    (3) ${\sim}S$
    (4) $E \lor V$
    ___
    ∴V
    (5) ${\sim}C \cdot {\sim}O$ (2), (3)   MP
    (6) ${\sim}(C \lor O)$ (5)   DeM
    (7) ${\sim}E$ (1), (6)   MT
    (8) V (4), (7)   DA

12. Invalid

F	P	V	C	A	F·~P	F∨C	(F·~P) ⊃ V	~(F∨C)	C ⊃ A	~P∨A	/∴V
F	F	F	F	F	F	F	T	T	T	T	F

14. (1) $(R \cdot C) \supset D$
   (2) $(C \supset D) \supset V$
   (3) $\sim V$
   (4) $(R \lor D) \lor M$
   _____
   $\therefore D \lor M$
   (5) $R \supset (C \supset D)$ (1) Exp.
   (6) $R \supset V$ (5), (2) HS
   (7) $\sim R$ (6), (3) MT
   (8) $R \lor (D \lor M)$ (4) Assoc.
   (9) $D \lor M$ (8), (7) DA

EXERCISES ON PP. 241–245

A.

2. (1) $\sim A \lor B$
   (2) $\sim (B \cdot \sim C)$
   (3) $\sim C$
   _____
   $\therefore \sim A$
   (4) A **AP**
   (5) B (1), (4) DA
   (6) $\sim \sim C$ (2), (5) DCA
   (7) C (6) DN
   (8) $C \cdot \sim C$ (3), (7) Conj.
   (9) $\sim A$ (4)-(8) **IP**

4. (1) $(\sim A \lor B) \cdot (\sim A \lor C)$
   (2) $\sim B \lor \sim C$
   (3) $\sim A \supset (D \cdot \sim E)$
   (4) $(\sim D \lor E) \lor F$
   _____
   $\therefore F$
   (5) $\sim A \lor B$ (1) Simp.
   (6) $(\sim A \lor C) \cdot (\sim A \lor B)$ (1) Comm.
   (7) $\sim A \lor C$ (6) Simp.
   (8) $F \lor (\sim D \lor E)$ (4) Comm.
   (9) $\sim F$ **AP**
   (10) $\sim D \lor E$ (8), (9) DA
   (11) $\sim (D \cdot \sim E)$ (10) DeM
   (12) A (3), (11) MT & DN
   (13) B (5), (12) DA
   (14) C (7), (12) DA
   (15) $B \cdot C$ (13), (14) Conj.
   (16) $(B \cdot C) \cdot (\sim B \lor \sim C)$ (2), (15) Conj.
   (17) $(B \cdot C) \cdot \sim (B \cdot C)$ (16) DeM
   (18) F (9)-(17) **IP**

6. (1) $A \cdot (B \supset C)$
    (2) $C \supset D$
    (3) $\sim(\sim B \cdot A)$
    (4) $\sim D \lor (\sim E \lor F)$

    $\therefore E \supset F$

(5)	$(\sim E \lor F) \lor \sim D$	(4)	Comm.
(6)	A	(1)	Simp.
(7)	$(B \supset C) \cdot A$	(1)	Comm.
(8)	$B \supset C$	(7)	Simp.
(9)	$\sim(E \supset F)$		AP
(10)	$\sim(\sim E \lor F)$	(9)	MC
(11)	$\sim D$	(5), (10)	DA
(12)	$\sim C$	(2), (11)	MT
(13)	$\sim B$	(8), (12)	MT
(14)	$\sim A$	(3), (13)	DCA
(15)	$A \cdot \sim A$	(6), (14)	Conj.
(16)	$E \supset F$	(9)–(15)	IP

8. (1) $\sim(O \cdot \sim F)$
    (2) $F \supset (P \cdot D)$
    (3) $\sim D$
    (4) $O \lor S$

    $\therefore S$

(5)	$S \lor O$	(4)	Comm.
(6)	$\sim S$		AP
(7)	O	(5), (6)	DA
(8)	F	(1), (7)	DCA &DN
(9)	$P \cdot D$	(2), (8)	MP
(10)	$D \cdot P$	(9)	Comm.
(11)	D	(10)	Simp.
(12)	$D \cdot \sim D$	(11), (3)	Conj.
(13)	S	(6)–(12)	IP

10. (1) $(A \lor \sim K) \supset D$
     (2) $\sim D$
     (3) $(K \cdot \sim A) \supset I$

     $\therefore I$

(4)	$\sim I$		AP
(5)	$\sim(K \cdot \sim A)$	(3), (4)	MT
(6)	$\sim K \lor A$	(5)	DeM & DN
(7)	$A \lor \sim K$	(6)	Comm.
(8)	D	(1), (7)	MP
(9)	$D \cdot \sim D$	(8), (2)	Conj.
(10)	I	(4)–(9)	IP

B.

2. (1) $B \supset (P \cdot S)$
   (2) B
   (3) $\underline{\sim S \lor F}$

   $\therefore F$
   (4) $P \cdot S$ (1), (2)   MP
   (5) $S \cdot P$ (4)   Comm.
   (6) S (5)   Simp.
   (7) F (3), (6)   DA

4. (1) $D \supset (\sim T \lor \sim A)$
   (2) $A \lor E$
   (3) $\underline{D \cdot T}$

   $\therefore E$
   (4) D (3)   Simp.
   (5) $T \cdot D$ (3)   Comm.
   (6) T (5)   Simp.
   (7) $\sim T \lor \sim A$ (1), (4)   MP
   (8) $\sim A$ (6), (7)   DA
   (9) E (2), (8)   DA

6. (1) $\sim(Z \cdot \sim A)$
   (2) $A \supset M$
   (3) $S \lor \sim M$
   (4) $\sim(S \cdot \sim R)$
   (5) $\underline{Z}$

   $\therefore R$
   (6) A (1), (5)   DCA & DN
   (7) M (2), (6)   MP
   (8) $\sim M \lor S$ (3)   Comm.
   (9) S (8), (7)   DA
   (10) R (4), (9)   DCA & DN

8. (1) $A \lor C$
   (2) $A \lor M$
   (3) $\underline{[A \lor (C \cdot M)] \supset R}$

   $\therefore R$
   (4) $(A \lor C) \cdot (A \lor M)$ (1), (2)   Conj.
   (5) $A \lor (C \cdot M)$ (4)   Dist.
   (6) R (3), (5)   MP

10. Invalid

S	O	A	M	$S \cdot O$	$A \supset O$	$\sim(S \cdot O)$	$S \supset M$	$/\therefore A \supset M$
F	T	T	F	F	T	T	T	F

12. (1) $\sim(A \cdot \sim D)$
    (2) $\sim[D \cdot (\sim I \lor \sim N)]$
    (3) $(N \cdot I) \supset M$
       $\therefore \sim M \supset \sim A$

(4)	$A \supset D$	(1)	DeC
(5)	$D \supset \sim(\sim I \lor \sim N)$	(2)	DeC
(6)	$D \supset (I \cdot N)$	(5)	DeM
(7)	$A \supset (I \cdot N)$	(4), (6)	HS
(8)	$A \supset (N \cdot I)$	(7)	Comm.
(9)	$A \supset M$	(8), (3)	HS
(10)	$\sim M \supset \sim A$	(9)	Contrap.

14. (1) $\sim F \supset (L \lor I)$
    (2) $(E \lor C) \supset \sim F$
    (3) E
       $\therefore \sim(\sim L \cdot \sim I)$

(4)	$E \lor C$	(3)	Add.
(5)	$\sim F$	(2), (4)	MP
(6)	$L \lor I$	(1), (5)	MP
(7)	$\sim(\sim L \cdot \sim I)$	(6)	DeM

16. (1) $M \lor (J \cdot S)$
    (2) $(M \lor S) \supset D$
       $\therefore (D \cdot M) \lor (D \cdot J)$

(3)	$(M \lor J) \cdot (M \lor S)$	(1)	Dist.
(4)	$M \lor J$	(3)	Simp.
(5)	$(M \lor S) \cdot (M \lor J)$	(3)	Comm.
(6)	$M \lor S$	(5)	Simp.
(7)	D	(2), (6)	MP
(8)	$D \cdot (M \lor J)$	(7), (4)	Conj.
(9)	$(D \cdot M) \lor (D \cdot J)$	(8)	Dist.

18. (1) $R \equiv L$
    (2) $L \supset I$
    (3) $\sim(\sim B \cdot I)$
    (4) $\sim B$
       $\therefore \sim R$

(5)	$(R \supset L) \cdot (L \supset R)$	(1)	MBC
(6)	$R \supset L$	(5)	Simp.
(7)	$\sim B \supset \sim I$	(3)	DeC & DN
(8)	$I \supset B$	(7)	Contrap.
(9)	$R \supset I$	(6), (2)	HS
(10)	$R \supset B$	(9), (8)	HS
(11)	$\sim R$	(10), (4)	MT

20. Invalid

H	O	C	S	D	$C \vee S$	$H \vee \sim O$	$\sim O \supset (C \vee S)$	$(C \vee S) \supset \sim D$	$\sim D$	$/\therefore H$
F	F	T	T	F	T	T	T	T	T	F

EXERCISES ON PP. 256–257

A.

2. $(\exists x)(Ox \cdot \sim Rx)$
4. $(x)(Bx \supset \sim Tx)$
6. $(\exists x)(Tx \cdot Px) \vee (\exists y)(Cy \cdot \sim Gy)$
8. Gj
10. $Ij \supset Bt$
12. $(x)(y)[(Lx \cdot Wy) \supset Hxy]$
14. $(x)(y)(z)\{(Dx \cdot Yy \cdot Mz) \supset [(Cxy \cdot Czx) \supset Czy]\}$
16. $\sim (x)(Ix \supset \sim Sx)$
18. $(\exists x)Hx$
20. $(\exists x)(y)Axy$

B.

2. Some language users are rational.
4. Some language users are not human.
6. Sue is not a friend of Mary.
8. If Joe is the spouse of Mary, then Mary is the spouse of Joe.
10. If Sue is the spouse of Joe, then Mary is not the spouse of Joe.
12. Every human is rational and every teacher is a language user.

C.

BV = Bound variable
FV = Free variable
PC = Property constant
PV = Property variable
OS = Open sentence
CS = Closed sentence
2. OS. F and G are PV. y is FV.
4. OS. L and M are PC. x and y are FV.
6. OS. N is PC. z is FV. y is BV.
8. OS. F, G, and H are PV. y is FV.

EXERCISES ON PP. 271–273

A.

2. **UG** cannot be used on a line introduced in the proof by the use of **EI**. (Line (9))
4. In **UI** the **w** in $\phi\textbf{w}$ must replace each **u** free in $\phi\textbf{u}$. (Line (2))
6. **EI** cannot be used since the "~" is not within the scope of the quantifier. (Line (2))

B.

2. (1) $(\exists x)(Fx \cdot Gx)$
   (2) $\underline{(x)(Gx \supset Hx)}$
        $\therefore (\exists x)(Fx \cdot Hx)$

(3)	$Fy \cdot Gy$	(1)	**EI**
(4)	$Gy \supset Hy$	(2)	**UI**
(5)	Fy	(3)	Simp.
(6)	Gy	(3)	Comm. & Simp.
(7)	Hy	(4), (6)	MP
(8)	$Fy \cdot Hy$	(5), (7)	Conj.
(9)	$(\exists x)(Fx \cdot Hx)$	(8)	**EG**

4. (1) $(x)[Cx \supset (Dx \vee Ex)]$
   (2) $\underline{(\exists x)(Cx \cdot {\sim}Dx)}$
        $\therefore (\exists x)(Cx \cdot Ex)$

(3)	$Cy \cdot {\sim}Dy$	(2)	**EI**
(4)	$Cy \supset (Dy \vee Ey)$	(1)	**UI**
(5)	Cy	(3)	Simp.
(6)	$Dy \vee Ey$	(4), (5)	MP
(7)	$\sim Dy$	(3)	Comm. & Simp.
(8)	Ey	(6), (7)	DA
(9)	$Cy \cdot Ey$	(5), (8)	Conj.
(10)	$(\exists x)(Cx \cdot Ex)$	(9)	**EG**

6. (1) $(x)[(Lx \cdot Mx) \supset Nx]$
   (2) $\underline{(x)[(Mx \supset Nx) \supset Ox]}$
        $\therefore (x)(Lx \supset Ox)$

(3)	$(Ly \cdot My) \supset Ny$	(1)	**UI**
(4)	$(My \supset Ny) \supset Oy$	(2)	**UI**
(5)	$Ly \supset (My \supset Ny)$	(3)	Exp.
(6)	$Ly \supset Oy$	(5), (4)	HS
(7)	$(x)(Lx \supset Ox)$	(6)	**UG**

8. (1) $(x)[(Px \lor Qx) \supset (Rx \lor Sx)]$
 (2) $(\exists x)(Px \cdot \sim Rx)$

  $\therefore (\exists x)(Px \cdot Sx)$

 (3) $Py \cdot \sim Ry$ (2) **EI**
 (4) $(Py \lor Qy) \supset (Ry \lor Sy)$ (1) **UI**
 (5) Py (3) Simp.
 (6) $Py \lor Qy$ (5) Add.
 (7) $Ry \lor Sy$ (4), (6) MP
 (8) $\sim Ry$ (3) Comm. & Simp.
 (9) Sy (7), (8) DA
 (10) $Py \cdot Sy$ (5), (9) Conj.
 (11) $(\exists x)(Px \cdot Sx)$ (10) **EG**

10. (1) $\sim(x)(Px \supset Qx)$
 (2) $(x)[(Rx \cdot Sx) \supset Qx]$
 (3) $(x)[(Px \lor Tx) \supset Rx]$

  $\therefore (\exists x) \sim Sx$

 (4) $(\exists x) \sim (Px \supset Qx)$ (1) **QE**
 (5) $(\exists x)(Px \cdot \sim Qx)$ (4) DeC
 (6) $Py \cdot \sim Qy$ (5) **EI**
 (7) $(Ry \cdot Sy) \supset Qy$ (2) **UI**
 (8) $(Py \lor Ty) \supset Ry$ (3) **UI**
 (9) Py (6) Simp.
 (10) $\sim Qy$ (6) Comm. & Simp.
 (11) $\sim(Ry \cdot Sy)$ (7), (10) MT
 (12) $Py \lor Ty$ (9) Add.
 (13) Ry (8), (12) MP
 (14) $\sim Sy$ (11), (13) DCA
 (15) $(\exists x) \sim Sx$ (14) **EG**

12. (1) $(x)(Tx \supset Lx)$
 (2) $(x)(Lx \supset Ux)$
 (3) $(x)(Ux \supset Px)$
 (4) $(\exists x)(Tx \cdot Sx)$

  $\therefore (\exists x)(Px \cdot Sx)$

 (5) $Ty \cdot Sy$ (4) **EI**
 (6) $Ty \supset Ly$ (1) **UI**
 (7) $Ly \supset Uy$ (2) **UI**
 (8) $Uy \supset Py$ (3) **UI**
 (9) Ty (5) Simp.
 (10) Sy (5) Comm. & Simp.
 (11) Ly (6), (9) MP
 (12) Uy (7), (11) MP
 (13) Py (8), (12) MP
 (14) $Py \cdot Sy$ (13), (10) Conj.
 (15) $(\exists x)(Px \cdot Sx)$ (14) **EG**

14. (1) $(x)[Vx \supset (Dx \lor Fx)]$
    (2) $(x)[(Dx \lor Fx) \supset Rx]$

    $\therefore (x)[Ax \supset (Vx \supset Rx)]$

    (3) $Vy \supset (Dy \lor Fy)$ (1) **UI**
    (4) $(Dy \lor Fy) \supset Ry$ (2) **UI**
    (5) $Vy \supset Ry$ (3), (4) HS
    (6) $(Vy \supset Ry) \lor \sim Ay$ (5) Add.
    (7) $\sim Ay \lor (Vy \supset Ry)$ (6) Comm.
    (8) $Ay \supset (Vy \supset Ry)$ (7) MC
    (9) $(x)[Ax \supset (Vx \supset Rx)]$ (8) **UG**

C.

2. In **UG** there must be a comparable variable free in ϕ**u** for each variable free in ϕ**w**. (Line (2)). A quantifier such as (x) cannot capture in **UG** two different variables such as y and x in ϕ**w**.

4. The error is in line (4). (Line 3 is correct.) **UG** cannot be used on a variable free in a line introduced in the proof by the use of **EI**.

D.

2. (1) $(\exists x)(y)Oxy$

    $\therefore (\exists x)Oxx$

    (2) $(y)Ozy$ (1) **EI**
    (3) Ozz (2) **UI**
    (4) $(\exists x)Oxx$ (3) **EG**

4. (1) $(x)(y)(Sxy \supset Syx)$
   (2) $\sim Sba$

    $\therefore \sim Sab$

    (3) $(y)(Say \supset Sya)$ (1) **UI**
    (4) $Sab \supset Sba$ (3) **UI**
    (5) $\sim Sab$ (4), (2) MT

6. (1) $(x)(y)Rxy$

    $\therefore (\exists x)Rxx$

    (2) $(y)Rzy$ (1) **UI**
    (3) Rzz (2) **UI**
    (4) $(\exists x)Rxx$ (3) **EG**

8. (1) $(x)[Hxj \supset (\exists y)Lyj]$
   (2) Hgj

    $\therefore (\exists y)Lyj$

    (3) $Hgj \supset (\exists y)Lyj$ (1) **UI**
    (4) $(\exists y)Lyj$ (3), (2) MP

10. (1) $(x)(y)(z)[(Sxy \cdot Syz) \supset \sim Sxz]$
   (2) $Sjt \cdot Stb$
   ————————————
     $\therefore \sim Sjb$
   (3) $(y)(z)[(Sjy \cdot Syz) \supset \sim Sjz]$ (1) **UI**
   (4) $(z)[(Sjt \cdot Stz) \supset \sim Sjz]$ (3) **UI**
   (5) $(Sjt \cdot Stb) \supset \sim Sjb$ (4) **UI**
   (6) $\sim Sjb$ (5), (2) MP

EXERCISES ON PP. 283–286

A.

2. Invalid.

			$(x)(Px \supset Qx)$	$(x)(Rx \supset Qx)$	$/\therefore(x)(Px \supset Rx)$
Pa	Qa	Ra	$Pa \supset Qa$	$Ra \supset Qa$	$/\therefore Pa \supset Ra$
T	T	F	T	T	F

4. Invalid

										$(x)(Mx \supset Nx)$	$(x)(Nx \supset Ox)$
Ma	Mb	Na	Nb	Oa	Ob	Pa	Pb	Ra	Rb	$(Ma \supset Na) \cdot (Mb \supset Nb)$	$(Na \supset Oa) \cdot (Nb \supset Ob)$
T	T	T	T	T	T	T	F	F	T	T	T
										T T	T T

$(x)(Px \supset Ox)$	$(\exists x)(Mx \cdot Rx)$	$/\therefore(\exists x)(Px \cdot Rx)$
$(Pa \supset Oa) \cdot (Pb \supset Ob)$	$(Ma \cdot Ra) \lor (Mb \cdot Rb)$	$/\therefore(Pa \cdot Ra) \lor (Pb \cdot Rb)$
T	T	F
T T	F T	F F

6. (1) $(\exists x)(Kx \cdot Lx)$
   (2) $(x)(Lx \supset Mx)$
   (3) $(x)(Kx \supset Nx)$
   ————————————
     $\therefore(\exists x)(Mx \cdot Nx)$
   (4) $Ky \cdot Ly$ (1) **EI**
   (5) $Ly \supset My$ (2) **UI**
   (6) $Ky \supset Ny$ (3) **UI**
   (7) Ky (4) Simp.
   (8) $Ly \cdot Ky$ (4) Comm.
   (9) Ly (8) Simp.'
  (10) My (5), (9) MP
  (11) Ny (6), (7) MP
  (12) $My \cdot Ny$ (10), (11) Conj.
  (13) $(\exists x)(Mx \cdot Nx)$ (12) **EG**

8. Invalid

			$(x)(Px \supset Sx)$	$(x)(Px \supset Ax)$	$/\therefore(x)(Ax \supset Sx)$
Pa	Sa	Aa	$Pa \supset Sa$	$Pa \supset Aa$	$/\therefore Aa \supset Sa$
F	F	T	T	T	F

10. Invalid

						$(x)(Ex \supset Ax)$
Ea	Eb	Aa	Ab	Ma	Mb	$(Ea \supset Aa) \cdot (Eb \supset Ab)$
T	F	T	F	T	T	T
						T T

$(\exists x)(Mx \cdot Ex)$	$/\therefore(x)(Mx \supset Ax)$
$(Ma \cdot Ea)V(Mb \cdot Eb)$	$/\therefore(Ma \supset Aa) \cdot (Mb \supset Ab)$
T	F
T F	T F

B.

2. (1) $(\exists x)(Dx \cdot \sim Ex)$
   (2) $(x)(Fx \supset Ex)$
        $\therefore(\exists x)(Dx \cdot \sim Fx)$

(3)	$Dy \cdot \sim Ey$	(1)	**EI**
(4)	$Fy \supset Ey$	(2)	**UI**
(5)	Dy	(3)	Simp.
(6)	$\sim Ey \cdot Dy$	(3)	Comm.
(7)	$\sim Ey$	(6)	Simp.
(8)	$\sim Fy$	(4), (7)	MT
(9)	$Dy \cdot \sim Fy$	(5), (8)	Conj.
(10)	$(\exists x)(Dx \cdot \sim Fx)$	(9)	**EG**

4. (1) $(x)[Ax \supset (Bx \lor Cx)]$
   (2) $(x)[\sim(Bx \lor Cx) \lor (y)Dyx]$
        $\therefore(x)[Ax \supset (y)Dyx]$

(3)	$Az \supset (Bz \lor Cz)$	(1)	**UI**
(4)	$\sim(Bz \lor Cz) \lor (y)Dyz$	(2)	**UI**
(5)	$(Bz \lor Cz) \supset (y)Dyz$	(4)	MC
(6)	$Az \supset (y)Dyz$	(3), (5)	HS
(7)	$(x)[Ax \supset (y)Dyx]$	(6)	**UG**

6. (1) $(x)(Cx \supset Dx) \supset (y)(Ey \supset Fy)$
   (2) $(\exists y)(Ey{\cdot}{\sim}Fy) \vee (z)(Hz \supset Iz)$
   (3) $\underline{(\exists z)(Hz{\cdot}{\sim}Iz)}$

      $\therefore(\exists x)(Cx{\cdot}{\sim}Dx)$
   (4) ${\sim}(z) \sim (Hz{\cdot}{\sim}Iz)$ (3) **QE**
   (5) ${\sim}(z)(Hz \supset Iz)$ (4) DeC
   (6) $(\exists y)(Ey{\cdot}{\sim}Fy)$ (2), (5) Comm. & DA
   (7) ${\sim}(y) \sim (Ey{\cdot}{\sim}Fy)$ (6) **QE**
   (8) ${\sim}(y)(Ey \supset Fy)$ (7) DeC
   (9) ${\sim}(x)(Cx \supset Dx)$ (1), (8) MT
  (10) $(\exists x) \sim (Cx \supset Dx)$ (9) **QE**
  (11) $(\exists x)(Cx{\cdot}{\sim}Dx)$ (10) DeC

8.

                                  $(\exists x)(Px{\cdot}Ex)$

Pa	Pb	Ea	Eb	Ia	Ib	${\sim}Ia$	${\sim}Ib$	$(Pa{\cdot}Ea) \vee (Pb{\cdot}Eb)$	
T	T	T	F	T	F	F	T	T	
								T	F

$(\exists x)(Px{\cdot}{\sim}Ix)$		$/\therefore(\exists x)(Ex{\cdot}{\sim}Ix)$	
$(Pa{\cdot}{\sim}Ia) \vee (Pb{\cdot}{\sim}Ib)$		$/\therefore(Ea{\cdot}{\sim}Ia) \vee (Eb{\cdot}{\sim}Ib)$	
T		F	
F	T	F	F

10. (1) $(x)(Fx \supset Cx)$
   (2) $\underline{(x)[(Hx \vee Tx) \supset Fx]}$ Assumed
      $\therefore(x)[(Hx \vee Tx) \supset Cx]$ premise
   (3) $Fy \supset Cy$ (1) **UI**
   (4) $(Hy \vee Ty) \supset Fy$ (2) **UI**
   (5) $(Hy \vee Ty) \supset Cy$ (4), (3) HS
   (6) $(x)[(Hx \vee Tx) \supset Cx]$ (5) **UI**

12. (1) $Dg \vee Dj$
   (2) $(x)(Dx \supset Lx)$
   (3) $(x)(Lx \supset {\sim}Ix)$
   (4) ${\sim}Ij \supset {\sim}Dg$
   (5) $\underline{Dj}$

      $\therefore{\sim}Dg$
   (6) $Dj \supset Lj$ (2) **UI**
   (7) $Lj \supset {\sim}Ij$ (3) **UI**
   (8) $Dj \supset {\sim}Ij$ (6), (7) HS
   (9) ${\sim}Ij$ (8), (5) MP
  (10) ${\sim}Dg$ (4), (9) MP

14. (1) $(x)(Wx \supset Cx) \supset (\exists y)(Fy \cdot Py)$
    (2) $\sim(y)(Fy \supset \sim Py) \supset (\exists z)(Lz \cdot Rz)$

$\therefore (x)(Wx \supset Cx) \supset \sim(z)(Lz \supset \sim Rz)$

(3) $(\exists y) \sim (Fy \supset \sim Py) \supset (\exists z)(Lz \cdot Rz)$	(2)	**QE**
(4) $(\exists y)(Fy \cdot Py) \supset (\exists z)(Lz \cdot Rz)$	(3)	DeC
(5) $(x)(Wx \supset Cx) \supset (\exists z)(Lz \cdot Rz)$	(1), (4)	HS
(6) $(x)(Wx \supset Cx) \supset \sim(z) \sim (Lz \cdot Rz)$	(5)	**QE**
(7) $(x)(Wx \supset Cx) \supset \sim(z)(Lz \supset \sim Rz)$	(6)	DeC

16. (1) $(\exists x)(Px \cdot Sx) \supset (\exists y)(Jy \cdot Cy)$
    (2) $(z)(Nz \supset Iz) \supset (y)(Jy \supset \sim Cy)$
    (3) $(z)(Nz \supset Iz) \lor (\exists w)(Aw \cdot Tw)$

$\therefore (w)(Aw \supset \sim Tw) \supset (x)(Px \supset \sim Sx)$

(4) $\sim(z)(Nz \supset Iz) \supset (\exists w)(Aw \cdot Tw)$	(3)	MC
(5) $\sim(\exists w)(Aw \cdot Tw) \supset (z)(Nz \supset Iz)$	(4)	Contrap.
(6) $\sim(\exists w)(Aw \cdot Tw) \supset (y)(Jy \supset \sim Cy)$	(5), (2)	HS
(7) $\sim(\exists w)(Aw \cdot Tw) \supset \sim(\exists y) \sim (Jy \supset \sim Cy)$	(6)	**QE**
(8) $\sim(\exists w)(Aw \cdot Tw) \supset \sim(\exists y)(Jy \cdot Cy)$	(7)	DeC
(9) $\sim(\exists y)(Jy \cdot Cy) \supset \sim(\exists x)(Px \cdot Sx)$	(1)	Contrap.
(10) $\sim(\exists w)(Aw \cdot Tw) \supset \sim(\exists x)(Px \cdot Sx)$	(8), (9)	HS
(11) $(w) \sim (Aw \cdot Tw) \supset \sim(\exists x)(Px \cdot Sx)$	(10)	**QE**
(12) $(w)(Aw \supset \sim Tw) \supset \sim(\exists x)(Px \cdot Sx)$	(11)	DeC
(13) $(w)(Aw \supset \sim Tw) \supset (x) \sim (Px \cdot Sx)$	(12)	**QE**
(14) $(w)(Aw \supset \sim Tw) \supset (x)(Px \supset \sim Sx)$	(13)	DeC

C.

2. $(\exists x)(Fx \lor Gx) \supset [(\exists x)Fx \lor (\exists x)Gx]$

(1) $(\exists x)(Fx \lor Gx)$	Given as premise	
(2) $\sim(\exists x)Fx$	**AP**	
(3) $(x) \sim Fx$	(2)	**QE**
(4) $Fy \lor Gy$	(1)	**EI**
(5) $\sim Fy$	(3)	**UI**
(6) Gy	(4), (5)	DA
(7) $(\exists x)Gx$	(6)	**EG**
(8) $\sim(\exists x)Fx \supset (\exists x)Gx$	(2)–(7)	**CP**
(9) $(\exists x)Fx \lor (\exists x)Gx$	(8)	MC

4. $[(x)Fx \cdot (x)Gx] \supset (x)(Fx \cdot Gx)$

(1) $(x)Fx \cdot (x)Gx$	Given as premise	
(2) $(x)Fx$	(1)	Simp.
(3) $(x)Gx$	(1)	Comm. & Simp.
(4) Fy	(2)	**UI**
(5) Gy	(3)	**UI**
(6) $Fy \cdot Gy$	(5)	Conj.
(7) $(x)(Fx \cdot Gx)$	(6)	**UG**

6. $[(x)Fx \cdot P] \supset (x)(Fx \cdot P)$

    (1) $(x)Fx \cdot P$ Given as premise

    (2) $(x)Fx$ (1) Simp.

    (3) P (1) Comm. & Simp.

    (4) Fy (2) **UI**

    (5) $Fy \cdot P$ (4), (3) Conj.

    (6) $(x)(Fx \cdot P)$ (5) **UG**

8. $[P \supset (x)Fx] \supset (x)(P \supset Fx)$

    (1) $P \supset (x)Fx$ Given as premise

    ⌈(2) P **AP**

     (3) $(x)Fx$ (1), (2) MP

    ⌊(4) Fy (3) **UI**

    (5) $P \supset Fy$ (2)-(4) **CP**

    (6) $(x)(P \supset Fx)$ (5) **UG**

10. $(\exists x)Fx \supset \sim(x) \sim Fx$

    (1) $(\exists x)Fx$ Given as premise

    ⌈(2) $(x) \sim Fx$ **AP**

     (3) Fy (1) **EI**

     (4) $\sim Fy$ (2) **UI**

    ⌊(5) $Fy \cdot \sim Fy$ (3), (4) Conj.

    (6) $\sim(x) \sim Fx$ (2)-(5) **IP**

EXERCISES ON PP. 301–304

A.

2. Argumentative
   (1) Number of cases—highly limited.
   (2) Relevance of properties—analogy is weak.
   (3) Differing contexts—missing to a significant degree.
   (4) Restraint in conclusion—appears to be missing.
   (5) Significant disanalogies—appear to be present. The relation and responsibility of a student in these cases appears to require that he or she do his own work. In the other cases one can argue that the parties are fulfilling an obligation that provides for an exception to a general rule. But this kind of exceptional situation is not present in the case of the student.
4. Illustrative
6. Argumentative
   This argument is circumstantial. There is need for more evidence.
   (1) Number of instances—too few.
   (2) Relevance of properties—The properties listed have some relevance for identifying the person who committed the crime. Yet having these properties is not sufficient to identify the person committing the crime.

(3) Differing contexts and conditions—The analogy presents a set of differing contexts and conditions. But others are needed.

(4) Restraint made in claim—The analogy does not exercise restraint. It would have been stronger if there was a recommendation to search for further evidence.

(5) Significant disanalogies—None are given in this example.

8. Illustrative but with some elements of an argument

10. Illustrative

12. Illustrative

B.

2. (1) Weaker—There is a difference that can be significant.

(2) Weaker—There is a difference that can be significant.

(3) Not affected.

(4) Stronger—New conditions that are favorable together with an increase in the number of instances.

(5) Weaker—Significant disanalogies—The car may not be in proper running condition.

EXERCISES ON PP. 324–328

2. Hypothesis: There is some variation between the density of an object and the degree to which x-rays penetrate such objects.
Tests:

(1) Greater penetration of glass without lead than of glass with lead

(2) Greater penetration of metals like copper, silver, and gold than of lead

Other tests:

(1) Greater penetration of pottery without lead than of pottery with lead

(2) Greater penetration of iron and of zinc than of lead

4. Hypothesis: The taking of both alcohol and of a sweet drink on an empty stomach results in a wider range of behavioral modification than either the taking of the alcohol without the sweet drink or the taking of the sweet drink without the alcohol.
Tests:

(1) There will be a greater increase in the rise of the blood sugar the first hour after the drinking of the alcohol and sweet drink than in the case in which the sweet drink is taken without the alcohol or in which the alcohol is taken without the sweet drink.

(2) There will be a sharper decrease in the amount of blood sugar within two to three hours in the case of those taking the alcohol and sweet drink in comparison to those who do not.

(3) There will be a greater tendency toward depression, grief reaction and sleepiness on the part of those taking the alcohol and tonic in comparison with those who take only one of these drinks.

6. Hypothesis: Rats that grow up in a highly stimulating living environment will

develop larger anterior brains than those that grow up in isolation and with highly restricted living quarters.

Tests:

(1) There is need to find an appropriate species of rats and select a group that is sufficiently large to have a control group and an experimental group.

(2) There is need to divide the larger group into a control group and an experimental group. The experimental group is provided with a living environment with facilities for group living and with toys. Individual rats in the control group are kept in isolation and in restricted living conditions.

(3) The amount of growth of the brains of rats in each group is weighed at the end of the experiment.

(4) There is a repetition of the experiment with different sets of rats using different time periods for exposure to these two different kinds of living conditions.

8. Hypothesis: The degree of intellectual stimulation and of emotional support found within a family is a more reliable instrument in predicting the performance on I.Q. tests than the socioeconomic status of the family is.

Tests:

After identifying factors that characterize intellectual stimulation and emotional support within a family on the one hand and that characterize socioeconomic status on the other there is need to compare the I.Q. scores of children with their family background.

The hypothesis would require that there is a higher correlation between strong family intellectual stimulation and emotional support and scores on I.Q. exams for children in these families than between the socioeconomic background of the family and the performance on such tests.

10. Hypothesis: Left-handed persons who write in an inverted manner will have the left hemisphere of the brain dealing primarily with language development. And left-handed persons who write with their hands below the line will have the right hemisphere of the brain dealing primarily with language specialization.

Tests:

(1) Measure for the side of the brain for language specialization for groups of left-handed persons who write in an inverted manner and for those who do not.

(2) There should be a strong and predominant tendency for the left-handed persons who write with an inverted hand to have language specialization on the left side of the brain and for the others to have such specialization in the right side of the brain.

EXERCISES ON PP. 341–344

2. Method of concomitant variations—The evidence is strong.

4. Method of difference—The evidence supports the hypothesis. There is need for further testing.

6. Method of agreement and negative use of method of difference—The evidence supports the hypothesis. There is need for additional testing.
8. Method of difference—The evidence is strong. There is need for further testing.
10. Method of difference—The evidence is strong but there is need for further testing.
12. Methods of difference and of concomitant variations—The evidence appears significant but there is need for additional testing.

EXERCISES ON PP. 346–347

2. Oversimplified conditions treated as causes.
4. Confusion of reasons and causes.
6. Misuse of common factors.
8. Joint effects of a common cause.
10. Joint effect of a common cause.

EXERCISES ON PP. 360–361

2. (a) 5/36
   (b) 5/36 + 4/36 or 9/36
   (c) 3/36 + 4/36 + 5/36 + 5/36 + 4/36 + 3/36 or 24/36
   (d) $1 - 6/36$ or 30/36 or 5/6

4. (a) $1/20 \times 1/20 \times 1/20 = 1/8000$
   (b) $1/1 \times 1/20 \times 1/20 = 1/400$
   (c) $1 - 1/20$ or 19/20

EXERCISES ON PP. 384–386

A.

2. Any conclusion based on information gathered in this manner is highly questionable. The way the survey is carried out introduces bias in the survey.
4. The conclusion is questionable. There is a bias in the sample since each person in the neighborhood did not have a chance for inclusion in the sample. Likewise, the use of bars and a particular time of day excluded those who do not frequent bars at that particular time of day from being included in the sample.
6. The data can represent a general finding about a given group of students. But given the manner in which the data are gathered, the proposed conclusion is more precise than the data warrant. Furthermore, the data base is too restrictive either to make generalizations about all freshman English students in a given academic setting or about freshman English students in general.

B.

2. Null Hypothesis: There is no difference in the number of toys sold at supermarkets where toys are (1) dispersed throughout the store, (2) collected together in one aisle, or (3) concentrated at the checkout counters.
Alternative Hypothesis: There is a difference in the number of toys sold at supermarkets where toys are (1) dispersed throughout the store, (2) collected together in one aisle, or (3) concentrated at the checkout counters.

EXERCISES ON PP. 443–445

2. One can claim that the evidence is faulty or that there is need to make distinctions within the different programs that form our foreign policy.
4. In this argument there is an appeal to an infinite regress.
6. There is need to make distinctions. For example, the claim can be made that in opposing the official Cuban regime in 1958 the State Department was seeking to encourage the development of a democratic regime in Cuba.
8. The notion of class consciousness in this argument is vague. One also can challenge the truth of some of the premises. There are grounds for holding that conflicts develop between government bureaucracies and bureaucracies in finance and industry. Likewise, conflicts develop between different bureaucracies within government and between different bureaucracies in the private sector.
10. The method of collecting evidence is defective.
12. One can argue that a different outcome than the expected one would result. There could be a lowering of production and a decrease in employment and tax revenue.
14. One can appeal to a faulty model. The state has only some characteristics of an organism. And there are grounds for questioning that a political body develops into a wholly rational entity. Furthermore, the notion of "wholly rational" is vague.
16. The argument appears to have some merit. But one can use both counterarguments and different arguments. Counterarguments would use the premises to show many new programs that have developed in the United States including movements supporting human rights and social welfare that were other than a mere repetition of conservative tendencies of the past. Different arguments would seek to show that some of these programs have been innovative.
18. One can claim that the expenditure of public funds in such cases makes possible a greater demand for goods and hence stimulates the economy. One also can appeal to a different argument by claiming a public responsibility for dealing with unemployment based on the structure taken by the economy and by the forces of production.
20. The methods used to gather this information are defective.

GLOSSARY

Absorption (Abs.) A basic argument form expressed as $p \supset q$, thus, $p \supset (p \cdot q)$.

Absurdity An argument with premises that are contradictory. In common sense, an argument with an essential premise that on its face appears highly unlikely.

Accent The placing of improper emphasis upon a word, phrase, or a sentence to distort the meaning of an expression in a given context.

Accident An informal fallacy in which one applies a general principle to exceptional or accidental cases to which the given general principle does not apply.

Addition (Add.) A basic argument form expressed as p, thus, $p \vee q$.

***Ad Hoc* Hypothesis** A hypothesis that accounts only for one kind of event or one set of facts. It does not interlock with other hypotheses or laws into a system.

Affirmative Statement In syllogistic logic, a statement that holds that all or some of the members of the class expressed by the subject term are included in the class expressed by the predicate term.

Ambiguity The property of an expression that can have more than one meaning in a given context.

Ambiguity of Significance A statement whose various meanings derive from unexpressed relevant factors found in the broader context in which such a statement occurs.

Amphiboly   An ambiguity that is attributable to errors of syntax or of punctuation in a sentence.

Antecedent   In a conditional statement, the part of the statement expressing the condition and introduced by "if."

Appeal to Common Consensus   An appeal to misplaced authority that seeks to resolve a point at issue in an argument by introducing evidence based on an alleged general belief of humankind.

Appeal to Force (*Argumentum ad Baculum*)   Use of force or the threat of its use rather than rational evidence in the support of a conclusion.

Appeal to the Gallery (*Argumentum ad Populum*)   An effort to seek acceptance of a conclusion merely by appealing to the emotional values, traditions, interests, or provincial concerns shared widely by members of an audience.

Appeal to Ignorance (*Argumentum ad Ignoratiam*)   An informal fallacy in which one makes the claim that if the conclusion of an argument cannot be shown to be false then the conclusion needs to be accepted as true.

Appeal to the Man, Abusive (*Argumentum ad Hominem*)   An informal fallacy in which one seeks to discredit an argument by verbal attacks on the character or reputation of the person advancing the original argument.

Appeal to the Man, Circumstantial (*Argumentum ad Hominem*)   An informal fallacy in which one seeks to discredit an argument by attacks on the particular situation of a person advancing an argument rather than by showing that the evidence given to justify a conclusion is faulty.

Appeal to Pity (*Argumentum ad Misericordiam*)   An informal fallacy that attempts to elicit a feeling of sympathy as the grounds for accepting a conclusion.

Arguing in a Circle   An informal fallacy in which a premise provides evidence to support a conclusion, which one then uses as evidence to claim that the original premise is true.

Argument   A set of statements given to justify an additional statement that is a conclusion.

Argument by Analogy   A claim that since two or more objects share one or more known properties in common, they also must share an additional property known to hold for only one of the objects.

Argumentive Leap (*Non Sequitur*, it does not follow, or jumping to a conclusion)   An informal fallacy that is due to an internal irrelevance found in an argument. The evidence of the argument has some relevance to a proposed conclusion. But the evidence is insufficient to establish the claim of an argument. Some writers use *non sequitur* to apply to any invalid argument.

Aristotelian Logic   An analysis of arguments using only two categorical statements as premises and a categorical statement as a conclusion. We also refer to Aristotelian logic as syllogistic logic.

Aristotelian Sorites   A chain argument using categorical statements in which the predicate term of an original premise becomes the subject term of each succeeding premise. The subject term of the conclusion is the subject term of the first premise in an Aristotelian sorites.

Arithmetic Mean   A measure of central tendency, calculated by adding the sum of scores in a unit and dividing this total by the number of scores entered in the unit.

Assertion   A sentence which makes a claim that certain conditions, happenings, states of affairs, relations, or connections expressed by the ordering of the elements in the sentence hold in a domain of discourse.

Association (Assoc.)   A basic statement equivalence used in extended proofs and expressed as $[p \lor (q \lor r)] \equiv [(p \lor q) \lor r]$ or as $[p \cdot (q \cdot r)] \equiv [(p \cdot q) \cdot r]$.

Asymmetrical Relation   The relation of one individual or class to a second, requiring that the second individual or class cannot have the same relation to the first. For example, "x is older than y."

Atomic Statement   A statement that has a single and complete unit of meaning. Two or more atomic statements joined by a statement connective form a compound or molecular statement.

Attack by Going through the Horns   The attack on a dilemma by adding another disjunct to the minor premise.

Attack by Proposing a Counterdilemma   The attack on a dilemma by interchanging and negating the consequents of the original conditional statements found in the major premise. (The minor premise remains the same. The disjuncts in the conclusion become interchanged and denied.)

Attack by Taking the Dilemma by the Horns   Attack on a dilemma which claims that at least one of the conditional statements in the major premise is false.

Authority, Misusing Appeals to (*Argumentum ad Verecundiam*)   An informal fallacy in which the basic evidence given to support a conclusion quotes a source that is not germane to or qualified to deal with the point at issue.

Begging the Question (*Petitio Principii*)   In a general sense, any faulty assumption of the point of issue in an argument. In a limited meaning, it is the use of an argument whose premises have an unexpressed assumption and whose conclusion makes this assumption explicit.

Behavioral Theories of Meaning   The view that an expression signifies those activities and dispositions which tend to evoke an utterance, and the range of responses or tendencies to respond that an utterance tends to evoke.

Biconditional Statement   A compound sentence with the form "p if and only if q."

Boolean Analysis   For categorical statements, the use of the notion of null classes to specify the relation of the class expressed by the subject term to the class expressed by the predicate term. **A**, the class of F and not G is null. **E**, the class of F and G is null. **I**, the class of F and G is not null. **O**, the class of F and not G is not null.

Bound Variable   In the logic of quantification, a variable whose quantifier includes it within its scope.

Burden of Proof   The obligation on the part of the maker of an argument to show that adequate evidence justifies that argument's conclusion.

Bureaucracy   A group of persons who have as their primary job directing and overseeing at intermediate and higher levels the way in which an organized group carries out its policies.

Categorical Statement   In syllogistic logic, a statement that affirms (or denies) that all or some of the members of the class expressed by the subject term are included in (or excluded from) the members of the class expressed by the predicate term.

Categorical Syllogism   An argument having three and only three terms with two categorical statements as premises and a third categorical statement as a conclusion.

Cause   Any combination of essential and sufficient conditions in whose presence an additional and relevant specified event always follows. (But such conditions cannot be joint effects of a common cause.)

Circular Definition   An expression defined by use of a second expression, which in turn is defined by use of the original expression.

Claim of an Argument   A conclusion that someone advances on the basis of reasons or evidence given to justify it.

Class   A group (or set) of individuals or objects having one or more identifiable properties in common.

Class Term   A unit of discourse that stands for a set of individuals which have one or more properties in common.

Closed Sentence   A sentence in which all variables are bound.

Column   In a truth table, all of the entries found in a vertical reading of entries of **T** or **F** under any simple sentence or place holder for such a sentence in the table.

Commutation Equivalents (Comm.)   A basic statement equivalence used in extended proofs and expressed as $(p \lor q) \equiv (q \lor p)$ or as $(p \cdot q) \equiv (q \cdot p)$.

Complementary Class Term   A unit of discourse that stands for everything not covered by an expression used as a class term for which it is the complementary term. (If a class term is "numbers," its complementary class term is "non-numbers.")

Complex Constructive Dilemma   An argument with the form $(p \supset q) \cdot (r \supset s)$, $p \lor r$, thus, $q \lor s$.

Complex Destructive Dilemma   An argument with the form $(p \supset q) \cdot (r \supset s)$, $\sim q \lor \sim s$, thus, $\sim p \lor \sim r$.

Complex Question   The forming of a question in a way that assumes that a certain state of affairs holds when the point at issue is what holds with regard to such a state of affairs.

Composition An informal fallacy with the faulty assumption that the characteristics of the parts of a whole also apply to the whole.

Compound Sentence One whose component parts are two or more sentences.

Compound Statement A true or false sentence with two or more statements as component parts.

Conditional Proofs A series of steps within a proof in which one assumes a statement and then derives within the proof other statements that also hold, provided that the assumed statement is true.

Conditional Statements Statements that use the connective "if . . . then _____." The symbol for this connective is the horseshoe, "⊃."

Conjunct The sentence preceding or following the "and" in a conjunctive statement.

Conjunction (Conj.). A basic argument form expressed as p, q, thus $p \cdot q$.

Conjunctive Contrary A statement joined to another statement by "and" in a denial-of-conjunction statement. In the statement form $\sim(p \cdot q)$, p and q are each conjunctive contraries.

Conjunctive Statement A compound sentence with the form "p and q."

Connectives of Statements Expressions used to join together two statements. Examples of statement connectives used in logic are "and," "if . . . then _____," "either . . . or _____," "It is not the case that" and ". . . if and only if _____."

Connotation of a Word Used as a class term, the properties held in common by the objects to which the class term applies.

Connotative Definition A definition in which the definiens states the meaning of a word by specifying both a general class term and an identifying and essential property held by the members of the class specified by the definiendum. A connotative definition is sometimes called a "definition by genus and difference."

Consequent In a conditional statement, the part of the statement expressing what follows by meeting the conditions of the antecedent. It is usually preceded by "then."

Constructive Complex Dilemma (CCD) A derivable elementary argument form expressed as $(p \supset q) \cdot (r \supset s)$, $p \vee r$, thus, $q \vee s$.

Context Theory of Meaning As used in this work, the view that the meaning of a linguistic expression is the range of what it connotes, of what it denotes, of what it relates, of what it connects, and of how it functions in the situation of its use.

Contingent Statement Has a logical form yielding statements that may be true in some cases and false in others.

Contradiction One statement is the contradiction of another by meeting these two conditions: The truth of either statement requires the falsity of the other. And the falsity of either statement requires the truth of the other.

Contradictory Statement   Has a logical form that yields only statements that are false.

Contraposition (Contrap.)   In extended proofs, a basic statement equivalence used in extended proofs and expressed as $(p \supset q) \equiv (\sim q \supset \sim p)$. In categorical statements, a logical operation of interchanging and negating the subject terms of an **A**- or an **O**-type statement. There is no contrapositive for an **I** statement. And there is only a partial contrapositive for an **E** statement.

Contrariety   A relation holding between two statements such that both statements cannot be true, but both can be false.

Contrary Class Terms   A linguistic unit that meets two conditions: (1) it has no overlapping members with the original class term for which it is a contrary term, and (2) a class term and its contrary term together do not exhaust all objects in a universe of discourse.

Controvert an Argument   To provide justification for holding that in some way an argument's evidence does not justify its conclusion.

Conventional Nonlinguistic Sign   An object whose meaning one conveys by acts based on social practices other than by direct language expressions.

Conventional Sign   A sign whose meaning one derives from social usage and custom.

Converse Accident   An informal fallacy of deriving a general principle from exceptional or accidental cases that do not provide the basis for forming such a general principle.

Conversion   A logical operation of a categorical statement in which the subject term and the predicate term are interchanged without increasing the distribution of any term. Only the **E** and **I** statements have full conversions.

Copula   In a categorical statement, the use of some form of the verb "to be" in the present tense ("is" or "are") with the meaning of "is included in the class of" (or with "not": "is not included in the class of").

Counterargument   Uses the premises of an original argument to construct an argument that derives a conclusion opposed to the conclusion found in the original argument.

Cross-Section of a Truth Table   The entering of only those rows of a truth table that are sufficient to prove the validity or invalidity of an argument or argument form.

Deductive Explanation   Has premises (the explicans) which state a general principle or law (or laws) and specify a given set of conditions covered by the general principle as holding. These two premises provide a reason for expecting that another event, condition, or principle also will be the case.

Deductive Logic   The logic of necessary inference. It is the analysis of arguments whose form requires that in all cases in which the conclusion is false at least one premise also is false.

Definiendum   The expression whose meaning a definition clarifies.

Definiens   The part of a definition that clarifies the meaning of an expression. It is the defining part of a definition.

Definite Description   An expression using a general class term that has a word or phrase that limits the scope of the expression to a singular entity.

Definition   A way of clarifying and making explicit the meaning of an expression in a given context.

Definition by Classification   The procedure of making definitions by ordering the major types of objects that one finds covered by the word being defined.

DeMorgan's Law (DeM)   A basic statement equivalence used in extended proofs and expressed as $(p \lor q) \equiv \sim(\sim p \cdot \sim q)$.

DeMorgan's Law and Material Conditional (DeC)   A basic statement equivalence used in extended proofs and expressed as $(p \supset q) \equiv \sim(p \cdot \sim q)$.

Denial-of-Conjunction Argument (DCA)   A derivable elementary argument form expressed as $\sim(p \cdot q)$, p, thus, $\sim q$.

Denotation of a Word   Used as a class term, consists of each separate entity designated by that word.

Denotative Definition   A definition that points to or gives examples of objects to which an expression applies.

Determinism, Hard   Holds that every human action is a part of a network or a chain of events in which each link is a result only of what already has occurred in the preceding links in the series.

Determinism, Self-   Holds that within a causal interpretation of human acts a moral agent can act on the basis of intelligible reasons by means of which such an agent can choose to make some things happen or prevent other things from happening.

Determinism, Soft   Holds that (1) all human actions are a part of a cause-and-effect sequence of events, and (2) a person is morally responsible for a given moral act provided that he or she has the power or ability either to do or not to do such an act in a given context, and that such an act is not the result of coercion.

Difference   In a connotative definition, an essential and identifying property of the specific subclass of the definiendum in relation to the more general class designed by the genus.

Dilemma   An argument presenting alternative choices or courses of action such that in choosing either course of action a given set of consequences (usually unfavorable) is to be expected. A complex constructive dilemma has the form $(p \supset q) \cdot (r \supset s)$, $p \lor r$, thus, $q \lor s$.

Disjunct   The sentence preceding or following the "or" in a disjunctive statement.

Disjunctive Argument (DA)   A derivable elementary argument form expressed as $p \lor q$, $\sim p$, thus, q.

Disjunctive Statement   Has the form "either p or q." See **Inclusive Disjunction** and **Exclusive Disjunction**.

Dispute   A disagreement between two or more persons or groups about the preferred resolution of a discussed issue.

Dispute about Relevance of Evidence   In an argument, a disagreement about what facts or notions are essential and sufficient to justify the claim of an argument.

Dispute over Expectancies   A disagreement in an argument in which the disputants hold different views about the future consequences of a set of conditions or of acting on different live options.

Distributed Term   An expression, used as a class term, that refers to all members of its class.

Distribution (Dist.)   A basic statement equivalence used in extended proofs and expressed as $[p \lor (q \cdot r)] \equiv [(p \lor q) \cdot (p \lor r)]$ or $[p \cdot (q \lor r)] \equiv [(p \cdot q) \lor (p \cdot r)]$.

Dividing a Question   A separating of different meanings that either can occur in any given interrogative sentence or can be distinguished in any statement that purports to resolve an issue.

Division   As an informal fallacy, an argument with the faulty assumption that a characteristic of a whole also applies to the separate parts of the whole.

Domain of Discourse   An area of talk with a common set of language meanings and rules for language use. (A domain of discourse makes possible the testing of a set of concepts and statements for clarity and consistency.)

Double Negation Equivalents (DN)   A basic statement equivalence used in extended proofs and expressed as $p \equiv \sim\sim p$.

Duty Claim   A moral rule that has relevance to a person making moral decisions.

Duty Obligation   A binding moral rule having priority, that a person must try to make certain things happen or not happen in a given situation.

Empirical or *A Posteriori* **Probability**   Of a given type of event, the relative frequency with which a stated event or condition is known to occur in a given context. The basis for determining empirical probability is past experience.

Enthymeme   An argument that has an unexpressed but implicit premise or conclusion.

Equivalence   Two statements have a relation of equivalence in truth values if in any case in which one statement is true, the other also is true, and if in any case one is false, the other also is false.

Equivocation   The use of a word or phrase in a given context with a shift in the meaning of the word from one occurrence to another.

Essential Condition   A state of affairs that needs to be present for another event or sequence of events to occur. However, the essential condition can be present and the indicated event fail to occur.

Ethics   In a historical and philosophical sense, a critical analysis of rational ways to justify moral judgments about the good life or about human conduct judged as good or bad, as right or wrong, as obligatory or not obligatory.

Evaluative Dispute   A disagreement in an argument about the properties attributed to an object and appraised as good or bad, commendable or not commendable, or desirable or undesirable.

Exclusive Disjunction   The exclusive and strong sense of "or," requiring that one disjunct in a disjunctive statement be true and that the other statement be false. The form of exclusive disjunction is $(p \lor q) \cdot (\sim p \lor \sim q)$ as used in this work.

Existential Import   The property of some categorical statements in which one requires that the class of the subject term has members in order for the statements to be true.

Existential Quantifier ($\exists x$)   Uses the form $(\exists x)$ and expresses the notion of "there is at least one thing x" or "there exists at least one thing x."

Explanation   A statement of the reason for an event happening or for a relation, condition, or principle holding. Explanations for events usually refer to causal relations.

Explicandum   The event, relation, or principle for which one seeks to account in an explanation.

Explicans   The part of an explanation that accounts for the occurrence of another event or for the holding of another relation, condition, or principle.

Explicative Definition   Statement of some conventional characteristics associated with the use of a word, together with a placing of added restrictions on the use of a word in a given context.

Exportation (Exp.)   A basic statement equivalence used in extended proofs and expressed as $[p \supset (q \supset r)] \equiv [(p \cdot q) \supset r]$.

Extended Proofs   Proofs that use a step-by-step combination of valid argument forms and equivalent statement forms used to construct proofs of arguments.

Extension   In an expression used as a class term, the individuals who are members of the class signified by an expression.

Factual Dispute   A disagreement about what happens, what characterizes a state of affairs, or what relations hold in the world about us.

Fallacy   An error in an argument that results from a flaw in the structure of the argument, a lack of relevance of the evidence to the conclusion, or inadequate evidence.

Fallacy of Affirming the Consequent   A faulty argument that uses a conditional statement as a premise, affirms the consequent of the conditional statement as a second premise, and affirms the antecedent in the conclusion.

Fallacy of Affirming a Disjunct   A faulty argument using an inclusive disjunctive statement as a premise and holding that since one disjunct is true, the other disjunct must be false.

Fallacy of Denial of a Conjunctive Contrary   A faulty argument having as one premise a statement with two conjunctive contraries and as a second premise a statement denying one of the conjunctive contraries. The conclusion erroneously affirms the other conjunctive contrary.

Fallacy of Denying the Antecedent   An argument in which one premise is a conditional statement and a second premise holds that the antecedent of the conditional statement (the "if" part) is false. And one makes the error of holding in the conclusion that the consequent of the conditional statement (the "then" part) is false.

Fallacy of Equivocation   The use of a key expression that has more than one possible meaning in a context to justify the claim of an argument.

Fallacy of Misuse of Appeal to Emotions   An informal fallacy in which an argument makes an appeal to emotion as the primary evidence to justify a conclusion.

Fallacy of the Misuse of a Relational Expression   The use of a relational expression as a basis to derive a conclusion that cannot be justified by the logical meaning of that expression in a given argument.

Fallacy of Reification   A faulty argument whose claim rests on the mistaken belief that a given object has some kind of physical existence on the basis that there is a word or phrase for such an object.

Fallacies of Relevance   Faulty arguments in which the evidence fails to provide the kind of material evidence needed to establish a conclusion.

Fallacy of Simple Ambiguity   Use of an expression which can have several meanings to justify a conclusion derived from an improper interpretation of an ambiguous expression.

Figure   In a categorical syllogism, the placement of the middle term in a proper ordering of the major and minor premises.

Fig. I   Fig. II   Fig. III   Fig. IV

$M \quad P$ $P \quad M$ $M \quad P$ $P \quad M$

$S \quad M$ $S \quad M$ $M \quad S$ $M \quad S$

Finite Population   In statistics, one whose total membership could be counted if one had the time and means to do so.

Formal Proof   In an argument in the logic of truth functions, a statement or series of statements serving as premises with an added statement or series of statements derived from the premises by use of elementary argument forms and equivalent statement forms to justify a conclusion.

Form of an Argument   The way in which the ordering and connecting of statements and of statement elements occur in an argument.

Freedom in Moral Action   To have human freedom in moral action one expects the following conditions to be present: (1) the moral agent must be able to act voluntarily and without coercion in choosing between alternative courses of action; (2) the moral agent must have the ability or power to carry out the indicated act; and (3) the moral agent must be able to set himself or herself to initiate the action chosen and to have reasonable expectancies of making headway in carrying out the intended action.

Free Variable   In the logic of quantification, a variable that in a given context does not fall within the scope of a quantifier appropriate for it.

Function in a Correlation   A property found in a given population that has relevance for predicting the occurrence of a second property in that population. If x is a function of y, y has relevance in predicting the occurrence of x.

Generalization by Enumeration   Identifying a property or a group of properties found in a limited number of individuals of a larger set and holding either that another specified ratio or that all members of the larger set also have such properties.

Generalization in the Logic of Quantification   The procedure of deriving a quantified expression from an appropriate instance of that expression.

Genetic Explanation   Accounting for events or conditions by reference to the context out of which they develop.

Genus   The general class to which a word used as a class term applies. In a definition such as "Man is a rational animal" the genus is "animal."

Goclenian Sorites   A chain argument using categorical statements in which the subject term of an original premise becomes the predicate term of each succeeding premise. The predicate term in the conclusion of a Goclenian sorites is the predicate term of the first premise.

Going through the Horns   A way of rebutting a dilemma by adding another disjunct to the disjunctive premise. If the disjunctive premise has the form $p \lor r$, then the form $p \lor r \lor t$ would provide a way of going through the horns.

Hasty Generalization   A fallacy in which one derives a general principle from a sample that is too small to justify such a conclusion.

Hempel's Paradox   Pointing out that by using one statement and an equivalent form (such as contraposition) anything can account as a confirming instance of some hypotheses.

Historical Definition   A definition that states the meaning that an expression has had in a previous period.

Horseshoe   "⊃," a symbol used as a connective in expressing a conditional statement.

Hypotheses, Laws, and Theories   A hypothesis is a statement tentatively set forth to try to account for another set of facts or conditions or principles. Hypotheses are attempts to account for the way things are or how they got as they are. A law is a well-confirmed hypothesis in a set of related and consistent well-confirmed hypotheses. A theory is a principle that helps to unify a set of well-confirmed laws. A theory also has nonobservable or theoretical entities such as mass or energy.

Hypothesis in Statistical Studies   A statement to guide a testing procedure about some observable and measurable difference holding between two or more populations or about some measurable relationship holding between two or more properties.

Hypothetical Syllogism (HS)   A basic argument form expressed as $p \supset q$, $q \supset r$, thus $p \supset r$.

Idea Theory of Meaning   The view that words are the sensible marks of ideas.

Immediate Inference   An act of deriving directly a conclusion on the basis of using only one premise as evidence. Given an original statement as true, one can know directly the truth or falsity of a second statement by use of only one step in a proof.

Inclusive Disjunction   A statement with the form $p \vee q$. At least one disjunct is true if an inclusive disjunctive statement is true. But both disjuncts also may be true in such cases.

Independence   A relation holding between two statements in which the truth or falsity of either statement does not permit one to derive the truth or falsity of the other.

Individual   In logic, a discrete unit of any kind to which one can ascribe a property. A set of individuals sharing one or more identifiable properties in common is a class.

Inductive Logic   The logic of probable inference. A good inductive argument leads into a conclusion whose falsity is unlikely.

Inference   The act a person takes in deriving a conclusion of an argument.

Inferential Statistics   A procedure of using tests, manipulations, and probability theory to derive conclusions about differences or relations found in a total population on the basis of factors known about a random sample of that population.

Infinite Regress, Harmless   A presentation of a possible infinite series of facts within which it is possible to begin an explanation at any point in the series.

Infinite Regress, Vicious   An argument which introduces premises for holding to a view, within a series of similar kinds of premises, which have no originating point that can justify the subsequent premises given in the argument.

Informal Fallacy   An error in an argument that is due to faulty assumptions or to irrelevances occurring in presenting evidence for a conclusion.

Instantiation   In the logic of quantification, the procedure of specifying cases (instances) to which a quantified expression may apply.

Intension   In an expression used as a class term, the set of properties held in common by the objects found in the class covered by the expression.

Interval Scale   In statistics, a level of measurement that uses an identifiable and equal distance (or interval) between the categories used to measure a variable.

Intransitive Relation   A relation is intransitive if it meets these conditions. One knows that one individual or class has a stated relation to a second. One also knows that the second individual or class has the same relation to a third. The relation is intransitive if one also can derive the conclusion that the first individual or class cannot have that relation to the third. For example, "*A* is the mother of *B* and *B* is the mother of *C*. Thus, *A* cannot be the mother of *C*."

Invalid Argument Form   In deductive logic an argument form in which it is possible for all premises to be true with a conclusion that is false.

Invalid Deductive Argument   One having a logical form that permits a false conclusion with true premises.

Irreflexive Relation   A relation expressed by a relational term that cannot hold when it is used to refer back to an individual or class used as a subject term. For example, "*A* is greater than *A*" cannot hold.

Joint Method of Agreement and Difference   Mill's method holds: "If two or more instances in which the phenomenon occurs have only one circumstance in common, while two or more instances in which it does not occur have nothing in common save the absence of that circumstance, the circumstance in which alone the two sets of instances differ is the effect, or the cause, or an indispensable part of the cause, of the phenomenon."

Law   See **Hypotheses**.

Leading Question   A form of complex question stated in a manner that suggests a preferred answer.

Lexical Definition   A definition that states in some detail the traditional meaning or meanings of a word.

Linguistic Sign   A language expression, such as words or phrases, that one uses to indicate or communicate meanings about objects of discourse.

Logic   A study of ways to justify and evaluate arguments and to analyze the elements found in arguments and argument forms.

Logical Operators   An expression (or a symbol for an expression) in a statement (or statement form) that indicates a property or a relation that makes possible the deriving of other statements in an argument.

The following expressions can function as logical operators: "all," "some," "is," "are," "no," "not," "and," "if . . . then _____," "either . . . or _____," and "_____ if and only if. . . ."

Logic of Truth Functions   The logic of arguments using compound statements whose truth value is determined (1) by the values assigned to its simple statements and (2) by the logical meaning of the statement connectives used in such compound statements. Propositional logic or sentential calculus are other names for this kind of logic.

Major Premise   In a categorical syllogism, the premise that has the major term.

Major Term   In a categorical syllogism, the predicate term of the conclusion.

Material Biconditional (or **Material Equivalence**) (**MBC**)   A basic statement equivalence used in extended proofs and expressed as $(p \equiv q) \equiv [(p \supset q)\cdot(q \supset p)]$ and $(p \equiv q) \equiv [(p\cdot q) \vee (\sim p\cdot\sim q)]$.

Material Conditional (MC)   A basic statement equivalence used in extended proofs and expressed as $(p \supset q) \equiv (\sim p \vee q)$.

Material Statement   A statement whose truth or falsity can be determined only by examining the state of affairs to which the statement applies. The truth of a material statement cannot be determined merely by analyzing the form or the meaning of the component parts of a statement.

Mathematical or *A Priori* **Probability**   The estimate of the likelihood of the occurrence of a given type of event on the basis of the number of times that such an event can occur in relation to the total number of events of that kind that may occur. In such cases one holds that the occurrence of any event of the set under review is as equally probable as any other single event of that set.

Median   A measure of a central tendency determined by the point occurring midway in the distribution of the entries of a unit.

Mediate Inference   An act of deriving a conclusion by use of more than one premise as evidence or by use of more than one step in a proof.

Mention of a Word   The occurrence of a language expression whose referent is itself. (For example, " 'Red' has three letters.")

Metaethics   An analysis of the meaning of the language of morals and of ways used to justify rationally the logic, methods, and standards used in advancing moral claims.

Method of Agreement   Mill's method holds: "If two or more instances of the phenomenon under investigation have only one circumstance in common, the circumstance in which alone all the instances agree is the cause (or effect) of the given phenomenon."

Method of Concomitant Variations   Mill's method holds: "Whatever phenomenon varies in any manner whenever another phenomenon varies in some particular manner, is either a cause or an effect of that phenomenon, or is connected with it through some fact of causation."

Method of Difference   Mill's method holds: "If an instance in which the phenomenon under investigation occurs, and an instance in which it does not occur, have every circumstance in common save one, that one occurring only in the former; the circumstance in which alone the two instances differ is the effect, or the cause, or an indispensable part of the cause, of the phenomenon."

Method of Residues   Mill's method holds: "Subduct from any phenomenon such part as is known by previous inductions to be the effect of certain antecedents, and the residue of the phenomenon is the effect of the remaining antecedents."

Middle Term   Of a categorical syllogism, the term common to each of the premises. It does not occur in the conclusion.

Minor Term   Of a categorical syllogism, the subject term of the conclusion.

Missing the Point at Issue (*Ignoratio Elenchi*—ignoring the point at issue)   An informal fallacy based on an external irrelevance found in an argument. The evidence of the argument supports a claim other than the issue at hand and ignores the point at issue.

Mode   A central tendency determined by the value of the entry occurring with greatest frequency in a unit.

***Modus Ponens* (MP)**   A basic argument form expressed as $p \supset q$, p, thus, q.

***Modus Tollens* (MT)**   A derivable elementary argument form expressed as $p \supset q$, $\sim q$, thus, $\sim p$.

Molecular Statement   A statement with two or more simple sentences as elements. Molecular statements are also called compound statements.

Mood   In a categorical syllogism, the order of occurrence of **A, E, I, O** statements found in the syllogism with properly ordered premises and conclusion. In a categorical syllogism with proper ordering, the major premise occurs first, the minor premise second, and the conclusion last.

Moral Issue   A state of affairs about which one can make a duty claim, assert a duty obligation, or hold to be morally good or bad. (See **Morality**)

Morality   In ethics, the character of human conduct that relates to reducing conflicting interests in a way consistent with justice and to attaining the enlightened interest and well-being of all persons.

Morality, Social   The set of actions, group habits, and customs subject to a group's approval and disapproval on the basis of beliefs held about preserving that group's social identity and advancing its well-being.

Morally Good Acts   Those human actions that are chosen for moral reasons and that result in supporting or attaining the enlightened interest of a society.

Morally Obligatory Act   A moral act that has the highest priority on a person's action in a rational ordering of duty claims on a person's conduct in a given context.

Morally Right Act   Giving expression to a duty claim that has as great a priority in a rational ordering of duty claims on a moral agent's conduct as any other duty claim.

Moral Principle   A moral rule that tends to apply to all or to almost all moral evaluations or decisions.

Natural Signs   A sign whose meaning one derives from the relation of its physical character to its physical environment.

Necessity   Logical necessity relative to a deductive argument is a relation holding between premises and a conclusion such that if the conclusion is false at least one premise also is false. Logical necessity relative to a statement or statement form is a relation holding between the component parts of such a statement so that in the system in which such a statement occurs it has one and only one truth value. (It is logically necessary in truth-functional logic for a statement with the form "p v $\sim p$" to be true.)

Negative Statement   In syllogistic logic, a statement that holds that all or some of the members of the class of the subject term are excluded as members of the class of the predicate term.

Neutral Words   A language expression that tells how things are or at least how things are believed to be. (It is not in itself the kind of utterance that usually gives direct expression to how one feels about things or how one would like others to feel.)

Nominal Scale   In statistics, a level of measurement that distinguishes categories based solely on the notions of sameness or of difference.

Nondeductive Argument   An argument whose form yields conclusions that one can appraise as probably true rather than as necessarily true if the premises are true.

Nonreflexive Relation   The relation expressed by the relational term may or may not apply to a given individual or class expressed as a subject term. For example, "A is an admirer of A."

Nonsymmetrical Relation   The relation of one individual or class to a second that does not provide a basis to derive any conclusion about the same relation holding or not holding between the second individual or class to the first. For example, "A is the sister of B."

Nontransitive Relation   Holds that if R is a relational expression and aRb and bRc hold in a given field, then the truth or falsity of aRc cannot be determined merely by the meaning assigned to R. For example, "is a cousin of" is a nontransitive relational expression.

Null Class   A class that has no members. It also is an empty class.

Null Hypothesis   A statement holding that there is no difference between samples studied in a statistical analysis and that chance can account for any observed differences or relationship in the samples.

Object   In its broadest sense, any subject of discourse and anything one says about a subject of discourse.

Objective Connotation   Of a word used as a class term, the properties that a qualified person can recognize as applicable to the members of the class for which the expression is used.

Obversion   A logical operation using negation, in which there is a denial both of a categorical statement as a whole and of the predicate term. (The subject term remains the same.)

Open Sentence   A sentence that has at least one free variable.

Operational Definition   A definition that specifies a set of actions or operations that need to be satisfied in order to apply a word or concept to a given situation.

Ordinal Scale   In statistics, a level of measurement that provides for the assigning of an order or rank in the scales as well as for the identifying of sameness or difference.

Ostensive Definition   An example given for the meaning of a word by the act of pointing to an object or to a series of different objects that count as instances of an object to which the word applies.

Parameter   In statistics, a summary measure whose calculations refer to the total population covered by a study.

Particular Statement   A particular categorical statement is a statement whose subject term includes at least one, but less than all, of the members of its class. A particular categorical statement has an undistributed subject term.

Persuasive Definition   A proposed definition of a word in a biased way so as to condition the attitudes of an audience in a way sought by the language user.

Place Holder   A symbol used in a sentence form to occupy the position (or to take the place) of an expression by which it may be replaced. Another name for "place holder" is "variable."

Point of Reference   In analyzing central tendencies, the total population covered by a central tendency in a given statistical study.

Policies   Of an organization, the general guidelines or principles which it uses to govern both its overall operations and its more specific operations to attain its primary objectives.

Population in Statistics   All the members of specifiable groups or of aggregates of any measurable kind of entity, event, or process.

Post Hoc **Fallacy**   The unwarranted claim holding that in a series of two events, the event occurring prior in time is the cause of the second, solely on the basis of the priority in time of the first event.

Practical or **Applied Ethics**   An analysis of proposals for resolving specific moral issues in a society.

Predicate Term   In syllogistic logic, the term which occurs after the copula of a categorical statement.

Premises   The statements which provide evidence as a basis for deriving a conclusion for an argument.

Principle of Contradiction   The truth value of any given statement cannot have two different truth values in a given context. A statement cannot have both the value of true and the value of false in a given context.

Principle of Excluded Middle   Restriction of the truth value of a given statement to only one of two truth values. Either the statement is true or it is false in a given context.

Principle of Existential Generalization (EG)   An existentially quantified statement can be inferred from any of its instances.

Principle of Existential Instantiation (EI)   The deriving of an instance of an ambiguous name (or a free variable) from an existentially quantified expression, provided that the variable chosen does not occur free either in a premise or in a previous step in the proof.

Principle of Identity   The truth value of a given statement (in a given context) remains constant.

Principle of Quantifier Equivalence (QE)   In its more inclusive use it is expressed by the following forms: (a) $\sim(x)Fx = (\exists x) \sim Fx$; (b) $\sim(\exists x)Fx \equiv (x) \sim Fx$; {it also covers expressions having the form (c) $[(x)Fx\cdot(x)Gx] \equiv (x)(Fx\cdot Gx)$; (d) $[(\exists x)Fx \lor (\exists x)Gx] \equiv [(\exists x)(Fx \lor Gx)]$}.

Principle of Replacement   In truth-functional logic any two statements that are logically equivalent may replace each other wherever they occur in an argument or in a proof.

Principle of Universal Instantiation (UI)   From a universally quantified statement we can derive instances of that statement.

Probabilistic Explanations   Use of premises that express the frequency with which an original set of conditions are followed by a second set of conditions or events. Since the original conditions are then affirmed as holding in a given case, one has grounds to expect the second set of conditions will occur in the latter case with their stated frequency.

Probability of Commonsense Generalizations   The degree of confidence that is warranted in the reliability of such generalizations as is attestable by their serving as good guides for decision making.

Property   Anything ascribed to an object or to a set of objects. We ascribe a property to a class or to an individual member of a class. A property is a characteristic or an attribute of something.

Property Term   A unit of discourse that stands for an expression that ascribes anything to a class or to an individual member of a class.

Proposition   A meaningful declarative sentence which is either true or false and which makes an assertion. A proposition also is a statement.

Quality   In a categorical statement, reference to such a statement as a whole as affirmative or negative.

Quantification Logic   The analysis of sentence elements through the use of the quantifiers (x) and $(\exists x)$, as well as the use of the logic of truth functions, and the rules of instantiation (UI and EI), of generalization

(EG and UG), and of quantifier equivalence (QE) to analyze and develop argument forms and arguments.

Quantifiers in a Categorical Statement   Expressions such as "all," "some," "no," or "not," designate the distribution of an expression used as a class term.

Quantifiers in Logic of Quantification   The symbols "(x)" and "$(\exists x)$." The symbol used for universal quantification is "(x)." The symbol used for existential quantification is "$(\exists x)$."

Random Errors   In a statistical study, mistakes in measuring precisely the degree to which a given property applies to an object as a result of chance. (Random errors tend to cancel each other out.)

Random Sampling   A representative group within a larger population. In choosing a random sample the following conditions need to be met: (1) The method of choosing a member of the sample gives every member of the population studied an 'equal chance of being included in the sample. (2) The method used in such cases assures that the choice of any given member of the sample has no predictive effect on the next choice.

Ratio Scale   In statistics, a level of measurement that uses an absolute zero as well as intervals to show the degree of difference holding between different observations.

***Reductio ad Absurdum* Proof**   The denial of the conclusion of an argument results in the occurrence of a contradiction within the set of statements used as premises.

Reference Theory of Meaning   The view that the meaning of a word is the object which such a word designates.

Referent   The thing, event, condition, relation, or object signified by a language expression in a given context.

Reflexive Relation   A relation that an individual (or class) holds to itself such that such an individual (or class) must have such a relation to itself. For example, "A is equal to A."

Relation   Anything which ascribes a logical order or a logical connection to classes or to individuals.

Relational Term   A unit of discourse that stands for a language expression that orders individuals or classes to each other.

Relativism, Cultural   An ethical theory which holds that moral evaluations are merely an expression of group approval or disapproval for given types of human actions in a given time, place, or situation.

Relativism, Ethical   A subjective view of ethics which holds that moral judgments are expressions of personal tastes and preferences.

Repetition (Rep.)   A basic statement equivalence used in extended proofs and expressed as $(p \lor p) \equiv p$ or $(p \cdot p) \equiv p$.

Reportive Definitions   A definition that provides information about a past or present usage of an expression.

Reversal of Cause and Effect   The mistake of identifying an effect in a given context by labeling it the cause.

Row   In a truth table, all of the entries for truth values found on any one horizontal set of entries in the table.

Rule of Replacement   In truth-functional logic, one equivalent statement (or statement form) can replace another equivalent statement (or statement form) either as a complete line in a proof or as part of a line in a proof.

Scope   Of a quantifier, all elements in a statement form that are governed by that quantifier. Parentheses and other such marks serve to make explicit those parts of an expression to which a quantifier applies.

Scope of Logical Operator   The elements in a statement form which are covered by the operator's function.

Self-Realization View   An ethical view that the morally good is that action which develops one's intellectual, moral, spiritual, and aesthetic capacities in the highest degree.

Set   Frequently an undefined term. Any actual or purported group, collection, or class of individuals or objects (which can be actual, abstract, or fictitious).

Sentence   The smallest grammatically independent linguistic unit that makes a complete utterance within a given system of grammar.

Sign   An object that is used to convey some meaning related to some object other than itself.

Significance Level   In statistics, the point selected as a basis for rejecting a null hypothesis. If the null hypothesis is rejected, the alternative hypothesis holding that the observed differences in a sample are actual differences in the sample is not rejected.

Simple Constructive Dilemma   An argument with the form $(p \supset q) \cdot (r \supset q)$, $p \vee r$, thus, q.

Simple Destructive Dilemma   An argument with the form $(p \supset r) \cdot (p \supset s)$, $\sim r \vee \sim s$, thus, $\sim p$.

Simple Sentence   A sentence with one and only one sentence as an element. It does not have two or more sentences as components.

Simplification (Simp.)   A basic argument form expressed as $p \cdot q$, thus, p.

Singular Term   A unit of discourse that stands for a single individual or entity, actual or fictitious.

Solipsism   The view that the self essentially is a bundle of its own sensations and that nothing other than the self and its sensations can be known as existing objects.

Sorites   Chain arguments which have several categorical syllogisms telescoped or condensed into a single argument.

Sound Argument   An argument that has a valid form and true premises.

Square of Opposition   A scheme that uses a square figure to provide an

Tu Quoque **Argument**   A special case of a circumstantial *ad hominem* argument in which one seeks to discredit views of an opposing party by charging that the person advancing an argument does or has said the kind of thing he or she rejects in the original argument. (*Tu Quoque*— you also, or you are another one.)

Undistributed Term   An expression used as a class term to refer to at least one member of its class but to less than all members of such a class.

Uniform General Hypothesis   A principle that accounts for a property or relation that holds without exception to all members of a set.

Universal Categorical Statement   In syllogistic logic any categorical statement whose subject term includes all members in its class.

Universal Quantifier (*x*)   Uses the form "(*x*)" and expresses the notion "for anything *x*," "for any *x*," and "for everything *x*."

Univocal Use of a Word   The case of a word having a constant meaning throughout a given context.

Use of a Word   The occurrence of a language expression to signify something other than the word used in such an expression.

Use Theories of Meaning   The view that the meaning of a linguistic expression is its use. "Use" refers to the function that language fulfills in human activities and includes the purpose of a language user in making an utterance in a social setting.

Utilitarianism, Act   An ethical view holding that the morally right act is that act in a given context which results in the greatest happiness for the greatest number.

Utilitarianism, Hedonistic   The ethical view holding that the morally good is what maximizes pleasure and minimizes pain.

Utilitarianism, Ideal   The ethical view of G. E. Moore holding that a morally right act is one that maximizes the good. But in this view the good is a moral and nonnatural property that one cannot define.

Utilitarianism, Rule   An ethical view holding that the morally right act is that act which is based on a moral rule, that tends to result in the greatest happiness for the greatest number.

Utterance   Any human talk originating from a common source and having pauses or sequences of pauses before and after the sounds that are made. In a derived sense an utterance also includes the written form of such talk.

Vagueness   The property of an expression that makes it impossible to determine the precise range of entities to which the expression applies in a given context.

Valid Deductive Argument   A deductive argument with a valid argument form.

Valid Deductive Argument Form   A deductive argument form in which in all cases where the conclusion is false there also is at least one false premise.

Variable, in Logic   See **Place Holder**.

Variable, in Statistics   Any given identifiable characteristic whose value differs among members in a population.

Venn Diagram   A scheme that uses Boolean analysis of categorical statements to prove the validity or invalidity of a categorical syllogism. A categorical syllogism is valid if the marking of the major and minor premise on the diagram also draws the marking required by the conclusion. The argument is otherwise invalid.

Verbal Denotative Definition   A definition that uses words to identify objects to which the defined word applies.

Verbal Dispute   A disagreement based on the use in an argument of a key word or phrase to which the disputants give different meanings.

Verbal Token   The physical character of a language expression. (It may be spoken or written.)

Virtue   In historical ethics, an excellence of character developed through habit, particularly the habit of exercising rational control over desires.

Wedge   The symbol, "V," used to express inclusive disjunction.

INDEX